D1570756

THE NEW CHAUCER SOCIETY

Studies in the Age of Chaucer, the yearbook of The New Chaucer Society, is published annually. Each issue contains substantial articles on all aspects of Chaucer and his age, book reviews, and an annotated Chaucer bibliography. Manuscripts, in duplicate, accompanied by return postage, should follow the *Chicago Manual of Style,* 14th edition. Unsolicited reviews are not accepted. Authors receive free twenty offprints of articles and ten of reviews. All correspondence regarding manuscript submissions should be directed to the Editor, Larry Scanlon, Department of English, Rutgers University, 510 George Street, New Brunswick, NJ 08901-1167. Subscriptions to The New Chaucer Society and information about the Society's activities should be directed to Susan Crane, Department of English, Rutgers University, 510 George Street, New Brunswick, NJ 08901-1167. Back issues of the journal may be ordered from The Ohio State University Press, 180 Pressey Hall, 1070 Carmack Road, Columbus, OH 43210; phone: 614-292-6930; fax: 614-292-2065.

Studies in the Age of Chaucer

Studies in the Age of Chaucer

Volume 21
1999

EDITOR

LARRY SCANLON

PUBLISHED ANNUALLY BY THE NEW CHAUCER SOCIETY

RUTGERS, THE STATE UNIVERSITY OF NEW JERSEY

The frontispiece design, showing the Pilgrims at the Tabard Inn, is adapted from the woodcut in Caxton's second edition of *The Canterbury Tales*.

ISBN 0933784–24–4

ISSN 0190–2407

CONTENTS

REVIEWS

Studies in the Age of Chaucer

THE PRESIDENTIAL ADDRESS
The New Chaucer Society
Eleventh International Congress
July 17–20, 1998
Université de Paris IV–Sorbonne
Paris

The Presidential Address

"Micrological Aggregates": Is the New Chaucer Society Speaking in Tongues?

Mary Carruthers
New York University

Off and on during the last two years I have worried over this occasion, required of the holder of this office: making a speech to a group of friends and colleagues all of whom have far more interesting and clever opinions about the meaning of Chaucer than I do, especially at this point in my life when I've changed my mind so often about what he might have meant. And so I have decided not to speak about the meaning of Chaucer, or indeed the meaning of any poets at all, but to talk instead about our society, the New Chaucer Society, and what it might possibly be up to now that we are rapidly approaching the 600th anniversary of Chaucer's death. I have no opinions to offer about what directions I think our research work in Chaucer studies, Middle English studies, or medieval studies should take. I think, in fact, that during the twenty-five years or so that the NCS has been in existence, published work in these areas, much of the best by members of this society, has flourished as rarely before. It has been diverse, imaginative, fruitful— open to all sorts of new subject matter, approaches, and themes and, compared especially to other work in the humanities, notably well argued and carefully presented. There is, it seems to me, nothing very wrong with the state of scholarship on the Middle Ages.

I want rather to talk about the New Chaucer Society in the context of teaching English literature generally, especially to undergraduates, and of what medieval English studies might bring to the humanities and to the social science spun out from literary study, that of linguistics. I do not speak of these matters as any sort of expert, but as a fellow citizen of the *polis* of academic literary study. This is a dangerous position to be in, but also a liberating one. As I prepared this talk, I realized how I too often have hidden behind and within my own certification as expert, as a learned observer of objects of study. I found myself wishing over and over again for some measurements to cite, somebody else's conclusions to quote. But doing that was an evasion of the problem I wanted to address, which is essentially a political one, because it has to do with our institutional place. A society made up entirely of experts is also one without the means or the will for self-governance, the sort of techie-dystopia science fiction so often depicts.

As is also customary in composing this genre of oratory, I looked back over the elegant addresses of my immediate predecessors in this office, Jill Mann and Del Kolve, to recall what they had talked about.[1] And what struck me was how both of these scholars had raised the specter of apostasy in their own relationship to Chaucer studies—Jill Mann in wondering how well a postmodern atheist could engage the mentality of a thoroughly Christian poet when to do so required a constant measure of personal hypocrisy, and Del Kolve in modulating that theme brilliantly into the motif of "God's fool." Apostasy is an abandonment of beliefs, and both these talks addressed the uneasy feeling that haunts many of us now, working as so many of us do in universities that have become in many respects public and private venture corporations governed to serve the immediate needs and interests of other corporations, private, state, and multinational. Must we not in some measure have deserted our beliefs in what we do when we continue to draw salaries from such a hostile academy, whose interests have been defined to elevate technology and exclude "the arts," except as the arts serve some corporation's dreams of "culture" and "values"? In our corporate academic culture now, the most pressing question the members of this society all face is surely this: why should anybody, other than for motives of simple sentimentality, continue to sponsor the teaching of Middle English literature, even including Chaucer? That is the question I want to explore today.

A major source of our disciplinary malaise is certainly the century-long academic "quarrel" between "philology" and "criticism," long since dead-ended. Literary criticism reigns supreme in Anglo-American de-

---

[1] Jill Mann, "Chaucer and Atheism," *SAC* 17 (1995): 5–19; V. A. Kolve, "God-Denying Fools and the Medieval 'Religion of Love,'" *SAC* 19 (1997): 3–59.

partments, even after "the death of theory," and now the heralded move (there's been a conference) "beyond the New Historicism." In many European universities the quarrel was enshrined in the separate departments of "language" (the medievalists) and "literature" (written works from the Renaissance on). This quarrel was from the beginning fundamentally flawed in conception, largely pointless and incoherent on both sides in its execution, and on balance more destructive than not of our field of study. We should not "return to philology," as some have suggested, because academic philology itself was always a flawed science.[2] And so was academic literary criticism. It was incoherent and destructive to have divided the study of literature and language from one another as this quarrel did. For we cannot study English literature without studying all those various Englishes written down in consciously crafted texts from many times and places. These varieties are completely embedded both in historical particularities and in cross-temporal social relationships of interpretation and practical use, from which they cannot and should not be abstracted.

Which brings me to my title, "Micrological Aggregates." I discovered this phrase in a letter of recommendation written on behalf of a distinguished professor of modern European literary theory. He was described as being a "real intellectual leader" among the "micrological aggregates" of his university. I was intrigued. The type of aggregate with which I was most familiar—having spent many years in a high-rise university building clearly constructed from substandard materials—was the gravel aggregate that is mixed with cement to make concrete. I used to be able to examine this material very closely as large chunks of it fell some twenty stories nearly every night to the sidewalk just by the entrance to my office. That aggregate was evidently macro-, but perhaps

[2] The call to return to philology was issued by Paul de Man; see Lee Patterson, "Return to Philology," in John van Engen, ed., *The Past and Future of Medieval Studies* (Notre Dame: University of Notre Dame Press, 1994), pp. 231–44. On the history in America of the philology-criticism quarrel (which, unlike me, Graff assumes was waged on valid grounds), see Gerald Graff, *Professing Literature: An Institutional History* (Chicago: University of Chicago Press, 1987), and more recently, Robert Scholes, *The Rise and Fall of English* (New Haven, Conn.: Yale University Press, 1998). On the late Renaissance conceptualization of "literature" as a separate category of value, wholly unlike "ordinary" language, see the interesting history by Timothy Reiss, *The Meaning of Literature* (Ithaca, N.Y.: Cornell University Press, 1992). In all these matters concerning the social valuations of a language and its literature, Erich Auerbach's *Literary Language and Its Public in Late Latin Antiquity and in the Middle Ages* (Princeton, N.J.: Princeton University Press, 1965) has much to teach us again.

"micrological aggregate" was used in buildings designed by academic architects for particularly refined literature departments, those specializing in the really exquisite aesthetic theories.

Or maybe a micrological aggregate was a group of people all of whom used only words of one or two syllables. The prospect of any academic group (let alone several on the same campus) being able to converse in such a fashion was truly astonishing—so much so that I instantly rejected this as a possible meaning for the phrase. Eventually I had to admit that I had no idea what a "micrological aggregate" could be, though from the context it ought to refer to a "clique." But if that were the case, the phrase should rather have been something like "logical microaggregates." I was very disappointed when I realized that the phrase simply fizzled, for what I had hoped might be wit turned out to be merely another case of modern pseudospeech, a pretense of technical precision wrapped in a phrase of bad Latin, a pretense of transparency that on closer inspection was only confusing—all the worst features of English technobabble, or rather "techno-Babel," a contemporary version of that tower built of and by micrological aggregates.

At about the same time I was happily distressing myself with this meditation, I was teaching Sir Philip Sidney's *The Defence of Poesy,* which ends, you remember, with a lengthy reflection on the merits of the English language and its then new literature. And to characterize the particular merit of English, Sidney contrasts it to other better-regarded European languages:

I know some will say [English] is a mingled language. And why not so much the better, taking the best of both the other? Another will say it wanteth grammar. Nay truly, it hath that praise, that it wants grammar: for grammar it might have, but it needs it not, being so easy in itself, and so void of those cumbersome differences of cases, genders, moods, and tenses, which I think was a piece of the Tower of Babylon's curse, that a man should be put to school to learn his mother-tongue.[3]

For Sidney, the world before Babel (and notice how, in the medieval manner, he has conflated Babel and Babylon) was a place of easy language, one without grammar (at least without inflections), all the earth's

[3] Sir Philip Sidney, *The Defence of Poesy,* ed. J. A. Van Dorsten (New York: Oxford University Press, 1966), pp. 72–73.

peoples using a single language of grace, of purity, of sense—using in fact a sort of English!

This dream of a single universal language—a "deep structure," as Noam Chomsky called it, into which all languages can be resolved—began as a late-medieval scholastic pursuit.[4] The *modistae* and speculative grammarians of Oxford and Paris thought of Latin as the exemplary language, and whereas Augustine believed that Adam and Eve spoke no known human language with God, the labors of the *modistae* helped to locate the universal language as Latin, a labor capped when some fifteenth-century humanists, Pietro Bembo for instance, made of Cicero the "universal writer." *Plus ça change* . . . Chomsky and other linguists have located the universal language as English—or at least implied as much, since they have seen no reason to employ evidence or examples from languages other than English. And Shakespeare has become so timeless and universal that he scarcely needs to be read at all (indeed, less and less as fewer and fewer people can understand his English). But his mere listing on a syllabus guarantees that a department is maintaining high standards of English.

Such universalist views are of course also transparently imperialist. We have all witnessed English-speakers in a foreign country trying to ask questions of the locals by speaking English to them very slowly and very loudly, obviously in the expectation that eventually some variety of Platonic reminiscence will occur, so they will abandon their own grammar and recall the "true" language. This characteristic is by no means peculiar to English imperialism—many of the Spanish missionary clergy, teaching the faith to the Indians of Mexico, catechized them in Spanish! Just this year, when the President from Beijing, Jiang Zemin, accepted the return of Hong Kong to the mainland, he spoke in Mandarin to his audience of Cantonese speakers: whether he also spoke loudly and slowly wasn't recorded in the accounts I read, but it was certainly an imperial gesture. And just a few years ago, during one of the more delightful hours I have ever spent in this grand city of Paris, a gentleman of a certain age explained to me in French, at length and with many examples, just how English, historically, is really a dialect of French!

[4] Chomsky's most succinct statement of this view is probably in his *Language and Mind,* enl. ed. (New York: Harcourt, Brace, 1972); see also M. A. K. Halliday, "Categories of the Theory of Grammar," *Word* 17 (1961): 241–92. On the *modistae,* see still especially G. L. Bursill-Hall, *Speculative Grammars of the Middle Ages* (The Hague: Mouton, 1971).

Et pourquoi pas? Indeed, I learned yesterday that the French minister of education, Claude Allegre, recently announced that English is not a foreign language in France.

Last year the British Council published a large, graphically handsome booklet called *The Future of English?* It was put together by something called The English Company at the commission of the British Council's "English 2000" project, under the patronage of Prince Charles. This publication stirred considerable interest in Britain and was even briefly noticed by the smaller (the "micrological") journals in the U.S. (where it is probably un-American to question the future of "our native tongue"). I would like to share with you some of the points made in this provocative and disquieting study.

For example, of the 6,000+ languages currently spoken in the world (many by a handful of living speakers), approximately five-sixths are likely to disappear within the next fifty years, and much of what linguistic diversity remains will be the direct result of institutionalized sponsorship, usually as a matter of politically supported concepts of national honor that have indissolubly linked "culture" to a particular form of "language" and seek to protect the one by preserving the other. Only five or six languages are predicted to be in use as regional linguae francae by large numbers of people, most likely including Chinese, Hindi/Urdu, Spanish, Arabic—and English.[5]

Who speaks English? There are three groups (of course there are three: this is a social science paper). These are "native speakers," for whom English is their first and very often only language (they live in countries that rarely encourage the acquisition of "foreign" tongues, except for specific purposes such as diplomacy, and even those are suspect); those for whom English is a second language (certain of the educated elite in India and Pakistan, for example); and those who acquire English as a foreign language in school—the EFL speakers. "Competence in English among second-language speakers, like that of EFL speakers," notes the British Council, "varies from native-like fluency to extremely poor"[6] (when I read this I wondered why the native speakers weren't also described as subject to a range of competency—clearly the linguists and I had different conceptions of "fluency"). Second-language speakers are distinguished from EFL speakers mainly by the fact that they live in

---

[5] See David Graddol and The English Company, *The Future of English?* (London: British Council, 1997), esp. pp. 12–13, 39, 59.
[6] Ibid., p. 11.

countries where English is sponsored for internal administration (for the time being at least, because the sponsorship that validates this situation is a historical result of colonialism, British and U.S.). The greatest increase and greatest change in numbers and sorts of English speakers will come among these two groups of speakers, the non-native speakers who now outnumber native speakers and will soon greatly outnumber them by some 3 or 4 to 1. English has become the official language of publication and conferences in the natural sciences, of international safety and security in airports and terminals, of international advertising, tourism, technology transfer, Internet communication, global organizations, banking and trade, TV, and international law. The English Company explains "why economic development encourages English":

1. Joint ventures (e.g. Sino-Swiss and German) tend to adopt English as their lingua franca, which promotes a local need for training in English.

2. Establishment of joint ventures requires legal documents and memoranda of understanding. International legal documents are written in English because there exists international consensus about the meanings of terms, obligations, and rights.

3. Joint ventures will in most cases be involved in international trade. . . . This will create a need for back-office workers, sales, and marketing staff with skills in English.[7]

"Skills in English." But what is this English in which one is supposed to acquire "skill"? It is not one language at all but the sociolects and technolects of institutionalized, corporate communications—simplistically "correct" in its syntax, limited and fixed in its lexicon.[8] No sort of change, of invention, is predicted in such skilled Englishes; instead, The English Company predicts an increasing number of what it calls "hybrid" Englishes, creoles, and pidgins found among the great diversity of EFL users. They also urge that British English, one among the world's Englishes, maintain its "brand name advantages" by keeping control over the production of EFL instructors and teaching materials. No-

---

[7] Ibid., p. 32.

[8] See H. G. Widdowson, "The Ownership of English," *TESOL Quarterly* 29 (1994): 377–89. In this 1993 plenary address to the TESOL Association, Widdowson stresses the obvious, but conveniently overlooked, point that all the new Englishes are a product of the wholly historical processes of language adaptation, and therefore that everybody and nobody "owns" English, most particularly not its native speakers, for English "is only international to the extent that it is not their language. It is not a possession which they lease out to others, while still retaining the freehold" (p. 385).

where—not even once—is the word *literature* mentioned. Apparently, as English takes over the globe, literature in English will remain incidental, even irrelevant to it.

But I read about this predicted future of English with an increasing sense of skepticism and disappointment. What was most striking to me was the obvious point that this was a document produced by linguists and other social scientists, and "educationists"—experts all, no doubt. It is theory-driven, even while it makes obeisances in the direction of language history: it thus cannot help flattening out its subject matter, dehistoricizing and departicularizing it (despite all its charts and numbers). It is thus in its way an expression of a certain kind of academic imperialism. The technolects of the English it describes take as their stylistic goals "transparency" and "clarity." Thus, it is concluded that English is now the language of international law *because* "there exists international consensus about the meaning of [its] terms," a consensus about syntax and lexicon hostile toward two of a living language's great inventive engines: translation and importation.[9]

It is a vision of English triumphant that reminds me very much of Jell-O®, a material artifact of American culture that many of you know well (certainly any of you who have ever eaten in the dining room at "Kalamazoo"). Jell-O® was a product of turn-of-the-century American academic domestic science and the "pure food" movement. It is completely a product of institutionally sponsored laboratories, made according to the theories of an enlightened and rationalized science, and foisted upon the public for their imagined betterment and/or convenience. Jell-O® was advertised as healthy and future-oriented, the basis of something called "perfection salad"; its development considered no known human palate and deliberately owed nothing to any human cuisine.[10] But it took minimal "skills" to prepare and always tasted exactly the same. It is a truly universal food, all calories, nothing to digest. Like

---

[9] Graddol, *The Future of English?*, p. 32.

[10] On the early history of granulated gelatin (made by the Knox Company) in salads, see Laura Shapiro, *Perfection Salad: Women and Cooking at the Turn of the Century* (1986; rpt. New York: North Point Press, 1995), esp. pp. 71–105. The original recipe for "perfection salad" (ca. 1900) called for finely chopped cabbage, celery, and red peppers in a clear aspic, but fruit-flavored gelatins soon swept the field in American scientific cooking. After World War II, "perfection salad" gave way to the classic 1950's molded vegetable salad: finely chopped celery, green peppers, and pineapple or tiny marshmallows, set in lime- or lemon-flavored gelatin and served in a leaf of iceberg lettuce. As Shapiro observes, "Salads that were nothing but a heap of raw ingredients in disarray plainly lacked cultivation"; molded gelatin made possible "a salad at last in control of itself" (pp. 98, 100).

Sidney's idealized English, it is easy and no one needs schooling in it. But it does come in slightly different flavors ("sociolects" of a sort) and can have different things mixed into it ("hybrids").

The Future of English? tries sporadically to be both particular and historical. It has a one-page summary of "The Seven Ages of English"— beginning with the Celts and the Romans.[11] I actually read over this bit twice before I realized what was so obviously wrong with it. This first "age" of English is labeled "pre-English" English, and the implication is clearly that Celtic and even Latin were really a sort of "English" too, but a sort spoken by people still befuddled by grammar and who mumbled their words. Certainly the Old English (an untranslated snatch of *Beowulf* is quoted as a sample) not only mumbled badly but also couldn't spell. After all of this I had much sympathy with my students who, when I cheerfully assure them "But it really is English" the first time they look at a passage of Chaucer, always fix me with a rightfully skeptical eye.

"The" English language posited by the evolutionary model charted on that page about "the seven ages of English"—and also in traditional academic philology—has never existed. There have always been many Englishes, none of them with a claim to primacy or ascendency that can be based on anything but localized custom and political will. A Chaucerian could only rejoice, I think, at the prospect of highly diverse, highly mixed and hybrid forms of Englishes—this after all describes the situation in England between at least 1100 and about 1450. A very fortunate decision (from my point of view) was made early on with respect to the pedagogy of Middle English texts when schoolbook editors did not "normalize" them to one dialect and time. But Old English was normalized in such a manner, with the result that nonexperts, students for instance, tend to think of it as a single ancestral form of English— its chimpanzee stage perhaps—from which it is a straight evolutionary shot to the completely normalized and standardized language of their contemporary printed books. A student of mine using the Burrow and Turville-Petre anthology of Middle English texts[12] wondered aloud at how "irrational" Middle English seemed to be when compared to the Old English texts he had studied—as he said, "Middle English has all

---

[11] Graddol, *The Future of English?*, p. 7.
[12] J. A. Burrow and Thorlac Turville-Petre, *A Book of Middle English,* 2d ed. (Oxford: Blackwell, 1996).

those dialects," and all those French words. Old English, he had learned, is clear, once you get the hang of it—Middle English is not and never can be. It is an evolutionary muddle, full of hybrids and wrong turns.

Except of course for Chaucer. And here I want to turn my main attention to my second opinion, that literary criticism as we have defined it in the academy is just as incoherent and hurtful to English as academic philology has been. I now believe that an exclusive focus on hermeneutics, on the "valid" interpretation of texts and how they express "values" (positive and negative), is doing those of us who teach literature more intellectual harm than good; and, I also believe, it guarantees our further marginalization and reduced social and political influence, both as medievalists and as members of humanities faculties.[13] Medievalists were probably the first to feel the chill of marginalization, from their very own colleagues allocating resources within their very own departments, who wondered aloud about the "relevance" of Chaucer and altered the curriculum accordingly. "Relevance," I need hardly tell you, is a judgment concerning value.

I do not think we medievalists do well politically (let alone intellectually) to try simply to climb aboard the cultural studies wagon: we have been and will always be the first to be pushed off, no matter how cleverly we disguise ourselves. But the canon debates woven into our colleagues' cultural studies have themselves now reached a state of frustrated exhaustion, at least in America. And we medievalists are in a particularly strong position to appreciate why and perhaps to help find a way out. There are intellectual advantages to having been marginalized first.

Members of this society, especially over the past two decades, have rewritten the history of Chaucer's canonization compellingly, coherently, and even eloquently. It is a sorry fact that so few of our colleagues in more modern periods—who assuredly teach the "survey of English literature" alongside us—have not seen fit to pay much attention to the implications of this work for their own canon debates, for (as we all know) Chaucer provides one of the most thorough-going, best documented, and precedent-setting instances of an author entering canonical status.[14] And this special place is signaled by the way in which his lan-

---

[13] *Valid* and *value* both derive ultimately, of course, from Latin *valeo.*

[14] So many Chaucerians have been part of telling this story, that I cannot single out any one individual *auctor,* but various works dating to the 1970s by Patricia Kean, Richard F. Green, John H. Fisher, Derek Pearsall, Elizabeth Salter, and Paul Strohm all come readily to mind. There are a great many others. For a very brief overview, see my review of Seth Lerer's *Chaucer and His Readers,* in *MP* 93 (1995–96): 375–78.

guage has been treated, both editorially and visually. The general conclusion is evident: Chaucer was made into "the father of English poetry,"
well after his death, as a deliberate act of national policy. He was suitably
"antiqued," becoming more and more old-fashioned and quaint-seeming
as knowledge of his English and with it his prosody recessed in time,
and thus he became the icon not of "old English" but of "old England."
This national identification was from the start the purpose of his canonization by Henry's court—not primarily as a model of style but as an
embodiment of national virtue. And that identification with mytholo-
gized national history is surely what enabled Sidney to overlook what
he called Chaucer's "great wants" in language, and encouraged as well
the modernized dress he acquired from Dryden, Pope, and (yes) John
Urry. Chaucer's value to the cultural ambitions of an imperial nation
was what saved him: it was never the purity of his English.

The fifteenth- and sixteenth-century canonization of Chaucer shows
with great clarity how the reference of "canonicity" had shifted since
antiquity from models of language to models of virtue. And despite all
our current sophistication about canon formations and re-formations,
Chaucer's "value" to us now (positive and negative) is still being argued
largely in terms of his worth as a cultural artifact. While I have sympathy with this position, and it has certainly led to much valuable work,
I am coming to think of it as insufficient to gain the sponsorship we
need, academic and general, to keep going. Simply being canonical, as
we all now know, is a curse more than a blessing in a world of many
Englishes. Thus, I do not think that worrying the issue of Chaucer's
place in the canon is a necessary or even a very helpful phenomenon any
longer. "Ye, baw for bokes!" says the emperor Trajan in *Piers Plowman*
(B.11.140). He makes a strong case. For canonizing books will not, I
think, suffice for our salvation.

When preparing this talk, I found, gently yellowing away on my
shelves, another report, this one prepared in 1978 by a U.S.-sponsored
Commission on the Humanities and called *The Humanities in American
Life*. It took a familiar American line, noting as a premise that "American society, among the world's most diverse in its cultural origins,
should cherish that diversity as a source of constantly renewed strength.
But there is danger in diversity when it is carried to extremes."[15] To

[15] Commission on the Humanities, *The Humanities in American Life* (Berkeley and Los Angeles: University of California Press, 1980). All quotations are from pages 10–11. "Common humanity" remains a prime justification for studying literature: see Sandra Gilbert's 1996 presidential address to the Modern Language Association, "Shadows of

13

effect a cure against the evil of *extreme diversity* (a concept, you must admit, that only a committee could have created), the report next called for redefining "the canon of classics" while continuing to maintain "high standards" in doing so, though, needless to say, no means to define such "standards" is identified. But there is no need to worry about that, for "[t]he humanities, by emphasizing our common humanity, contribute especially to the social purpose of learning—to education for civic participation." And then the usual history lessons are repeated:

No conception of the humanities is complete if it omits humanism as a civic ideal. In the European Renaissance many humanists connected learning with civic duty and decried what they took to be the pedantic, unworldly attitudes of medieval scholasticism. Since the Renaissance the connections between education and public life have multiplied.

It is very easy to take a dismissive view toward such pieties and such historically wrongheaded platitudes, but that would not get us very far. The myth of the medieval dystopia is too basic to formulations of "modern history" to be easily dispelled. Indeed, we medievalists have long been accustomed to having our work ignored and unread by the early modernist literary historians whom we particularly seek among our audiences. There is a reason for this studied, intransigent ignorance— utopias require dystopias for their definition. The "dream of a common language" and of a common rationalized "culture" needs its nightmares, its Babels and its Babylons, and what is "medieval" provides these. With respect to most of my modernist colleagues, even those who smile upon me kindly in department meetings, when I try to argue the intellectual value or benefit of studying medieval languages and cultures I might as well spit into the wind. I realized the futility of trying to dispel such willed ignorance some years ago when I attended a lecture by Carolyn Walker Bynum during which she gave her usual magisterial, witty presentation of some point in medieval resurrection theology, and was roundly chastised by a questioner in the audience because her presentation of medieval thought was too clear, too reasonable, too amusing. This questioner, who identified herself as "not a medievalist," liked "her" Middle Ages arbitrary, totalitarian, irrational, otherworldly, pedantic,

Futurity: The Literary Imagination, the MLA, and the Twenty-First Century," *PMLA* 112 (1997): 370–79.

and monstrous, and she told Bynum that she did not appreciate having this view messed with.

There is so much that is simply wrong with the humanist, "Renaissance" (sorry, "early modern") story that one hardly knows where to begin to correct it. But I am convinced by now that trying to dispel it with facts or alternative analyses, or trying to redraw the chronology of "the Renaissance" to include all awakenings of Culture (note the phrase) from the eighth century onward—these are not effective strategies of argument. Nor is an effort to analyze the phenomenon as an instance of the common psychology of "otherness." We are dealing not with expressions of human psychologies or human narratives subject to demonstration, but with a system of beliefs on the part of our colleagues that have the status of religious orthodoxy.[16] Postmodern academic critics are the people obsessed by literary canonization, after all, and by schools of dogma, orthodoxies and heterodoxies, disciplineships and apostasies. The High Modern inventors of literary criticism like Eliot and Leavis have been excoriated for using such words, but the language commonly used within the field of academic criticism continues to be the language of dogmatic religion. And yet we medievalists are the ones who are characterized as priest-ridden!

An essential flaw in the whole task of formulating literary canons, traditional or revised, is that it rests on an unchallenged assumption that things called "values" are located in literary works, and that one acquires "values" from them rather in the way one gets other sorts of "information." This is indeed a common fifteenth- and sixteenth-century humanist position. Cardinal Pietro Bembo, for instance, wanted to reform the basic reading curriculum ("the canon") by limiting it entirely to the works of Cicero.[17] In this fashion, the thought was, "pure" Latin style would of necessity be inculcated in every boy, rather like taking a daily Cicero pill against all vulgar influences, such as those coming from one's family and household. Ingesting Cicero brought not only eloquence but virtue, that is, "values."

---

[16] David Wallace, in *Chaucerian Polity: Absolutist Lineages and Associational Forms in England and Italy* (Stanford, Conn.: Stanford University Press, 1997), makes some cogent observations on the chief *auctores* of this modernist orthodoxy and its intimate enfolding within the greater dogma of individualism; see esp. pp. 54–62.

[17] See especially the correspondence of Bembo and Pico della Mirandola, translated in Izora Scott, *Controversies over the Imitation of Cicero in the Renaissance* (1910; rpt. Davis, Calif.: Hermagoras Press, 1991), 1: 22–23, 2: 1–18.

Grafting the doctrinal need for canonicity onto the syllabus of trivium authors was a task of humanism, not a belief shared by those "pedantic, unworldly" medieval scholars whose backwardness the Humanities Commission so deplored. In applying the metaphor of "canon" in this way, the early humanists were reviving a term used by their beloved Greeks for the authors whose works provided models of correct and elegant language and in this way added "value" to education. "Value" has to do with money and social standing, how other people judge one's "dignity" in relationship to things that matter to them. As such, values are socially and historically localized in much the way language is. It is only modern usage that has treated "value" as absolute and intrinsic, "timeless" even, and in this shift of meaning religion has played its large part. But we in English departments aid and abet this lexical deception by adopting without question the term "canon," and seeking to do little more than add or subtract names from a list. The purpose of making such lists in the first place is what is at issue, and that subject, it seems to me, has been too little considered in the various "canon" debates. As one contemporary critic has recently—astutely—observed, "it is unquestionably the case that the several recent crises of the literary canon . . . amount to a terminal crisis, more than sufficient evidence of the need to reconceptualize the object of literary study."[18]

A number of academic critics have proposed, as a solution to this crisis, revitalizing the conception of "the aesthetic" as the essential value of "literature" by freeing it from its identification with the tastes of particular social classes and from the "micrological" political agendas these imply.[19] Instead literary study would focus on issues of access through education to this universal value in literature. As one such critic writes, canon formation, in this utopia, would be seen as "a much larger part of social life, because not restricted to the institutions of the materially

[18] John Guillory, *Cultural Capital: The Problems of Literary Canon Formation* (Chicago: University of Chicago Press, 1993), p. 265.

[19] See, for example, Wendy Steiner, *The Scandal of Pleasure: Art in an Age of Fundamentalism* (Chicago: University of Chicago Press, 1995), and the essays in Stephen Regan, ed., *The Politics of Pleasure: Aesthetics and Cultural Theory* (Buckingham, England: Open University Press, 1992). I have no quarrel with "the aesthetic" as a value, so long as it is recognized as historically conditioned and indeed (re-)invented at discontinuous historical moments, now as a mainly post-Romantic aspect of Western individualism. There is, it seems to me, no really comparable "value" in medieval literatures; their operative values are derived from social and rhetorical categories constantly relating composer and text with an actively engaged, changing and changeable audience, and expressed in terms like *utor* and *fruor, delight* and *instruct*—and *sentence* and *solaas*.

16

advantaged." And, he concludes, "[i]n such a culture of universal access, canonical works could not be experienced as they so often are, as . . . proofs of class distinction." [20] But once again, some "universal" quality is taken as a good inherent in literature.

Moreover, "the aesthetic," like "the Renaissance" and "the literary canon," is a creation of modernism. I do not think it holds much promise for those of us seeking sponsorship (vitally including monetary support) for the continued teaching of English medieval literature. Finding Chaucer's (or Langland's or Gower's) "aesthetic" qualities will, I suspect, be as illusory and disappointing as finding his essential Englishness has proven to be.

The "values" that Chaucer has been said to teach are defined in so various and contradictory a manner that I don't see how anyone can— or should try to—claim universality (let alone "timelessness") for any of them. We are fortunate to have recorded responses to Chaucer's work over the period of six hundred years, and with that evidence it is impossible (I think) not to conclude that the "values" found in him are a barometer of his readers' opinions and beliefs and judgments rather than something "in" his works. A concept like "our common humanity" is as analytically mushy as is "our common language," and for most of the same reasons.

In my darker moments I recall the visit I once made to the literature department of a famous and exceptionally well endowed American technical university. Its lush campus was next to a famous library, it had beautiful, well-maintained buildings, a department small in numbers but lavishly appointed, all the latest technical equipment, new office furniture, a secretary assigned to every two faculty members. I asked about its political power on that campus, and of course the department had none. It dispensed "culture" and "values" to the young engineers, and all its money was assigned to it from the budgets of the science departments, all holders of multimillion dollar externally funded grants. The department was regarded by the university's corporate institutional sponsors (the U.S. government chiefly) as "resource-consuming," not "resource-generating." Its budgets could be modified or even withdrawn at any time, and there would be no recourse because it had no independent resources, political or monetary. The situation presented a great irony: a department charged with teaching cultural "values" but deemed

---

[20] Guillory, *Cultural Capital*, pp. 339–40.

by its own institution to have no value in itself. I thought of Tennessee Williams's Blanche Dubois: "I have always depended on the kindness of strangers."

So if, as I am arguing, medieval literature should not be included in the curriculum principally so that our students will learn the values all great literature teaches, and if it is, as I believe, distinctly *not* in our long-term interest to teach these poems for the sake of their (or our) "values" alone, is there still a way in which reading this literature can be seen to be "of value"? I seek an argument more compelling to our institutional sponsors than the obvious but, alas, trivial reply, "Yes, Chaucer is of value, because Chaucer is great stuff and some people, fit though few, will always love reading him." At one time, its admirers probably said that about the story of Wade and his boat.

Arguing over book lists is not an activity much valued either by our general university colleagues or by the professional, managerial, and technical general public—who are after all our basic sponsors. And yet learning to use English with true fluency, elegance, and imagination is highly valued by those same university colleagues and especially by that same public. I find it an extraordinary irony that at the very historical moment when mastering English—and not just wrestling it to the ground but commanding it flexibly, creatively, with wit—has such a high social, even commercial, value, so many university departments of English language and literature have cut themselves off from their legitimate share in teaching it.

We medievalists have been among the first to use new technology inventively and productively. Actually, in doing so we are imitating those we study, who throughout the long history of the Middle Ages explored new technologies successfully. This medieval tradition goes back at least to Cassiodorus's exploitation of the superior archival properties of parchment codices over papyrus rolls. Cassiodorus was also the man who coined the word *modernus*.[21] He didn't intend it as a compliment. There is no question in my mind that much of the most innovative and important work in medieval literary study—work that has done much to produce the "new Middle Ages" we've enjoyed shaping over the past quarter century—has come from material studies of manu-

---

[21] A spirited defense of Cassiodorus's technological judgments is in James J. O'Donnell, "The Pragmatics of the New: Trithemius, McLuhan, Cassiodorus," in Geoffrey Nunberg, ed., *The Future of the Book* (University of California Press, 1996), pp. 37–62.

scripts and early books, and the greatly sophisticated theorizing of editing procedures that these have enabled. This study has significantly profited from the sponsorship of academic computing specialists, who have found able partners among medievalists wanting to use computer technologies in just such research. We can see this as an instance of academic venture capitalism at work, wherein a wealthy, much more powerfully capitalized entity (computer science) sponsors the work of one weak and marginalized, but enterprising enough to deliver a great product to develop. And it has worked brilliantly—for now.

But I'm still looking for some practical "hook" that will persuade nonspecialists, our ultimate social and financial sponsors, of the ways in which medieval literary study itself, without intermediate patrons in the sciences and social sciences, can be "of value" to them. And so I come back to the subject of "the future of English."

It seems to me that, as a place to start, the essential argument needs to be made clearly that "English" has no academic future except in English departments. The necessary relationship of English literature to English language should be self-evident, but it obviously is not. I recently read, in a chatty article in the *Cambridge Alumni Magazine,* a glossy publication designed for corporate sponsors and important alumni, that "[i]t is easy to overestimate the extent to which literature shapes language." But the author hastens to add, "That said, the contributions of literature remain—and they influence culture in subtle ways. [For example,] until the era of European contact, Australian Aborigines had no written literature: communication was by language" and by gesture.[22] This author, an alumnus, evidently assumes it is reasonable to distinguish "language" from "literature" because language and literature are separate subjects. I don't mean to single out Cambridge here; the author could have learned this in any English department in the world.

What we teach of importance, I think, is neither values nor a material list of texts, but the crafts of reading and composing in English. And English is not a thing separate from those who write and speak it; it doesn't have "seven ages," like some slouching creature gradually but certainly evolving toward a linguistic uprightness commensurate with its "universal grammar." We've pursued for too long the chimera of adapting scientific methods to our subject, again and again searching

[22] Ross Clark, "Best of All Worlds," *CAM: Cambridge Alumni Magazine* (Lenten Term, 1998): 15.

for academic acceptance and sponsorship by seeking to demonstrate that we too are "theoretically rigorous"—at least we can establish a "method" that can be "universally" applied, like all good science. This too was a modernist dream. But we are not theoretically rigorous; we aren't even all that good at flabby theory. It isn't in the nature of what we do. Our theories dissolve almost instantly into the particularities of language and its interpretation—and they should. That is where our intellectual strength lies.[23]

So instead of modeling what we do on scientific methods, in a futile spirit of "we can do it too," we might ask ourselves what it is that *we* do. How *do* we in fact proceed in literary study that is different from what our scientific colleagues do? A place to start is the different way in which we use theory. The role of theory in natural science is predictive and normative. Theories and methods in our disciplines, however, are descriptive and useful when they account for particularities. In the words of one medieval historian, "[I]n history . . . our focus is on particular events or trends rather than on general laws. The events we deal with are not like the orbits of the planets . . . but are more like car accidents which, although totally in accord with the laws of physics, cannot be

---

[23] It is on this point, the practical particularities of making language craft the core of our undergraduate teaching, that I find recent analyses by academic literary critics most wanting and most silent. Neither Stanley Fish in *Professional Correctness: Literary Studies and Professional Change* (New York: Oxford University Press, 1997), nor Bill Readings in *The University in Ruins* (Cambridge, Mass.: Harvard University Press, 1997), put practical language mastery at the center of their critiques—Fish, self-defensively, argues that the pleasure of analytical reading is a wholly private one, and like virtue, its own reward (pp. 93–114); and Readings, more earnestly, calls for Thought as the basis of university pedagogy, which, being an activity and not a subject, will thus always be a problem to itself. Neither of these justifications, I suspect, will be widely understood by those outside the field wondering why literature should continue to be sponsored as a core university subject, though I hope, in calling for an emphasis on reading *crafts* (not skills), my proposal will not be judged inimical either to thought or to pleasure. Robert Scholes's *The Rise and Fall of English* is exceptional in that it does emphasize a new kind of reading-centered trivium at the core of secondary and undergraduate curricula, one that includes reading visual as well as verbal rhetorical texts. But all focus on imparting "values" of some kind as the ultimate, justifying reason for studying literature. It seems to me that this emphasis reflects yet again the imperial Roman hope, best articulated by Quintilian, that rhetorical study produced *vir bonus dicendi peritus*—that is (as humanists like Erasmus understood this aphorism), that studying literature made a man wise and good. Alas, English faculty are particularly well positioned to observe, on a daily basis, the fallacy of this idealistic belief. An engaging analysis of this matter is Richard A. Lanham, "The 'Q' Question," in his *The Electronic Word* (Chicago: University of Chicago Press, 1993), pp. 155–94.

predicted or deduced from such laws. . . . [They] require some particular *post factum* explanation[s]."[24] It would, I think, be very useful for undergraduates not only to know that theories play different roles in different disciplines, but to learn to respect the reasons why.

But continuing to confine ourselves to the uses of theory, even in multiple ways, will not take us far enough. In the United States at any rate—and as capitalist-inspired "privatization" takes hold internationally, this will be true in other countries also—we need to show some practical benefit to earn the kind of general, public support we require. After all, in an allegorical mnemonic we all here remember, that of Lady Philosophy's robe, *praxis* and *theoria* are related as clearly marked out stages, "like a staircase," Boethius observes—only the hands of violent men have ripped pieces of it away (book 1, prosa 1.18–24). You also recall that the Lady explains to Boethius how this destructive division of theory from practice was caused by the quarrels of a vulgar mob of scholars, each seeking his or her own interest (book 1, prosa 3.21–27).

I think the moment is right for us to think and speak again in terms of craft mastery as a governing model for how and what we teach in departments of literature. The model that now regulates us all in higher education is a competency one, based upon mass testing. It evidently derives from scientific method, because the "competency" it purports to measure is a reality ("the norm") that is a statistically created fiction. It works wonderfully for predicting the overall behavior of atoms in a particle accelerator or how many fruit flies in a jar will have white eyes. But for measuring whether a particular undergraduate, native speaker or not, has mastered English well enough to be able to analyze a simple sentence in one of Wordsworth's sonnets or to write a brief essay in ordered, coherent paragraphs, it is wholly, painfully inadequate. Nor can its inadequacies be corrected by adjusting the test—the very method is simply wrong. That is one thing we need to convey to our sponsors.

In a craft model of teaching language, as distinguished from a competency model, the function of literary works is quite straightforward, though it is also variable, flexible, and complex—highly particular. These works provide the materials and "hands-on experience" all apprentices need in order to begin to master their craft. Their importance

---

[24] S. H. Rigby, *English Society in the Later Middle Ages: Class, Status, and Gender* (London: Macmillan, 1995), pp. 13–14.

is not as canons of correctness but as matter for the imagination, furnishing the reading and thinking mind.[25]

The last several decades in American higher education have seen the withdrawal of the teaching of writing from the teaching of reading, to the point where, while some degree of composition craft is required of all students, an equivalent mastery of reading craft is not. One influential school of thought holds in fact that students of composition should not read literature at all, because literature will simply confuse and distract both students and teachers. Instead, students use as models only their own class-generated essays.

Yet we all know that reading and writing cannot be successfully taught in isolation from one another. As teachers of English we would never consider teaching our own departmental undergraduates to read literature without writing about it: the essay analyzing literary material is fundamental to how we teach the craft of reading in all its variety. And yet the majority of my department colleagues are perfectly happy to give over the task of teaching writing to other university units, regarding the composition courses as fit only for graduate assistants, adjuncts, and the common run of students (the laity, as it were). The result has been the great impoverishment and weakening of English and composition both, a failure, as economists would describe it, to make capital of our value.[26]

Yet the study of English has immense value. On this point everyone is agreed. So why can't English faculties, professors of "English Language and Literature," capitalize on this? For they must do so or they

[25] I have written extensively on the ethical and social valuation of literature in medieval cultures as "furnishing the mind" by giving it things and places to think with, both in *The Book of Memory* (Cambridge: Cambridge University Press, 1990) and in *The Craft of Thought: Meditation, Rhetoric, and the Making of Images, 400–1200* (Cambridge: Cambridge University Press, 1998).

[26] Many people both within and outside of composition and English have decried this situation. Two critiques helpful to me early on were Susan Miller, *Textual Carnivals: The Politics of Composition* (Carbondale: Southern Illinois University Press, 1991), and Mark Turner, *Reading Minds: The Study of English in the Age of Cognitive Science* (Princeton, N.J.: Princeton University Press, 1991). In addition, I was privileged to read in manuscript parts of John Guillory's fine analysis *Literary Study in the Age of the New Class* (Chicago: University of Chicago Press, forthcoming). Nothing substituted, however, for the decade and more I spent at the University of Illinois at Chicago, planning, implementing, and teaching in a three-headed Ph.D. program in English that attempted, with mixed success and many revisings, to marry up rhetoric and composition, language and literature, and creative writing.

will not survive. In considering how "value" is defined, we need to keep in mind an important distinction made long ago by Adam Smith, as follows:

The word VALUE, it is to be observed, has two different meanings, and sometimes expresses the utility of some particular object, and sometimes the power of purchasing other goods which the possession of that object conveys. The one may be called "value in use"; the other, "value in exchange." The things which have the greatest value in use have frequently little or no value in exchange; and on the contrary, those which have the greatest value in exchange have frequently little or no value in use.[27]

The example Smith gives is of water, than which "nothing is more useful," but it purchases very little; diamonds, however, have little value in use but considerable value in exchange. It should also be noticed that these valuations are relative: water can have great "exchange value" in a desert, and industrial diamonds have much use-value but little exchange-value. In these terms, English is accorded solely use-value now, except in some EFL situations; we need to find ways to give it exchange value as well, in the context of our institutions and the corporate publics they serve.[28]

It is time to stop pretending that English lacks a complex grammar and thus does not need to be studied by its native speakers; that English speakers are born with a built-in, God-given fluency not just in English

[27] Adam Smith, *An Inquiry into the Nature and Causes of the Wealth of Nations,* book 1, chapter 4 (quoted from the text published in the Irwin Paperback Classics in Economics series, Homewood, Ill.: R. D. Irwin, 1963). John Guillory discusses this distinction as the basis of his effort to define what he (following the French sociologist, Pierre Bourdieu) calls "cultural capital"; see his *Cultural Capital,* esp. pp. 298–340. In this discussion, however, Guillory confines himself to defining a value in literature (and so comes up with "the aesthetic"), rather than considering the function of literary study in the larger context of English language mastery, a limitation he has corrected in *Literary Study in the Age of the New Class.*
[28] A crude but telling example of how languages can lose and acquire "exchange value" came when the late, unlamented tyrant of Nigeria, General Sani Abacha, approached Jacques Chirac, the president of France, with a promise to make Nigeria "virtually overnight" into a bilingually Francophone country, rather than the bilingually Anglophone one its colonial and postcolonial history had actually produced. General Abacha apparently was angered by the failure of the U.S. and Britain to support him because of his abuses of human rights: he decided to go shopping for better sponsorship and to use French as his currency. See Howard W. French, "Lagos Journal; Nigeria Hangs Out a Banner: Ici on parle français," *New York Times,* May 4, 1998, Foreign Desk section.

but in "language" itself (whatever that is). The teaching of English needs to be reinvented as a particular craft that deals effectively with the immensely practical, publicly recognized need for mastery (not competency) in the arts of a new sort of trivium, that is, reading, reasoning, and writing in all forms of English, learned through all of its many literatures. As in the case of the trivium, these arts must be mastered together, not as separate and separable "skills" or (God help us) disciplines. And mastering the variety of reading craft—"grammar" in its original, broadest, and least disciplined sense—is the ground of it all.[29] It seems idiotic to stand in front of a group of English scholars to say so obvious, so basic a thing. But we must learn again how to articulate what we do persuasively to our institutions, in the face of now-entrenched skepticism and competition from other, better-connected divisions.

What can the New Chaucer Society do? Well, for one thing, we medievalists must be among the few people left in English who still understand both the intellectual power and the severe limitations of the old philology, and who therefore might be in a position to reinvent English as the study of language through literature. At least we know the difference between "English," the ever-various language, and "the English," people who have lived at various times in Britain. As medievalists we also can appreciate the presence of "hybrids" and "dialects" of English—in our period, there wasn't anything else. We don't mind Babel: in fact, that's not a bad way to describe the speaking and writing of English in thirteenth-, fourteenth-, and fifteenth-century Britain.

As medievalists we are also about the only people in our departments who can teach English as a subject imbedded in a particular, complex language. We can counter universalist notions about our language and its literature—the Jell-O® model—with our knowledge of its histories, its diversities and change, including the manifold "long histories" of its interpretation. And I remind you that the current mood in many countries is to engage what is particular, historically situated, and regional rather than what is "new" and universal. That desire in our students is often inchoate and crude, but we would be foolish to ignore it.

The first Chaucer Society was founded not as a talking group but for the purpose of sponsoring publications of materials relevant to Chaucer scholars. When it had published the Six-Text edition of Chaucer, it had

---

[29] I am, of course, alluding to *Piers Plowman* B.15.371.

essentially finished its business, and it left as we all have seen a material legacy of uniform printed and bound volumes. When this New Chaucer Society was formed in the late 1970s, its members evidently had a similar mission in mind, because it began as an off-shoot of the Variorum Chaucer project. Yet during the past two years, when I asked a number of you about the future of this society, not a single person to whom I spoke mentioned sponsoring publications (other than *Studies in the Age of Chaucer*) as its most important activity. Instead, its function as a forum for conversations has now become primary: we are a society of "logical microaggregates," of intellectual hybrids and various sociolects, and we clearly want our Society to stay that way. While I would like to see the New Chaucer Society members in their own various countries and institutions take an active role in reinventing English for our colleagues in ways that will gain us monetary sponsorship and broad intellectual alliances, and while I hope that this Society will continue to rethink the role of Chaucer and Middle English studies in the larger context of higher educational priorities and goals, I do not foresee us issuing position papers. Rather I would like the New Chaucer Society, as it can, to support various projects related directly to teaching; the identification and production of teaching materials including those for computer-based instruction; the continued support of young scholars; the continued growth of our multinational membership. We also need to recognize that, for the foreseeable future, fewer and fewer of us will be assigned annually to teach something called "the Chaucer course," or indeed much of anything specifically labeled "medieval literature," and we need to reinvent our pedagogy in light of this fact.

We might all remember that while the loss of a universal language through a confusion of multiple tongues was a sign of apostasy at Babel, one of the gifts of the Holy Spirit at Pentecost was the ability to speak in the languages "of all nations under heaven": Galileans, Parthians, Medes, Cretes, and Arabians (Acts 2:1–11). I wouldn't presume to say which type of multiglossia is at work among the aggregates who make up this Society, though I hope ours is a mark of grace. A good exegete looks for distinguishing features. Perhaps one way to judge is this: The confusion of Babel fell upon people engaged in building a tower transcending any that had been built before, all the way up to God. By contrast, when the apostles were filled with the Spirit, they ran down into the public streets speaking in human tongues. Evidently, in order to determine in which language to speak, they had first to listen to the speech of those with whom they wished to converse. I hope that we do not become immured in a cantankerous, bitter tower of our own making, but have enough conviction in what we are doing to run into our own institutional and public streets, and discuss what we do and why we do it with people other than just ourselves.

THE BIENNIAL CHAUCER LECTURE
The New Chaucer Society
Eleventh International Congress
July 17–20, 1998
Université de Paris IV–Sorbonne
Paris

The Biennial Chaucer Lecture

"And countrefete the speche of every man / He koude, whan he sholde telle a tale": Toward a Lapsarian Poetics for *The Canterbury Tales*

R. W. Hanning
Columbia University

A s I thought about how to begin these remarks, my mind was
repeatedly drawn to a famous line from the Proem to book 2 of *Troilus
and Criseyde:* "Myn auctour shal I folwen, if I konne."[1] This narratorial comment strikes me as apt because it describes as well as any few
words can my credo over thirty-five years of speaking and writing about
Chaucer—or, differently put, as a stand-up and sit-down Chaucerian—
although honesty requires me to add, in Pandar's voice, "By God, quod
he, I hoppe alwey byhynde" (*TC* 2.1107).

Such personal considerations aside, the notion of following one's *auctor,* if one can, matters to me—and perhaps I can make it matter to
you—because it embodies a thematic concern in much of Chaucer's poetry about the implications of "following," in two dialectically opposed
senses of that term, which might be paraphrased respectively as "taking

I wish to express my gratitude to the Trustees of the New Chaucer Society for inviting
me to give this lecture. I also wish to acknowledge the many Chaucerian and other
scholars from whose insights the following pages profit, and the accomplished research
assistance of three Columbia graduate students, Lisa Cooper, Nicole Rice, and Elizabeth
Weinstock. This lecture is dedicated to the memory of Howard H. Schless and Richard
Tristman. The quotation is from *The Manciple's Tale,* lines 134–35.

[1] *Troilus and Criseyde* [hereafter *TC*] 2.49. All references to Chaucer's text are from
Larry D. Benson, gen. ed., *The Riverside Chaucer,* 3d ed. (Boston: Houghton Mifflin,
1987). Subsequent references will be made parenthetically within the text.

after," i.e., imitating or living up to the challenge, and "coming after," i.e., in temporal sequence.

Central to my argument is that throughout his poetic career before *The Canterbury Tales*, "following" is an anxious situation for Chaucer, for two understandable reasons. One is that he is a "modern" poet engaged in translating and adapting illustrious predecessors, both ancient (such as Ovid, Vergil, or Boethius) and more recent (Dante, Petrarch, Boccaccio). The other is that he is composing and translating in an English vernacular still relatively without status in a culture where Latin dominates learned, and French courtly, discourse.

In *The Canterbury Tales*, however, this anxiety (which didn't stop Chaucer, to be sure, from adapting poets such as Dante and Ovid freely, even disrespectfully) appears to give way to a new perception that following is at least as much an opportunity as a problem. This change in outlook coincides, I believe, with the expansion of the poet's interest toward a major new type of belatedness, that which involves established discourses rather than established *auctores*.

The condition of inheriting established, authoritative discourses—a condition inevitably shared by all people—gives the legatee the chance, Chaucer realized, not simply to repeat them for purposes of communication or of adherence to the interests such discourses often represent, but rather to appropriate and manipulate them in one's social intercourse, for purposes of competition and negotiation.

This self-aggrandizing appropriation of established discourses, functioning in tandem with the telling of traditional stories adapted to competitive situations both "official" (Harry Bailly's contest) and "unofficial" (professional rivalries or personal animosities), constitutes what I call the ***social eloquence*** of Chaucer's Canterbury pilgrim *compaignye*.[2] *The Canterbury Tales*, I believe, represents Chaucer's model of a socially eloquent ad hoc polity, and as such it stands in both metaphoric and metonymic relation—and, I might add, in prudentially displaced rela-

---

[2] Bonnie Irwin, "What's in a Frame," *Oral Tradition* 10, no. 1 (1995): 46, notes that in frame-tale collections based in, or mimicking, oral-traditional tale telling, "narrators are always competing against each other or against the standards of a very demanding audience that holds the life of the narrator in its hands." The most famous instance of the latter type of competition is the situation of Scheherezade in *The Thousand and One Nights*; oddly (and, it would seem, inappropriately, given his role as judge rather than competitor), Harry Bailly recalls that situation when he promises the pilgrims whom he is organizing into a tale-telling competition, "But ye be myrie, I wol yeve yow myn heed!" (*GP* 782).

tion—to the world of political faction and economic competition which Chaucer experienced throughout his adult life, both within and outside London.

The competitive use of language, standing for social competition per se at the levels of both constituent and framing fictions, distinguishes the *Tales* from its most likely model, Boccaccio's *Decameron*. It's the contention of my remarks today that to depart from the *Decameron* in this way, the *Tales* had to receive the *centonovelle* through the mediation of John Gower's major poetry.

My argument is that Gower's trilingual *opera* offered Chaucer a prime example of the authority of the late-medieval European discourse of penance. Responding resistantly to Gower, Chaucer embodies his new understanding of the advantages of poetic belatedness (and of its partner in crime, linguistic instability) in a text that appropriates and subverts discourses of estates criticism and confession, both subdivisions of the overall discourse of penance, and both foundational for the *Tales*'s social eloquence and peculiar agonic cohesiveness. The fact that this Chaucerian poetic of social eloquence is at once influenced by and "fallen away" from Gower's penitential poetic doubly justifies my calling it, as I shall henceforth, *The Canterbury Tales*'s **lapsarian poetic.**

What follows are only a few points in a complex argument, and those treated more cursorily than I would like. After establishing the pre-Canterbury importance to Chaucer of the issue of poetic following, I'll consider a passage in the *Tales* that dramatizes a reorientation in the poet's view of belatedness, then sketch Gower's penitential poetic, and finally suggest a few of the ways in which the *Tales* responds creatively to the established discourses and outlooks mediated to him by Gower.[3]

Return with me first to line 49 of the Proem to book 2 of *Troilus and Criseyde*: "Myn auctour shal I folwen, if I konne." When the narrator says he will "follow" his *auctor,* he uses the verb in the double sense of translating "out of Latyn in my tonge" (line 14) and of doing justice in English, despite his own lack of amatory experience, to the love story told in Lollius's Latin original. This double meaning corresponds to

---

[3] For different assessments of the poetic relationship between Chaucer and Gower, see John H. Fisher, *John Gower: Moral Philosopher and Friend of Chaucer* (New York: New York University Press), ch. 5; Donald R. Howard, *The Idea of the Canterbury Tales* (Berkeley and Los Angeles: University of California Press, 1976), pp. 45–56; and the essays in Robert F. Yeager, ed., *Chaucer and Gower: Difference, Mutuality, Exchange* (Victoria, B.C.: University of Victoria, English Literary Studies, 1991).

definition 2b of *folwen* in the *Middle English Dictionary* (hereafter *MED*): "to be guided by (an authority), to translate (a book)."[4]

But when the narrator adds, "if I konne," he suggests the real possibility that he can't, or can't always do the job. That is, an acceptance of the status of follower opens into a poetics of anxiety and shortfall, haunted by the specter of an inadequacy or failure analogous to that expressed, however self-parodically, by Pandar, when he tells Criseyde, in the other line I quoted earlier, that he hops "alwey byhynde" in "loves daunce" (2.1106–7). This anxiety in fact frames the narrator's entire retelling of the story: in starting out, he describes himself as "the sorwful instrument, / That helpeth loveres, *as I kan,* to pleyne" (1.10–11), and in concluding he reaffirms both his task and his uncertainty about having fulfilled it: "But for that I to writen first bigan / Of his [i.e., Troilus's] love, I have seyd *as I kan*" (5.1768–69; emphases mine).

Ironically, a major obstacle to the narrator's following his *auctor* faithfully results from following him, as he must, temporally (as in *MED* definition 1b of "folwen"[5]), and especially at the distance in time that separates a classical *auctor* from a modern *actor.*[6] The narrator alludes to the effect of this temporal gap earlier in the Proem to book 2, in a passage traceable back through Dante's *Convivio* to Horace's *Ars poetica:* "Ye knowe ek that in forme of speche is chaunge / Withinne a thousand yeer, and wordes tho / That hadden pris, now wonder nyce and straunge / Us thinketh hem, and yet thei spake hem so, / And spedde as wel in love as men now do" (2.22–26).[7] To "come after" in time is to be hindered in "taking after" in poetry, thanks to the unstable, because inevitably

---

[4] *The Middle English Dictionary,* ed. Hans Kurath et al. (Ann Arbor: University of Michigan Press, 1954–), vol. F3, pp. 687–88. That Chaucer is also thinking of (and parodying) Dante's literally "following" Vergil through Hell and Purgatory is suggested by the opening lines of the legend of Dido in *The Legend of Good Women* [*LGW*]: "Glorye and honour, Virgil Mantoan, / Be to thy name! And I shal, as I can, / Folwe thy lanterne as thou gost byforn" (lines 924–26). (The "lanterne" reference recalls Statius's comparison, in *Purgatorio* 22.67–69, of Vergil, the pagan poet who led him to Christianity, to one who walks carrying a lantern behind him that lights the way for others, though not for himself.)

[5] Ibid.

[6] On the distinction between *auctor* and *actor,* see A. J. Minnis, *Medieval Theory of Authorship: Scholastic Literary Attitudes in the Later Middle Ages* (London: Scolar Press, 1984), pp. 26, 157.

[7] See Dante Alighieri, *Il Convivio,* ed. Maria Simonelli (Bologna: Pàtron, 1966), 1.5.8–9, 2.13.10; Horace, *Ars poetica,* ed. and trans. H. Rushton Fairclough, Loeb Classical Library (Cambridge, Mass.: Harvard University Press; London: William Heinemann, 1961), lines 60–72.

mutable, medium of language that links present to past. That very mutability puts the narrator's efforts, already in danger of falling short of their exemplar, at the further risk in the hands and mouths of those who follow *him*. Hence the new anxiety that intrudes on his valedictory prayer over his "litel boke":

> And for ther is so gret diversite
> In Englissh and in writyng of oure tonge,
> So prey I God that non myswrite the,
> Ne the mysmetre for defaute of tonge;
> And red wherso thow be, or elles songe,
> That thow be understonde, God I biseche! (5.1793–98)

Translation and transmission share a similar fate: to come after is either to fall short or to get it wrong.

I turn now to a moment in the *Tales* that provides a fictive etiology for a basic change in Chaucer's thinking about the implications of following. The introduction to *The Man of Law's Tale* offers an account of how a member of the pilgrim *compaignye*, faced with what R. A. Shoaf has called "the inexorable fact of belatedness,"[8] moves from a defensive posture of anxiety to the embrace of an oft-told tale (hence, one lacking both auctorial point of origin and cultural authority), which he subsequently ornaments eloquently, with embellishments appropriated from a variety of established discourses, in an aggressive strategy of poetic and social competition.[9] I believe it's no coincidence that only at this point in the *Tales* is Chaucer mentioned by name, by a pilgrim teller who must follow him—in the sense of coming after—but refuses to follow him—in the sense of taking after.

Ordered by the Host to tell a tale, the Man of Law begins to obsess about Chaucer as an impoverishing poetic predecessor. Both the Sergeant's self-described situation and the Chaucer he constructs to explain it recall the poet who worries about following (*MLH* 46–50):

---

[8] R. A. Shoaf, "'Unwemmed Custance': Circulation, Property, and Incest in the Man of Law's Tale," *Exemplaria* 2, no. 1 (1990): 298.

[9] I have more to say about this aspect of the Man of Law's performance in "Custance and Ciappelletto in the Middle of It All: Problems of Mediation in *The Man of Law's Tale* and *Decameron 1.1*," in Leonard Michael Koff and Brenda Deen Schildgen, eds., *The Decameron and the Canterbury Tales: New Essays on an Old Question* (Cranbury, N.J.: Associated University Presses, 1999 [forthcoming]).

> "I kan right now no thrifty tale seyn
> That Chaucer, thogh he kan but lewedly
> On metres and on rymyng craftily,
> Hath seyd hem in swich Englissh as he kan
> Of olde tyme. . . ."

But the Man of Law's subsequent remarks on the theme of belatedness mark an important shift of perspective (*MLH* 90–95):

> "But of my tale how shal I doon this day?
> Me were looth be likned, doutelees,
> To Muses that men clepe Pierides—
> *Methamorphosios* woot what I mene;
> But nathelees, I recche noght a bene
> Though I come after hym with hawebake."

In rapid succession, the crisis of having nothing new (or left) to say becomes a fear of being considered a mere imitator, then moves to a defiant readiness to "come after" Chaucer with inferior goods.

The key to this moment is the reference to the Pierides, nine daughters of Pierus who challenge the Muses to a singing contest in book 5 of Ovid's *Metamorphoses* and for their presumption are turned into magpies—birds who imitate human voices, but whose "hoarse garrulity [and] boundless passion for talk" lacks human art or intelligence.[10] (Dante cites this story in the *De vulgari eloquentia* to distinguish between birds who can imitate the sound of human voices and humans, who alone can use language as an instrument of communication and referentiality.[11]) But the Pierides are also figures of rivalrous subversion: in their competition with the Muses, they offend the goddesses by "ascribing undeserved honour to the giants, and belittling the deeds of the mighty gods."[12]

---

[10] "*rauca garrulitas studiumque inmane loquendi*"; Ovid, *Metamorphoses,* ed. Rudolph Ehwald, trans. Frank Justus Miller, Loeb Classical Library (Cambridge, Mass.: Harvard University Press, 1916; rpt., 1971), 5.678. When Minerva hears a magpie's voice, "she thought some human being spoke; but it was a bird" ["*hominemque putat Iove nata locutum; / ales erat*" (5.297–98)]. The contest is recounted in 5.294–678.

[11] See Dante Alighieri, *De vulgari eloquentia,* ed. and trans. Warman Welliver (Ravenna: Longo, n.d.), 1.2.35–44.

[12] "*Bella canit superum falsoque in honore gigantas / ponit et extenuat magnorum facta deorum*"; Ovid, *Metamorphoses,* 5.319–20.

By having the Man of Law evoke the Pierides, Chaucer suggests that all telling is retelling, and as such is forever open to the punishing judgment of being merely unintelligent imitation (a charge in fact often leveled in the past at Chaucer's Ovidian appropriations—or, in Rita Copeland's term, secondary translations—in *The Legend of Good Women*).[13]

As an alternative to imitating *auctores,* there is "coming after with hawebake," specifically, retelling a tale the Man of Law once heard from a merchant (*MLP* 131–33):

> I were right now of tales desolaat,
> Nere that a marchant, goon is many a yeere,
> Me taughte a tale, which that ye shal heere.

This merchant, who here replaces *auctors* or makers as the source of narrative fictions, has multiple significance for *The Canterbury Tales.* He represents its internal economy based on the competitive circulation (actually recirculation) of established stories and discourses. He dramatizes Chaucer's reception of new poetic models, and he stands for the *Tales*'s role in mediating important cultural concerns. I'll say a few words about each of these levels of significance.

It transpires that the Man of Law can't be faithful to his announced ban on retelling ("What sholde I tellen hem, syn they been tolde?" [*MLH* 56]), but in choosing what is clearly an oft-told tale—merchants were famous for circulating news, rumors, and stories as they circulated merchandise—he confirms his unwillingness to follow "Chaucer" as Chaucer has followed Ovid. That is, he abandons the anxiety-causing model of following an *auctor,* choosing instead to become part of a network of always already-told tales, a network of universal belatedness in which all are followers and imitators, but there is no *auctor* going before, only a merchant who told the last version, i.e., kept the tale in circulation.

Thus stripped of anxiety, "coming after" becomes the Man of Law's opportunity to engage in effective "Pieridean," i.e., imitative yet rivalrous, storytelling. In fact, in the world of stories without origins into which the Sergeant enters, all are at once imitators and innovators, Muses and magpies, or, as he in fact puts it, "Muses that men clepen

---

[13] See Rita Copeland, *Rhetoric, Hermeneutics, and Translation in the Middle Ages* (Cambridge: Cambridge University Press, 1991), pp. 93–95; and, on *LGW*, pp. 186–202.

Peirides."[14] And just as merchants, in their role as purveyors, transmit goods from maker to buyer for personal profit, so those, like the Man of Law, who retail (and retell) oft-told stories can be expected to deploy them for personal advantage, at least in situations like the tale-telling competition to which the Host has just summoned the Sergeant.

The means whereby the Man of Law seeks the profit of impressing his fellow pilgrims, as well as winning the free dinner at the Tabard, is to add narrational value to his inherited story by means of rhetorical heightening and ornamentation—like patched-in material on second-hand clothes—derived from established discourses such as those of astronomy, theology, and devotional pathos, as well as by highly selective quotation from—one might more accurately say vandalizing of—authoritative texts such as the *De miseria humanae conditionis* by the future Pope Innocent III.[15]

Such rhetorical variety and virtuosity are the traditional province of the lawyer, the master of forensic strategies. In this case the Sergeant undertakes to demonstrate that the trials of Custance, his saintly and much-imperiled heroine, offer evidence *for* rather than, as one might expect, *against* the justice of the divine providence in permitting her to be so severely tested.[16] But he also seeks to demonstrate, by his discursive appropriations and his affective manipulations of his audience, that he is a wise as well as an eloquent advocate, worthy of respect and reward.

The Man of Law's performance of the Custance tale suggests two ways in which the process of transmitting or mediating stories is not a neutral one. First, the narrative is inflected in the (re)telling in accord with the professional, ideological, or institutional concerns and outlook of the teller; and second, storytelling profits from the teller's having at his disposal a variety of always already-formulated discourses, not just stories, that he can lay under contribution without concern for their integrity,

[14] Helen Cooper has astutely observed that in the classical tradition "Pierides" was also a name given the "true" Muses, though she draws from this a conclusion somewhat different from my own; see *Oxford Guides to Chaucer:* The Canterbury Tales (Oxford: Oxford University Press, 1989), p. 123: "It seems to be an irony not lost on Chaucer that Muse and magpie share the same name, just as the true poet is the ventriloquist for the Man of Law as he declares himself capable of producing only the most miserable fare."

[15] See further Cooper, *Oxford Guides,* p. 128; as she puts it, "a large proportion of the Man of Law's Tale is devoted not to story but to comment, explanation, and rhetorical question."

[16] See, for example, Walter Scheps, "Chaucer's Man of Law and the Tale of Constance," *PMLA* 89 (1974): 285–95.

referentiality, or mutual compatibility. This is, of course, the world of Bakhtin's heteroglossia, a farrago of "social dialects, . . . professional jargons, generic languages, . . . tendentious languages, languages of the authorities, of various circles and passing fashions, languages that serve the specific sociopolitical purposes of the day, even of the hour." [17] To adapt the Sergeant's metaphor, he doesn't just come after Chaucer with the "hawebake" of a traditional story; he makes that hawebake more palatable—if arguably no more nutritious—by decorating it with the fruits of his belatedness, a belatedness he shares with all who live, move, and have their being in a universe of preexistent discourses.

But with opportunity comes moral dilemma: at what point does the self-interested appropriation of tales and discourses become reprehensible? At what point does imitation become fraud? The cultural ambiguities of belatedness are encapsulated in the word "countrefete," which in Chaucer's English, and in *The Canterbury Tales,* has connotations from positive to neutral to highly pejorative. [18] The practical dangers of counterfeiting are exemplified by Phebus's crow in *The Manciple's Tale,* often identified with the poet of the *Tales* because "countrefete the speche of every man / He koude, whan he sholde telle a tale" (*ManT* 134–35). As a figure of universal mimickry, the crow would seem to make a virtue of belatedness, but his gift causes him no end of trouble when he uses it to counterfeit inopportunely the song of the cuckoo—or, as William Askins suggests, a song in which human beings counterfeit the song of a cuckoo[19]—and to appropriate the Manciple's own discourse of plain speaking (actually nasty verbal abuse), a strategy that works with a drunken cook but not a cuckolded Phebus Apollo. [20]

Counterfeiting's threat to Christian faith itself underlies the villainy of Donegild, Custance's Northumbrian mother-in-law, who intercepts and counterfeits letters between King Alla on the battlefield and his constable, at home with Custance, in order to effect the banishment of

[17] M. M. Bakhtin, "Discourse in the Novel," in *The Dialogic Imagination,* ed. Michael Holquist, trans. Caryl Emerson and Michael Holquist (Austin: University of Texas Press, 1981), p. 263.

[18] See *Middle English Dictionary,* vol. C3, s.v. *countrefete,* pp. 657–59.

[19] See William Askins, "The Historical Setting of *The Manciple's Tale,*" SAC 7 (1985): 93 and n. 23.

[20] See further V. J. Scattergood, "The Manciple's Manner of Speaking," *Essays in Criticism* 24 (1974): 124–46; Louise Fradenburg, "The Manciple's Servant Tongue: Politics and Poetry in *The Canterbury Tales,*" ELH 52 (1985): 85–118; and, for a divergent perspective, John J. McGavin, "How Nasty is Phoebus's Crow," *ChauR* 21 (1987): 444–58.

Custance and her infant son. When Custance and Alla identify Donegild's phony messages as "Goddes Sonde"—meaning God's providence,
but also his messages and messengers—they not only show themselves
helpless against those who take advantage of their piety, but also embody, through the Man of Law's fiction, some of the tensions in Chaucer's
England surrounding the status of the clergy, and of the sacraments, as
"Goddes sonde," that is, the mediating instruments of his grace.[21]

The Man of Law claims to be following a merchant in his tale telling,
but in fact the tale of Custance is the only "Canterbury Tale" that has
equivalents in both Boccaccio's *Decameron* and Gower's *Confessio Amantis*.
More important than this fact is how *The Man of Law's Tale* renders each
of these writers present in its text, thus offering a clue to how Chaucer
has undertaken to "follow" them in his last major poem.

Gower is implicitly rebuked (whether teasingly or earnestly need not
concern us here) at two points that more or less frame the Man of Law's
effort: his introductory comments about incest stories refer to tales in
the *Confessio*,[22] and in the last movement, as it were, of his Custance

---

[21] Alla's response to the letter that falsely describes his newborn son as "a feendly
creature" (*MLT* 751) is to write in return, "Welcome the sonde of Christ for everemoore /
To me that am now lerned in his loore!" (lines 760–61); Custance, about to embark on
her banishment with her son, "nathelees . . . taketh in good entente / The wyl of Crist,
and knelynge on the stronde, / She seyde, 'Lord, ay welcome be thy sonde!'" (lines 824–
26). On the Wycliffite attack on the role of the clergy as necessary and exclusive mediators of the sacraments of penance and the Eucharist, see, e.g., the confession attributed
to Hawisia Moone in the heresy trials of the diocese of Norwich in 1430, in R. N. Swan-
son, trans., *Catholic England: Faith, Religion, and Observance before the Reformation* (Manchester and New York: Manchester University Press, 1993), pp. 270–73, and the analysis of Lollard beliefs in Anne Hudson, *The Premature Reformation* (Oxford: Clarendon
Press, 1987), ch. 6, "The Ideology of Reformation: (i) Theology," and ch. 7, "The Ideology of Reformation: (ii) Ecclesiology." But cf. Steven Justice, "Inquisition, Speech, and
Writing: A Case from Late Medieval Norwich," in Rita Copeland, ed., *Criticism and
Dissent in the Middle Ages* (Cambridge: Cambridge University Press, 1996), pp. 308–19,
for a caveat about Hudson's assumption that "the fractured and apparently random assertions [of Lollardy] found in vernacular treatises, episcopal registers, and first-person tes-
timonies can be shown to be a coherent and reasoned set of beliefs if they are fit to the
template of Wyclif's teaching" (p. 309).

[22] See the introduction to *The Man of Law's Tale* (*MLH* 77–89) on "thilke wikke en-
sample of Canacee, / That loved hir owene brother synfully" and "of Tyro Appollonius, /
How that the cursed kyng Antiochus / Birafte his doghter of hir maydenhede"; cf. John
Gower, *Confessio Amantis,* ed. G. C. Macaulay, vols. 2–3 of *The Complete Works of John
Gower* (Oxford: Clarendon Press, 1899–1902) 3.143 ff. (Canace and Macharius); 8.271
ff. (Apollonius of Tyre). The reference to Gower was first noted by Thomas Tyrwhitt in
his edition of Chaucer (1775–78); John H. Fisher, *John Gower,* p. 289, agrees with such
a reading, while Patricia Eberle, in the notes to *The Riverside Chaucer* (p. 856), is more
skeptical. Larry Scanlon, *Narrative, Authority, and Power: The Medieval Exemplum and the
Chaucerian Tradition* (Cambridge: Cambridge University Press, 1994), p. 247, reads the

version he takes issue with "som men" (that is, with Gower's telling of the story of Constance) over the decorum of King Alla's sending his young son to the Roman emperor as an messenger—once again, we note, the issue is one of appropriate mediation.[23] In addition, the troweled-on pathos of *The Man of Law's Tale* represents, in Hope Weissman's conclusive formulation, Chaucer's "magniloquent outdoing of Gower's pathetic heroine."[24] Finally, I can't help suspecting that the Sergeant's prologial lament over the "hateful harm, condicion of poverte" (*MLP* 99), appropriated from the *De miseria humanae conditionis* and linked most un-Innocently to a praise of rich merchants, may constitute Chaucer's tongue-in-cheek comment on Gower's traditional, moralizing praise of poverty in the *Mirour de l'Omme* as "a sort of commerce in which one cannot lose anything."[25]

By contrast, *The Man of Law's Tale* contains less judgmental borrowings from Boccaccio's *novelle* of Gostanza and Alatiel,[26] but more significant than these is the Sergeant's debt to a tale-carrying merchant for a story in which the heroine journeys from the Mediterranean to England along widely known Italian commercial routes. This situation seems to me to constitute Chaucer's sly acknowledgment of the influence of the *Decameron* on the trajectory of his poetic career, since Boccaccio's text may well have been purveyed to him by the Italian merchant

---

passage as a "playful" indication of "a significant difference between the two poets within their shared project" of using poetry as a medium for claiming lay moral and political authority: Chaucer proceeds indirectly and decorously, while a "taste for the lurid is only the more spectacular aspect of Gower's general predisposition toward explicitness." On the irony of the Sergeant's condemning tales of incest and proceeding to tell a tale the antecedents of which tell of a daughter's flight from her father's incestuous desires, see Carolyn Dinshaw, *Chaucer's Sexual Poetics* (Madison: University of Wisconsin Press, 1989), ch. 3.

[23] *MLT* 1086 ff. See Fisher, p. 292, for a similar interpretation, and Derek Pearsall, "The Gower Tradition," in A. J. Minnis, ed., *Gower's* Confessio Amantis: *Responses and Reassessments* (Cambridge: D. S. Brewer, 1983), p. 180, for a dissent.

[24] See Hope Weissman, "Late Gothic Pathos in *The Man of Law's Tale,*" *JMRS* 9, no. 1 (1979): 133–53, at p. 151.

[25] John Gower, *Mirour de l'Omme* [*The Mirror of Mankind*], trans. William Burton Wilson, rev. Nancy Wilson Van Baak (East Lansing, Mich.: Colleagues, 1992), p. 217: "celle Marchandie, / Don't perdre l'en ne porra mye"; John Gower, *Mirour de l'Omme,* lines 15865–66, in G. C. Macaulay, ed., *The French Works,* vol. 1 of *Complete Works.*

[26] On the reminiscences of these *novelle,* and a reference to Dioneo's choice of subject for the storytelling of the seventh day of the *Decameron* in the Sergeant's performance, see the essay "Custance and Ciappelletto in the Middle of It All," referred to in n. 8, above. See also the brief discussion of the parallels between *MLT* and *Dec* 5.2 (the *novella* of Gostanza) by Cooper, *Oxford Guides,* p. 128.

colony in London, whom he would have known through both family and professional connections. (As Vittore Branca has documented, the *Decameron* was particularly popular among Italian merchants, who circulated copies of it among themselves throughout Europe.[27])

The *novelle* that comprise the *Decameron* vary widely in their often parodic exploitation of the resources of Boccaccio's Italian vernacular: dialects, class-based argots, religious and political discourses, sexual euphemisms and doubles entendres. But while the one hundred stories express the aspirations, or disguise the problems, of *trecento* Florence, so perspicaciously analyzed by David Wallace,[28] the brigata of well-to-do young folk that tells them distances itself by laughter and aestheticized rituals of good living from both the turbulence and class tensions of many of its fictions, even as it has removed itself from the plague-ravaged city.

Chaucer transforms the *Decameron* by reconceiving the framing fiction at the same level of social competition that he found limned in many of the *novelle*. To this end, he broadened the complement of tale tellers to include a social range from gentry to lower artisans, and established rivalries between them based on estate, that is, on profession, rank, or social status. The Canterbury pilgrims express these rivalries in the tales they tell and in the discourses of complaint and satire which they deploy against each other, not only in the tales but in the interstitial confrontations for which *The Canterbury Tales* is justly famous. And now it is time for me to explain further my contention that Gower's penitential poetic is, in a sense, the poetic midwife bringing the *Tales* to birth out of *Decameron*.

It is not, however, the time or place, nor am I the person, to offer a thorough consideration of the doctrinal bases or cultural implications of penance. I will simply call your attention to a few points salient to my argument. The doctrine of penance is constructed on the assumption that each human being recapitulates in his or her life the original fall of humanity, and can, through proper use of the sacrament of penance,

---

[27] On Chaucer's probable familiarity with Italian through contacts with the Italian merchant colony of London, see Howard Schless, "Transformations: Chaucer's Use of Italian," in Derek Brewer, ed., *Geoffrey Chaucer: Writers and Their Background* (Athens: Ohio University Press, 1975), pp. 190–96. On the diffusion of the *Decameron* via the network of Italian commerce, see Branca, *Boccaccio medievale* (Florence: Sansoni, 1956), ch. 1, "Tradizione medievale."

[28] See David Wallace, *Boccaccio's* Decameron, Landmarks of World Literature (Cambridge: Cambridge University Press, 1991), passim; *Chaucerian Polity: Absolutist Lineages and Associational Forms in England and Italy* (Stanford, Conn.: Stanford University Press, 1997), chs. 1, 2, 6, and 10, passim.

individually enjoy the redeeming grace made collectively available to humanity by the sacrifice of Christ. As formulated by theologians during the twelfth century, the core of the sacrament consisted in a three-stage movement from contrition, through confession, to satisfaction (the performance of compensatory prayers or works assigned by the priest confessor). According to its most usual explication, the efficacy of the sacrament depended on an absolute accord between thought, word and deed, that is, between exhaustive self-scrutiny and genuine contrition for all sins thereby uncovered; full and accurate disclosure of the sins in confession; and complete and willing performance of the assigned penance.[29]

In mandating annual confession for all Catholic Christians, the twenty-first canon of the Fourth Lateran Council also required of confessors that they "carefully inquire about the circumstances of both the sinner and the sin" [*diligenter inquirens et peccatoris circumstantias et peccati*]. In confessional theory and practice, the rhetorical concept of *circumstantiae* came to mean that members of particular estates, professions, or ranks (and, for women, genders) should be especially examined for the sins to which their respective groups were susceptible (e.g., merchants and avarice, nobles and pride, courtiers and envy, women and vanity or lechery).[30]

---

[29] On the development of the theology of penance see Paul Anciaux, *La théologie du sacrament de penitence au xiie siècle* (Louvain: Nauwelaerts, 1949); Amadée Teetaert, *La confession aux laïques dans l'église latine depuis le VIIIe jusqu'au XIVe siècle* (Paris: Gabalda, 1926); Paul F. Palmer, *Sacraments and Forgiveness: History and Doctrinal Development of Penance, Extreme Unction, and Indulgences* (Westminster, Md.: Newman, 1959). Major twelfth-century discussions include Hugh of Saint Victor, *De sacramentis*, trans. Roy J. Deferrari (*On the Sacraments of the Christian Faith* [Cambridge, Mass.: Medieval Academy, 1951]), pt. 14, "On Confession," pp. 401–30; Peter Lombard, *Sententiae in IV libri distinctae*, ed. Collegium Sancti Bonaventurae (Grottaferrata: Collegium S. Bonaventurae ad Claras Aquas, 1971–81), book 4, dist. 14–22; pseudo-Augustine, *De vera et falsa penitentia*, PL 40, cols. 1113–30. After the Fourth Lateran Council, there was a flood of manuals and legislation concerning penance, on which see Leonard Boyle, O.P., "The Fourth Lateran Council and Manuals of Popular Theology," and Judith Shaw, "The Influence of Canonical and Episcopal Reform on Popular Books of Instruction," both in Thomas J. Heffernan, ed., *The Popular Literature of Medieval England* (Knoxville: University of Tennessee Press, 1985), pp. 30–43, 44–60. One of the most influential post-Lateran IV compendia on the theology of penance was Raymond of Pennaforte, *Summa casuum poenitentiae* (1222–29), an ultimate source for parts of *The Parson's Tale*.

[30] Canon 21, quoted from Norman P. Tanner, S.J., ed., *Decrees of the Ecumenical Councils. Volume One: Nicaea I to Lateran V* (Washington, D.C.: Georgetown University Press, 1990), p. 245. On the *circumstantiae*, see Johannes Gründel, *Die Lehre von den Umständen der menschlichen Handlung im Mittelalter* (Muenster: Aschendorf, 1963); D. W. Robertson Jr., "A Note on the Classical Origin of 'Circumstances' in the Medieval Confessional," *SP* 43 (1946): 6–14, and "The Cultural Tradition of *Handlyng Synne*," *Speculum* 22 (1947): 162–85, esp. pp. 172 ff.; on how the "who" of the *circumstantiae*—the categories were *who, what, where, by what means, why, how,* and *when,* and sometimes *with whose help*—

In addition to mediating the sacrament of penance as skillful confessors, the clergy were also assigned the task—for which many were poorly trained—of mediating to the laity, through preaching, the information about the categories of sin and the procedures of repentance deemed essential for making a proper confession. This preaching office, buttressed by ecclesiastical legislation that set the clergy apart from the laity in dress and behavior, constructed for late-medieval Europe an authoritative, quasi-prophetic voice thundering, as if from above or outside the human condition, against fallen humanity in its varied, estate-defined manifestations.[31]

As Colin Morris has put it, "the new [penitential] discipline was both an individual one which required all adults to answer for their personal sins, and a recognition of the variety of social ranks into which the population, especially in cities, was now divided."[32] Accordingly, aspects of penitential theory and practice came to underlie a highly influential late-medieval social model, which proposes as an ideal the harmonious accord between the different parts of the polity, identified as clearly demarcated and stably, hierarchically interconnected estates. Conversely, this paradigm tends to present actual, dynamic social relations—for example, political faction or commercial competition—as culpable instances of discord, resulting from fallen humanity's sinfulness. The remedy for such discord is individual repentance, through which a prelapsarian state of social harmony can be recuperated.

The penance-based discourse of social analysis passed from preaching into texts of complaint and estates satire, the admonitory, prophetic voice of which bewails the sins of the times, usually group by group,

---

came to "express the social dimension [of the penitent] more explicitly"; see John Baldwin, *Masters, Princes, and Merchants: The Social Views of Peter the Chanter and His Circle*, 2 vols. (Princeton, N.J.: Princeton University Press, 1970), 1: 49–59 (quotation from p. 56); and W. A. Pantin, *The English Church in the Fourteenth Century* (Cambridge: Cambridge University Press, 1955), p. 206 ff. For the failings attributed to the "status" of woman, see Mary Flowers Braswell, "Sin, the Lady, and the Law: The English Noblewoman in the Late Middle Ages," *M&H*, n.s., 14 (1986): 81–101.

[31] See Thomas J. Heffernan, "Sermon Literature," in A. S. G. Edwards, ed., *Middle English Prose: A Critical Guide to Major Authors and Genres* (New Brunswick, N.J.: Rutgers University Press, 1984), pp. 177–207; Roberto Rusconi, "De la prédication à la confession: Transmission et controle de modèles de comportement au XIIIe siècle," in André Vauchez, ed., *Faire croire: Modalités de la diffusion et de la reception des messages religieux du XIIe au XVe siècle* (Rome: Ecole française de Rome, 1981), pp. 67–85; H. Leith Spencer, *English Preaching in the Late Middle Ages* (Oxford: Clarendon Press, 1993), ch. 5, "The Preaching of *Pastoralia*"; and for texts of preaching manuals, Th.-M. Charland, O.P., *Artes praedicandi: Contribution à l'histoire de la rhetorique au moyen âge* (Paris: Vrin, 1936), pt. 3 (editions of preaching manuals by Robert of Basevorn and Thomas Waleys).

[32] Colin Morris, *The Papal Monarchy* (Oxford: Clarendon Press, 1989), p. 493.

and adduces the final judgment as a warning to the errant that they repent before it is too late.[33] And both the voice and the perspective of the traditions of complaint and satire achieve full, and repeated, articulation in the major poetry of John Gower. Much recent Gower scholarship, operating in accord with cultural studies paradigms, has achieved an understanding of Gower's cultural positioning, political agenda, and poetic accomplishment more complex (and thus more just) than that which obtained among earlier students of medieval English literature. In what follows I have no intention of denigrating or disputing such insights; my sole concern is to provide a brief account of aspects of Gower's poetry relevant to my argument here, as I believe they registered with Chaucer.[34]

The *Mirour de l'Omme* and *Vox Clamantis* focus on the structure of social relations and the state of the body politic obtaining in Gower's England, but very much through a penitential lens. The tropological relationship of personal sin and repentance to humanity's fall and redemption defines the structure of the *Mirour,* the earliest of Gower's three major works. Its opening, historical account of the fall of Lucifer and of Adam and Eve serves as preface to an allegorical retelling, based on penitential preaching and confession manuals, in which the World's marriage to the seven daughters of Sin and Death (i.e., the Seven Deadly Sins) leads to catastrophe for humanity, despite the Soul's temporary establishment of control over the Flesh with the aid of Reason and the Fear of Death.[35] And although the Passion, Death, and Resurrection of Christ together constitute the central Christian mystery, they are displaced from the structural center of the *Mirour,* their place taken by an account of the proper form of contrition, confession, and satisfaction.[36]

In book 1 of *Vox Clamantis,* Gower's account of the Great Rising of

---

[33] See John D. Peter, *Complaint and Satire in Early English Literature* (Oxford: Clarendon Press, 1956), and Jill Mann, *Chaucer and Medieval Estates Satire* (Cambridge: Cambridge University Press, 1973).

[34] On Gower see, e.g., Minnis, ed., *Gower's* Confessio Amantis; R. F. Yeager, ed., *John Gower: Recent Readings* (Kalamazoo, Mich.: Medieval Institute Publications, 1984); Yeager, *John Gower's Poetic: The Search for a New Arion* (Cambridge: D. S. Brewer, 1990); Yeager, ed., *Chaucer and Gower;* Larry Scanlon, *Narrative, Authority, and Power,* ch. 9, "Bad Examples: Gower's *Confessio Amantis*"; Judith Ferster, *Fictions of Advice: The Literature and Politics of Counsel in Late Medieval England* (Philadelphia: University of Pennsylvania Press, 1996), ch. 7, "O Political Gower."

[35] *Mirour* 49–187 (fall of Lucifer and of Adam and Eve); 193–276 (birth of Seven Deadly Sins); 529–750 (the soul separates the flesh from the Devil's control with the aid of reason and fear); 841 ff. (the marriage of the World to the Seven Deadly Sins).

[36] *Mirour* 14797–15096.

1381 analogously displaces contemporary history into a double allegory by describing the rebels as domestic animals transformed into wild beasts, a technique recalling the allegorical representation of the Seven Deadly Sins as animals in many post-Lateran IV treatises.[37] At the end of book 1, a wise old man tells the terrified narrator—Gower in conversation with himself, as it were—that the inhabitants of the island of Britain are always at strife, "yet I do not think there is a worthier people under the sun, if there were mutual love among them."[38] The lesson drawn from the Rising is thoroughly penitential: wrath transforms men into beasts; and the key to solving England's social and political problems is the remediation of anger by *caritas*—again a reflection of the pairing, in confession manuals, of capital sins and their countervailing *remedia*.[39]

The same binary governs the opposite end of the *Vox Clamantis,* a "*Cronica tripertita*" recounting the deposition of Richard II (and thus a text doubtless not known to Chaucer). The *Cronica's* prefatory verses label its three parts as, respectively, the work of humanity (*opus humanum*), of hell (*opus inferni*), and in Christ (*opus in Christo*). Gower's marginal gloss explains that it is "the work of humanity to pursue and seek out peace, . . . the work of hell to disturb peace and slay a kingdom's just men, . . . [and] the work done in Christ to depose haughty men from the throne and exalt the humble." And the text proper asserts that the attentive reader will learn from this account "what love is, and what wrath is, and finally [that] 'love conquers all things.'"[40] History travels along a trajectory of fall and redemption, and offers to the Christian exempla of deadly sins and their remedies.

[37] See John Gower, *Vox Clamantis,* in Macauley, ed., *The Latin Works,* vol. 4 of *Complete Works,* bk. 1, chs. 2–8; on the Seven Deadly Sins as animals, see Morton W. Bloomfield, *The Seven Deadly Sins* (East Lansing: Michigan State University Press, 1952; rpt., 1967), *passim,* and appendix 1, "The Association of Animals and Sins," pp. 245–49. For an instance, see pt. 4 of *Ancrene Wisse* (ca. 1225), a text whose wide diffusion suggests Gower's knowledge of it.

[38] *Vox,* bk. 1, ch. 20; trans. Eric W. Stockton, in *The Major Latin Works of John Gower* (Seattle: University of Washington Press, 1962), p. 92. The Latin reads, "*Non magis esse probos ad finem solis ab ortu / Estimo, si populi mutuus esset amor*" (1.1980–82).

[39] On the Seven Deadly Sins and their remedies, see, e.g., the apposite section of *The Parson's Tale* in *CT* (line 387 ff.), in which the description of each sin is followed by a subsection headed, "*Remedium contra*" that sin.

[40] See *Major Latin Works,* p. 289. The Latin reads, "*Opus humanum est inquirere pacem et persequi eum. . . . Opus inferni est pacem turbare, iustisque regni interficere. . . . Opus in Cristo est deponere superbos de sede et exaltare humiles*"; "*Vir qui bene sentit in isto / Scire potest mira, quid amor sit, quid sit et ira: / Est tamen hoc clamor, 'Omnia vincit Amor'*" (p. 314).

In both *Mirour* and *Vox,* sacred and secular history are marginalized, placed at the outer edges of the text. The center is claimed by the penitential discourse of sins and remedies, as we've seen, but also by the estates discourse that castigates the characteristic shortcomings of each vocational and occupational group, thus underscoring the link between personal sinfulness and the social disharmony present in the polity at each level from the sovereign on down.[41] (In the *Confessio,* an estates analysis precedes the establishment of confession as itself the framing fiction of Gower's English tale-collection.[42])

The fall of humanity from Eden—the ultimate basis of penitential theology—underlies Gower's formulation of estates criticism as a past-present binary. In the prelapsarian state, Gower explains in the Prologue to the *Confessio,* perfect accord between thought, word, and deed—the foundation, we recall, of the sacrament of penance—obtained at personal and social levels (lines 106–14):

> The cites knewen no debat,
> The peple stod in obeisance
> Under the reule of governance,
> And pes, which ryhtwisnesse keste,
> With charite tho stod in reste:
> Of mannes herte the corage
> Was schewed thanne in the visage;
> The word was lich to the conceite
> Withoute semblant of deceite."

The "divisioun" that now characterizes relations between estates of the realm and also between body and soul began in Paradise (line 991 ff.) and can only be ended by personal repentance, since "Senne of his condicioun, / Is moder of divisioun / And tokne whan the world schal faile" (lines 1029–31); if love and reconciliation do not come soon, a terrible final judgment is in store for all.

Gower's nostalgic narrative of social deterioration—which is indebted to classical "golden age" topoi as well as to penitential thought and preaching—attempts no analysis of the process by which an estate falls into collective error. Instead, in *Vox* and *Confessio* he borrows from

---

[41] See *Mirour* 18, 412–26, 604; *Vox,* bks. 3–6, ch. 7.
[42] See *Confessio,* Prol. 93–519.

the Book of Daniel its powerful and authoritative image of universal decline: Nebuchadnezzar's dream of a statue whose constituent body parts descend from head of gold through increasingly base materials to feet of steel and clay.[43] On the other hand, in all three of his major texts Gower rejects the idea that God or fortune is responsible for universal decline—an idea in fact implicit in the Danielic dream—by insisting that human sin is responsible for the sad state of both the political and the natural world, since humanity is the crucial microcosm: "and thus stant al the worldes werk / After the disposicioun / Of man and his condicioun" (*Confessio* Prol. 942–44).[44]

As the title of his Latin text *Vox Clamantis* suggests, Gower casts himself in the role of a famous namesake, John the Baptist, by calling for repentance and warning of the coming judgment. This prophetic voice, derived more immediately from the preaching voice of the post-Lateran IV clergy,[45] appears to originate from a position of moral superiority and omniscience. As Patricia Eberle has noted, Gower "presents himself, and by implication invites the audience to identify with him, as removed from the corrupt world he is attacking"; she calls attention to the poet's self-portrayal, in a headnote included in several manuscripts of the *Vox*, as "an archer, standing somewhere in space and aiming his shafts at the world."[46] But in an instance of rhetorical strategy triumphing over logical consistency, Gower also, in Steven Justice's words, "imagines himself a prophet who declares a consensus of the realm"[47] when he appeals for authority to the "common vois" and insists that he not be held responsible for the judgments he makes on the estates of the realm, since he merely echoes the *vox populi*.[48]

---

[43] For Nebuchadnezzar's dream, see Daniel 2: 31–45. Cf. *Vox,* bk. 7, chs. 1–4; *Confessio* Prol. 585–880.

[44] Cf. *Mirour* 26605–7360; *Vox,* bk. 7, chs. 5–8.

[45] See, e.g., Thomas Wimbledon's sermon, *"Redde rationem villicationis tue"* (1388?), addressed to the errant estates of the realm. The sermon has been edited by Ione Kemp Knight (Pittsburgh: Duquesne University Press, 1967).

[46] Patricia Eberle, "Commercial Language and the Commercial Outlook in the *General Prologue,*" *ChauR* 18, no. 2 (1983): 167. See the illustration of this rubric in BL MS Cotton Tiberius A.4, fol. 9, showing the poet taking aim with bow and arrow at a world divided into three parts, somewhat as in a medieval *mappa mundi,* but here representing the three estates. This image is reproduced opposite the title page of vol. 4 of the *Complete Works.*

[47] Steven Justice, *Writing and Rebellion: England in 1381* (Berkeley and Los Angeles: University of California Press, 1994), p. 209.

[48] See Stockton's note to *Vox,* 3.Prol. 11–13 (*Major Latin Works,* p. 386) which reproduces, with additions, Macaulay's list of the passages in *Mirour* and *Vox* where Gower

I have already agreed with those who argue that Gower is present as an object of parody or disagreement in the Man of Law's performance. He figures similarly in several other tales, including *The Wife of Bath's Tale,* which, in "following" the "Tale of Florent" from the *Confessio,* adds an initial, brutal rape derived (minus Gower's sadistic tone) from *Mirour,* where it is included in the description of virginity as a *remedium* to the sin of rape: ". . . the strength of a feeble woman (whether she be right or wrong) cannot resist a strong man, and she must suffer without mercy his delight and his pleasure if he succeeds in finding her alone."[49] Moreover, Gower's appeal to the "common vois" to justify his estates criticism, which Anne Middleton has identified as a component of a new Ricardian "public poetry," seems to me to have struck Chaucer as something closer to a self-exculpatory ploy, which he sends up via a number of dubious narratorial apologies, such as the Nun's Priest's comic attempt to avoid the consequences of his mysogynistic statements by claiming, "Thise been the cokkes wordes, and nat myne," or the narrator's famous caveat to his page-turning readership, "Blameth nat me if that ye chese amys."[50]

In responding more specifically to Gower's penitential poetic, Chaucer first (to borrow a term from Teodolinda Barolini's Dante criticism[51]) detheologizes social time, substituting for the Edenic-then/fallen-now binary of Gower's estates criticism the entirely contingent then/now of the Chaucerian narrator: "then" is the period of some days in an April of the indefinite past during which he went on pilgrimage as one of thirty "sondry folk"; "now" is the equally indefinite present, during the "time and space" of which he will recount the tales told "then" as well as the "condicioun" and the behavior of those who told them (*GP* 1–42). Furthermore, the narrator faces the same problems *then* and *now:* on the pilgrimage, he had to deal with having his first attempt at tale telling rudely interrupted by the Host; as he recreates the pilgrimage, he

---

describes his estates satire as a reproduction of the *vox populi* or what *"l'en dist communement"* (*Mirour* 19057).

[49] *Mirour* 16945–50; "La femme fieble a l'omme fort, / Ou soit a droit ou soit a tort, / Sa force ne puet resister, / Ainz son delit et son desport / Souffrir l'estuet sanz nul desport."

[50] Anne Middleton, "The Idea of Public Poetry in the Reign of Richard II," *Speculum* 53 (1978): 94–114; *NPT* 3265; *MilP* 3181. A. J. Minnis, *Medieval Theory of Authorship* (London: Scolar, 1984), pp. 197–98, links these passages to the "disavowal of responsibility trope" (p. 198) resorted to by "compilators" of collections of excerpts from *auctores.*

[51] Teodolinda Barolini, *The Undivine Comedy: Detheologizing Dante* (Princeton, N.J.: Princeton University Press, 1992).

engages in elaborate strategies of self-exculpation—including appeals to the example of Christ and the authority of Plato (*GP* 725–42)—in order to prevent being cut off again by his audience, this time for speaking "rudeliche and large" (*GP* 734) and retelling "cherles tales" of "harlotrie" (*MilP* 3169, 3184).

As part of his lapsarian reconception of Gower's penitential poetic, Chaucer separates social analysis from penitential exhortation, and assigns chief responsibility for them to two separate voices placed at opposite ends of the *Tales*. The narrator of the entire pilgrimage, who is most before us at the beginning of the fictive journey, is the voice that corresponds to Gower's estates complaint and satire. But as opposed to Gower's narrator, Chaucer's is immediately and firmly located within the world he is describing; his is an act of memory, not prophecy: "Bifil that in that seson on a day" (*GP* 19). And the text insists on his immediate inclusion in the group he will subsequently chronicle, an inclusion that results from eloquence, from his saying appropriate things to each individual pilgrim: "And shortly, whan the sonne was to reste, / So [I emphasize the key word] hadde I spoken with hem everichon / That I was of hir felaweship anon" (*GP* 30–32).[52] The "felaweship" proceeds to make practical, limited agreements—"And made forward erly for to ryse / To take oure wey ther as I yow devyse" (*GP* 33–34)—rather than embracing a broad ideal of social or religious accord characteristic of the Edenic "then" of Gower's estates analysis.

It is from this twin perspective of recollection and a position inside the event recollected that the narrator undertakes to reconstruct composite portraits of his fellow pilgrims. Following E. Talbot Donaldson and, more recently, H. Marshall Leicester Jr., I believe it is extremely important to stress the mediating agency of the narrator in assessing the impact of *The General Prologue*'s "portrait gallery."[53] That I continue to

---

[52] I read "so" as encapsulating the rhetorical doctrine of *circumstantiae* as applied to persuasive speech having as its goal the narrator's inclusion among the pilgrim *compaignye*. On the circumstantiae, see n. 29 above.

[53] E. Talbot Donaldson, "Chaucer the Pilgrim," *PMLA* 69 (1954): 928–36; and especially H. Marshall Leicester Jr., "The Art of Impersonation: A General Prologue to the *Canterbury Tales*," *PMLA* 95 (1980): 213–24, and *The Disenchanted Self: Representing the Subject in the* Canterbury Tales (Berkeley and Los Angeles: University of California Press, 1990), conclusion, "The Disenchanted Self." I should add that Leicester's view of what happens in *The General Prologue* is a good deal more "disenchanted" than mine, though I am greatly indebted to it. As he puts it, "[T]he *General Prologue* . . . is in fact not an estates satire but a critique of an estates satire in the mode of deconstruction"; *Disenchanted Self*, p. 404.

use this metaphor despite David Wallace's recent caveat[54] reflects my conviction that, as J. V. Cunningham argued some years ago, the portraits on the wall of the Garden of Mirth in Guillaume's *Roman de la rose* provide one half of the narrator's inspiration.[55] Faced with the task of mediating the pilgrimage to his audience, he decides to follow two models: the *Roman de la rose,* which he is far from the only pilgrim to be acquainted with, and—can I possibly persuade you of this?—the tale of the Miller, a pilgrim for whom he has an obvious, almost racist, dislike but from whom he is quite willing to steal the idea of prefacing a story with elaborate *effictiones* of its characters.[56]

As Jill Mann's classic study has taught us, the resultant descriptions both participate in and depart from, sometimes strikingly, the conventions of estates satire.[57] These conventions, as they energize the framing fiction of the *Tales,* distinguish it from the analogous frame of *Decameron,* inhabited by the socially monochromatic brigata. Since Chaucer would have found the estates model dominating the social analysis of Gower's trilingual poetry, it seems to me "accordaunt to resoun" to understand the modifications of estates satire in *The General Prologue* portraits as yet another instance of his resistance to Gowerian models.

The portraits variously combine the narrator's commitment to an estates model of analysis with what we might call the erotics of memory, the recollection of his attraction to, or revulsion from, individual pilgrims that affects both the contents and order of his re-creations of them. (We remain in Donald R. Howard's debt for his insistence on the importance of memory for the *Tales.*[58]) The resultant uneven, unpredictable synthesis of ideology and personal response, which has made portraits such as that of the Prioress and, in a very different way, the Pardoner the object of so much critical debate, effectively subverts the Gowerian *prise de position* as a prophetic voice analyzing society from an external, implicitly superior position. One may, in fact, characterize *The*

[54] Wallace, *Chaucerian Polity,* p. 65: "By dedicating so much space to the *Prologue*'s middle section, Chaucer criticism unconsciously evokes an institutional setting that has no contemporary relevance: the pilgrim *descriptiones* are figured as portraits hanging for leisurely scrutiny in a Tennysonian palace of art. It is time to forget the master metaphor of the art gallery. . . ."
[55] J. V. Cunningham, "Convention as Structure: The Prologue to the *Canterbury Tales,*" *MP* 49 (1952): 172–81.
[56] Cf. *The Miller's Tale* 3191–270, 3312–38.
[57] Mann, *Chaucer and Medieval Estates Satire* (see n. 34 above).
[58] See Howard, *The Idea of the Canterbury Tales,* ch. 4, "Memory and Form," esp. pp. 139–58 on *The General Prologue.*

General Prologue narrator, in his role as purveyor of pilgrim descriptions, as Gower come down from his prophetic mountain or preacher's pulpit to ride the dusty road to Canterbury.

Chaucer also wants us to understand that his narrator is mimicking the pilgrims themselves, who use estates-satire commonplaces against each other, capitalizing on them for agonic purposes—to outrage, put down, disgrace—rather than to correct or reform. (The Summoner's attack on his rival, Friar Huberd, using the tropes of antifraternal satire, comes immediately to mind.) In this way the discourses of complaint and satire are absorbed into social eloquence and the social agon, in the process losing their Gowerian status as objective, moral statements.

The undoubted triumph of Chaucer's "lapsarian" response to Gower's penitential poetic is the relationship the *Tales* establishes between the Parson's exposition of penance, on the one hand, and on the other the ostensibly confessional prologues of the Wife of Bath and the Pardoner, surely the single feature that most distinguishes *The Canterbury Tales* from the *Decameron*.

The Parson's "tale" is actually a belated hybrid of manifestations of the late-medieval discourse of penance. It combines elements from treatises on the parts and circumstances of penance, on the seven deadly sins, and on their remedies; and it frames them, at least intermittently, in a preaching rhetoric and voice.[59] But the Parson prefaces this synthetic, textual-*cum*-oral construct with a reference that identifies him as the inheritor, and thus follower, of yet another discursive component of institutionalized penitence. This is the discourse that constructs the ideal priest and preacher, the necessary mediator of the sacraments of penance and the eucharist and the inculcator by word and example of the perfect Christian life. By general ecclesiastical agreement, the compendium of advice and warnings incorporated in the two Pauline (or pseudo-Pauline) epistles to Timothy provided the theoretical basis for clerical formation in the late-medieval institutional church.[60] Hence the Par-

---

[59] See Kate Oelzner Petersen, *The Sources of* The Parson's Tale (Boston: Ginn, 1901); Siegfried Wenzel, "The Source for the 'Remedia' of the Parson's Tale," *Traditio* 27 (1971): 433–53; "The Source of Chaucer's Seven Deadly Sins," *Traditio* 30 (1974): 351–78; "Chaucer and the Language of Contemporary Preaching," *SP* 73 (1976): 155–61; and the explanatory notes to *The Parson's Tale* in *Riverside Chaucer*, p. 956. On the *Tale's* generic associations, see Lee Patterson, "The 'Parson's Tale' and the Quitting of the 'Canterbury Tales,'" *Traditio* 34 (1978): 334–40.

[60] As Henry Wansborough puts it in *A New Catholic Commentary on Holy Scripture,* rev. ed. (London: Nelson, 1969), "[T]he Pastoral Epistles [1 and 2 Timothy and Titus] form the *locus classicus* in the New Testament for the ministry" (p. 1210). For a medieval testimony, see, for example, Jacopo Passavanti, *Lo specchio di vera penitenza* (ca. 1355),

son's dismissive reply to the Host's request that he "[t]elle us a fable anon" tells us instead that he has cast himself in the Timothean mold: "Thou getest fable noon ytoold for me, / For Paul, that writeth unto Thymothee, / Repreveth hem that weyven soothfastnesse / And tellen fables and swich wrecchednesse" (*ParsP* 29, 31–34).

The Parson, then, is Gower's penitential voice traced back to both its proximate and ultimate origins, in Lateran IV–induced and Pauline discourse, respectively. The fact that he aggressively eschews the "ha-webake" of traditional stories—the kind the Host assumes the priest carries with him in the "male," or coffer, of his memory[61]—implies Chaucer's judgment of the ultimate opposition between the social eloquence of the rest of the pilgrims and a penitentially-based poetic such as Gower's. The Parson seeks instead to transcend and transform the particularity of the Canterbury pilgrimage, by proposing to show the pilgrims "the weye, in this viage, / Of thilke parfit glorious pilgrymage / That highte Jerusalem celestial," specifically the "ful noble wey and a ful convenable . . . [that] is cleped Penitence" (*ParsP* 49–51, 80–81).

But the Parson is also located firmly within, not outside, the pilgrim compaignye, like the *General Prologue* narrator whose role as commentator he complements at the other end of the *Tales*. (Traugott Lawler has in fact referred to *The Parson's Tale* as "a kind of General Epilogue" that bears "a special relation to the General Prologue."[62]) He is accused of Lollardy and prevented from giving a "predicacioun" after he complains about the Host's swearing in the interstitial passage connected in some manuscripts to *The Man of Law's Tale*.[63] And when Harry, noting that only one tale is lacking, commands the Parson, "ne breke thou nat oure pley" (*ParsP* 24), the latter, in counterproposing his "myrie tale in

---

ed. Maria Lenardon (Florence: Libreria editrice fiorentina, 1925), dist. 5, ch. 4, p. 154: "Chi vuole sapere chente dee essere colui, che ha cura d'anime, legga nella prima Pistola di San Paulo a Timoteo, quello capitolo dovè dice: *Oportet episcopum inrepreheibilum esse* . . . , e quello che seguita. Il quale capitolo esponendo santo Agostino e santo Ambrugio, come si contiene nel Decreto, dicono che avvegna che paia che l'Apostolo parli dei Vescovi, ma quella regola s'intende di tutti coloro, che sono preti ordinati e hanno cura d'anime."

[61] See Mary Carruthers, *The Book of Memory* (Cambridge: Cambridge University Press, 1990), p. 34, on this use of "male" to stand for a "memorial storehouse or *thesaurus*."

[62] Traugott Lawler, *The One and the Many in the* Canterbury Tales (Hamden, Conn.: Archon, 1980), p. 156.

[63] The so-called *Man of Law's Epilogue* (Fragment 2 of *CT*, lines 1163–90) does not appear in the Hengwrt or Ellesmere manuscripts; for a sensible conjecture about its history within Chaucer's authorial project, see Cooper, *Oxford Guides*, pp. 136–37.

prose" (line 46), feels obliged to ask the permission of the compaignye —permission granted on the grounds of rhetorical appropriateness rather than religious conviction: "For, as it seemed, it was for to doone— / To enden in som vertuous sentence" (lines 62–63).[64] Furthermore, although he disdains fables, the Parson undertakes to capitalize on his position following all the other tales—a truly "lapsarian" maneuver— by referring to several of them indirectly as examples of sin, especially sins of the tongue, thus characterizing as sinners his fellow pilgrims even as he appropriates their stories for his own use, as if he were Gower's Genius in the *Confessio.*[65]

One of the main strands linking the post–Lateran IV discourse of penance and the discourse of apostolic formation in the Timothean epistles is the shared notion of an accord between thought, word, and deed. In penitential terms, the accord must underlie the sacramental sequence of contrition (*contritio cordis*), confession (*confessio oris*), and satisfaction (*satisfactio operis*); in the Pauline instruction, the analogous continuum flows from *caritas de corde puro* to *sermo fidelis* to *omne opus bonum.*[66] The *Parson's Tale* exemplifies this accord in its exposition of the sacrament,[67] but Chaucer places it under great—one might say fatal—stress in the confessional performances of the Wife of Bath and the Pardoner.

Just as the Parson embodies Chaucer's understanding of the inter-

---

[64] See Spencer, *English Preaching,* p. 110: "A new covenant has to be made between the Parson and the pilgrims before they agree to 'enden in som vertuous sentence'"; Spencer links this negotiation to the English laity's resentment of serious talk on occasions of recreation. Cf. the negative reaction of Margery Kempe's fellow pilgrims to her insistence on speaking at the dinner table about her religious devotions and experiences; *The Book of Margery Kempe,* ed. Sanford Meech and Hope Emily Allen, EETS, o.s., 212 (London: Oxford University Press, 1940), bk. 1, chs. 26–27.

[65] On the relationship between *The Parson's Tale* and the rest of the tales, see the divergent hypotheses of Ralph Baldwin, *The Unity of the Canterbury Tales* (Copenhagen: Rosenkilde and Bagger, 1955), pp. 95–105; Patterson, "The 'Parson's Tale,'" pp. 356–70; and Traugott Lawler, *The One and the Many,* pp. 159–67. Chauncey Wood, "Chaucer's Most 'Gowerian' Tale," in Yeager, ed., *Chaucer and Gower,* pp. 75–84, sees a connection between *The Parson's Tale* and Gower, but for very different reasons, as he denies that Gower is interested in penance and confession.

[66] For the penitential sequence, see, e.g., Peter Lombard, *Sentences,* bk. 4, dist. 17, para. 1; for the Timothean sequence, see, e.g., 1 Tim. 1:5 [*caritas de corde puro et conscientia bona et fide non ficta*], 1 Tim. 1:15, 3:1, 4:9 [*fidelis sermo (et omni acceptione dignus)*], and 1 Tim. 2:10 [*opera bona*], 3:1 [*bonum opus*], 5:10 [*omne opus bonum*].

[67] See esp. ParsT 107–14, which explains the interconnection of "Contricioun of Herte, Confessioun of Mouth, and Satisfaccioun" (line 108), through quotation and metaphor (penance as a tree with contrition as its root, confession as its branches and leaves, and satisfaction as its fruit.

twined institutional church imperatives of sacramental penance and clerical formation, represented respectively by penitential and Timothean discourses, so the Wife of Bath and the Pardoner embody the poet's recognition of the linked and prevalent anxieties about the sacrament and its mediators within late medieval European culture, and his appropriation of these anxieties as the basis for quintessential performances of competitive social eloquence by the two Canterbury pilgrims whom I like to think of, respectively, as Mother Tongue and Father Confesser (spelled for my purposes "er" rather than "or"), the parents of Chaucer's lapsarian poetic.

It's important to realize that the Wife of Bath and the Pardoner are "Pauline nightmares." That is, Alisoun of "biside BATHE" (*GP* 445) is a compendium of behavior condemned by Paul (or pseudo-Paul) in his admonitions to Timothy: she is a widow who wanders from place to place, insists on speaking in the assembly, will not subject herself to men, and, as a consummate gossip whose battle cry is *"wol ye heere the tale?"* (*WBT* 951; my emphasis), the arch-practitioner of precisely those *"ineptas aniles fabulas"* (silly old wives' tales) that Paul specifically warns Timothy to avoid.[68] As for the Pardoner, his "theme is alwey oon, and evere was— / *Radix malorum est cupiditas,"* whereby, he contends, "I preche agayn that same vice / Which that I use, and that is avarice" (*PardP* 333–34, 427–28). The text, of course, comes from that same Timothean corpus that generates Alisoun (specifically, 1 Tim 6:10).

Others—e.g., Alcuin Blamires and Alastair Minnis—have called these characters nightmares or, like Frank Cespedes, traced their Timothean roots.[69] My further claim is that both the Wife of Bath and the

---

[68] For *ineptas aniles fabulas,* see 1 Tim. 4:7; on widows with bad habits (ironically, Paul generalizes that they are the "younger" [*adolescentiores*] widows) see 1 Tim. 5:11–13: *"simul autem et otiosae discunt circuire domos; non solum otiosae sed et verbosae et curiosae, loquentes quae no oportet."* On women not being allowed to speak in meetings and having to dress decorously in public, see 1 Tim. 2:9–15.

[69] A. J. Minnis, "Chaucer's Pardoner and the Office of Preaching," in Piero Boitani and Anna Torti, eds., *Intellectuals and Writers in Fourteenth-Century Europe,* in *Tuebinger Beitraeger zur Anglistik* 7 (1986): 88–119; Frank V. Cespedes, "Chaucer's Pardoner and Preaching," *ELH* 44 (1977): 1–18; noteworthy in this regard are Hope P. Weissman, "Antifeminism and Chaucer's Characterization of Women," in George D. Economou, ed., *Geoffrey Chaucer* (New York: McGraw-Hill, 1975), pp. 105–6, who argues that the Wife's portrait in *The General Prologue* is "a parody of the Virtuous Woman (*mulier fortis*) of Proverbs 31" (p. 105), and Paule Mertens-Foncke, "Tradition and Feminism in Middle English Literature," in Hena Maes-Jelinek, et al., eds., *Multiple Worlds, Multiple Words: Essays in Honour of Irène Simon* (Liège: University English Department, 1987), pp. 178–82, who notes the similarities between Alisoun and "the Adulterous Woman in

Pardoner take advantage of their belatedness, vis-à-vis both Pauline and penitential traditions and discourses, to construct eloquential selves in a pseudo-confessional mode for specifically agonic purposes within the overall poetic and social competitions concurrently staged by the *Tales*.[70] The effect of their performances is to provide the ultimate example of a "lapsarian" peculiarity of the *Tales:* all its tales appear to be equally belated. Before we hear the Parson speak, Mother Tongue and Father Confesser have already subverted his contribution—not doctrinally but eloquentially—by seizing on the Pauline connection he establishes for himself in his Prologue.

In addition to being Pauline nightmares, the Wife of Bath and the Pardoner become "penitential nightmares" by following—that is, taking after, as well as coming after—major allegorical characters drawn from Jean de Meun's *Roman de la rose*—La Vieille and Fals Semblant, respectively—as models for their respective scandalous confessions. Their familiarity with, and willingness to exploit, this text becomes clear at the moment of dialogue between them, when the Pardoner interrupts Alisoun's parodic exercise in self-interested scriptural exegesis (*WBP* 20–162) to offer mock praise for the power of her "preaching" to dissuade him from marrying (lines 165–68):

> "Ye been a noble prechour in this cas.
> I was about to wedde a wyf; allas!
> What sholde I bye it on my flessh so deere?
> Yet hadde I levere wedde no wyf to-yeere!"

When the Wife proposes to offer "ensamples mo than ten" of the "wo that is in mariage," the Pardoner replies, "Telle forth youre tale, spareth for no man, / And teche us yonge men of youre praktike" (*WBP* 179, 3, 186–87). That is, he offers to assume the role of *Bel acceuil* in Jean's *Roman* if Alisoun will play the part of La Vieille, an offer she cannot and does not refuse.

The result of the performances by the Wife of Bath and the Pardoner is to create "confessions"—albeit not contrite ones—that by their li-

---

the *Book of Proverbs* 7" (p. 178)—a passage that underlies much of the misogynistic rhetoric in the Timothean epistles.

[70] Jerry Root has recently made a similar argument about the Wife of Bath from a more Foucauldian perspective: "'Space to Speke': The Wife of Bath and the Discourse of Confession," *ChauR* 28, no. 3 (1994): 252–74.

terariness fatally destabilize the accord between thought, word, and deed on which penance depends. Alisoun admits of her eloquence on two occasions—once in harrassing her first three husbands, once in wooing her fifth—that "al was fals" (*WBP* 382, 582); while the Pardoner, in claiming that he is about to marry and that he prefers "a joly wenche in every toun" (*PardP* 453) to apostolic poverty, is at the very least challenging assumptions either as to his sexuality (a matter of uncertainty, we recall, to the *General Prologue* narrator)[71] or his veracity. The Pardoner also radically challenges the post–Lateran IV institutional church's closely related enterprises of penitential discipline and clerical reform by showing himself equally adept at reproducing the admonitory preaching discourse of the deadly sins and (to follow but revise Cespedes) at applying to himself the admonitory discourse of the *artes praedicandi* about the dangers posed to the system of preaching and penance by clerics who do not practice what they preach, and make of preaching an overly theatrical, as well as hypocritical, performance.[72] The Pardoner may be, in Kittredge's famous phrase, "the one lost soul on the pilgrimage"[73]—or, instead, his Prologue may be a late-fourteenth-century version of a bumper sticker I saw recently on a car moving sedately down a New York City avenue: "Warning: I swerve and hit people at random."

In other words, I would argue that it is impossible to tell where the Wife of Bath and the Pardoner really stand, morally or autobiographically. But if they are personal enigmas, they still carry social meaning. Even as the bumper sticker I just mentioned functions not only as comic relief but as a tart comment on the self-righteousness implicit in bumper stickers announcing that the driver brakes for animals or wishes to save the whales, so the belated, "lapsarian" eloquence of Mother Tongue and Father Confesser articulates or alludes to a range of late-medieval cultural anxieties and crisis points.

For example, Alisoun embodies worries about the imagined power of the female voice to seduce and corrupt men—a power adduced, as

---

[71] See *GP* 691: "I trowe he were a geldyng or a mare."

[72] See Cespedes, "Chaucer's Pardoner," pp. 6–7, quoting a post-Lateran IV *ars praedicandi* translated by Harry Caplan. Cf. Thomas Waleys, *De modo componendi sermones,* ed. Charland, *Artes Praedicandi,* ch. 1, *De qualitate praedicatoris, "quintum documentum,"* p. 332, on improper motions and gestures in the pulpit, all of which the Pardoner employs.

[73] G. L. Kittredge, *Chaucer and His Poetry* (Cambridge, Mass.: Harvard University Press, 1915; rpt., 1970), p. 180.

Alcuin Blamires has demonstrated, in contemporaneous scholastic polemics against allowing women to preach, a practice countenanced in some Lollard communities.[74]

In addition, her famous "wandrynge by the weye," (*GP* 467) which literally refers only to her love of traveling (itself a Pauline no-no for widows,)[75] suggests her symbolic identification with errant female sexuality, but also with the errant vernacular, the medium of Wycliffite Bible translations and other forms of religious textuality increasingly worrisome, as Nicholas Watson has recently reminded us, to the institutional church in the decades leading up to Archbishop Arundel's draconian *Constitutions* of 1409.[76] I believe, in fact, that Chaucer constructed the Wife of Bath as an embodiment of the errant vernacular—Mother Tongue, as I call her—in seriocomic response to Dante's more pompous elevation of the vernacular in *De vulgari eloquentia* (if he knew that text) and the *Convivio*. Dante uses the same gospel image—Christ refreshing the multitudes with coarse bread—for the *Convivio*'s vernacular commentary that the wife appropriates, more scandalously, to describe her goal of multiple marriages;[77] in addition, when Dante notes that he owes his existence to the fact that his father wooed his mother in the vernacular, he makes a connection between the vernacular and sexual desire that Chaucer must have found highly suggestive.[78]

[74] See Alcuin Blamires, "The Wife of Bath and Lollardy," *MÆ* 58, no. 2 (1989): 230–31; Alcuin Blamires and C. W. Marx, "Women Not to Preach: A Disputation in British Library MS Harley 31," *Journal of Medieval Latin* 3 (1993): 34–63, including an edition of the *Questio, "Utrum liceat mulieribus docere viros publice congregatos"* (pp. 55–63), translated by Marx in Blamires, ed., *Women Defamed and Women Defended* (Oxford: Clarendon Press, 1992), pp. 251–55. For the Lollard Walter Brut's arguments (1393) that women could preach and administer the sacraments, see Margaret Aston, "Lollard Women Priests," *Journal of Ecclesiastical History* 31 (1980): 444–51.

[75] 1 Tim. 5:11 (cf. n. 69 above); Mertens-Foncke, "Tradition and Feminism," p. 179, following the lead of G. R. Owst, *Literature and Pulpit in Medieval England* (Cambridge: Cambridge University Press, 1933), pp. 385–86, who traces the condemnation to Proverbs 7:10–12, which describes the *"mulier . . . praeparata ad capiendas animas, garrula et vaga, quietis impatiens, nec valens in domo consistere pedibus suis, nunc foris, nunc in plateis, nunc iuxta angulos insidians."*

[76] See Blamires, "The Wife of Bath and Lollardy," pp. 229–30, and Nicholas Watson, "Censorship and Cultural Change in Late Medieval England: Vernacular Theology, The Oxford Translation Debate, and Arundel's Constitutions of 1409," *Speculum* 70 (1995): 822–64.

[77] *The Wife of Bath's Prologue* 145–46; cf. *Convivio* 1.13.12. The source of the image is the feeding of the multitudes in John 6:9–13, and Alisoun is also parodying Jerome's misogamist gloss on it in *Adversus Jovinianum* 1.7. The Wife of Bath draws on *Convivio* 4.15.1–5 in her *Tale*, lines 1133–38.

[78] *Convivio* 1.13.4: "questo mio volgare fu congiugnatore de li miei generanti, che con esso parlavano. . . . Per che manifesto è lui essere concorso a la mia generazione, e così essere alcuna cagione del mio essere"; trans. Richard H. Lansing (New York: Garland,

As for the Pardoner, his outrageous self-characterization acts out widespread popular worries, and reformers' complaints, about the mediational and disciplinary power vested by the institutional church in clergy, both secular and regular, who may well be hypocrites intent on using that power to sell the sacraments for personal gain.[79] Even more fundamentally, he serves as an emblem of the ultimately indeterminate truth value of confessional speech—a reason why some Wycliffites argued against the priest's authority to absolve confessed sins—and this emblematic status is reinforced by his analogous sexual and professional indeterminacy.[80] With respect to the latter, the documents about pardoners assembled by Chaucerians during this century make it clear that it was notoriously difficult to distinguish between true and false pardoners, or between real pardoners selling authorized or unauthorized indulgences.[81]

Furthermore, the eloquential, "lapsarian" confession serves both Alisoun and the Pardoner as a weapon for combating discourses and practices that marginalize and punish them for who they are. The Wife attacks the self-interested misogyny and misogamy of the clerical establishment and the discursive monopoly by which it disseminates such views; the Pardoner, the stereotypical thinking of all those who assume that a man with physical characteristics culturally deemed effeminate is both sexually and morally deformed or monstrous. Both attempt to ex-

---

1990), p. 31: "This vernacular of mine was what brought my parents together, for they conversed in it . . . and so it is evident that it has contributed to my generation, and so was one cause of my being."

[79] The institutional church's worry about these abuses, and about the complaints they generated, is reflected in the repeated injunctions, in English synodal documents issued during the decades after the Fourth Lateran Council, against selling the sacraments or appearing to (e.g., by assigning as penance having masses said, since that involved a fee paid to the same priest hearing the confession). See, for example, The Council of Oxford, 1222, canon 31; Bishop Robert Grosseteste's Statutes for the Diocese of Lincoln, 1239(?), statute 27; Bishop Walter of Cantilupe's Statutes of Worcester, 1240, statutes 33 and 56; etc. These documents are published in F. M. Powicke and C. R. Cheney, eds., *Councils and Synods with Other Documents Relating to the English Church*, vol. 2, A.D. 1205–1313, pt. 1, 1205–1265 (Oxford: Clarendon Press, 1964). On Wycliffite objections to the selling of penance, see Anne Hudson, *Premature Reformation*, pp. 295–96 and n. 101.

[80] See Hudson, *Premature Reformation*, pp. 294–301, for Wyclif's and Wycliffite problematizing of confession and absolution. Cf. Dinshaw, *Chaucer's Sexual Poetics*, pp. 156–60, who speaks of the "eunuch hermeneutics" of indeterminacy represented by the Pardoner's fragmented body.

[81] See, e.g., Arnold Williams, "Some Documents on English Pardoners, 1350–1400," in John Mahoney and John E. Keller, eds., *Medieval Studies in Honor of Urban Tigner Holmes, Jr.* (Chapel Hill: University of North Carolina Press, 1965), pp. 197–207.

pose the ideological interests driving, and the contradictions embedded in, such marginalizing discourses by pushing them to outrageous extremes: the Wife through her posture as sexpot and husband-tamer, the Pardoner through his campy behavior and verbal insults addressed to the pilgrim compaignye. And while the Pardoner is finally out-insulted by the Host (*PardT* 946–55) (Chaucer has no illusions about the cultural power of marginalizing discourses), Alisoun of Bath succeeds in generating a broad spectrum of stories from male pilgrims whose masculine authority she has somehow threatened. In a sexual reversal he clearly enjoys, Chaucer has the Mother Tongue of *The Canterbury Tales* implant, by her agonic eloquence, the seeds of these, her verbal offspring, in men as diverse as the Clerk of Oxford, the Merchant, and the Nun's Priest, who must now come after her (in both senses of that locution) on the road to Canterbury. (After writing this sentence, I discovered David Wallace's comment that "[t]he Wife might be seen as the only motherly begetter of the Clerk's Tale."[82] And then some!)

Nothing could be further removed from the golden decorum and harmless verbal ripostes of the aristocratic and like-minded *Decameron* brigata. And to think we owe this wonderful innovation in Chaucer's adaptation of Boccaccio's frame-tale collection to the mediation of Gower's penitential poetic, as understood, resisted, and transformed by Chaucer. Or do we? I must leave it to you to decide.

[82] Wallace, *Chaucerian Polity,* p. 292.

Desire for the Past

Nicholas Watson
University of Western Ontario

In the same way love grows between these two, so grows a fear there. And this fear is twofold. The first fear is that they fear they are not worthy of such a love and cannot do enough for it. This fear is noblest of all. Here one grows the most, and here one submits to love. . . . This fear makes a person noble . . . it makes one's thought sparkle, teaches the heart, clarifies one's knowledge, makes the mind wise, unifies the memory, watches over one's words and works, and allows one to fear no death. All this does the fear that fears it cannot do enough for love.

The second fear is, someone fears that love does not love them enough. For she binds them so painfully that they think love always oppresses them and helps them too little, and that they alone love. . . . But this noble unfaith has such expanded knowledge! Even if anybody loves so violently that they fear to go mad, and their heart feels crushed, and their veins always stretch and rupture, and their soul melts—even if anyone loves love so violently, nevertheless this noble unfaith can neither feel nor trust love, so expansive do unfaith and desire make each other. . . . So high is unfaith, which always fears either that she does not love enough or that she is not enough loved.

—Hadewijch

Me thought I had sumdeele feelyng in the passion of Christ, but yet I desyred to have more by the grace of God. Me thought I woulde have ben that tyme with Magdaleyne and with other that were Christus lovers, that I might have seen bodilie the passion that our Lord suffered for me, that I might have suffered with him, as other did that loved him. And therfore I desyred a bodely sight, wher in I might have more knowledge of the bodily paynes of our Saviour, and of the compassion of our lady and of all his true lovers that were lyvyng that tyme and saw his paynes; for I would have be one of them and have suffered with them.

—Julian of Norwich

I n this paper, I want to think along a zigzag line about how and why we study the past, about the ways in which it is a good or bad thing that we do, and especially about the role of feeling in our study. The zigzag line begins with a famous book, Caroline Walker Bynum's *Holy Feast and Holy Fast: The Religious Significance of Food to Medieval Women,* a book whose paradoxes I return to again and again in the following pages.[1] The line then snakes back to puzzle over a critique of the book by Kathleen Biddick and, more briefly, another by David Aers, before pushing on with some thoughts of my own about the relations between the desire for the past Bynum's book evokes and the past's own expressions of desire that are her subject.[2] These thoughts are partly developed through a reading of another book, Karl Morrison's *"I Am You": The Hermeneutics of Empathy in Western Literature, Theology, and Art,* which lends the later parts of my discussion a justification for their methodology, or at least their poetics. Morrison's explorations of the history of empathy as a mode of understanding, especially his analyses of the role of "hermeneutic suspicion" as an integral part of empathetic understanding, form an important general basis for the remarks about scholarly feeling I want to make.[3] But my particular sources are the writings of medieval women visionaries like the two quoted above, the thirteenth-century Dutch beguine Hadewijch and the fourteenth-century English anchoress Julian of Norwich. By reading Bynum's account of medieval women's spirituality alongside writers like these, the later parts of the paper formulate my own critique of *Holy Feast and Holy Fast,* arguing that, far from repudiating Bynum's empathetic approach to the past, as Biddick would have us do, we need to go even further than Bynum in systematizing the role desire plays in historical scholarship. Indeed, I end by proposing that we adapt Hadewijch's and Julian's insights about the relationship between desire and knowledge in the religious sphere to our own pursuit of historical knowledge: that we explicitly set out to learn from the past how our desire for it can be used.

[1] Caroline Walker Bynum, *Holy Feast and Holy Fast: The Religious Significance of Food to Medieval Women* (Berkeley: University of California Press, 1987).

[2] Kathleen Biddick, "Gender, Bodies, Borders: Technologies of the Visible," *Speculum* 68 (1993) [*Studying Medieval Women: Sex, Gender, Feminism,* ed. Nancy F. Partner]: 389–418: revised and reprinted in her *The Shock of Medievalism* (Durham, N.C.: Duke University Press, 1998), pp. 135–62. David Aers, ch. 1 of David Aers and Lynn Staley, *The Powers of the Holy: Religion, Politics, and Gender in Late Medieval English Culture* (University Park: Pennsylvania State University Press, 1996): an essay based on his earlier "Figuring Forth the Body of Christ: Devotion and Politics," *Essays in Medieval Studies* 11 (1994) [*Figures of Speech: The Body in Medieval Art, History and Literature,* ed. Allen J. Frantzen and David A. Robertson]: 1–14.

[3] Karl F. Morrison, *"I Am You": The Hermeneutics of Empathy in Western Literature, Theology, and Art* (Princeton, N.J.: Princeton University Press, 1988).

The "past" of this essay is the medieval Western past, especially the part of it inhabited in fact and in the modern scholarly imagination by Christian holy women: the nuns, beguines, anchoresses, and laywomen from all corners of Catholic Europe whose lives were recorded or whose writings have come down to us. These are the women Bynum has done so much to transform from the crazed anorexics depicted by earlier historians into the foremothers of modern feminism eulogized—in a flood of publications—by most of her successors. What drives the essay is not exactly the need to justify the study of the past, but rather the need to think clearly about the way all such study has emotional designs on its object, whether the emotions are of love, anger, guilt, or anything else. I believe this need may be especially strong now, when those of us who work in historical disciplines often see ourselves—rightly or wrongly— as members of an endangered profession whose role is to reaffirm the urgency of the past to an indifferent or hostile present. Especially if we work outside the geographical region we study, we have in our teaching and our scholarship to *represent* the past in the present, straddling the centuries in the intense but usually undefined belief that we enrich the self-understanding of our communities in the process. Since this self-conception is so much an emotional one—and since the task we assign ourselves, if we do view ourselves like this, largely depends on our ability to arouse emotion in others—it matters that historical scholars learn to theorize the affective component of their projects: or, to translate this, that we discuss whether we are right to care for or about the past, what this caring is, and what impact our feelings legitimately have on our scholarship. In a way, I am retreading ground Louise O. Fradenburg has explored in several articles over the last few years in which she discusses the role of desire in modern and postmodern representations of the middle ages in psychoanalytic terms.[4] But while many parts of my discussion could readily be framed around a similar model, and perhaps will be by some readers, the discourse around which this essay is organized is not psychoanalytic but mystical. Here, for better or worse, the scholarly quest I use *Holy Feast and Holy Fast* to imagine shamelessly

[4] See, for example, Louise O. Fradenburg, "Voice Memorial: Loss and Reparation in Chaucer's Poetry," *Exemplaria* 2 (1990): 169–202, and "'Be not far from me': Psychoanalysis, Medieval Studies and the Subject of Religion," *Exemplaria* 7 (1995): 41–54, two fine essays. For a very different study of affective interaction between present and past, see Carolyn Dinshaw, *Getting Medieval: Sexualities Pre- and Postmodern* (Durham, N.C.: Duke University Press, 1999). See also Gayle Margherita, *The Romance of Origins: Language and Sexual Difference in Middle English Literature* (Philadelphia: University of Pennsylvania Press, 1994).

(*inverecunde*) takes the past as the object of a desire we can only partly satisfy but which we also cannot set aside. Here, in other words, Richard of St. Victor's *amor insatiabilis,* not Lacanian lack, is my lodestar.[5]

1. The Redemption of History

Bynum's *Holy Feast and Holy Fast,* published in 1987, revealed to English-speaking readers a religious culture many had not known existed: a culture centered on the symbolism of food—on eating and being eaten, on assimilation and incorporation, on wine, blood, and flesh—in which Christian women are said to have found a sense of gendered identity and even quasi-institutional authority through passionate identification of their bodies with the crucified body of Christ. Taking much of western Europe and four hundred years as her notional canvas, Bynum paints a picture of this culture in which the category of gender is taken to be separate from, and implicitly more important than, all other categories, whether of class, profession, language, region, period, or race (the exception is religion). In this picture, the consuming, consumed, suffering, and endlessly signifying bodies of women are seen to form the basis of an intensely imagined female community, a community bound together not by the networks of communication that might be said typically to cement masculine institutions but by common desires lived out in common ways. *Holy Feast and Holy Fast* evokes these desires anecdotally, incrementally, and at great length, describing what Bynum often calls the "richness" of food symbolism in the lives of medieval women in ways that insist on an absolute gulf between the culture that gave these lives meaning and the symbolic poverty of the present, while also claiming to give access to this past by translating its voices to readers in the present (p. xvi).

On the face of it, this double move (toward and away from a sense of the past's relevance) seems self-thwarting, making the past into a museum display we can wonder at but never use, both because "the practices and symbols of any culture are so embedded in that culture as to be inseparable from it" (p. 299) and because Bynum takes our culture

---

[5] See Richard of St. Victor's late work *De quattuor gradibus violentae caritatis,* in *Ives: Epître a Sévérin sur la charité, Richard de Saint-Victor: Les quatres degrés de la violente charité,* ed. and trans. Gervais Dumeige, Textes philosophiques du moyen âge 3 (Paris: Librairie Philosophique J. Vrin, 1955), pp. 127–77, a major source-text for the whole tradition of affective theological writing by women that this essay, in one aspect, explores. The notion that burning love for God is "shameless" is, of course, a topos of this tradition.

to be so irredeemably fallen from symbolic grace. But the evocative quality of the writing makes this pessimism hard to feel. Affinity between past and present haunts the book's rhetoric, as Bynum woos us into participation with the community she describes. Indeed, after warning against drawing "lessons" from the past, the book ends with a discussion of modern anorexia in which Bynum speaks as a public intellectual, calling on our age to recognize its need to recapture "something of the medieval sense . . . that generativity and suffering can be synonymous" (p. 301), by allowing the "images and values" of medieval holy women to "teach us that we need richer images and values" (p. 302). Even the book's dedication to Bynum's mother suggests that a complex mixture of feelings informs every aspect of its composition:

This book is dedicated to the memory of my mother, Merle Walker. A brilliant philosopher, poet, scholar, and teacher, she was as circumscribed as any fourteenth-century woman by her society's assumptions about female nurturing and self-sacrifice. Only those who knew her will understand fully the ways in which this book is a tribute to her and an exploration of the pain and triumph of her life. But this book is more. For the books my mother might have written never appeared. My act of writing is therefore my pledge to her granddaughter, Antonia Walker, and to her granddaughter's generation that women's creativity shall not in the future be silenced. It is also an expression of hope that those future generations of women will not lose the compassion, the altruism, and the moral courage that made Merle Walker's life not a tragedy of self-abnegation but a triumph over meaninglessness and suffering. (p. xvi)

To reflect for a moment on the moving contradictions in what is implied here about abnegation and triumph, silent suffering and women's creativity, a circumscribed past and a hopeful new future, is to see how entangled the relationship between past and present *Holy Feast and Holy Fast* evokes must be, beyond all possibility of straightforward argument or paraphrase.

Like some other women medievalists (an outstanding example is Barbara Newman), Bynum writes as a feminist who is also a historian with a real sense of belonging *within* Western culture, as a full member of intellectual institutions—the academy and the Christian church—whose attitudes toward women through the centuries have been, to say the least, problematic.[6] By helping to write women back into the history

[6] See Barbara Newman, *From Virile Woman to WomanChrist: Essays in Medieval Religion and Literature* (Pennsylvania: University of Pennsylvania Press, 1995).

of the church, she cannot avoid drawing implicit attention to her own role as a pioneering woman scholar who still does battle against the institutional power wielded by misogyny, and whose career poses the problems of self-definition that face all feminists. Reacting against the equal-opportunities feminism of the seventies, with its millenarian-utopian tendency to deny gender difference and history, Bynum, like Newman, wants to help readers find roots in a past when patriarchy never even came close to squeezing Western systems of value wholly into its own shape. The pervasiveness of misogyny is not the meaning of this past, its one melancholy lesson about the way culture works—as it is for feminist historians like Margaret Miles—but (in Newman's bold words) a mere "cliché [. . .] always present, sometimes loud, but easy to tune out if one is intent on the more interesting harmonies and discords that are woven above and around it."[7] Despite the tensions within the book, it is not much of an exaggeration to suggest that the project of *Holy Feast and Holy Fast* is thus to *redeem* the past, with its institutions, beliefs, and stories, for feminists—or, at least, for educated Western feminists with Christian leanings—seeking to realign themselves with their culture. And for many of Bynum's thousands of readers, *Holy Feast and Holy Fast* has been what it set out to be: a book that, like Christine de Pizan's *Livre de la cité des dames* nearly six hundred years earlier, finds meaning in women's lives in the past, and so helps women and men now to think of their culture as belonging to women as well as to men and "their" institutions.

The importance readers attach to *Holy Feast and Holy Fast* helps explain why Kathleen Biddick's critique of Bynum aroused such intense feelings. This critique, published in 1993 in an issue of the journal *Speculum* devoted to women's studies—and immediately reasserted, debated, condemned, and praised at conferences across the United States, sometimes in specially organized sessions—was one of the earliest articles to bring postcolonial studies to bear on the Middle Ages. Outflanking feminism by appealing to the neglected categories of race and class, Biddick's article is as emotionally driven as *Holy Feast and Holy Fast* and shares the ambition and the desire to make large cultural generalizations of the book it critiques. Yet for all its rebarbative difficulty, Biddick's critique is powerful because she puts pressure on the ideological

---

[7] Margaret Miles, *Carnal Knowing* (Boston: Beacon Press, 1989); Newman, *From Virile Woman to WomanChrist*, p. 2.

center of *Holy Feast and Holy Fast:* the book's reification of the terms "women" and "experience," and the ways it makes these terms serve, in all their silent lack of differentiation, as channels between past and present.

Biddick works her way out from Bynum's use of Victor Turner, extending to *Holy Feast and Holy Fast* a critique of one of Turner's essays by Michael Taussig.[8] Just as Taussig claims that Turner appropriates, rather than analyzes, the power of the magical practices he describes— with the result that "his ethnography becomes a form of magic"—so Bynum's empathetic interpretation of medieval holy women is said to conflate the role of the historian with that of the shaman, speaking for, not about, her subjects ("Genders, Borders, Bodies," pp. 394–95). Sharing with Turner a structuralist methodology that encourages her to treat the "past" she is considering as a united phenomenon, wholly distanced from the present, Bynum reclaims the connection between past and present by positing an undifferentiated "human essence," women's experience of the maternal (p. 397). I take it Biddick is implying that this is Bynum's real agenda: structuralism creates a single "community" out of the mass of phenomena Bynum analyzes *so that* essentialism can fuse her, her prose, and its readers with that community. Biddick then focuses on the groups that Bynum's recuperative project must exclude, drawing on R. I. Moore's study of the high Middle Ages, *The Formation of a Persecuting Society,*[9] to show how *Holy Feast and Holy Fast* accepts as normative a view of Christendom that depends on its violent self-differentiation from Jews, heretics, and others inside and outside its "fluid boundaries." This view, she implies, still underlies, with terrible potency, modern Western hegemony. Because Bynum's holy women were central to the development of a cult that provided Christendom with one of its most seductively organic self-definitions, Corpus Christi, Biddick accepts Bynum's claim that medieval women were agents of cultural production, not passive consumers. But she does so to urge a decisive break with the values they represent, adopting a "transformative ethic for medieval gender studies" (p. 418). For Biddick, quoting Toni Morrison's *Beloved,* the story told by *Holy Feast and Holy Fast* is "not a story to pass on" (p. 418).[10]

---

[8] Michael Taussig, "Homesickness and Dada," in *The Nervous System* (New York: Routledge, 1992), pp. 149–82.

[9] R. I. Moore, *The Formation of a Persecuting Society: Power and Deviance in Western Europe, 950–1250* (Oxford: Basil Blackwell, 1987).

[10] Toni Morrison, *Beloved* (New York: Alfred A. Knopf, 1987).

One way of clarifying the implications of Biddick's analysis of Bynum's book is by briefly juxtaposing it with another critique, made by David Aers in a book written with Lynn Staley, *The Powers of the Holy: Religion, Politics, and Gender in Late Medieval English Culture.*[11] Unlike Biddick, Aers is sympathetic to Bynum's project. But he takes issue with Bynum's claim that medieval holy women were empowered through suffering identification with Christ (a claim Biddick does not challenge). Bynum argues that such an identification enabled women to align their supposed feminine carnality with Christ's crucified human flesh, and thus to redefine weakness as power. After noting parallels with the writings of Luce Irigiray, Aers points out that the equation Bynum assumes of Christ's humanity with his Passion is not a necessary one. Indeed, it is an ecclesiastical invention that dates from the very historical period under study. The Gospels, says Aers, citing the Catholic theologian Edward Schillebeeckx,[12] treat the incarnate Christ as a teacher and social activist more than as a victim, and the tendency in Western Christianity since the Middle Ages to emphasize his passivity has given suffering an illusory meaningfulness that is often used to aggrandize those who control a society's cultural symbols. By treating this depiction of Christ as natural, Bynum fails to think through a situation where what *looked like* female empowerment was promoted by the masculinist institution of the church as it struggled to assert ideological control. Aers finds protest against this situation in the Lollard movement of the English fifteenth century, with its refusal of Passion meditation and image veneration as devotional practices, and its assertion of Christ's humanity as summed up by his teaching, not his death. It might be as plausible to look for it in earlier continental heresies, such as the Waldensians or the Cathars, whose dualism was attacked (according to Jacques de Vitry) by the devotional practices of Marie of Oignies; or even to point to orthodox reformist movements contemporary with the Lollards, such as the *Devotio moderna.*[13] Either way, any power medieval

---

[11] For other discussions of Aers's critique of Bynum, which I have found most preoccupying, see my review in *SAC* 20 (1998): 219–26, and my "Conceptions of the Word: The Mother Tongue and the Incarnation of God," *New Medieval Literatures* 1 (1997): 85–124, an article whose argument often parallels the present discussion, although in a different mode.

[12] See especially Edward Schillebeeckx, *Jesus: An Experiment in Christology,* trans. H. Hoskins (New York: Seabury, 1979), and *Christ: The Experience of Jesus as Lord,* trans. J. Bowden (New York: Crossroad, 1990), both cited by Aers.

[13] On the Waldensians and Cathars, see M. D. Lambert, *Medieval Heresy: Popular Movements from the Gregorian Reform to the Reformation,* 2d ed. (Oxford: Basil Blackwell, 1992).

holy women may have believed they had—or, at least, any power that Bynum's argument seeks to attribute to them—turns out, according to Aers, to be illusory.

Where Bynum finds cultural meaning for feminists in the devotions of medieval Christian women, Biddick and Aers thus find compliance or victimization. Biddick emphasizes the first of these, Aers the second, and their arguments work in different ways. But there is common ground between their positions. Biddick sees medieval Christendom as an institution in the process of defining itself by pushing all it could not accommodate outside its physical or conceptual boundaries; Aers focuses his attention on the pressure toward subordination and hierarchization *within* the Christian church. But according to both these scholars, to seek to recuperate the Christian past represented by medieval holy women as Bynum does is to set out along a road at the end of which feminists must find, yet again, that they have defined themselves in the same exclusive yet ultimately self-excluding terms in which medieval holy women turn out to have been complicit; it is to accept a definition of feminist community that might be able to include, for example, the male author of this article, but could not incorporate anyone whose communion with medieval holy women is as troubled as we are told it should be. For all the importance Aers and Biddick attribute to Bynum's book, both imply that the past with which *Holy Feast and Holy Fast* would unite us not only cannot redeem the present but actually threatens to harm us.

2. The Marriage of Past and Present

The controversy over Biddick's critique of Bynum, which raged for a while through conferences and e-mail discussion groups, generated some of the ferocity of the larger debate the controversy parallels, between straight, white, middle-class feminism and its queer, black, third-world, and postcolonial counterparts. My own first reaction, shared with many and never wholly overcome, was of defensive anger: for Biddick's critique struck me, and still partly strikes me, as reducing medieval Christendom to a totalizing worldview that *ought not to have been*. While it makes some brilliant observations, I am also uneasy about Aers's cri-

---

On Marie of Oignies, see references in note 21 below. For the *Devotio moderna,* see John van Engen, *The Devotio Moderna,* Classics of Western Spirituality (New York: Paulist Press, 1988).

tique, especially its collapse of Bynum's model of female resistance into a generalized model of compliance to make space for a picture of Lollard heroism that seems as idealizing as what it replaces. But while I still regard *Holy Feast and Holy Fast* as a remarkable book, and want to believe its redemptive rewriting of the past, I have come to think that Biddick and Aers are partly right about it, and that, if nothing else, the sheer ferocity of the resistance to Biddick's critique from some quarters demonstrates the critique's importance. In what follows, then, I want to rethink Biddick's account of Bynum, sketching an approach to *Holy Feast and Holy Fast* that takes the critique seriously but argues that it can be used to help refine the historiographic mode the book represents, rather than simply disputing the book's right to be. The starting point of this recuperative enterprise is Biddick's description of Bynum as a "shaman" (p. 394). Biddick's analysis assumes that to call Bynum by this name and so imply that her methodology is "magical" is to strike an unanswerable blow against her absorption or appropriation of the past, by defining her as unable by definition to think critically about it. But there is no reason to accept this slur on the shaman. As we shall see, if we translate Biddick's metaphoric accusation into terms more familiar to medievalists by thinking of Bynum's voice in *Holy Feast and Holy Fast* as a *mystic's*—and if we decide to explore, instead of rejecting out of hand, the relationship between past and present that this word implies—a very different argument, and a whole new terminology in which to couch it, is suddenly available to us.

As has often been pointed out, *Holy Feast and Holy Fast* is famous for its lyrical evocations of the gruesome ascetic practices attributed to holy women. Aers (*Powers of the Holy,* p. 33) culls this representative example (from *Holy Feast and Holy Fast,* pp. 209–10, where the last two clauses are an inset quotation from one of the fourteenth-century German *Nonnenbücher,* from Unterlinden):

Deliberate and systematic physical punishment was part of the daily routine for many religious women. [. . .] Alda of Siena, for example, [. . .] whipped herself with chains, wore a crown of thorns [. . .] Dorothy of Montau put herself through a pantomime of the Crucifixion that involved praying with her arms extended in the form of a cross and later, in imitation of Christ's burial, lying prostrate with the entire weight of her body supported only by toes, nose, and forehead. Jane Mary of Maillé stuck a thorn into her head in remembrance of Christ's crown of thorns. Reading the lives of fourteenth- and fifteenth-century women saints greatly expands one's knowledge of Latin synonyms for whip, thong, flail, chain etc. Ascetic practices commonly reported in these *vitae* include wearing hair shirts, binding the flesh tightly with twisted ropes, rubbing lice into self-inflicted wounds [. . .] thrusting nettles into one's breasts, [. . .] rolling in broken glass, jumping into ovens, hanging from a gibbet . . . lacerating their bodies until the blood flows, with all kinds of whips.

Bynum calls this kind of writing storytelling (p. 5) in which medieval women, not men or modern feminists, "generate questions as well as answers" (p. 30). Elsewhere, analyzing writings by women, she speaks of listening to their "voices" as they tell "how they gave meaning to their experiences" (p. 152). This is what Biddick correctly calls Bynum's rhetoric of fusion (p. 417), which tempts her into using the pronoun "we" in such a way as to conflate the author, her readers, and medieval holy women into a single devout entity ("Genders, Bodies, Borders," p. 396, citing, e.g., *Holy Feast and Holy Fast,* p. 159). It is the audacity of this strategy that accounts for so much of the book's texture: for its accumulative rather than argumentative structure; for its tendency to homogenize its wide-ranging material; for its policy of working within, rather than questioning, the categories it describes; and for its attempt to think of women's bodies as speaking through suffering, even when that "speech" is mediated to us through hagiographic writing, most of it by men. It is as though *Holy Feast and Holy Fast* were a verbal analogue of the singular medieval woman's body—distanced but yet immediate, suffering but yet powerful—that the book depicts.

Yet there are two aspects of things Biddick seems not to consider. First, Bynum's book is more thorough in deriving its rhetoric of fusion from the vitae and writings of medieval women than either Bynum or Biddick makes explicit. The book's textual strategies imitate the bodily and writing strategies with which it is concerned *systematically.* Not only does the book present itself as a product of anthropological fieldwork, based on a historian's version of extended discussions with her subjects, and written along lines suggested by those subjects. The way the book's subjects are taken to understand their lives has penetrated deep into the book's own mode of understanding. If *Holy Feast and Holy Fast* seeks to celebrate—and so assimilate, rather than critique—the past, it does so because it is describing a cultural practice itself centered on assimilation. Bynum's women seek union with Christ through the labor of suffering identification with him, a labor through which they hope to annihilate space, time, and difference. Denaturalizing their bodies in order to sacralize them, they live their lives in a deliberately heightened tension between bodily need and its fulfillment, a tension to which they assign many meanings. Bynum's book seeks union with these women through the labor of its making and the intensity of its desire to occupy a subject-position far from the author's: a desire that places the book's language under a strain that figures both the difficulty and the ineffable value of the fusion of past and present it attempts. The book is a historian's version of a mystical journey into the abyss like those described by Mechtild of Magdeburg, an instrument of mediation between a revelation and its public like Julian of Norwich's *Revelation of Love*.

This set of equations explains why *Holy Feast and Holy Fast* treats its subjects so much as a single entity. It explains why this entity is described so positively; why Bynum is uninterested in problematizing her own strategies, despite her awareness of the book's radical agenda; why the book focuses on women's bodily experiences and the value of suffering in ways that seem to Aers to reinscribe misogynist definitions of women's "nature"; and, above all, why the book has been able to make so powerful an emotional impact on readers. For the mystical theology Bynum is imitating emerges from her book as directed toward an affective, quasi-bodily union between a lover and a singular beloved, in whom (as Song of Songs 4:7 has it) no spot or blemish is seen, and in aspiring to attain whom there can be no hesitation or compromise.

Second, if Biddick chooses to ignore the logic underlying the *Holy Feast and Holy Fast*'s hermeneutic, she seems actively unaware that anything might link this hermeneutic with her own. Her article stakes everything on its postmodernity, its place as part of a revolutionary moment in intellectual history. Yet despite its secularism, its insistence on deconstructing, rather than seeking to create, meaning, and its determination to expose the agendas hidden in historical study, "Genders, Bodies, Borders" still dreams its own desiring dream about past and future. And if we evoke this dream in theological language, it suddenly appears as if the taproot of feeling that gives Biddick's critique its own emotional power reaches down into the same medieval subsoil as *Holy Feast and Holy Fast,* with the same hunger for life. The mode of the dream is expressed in the article's subtitle, "Technologies of the Visible." Despite Biddick's attempts to distance her prose from the rhetoric of visualization, here, says this phrase, we are to be taught to frame our view of the past aright, to reject spurious modes of contemplation, and to recreate the manner of our gaze and its object; here, in other words, we are to be led along a path tracked by Dante's *Paradiso* or Bonaventure's *Itinerarium*. No longer must we look at medieval holy women with compassion. Instead, we must learn *contemptus,* the world-weariness that functions as a first step on the road to holiness in ascetic texts like Innocent III's *De miseria condicionis humane.* How are we to use *contemptus,* once gained? To despise what once we loved—the bodies of medieval holy women, and the myth of maternity that is the essentialist aura those bodies cast for us; and to love what we despised—the faces of those our sin has made invisible, and the hope of a better world. How is such a hope realized? Through a process that begins when we gaze on the "fearful interconnectedness" between spirituality and oppression, "the interior Christian" and "the exterior Jew," as these characters people the unredeemable past (pp. 417–18): a process that comes to fruition through an apophatic forgetting of the meaning we once ascribed to the past, as all it seemed to have of value is revealed soaked in the "excluded blood of the Other" (p. 409). And where does this revelation lead? To an eschatological "transformation" that Biddick can depict only in negative form, through gazing at the fallen world of the present; but that putatively— in the rhetoric of the article's conclusion—has the power to leave the past behind as the soul sheds the body at death, or as the New Jerusalem sloughs away the old.

In some way, then, Biddick's article effects its own fusion of present and medieval past, and does so in the very act of seeming to reject that past as a possible site on which to build meaning. The notion of transformation, the longing to escape the essentialized body, the insistence that history respond to ethical imperatives—all are part not just of the postmodern present in which Biddick writes but of the same affective culture that frames *Holy Feast and Holy Fast:* a culture whose own desire for the past was offset by a hope in the coming *renovatio* of the world, in which (according to some of the followers of Joachim of Fiore) the destruction of old meanings and long-accepted truths was to usher in the final phase of history, the kingdom of the Holy Spirit.[14] As with *Holy Feast and Holy Fast,* the affective framework underlying "Genders, Bodies, Borders" is as much medieval and religious as postmodern and polit-

---

[14] See Marjorie Reeves, *The Influence of Prophecy in the Later Middle Ages: A Study of Joachism* (Oxford: Clarendon Press, 1969); Bernard McGinn, *The Calabrian Abbot: Joachim of Fiore in the History of Western Thought* (New York: Crossroads, 1985).

ical; indeed, Biddick's prose is rich with the eerie and densely metaphorical language of apocalypse. This is not to say that Biddick and Bynum are in theological agreement, despite their common hope for a transformed future. But it is to say that both scholars seem equally haunted by echoes of a past that finds ghostly ways of speaking through them *whether they like it or not,* curiously shaping the desires they express and the language they use to express it. From this viewpoint, Bynum's belief in her abilities to translate past lives seems less naive than Biddick's seeming confidence that she might be able to separate herself by sheer self-awareness from the past's systems of value. Perhaps we can even conclude that Biddick's predicament is inevitable: that the past will always push through in this emotion-laden way in our accounts of it—isn't this in fact the very point made over and over again in Toni Morrison's *Beloved?*[15]—a story that passes itself on into the future whether or not it is the story we want to be telling.

"Genders, Bodies, Borders" is thus at least as susceptible to the charge of shamanism as *Holy Feast and Holy Fast,* and while this fact does not invalidate the article's argument—although Biddick herself would seem to think it did—it does suggest that we need to reevaluate the role of affect in thinking about the past, and devise historiographic models that are self-conscious about their incorporation of affect, rather than seeking to exclude it. It seems, too, that such models need to be especially sensitive to how moderns inherit modes of feeling, as well as institutional and intellectual structures, from the past, and how this fact may constitute much of the past's urgency for us: both Bynum's book and Biddick's critique testify to the intricacy with which present urgencies can prove to be grounded in past ones. In the next three sections of this paper, I therefore want to offer some further reflections on the relation between history writing and affect that arise from Bynum's clear, but inexplicit, use of a shamanistic or mystical model of historiography. The discussion begins with an account of a book by another medieval historian, Karl Morrison's *"I Am You,"* before going on to reread *Holy Feast and Holy Fast* from the imagined viewpoint of some of its medieval subjects, and then, finally, to ask these subjects to offer some suggestions of their own.

---

[15] I owe this observation to Jennifer Summit, who referred me to an analysis of "it was not a story to pass on" by Shavoldalyn Givens, "In Her Own Words: the Chicana and African American Woman Author (Re)writes Her Mother, Her Self" (unpublished honors thesis, Stanford University, 1998).

3. Empathy and Knowledge

Karl Morrison's *"I Am You": The Hermeneutics of Empathy in Western Litera-ture, Theology, and Art* is a study of the uses to which Western Christian culture has put the imagery of assimilation and union, and, in particular, of the intellectual tradition that regards empathy or affect as a mode of understanding. While there are many aspects of this tradition—partic-ularly political ones—he does not explore and that need to be taken into account, Morrison is the only historian I know to have organized into one frame the discourses of erotic and mystical love, alchemy and sci-entific understanding, assimilation through colonization and discovery through academic research, artistic endeavor, or the practice of *imitatio Christi*. His analysis is important to my argument in several ways. First, he provides a vocabulary for analyzing affect. This can be used to make explicit the connections I have been implying exist between, for ex-ample, desire for historical knowledge, desire for transformation of the present, and desire for union with God. Second, he describes a set of rules for the use of affect as a mode of understanding, which are valuable in helping to sort out what is happening when an exchange between past and present becomes as emotionally invested as it does in *Holy Feast and Holy Fast* and "Genders, Bodies, Borders." Third, Morrison's analysis suggests that there are continuities between our desire to understand the medieval past and that past: in other words, that the desire a text like *Holy Feast and Holy Fast* expresses for discursive union with medi-eval holy women belongs in a common tradition with these women's desire for union for God. Thus, a reading of *"I Am You"* gives grounds for hope that to write emotionally about the past is not necessarily to displace it in solipsistic self-enjoyment, but to allow it to live again in constructive textual engagement with the present.

"I Am You" traces two historical patterns. The most important of these is the history of the phrase "I am you" itself, a phrase perhaps originally Vedic, which Morrison characterizes as "the signature of a long and many-formed hermeneutic tradition" (p. 3) in Western culture since the antique period. Whereas the empiricist intellectual tradition to which the modern academy primarily belongs takes as its theoretical starting point the separation of intellect from emotion, this other tradition con-ceives of understanding as affective, imitative, progressive, and assimila-tive. That is, in this model you come to understand something by desir-ing it, setting out to be like it, becoming like it, and, finally, seeking to

fuse with it. The phrase "I am you" is first found in texts written as late as the second century after Christ. But it was from the first interpreted in the light of older ideas about selfhood, especially Neoplatonic ones. The phrase persisted through the Middle Ages, pervades the thought of John Donne, and underwent a revival with nineteenth-century romanticism, especially in Germany; indeed, Morrison's defense of the "hermeneutics of empathy" can be thought of as forming part of this revival, indebted to figures such as Hans-Georg Gadamer.[16] At the same time, however—and this is the second pattern the book traces—the tradition encapsulated by the phrase came under increasing fire from proponents of empiricism, especially after the Enlightenment, and the claims it makes for itself have progressively narrowed over the last two hundred years as a result. Empiricist hermeneutics now dominate the sciences and social sciences and have radically influenced the study of theology, philosophy, history, literature, and the visual arts, despite the difficulty of applying strictly empirical criteria in these fields. "It is not," says Morrison, boldly declaring his own sympathies from the outset, "the first, or the last, instance in which one art has been seduced by another" (p. xx).

In elucidating the phrase "I am you," Morrison focuses on a dichotomy between what he calls the "positive" or "amorous" content of the phrase and its "negative" or "malevolent" content. In broad outline, this dichotomy demands that we see the phrase "I am you" as simultaneously asserting and denying the fusion of the self with the other it appears to announce. At its positive or amorous extreme, "I am you" is equivalent to the equation "I = you," which in turn gestures toward the solipsistic "I am I"; at its negative or malevolent one, the phrase is an oxymoron that, as such, encodes the opposite phrase "I am not you," or "you are you," which implies that all communication is impossible. Yet according to Morrison, the phrase, and the movement toward union that it depicts, always contains positive and negative elements. There are many modes in which a subject might desire to fuse wholly with another, whether the subject is God, the lover, the parent, the ruler, or the imperialist power, and whether the other is the soul, the beloved, the child, the ruled, or the conquered people (and all these terms can be reversed). But even an amorous and mutually desired attempt to "occupy" another involves conflict: Walter's desire for full knowledge of Griselda in Chau-

[16] See Hans-Georg Gadamer, *Truth and Method,* trans. G. Barden and J. Cumming (New York: Seabury, 1975).

cer's *Clerk's Tale,* despite being abetted by Griselda, only emphasizes the gap between them by expressing itself through violent coercion; and the tale seemingly shows no interest in the question of Griselda's knowledge of Walter. (Indeed, the only discourse within which the phrase "I am you" does not involve an explicit relation of power is that of friendship: as Morrison insists, other kinds of discussions of empathetic knowing consistently invoke images of subordination, paradigmatically that of female subordination to the male.) There are also modes in which any of these subjects might refuse likeness with the other, in a child's self-differentiation from a parent, a people's revolt against a ruling power, or a soul's revolt against God. Yet conflicts such as these also partake of the amorous; as David Hume declared in the *Treatise of Human Nature,* contrariety is only another "mode of likeness" (*"I Am You,"* p. 37) that leads inevitably to a "coincidence of opposites."

As a result of the contradictions and the potential for violence involved in the movement toward fusion expressed by "I am you," thinkers within the empathetic tradition from Augustine on emphasized that empathy is a responsible mode of understanding only when the phrase's positive and negative implications are felt at the same time: that is, when the two are in irreconcilable tension with one another. Only through such tension—a tension, one might say, between intuition and suspicion, in which understanding is always conscious of the persistence of a "hermeneutic gap" that separates it from its desired object—can empathy aspire to a union that does not involve coercion or solipsism, retaining difference in likeness, acknowledging that the other remains other, however carefully it is understood. This is the hermeneutic system Morrison calls "play." Play, in this special sense, leads to understanding, and the process by which it does so is often systematized in the Middle Ages as a ladder or set of stages, culminating in full understanding of the beloved. But accounts of this culmination, in which the self is sometimes taken to be all but annihilated, still find metaphoric or other ways to emphasize the persistence of difference, and even do so when they are speculating about a union that cannot occur, except in momentary flashes, in the present life:

As a drop of water seems to disappear completely in a big quantity of wine, even assuming the wine's taste and colour; just as red, molten iron becomes so much like fire it seems to lose its primary state; just as the air on a sunny day seems transformed into sunshine instead of being lit up; so it is necessary for the saints that all human feelings melt in a mysterious way and flow into the will of God. Otherwise, how will God be "all in all" (I Corinthians 15:28), if something human survives in man?[17]

So Bernard of Clairvaux writes in the *De diligendo Deo* of the fourth degree of love, in which the deified soul loves God only for God's sake, but still retains a real distinctiveness as water, not wine; iron, not fire; sustained in its createdness by the very will of God to which it is wholly united. And as Richard of St. Victor speculated in calling his rather different version of this fourth degree *amor insatiabilis* (insatiable love), the nearest state to this final union that can be attained in this life is characterized more by frustration than by consummation, as the very process of fusion with the beloved object leads to the ever more intense recognition that full union is impossible. At least in this life, according to most mystical theologies, the oxymoron "I am you" can never be resolved.

4. The Mother's Body, the Daughter's Mind

Morrison's book leaves many questions unexplored, and despite its interest in this theme, may still understate the potential for violence within the hermeneutics of empathy: a potential underscored by the way post-colonial studies has adopted certain terms associated with mysticism ("assimilation," "appropriation") to describe the relationship between colonizer and colonized. Accepting that this leaves any argument based on *"I Am You"* vulnerable to the same charge, what happens if we now return to *Holy Feast and Holy Fast* with Morrison's empathetic hermeneutic in mind? A number of things become clear. First, it is immediately obvious that the book employs a version of this empathetic hermeneutic, involving Bynum in a sustained repetition of the past that unites her and her readers with her subjects. Second, even though the whole book is drenched in the rhetoric of passion, this hermeneutic is not explicitly acknowledged. Third, and this is my major claim, Bynum's failure to clarify the role of empathy means that she also fails to systematize its uses. This has important consequences, for it allows her book to con-

---

[17] Quoted from *Bernard of Clairvaux: Treatises II: The Steps of Humility and Pride, The Book on Loving God,* trans. Robert Walton, Cistercian Fathers Series, no. 13 (Kalamazoo, Mich.: Cistercian Publications, 1980), p. 120. The translation is fairly free. For the Latin, see *Sancti Bernardi Opera,* ed. J. Leclerq, C. H. Talbot, H. M. Rochais, vol. 3 (Rome: Editiones Cistercienses, 1963), pp. 119–54.

struct itself around deep feelings about the past without applying hermeneutic suspicion to these feelings. In Morrison's terms, there is empathy, but little of the hermeneutic play that makes empathy a mode of understanding as well as of feeling.

I have already suggested that one consequence of this failure is the tendency of *Holy Feast and Holy Fast* to homogenize the devotional practices it considers, presenting a single mode of female spirituality as the object of its quest into the past, because the meaning of that quest has been infused with the medieval mystical quest for the singular object that is God. I now want to argue that there are two other consequences: first, that the book finds its closest point of identification in the past not in the feelings of holy women, but in those of the men who described them; second, that *as a direct result* of this unintended identification with a medieval masculine viewpoint, the desire for the past expressed in *Holy Feast and Holy Fast* significantly underrates the capacity of holy women for hermeneutic suspicion of their own.

As we saw, Bynum's dedication of her book positions it at a cultural watershed between past generations of mothers, whose achievements are bodied forth through the medium of silence and suffering, and future generations of daughters, who, for almost the first time in Western history, have the chance to speak and act directly. Remarkably, though, the book presents this moment of triumph most powerfully as a moment of loss. Suffused with the urgent hope that the daughters to whom it is addressed learn from the mothers they are leaving behind, *Holy Feast and Holy Fast* plunges us into the very past these daughters might be most likely to scorn—a past of pain and silence—insisting on its richness, even its partial superiority to the present. After all, as Bynum's final chapter points out, this is the same present in which certain anorexic daughters still act out versions of medieval food practices, but with all their suffering rendered meaningless (so it is suggested) by the very cultural forces that have, in another and perhaps suspect sense, been instrumental in empowering them.

Given this framing, it is not surprising, then, that the book's argument makes more use of the vitae of holy women than of their writings. The vitae have the necessary emphasis on food *practices,* not literary imagery; on the bodies of women, not their words; on the memorializing of the dead, not the living presence of their voices; and so it is there Bynum turns in her effort to avoid "presentist concerns" and "male perspectives," and to allow "the women themselves to generate questions as well as answers" (p. 30). (Bynum does analyze writing by women, but more in terms of its imagery than its ideas, fitting her analysis to a framework already evolved from her study of the vitae.) The obvious problems here are that most vitae are by men, and that hagiography is a poor source of accurate historical information. Bynum confronts the second problem head-on in her introduction by insisting that, as a cultural historian, her interest is in attitudes toward what happened—as she says, with "what medieval people *experienced*" (p. 8)—not with what did happen. But this only exacerbates the first problem, since it is not clear either that "stories" contained in the vitae do express "a way of finding value and giving meaning that holy women, their chroniclers, and their admirers all shared," or that in such stories it is women, not men, who generate "questions as well as answers." These problems are patchily acknowledged in the early parts of *Holy Feast and Holy Fast,* where, for example, Bynum admits that "we sometimes find that the further an account of a saint is from the saint herself, the more her food ascetiscm . . . [is] emphasized," so that it is easier to learn about "the stereotypes of holiness held by different audiences" than about actuality (p. 84). But later in the book, the emphasis is increasingly on *women's experience,* and the raw data for this experience is mined from the vitae with small regard for matters of historicity or viewpoint. As a result, the book itself sometimes takes on the appearance of a composite saint's life, representing the Middle Ages, yet again, as a time of legends. As we have seen, it even closes with a version of the old hagiographic trope about how we should admire, not imitate, the extreme ascetic practices it describes.

Bynum builds her argument with enviable resourcefulness, and the ad hoc way in which she treats certain questions of evidence often pays off. But I still think the elisions just mentioned matter, and that it becomes obvious they do if you begin asking awkward questions of the vitae themselves. For example, Philip of Clairvaux's mid-thirteenth-century life of Elizabeth of Spalbeek, which merits a half-dozen references in *Holy Feast and Holy Fast,* describes the routine of a paralytic who, several times a day, would arise from her bed and publicly perform certain ritualized gestures. In Philip's account, these gestures enacted Christ's Passion, and did so in a liturgically appropriate order:

At mydnyghte . . . sche ryseth, to knowleche wonderfully the begynnynge of oure Lordes passyone, that is to saye, how hee was taken and drawen hyder and thyder ful cruelly with wicked mennes handys . . . And whanne sche is up . . .

than sche walketh ful honestly in hir chaumbyr, and withoute blynnynge, as sche goth and commith ageyn, sche swappeth hirselfe upon the chekys with booth handys, and of hir strokes maye be herde acordaunte sowne and cleer; and so in the steed of psalmes as in tymbyrs and wele sownynge cymbals, she solempnyes the watches of the firste nocturne. After that, soothly, as for lessuns, sche makith a bigynnynge of oure lordys passyone, how he was taken and with a feerful cruelte drawen. Than it is to se how sche takith her owne clothes byfore her breste with her right hande and drawith hirself to the righte syde, and thanne with her lefte hande to the lefte syde, and otherwhyle sche berith over hirselfe even forwarde dyvers tymes, as sche were drawen with vyolens.[18]

By the time Philip visited Elizabeth and wrote this account, her cult was well established, and many of the interpretations of her actions given here were probably in place, evolved by her, her family, and the local Cistercians who promoted her. The account is clear, has an ethnographer's eye for detail, and surely does reveal a situation in which, on a local level, a woman's bodily and ascetic practices had social advantages and communally accepted meanings. But two other points need making. First, the account tells us nothing of Elizabeth's attitude toward her performance and is carefully uninterested in the question of whether she was *conscious* of enacting the Passion herself. Second, all the pressure in the text to read her gestures as meaningful, to disregard her own thoughts about them, and above all to emphasize the literalness (as distinct from the rhetoricity) of her *imitatio Christi,* comes from the monk, Philip. This is why he makes so much of her physical inability to do what she does without divine aid; indeed, he even finds it necessary to excuse his use of active verbs to describe her gestures:

But sothely, that at I sey heer and have byfore seide, that sche "leyth hir downe," "stirith," and "bowith," and other doynge lyke to thees, I refere it to outwarde sighte, thof it be leve that sche doth it not with strengthe of hirselfe but with othere vertue that God woot.[19]

---

[18] Carl Horstman, ed., "S. Elizabeth of Spalbeek," in "Prosalegenden: Die legenden des ms. Douce 114," *Anglia* 10 (1888): 107–17; quotation from pp. 107.42–108.37. For the Latin, see Hagiographi Bollandiani, ed., *Catalogus codicum hagiographicorum bibliothecae regiae Bruxellensis,* vol. 1, pt. 1, published as *Analecta Bollandiana* 2 (Brussels: Typos Polleunis, Ceuterick et Lefébure, 1886), pp. 362–78.

[19] See Horstman, "S. Elizabeth," p. 113.23–26. The Latin original is even more explicit here: "Quod autem dico et supra dixi seipsam provolvit, exagitat et inclinat, et his similia, ad id quod extra videtur refero: quamvis haec non sua, sed aliena virtute, ut supra memini, facta credantur" (p. 370.27–30).

Elizabeth can thus be a *miraculum* in this text only insofar as she is not an agent. While Philip knows he is watching a performance, it is God who is the real actor, inspiring a reenactment of Christ's Passion which "this virgyne . . . figures and expounes . . . in hir body"; what fascinates him, in this life that is "alle mirakill," is the fusion of sign and signified, text and exposition, body and word.

The fusion of sign and signified is also what fascinates Bynum, and the second part of *Holy Feast and Holy Fast* is full of claims that women were "intensely literal in their *imitatio Christi*" (p. 119), so that "Colette *became* food" (p. 139), or "God is food and self is food" (p. 135). As a result, medieval holy women emerge from the book as committed to a version of the dictum "I am you" from which the pressure of oxymoron is largely absent. While they think largely in paradoxes, their interest is consistently in affirming identity with Christ's humanity, the totality of union between it and Christ's divinity, and the possibility of reaching union with that divinity through their bodiliness. There is little herme-neutic play, suspicion, or negative theology in this spirituality, as By-num reenacts it. Admittedly, it could be claimed, and may be true, that such qualities were absent in reality from many medieval women's con-sciousnesses; even Amy Hollywood's careful critique of Bynum, which partly parallels this one, is willing to imagine that fourteenth- and fifteenth-century women were more literalistic in their attitudes than their twelfth- and thirteenth-century predecessors.[20] But there is some-thing suspect about an analysis that conforms so well to the medieval stereotype associating women and the uneducated with the inability to conceptualize except in "carnal" terms. And the case of Philip of Clairvaux and Elizabeth of Spalbeek suggests that often, at least, holy women gave educated men a chance to think quasi-literalistically them-selves—to return briefly with relief to the sweet spiritual milk of the literal level after years of chewing away at the tough spiritual meat of theological abstraction—rather than that holy women did so. We have no way of telling what Elizabeth thought as she moved through her routine in front of the day's audience, and the fact that we do not and never will is precisely the cost of Philip's actually highly abstract preoc-cupation with the literal. But we have no reason to believe she thought what Philip did about her agency, or failed to realize she was *acting*

[20] Amy Hollywood, *The Soul as Virgin Wife: Mechtild of Magdeburg, Marguerite Porete, and Meister Eckhart* (Notre Dame: University of Notre Dame Press, 1995), esp. ch. 2.

something. Quite a bit of Bynum's material could be recast as stories about educated men taking refuge from scholasticism by imagining in holy women a simplicity of feeling and a focus on the body that was not necessarily there, or not in the "literal" form attributed to them. So even Jacques de Vitry, whose friendship with Marie of Oignies was full of talk and respect, is more interested in her tears than her ideas in his vita, and creates a picture of her that must leave out much of what made her so powerful. Marie *integrated* things for Jacques, rather as the notion of women's bodiliness gives *Holy Feast and Holy Fast* its coherence, and her vita testifies movingly to this, but by the same token does not notice other aspects of Marie's mind. Love is a mode of knowing in Jacques's vita, but love also blinds.[21] So it is, I think, with *Holy Feast and Holy Fast.*

The book's longing for fusion with holy women as mothers thus finds its closest medieval analogue not in the women it describes but in the attitudes of male hagiographers. These men tell us much, and Bynum's empathetic reading of them in some ways tells us more; after all, *Holy Feast and Holy Fast* attempts a synthetic understanding of women's food practices more ambitious than any we know to have been made at the time, whether by men or women intellectuals. Yet her book gives little sense of how hagiography irons out the variety of women's attitudes to suffering and the body, and actively occludes the status of many women as intellectuals, more than capable of the realization that "I am you" is meaningful only if it also affirms its opposite. Quite a number of the women her book discusses are more like the daughters of its dedication than like the mothers. As such, they were as likely to react *against* the theological logic that attributed to them a special bodiliness—or, at least, to insist on thinking it through in their own way—as they were to define themselves in these terms.[22]

---

[21] See *Vitae Mariae Oigniacensis,* ed. D. Paperbroeck, in *Acta Sanctorum,* June 5 (1867): 542–572; Jacques de Vitry, *The Life of Mary d'Oignies,* trans. Margot King, Matrologia Latina 2 (Saskatoon: Peregrina Publishing, 1986).

[22] Hollywood, *The Soul as Virgin Wife,* gives examples of this reaction, e.g., in Marguerite Porete's *Mirouer des simples ames anientiés,* which accuses Porete's beguine contemporaries of too great a focus on the delights of spiritual inebriation (p. 98, quoting from ch. 122, a passage preserved only in the French version). (I have not yet seen a book which is also relevant here: Catherine M. Mooney, ed. *Gendered Voices: Medieval Saints and Their Interpreters,* Philadelphia: University of Pennsylvania Press, 1999.) See Romana Guarnieri and Paul Verdeyen, eds., *Marguerite Porete: Speculum simplicium animarum/Mirouer des simples ames,* Corpus Christianorum, Continuatio Medievalis, vol. 69 (Brepols: Turnhout, 1986); Margaret Porette, *The Mirror of Simple Souls,* trans. Edmund Colledge and Judith Grant (South Bend, Ind.: Notre Dame University Press, 1999).

Occasionally, we can watch what happens when a woman's thoughts and a man's idea of what they should be meet. The anonymous author of the vita of the thirteenth-century Dutch Cistercian nun, Beatrice of Nazareth, based the final part of his book on her treatise *Van seven manieren van minne,* which has also survived independently in Dutch and Latin.[23] A close reader of Richard of St. Victor, Bernard, and other pioneers of affective theology, Beatrice took over the notion of *amor insatiabilis* from Richard's *De quattuor gradibus violentae charitatis,* and used it to develop a severe argument about the fact of God's incomprehensibility, and the suffering the loving soul must undergo in its inability to accept this fact. Since "what the soul desires is impossible and improper for any creature," all the life of the soul is "hellish, misfortune and affliction because of the horror of this dreadful desire which it can neither satisfy, nor appease, nor calm" (pp. 301–3). Beatrice writes as a theological theoretician of affectivity, boldly exploring an analogy between spiritual love and hell from which even the brilliant Richard, a century earlier, had retreated.[24] While it uses images derived from bodily existence, and may be a reflection of Beatrice's experience, her book says nothing directly about the body, and nothing about herself. Her hagiographer, on the other hand, completely relaxes the intellectual tension in her analysis, omitting the logical steps that make her treatise into an *argument* about love as a mode of knowing, and staging the simplified account of love-pain that survives his ministrations as a drama that takes place solely in Beatrice's body—as her soul waits for its release into the holy death that allows the hagiographer to begin the work of reconstructing her. Here, a vita full of admiration for its female protagonist unselfconsciously bundles her mind back into her body. Bynum finds the hagiographer "essentially truthful" (*Holy Feast and Holy Fast,* p. 161), and

[23] See *Seven Manners of Love,* in Roger de Ghanck, ed. and trans., *The Life of Beatrice of Nazareth,* Cistercian Fathers Series, no. 50 (Kalamazoo, Mich.: Cistercian Publications, 1991), pp. 288–331, a parallel-text edition and translation of part of Beatrice's vita and a Latin translation of its source, the *Seven manieren.* (I have not seen the Middle Dutch original.) Some of the observations in this paragraph are indebted to Hollywood, *The Soul as Virgin Wife,* pp. 26–39, and especially to Else Marie Wiberg Pedersen, "The Incarnation of Beatrice of Nazareth's Theology," in Juliette Dor, Lesley Johnson, and Jocelyn Wogan-Browne, eds., *New Trends in Feminine Spirituality: The Holy Women of Liège and Their Impact,* Medieval Women: Texts and Contexts 2 (Turnhout: Brepols, forthcoming 1999), 25.

[24] Beatrice's description of the third manner of loving quoted here draws on material from the first sections of Richard's *De quattuor,* where hell is the endpoint of *amor insatiabilis* only in its secular version. For Richard, spiritual *amor insatiabilis* is characterized by frustration and pain, but never merits the term "hell," which accordingly disappears from the latter part of the treatise.

describes Beatrice's thought entirely in terms of Jesus' eucharistic blood and her painful woman's bleeding as an image of that blood:". . . a bodily function of the woman mystic who lay in bed, out of her senses with inebriation, and who rose to advise troubled sisters and visitors from the world outside the convent" (p. 165). But despite her hagiographer's love of the language of love-sickness, spiritual drunkenness, and frenzy, there is no particular reason to think that Beatrice was really "inebriated." More likely, on the evidence, she was *thinking*.

Beatrice's treatise is written in a specific milieu, as part of a rethinking of pseudo-Dionysian theology in affective terms to which Barbara Newman gives the nickname *la mystique courtoise*.[25] Obviously, we cannot confidently form any generalization about holy women, or even women writers, on a single example: indeed, it is important that we acknowledge, against Bynum's powerful generalizing narrative, the *variety* within medieval women's spirituality. However, I venture the opinion that many writings by women do not correspond directly to Bynum's model of their spirituality, and that the more control women had over the production of the texts attributed to them, the less committed they may have been to affirming their bodiliness, or at least to doing so in the literalistic fashion Bynum's rhetoric tends to attribute to them. Gertrud Lewis's study of the early-fourteenth-century German *Nonnenbücher,* for example—a group of texts long held up to ridicule by Protestant medievalists for their copious descriptions of miracles and visions—reveals a world much less ostensibly intellectual than that of Beatrice or the nuns of Helfta, but one in which theological ideas were apparently discussed without any special emphasis on bodiliness or food symbolism.[26] Catherine of Siena, one of Bynum's test cases (*Holy Feast and Holy Fast,* pp. 165–82), is not at all the same in her letters or her theological treatise, the *Dialogo della divine providenzza,* as she is in Raymond of Capua's garish account of her life, for all Bynum's assertions to the contrary; indeed, her thinking is severe in its containment of the language of affectivity within a balanced theological framework.[27] And while Julian of Nor-

---

[25] Newman, *From Virile Woman to WomanChrist,* ch. 3.

[26] Gertrud Jaron Lewis, *By Women, For Women, About Women: The Sister-Books of Fourteenth-Century Germany* (Toronto: Pontifical Institute of Mediaeval Studies, 1996).

[27] See *Catherine of Siena: "The Dialogue,"* trans. Suzanne Noffke, Classics of Western Spirituality (New York: Paulist Press, 1980), and the analysis of Raymond of Capua's *Vita* of Catherine by John Coakley, "Friars as Confidants of Holy Women in Medieval Dominican Hagiography," in Renate Blumenfeld-Kosinski and Timea Szell, eds., *Images of Sainthood in Medieval Europe* (Ithaca, N.Y.: Cornell University Press, 1991), pp. 222–46.

wich and Margery Kempe both insist on their loyalty to the body (that is, the humanity) of Christ, rejecting the offers they receive to turn aside in abstract contemplation of the divinity, this is, in both cases, an intellectual and self-conscious, not a "literalistic," stand.[28] Hollywood may be wrong to suggest that there is a gulf between the thirteenth- and early-fourteenth-century women theologians with whom her own study is concerned and their successors.

I will analyze other examples of hermeneutic suspicion in women writers in a moment. But by way of concluding this long critique of Bynum's book, I first offer the following recapitulation. The desire *Holy Feast and Holy Fast* sets out to track is the desire of medieval holy women for Christ. However, the desire it most closely resembles, and the findings to which it comes, have more to do with a male hagiographic tradition in which holy women are presented as bodies that feel, not minds that think, and which often has the same kind of desiring relationship with its subject that *Holy Feast and Holy Fast* has with the vitae. It is also partly the vitae that validate the book's separation of the devotional from the political. Bynum's empathetic approach yields brilliant results, and she is probably often right: clearly, holy women and their hagiographers, reality and topoi, influenced one another; clearly, holy women did act as some of medieval culture's most important representatives of sanctified bodiliness. Yet in some ways *Holy Feast and Holy Fast* offers an unsatisfactory model for a historical project founded on empathy, for however much love reveals in this book, there is too much it has been unable to see. Not only is the play of intuition and suspicion that characterizes empathetic understanding absent from the book's hermeneutic, it is also missing from the book's account of how holy women thought. If *Holy Feast and Holy Fast* is to remain a touchstone and beacon to future scholars of women's spirituality, Biddick and Aers are right to urge that we read it with caution. The community of its readers must provide the hermeneutic suspicion the book itself lacks.

5. Noble Unfaith and the Desire for a Bodily Sight

Bynum's work since *Holy Feast and Holy Fast* has never reattained that book's intensity, and may have set out to avoid it. Despite their lyrical passages, the collection of essays titled *Fragmentation and Redemption* and

[28] On Julian, see my "'Yf wommen be double naturelly': Remaking 'Woman' in Julian of Norwich's *Revelation of Love*," *Exemplaria* 8 (1996): 1–34. On Kempe, see a paper in progress, currently entitled "Margery Kempe and Writing."

the intellectual history *The Resurrection of the Body* continue her lifelong exploration of Christianity as a religion of embodiment in a more conventional mode.[29] In these books, empathy is recontained, in a celebration of the difference of the past whose tone resembles that of Peter Brown's writings on late antiquity, and the focus is firmly on ideas, not on feelings.[30]

But while this return to something not too far from the old ideal of scholarly neutrality may have been welcomed by some, it does represent a retreat from much of what Bynum imagined in *Holy Feast and Holy Fast,* into an academicized conception of scholarly writing that sets out to achieve specific intellectual goals for the benefit of a select audience, rather than attempting, with blazing ambition, to reconfigure modern Western society's entire conception of its history. Although I am an admirer of all Bynum's work, in some ways this retreat seems a pity, not only because I think it was unnecessary but because her newer mode of writing seems less likely to be of help in making the study of the Middle Ages matter to the larger world than her earlier mode. Because I think there are more positive lessons to be learned from *Holy Feast and Holy Fast,* I thus want to push my discussion here in exactly the opposite direction. Rather than trying to rid ourselves of empathetic entanglements, as Bynum now seems (on the whole) to want to do, my thought is that it might be to our advantage instead to explore them more thoroughly, and in doing so hope to recapture the *hermeneutic* power that, as Morrison shows, many of our intellectual ancestors attributed to empathy.

Earlier, I implied a way of reading Beatrice of Nazareth's *Van seven manieren van minne* as though it were a preemptive critique both of her hagiographer's rewriting of her text and of Bynum's empathetic historiography. Beatrice's treatise describes what Richard of St. Victor terms the "insatiable" to-and-fro of love's knowledge, as the soul, pushing its

---

[29] Caroline Walker Bynum, *Fragmentation and Redemption: Essays on Gender and the Human Body in Medieval Religion* (New York: Zone Books, 1991), and *The Resurrection of the Body in Western Christianity, 200–1336,* Lectures on the History of Religions, n.s., 15 (New York: Columbia University Press, 1995).

[30] See especially Peter Brown, *The Body and Society: Men, Women, and Sexual Renunciation in Early Christianity,* Lectures on the History of Religions, n.s., 13 (New York: Columbia University Press, 1988), a book that seems to have provided Bynum with a model for *The Resurrection of the Body,* written and published as part of the same lecture series. Brown's writing is, of course, famously evocative, and Bynum's recent scholarship has not lost this quality, but the emphasis in both *The Body and Society* and *The Resurrection of the Body* is firmly on the variety and "richness" of the intellectual history of the past, and I see no sign of the extreme complexity of the relationship between past and present evident in *Holy Feast and Holy Fast.*

way with many setbacks through the modes of loving, finds over and over again that what it has learned is merely a new and profounder awareness of its ignorance. Like Marguerite Porete, whose account of the *sept estaz* of love often resembles Beatrice's of the *seven manieren* and may even be based on it, Beatrice is especially suspicious of the moments of rest where it seems that God has been attained: those solipsistic times when, as Porete puts it, "Love's great clarity has blinded her so completely that she can see nothing but her love."[31] Since it is exactly the scholarly equivalent of this state of ravishment that dominates *Holy Feast and Holy Fast*—a state that, Porete informs us, has the tricky tendency to disguise itself as the goal of love's journey, not a mere stage on the way—it seems we could do worse than to turn to medieval holy women themselves for help in understanding the pitfalls involved in empathetic identification with the object of desire. After discussing a contemporary historian as though she were a medieval mystic, in the present section of this essay I will thus track the relationship between past and present in the opposite direction, by treating the two medieval mystics quoted in the epigraphs to this essay as though they were contemporary historians.

The first epigraph, from a letter written by the thirteenth-century Dutch beguine Hadewijch, is an extended fugue on the topic of hermeneutic suspicion.[32] Another passionate experimental thinker in the tradition of Richard of St. Victor's *De quattuor gradibus,* Hadewijch resem-

---

[31] Porete, *Mirouer des simples ames,* ch. 118, *quart estaz,* p. 322.

[32] "Altermet dat minne wast tussen hen tween, soe wastere een vreese in. Ende dese vrese es tweerande. Die ierste vrese es: si vresen datsi niet werdich en sijn selker minnen, noch daer toe niet ghenoech en conen ghedoen. Deze vrese es alre edelst. Hier met wastmen meest, ende hier met wertmen der minnen onderdaen. Met deser vresen steet men haren gheboden te dienste. . . . Dese vrese maectene vri. . . . Si claert hem sinen sin, si leert sijn herte, si suvert sine conscientie, si maect sinen gheest wijs, si enicht sine memorie, si hoeder sine werke ende sine worde, si en laettene ghene doet ontsien. . . . Die ander vrese es, dat een vreset dattene minne niet ghenoech en mint. Omme datsine soe sere bendet, soe duncket hem dattene minne altoes verladet ende hem te luttel hulpet, ende dat hi allene mint. . . . Mer dese edele ontrouwe hevet de conscientie soe wijt. Al mint een soe dat hi ontinnen waent, ende dat sijn herte versuchtet, ende zijn aderen altoes recken ende scoren, ende sine ziele smeltet, nochtan datmen dus de minne mint, nochtan en can die edele ontrouwe minnen ghevoelen noch trouwen, soe wijt maect begherte ontrouwe. Ende ontrouwe en laet begherten niewers ghedueren, in gheenre trouwen, sine mestrout hare altoes, datse niet ghenoech ghemint en es. Dus hoghe es ontrouwe die hare altoes vervaert, och dat sie niet ghenoech en mint, ochte dat si niet ghenoech ghemint en es"; Hadewijch, *Achtse brief,* from *Brieven,* ed. Jozef Van Mierlo, 2 vols. (Antwertp: Staandard, 1947), 1:59–60; translation adapted, with the very necessary and patient help of Saskia Murk Jansen, from *Hadewijch: The Complete Works,* trans. *Columba Hart, Classics of Western Spirituality (New York: Paulist Press, 1980),* pp. 64–65.

bles Beatrice of Nazareth, Marguerite Porete, and perhaps Mechtild of Magdeburg both in her desire to know the truth of love as immediately as possible and in her principled rejection of most of what is actually offered her. The word *minne,* or love, jumps out everywhere in her writing, here signifying human love, there divine, here identified with Hadewijch herself, there seen as a power within the Godhead, here a force that drives two entities toward union, there a source of struggle that makes them clash and divide. Indeed, Hadewijch's tendency to personify *minne* and so give her a measure of rhetorical freedom from both lover and beloved—as the third term that unites and divides them—turns *minne* into a figure of the unpredictable play of empathy itself, and of the dangers within empathetic identification; for it is easy, as Porete also notices, to love a personified Love for itself, not for the knowledge to which it can lead.[33] In this passage, *minne* is aided by another emotional entity who unexpectedly turns out to be her kin, *vrese* or fear. *Vrese* is first seen as a principle of self-suspicion, closely associated with traditional Christian understandings of *humilitas,* although here imagined in a typically positive light: this noblest (*edelst*) fear does not subdue, but clarifies, teaches, integrates (*Si claert . . . si leert . . . si enicht*). (An ancestor may be the concept of *puritas cordis* in Cassian's *Collations.*[34]) We are still close enough to the thought structures of medieval Christianity that *vrese* in this form is recognizable as a scholarly virtue as well: the principle of intellectual caution that checks evidence, worries over details, and automatically suspects bold hypotheses, especially one's own. *Vrese* in this form is much in evidence throughout *Holy Feast and Holy Fast,* for all the book's passionate dedication to *minne.*

But then Hadewijch defines *vrese* in a more daring way, pushing the concept much further than the usual boundaries of medieval discussions of spiritual fear—which in general extend only from the self-interested but necessary *timor servilis* to the reverential and disinterested *timor filialis*—and further than our usual understanding of scholarly caution.[35] Now *vrese* becomes an angry fear at the object of desire—at its recalci-

---

[33] Hadewijch and Porete may here be taking a cue from Hugh of St. Victor's *De laude charitatis* (PL. 176, cols. 968–76), one of the main influences on Richard of St. Victor's *De quattuor gradibus.*

[34] John Cassian, *Conferences,* trans. Colm Lubheid, Classics of Western Spirituality (New York: Paulist Press, 1985).

[35] See, e.g., Hugh of St. Victor, *De sacramentis Christianae fidei,* PL. 176: cols. 173–617, at 2.13 (cols. 527–28).

trance, its apparent indifference, its refusal to yield itself up to the lover. This anger, which also extends to desire itself—since *minne* loves (*minne mint*), and *minne* is the beloved—is given the neologistic name *ontrouwe*, or unfaith. *Ontrouwe* can be defined as the principle of dissatisfaction not with the lover's worthiness to undertake the quest but with the quest and its object themselves. And where *vrese* in its first sense acts as a force for integration, this noble (*edele*) gift of *ontrouwe* distends and ruptures (*recken ende scoren*), expanding desire as desire expands it (*soe wijt maect begherte ontrouwe*, a clause in which *begherte* and *ontrouwe* can each be read as subject or object). *Ontrouwe* thus represents the endless struggle with any settled enjoyment of love, born of an endless desire to expand the understanding (*Mer dese edele ontrouwe hevet de conscientie soe wijt*). Porete's warning about the dangers of "Love's great clarity" runs along similar lines to Hadewijch's thought here, which in part has to do with love's tendency to mistake images of the beloved for the reality, and the need to use *ontrouwe* to strip away these false havens in a gesture of apophatic denial—although for Hadewijch, as not for Porete, God apparently cannot be trusted to reveal himself in full, but must be fought to be found, as Jacob fought the angel.[36] *Ontrouwe*, then, can be seen as a facet of the larger principle of suspicion by which Hadewijch's writings as a whole seek to guide the reader, making her disciples into exiles in relation not only to this world but just as profoundly to their earthbound conceptions of the next one. For the final consummation of understanding toward which the lovers of God yearn can be achieved only if their premonitions of eternity—all but the very highest of their ecstatic experiences of union with the object of desire—are refused, or enjoyed only under erasure, as long as they are still subject to the order of time.

Ontrouwe, dissatisfaction over the experience of desire or anger at desire's inability to identify its object correctly, is also the principle that governed both my own critique of *Holy Feast and Holy Fast* in this essay and the critique by Kathleen Biddick out of which mine developed. But where Biddick's attempt to redirect the goal of the scholarly quest understands *ontrouwe* as the rejection of desire for the past, in yearning for an almost unimaginable future, Hadewijch understands the concept as an integral part of desire and love, one that grows painfully (*recken ende scoren*) with them and spurs them toward further growth. In my comments on *Holy Feast and Holy Fast*, I tried to suggest ways to make

[36] See *Hadewijch: The Complete Works*, Letter 12 (pp. 70–74).

expansive (*wijt*), rather than deny, the desire that impels the book, by using *ontrouwe* in Hadewijch's sense: to show how the book does in part misidentify the object of its desire—finding its way as much to male topoi about holy women as to the knowledge of women's "experiences" toward which it yearns—but then to use this insight to further, not to abandon, the quest for a loving understanding of the past (exemplified by the analyses I offered of Elizabeth of Spalbeek and Beatrice of Nazareth). In sorting our way through the complexities of thinking about the past, Hadewijch's conviction that *ontrouwe* is integral to *minne* makes her work an essential reference point for explorations into both the topic of medieval women's religiosity and our modern scholarly investments in the topic.

Although there was probably no direct connection between Hadewijch and Julian of Norwich, something akin to Hadewijch's version of *ontrouwe* also emerges from the exploration that begins in the passage that provides my second epigraph. This passage from the opening of the Long Text of Julian of Norwich's *Revelation of Love* describes the origin of the visions on which the text is based in what Julian stresses was an unusual desire to engage in a version of time travel.[37] Longing for a closer identification with the past, her desire was to occupy physically the same ground and moment as those who saw Christ die, to be there with all who were, or would be, "Christus lovers" throughout time: a mighty company gathered together to assist through suffering in the turning point of world history. What determined the course of her thinking, however, was that so little of this plenitude of presence was ever given her. The "bodely sight" of Christ's death her revelation did afford, as it is described in subsequent chapters of her book, was firmly tied to her present, and came through to her only as shards of doubtful meaning: images of drops of blood that made her think of rainstorms or fish scales; a terrible apprehension of the leathering of Christ's skin; the subvocal mutterings of demons. The death itself could not even be seen, perhaps because it could not be repeated or borne.

But where Julian's visions entirely failed to measure up to the detailed story visions of fourteenth-century visionaries like Elizabeth of Hungary or Julian's colleague, Margery Kempe, there were real compensations:

[37] Julian of Norwich, *A Revelation of Love,* Long Text, MS Paris, Bibliothèque Nationale, fonds anglais 41, ff. 3r–v; see Edmund Colledge and James Walsh, eds., *A Book of Showings to the Anchoress Julian of Norwich,* 2 vols. (Toronto: Pontifical Institute of Mediaeval Studies, 1978), 2: 285–86.

"ghostly" sights of a less clear but more potent kind, whose meaning proved inexhaustible; words of hope, such as that "all shall be well" (chapter 27), pointed with anxious conviction at a future in an utterly different mode from the one we occupy; and, most of all, gaps, blurs, absences, or witholdings that Julian learned to take as hints of meanings previously unguessed at. After two decades of sifting the evidence provided by her memory of the thirty hours of her revelation, she at last came to an understanding of the hermeneutic underlying her experience that enabled her to finish her great research project into the meaning of the divine. This is what I term the "trinitarian hermeneutic," founded not only on the divine Trinity but on the insights provided by the trinity of faculties of her mind: the memory, which grounded her in "the begynnyng of techyng that I understode therin in the same tyme"; the reason, which furthered "the inwarde lernyng that I have understonde therein sythen"; and the *affectus* or will which enabled her to grasp the totality of the vision, "the hole revelation fro the begynnyng to the ende" (chapter 51), whose meaning as a whole ("love was his menyng," chapter 86) could be used as a further guide to its individual parts. In the end, the three proved "so onyd" that, as she says, "I can nott nor may deperte them": textual evidence, the rational pursuit of its implications, and the passionate intuition of its meaning all joining together in a single, but still self-reflexive, mode of understanding that, mirroring her revelation's message, is also called by the name love.[38] The divine and human trinities also join together in these formulations as a guarantee of their truth, which God and the soul together have labored to produce: mystics do, in the end, have this advantage over historians. But as a good scholar, Julian knew that her own version of this truth, divinely inspired though it may have been, was not necessarily correct in every detail. Not only was there more to be said, and many secrets ("privities") God conceals from humanity until death or even until the Day of Judgment (chapters 30–32); there would also be some who would be able to understand her revelation more fully than she could herself (chapter 9), or be better able, standing on her shoulders, to realize its place in the

---

[38] MS Paris, Bibliothèque nationale, fonds anglais 41, ff. 96r, 173v (Colledge and Walsh, eds., *A Book of Showings,* pp. 519–20). See my "The Trinitarian Hermeneutic in Julian of Norwich's *Revelation of Love,*" in Marion Glasscoe, ed., *The Medieval Mystical Tradition in England,* 4 (Cambridge: D. S. Brewer, 1991), pp. 79–100; reprinted in Sandra McEntire, ed., *Julian of Norwich: A Book of Essays* (New York: Garland Press, 1998), pp. 61–90.

larger world of Christian teaching. As she begins her last chapter (chapter 86), she confesses that "this boke is begonne by Goddys gyfte and his grace, but it is nott yett performyd, as to my syght," issuing what we can take as an invitation extended even to ourselves to assist in this process, one part of the past's always incomplete attempt to understand itself.[39] Where Hadewijch's *ontrouwe* is part of a fiercely exclusive mode of understanding, in which the rejection of meaning plays a large part, Julian's *love was his menyng* opens her book up to as wide a community of interpreters as is prepared to engage in her quest for truth with her. If Hadewijch is among our best guides to the operations of hermeneutic suspicion, which focuses on the negative valencies of the statement "I am you," Julian's extraordinarily detailed but integrated line-by-line exposition of her revelation provides as good a model as we are likely to get for positive or intuitive applications of the hermeneutics of empathy. In her visionary theology, in which God and the soul already lie kerneled within one another, truth is not too distant to grasp but too close to know clearly. Here, scholarly discovery is a truly an act of recovery, a recuperation.

6. Recapitulation: The Past in the Present

Historical scholarship—the kind that seeks to build stories out of textual and material remains and even the kind that critiques this storytelling tends to find itself paraphrasing or repeating the past, as its language and assumptions are pulled magnetically toward those of the subject under discussion. One reason for this process is love, or its contrary, hate—names we can give to the kinds of understanding that involve more than strictly empirical judgments; to the intuitions that link fragments into patterns, or names and dates into stories. A larger but more shadowy reason is that studying the past reawakens it. Insofar as the past comes to matter to historians and their readers, this is partly because ideas and feelings, as well as institutions, have successfully translated themselves into the present, giving a sense of urgency to the process of understanding the past whose source often goes unnoticed. A third reason, applicable to all the human sciences, is simply that what matters most to people, broadly defined, may not vary all that much: as

---

[39] Paris MS, fols. 172v–174r (Colledge and Walsh, eds., *A Book of Showings,* pp. 731–33).

the work of George Devereux makes clear, cultural anthropologists can succumb to the same sympathies as do historians.[40]

Faced with the problem of sympathy, medieval historians have traditionally responded by *not* facing the problem, emphasizing the "otherness" of the past (as though there were no "coincidence of opposites"), worrying about anachronism, and in other ways building up the walls of their magic garden.[41] Only when safe inside that garden, envisioning a beloved wholly unlike themselves (*nigra . . . sed formosa* [Song of Songs 1:4]), have they indulged their donnish versions of love's delights (*veniat dilectus meus in hortum suum et comedat fructum pomorum suorum* [Song of Songs 5:1]). One consequence of this may be that outside fields such as constitutional and doctrinal history, the Middle Ages has been accepted as "other" by scholars of later periods, a notion that may yet bring about institutional disaster for medievalists. A second consequence is that since the Middle Ages is not only "other" but is also indissolubly tied to the present, neither medieval studies nor modern cultural studies can operate in all the dimensions they should. All of us grumble about both these problems all the time.[42] *Holy Feast and Holy Fast* is important because, as Biddick shows, Bynum could not contain her thinking within the *hortus conclusus* of the past, overflowing the boundaries she set with a passion resembling the love Bernard calls *modus sine modo* in his *De diligendo Deo.* She could not do it because neither past nor present would let her. As the book's reception shows, what she was describing was too important for containment—with the result that a book about a medieval phenomenon has become one of the most influential analyses of women in history ever written.

Bynum's success was not without heavy costs—both the costs counted by Biddick and Aers and the others I have reckoned here with the help of scholars like Amy Hollywood—and there are plenty of respectable grounds for concluding that her scholarly experiment should not be repeated. My whole argument is that it should be, and that it can be once our thinking about present and past, and about the role of affect in scholarship, has achieved a greater flexibility than it has now. To that

[40] See, e.g., George Devereux, *From Anxiety to Method in the Behavioural Sciences* (The Hague: Mouton, 1967).
[41] On this tendency, see again Fradenburg, "'Voice Memorial.'"
[42] Nancy Partner's "Did Mystics Have Sex?," in Jacqueline Murray and Konrad Eisenbichler, eds., *Desire and Discipline: Sex and Sexuality in the Premodern West* (Toronto: University of Toronto Press, 1996), pp. 296–312, is only one of the more recent in what has become a medievalist genre of discussions of the field's marginalization.

end, I raised the banner of Karl Morrison's synthetic study of affect as a mode of knowing, and then showed how this mode might work by reading texts we would normally expect to approach as objects of study as though they were theoretical essays in affective historicity. Fusing past and present in this way, I confirmed Morrison's implied claim that affect is still a mode of knowing, as it was in the Middle Ages—albeit a mode that scholars seldom recognize—while submitting myself and my readers to a pair of *collationes,* or instructive discussions, conducted in the imagined voices of two medieval women intellectuals, Hadewijch and Julian of Norwich. It is important to the success of this essay that I have reproduced these voices well enough for them to be heard as at once "other"—part of an enterprise that is no longer at all the same as it was—and as unexpectedly familiar—part of a thinking and feeling life that still goes on. Marguerite Porete personifies the relationship between the soul and God as *Loingprès,* Farnear, which states in a succinct oxymoron the effect I intend.[43] If this has more or less worked, or if readers can at least imagine how it *ought* to have worked, a way may be open to adapt the hermeneutics of empathy as described by these medieval mystics, and of course by many others, to our own ends as modern historians: a project that, taken seriously, will force us to think over and over again about our investments in the past, but in a manner that can include those investments as part of our study, as traces of the past in the present. The inherent unlikeliness of this project—the manner in which it confronts us constantly with the "hermeneutic gap" that is integral to empathetic understanding, as we imagine our writing as an expression of *la mystique courtoise,* or Julian's desire for a bodily sight— is part of what may make it worth pursuing. But much more important, perhaps a project like this could also help us to find the powerful new means of exploring the relevance of our field to the human sciences as a whole that medieval studies so badly needs if it is to make its way in the world.

At the end of it all, though, where in this long zigzag of argument am I? While there is a way in which this paper wears its author's own feeling relationship with the past on its sleeve (for why else would he have written it?), the overt stance it has taken has been anything but confessional. Its readings of modern and medieval texts are represented as thought experiments; its appeals are all made as if on behalf of a community of scholars whose values and self–conceptions the paper is simul-

[43] Porete, *Mirouer des simples ames,* e.g., ch. 80.

taneously trying to refocus—and whom it has just followed Bynum and Biddick in drawing into a potentially coercive collective "we." If I end in this generalized mode, after so many pages of discussion of the attitudes of others, I think I turn into a version of one of the sympathetic male interpreters of women visionaries—Jacques de Vitry, Philip of Clairvaux, the anonymous author of the *vita* of Beatrice of Nazareth— whose lack of deep understanding of their subjects this paper has criticized: more a voyeur or stereotyper than a true imitator of the way of feeling thinking I advocate.

It is important to me to be clear, then, that I do not want simply to point to affective historiography as a possibility or an interesting experiment, but actually to imagine myself as practicing it. Indeed, the building I have put up here has foundations at least as firmly sunk in my own experience of absorption into the medieval religious texts that are my long preoccupation as they are in the admiring reading of Bynum I have used for bricks and mortar. It was Julian of Norwich who made me see, with shock, how much I had learned *as a scholar* from her and others like her—how far my approach to the past had become infused, through a sort of hermeneutic osmosis, with her own. I had started out, not so very long before, as a crusading demystifier of medieval English mysticism, committed to teasing out the personal agendas, anxieties, and structural tensions behind writings that often justify themselves through the bland notion of *utilitas,* and equally committed to cutting through the sentimentality I saw as typical of mystics studies. I had not imagined learning from the past; it is astonishing how much trouble our discipline has framing this as a thinkable thought. I had not even seen clearly how my analysis of it—especially in my early work on the male mystic who became an *alter ego,* Richard Rolle—quite straightforwardly used a small part of the past to work through issues and anxieties associated with my present.[44] But, paradoxically because it was harder for me to make the identification with her that came so easily with Rolle, Julian would not even pretend to stay in place as an object of study, or leave me where I was, in charge of the investigation. I was slowly but surely swept away: first, as befitted the abstract nature of my preoccupations, by her long commitment to her own theological sort of history writing;

[44] See my *Richard Rolle and the Invention of Authority* (Cambridge: Cambridge University Press, 1991). When not busy inventing its author's own authority, the book is surreptitiously but persistently revisiting a painful early brush with evangelical religion.

next, by the way this commitment became part of a way of thinking through her vision that included her own evolving responses to it (she included *herself* in her investigation); then, by her desire to share not only her vision but her subject-position as a visionary woman with all her readers, with me; and, at last, by her refusal to admit the separation between desire and reason on which my historicist training—and, not coincidentally, my educated masculine identity—had been founded, and her insistence that bodies also think, minds also feel. It was as though Julian and I had come to mirror one another across the herme-neutic gap hidden in Morrison's signature phrase, "I am you."

The lowlander Hadewijch sometimes describes the experience of love as a flood, bursting the dikes of the soul, pushing out through its hills and valleys, invading its secret places.[45] Even so Julian's feeling thinking crept in around my edges, unsettled my belief in the sobriety of my projects, integrated things I had been taught to keep separate: reason and love, suspicion and belief, object and subject, past and present. She demanded new kinds of language, and a new sense of my role as a scholar, with which to talk about her. She made me revisit aspects of my earlier work and find them callow—my cavalier disregard, for example, of the experiential, as distinct from ambitiously rhetorical, sides of Rolle's writing—although I also found I could use what I learned from her to rethink what I had known about the past in a different mode. Julian taught me to think about more than Julian. Over a few years she rewrote—in ways I have yet fully to understand—my entire sense of what it is that scholars do, and set me in search of models to justify doing things in the new way she suggested. And in the end, however much I have learned from Caroline Bynum and Karl Morrison, it was Julian's *Revelation of Love* (as I studied it alongside the writings of Hade-wijch, Marguerite Porete, and a few others) that was instrumental in allowing me to develop the argument I have presented here.

I close, however, with a passage not of Julian but of my earlier com-panion Rolle: one which brings out as clearly as I could wish the possi-bilities and perils of the voice I assume in this paper:

Ego dormio et cor meum vigilat. The that lyste luf, held thine ere and here of luf! In the sang of luf I fynde it writen that I have sett at the begynnynge of my wrytynge: "I slepe and my hert wakes." Mykell luf he shewes that nevere is irke

---

[45] See Hadewijch, *Complete Works,* e.g. Letters (p. 63), 22 (pp. 100–2).

to luf, bot ay, standande, sittande, gangande, or any other dede doande, es ay
his luf thynkand, and oft-sithe therof dremand. Forthi that I luf the, I wogh
the, that I myght have the as I wilde—noght tille me, bot till my Lard. I wille
be comer and messager to bryng the till his bed that has made the and boght
the, Cryst the kynges son of heven. For he will wed the, if thou wille luf hym—
he askes the na mare bot thi luf. And my wille thou dose, if thou luf hym. Crist
covaytes thi faireheade in saule, that thou gyf hym halely thi hert. And I preche
noght ellys bot that thou do his will, and afforce the day and nyght to lefe alle
fleschely luf and al likyng that lettus the to luf Jhesu Crist verrayly. For i-whils
thi hert is heldande to luf of any bodyly thyng, thou may not parfitly be cupilde
wit God.[46]

In this romantic epistolary treatment of the degrees of love (usually referred to by its first phrase, *Ego Dormio*), Rolle imagines himself as a
spiritual mediator between Christ and a woman reader (probably a nun),
whom Christ loves so much that he has not only "boght" her but now
means to marry her, dowerless, if she will love him back. Rolle's nakedly
erotic interpellation of his own relationship with his reader—as the
means by which her union with God will come about—risks the collapse of the delicate structure of sexual sublimation that was integral to
fourteenth-century spirituality: the collapse of the figure of the saintly
guide into that of the seducer. But it does so in a deliberate act of trust
in the single–minded orientation towards God and the lack of possessive
jealousy towards one another both writer and reader must share for the
text to work. The reader already loves God, even if she wants to become
like Rolle in loving him more; only thus is it possible to write to her in
this vein. The risk is still real, not diminished by the fact that Rolle's
image of union with God always includes union with his fellow saints—
so that what he does here, theologically, is to anticipate the erotic solidarity that is to be his and his reader's for eternity. Yet the trust is what
should help us see the passage's sensuality as seductive, not patronizing,
and its privileging of the voice of a male hermit as incidental, not fundamental, to its logic. As in Julian's endlessly generous thought-world,
anyone here can play any of the available roles, and even Christ mingles
his desires with those his lovers feel for him—as the past in my account
of it mingles strangely with the present, or as the desire for the past I

[46] Richard Rolle, *Ego Dormio,* transcribed from MS Rawlinson A.389, f. 77, by C.
Horstman, *Yorkshire Writers: Richard Rolle of Hampole, an English Father of the Church and
His Followers,* 2 vols. (London: Swan Sonnenschein, 1895–96): I.50. This is the best
text of *Ego Dormio* (aside from its missing leaf), preserving the rare and presumably
authentic "comer."

declare here perhaps mingles with the desires of my readers, in the same way I catch fire from reading others.

Not everything in the passage translates into the new context I have for it here. For example, where Rolle assumes that he shares with all right-thinking readers a single path towards a single goal, any equivalent call made to scholars, not mystics, needs to be more open than he can conceive to being resisted, reformulated, multiplied, and diversified by those who hear it—for who is interested in working in a single way or towards a single model of the truth of the past? And none of us can have or even should have the exclusiveness of purpose, the lack of other preoccupations, these professional contemplatives claim to have won for themselves; abandonment of "the world" has nothing to do with our project. And there is in any case no possibility of being "parfitly cupilde" with anything in the past; all we ever have is fragments. But I still think there is much to be gained from taking into ourselves, as one of the ordinary tools we use in our research and writing, the full force of Rolle's passionate invocation of his reader here, the audacious intensity of what it is he wants, and wants her to want. I still think we should insist on our need to speak, in part, in the past's words; ask of it how it speaks both to and through us; demand of it—as not only Caroline Bynum but also Kathleen Biddick and David Aers indeed do demand of it—more than either the weakly satisfying confirmation of its "otherness" or the slender analogies and provisional points of origin that are all our current academic orthodoxies are willing to envisage.[47]

---

[47] Versions of this paper were given at the conference "Women and the Christian Tradition," sponsored by the European Science Foundation, Strasbourg, October 1995; at the conference "The Past at Present: Varieties of Historicism in Medieval and Early Modern Studies," University of Western Ontario, February 1996; at the University of Arizona, March 1996; as a plenary talk at the American Comparative Literature Annual Conference, Puerto Vallarta, Mexico, March 1997; and at the medieval seminar, Harvard University, February 1998. I want to thank all those who invited me to speak, or who responded to the paper. Special thanks are due to Amy Appleford, Claire Fanger, Saskia Murk Jansen, Larry Scanlon, Sarah Stanbury, Jennifer Summit, and Jocelyn Wogan-Browne; to my colleagues at Western, Richard Green, Richard Hillman, Fiona Somerset, and Leon Surette; and to the students in my seminar "Violent Love in Northern Europe, 1100–1400." The title of the paper owes an obvious debt to Allen J. Frantzen's book *Desire for Origins: New Language, Old English, and Teaching the Tradition* (New Brunswick, N.J.: Rutgers University Press, 1990). Its chief intellectual debts, besides the ones acknowledged in the paper itself, are to Anne Savage's essay "The Translation of the Feminine: Untranslatable Dimensions of the Anchoritic Works," in Roger Ellis and Ruth Evans, eds., *The Medieval Translator* 4 (Exeter: Exeter University Press, 1994), pp. 181–99; and to the novels and stories of the New Zealand fantasy writer Cherry Wilder, whose disciplined but impassioned imaginings of other worlds have brought me back and back to the topic explored here.

Langland's Musical Reader: Liturgy, Law, and the Constraints of Performance

Bruce W. Holsinger
University of Colorado

"Our songs have become laws."

—Plato, *The Laws*

Rarely has a literary work escaped the ideological grasp of its author as quickly as did William Langland's *Piers Plowman*. Within a few decades of their composition, the three versions of the poem attracted an astonishingly wide range of responses from a number of English writers who took the work as a justification for their own articulation of religious and political protest. The B-text initially circulated within what some have recently described as a "London coterie," the members of which included the bureaucratic functionary Thomas Usk and, perhaps, the increasingly prominent London poet Geoffrey Chaucer, who may have composed *The House of Fame* after encountering the work shortly before 1380.[1] Soon thereafter, however, allusions to *Piers Plowman* appear in two letters associated with the Peasants' Revolt of

I am grateful to the staff of the Students Room at the British Library for their assistance and to John Bowers, Anna Brickhouse, A. S. G. Edwards, Andrew Galloway, Richard Firth Green, Ralph Hanna, William Kuskin, Jana Mathews, Derek Pearsall, Wendy Scase, and Emily Steiner for their helpful suggestions.

[1] Ralph Hanna III, "On the Versions of *Piers Plowman*," in *Pursuing History: Middle English Manuscripts and Their Texts,* Figurae: Reading Medieval Culture (Stanford, Calif.: Stanford University Press, 1996), pp. 236–37; see also Hanna, *William Langland* (Aldershot, Hants.: Variorum; Brookfield, Vt.: Ashgate, 1993), pp. 23–24; and Kathryn Kerby-Fulton and Steven Justice, "Langlandian Reading Circles and the Civil Service in London and Dublin, 1380–1427," *New Medieval Literatures* 1 (1997): 59–83. A much more skeptical appraisal of the evidence for Usk's knowledge of Langland is forthcoming from John Bowers in *Yearbook of Langland Studies.* On Langland and the *House of Fame,* see most recently Frank Grady, "Chaucer Reading Langland: *The House of Fame,*" SAC 18 (1996): 3–23.

1381.[2] By the early fifteenth century, several heterodox writers had recruited *Piers Plowman* into what John Bowers terms a "renegade" textual community, attesting to a general tendency among later authors to view the work as primarily a political document that would lend prestige to their own critiques of church, law, and government.[3] While Langland's own positions on the controversies of his day have never been particularly easy to pin down, many of his poem's earliest readers sought to enlist its befuddled dreamer and laboring protagonist as vocal proponents for the necessity of dissent.

This essay proposes a new addition to the immediate vernacular legacy of *Piers Plowman*. I shall argue that the so-called "Choristers' Lament," a little-studied alliterative satire on the woes of musical learning within an English monastic institution, represents a sophisticated but hitherto unrecognized response to Langland's poem. (The "Lament" is newly edited and annotated in the Appendix.[4]) Provocative evidence for the argument that follows can be found in the notes to Skeat's 1886 parallel-text edition of *Piers,* and in fact the topic was first suggested to me by an entry in the *Middle English Dictionary.*

Among the most prominent obstacles that arguments for direct literary influence must inevitably confront are those of dating: while the earliest likely date of the B-text is 1377, the "Choristers' Lament" has been dated anywhere from circa 1300 to the middle of the fifteenth century.[5] A new estimate by Ralph Hanna, based in part on an assessment

[2] Steven Justice, *Writing and Rebellion: England in 1381* (Berkeley: University of California Press, 1994), p. 129. Recent work on *Piers Plowman* and the Rising includes John Bowers, "Piers Plowman and the Police: Notes Towards a History of the Wycliffite Langland," *Yearbook of Langland Studies* 6 (1992), esp. pp. 2–10; Susan Crane, "The Writing Lesson of 1381," in Barbara Hanawalt and David Wallace, eds., *Chaucer's England: Literature in Historical Context* (Minneapolis: University of Minnesota Press, 1992), esp. pp. 211–16; Richard Firth Green, "John Ball's Letters: Literary History and Historical Literature," in *Chaucer's England,* pp. 176–200; and Anne Hudson, "*Piers Plowman* and the Peasants' Revolt: A Problem Revisited," *YLS* 8 (1995): 85–106.
[3] John Bowers, "Piers Plowman and the Police," p. 34; Anne Hudson, " 'No newe thyng': The Printing of Medieval Texts in the Early Reformation Period," in Douglas Gray and E. G. Stanley, eds., *Middle English Studies Presented to Norman Davis* (Oxford: Clarendon Press, 1983), pp. 172–73. On *Piers Plowman* and Lollardy more generally, see especially David Lawton, "Lollardy and the 'Piers Plowman' Tradition," *MLR* 76 (1981): 780–93; Helen Barr, *Signes and Sothe: Language in the Piers Plowman Tradition,* Piers Plowman Studies 10 (Cambridge: D. S. Brewer, 1994), esp. ch. 4, pp. 95–132; and the numerous studies cited by Bowers on pp. 10–36.
[4] The poem has also been edited by Francis Lee Utley, "The Choristers' Lament," *Speculum* 21 (1946): 194–202.
[5] On the date of the B-text, see, for example, Hanna, *William Langland,* pp. 12–14; on the date of the "Lament," see the sources cited in note 47 below.

of the anglicana hand in which the unique copy of the "Lament" survives, places its composition "perhaps . . . as early as 1350."[6] Middle English paleographers have long cautioned against relying too heavily on the dating of individual hands, of course; L. C. Hector's warning in *The Handwriting of English Documents* that a range of fifty years counts as "close palaeographical dating" has recently been seconded by A. S. G. Edwards, who stresses the "limited evidence for dating that is afforded by script alone."[7] Indeed, I suggest that more conclusive evidence for the dating of the "Choristers' Lament" may lie in its allusions to the B-version of *Piers Plowman.*

More generally, the essay is intended to contribute to recent efforts by Anne Middleton, Kathryn Kerby-Fulton, Steven Justice, Hanna, Bowers, and others to broaden and complicate our view of Langland's influence upon his contemporaries. The "Choristers' Lament" may represent one of the earliest accretions to the literary afterlife of *Piers Plowman;* if so, the specific nature of its revisionism has significant implications for our understanding of the diverse character of Langland's reading public in the first decades of this readership's existence.[8] For while much of the vernacular writings inspired by *Piers Plowman* in the late fourteenth and early fifteenth centuries appropriate the poem to serve their own calls for broad reforms of church, crown, and government, the "Choristers' Lament" addresses its satirical critique to a much more mundane and seemingly less contentious arena: the discourses of musical pedagogy and liturgical performance. Though clearly distinct from the politically and religiously radical rewritings that characterize the early reception of *Piers Plowman,* the "Lament" nevertheless insists upon the social dimensions of musical practice by working against the legalistic conception of

---

[6] Ralph Hanna III, "Alliterative Poetry," in David Wallace, ed., *The Cambridge History of Medieval English Literature* (Cambridge: Cambridge University Press, 1999), pp. 509–10.

[7] L. C. Hector, *The Handwriting of English Documents,* 2d ed. (London: E. Arnold, 1966), p. 13: "The needs of scholarship are usually met if the date allotted to such material on the evidence of its handwriting can be taken to be correct to within fifty years, which by the wise student of archive hands is reckoned to be close palaeographical dating"; cited by A. S. G. Edwards with regard to book hands in "Manuscript and Text," in Vincent P. McCarren and Douglas Moffat, eds., *A Guide to Editing Middle English* (Ann Arbor: University of Michigan Press, 1998), p. 164, where he adds an "obvious general point: paleographical evidence is rarely clear-cut and, since it is open to various interpretations, needs to be used with caution."

[8] For an influential account of the breadth of Langland's imagined and actual readership, see Anne Middleton, "The Audience and Public of 'Piers Plowman,'" in David Lawton, ed., *Middle English Alliterative Poetry and Its Literary Background* (Cambridge: D. S. Brewer, 1982), pp. 101–23.

101

liturgical pedagogy and performance informing its most immediate source.

While there are any number of ways in which *Piers Plowman* gestures toward the diverse musical cultures of its day, only Langland's representations of minstrelsy have attracted more than a passing comment in the scholarship. In his 1949 study of the C-text, E. Talbot Donaldson demonstrated the poet's almost obsessive interest in defining and delimiting the role of minstrels as a professional class of musical and quasi-literary entertainers.[9] Yet Langland's explicit scrutiny of the peripatetic culture of minstrelsy coexists in *Piers Plowman* alongside an equally searching preoccupation with the musical culture of liturgy. The density of liturgical citation in the poem has been much studied, of course, but almost always in terms of the moral or religious significance of the interpolated liturgical texts at the expense of their performative embodiment in liturgical music.[10] The result has been an unspoken critical consensus in Langland studies upon what Herbert Marcuse would term the "affirmative character" of liturgical culture—that is, the unquestioning consent of liturgical performers and participants to clerical authority and ecclesiological orthodoxy.

Such a view of medieval liturgy inspires Eamon Duffy's widely acclaimed recent book, *The Stripping of the Altars: Traditional Religion in England 1400–1580,* in which he argues that the religious life of pre-Reformation England was characterized above all by "a remarkable degree of religious and imaginative homogeneity across the social spectrum, a shared repertoire of symbols, prayers, and beliefs, which crossed and bridged even the gulf between the literate and the illiterate."[11] For

---

[9] E. Talbot Donaldson, *Piers Plowman: The C-Text and Its Poet* (New Haven, Conn.: Yale University Press, 1949), pp. 136–55. Donaldson's careful delineation of the ways in which Langland self-consciously altered his poetic stance toward minstrels between the composition of the B- and C-texts remains one of the most forceful arguments for single authorship of the two versions. On Langland and minstrelsy, see also Wendy Scase, *'Piers Plowman' and the New Anticlericalism* (Cambridge: Cambridge University Press, 1989), pp. 147–49.

[10] The classic study of Langland's knowledge and use of liturgy is Greta Hort, *Piers Plowman and Contemporary Religious Thought* (New York: Macmillan, 1938); but see the critical overview of Hort's study in Robert Adams, "Langland and the Liturgy Revisited," *SP* 73 (1976): 266–84. More recent contributions include John A. Alford, *Piers Plowman: A Guide to the Quotations* (Binghamton, N.Y.: Center for Medieval and Early Renaissance Studies, 1992), esp. pp. 20–23; and M. Teresa Tavormina, "*Piers Plowman* and the Liturgy of St. Lawrence: Composition and Revision in Langland's Poetry," *SP* 84 (1987): 245–71.

[11] Eamon Duffy, *The Stripping of the Altars: Traditional Religion in England 1400–1580* (New Haven and London: Yale University Press, 1992), p. 3.

Duffy, in fact, Langland's "autobiographical" account in the C-text of the tools of his quasi-liturgical "labore"—"*pater-noster* and my prymer, *placebo* and *dirige,* / And my sauter som tyme and my sevene psalmes"— serves as useful literary evidence of what he terms the "bridge between lay piety and the liturgical observance of the church," one that "enabled lay people to associate themselves with the prayer of the clergy and religious."[12] More generally, liturgical practice stands at the center of what is perhaps Duffy's boldest act of historical homogenization: his working assumption, repeated even in the book's index, that liturgy represented the "basis of lay religion" in pre-Reformation England, that it was in "the liturgy and in the sacramental celebrations which were its central moments" that "medieval people found the key to the meaning and purpose of their lives."[13]

My own discussion will center not on lay liturgical practices, Duffy's main concern, but on representations of liturgical performance among the religious orders themselves, that branch of "medieval people" who, as David Aers points out, were responsible precisely for imposing ecclesiastical authority and religious orthodoxy upon the laity in their care.[14] As we shall see, however, even within the orthodox ranks of the religious orders, liturgical practice was riven with dissension and contradiction. No one discerned this more clearly than Langland's medieval revisers, several of whom responded to his poem's representations of liturgical performance by scrutinizing the various modes of authority that sustained it. As a simultaneously liturgical and *anti*-liturgical intervention into the literary afterlife of *Piers Plowman,* the "Choristers' Lament" in particular asks us to recognize the medieval English liturgy as the site of pedagogical and institutional conflict that it was.

[12] Duffy, *Stripping of the Altars,* p. 231; the Langland material is discussed on p. 220. Hanna has convincingly suggested that these "lomes" were intended by Langland to signal the dreamer's affiliation with eremitical *litterati,* and that the performance of the texts named in the "autobiographical" passage in C would have been considered among those "acceptable male clerical pursuits from which less fortunate hermits are debarred"; see Hanna, "Will's Work," in Steven Justice and Kathryn Kerby-Fulton, eds., *Written Work: Langland, Labor, Authorship* (Philadelphia: University of Pennsylvania Press, 1997), pp. 37–38.

[13] Duffy, *Stripping of the Altars,* pp. 641 and 11, respectively. For a particularly forceful response to Duffy's claims regarding the medieval English liturgy, see Katherine L. French, "Competing for Space: Medieval Religious Conflict in the Monastic-Parochial Church at Dunster," *Journal of Medieval and Early Modern Studies* 27 (1992), esp. pp. 231–38.

[14] David Aers, "Altars of Power: Reflections on Eamon Duffy's *The Stripping of the Altars: Traditional Religion in England 1400–1580,*" *Literature and History,* 3d ser., 3 (1994): 90–105.

Before turning to the "Lament" itself, it will be necessary to examine in some detail the particular strain of Langlandian musical representation with which the satire engages. The "Lament"-poet's clever send-up of the coercive dimensions of musical learning and performance responds to a remarkably explicit conflation of liturgical and legal authority in *Piers Plowman,* a conflation that figures as well in two other works more self-consciously indebted to Langland's poem. All three texts combine an anxious concern over legal protocol with a particular ideology of liturgical performance. For Langland and for at least some of his initial revisers, I argue, the law served both to mediate the institutional mechanisms and to control the social meanings of liturgical practice. It is by rejecting this venerable ideological alliance between liturgy and law that the "Choristers' Lament" reveals its historical and literary significance as an ingeniously crafted response to *Piers Plowman.*

Song Become Law

The interpenetration of music and law in the Western tradition is at least as old as Plato, whose writings collectively adumbrate a theory of musico-juridical subjection exemplified in the punning aphorism I have chosen as the epigraph to this essay. In his insistence that "songs" have become "laws"—the Greek *nomos,* which also denotes a variety of song accompanied by a cithar[15]—Plato assigns to music a fundamental role in the social regulation of the polis: "[L]et no one voice anything or make any dance movement contrary to the public and sacred songs, or the whole choral exercise of the young, any more than he would go against any of the other laws."[16] From his Pythagorean elaboration of the omniscient Demiurge in the *Timaeus* to his censorious rejection of certain musical instruments and modes in the *Republic,* Plato conceived of *harmonia as* obedience, an unheard but ubiquitous part of a "cosmic dance" in which the human performance of *mousike*—a mimetic discipline among the Greeks that embraced song, poetry, dance, and dra-

---

[15] See *The Laws of Plato,* trans. Thomas L. Pangle (New York: Basic Books, 1980), p. 526n.; and the remarks on this pun by Herbert Schueller, *The Idea of Music: An Introduction to Musical Aesthetics in Antiquity and the Middle Ages* (Kalamazoo, Mich.: Medieval Institute Publications, 1988), p. 51.

[16] Plato, *The Laws* 829e, p. 220; see Edward Lippman's discussion of such passages in *Musical Thought in Ancient Greece* (New York: Columbia University Press, 1964), pp. 83–86.

matic gesture[17]—would embody in miniature what Edward Lippmann terms "the ordered and ordering intelligence of the world soul."[18]

The confluence of musical terminology and legal diction assumed a striking variety of forms in the Middle Ages, which witnessed an extended encounter between music and law that scholars have examined only sporadically and can here be sketched only in its broadest outlines. In a now-classic lecture on canon law, Stephan Kuttner showed that the Platonic and Augustinian conception of *concordantia* was frequently employed by canonists as an analogy for the musical resolution of doctrinal "dissonance." The titular metaphor of Gratian's *Concordia discordantium canonum,* the great twelfth-century legal compendium, represents what Kuttner calls "the signal achievement of the medieval mind in organizing the law of the Church into a harmonious system out of an infinite variety of diverse, even contradictory, elements."[19] More recently, Jody Enders has proposed that the classical rhetorical canon of forensic *actio* exerted an originary influence on the development of medieval drama. As Enders points out regarding the performance of liturgical music specifically, "[T]he verbal antiphony of forensic oratory is a logical antecedent for the musical antiphony of troping," the embellishments that have traditionally been regarded as the performative impetus for liturgical drama.[20]

The conflation of legal and musical discourse reached what was surely its medieval apogee in a Latin theoretical treatise on music with the intriguing incipit *Ars cantus mensurabilis mensurata per modos iuris,* or "The art of mensurable song measured by the modes of law."[21] Written in Italy in the late fourteenth century, most likely by a Florentine monk,[22]

---

[17] On *mousike,* see Schueller, *The Idea of Music,* p. 45, and Jody Enders, "Music, Delivery, and the Rhetoric of Memory in Guillaume de Machaut's *Remède de Fortune," PMLA* 107 (1992): 450–51.

[18] Lippman, *Musical Thought in Ancient Greece,* p. 30. On the "cosmic dance" and its explicit conflation of *harmonia* and cosmic order, see James Miller's magisterial *Measures of Wisdom, The Cosmic Dance in Classical and Christian Antiquity* (Toronto: University of Toronto Press, 1986).

[19] Stephan Kuttner, *Harmony from Dissonance: An Interpretation of Medieval Canon Law,* Wimmer Lecture 10 (Latrobe, Penn.: The Archabbey Press, 1960), p. 10.

[20] Enders, *Rhetoric and the Origins of Medieval Drama* (Ithaca and London: Cornell University Press, 1992), p. 65; on liturgical troping and classical forensic oratory, see also pp. 56–57.

[21] *Ars cantus mensurabilis mensurata per modos iuris: The Art of Mensurable Song Measured by the Modes of Law,* ed. and trans. C. Matthew Balensuela, Greek and Latin Music Theory 10 (Lincoln and London: University of Nebraska Press, 1994).

[22] See Belensuela's introduction in *Ars cantus mensurabilis,* pp. 82–87.

this work represents an extended and particularly complex effort to apply the language and logic of medieval legal diction to the rules of musical time. Reflecting a sophisticated knowledge of both canon and civil law, the author enlists a dizzying array of allusions drawn from a variety of classical and medieval legal traditions in order to explicate musical phenomena. A maxim from the Justinian *lex regia,* for example, illuminates the varying use of red or hollow notation, while the closing lines of an 1177 decretal of Alexander III on the dispute between Becket and Henry II justifies a particular kind of mensural imperfection.[23] Though this treatise represents the densest use of legal terminology by a medieval writer on music, its deployment of juridical language is far from unique among the period's musical theorists and composers, a number of whom were trained in canon law or actually served as lawyers for a portion of their careers.[24]

More significant for the purposes of this essay are the many ways in which medieval vernacular writers register this terminological nexus in their diverse representations of liturgical and legal performances. A particularly striking example of this occurs in the fourteenth-century *Romans de Bauduin de Sebourc,* in which a judicial advocate is described as a performer "solefiant devant juges ses cas."[25] The term "solefiant" refers to the pedagogical practice of solmization, a medieval method of teaching plainchant in which each note of a scale was assigned a specific syllable, thus allowing chant melodies to be learned quickly and remembered easily (solmization survives today in the popularized gamut "Do-re-mi-fa-sol-la-ti-do"; the medieval Latin verb *solfare,* "to sing in solmization," was derived from the syllables "sol" and "fa").[26] The lawyer in *Bauduin de Sebourc,* then, is "sol-fa-ing his case before a judge." While I shall have much more to say below about literary representations of solmization, in this case the metaphor suggests that, in testifying before

---

[23] *Ars cantus,* pp. 234–36, 190 respectively; see Balensuela's informative discussion of the treatise's legal terminology on pp. 23–36 of the introduction.

[24] Balensuela, pp. 22–23 and notes.

[25] *Li Romans de Bauduin de Sebourc, IIIe Roy de Jhérusalem: Poëme du XIVe siècle, publié pour la première fois, d'après les Manuscrits de la Bibliothèque Royale,* Louis Napoleon Boca, ed. (Valenciennes: Impr. de B. Henry, 1841) 2.18.56; vol. 2, p. 173.

[26] On solmization, see Andrew Hughes, "Solmization I," in Stanley Sadie, ed., *The New Grove Dictionary of Music and Musicians* 17 (London: Macmillan, 1980), pp. 458–62; and Carol Berger, "The Hand and the Art of Memory," *Musica Disciplina* 35 (1981): 87–121.

a judge, a lawyer musically "performs" his case with the same discipline with which the liturgical performer learns to chant.[27]

A much more familiar example comes from *The General Prologue* to *The Canterbury Tales,* in which the Man of Law is a sonorous advocate very much like the singing lawyer in *Bauduin de Sebourc:*

> In termes hadde he caas and doomes alle
> That from the tyme of kyng William were falle.
> Thereto he koude endite and make a thyng,
> Ther koude no wight pynche at his writyng;
> And every statut koude he pleyn by rote.
> He rood but hoomly in a medlee cote. . . . [28]

While several commentators on the Man of Law's portrait have wondered whether a lawyer could possibly have memorized "every statut" enacted since the Norman Conquest,[29] equally significant may be Chaucer's suggestion that the lawyer *performs* the statutes he has learned. There is little evidence in fourteenth-century statutes to suggest that laws were actually composed for oral recitation, of course, and I do not mean to argue that Chaucer sought to resurrect a more archaic mode of juridical spectacle (as represented, for example, in the *Owl and the Nightingale,* perhaps the most dazzling conflation of musical and legal terminology in the English vernacular). Yet Chaucer's two other uses of the phrase "by rote" in *The Canterbury Tales* occur in the Prioress's description of the clergeon's learning and singing of the antiphon *Alma redemptoris* ("His felawe taughte hym homward prively, / Fro day to day, til he koude it by rote, / And thanne he song it wel and boldely, / Fro word to word, acordynge with the note" [*PrT* 544–47]) and in the

[27] I was initially led to this passage by a provocative comment in Leo Spitzer's *Classical and Christian Ideas of World Harmony* (Baltimore: Johns Hopkins Press, 1963), p. 170. The romance's portrait of the "singing lawyer" may well anticipate the performing advocates in the fifteenth- and sixteenth-century Theater of the Basoche as described by Enders, *Rhetoric and the Origins of Medieval Drama,* pp. 129–161; see also Howard Graham Harvey, *The Theatre of the Basoche* (Cambridge: Harvard University Press, 1941).

[28] *GP* 323–28. All citations of Chaucer's works are from Larry Benson, gen ed., *The Riverside Chaucer* (Boston: Houghton Mifflin, 1987). Subsequent references will be made parenthetically within the text.

[29] See, for example, the explanatory notes to *GP* in *Riverside Chaucer,* p. 812; and Muriel Bowden, *A Commentary on the General Prologue to the Canterbury Tales* (New York: Macmillan, 1948), p. 168.

Pardoner's account of the musical shape of his own rhetorical performance ("'I peyne me to han an hauteyn speche, / And rynge it out as round as gooth a belle, / For I kan al by rote that I telle" [*PardP* 330–32]). For Chaucer, perhaps, the law is as "performable" as liturgical song and sermon.

Such analogies between juridical and musical performance make perfect sense given the commonplace medieval notion of "the spiritual role of law as an earthly representation of God's rule."[30] As John Alford points out in an authoritative overview of law and literature in medieval England, many writers in this period consistently expressed what he terms "a profound faith in law as the tie that binds all things, in heaven and in earth."[31] A similar claim was frequently made for the Christian liturgy, which was commonly imagined as an all-embracing symbol of the divine plan for salvation. One of the central tenets of medieval liturgical commentary was that the liturgy constitutes an earthly embodiment of salvation history, a soteriological and typological reenactment in which liturgical performers represent significant actors from the Old Testament and the life and Passion of Christ.[32] Just as the ideal practitioner of the law is the earthly agent of God's authority, so the liturgical celebrant participates in the sacramental realization of divine omnipotence.

In this sense, popular twelfth-century liturgical treatises such as Honorius Augustodunensis's *Gemma animae* and the anonymous *Speculum ecclesiae* as well as later vernacular writings on the liturgy can be read as a kind of performative legislation. Thus, in a commentary on the Mass likely written for the laity and copied in the Vernon manuscript (which also contains one of the earliest A-texts of *Piers Plowman*), readers are reminded why even the Pope himself

> . . . bad wiþ ful good wille
> þat everi Mon schulde stonde stille,
> Whon he comeþ þe churche with-Inne.
> And þenne hou wel þat god may wreke

[30] Julian Wasserman, "Medieval Contracts and Covenants: The Legal Colouring of *Sir Gawain and the Green Knight*," *Neophilologus* 68 (1984): 598; cited in Barr, *Signes and Sothe*, p. 134.
[31] Alford, "Literature and Law in Medieval England," *PMLA* 92 (1977): 942.
[32] On the Latin liturgical commentary tradition see, most recently, Margot Fassler, *Gothic Song: Victorine Sequences and Augustinian Reform in Twelfth-Century Paris* (Cambridge: Cambridge University Press, 1993), pp. 18–37.

Euerich a word þat we speke,
We do ful muche synne;
A Prest miȝt be let of his mes,
Al þis world miȝt fare þe wers,
Vs alle to wo to wynne.[33]

The treatise freights each word uttered by the celebrant with a truly cosmological significance: as the priest performs the Mass, the "world" itself assumes a liturgical role, and "everi Mon" becomes responsible for maintaining silence and discipline in hopes of pleasing God by obeying his liturgical agent. The liturgy is, essentially and emphatically, "the law." In theory, at least, liturgy and law were perfectly suited to one another as ideological agents of Christian subjection.

But only in theory. For as social theorists from Durkheim to Pierre Bourdieu have insisted, every form of authority maintains itself in part through the public, rhetorical performances in which it reaches its subjects—in Bourdieu's influential formulation, the "symbolic violence" that seeks to legitimize the exercise of power by convincing the public that its subordination is natural and even desirable.[34] And the vagaries of performance must always raise more questions than the ideology of legitimation can answer. A powerful case in point is the medieval literary representation of law itself: what emerges from recent scholarship on law and literature in fourteenth-century England, for instance, is the gap between legal ideology and juridical practice, between the idealizing claims made on behalf of the law and the fallibility of legal institutions and agents in the public sphere.[35] In *Piers Plowman* and several of the alliterative writings it inspired, the thoroughgoing conflation of music and law paradoxically corrodes the authoritative bond between the juridical ideology of liturgical obedience and the social practice of liturgical performance. The result is a disciplinary collusion between

---

[33] "A Treatise of the Manner and Mede of the Mass," ed. Thomas Frederick Simmons, *The Lay Folks Mass Book,* EETS, o.s., 71 (London, 1879), appendix 4, p. 139 ln 392–400. The treatise appears in pt. 3 of Vernon, on which see A. I. Doyle, "The Shaping of the Vernon and Simeon Manuscripts," in Derek Pearsall, ed., *Studies in the Vernon Manuscript* (Cambridge: D. S. Brewer, 1990), pp. 4–5; and N. F. Blake, "Vernon Manuscript: Contents and Organisation," in *Studies in the Vernon Manuscript,* pp. 52–55.

[34] For the most extended treatment of symbolic violence, see Pierre Bourdieu and J.-C. Passerson, *Reproduction in Education, Society and Culture* (London: Sage, 1990).

[35] See, for example, Maura Nolan, "'With tresoun within': Wynnere and Wastoure, Chivalric Self-Representation, and the Law," *Journal of Medieval and Early Modern Studies* 26 (1996): 1–28.

law and liturgy that seeks but ultimately fails to hold liturgical practice to the same standards of consistency and "truth" supposedly embodied in the law—a failure upon which the "Choristers' Lament" will linger and capitalize.

Reading Langland Legally

The most extended intercalation of legal and liturgical performance in *Piers Plowman* occurs during the "dream within a dream" sequence of passus 11 of the B-text.[36] The passage in question appears near the end of the lengthy anticlerical harangue voiced by "oon . . . broken out of hell" that begins at line 140. The speaker of these lines (whose identity has been a matter of some contention[37]) has just outlined a series of objections to contemporary clerical abuses; after likening kings who make knights out of paupers to bishops who name unlearned laymen as clerics, the monologue concludes by indicting "preestes" who betray "lewed men" through their ignorance (B.11.303–14):

> A chartre is chalangeable bifore a chief Iustice:
> If fals latyn be in þat lettre þe lawe it impugneþ,
> Or peynted parentrelynarie, parcelles ouerskipped.
> The gome þat gloseþ so chartres for a goky is holden.
> So is it a goky, by god! þat in his gospel failleþ,
> Or in masse or in matyns makeþ any defaute:
> *Qui offendit in uno, in omnibus est reus.*
> And also in þe Sauter seiþ Dauid to ouerskipperis,
> *Psallite deo nostro; psallite quoniam rex terre deus Israel; psallite sapienter.*
> The bisshop shal be blamed bifore god, as I leue,
> That crouneþ swiche goddes knyȝtes, þat konneþ noȝt *sapienter*
> Synge ne psalmes rede ne seye a masse of þe day.

---

[36] Unless otherwise indicated, throughout the remainder of this essay all quotations from *Piers Plowman* will be taken from *Piers Plowman: The B Version,* ed. George Kane and E. Talbot Donaldson (London: Athlone, 1975), which will hereafter be cited internally. Although I cite from and discuss B only, all of the relevant passages occur with minor variation in C.

[37] See, for example, James Simpson, *Piers Plowman: An Introduction to the B-text* (London and New York: Longman, 1990), p. 127, who favors Trajan; and Scase, *Piers Plowman and the New Anticlericalism,* p. 167, who points out that in C the speaker is clearly identified as Rechelesnesse.

The passage draws a curious parallel between, on the one hand, charter makers who use "fals latyn" and "parentrelyn[ear]" glossing and thereby invalidate legal documents, and, on the other, liturgical performers who "maketh . . . defaute" in the performance of the liturgy, the "overskipperis" whom David advises to *psallite sapienter* as they perform from the Psalter. Both transgressions, legal and musical, render those who commit them "gokys": cuckoo-birds or, perhaps, simply fools.

Yet even as the speaker articulates his dogmatic conflation of improper legal and liturgical practices, Langland's text falters in its attempt to ground this critique convincingly in biblical authority. Below is the text of Psalm 46:7–8 from the Sarum Use:

> Psallite Deo nostro psallite
> *psallite regi nostro psallite*
> quoniam rex omnis terrae Deus psallite sapienter.

And here is Langland's rendition as it appears (a few single-word variants notwithstanding) in most copies of the B-text:

> Psallite deo nostro psallite
> quoniam rex terre deus Israel psallite sapienter.

As the italicized words indicate, the quotation from the Psalter omits the phrase "psallite regi nostro psallite." A seemingly insignificant skip, to be sure, perhaps an inevitable result of the poet's (or scribes') desire to fit the Latin quotation onto a single line. Given the surrounding context, however, it might be more fruitful to take this omission as revealing testimony to the fallibility of liturgical transmission. For at the very moment Langland draws on biblical authority to condemn "overskippers" in liturgical singing, his text itself performs just such an "overskip," deleting half a psalm-verse and thus performing the very transgression it condemns.

Of course, scholars have become increasingly aware of the difficulty of identifying the exact sources of Langland's biblical and liturgical citations, many of which are derived from patristic writings, florilegia, and biblical glosses. In his study of the Latin quotations in *Piers Plowman,* in fact, Alford warns explicitly against what I have just done: that is, citing a Latin passage from a modern printed edition and holding it up as an example of Langland's citational sloppiness.[38] Again, however, it may be the inevitability of what Langland calls "overskipping" that this liturgical "hiccup" registers in the poem. As the passus stumbles over its own pretensions to accuracy in liturgical citation, it necessarily subverts its own demands for consistency in liturgical performance. Collapsing under the weight of its claims to accurate representation, the poem forces the liturgically aware reader—anyone who has memorized the forty-sixth psalm: anyone, that is, who participates in the liturgy on a regular basis—to recognize the text's "overskip" for the error that it is. Indeed, at least one later reader of a B manuscript seems to have done just this (if on a somewhat smaller scale), erasing "terre" and inserting "omnis terre" in a different ink.[39] The emendation illustrates how difficult it can be to maintain liturgical consistency in a manuscript culture serving the needs of performers.

In their provocative juxtaposition of legal and liturgical fallibility, the lines above recall Langland's representation in an earlier passus of a self-consciously inept liturgical performer, an allegorical figure who virtually personifies the performative laxity that the speaker in B.11 critiques. In the confession scene in passus 5, Langland's portrait of Sloth clearly identifies a lack of musical proficiency with a corresponding lack of canonical legal skills (B.5.415–21):

> I haue be preest and person passynge þritty wynter,
> Yet kan I neyþer solue ne synge ne seintes lyues rede;
> But I kan fynden in a feld or in a furlang an hare
> Bettre þan in *Beatus vir* or in *Beati omnes*
> Construe clausemele and kenne it to my parisshens.
> I kan holde louedayes and here a Reues rekenyng,
> Ac in Canoun nor in decretals I kan noȝt rede a lyne.

In Langland's reference to "solue" or solmization, Sloth's inability to "solue" or "synge" represents his sinful resistance to clerical discipline. Just as he is inept at reading canon law (yet proficient at holding informal out-of-court settlements, or "louedayes"), he finds himself forever unable to learn or perform the liturgy. The passage creates a slightly different analogy than that informing passus 11: for Sloth, canon law

[38] Alford, *Piers Plowman: A Guide to the Quotations*, esp. pp. 17–19.
[39] See Kane and Donaldson's apparatus in *Piers Plowman: The B Version*, p. 456.

and liturgy are two components of a good parson's education; for the speaker in B.11, writing charters and performing the liturgy are similar kinds of tasks but are the responsibilities of two different occupations. In both cases, however, liturgical and forensic practices represent homologous discourses that, when performed inaccurately, can signify a certain measure of moral depravity.

Within the alliterative legacy of *Piers Plowman,* the specific association between "solue" and "song" in B.5 serves as the basis for passages in two—and, though with quite different implications, probably three—poems as a means of registering in liturgy certain performative abuses that come to attain the ideological status of legal transgressions. In *Mum and the Sothsegger,* the narrator describes the moral laxity of Mum's followers in the king's court of justice as a kind of musical failing:

> And in al the king-is court there coiphes been and other
> Mvm is maister there more thenne men wenen,
> For sum of tho segges wolle sich side-wayes,
> Whenne thay witen wel y-now where the hare walketh,
> Thay leden men the long waye and loue-dayes breken
> And maken moppes wel myry with thaire madde tales
> For to sowe siluer seede and solue ere thay singe,
> To haue ynne thaire harueste while the hete dureth.[40]

The explicit influence of the Sloth portrait from passus 5 is apparent in the Langlandian association of solmization with "song." Unlike Sloth in *Piers,* however—who, despite his inability to read Canon Law, emphasizes that he can in fact hold "love-days," or out-of-court settlements—the followers of Mum renegotiate (or better, perhaps, *pre*negotiate) such informal agreements, just as they attempt to practice solmization before they know how to sing and harvest their crops while the summer heat endures.

An ostensibly similar association between "solfe," "song," and the law figures in the mid-fifteenth-century "De veritate et consciencia," a 148-line moral verse from MS Wellcome 1493 that was shown by George

---

[40] *Mum and the Sothsegger,* lines 1141–48, in Helen Barr, ed., *The Piers Plowman Tradition* (London: Everyman, 1993), p. 178.

Kane to be a continuation of the search for Truth in *Piers Plowman*.[41] Although this poem has not been considered as a part of the *Piers Plowman* tradition by Helen Barr and others, its obvious resonance with many of the legal and political themes inspiring *Mum, Richard the Redeless, Pierce the Ploughman's Crede,* and *The Crowned King* suggests that it deserves consideration as a later extension of this post-Langland literary trajectory. The poem depicts a pilgrim seeking the whereabouts of the allegorical figures Truth and Conscience and, as Kane suggests, begins where *Piers Plowman* left off.[42] Consulting various sheriffs and "lyvers vppon londe" and inquiring at the "Benche Chekkyr and Chauncerye," the pilgrim includes in his search a bishop's palace and a consistory court. In the following stanzas, the pilgrim describes what he sees and hears at these two institutional sites. In doing so, he draws an implicit analogy between the musical sounds of liturgical performance produced by the bishop's auditors and the forensic sounds of the judicial oratory performed by the procurators in court (lines 101–24):

> By a bysshop ys paleys ther I was pight
> I herde a bischop holde his correccyoun
> Ther I saw a welfaire sight
> Of Clerkis þat were of Religyoun
> At his comynycacyoun þey knelid a downe
> Bothe lernyd lewde knyght & knave
> *Si dedero* was ther lessoun
> Who so cowde solfe þat songe shuld be save
> ffor all þat euer they cowde crave
> With penaunce they were vndernome
> Tonge ne tethe herde I none wave
> That cowde telle where conscyens was become
>
> But by a Concistorie as I come
> Procutours herd I plete full high
> I wend þat Conscyens had be come
> And they seide for symonye
> Ther was no dome but for whye

---

[41] See George Kane, "The Middle English Verse in Wellcome 1493," *London Mediaeval Studies* 2 (1951): 54–58; the poem is edited on pp. 61–65 and will here be cited internally.

[42] Kane, "Middle English Verse," p. 55.

Right othir wronge whedur euer hit were
The Prest the Persoun & the Vycarie
· Paide vp ther pensyoun for that yeve
ffor vowes disavowys & aduowtrie
With penaunce they were þer vndernome
Tonge ne tethe herd I non tell trewlye
Cowde wete where Conscyens were become

Curiously, these are the only two stanzas in the poem that specifically emphasize the *sound* of the characters encountered by the pilgrim. The vocal labors of the liturgical singers in the first stanza are echoed explicitly by the "full high" pleas of the forensic orators in the second. In both cases, the narrative emphasis on "tonge" and "tethe" constructs the musically or legally performing mouth as the site of both performers' exclusion from Truth and Conscience, effectively creating a debased notion of liturgical performance that provides for a similarly debased salvation.

In "De veritate et consciencia," however, we see a much more self-conscious deployment of this liturgical knowledge than in *Piers Plowman* or *Mum*. Unlike Langland, whose Sloth can *neither* "solue" *nor* "singe," or the *Mum* author, who carefully distinguishes between solmization and song, for this poet the measure of salvation from worldly desire and penitential want derives from the ability of "lernyd" and "lewde" to perform a specific Latin chant, the *Si dedero,* in solmization. For the first time recorded in the English vernacular, a writer uses "solfe" as a *transitive* verb. This verb's object, the fourth verse of Psalm 132, "si dedero somnum oculis meis," was a commonplace in both Latin and vernacular satirical writings from this period, many of them directed against poor legal practitioners.[43] In fact, the phrase is deployed in a very similar way in one of the 1381 letters transcribed in Henry Knighton's *Chronicon:*

> & trewþe hat bene sette vnder a lokke,
> And falsnes regneþ in everylk flokke;
> No man may come trewþe to,
> But he syng si dedero.[44]

---

[43] See Green, "John Ball's Letters," pp. 184 and 197–98n; and Justice, *Writing and Rebellion,* p. 73, where the phrase is termed a "mocking statement of necessity."
[44] Edited in Green, "John Ball's Letters," p. 194.

Although "De veritate et consciencia" participates in the larger satirical tradition that casts the singing of the *Si dedero* as salvational performance, the poet's use of "solfe" rather than the ubiquitous "sing" points to a quite specific concern with the liturgical resonances of the phrase. For as the author would have known very well, if one "sol-fas" a song—that is, if one performs a song in solmization—then one by definition does *not* pronounce the words, but rather sings the melody to a string of "nonsense syllables" that displace the original text in performance. At the same time, the phrase as it appears in "De veritate" suggests a pun of which Langland himself would surely have approved. Sloth's confessional "kan I neyþer *solue* ne singe" in the B-text became "kan y nother *solfe* ne synge" in many copies of C (the fourteenth-century Trinity College Dublin MS 212 reads "soolfe").[45] The result is a homophonic variant that highlights the lexical and connotative slipperiness of the term: even as the *Si dedero* is "solfed"—that is, fragmented into its constituent syllables so it can be learned more quickly and easily—the phrase is, ironically, transformed beyond recognition, rendering it simply impossible to be "solved."

With varying degrees of self-consciousness, then, the three texts considered thus far imply that within liturgical performance lies a legal test of moral worthiness. In a certain sense, liturgy and law have become so closely intertwined in these works that the liturgical subject has in turn become a veritable cipher for the legal subject, the Langlandian "agent" that Elizabeth Fowler locates at the intersection of the juridical, economic, and political forces that both enable and constrain the human person.[46] Indeed, while all three poems explore the music-law analogy's truth-claims in various ways, they leave uninterrogated the ideological terms of the analogy itself. When acquired correctly and performed with discretion, it seems, the liturgy remains both a privileged means of access to ecclesiastical authority and a discursive instrument of clerical control.

Yet there was another alliterative poet writing during this period whose revisionism of *Piers Plowman* presents us with a radically different notion of liturgical authority, one that resists the legalistic encrustations that had come to determine the Langlandian liturgical subject by calling

[45] *Piers Plowman: The C Version,* ed. George Russell and George Kane (London: Athlone; Berkeley: University of California Press, 1997), p. 329.
[46] Elizabeth Fowler, "Civil Death and the Maiden: Agency and the Conditions of Contract in *Piers Plowman,*" *Speculum* 70 (1995): 760–92.

attention to the very institutional practices and ideological mystifica-
tions upon which liturgical performance depends. If the remainder of
this essay leaves the law for the most part behind, it does so in the spirit
of the medieval poet who creatively eluded juridical constraints in rewriting the liturgical narrative he found in *Piers Plowman*.

Reading Langland Musically

The alliterative satire the "Choristers' Lament" records the agonized
complaints of two monastic singers, dubbed Walter and William, regarding the emotional and physical hardships entailed by the learning
and performance of liturgical music. The fifty-two-line satire in thirteen
stanzas of four long alliterative lines has been dated anywhere from circa
1300 to the early fifteenth century.[47] As we shall see, however, there are
compelling reasons for positing a *terminus a quo* of around 1377, the earliest likely date of Langland's B-text. I have argued elsewhere that the
"Choristers' Lament" presents a scene of institutionalized musical learning dramatically opposed to the pedagogical spectacle that figures so
prominently in Chaucer's *Prioress's Tale*; while the Prioress's clergeon ab-
sorbs the *Alma redemptoris* through rote repetition and with the help of
his "compeer," these students acquire their musical skills under the disciplinary surveillance of a "mayster," whose disgusted rantings at his
charges figure prominently in the poem.[48]

Because the "Lament" and its technical musical vocabulary will be
unfamiliar to most readers, a brief summary and explication are in order
(readers may wish to refer as well to the more complete annotations in
the Appendix). The poem commences with a first-person complaint by
Walter that moves from an abjectly confessional account of his own pedagogical woes to a remembered harangue from his teacher (lines 1–8,
13–20):

[47] See, for example, J. P. Oakden, *Alliterative Poetry in Middle English: The Dialectical
and Metrical Survey* (Manchester: Manchester University Press, 1930), p. 108, who proposes the range 1350–80; Rossell Hope Robbins, *Manual of the Writings in Middle English
1050–1500*, vol. 5 (Hamden, Conn.: Shoestring Press, 1975), p. 1472, who dates it to
the "later fourteenth century"; and the wildly inconsistent datings in the *MED* (compare, for example, *lurdan* n.d. and *solfen* v. [ca. 1380] with *donken* v. [after 1300]), the
majority of which date the "Lament" to around 1380.
[48] Bruce Holsinger, "Pedagogy, Violence, and the Subject of Music: Chaucer's *Prioress's
Tale* and the Ideologies of 'Song,'" *New Medieval Literatures* 1 (1997): 179–81.

> "Uncomly in cloystre   i coure ful of care,
> I loke as a lurdeyn   and listne til my lare.
> þe song of þe cesolfa   dos me syken sare,
> and sitte stotiand on a song   a moneth and mare.
>
> I ga gowlende abowte   also dos a goke,
> mani is þe sorwfol song   it singge vpon mi bok.
> I am holde so harde   vnneþes dar i loke;
> al þe mirthe of þis mold   for god i forsoke.
>
> . . . .
>
> Qwan i kan mi lesson   mi meyster wil i gon
> þat heres me mi rendre   he wenes i haue wel don.
> 'Qwat hast þu don dawn Water   sin saterdai at non?
> þu holdest nowt a note   by god in riht ton.
>
> Wayme leue Water,   þu werkes al til shame;
> þu stomblest and stikes fast   as þu were lame.
> þu tones nowt þe note,   ilke be his name,
> þu bitist asonder bequarre,   for bemol i þe blame.'"

From the beginning the satire derives much of its humor from the juxtaposition of Walter's proficient use of technical terms for musical pitch and notation with his inability to comprehend their meaning and perform accordingly. Despite Walter's extended devotion "in cloystre" to the song of the "cesolfa," his master likens the sound of his singing to the clanking of "an old cawdrun" (line 22). In the seventh stanza, Walter "wendes him til William," who begins a game of violent one-upmanship by boasting that Walter's pedagogical and performative nightmare pales in comparison to his own (lines 29–32, 37–44, 49–52):

> "Me is wo so is þe be   þat belles in þe walmes,
> I donke vpon dauid   til me tonge talmes.
> I ne rendrede nowt   sithen men beren palmes.
> Is it also mikel sorwe   in song so is in salmes?
>
> . . . .

Of bemol and of bequarre   of boþe i was wol bare,
Qwan i went out of þis word   and lifte til mi lare.
Of effauȝ and elami   ne coudy neuer are;
I fayle faste in þe fa,   it files al mi fare.

ȝet þer ben oþer notes,   sol and vt and la,
and þat froward file   þat men clipis fa.
Often he dos me liken ille   and werkes me ful wa;
miȝti him neuere hitten   inton for to ta.

.   .   .   .

Qwan ilke note til oþer lepes   and makes hem asawt,
þat we calles a moyson   in gesolreutȝ en hawt.
Il hayl were þu boren   ȝif þu make defawt.
þanne sais oure mayster,   'Que vos ren ne vawt.'"

Like Walter, William speaks the musical lingo of the cloister with fluency even while buried under an avalanche of unfamiliar notes and noises. By this point in the poem, moreover, these formal musical phenomena have become eerily anthropomorphized and objectified: the "fa" syllable is a "froward file" that "werkes" him "ful wa," while a note that he terms the "streinant" has been employed by his master to "horle" his "kayles" (lines 45–46). Though the vocabulary here refers mostly to the conventions of plainchant, several other terms used by William suggest that he may be referring to the performance of vocal polyphony. The note identified as a "streinant" with "two long tails" may be the *larga plicata,* a double-tailed note-form used in the mensural system in polyphony of the fourteenth-century Ars Nova.[49] Similarly, William's vivid memory of musical notes "leaping" and "hurling" at one another may be his oblique way of describing note-against-note polyphony, while "moyson" or "measure" refers to the practice of musical mensuration.[50]

[49] For a contemporary illustration of the *larga plicata,* see Thomas Walsingham, *Regulae de musica mensurabilis,* ed. Gilbert Reaney, Corpus Scriptorum de Musica 31 (n.p.: American Institute of Musicology, 1983), p. 74; the note is described as having "duas tractus descendentes vel ascendentes ex parte dextera longiorem." I would like to thank Oliver Ellsworth for his kind assistance in helping me interpret some of the poem's more puzzling terminology.
[50] See the discussion of these terms in Utley's notes, pp. 201–2, and below, pp. 139–41.

The "Choristers' Lament" is a remarkable work for any number of reasons, not the least of which is its explosive lexical inventory of first-recorded English usages, practically all of which result from direct translations of Latin musical vocabulary. Like Langland's "solfe," the terminology employed throughout the poem—including words and phrases like "cesolfa," "bequarre," "bemol," "sol and vt and la," and "gesol-reutȝ"—derives from the clerical discourse of solmization, a pedagogical method first developed by a Benedictine monk named Guido of Arezzo in the first half of the eleventh century and employed ubiquitously in subsequent Latin writings on the theory and practice of plainchant.[51] The opening passage from a late-fourteenth-century treatise in the Berkeley manuscript (ca. 1375) conveniently encapsulates the basics of this mnemonic system, in which the singing-master's hand served as a visual aid for his students. The letters A through G were each assigned a specific location on the palm or fingers, allowing for the elaboration of a gamut of individual pitches named for their location with respect to them (the terms from the gamut that appear in the "Choristers' Lament" are italicized):

Since the singer—to understand what is the mode or tone of any song—formulates beforehand a conception of it, for this understanding it must first be known that there are nineteen letters, joints, or pitch names in the hand and two outside, with all of which the song of the world is constructed. They are all written and initially named by these seven letters, repeated three times: A, B, C, D, E, F, G. Of the letters that exist outside the hand, one, F, is not in common custom, but according to art it may be placed at the middle of the thumb outside the hand. The other, E, is in common custom, and it is placed at the first joint of the middle finger outside the hand. Furthermore, common custom begins the hand or palm in the middle of the thumb, saying there Gamma-ut, which is written with the Greek letter Γ-ut, and ends it on the said letter E, where is said E-la; and it is reckoned this way: Γ-ut, A-re, *B-mi,* C-fa-ut, D-sol-re, E-la-mi, *F-fa-ut,* G-sol-re-ut, A-la-mi-re, b-fa-#-mi, C-sol-fa-ut, D-la-sol-re, *E-la-mi,* F-fa-ut, *G-sol-re-ut,* A-la-mi-re, B-fa-#-mi, *C-sol-fa,* D-la-sol, E-la.[52]

[51] On Guido see, most recently and concisely, David Hiley, *Western Plainchant: A Handbook* (Oxford: Clarendon Press, 1993), pp. 466–70.
[52] *Tractatus Primus,* in *The Berkeley Manuscript,* ed. and trans. Oliver Ellsworth (Lincoln and London: University of Nebraska Press, 1984), pp. 32–35.

Each musical pitch, then, receives its own "code name" that can be re-membered easily by the student for the purposes of rehearsal and perfor-mance. As with any highly technical discourse, of course, references to solmization depend upon the reader's insider's knowledge of the sys-tem itself as well as a close familiarity with the institutions that de-ploy it.

In the voices of the students portrayed in the "Choristers' Lament," we are witnessing the first significant incursion of this specialized clerical vocabulary into the English vernacular. In this respect, the poem's spir-ited musical vernacularity anticipates that of the English treatises on Fauburdon that begin to appear in the 1430s.[53] The "Lament" seems intended in part precisely *as* an extended act of vernacularization, the willful appropriation of an arcane and exclusively Latin pedagogical id-iom into an emergent literary language.

Despite its availability since 1845 in various anthologies, scholars have had little to say about the "Lament," usually relegating it to paren-theses or footnotes in wider treatments of fourteenth-century alliterative poetry.[54] By contrast, the alliterative poem adjacent to the "Lament" in the manuscript, the "Complaint Against Blacksmiths," has been widely hailed as an innovative and realistic satire on an often controversial me-dieval craft.[55] For Elizabeth Salter, who dates it to the last decade of the fourteenth century, the "Complaint" constitutes both a sophisticated response to conventional medieval representations of blacksmiths and a highly stylized literary intervention into contemporary debates over the practice of night-smithing. Thus, Salter identifies in the poem a concern with "the rapid skills and the massive energies of craftsmen and craft-processes" as well as a humane will on the poet's part to represent "the very substance and texture of the working life of the medieval Crafts."[56] Unlike the "Complaint Against Blacksmiths," however, the "Choristers'

[53] For these treatises, see Sanford B. Meech, "Three Musical Treatises in English from a Fifteenth-Century Manuscript," *Speculum* 10 (1935): 235–69.

[54] See, for example, Thorlac Turville-Petre, *The Alliterative Revival* (Cambridge: D. S. Brewer, 1977), p. 132; Derek Pearsall, "The Alliterative Revival: Origins and Social Backgrounds," in Lawton, ed., *Middle English Alliterative Poetry*, p. 39.

[55] See the studies cited by Elizabeth Salter, "The Complaint Against Blacksmiths," in Salter, *English and International: Studies in the Literature, Art and Patronage of Medieval En-gland,* ed. Derek Pearsall and Nicolette Zeeman (Cambridge: Cambridge University Press, 1988), p. 330.

[56] Salter, "Complaint," pp. 212 and 209, respectively.

Lament" represents for Salter a thoroughly conventional contribution to an established medieval genre:

> This wry and technically expert satirisation of the rigorous training imposed in monastic or cathedral song-schools presents no problems as an item in a miscellany of monastic provenance: moreover, the clerkly and essentially orthodox tradition of impudent criticism to which it subscribes provides it with a network of relationships in an established literary mode. But the relationships already proposed for the alliterative Complaint lead immediately into more controversial areas and prompt serious questions. . . . [57]

While Salter is certainly correct to associate the "Choristers' Lament" with the wider fourteenth-century genre of learned clerical satire, her assumption of the poem's unproblematically affirmative stance with respect to clerical authority must be revised. For despite its brevity and the ostensibly uncontroversial nature of its subject, the "Lament" draws much of its satirical energy from perhaps the most sustained and complex treatment of clerical authority in Middle English. The poet who wrote the "Lament," I would propose, knew *Piers Plowman* intimately enough to have responded in touching detail to Langland's legalistic constructions of liturgical music and its performance. Unlike *Mum* and "De veritate," however, the "Lament" reacts to the liturgical representations in *Piers* by emphatically removing the practices of musical learning and performance from juridical control, exposing the liturgical exercise of clerical authority as unnatural, violent, and ultimately unsuccessful. In its own humorous and self-satirizing way, the "Choristers' Lament" participates in what Wendy Scase has recently shown to be the widescale emergence of a "new anticlericalism" in the second half of the fourteenth century, a burgeoning of "new anticlerical making," primarily in the vernacular, whose central and most popular participant was Langland himself.[58] A signal contribution of this new anticlerical writing to Middle English literature was what Scase terms its "creation of a new vocabulary," a "new language" through which certain writers sought to bridge and ultimately to undermine the traditional gap between "lered" and "lewed" by appropriating Latinate clerical vocabulary for their own irreverent purposes. As Scase characterizes it, the new anticlericalism

---

[57] Salter, "Complaint," p. 200.
[58] Scase, *'Piers Plowman' and the New Anticlericalism.*

"was at once anti-intellectual and bookish," a remarkably fitting description of the "Choristers' Lament" in its simultaneously fluent but bewildered response to the clerical discourse of liturgical pedagogy its author found in Langland.[59]

The poem's initiating allusion to *Piers Plowman* appears in the first line of the second stanza, in which the speaker casts himself as a "goke"—a cuckoo-bird caught in a torturous relationship to the liturgical book, the "grayel" or gradual, that he holds while he sings. The term "goke," readers will recall, is the very label that Langland employs in passus B.11 to condemn both inept charter makers and lax liturgical performers:

> The gome þat gloseþ so chartres for a *goky* is holden.
> So is it a *goky*, by god! þat in his gospel failleþ,
> Or in masse or in matyns makeþ any defaute: (*Piers* B.11.306–8)

> I ga gowlende abowte   also dos a *goke*,
> mani is þe sorwfol song   it singge vpon mi bok.
> I am holde so harde   vnneþes dar i loke;
> al þe mirthe of þis mold   for god i forsoke. ("Lament" 5–8)

Casting himself as a liturgical "goke," Walter draws upon Will's "dream within a dream" in B.11 to articulate his own lament at the vagaries of liturgical performance. The poem amplifies a negative exemplum of liturgical performance in *Piers* by portraying for its readers living examples of just the sort of poor liturgical singer that Langland himself had critiqued in his vivid portrait of Sloth. Moreover, just as Langland in the lines above condemns liturgical singers who "*maketh* any *defaute*" in their performance of Mass or Office, the penultimate line of the "Lament" records William's dire warning that "il hayl were þu boren ʒif þu *make defawt*" (line 51) while singing. The song-master assumes the role of the speaker in B.11; he is not simply the representative of institutional authority within the monastery, but also the Langlandian arbiter of truth.

The second half of the stanza raises the stakes. So arduous is the speaker's musical labor that he scarcely dares glance anywhere but at the songbook already mentioned: "*I am holde so harde   vnneþes dar i loke / al þe*

---

[59] Ibid., p. 165.

mirthe of þis mold   for god i forsoke." The italicized line seems to be a
deliberate echo of Peace's complaint against Wrong near the beginning
of passus 4.[60] Peace, who has just entered the "parlement" and "putte vp
a bille," asserts that Wrong has taken away his wife—not only this, but
that he has "rauysshede Rose, Reignaldes looue, / And Margrete of hir
maydenhede maugree hire chekes." As Peace portrays it, Wrong's violence is simultaneously sexual and legal, a crime against person, property, and spirit (B.4.51–60):

> "Boþe my gees and my grys hise gadelynges feccheþ.
> I dar noȝt for fere of hym fiȝte ne chide.
> He borwed of me bayard and brouȝte hym neuer ayein,
> Ne no ferþyng þerfore for nouȝt I koude plede.
> He maynteneþ hise men to murþere myne hewen,
> Forstalleþ my feires, fiȝteþ in my Chepyng,
> Brekeþ vp my berne dores, bereþ awey my whete,
> And takeþ me but a taille for ten quarters Otes;
> And yet he beteþ me þerto and lyþ by my mayde.
> *I am noȝt hardy for hym vnneþe to loke."*

In Peace's complaint can be heard the indignance of the violated. Aside
from the rapes and ravishings of other women that he reports, Peace
himself is beaten and cuckolded, robbed and plundered by Wrong, the
"wikked luft" (line 62). The concluding line of Peace's speech—"Because of him, I am scarcely bold enough to show my face!" in A. V. C.
Schmidt's modernization—becomes in the "Choristers' Lament" an
equally abject complaint that enlists Wrong's physical and sexual viola-
tions into the more general pedagogical scenario satirized throughout
the poem.

For the most part, however, the poem's response to *Piers Plowman* confines itself to a learned amplification of Langland's scattered references
to liturgical culture. In at least three separate cases, entries in the *Middle
English Dictionary* adduce *Piers Plowman* and the "Lament" as the first
two recorded usages of specific words or phrases. While these lexical
coincidences alone are suggestive, especially given the brevity of the

---

[60] Thanks to Andy Galloway for pointing out this echo to me in a personal correspondence and thus adding to the list.

"Lament," in all three cases the terms or phrases in question relate explicitly to liturgical performance, and both poems employ them in remarkably similar ways.

First, in the third passus of the B-text, Conscience's polemic against Lady Meed anticipates the subsequent portrait of the personified Sloth as a cleric unable to learn or perform the liturgy:

> Ech man to pleye with a plow, Pykoise or spade,
> Spynne or sprede donge or spille hymself with sleuþe.
> Preestes and persons wiþ Placebo to hunte
> And *dyngen vpon Dauid* eche day til eue; (B.3.309–12)

> Me is wo so is þe be þat belles in þe walmes,
> I *donke vpon dauid* til mi tonge talmes.
> I ne rendrede nowt sithen men beren palmes.
> Is it also mikel sorwe in song so is in salmes? ("Lament" 29–32)

While the present-tense "dyngen" in Langland has become the past-tense "donke" in the "Lament," the phrases are otherwise identical—and, according to the *MED*, otherwise unattested in early English literature.[61] To "ding upon David" is to perform the Psalms repeatedly, incessantly, and obsessively: for Langland's Conscience, to sing all day until evening; for William in the "Lament," until his very tongue fails to perform. Through this particular allusive gesture, our poet demonstrates an adept ability to play upon Langland's wording. The phrases "sprede donge" and "dyngen vpon Dauid" in passus 3 of *Piers Plowman* proved perhaps irresistibly proximate and homophonic to the "Lament"-author: by shifting Langland's "dyngen" to the past-tense "donke," the poet may be asking the reader to recall Langland's own possible pun and imagine William himself spreading "donge" upon the Psalms as he repeats them. Liturgical psalmody represents nothing more than the mundane, arduous, but indispensable labor of manuring a field.

Next, in the stanza that immediately follows, the "Lament" reiterates the Langlandian association between "solfe" and "song" we have seen in *Mum and the Sothsegger* and "De veritate et consciencia." While Langland's Sloth in B.5 confesses his inability to perform through either sol-

---

[61] MED, *dingen* v.1b; and *donke* v.

125

mization or song, the "Lament"'s William, though clearly familiar with both performative techniques in some rudimentary way, nevertheless casts them as ultimately useless exercises within the pedagogical scenario. They serve only to highlight his liturgical incompetence:

> I haue be preest and person passynge þritty wynter,
> Yet kan I neyþer *solue ne synge* ne seintes lyues rede; (*Piers* B.5.415–16)

> > I *solfe and singge* after   and is me neuere þe nerre;
> > I horle at þe notes   and heue hem al of herre;
> > alle þat me heres   wenes þat i erre. ("Lament" 34–36)

Though forms of the verb *solfare* appear frequently in medieval Latin writings on musical pedagogy, once again the *MED* lists the passages above as the earliest two occurrences of a specifically liturgical English neologism, the vernacular "solfe" or "solue."[62] As it appears in *Piers Plowman,* Sloth's brief confessional phrase, "kan I neyther solfe ne synge," represents a momentary gesture toward a clerical/liturgical pedagogical institution and the vocabulary designed to serve it. In the "Lament," by contrast, we see a clever reversal of Langlandian liturgical representation, one that combines the Sloth portrait in B.5 with the extended legal-liturgical conflation in B.11 into an elaborate critique of liturgical authority. The representations of liturgical fallibility in Langland cast it as morally and ideologically suspect; the speakers in the "Lament," however, affiliate themselves and their musical labor not with the redemptive quest of *Piers Plowman*'s dreamer, but with the musical ineptness of the preconfessional Sloth in B.5 and the overskipping "goky" in B.11: in other words, they identify themselves with two reviled figures whose lack of liturgical knowledge and skill represents a quasi-legal transgression.

Finally, and perhaps most remarkably, the "Lament"-author recognized that a particularly explicit representation of pedagogical violence in passus B.10 of *Piers Plowman* also contained a technical vernacular reference to the dominant musical technique of the Ars Nova. He in turn incorporated the reference into his satire as a means of signaling the student's bewilderment at the violent musical spectacle in which he himself was participating:

[62] MED, *solfen* v.

Logyk I lerned hire, and al þe lawe after,
And alle þe *Musons* in Musik I made hire to knowe.
Plato þe poete I putte hym first to boke;
Aristotle and oþer mo to argue I tauȝte;
Grammer for girles I garte first write,
And bette hem wiþ a baleys but if þei wolde lerne. (*Piers* 10.176–81)

"Qwan ilke note til oþer lepes   and makes hem asawt,
þat we calles a *moyson*   in gesolreutȝ en hawt.
Il hayl were þu boren   ȝif þu make defawt.
þanne sais oure mayster,   'Que vos ren ne vawt.'" ("Lament" 49–52)

The terms "Musons" in *Piers* and "moyson" in the "Lament" are Anglo-Norman for *mensura* ("measure") or *mensionem* (accusative of *mensio*, "measuring"), terms common in the Latin theory of the Ars Nova to denote the general practice of musical mensuration (the variant "moysons" for Kane-Donaldson's "Musons" at line 177 appears in a mixed B-A text of East Anglian origin).[63] According to the English theorist Johannes Hanboys, writing around 1375 (and possibly in Norwich), "Mensura est habitudo quantitativa longitudinem et brevitatem cuiusliber cantus mensurabilis manifestans" [Measure is a quantitative attribute indicating the longness and shortness of some mensurable song].[64] As I have already suggested, the vivid image of notes "leaping at" and "assaulting" one another may also indicate that William is referring to note-against-note polyphony, as opposed to the less elaborate plainchant that Walter describes in the language of solmization.

The "Lament" thus recasts Langland's "all the Musons in musike"—that is, all the measures or note-forms in mensural polyphony pedagogically instilled by Dame Study—as a bewildering spectacle that William calls "moyson" and imagines as the violent outcome of a musical

[63] *Piers Plowman: The A Version,* ed. George Kane, rev. ed. (London: Athlone; Berkeley: University of California Press, 1988), p. 409 at line 129. The manuscript is H³ (British Library, MS Harley 3954); on its origin and provenance, see Kane's comments and notes in *Piers Plowman: The A Version,* pp. 7–8. On "moison" or "Musons," see MED *moisoun* n.a. Skeat cites a 1406 entry in Riley's *Memorials of London* regarding some boxes made "of nine different dimensions [orig. *mewsons*] in length, and breadth, and depth within"; Skeat, *Piers Plowman,* 2:153–54.

[64] Johannes Hanboys, *Summa,* cap. 1, in *Robertus de Handlo, The Rules and Johannes Hanboys, The Summa,* ed. and trans. Peter M. Lefferts, Greek and Latin Music Theory (Lincoln and London: University of Nebraska Press, 1991), pp. 182–83. Hanboys is here citing Franco of Cologne's *Ars cantus mensurabilis,* cap. 1.

"asawt." While Dame Study beats her students for failing to learn, the "Lament"-poet's William implies that the performed music actually contains the violence inherent in liturgical pedagogy. In other words, the poem relocates the pedagogical authority and terror of the "maister" into the very liturgical sonorities and note-forms that he forces upon his students. In the passage from Langland's B-text, the speaker learns the "Musons" immediately after learning "al þe lawe," suggesting once again the close parallel between liturgical and forensic performance informing *Piers Plowman*. The revision thus crystallizes the "Lament"-poet's response to Langland's conflation of law and liturgy. For the poet who wrote the "Choristers' Lament," Langland's "Musons" have become the *moyson* or "measure" that constantly demands obedience but ultimately fails to secure it.

Liturgical Culture and MS Arundel 292

It should come as no real surprise that a late-fourteenth-century English poem on practically any subject composed in long alliterative lines would reflect the influence of the most popular and controversial alliterative writing produced in the preceding century. But what historical sense are we to make of the subtle Langlandian allusiveness of the "Choristers' Lament"? What exactly motivated this poet to resist the liturgical ideology of *Piers Plowman* in the sneakily intertextual way that he did? I want to conclude by proposing some provisional answers to these questions, addressing briefly several codicological, institutional, and political factors that may shed some light on the act of poetic appropriation that I believe this poem represents.

The only known copy of the "Lament" survives in London, British Library MS Arundel 292, a trilingual miscellany originally written and compiled in the late thirteenth century. The contents of the manuscript include (among other items) Latin sermons and exempla, an English alliterative bestiary, Anglo-Norman religious verses, a Latin text of Henry of Saltrey's *St. Patrick's Purgatory,* and a bilingual *Distichs* of Cato.[65] A quire apparently containing a Latin work on the 1272 fire at the Norwich cathedral, which is listed in the table of contents on fol.

---

[65] For descriptions of this manuscript's contents, see H. L. D. Ward, *Catalogue of Romances in the Department of Manuscripts in the British Museum,* 2 vols. (London: British Museum, 1910), 2:452; and, more recently, Hanneke Wirtjes, ed., *The Middle English Physiologus,* EETS, vol. 299 (Oxford: Oxford University Press, 1991), ix–xvi.

114r, is missing; press-marks on two folios indicate that Arundel 292 was in the institution's possession by around 1300, and it has been assumed to have originated in the cathedral's Benedictine priory.[66] Along with the "Complaint Against Blacksmiths," the "Lament" was copied much later onto blank leaves at the end of the ninth quire.

The "Choristers' Lament" is not the only later accretion to Arundel 292 that registers an anxiety over the protocols of liturgical performance. On folios 68–70, immediately preceding the "Lament" near the end of the ninth quire, there appears a set of instructions in a fourteenth-century Latin hand informing liturgical celebrants what actions they are to take if, "per negligenciam," they are ever unlucky enough to drop consecrated bread or wine upon the floor during the performance of the Mass. The incipit puts it succinctly: "Quid agendum sit, si forte panis aut vinum in Eucharistia Domini caderet in terram" (fol. 69). Citing papal pronouncements (68v) and commonplaces from liturgical commentary (concerning, for example, the mystical inseparability of water and wine in the chalice [69]), the directions reveal that overriding, almost fetishistic concern with the regulation of liturgical ritual, action, and signification that Miri Rubin has identified as endemic to ecclesiastical treatises and legislation on the Eucharist in the Middle Ages.[67] While such sacramental anxieties were commonplace, they were nevertheless significant for those who harbored them: in the *Historia pontificalis,* John of Salisbury reports that an accidental spilling of eucharistic wine by a papal assistant during Mass was greeted with "general consternation" by those assembled, who believed "that such a thing could never happen in any church unless some serious evil threatened it."[68]

It is thus difficult to resist proposing an analogy between this ultra-clerical Latin entry in Arundel 292 and the "Choristers' Lament." Like the poem, which pokes fun at the clerical exercise of liturgical authority while steering clear of heterodoxy, the Latin directions avoid any suggestion that the Eucharist might not be substantially the body of Christ

---

[66] See N. R. Ker, "Medieval Manuscripts from Norwich Cathedral Priory," *Transactions of the Cambridge Bibliographical Society* 1 (1949–53): 1–28. See also Ker, *Medieval Libraries of Great Britain: A List of Surviving Books,* 2d ed. (London: Royal Historical Society, 1964), p. 138.

[67] See Miri Rubin, *Corpus Christi: The Eucharist in Late Medieval Culture* (Cambridge: Cambridge University Press, 1991), esp. pp. 12–82.

[68] John of Salisbury, *Historia Pontificalis* 5, ed. and trans. Marjorie Chibnall (London: Thomas Nelson and Sons, 1956), p. 11.

even as they treat the host like the *panis* it is: a piece of bread that a clumsy celebrant might easily drop as he holds it up for the assembled worshippers to venerate. Whether musical or sacramental, liturgical ritual remains ever-vulnerable to the vagaries of its embodied performance.

The survival of the "Choristers' Lament" in a Benedictine miscellany testifies as well to the specific intellectual and pedagogical sphere within which both Langland and the "Lament"-author may have been moving. Although Morton Bloomfield's suggestion that Langland himself was a Benedictine monk has been rejected, it has recently been suggested that part of the poet's early education may in fact have been acquired in a Benedictine institution (perhaps the cathedral school at Worcester, as John Bowers proposes).[69] A particularly striking testament to Langland's possible affiliations with the Black Monks is his deft use of medieval Latin riddles. Andrew Galloway has shown that Langland almost certainly knew such riddles both from the rhetoric section of the *Secretum philosophorum,* a late-thirteenth- or early-fourteenth-century treatise on the liberal arts, as well as from separate riddle-lists that circulated independently from the *Secretum.*[70] These riddle-lists achieved perhaps their widest readership "in the circles of Benedictine student-monks" at Oxford, and Galloway identifies five manuscripts, all of which date from the fourteenth and fifteenth centuries and several of which are of likely Benedictine origin, that contain such lists.[71]

The final quire of Arundel 292 (fol. 113v) contains a previously unstudied list of Latin riddles, a number of which correspond to those that occur in the five lists transcribed by Galloway.[72] The list in Arundel 292, however, appears to be much earlier than any of these lists; as an original part of (or a very early accretion to) the miscellany, the list may in fact predate the *Secretum* itself. If so, this would greatly strengthen Galloway's hypothesis that the Latin riddle-tradition exploited in the *Secretum philosophorum* and *Piers Plowman* had its origins among English

---

[69] John Bowers, *The Crisis of Will in Piers Plowman* (Washington, D.C.: Catholic University of America Press, 1986), pp. 21–23; see Morton W. Bloomfield, "Was William Langland a Benedictine Monk?" *MLQ* 4 (1943): 57–61.

[70] Andrew Galloway, "The Rhetoric of Riddling in Late-Medieval England: The 'Oxford' Riddles, the *Secretum philosophorum,* and the Riddles in *Piers Plowman,*" *Speculum* 70 (1995): 68–105.

[71] The riddle-lists are edited in Galloway, "The Rhetoric of Riddling," pp. 98–105; the citation is from p. 83.

[72] The Arundel 292 list includes the following riddles, keyed to Galloway's numberings: Harley 3362 nos. 15 and 20; Sloane 513 nos. 1, 8, 9 (but without the third line), and 13.

Benedictines; its survival in a miscellany containing texts in Latin, English, and Anglo-Norman speaks as well to the "playful trilingualism" that Galloway identifies as central to the pedagogical utilization of riddles in the *Secretum*.[73] Arundel 292 thus offers compelling and multilayered testimony to the intellectual past and ideological future of Langland's making, transmitting both an arcane rhetorical tool of the exact sort that would figure prominently in Langland's Latinate word-games and a vernacular satire that amplifies his representations of liturgical practice.

In a number of ways, however, the "Choristers' Lament" complicates somewhat the story of *Piers Plowman*'s reception within English monastic textual communities. The poem takes a more irreverent stance toward clerical authority and makes a more liberal assay at vernacular innovation than we might expect from an early monastic reader of Langland. That other English Benedictines read *Piers* less contentiously is suggested by the circumstances surrounding the production of the so-called Z-text in MS Bodley 851. The original owner of this book is identified in an inscription as "Fratri Iohanni de Wellis Monacho Rameseye," or John of Wells, a monk of the Benedictine abbey at Ramsey—the same John Wells of Gloucester College, Oxford, whose vehement anti-Wycliffism can be discerned in his enthusiastic participation in the Black Friars council of 1382 as well as in an approving chronicler's epitaphic description of him as a "malleus haereticorum."[74] As Hanna has shown in a review of George Rigg and Charlotte Brewer's Z-text edition, it is unlikely that John himself was responsible for adding *Piers Plowman* to the Latin works constituting the original codex, which Hanna describes as a "community product" of John's monastic successors.[75] Nevertheless, the Ramsey Benedictines who likely inherited John's Latin miscellany and added to it a version of *Piers* may have found in Langland's poem a comforting vernacular affirmation of doctrinal and ecclesiological orthodoxy, both their own and that of their more loudly orthodox predecessor.

The poet who wrote the "Choristers' Lament," by contrast, drew on *Piers Plowman* precisely to satirize the monastic clergy and its pedagogical severity. In doing so, he may have been reacting to specific contem-

---

[73] Galloway, "The Rhetoric of Riddling," p. 81.
[74] See the comments in *Piers Plowman: The Z Version,* ed. A. G. Rigg and Charlotte Brewer, pp. 3–5.
[75] Hanna, *Pursuing History,* p. 201.

poraneous transformations in the musical culture of Norwich. The final decades of the fourteenth century initiated a period of great musical expansion at the priory, during which the Lady Chapel enlisted the labor of more and more secular boys (probably from the institution's almonry) as well as monks to sing in the choir.[76] Although monastic choirs, unlike their secular equivalents, generally did not employ boys in the singing of the liturgy after the prohibition of child oblation in midcentury, Norwich was a likely exception to this rule.[77] Several thirteenth-century entries in the priory's customary, moreover, give explicit directions for the performance of polyphony in the liturgy, and it is reasonable to assume that the choir would have participated enthusiastically as well in the later musical changes that the "Lament"-poet playfully bemoans.[78]

At the same time, the poem adumbrates a more widespread insular sentiment in the later fourteenth century against liturgical excess and elaborate ecclesiastical music-making. The expansion of the Norwich Lady Chapel choir was part of a more general increase in the size and number of English choral institutions—monastic, cathedral, and royal/aristocratic household—beginning before 1390 and documented by scholars such as Frank Lloyd Harrison, Roger Bowers, and Andrew Wathey.[79] While the causes of this expansion remain a matter of speculation, several musicologists have been struck by the fact that it coincided with the emergence of Lollard polemic against liturgical excess (in his 1975 dissertation, Bowers went so far as to propose that the growth of English choral institutions in this period represented an "establishment backlash" against Lollardy).[80]

Though a little-studied aspect of the Lollard heresy, passages attacking musical display and liturgical profligacy appear with remarkable regularity in Wycliffite writings. Perhaps receiving their initial impetus from Wyclif's own condemnations of vain singing and from the entry on liturgical *cantus* in the *Floretum/Rosarium*, Lollards attacked the musical excesses of their day in sermons, biblical commentary, treatises

---

[76] See Roger Bowers, "Choral Institutions within the English Church: Their Origins and Development, 1340–1500," (Ph.D. diss., University of East Anglia, 1975), p. 4087.

[77] Frank Lloyd Harrison, *Music in Medieval Britain* (London: Routledge and Kegan Paul, 1967), pp. 39–40.

[78] See ibid., pp. 113–14.

[79] Ibid., esp. pp. 156–219; Bowers, "Choral Institutions," esp. pp. 4009a–4106; Andrew Wathey, *Music in the Royal and Noble Households in Late Medieval England: Studies of Sources and Patronage* (New York and London: Garland, 1989).

[80] Bowers, "Choral Institutions," p. 4001.

on clerical self-indulgence and pilgrimage, longer expository works such as *The Lanterne of Liȝt*, even in the midst of their interrogations by ecclesiastical officials.[81] The central tenets of Lollard anti-liturgicalism can be discerned with particular clarity in the vernacular treatise *Of feyned contemplatif lif*, which rails against both the obsessive observance of the daily hours and the polyphonic embellishment of liturgical music, both of which, so the author protests, distract the devotional subject from the "sentence" of Scripture.[82] The treatise's critique extends as well to the very size of the choir:

for whanne þer ben fourty or fyfty in a queer þre or foure proude & lecherous lorellis schullen knacke þe most devout seruyce þat noman schal here þe sentence, & alle oþer schullen be doumbe & loken on hem as foolis. & þanne strumpatis & þeuys preisen sire iacke or hobbe & williem þe proude clerk, hou smale þe knacken here notis.[83]

The more singers employed in liturgical performance, the writer suggests, the more difficult it becomes to "here þe sentence"; words are overwhelmed by music as the singers "knacken here notis," a phrase that

[81] Bruce Holsinger, "The Vision of Music in a Lollard Florilegium: *Cantus* in the Middle English *Rosarium Theologie* (Cambridge, Gonville and Caius College MS 354/ 581)," *Plainsong and Medieval Music* 8.2 (forthcoming, 1999). A systematic survey of dozens of Lollard writings on music will be included in a related essay (currently in progress), "Excitement and the Fifteenth Century: Lollards, Lancastrians, and the Liturgical Culture of Late-Medieval England," which will situate this material within the wider conflict between Lollardy and orthodoxy that emerged shortly after 1400 with the promulgation of the *De heretico comburendo* statute and the censorious enactment of Arundel's Constitutions. Examining the intimate relationship between cultural patronage and the suppression of dissent by the Lancastrian kings and upper nobility, the essay seeks to broaden and challenge the brilliant account of early-fifteenth-century English culture presented in Nicholas Watson's recent article "Censorship and Cultural Change in Late-Medieval England: Vernacular Theology, the Oxford Translation Debate, and Arundel's Constitutions of 1409," *Speculum* 70 (1995): 822–64. While literary scholars have long recognized the self-consciously cautious and derivative nature of much of this period's literature (attributed by Watson in large part to orthodox censorship of vernacular religious writing), it was the same period that witnessed what musicologists have long regarded as England's musical apogee; for a recent and authoritative statement, see John Caldwell, *The Oxford History of English Music*, vol. 1 (Oxford: Clarendon Press, 1991), pp. 108–10. I suspect that the remarkable dissimilarities between literary and musical production in fifteenth-century England may be in part a result of the widely divergent effects of orthodox suppression of Lollardy upon vernacular writers and liturgical composers.

[82] F. D. Mathew, ed., *The English Works of Wyclif Hitherto Unprinted*, EETS, o.s., 74 (London: Kegan Paul, 1880), pp. 187–96.

[83] *Of feyned contemplatif lif*, in Mathew, ed., *English Works*, p. 192.

likely refers to the mensural subdivisions that characterize the polyphony of the Ars Nova.[84] Even the liturgical books employed in the Salisbury Use come under attack as an economic and pedagogical distraction
from biblical authority:

A lord, ȝif alle þe studie & traueile þat men han now abowte salisbury vss wiþ
multitude of newe costy portos, antifeners, graielis, & alle oþere bokis weren
turned in-to makynge of biblis & in studiynge & techynge þer-of, hou moche
schulde goddis lawe be forþered & knowen & kept, & now in so moche it is
hyndrid, vnstudied & vnkept.[85]

In the Lollards' eyes, liturgical excess—whether in the sudden growth
of choirs, the expense lavished on the production of antiphonals, gradu-
als, and other service-books, and the emergence of spectacular new forms
of music-making—represents an ecclesiastical vanity comparable to the
wasteful decoration of churches and the idolatrous veneration of images.[86]

Though they are equally concerned with aesthetic change, however,
the "Choristers' Lament" and such iconoclastic polemics against liturgical excess launch their musical critiques from two very different directions. The Lollard writers are attacking an institutional practice with
which they are clearly familiar but in relation to which they are reso-
lutely and self-consciously external; the "Lament"-author presents himself as an active and longtime participant in the very practices he critiques. The poem survives, after all, in a Benedictine miscellany. It was
written or copied by a writer affiliated with—and perhaps performing
the liturgy within—a Benedictine institution. the "Choristers' Lament," I would suggest, exhibits a "gentle anticlericalism" that contrasts sharply with the explicit and no-holds-barred criticisms of contemporary liturgical culture found in Wycliffite writings. Even while
satirizing the institutionally sanctioned practice of liturgical pedagogy,
the speakers in the "Choristers' Lament" simultaneously satirize themselves.

For what distinguishes this poem from so many of the other works
constituting Langland's pre-Reformation legacy is its success in obscur-

---

[84] See Hudson, *The Premature Reformation*, p. 322.
[85] *Of feyned contemplatif lif*, in Mathew, ed., *English Works*, p. 194.
[86] On Lollard iconoclastic objections to church decoration, see Hudson, *The Premature Reformation*, pp. 305–6.

ing its affiliations with contemporary radicals and dissenters—and, for that matter, with *Piers Plowman*—under a clerical shroud of liturgical knowledge and satirical humor. In the voices of these pupils, we are hearing unique vernacular testimony to the negative emotional and somatic effects of orthodox liturgical music-making upon—crucially—*nonheterodox* liturgical performers. Drawing on the new anticlerical idiom of *Piers Plowman* while resisting the heterodox anticlericalism of the *Piers Plowman* tradition, the "Choristers' Lament" distances itself from these poems by imagining a realm of liturgical performance outside the ecclesiastical "law" of liturgical obedience.

Though it is unlikely that we shall ever learn the identity of its author, it is tempting to read the "Choristers' Lament" as a stylized vernacular response to the institutional and cultural transformations discussed above by a liturgical performer affiliated with the Norwich priory who had recently come across a copy of *Piers Plowman*. Perhaps our poet was a clerk in minor orders, a member of those "lower ranks of the clergy" whom Scase locates among the "non-professionals" constituting a significant portion of Langland's earliest readership.[87] Maybe he was himself a monk of Norwich, enjoying a sadistic Langlandian laugh at the youthful singers he heard and saw muddling through the cathedral's liturgy on a regular basis. Or a so-called secondary as described by Nicholas Orme: a former chorister standing on a relatively low rung of the city's ecclesiastical hierarchy, grinding away at the liturgy day in and day out while waiting for advancement.[88] Whatever the case, the "Choristers' Lament" gives us a momentary but poignant glimpse at the fractiousness of liturgical culture in late-medieval England. As a poetic representation of liturgy as a malleable cultural practice always in danger of eluding clerical control, the poem insists—perhaps despite itself—that liturgical performance is inherently resistant to juridical constraint.

Appendix

The following transcription and annotation of the "Choristers' Lament" is intended to complement rather than replace Utley's excellent edition and detailed explication of the poem in *Speculum* 21 (1946): 194–202.

---

[87] Scase, *'Piers Plowman' and the New Anticlericalism*, p. 170.
[88] See Nicholas Orme, *Education and Society in Medieval and Renaissance England* (London: Hambledon Press, 1989), pp. 192–95.

The poem has been edited previously by T. Wright and J. O. Halliwell in *Reliquae Antiquae,* vol. 1 (London, 1841), pp. 291–92; and by Celia and Kenneth Sisam for *The Oxford Book of Medieval English Verse* (Oxford: Clarendon Press, 1970), pp. 184–87. Drawing on a number of editions, dictionaries (most notably, of course, the *MED*), and several literary and musicological studies unavailable in 1946, I have attempted to expand the range of Utley's references, identify a number of previously unnoted analogues for certain passages, and solve a crux or two that eluded him. Most obviously for the purposes of the preceding essay, I have noted all possible echoes of *Piers Plowman.*

Nine musical terms used in the poem—*cesolfa, bequarre, bemol, effauȝ, elami, mi, fa, sol,* and *vt*—are taken directly from the technical Latin vocabulary of solmization; for the sake of brevity, I have simply identified each by its place in the Guidonian gamut. For slightly later vernacular usages of these and other musical terms that appear in the "Lament," see the works edited by Sanford B. Meech, "Three Musical Treatises in English from a Fifteenth-Century Manuscript," *Speculum* 10 (1935): 235–69, in which they are used for the explicit purposes of instruction in the performance of polyphony.

The poem's unique witness is London, British Library MS Arundel 292, where it is written in a fourteenth-century anglicana on folios 70v–71r as a later addition to fly-leaves at the end of the ninth quire. The manuscript has been described recently and at length by Hanneke Wirtjes, *The Middle English Physiologus,* Early English Text Society, vol. 299 (Oxford: Oxford University Press, 1991), pp. ix–xv, who doubts that it was originally compiled from booklets (p. xii). The dialect is Northern, as indicated by, for example, the end-rhymes in the first stanza (care/lare/sare/mare) and numerous other features throughout the poem ("til" in line 2, "ga" in line 5, etc.). The scribe likely came from near King's Lynn; on the poem's original dialect, however, see the brief comment by Angus McIntosh, "The Language of the Extant Versions of Havelock the Dane," *MÆ* 45 (1976): 48.

The four-line stanzas, written continuously in the manuscript, are separated below. All abbreviations are silently expanded, and punctuation has been added for the sake of clarity (on the difficulties of punctuating the poem, see Utley's comment in the "Choristers' Lament," p. 195). In the manuscript, most half-lines are separated by a *punctus,* for which I have substituted an em-space; a *punctus* is also used several times at the ends of lines. Original word divisions have been emended, though all editorial departures from the text (aside from punctuation) are recorded in the apparatus immediately below the edition.

The Choristers' Lament

"Uncomly in cloystre   i coure ful of care,
I loke as a lurdeyn   and listne til my lare.
þe song of þe cesolfa   dos me syken sare,
and sitte stotiand on a song   a moneth and mare.

5   I ga gowlende abowte   also dos a goke,
mani is þe sorwfol song   it singge vpon mi bok.
I am holde so harde   vnneþes dar i loke;
al þe mirthe of þis mold   for god i forsoke.

I gowle on mi grayel   and Rore als a Roke,
10   Litel wiste i þerof   qwan i þerto toke.
Somme notes arn shorte   and somme a long noke,
Somme kroken aweyward   als a fleshoke.

Qwan i kan mi lesson   mi meyster wil i gon
þat heres me mi rendre   he wenes i haue wel don.
15   'Qwat hast þu don dawn Water   sin saterdai at non?
þu holdest nowt a note   by god in riht ton.

Wayme leue Water,   þu werkes al til shame;
þu stomblest and stikes fast   as þu were lame.
þu tones nowt þe note,   ilke be his name,
20   þu bitist asonder bequarre,   for bemol i þe blame.

Wey þe leue Water,   þu werkes al to wondre
als an old cawdrun   bigynnest to clondre.
þu tuchest nowt þe notes,   þu bites hem on sonder;
hold vp for shame,   þu letes hem al vnder.'"

25   þanne is Water so wo   þat wol ner wil he blede,
and wendis him til William   and bit him wel to spede.
"God it wot," seys William,   "þerof had i nede.
Now wot i qwuo Iudicare   was set in þe crede.

Me is wo so is þe be   þat belles in þe walmes,
30   I donke vpon dauid   til me tonge talmes.
I ne rendrede nowt   sithen men beren palmes.
Is it also mikel sorwe   in song so is in salmes?

Ya bi god þu reddis   and so it is wel werre,
I solfe and singge after   and is me neuere þe nerre;
35   I horle at þe notes   and heue hem al of herre;
alle þat me heres   wenes þat i erre.

Of bemol and of bequarre   of boþe i was wol bare,
Qwan i went out of þis word   and lifte til mi lare.
Of effauȝ and elami   ne coudy neuer are;
40   I fayle faste in þe fa,   it files al mi fare.

ȝet þer ben oþer notes,   sol and vt and la,
and þat froward file   þat men clipis fa.
Often he dos me liken ille   and werkes me ful wa;
miȝti him neuere hitten   inton for to ta.

45   ȝet þer is a streinant   witȝ to longe tailes;
þerfore has vre mayster   ofte horled mi kayles.
Ful litel þu kenes   qwat sorwe me ayles.
It is but childes game   þat þu witȝ dauid dayles.

Qwan ilke note til oþer lepes   and makes hem asawt,
50   þat we calles a moyson   in gesolreutȝ en hawt.
Il hayl were þu boren   ȝif þu make defawt.
þanne sais oure mayster,   'Que vos ren ne vawt.'"

1 Vncomly] Vn comly   5 abowte] a bowte   7 vnneþes] vn neþes   8 forsoke]
for soke   10 litel] listel þerof] þer of   11 Somme] summe   12 aweyward] a
weyward   27 þerof] þer of had i] haddi   30 vpon] vp on   43 he dos]
hedos   46 þerfore] þer fore   49 asawt] a sawt

2 *listne til me lare:* "listen to my lesson." Perhaps proverbial, though
not listed in Whiting. A much earlier instance occurs in the *Ormulum*,
where close attention to teachings is a prerequisite for salvation: "et

whase wile borrʒ en beon, / He lisste till hiss lare" (lines 11026–27); *The Ormulum,* ed. Robert Holt (Oxford: Clarendon Press, 1878), 2:28.

3 *cesolfa:* a very high c; in the Guidonian system, c-sol-fa is the sol syllable in the hexachord built on f and the fa syllable in the hexachord built on g. Utley suggests that the term as employed here could refer to the totality of the system itself, though I see no evidence for this.

7 *I am holde so harde vnnepes dar i loke:* Compare *Piers Plowman* B 4.60: "I am noʒt hardy for hym vnnepe to loke." The phrase is not proverbial, and I have been unable to identify another instance in early English literature.

14 *pat heres me mi rendre:* Utley modernizes this phrase as "who hears my rendition for me," but I think the more likely meaning is "who hears me perform 'mi'." In other words, the master hears the student perform the "mi" or third syllable in the Guidonian gamut and reacts by sarcastically assuring him that he has "wel don."

20 *bequarre* is b-natural or b-mi, the third or mi syllable in the G hexachord; *bemol* is b-flat or b-fa, the fourth syllable (fa) in the F hexachord.

22 *to clondre:* to drone or hum (MED *clondren,* v.). The "Choristers' Lament" contains the unique recorded usage of the word.

28 *Qwuo Iudicare was set in þe crede.* A proverbial phrase implying "sudden instruction in the obvious," perhaps especially through violence. The phrase is first recorded in the "Choristers' Lament" and appears as well in, among others, "Friar Daw's Reply" and the Wakefield "Scourging"; see Francis Lee Utley, "How Judicare Came in the Creed," *Mediaeval Studies* 8 (1946): 303–9 (citation from p. 308).

29 *þe be þat belles in þe walmes:* according to Utley, "the bee that buzzes (half drowned) in the well." Walmes can mean "wave," but Utley favors the less frequent connotation, "water-source" (thus "well").

30 *donke vpon dauid:* a phrase apparently implying a repetitive beating at the Psalms during performance. (Utley modernizes the line "I hammer away at the Psalms until my tongue falters.") Compare *Piers Plowman* B.3.312: "And dyngen vpon Dauid eche a day til eue." *Piers* and the "Lament" contain the first two recorded usages of the phrase.

talmes: MED *talmes,* v.b., "to falter when singing." The *MED*'s definition is tautological, however, for it adduces only the "Lament" to support *talmes* as a specifically musical term. The more general v.a. definition seems more attractive: "to be overcome, faint; of the heart: weaken, become exhausted."

34   *solfe and singge:* "sol-fa and sing." A formulaic association between singing and the learning of plainchant through solmization. Compare the following instances:

> I haue be preest and person passynge þritty winter,
> Yet kan i neyþer solue ne synge ne seintes lyues rede
>   (*Piers Plowman* B.5.417–18)

> Forto sowe siluer seede and solue ere thay singe,
> To haue ynne thaire haruest while the hete dureth.
>   (*Mum and the Sothsegger* 1147–48)

> *Si dedero* was ther lessoun
> Who so cowde solfe þat songe shuld be save
> ffor all þat euer they cowde crave ("De veritate et consciencia" 107–9)

35   *heve hem al of herre:* that is, "heave [the notes] off of their hinges." Compare Chaucer's description of the Miller in *The General Prologue* (549–50): "He was short-sholdred, brood, a thikke knarre; / Ther was no dore that he nolde heve of harre."

39   *effauȝ:* F-fa-ut, the fourth or fa syllable in the C hexachord, the first or ut syllable in the F hexachord. *elami:* e-la-mi, the sixth or la syllable in the G hexachord, the third or mi syllable in the c hexachord.

40–42   *fa, sol, vt, la:* four of the six fundamental syllables in the Guidonian gamut ut-re-mi-fa-sol-la. Here the speaker seems to be truly losing it, for now he is unable to learn or perform even the most basic elements of the solmization system.

45   *streinant:* from the rare OF *estraignant,* which appears in an expanded translation of Ovid listed in Godefroy. The *streinant* referred to here may be the "strene" note, identified by Margaret Bent (with explicit reference to the "Choristers' Lament") as "a black breve with two descending (or occasionally ascending) tails"; "New and Little-Known Fragments of English Medieval Polyphony," *Journal of the American Musicological Society* 21 (1968): 149. However, given that the term does not appear again in English until Marbeck's *Book of Common Praier* in 1550, Bent's identification may be too confident. In Thomas Walsingham's *Regulae de musica mensurabilis,* a Benedictine musical treatise roughly contemporary with the "Lament," the *larga plicata* is described as having

"duas tractus descendentes vel ascendentes ex parte dextera longiorem" (see above, note 49).

48 *wit3 dauid dayles:* "have dealings with David" ("mess around with the Psalms," perhaps?). See MED *dailen* v.: "to have dealings with (sb.), be concerned with (sth.)."

50 *moyson:* "measure," from OF *moison, muison* or Latin *mensura,* a term closely associated with the advent of musical "mensuration" or measurement in the Ars Nova. Compare *Piers Plowman* B.10.176–77: "Logyk I lerned hire, and al þe lawe after, / And alle þe Musons in Musik I made hire to knowe."

gesolreut3 en hawt: the third g in the Guidonian system (the fifth or sol syllable on the second c hexachord, the second or re syllable on the second f hexachord, and the first or ut syllable on the third g hexachord). Like cesolfa in line 3, gesolreut3 *en haut* is an extremely high note; its quality when performed is perhaps best described by the author of the *Tale of Beryn,* who relies on it to convey the anger of the Host: "The hoost made an hidouse cry, in gesolreut þe haut, / And set his hond in kenebowe; he lakkid nevir a faute"; *The Tale of Beryn,* lines 1837–38, ed. F. J. Furnivall and W. G. Stone (London: EETS, e.s., 105, 1909), p. 57. The common echoes on hawt/defawt ("Choristers' Lament") and haut/faute (*Beryn*) are suggestive.

52 *que vos ren ne vawt:* OF phrase translating roughly "My, but you are worthless!", suggesting that the choristers are being instructed in French rather than in English.

Reading Gower in a Manuscript Culture: Latin and English in Illustrated Manuscripts of the *Confessio Amantis*

Richard K. Emmerson
Medieval Academy of America

T he so-called New Philology has given added impetus to the study of medieval literature within its manuscript context and has encouraged a genuine interdisciplinary examination of the dynamic ways in which the scribes, limners, and artists who produced manuscripts not only transmitted literary texts to, but also reinterpreted and even reformed them for, later medieval readers.[1] Although many manuscripts of vernacular literature were humble products, others visualized the text in brightly illuminated and lavishly illustrated manuscripts, whose folios are not only inscribed in inks of various colors highlighted with gold and elaborate colorful penwork, but also decorated with a hierarchy of paraphs, capitals, large initials, gilded frames, and floreated borders designed to aid and direct reading (see Fig. 1). If we are to understand the reception of a literary text in the later Middle Ages, then, we must not limit our investigations to textual matters alone. We must examine how the text was available to readers in particular manuscripts rather than how it is presented in a modern critical edition, and we must examine the miniatures that accompany the text in their manuscript context, not against the sanitized text of a critical edition.

Although providing their own set of symbols that constitute a modern scholarly apparatus, critical editions usually elide the matrix of signs

The research for this essay was supported by a Fellowship for College Teachers funded by the National Endowment for the Humanities. I wish also to express my gratitude for the hospitality of the Centre for Medieval Studies, University of York, and my thanks to its director, Felicity Riddy.

[1] See the essays in *Speculum* 65 (January 1990), particularly the introduction by Stephen G. Nichols, "Philology in a Manuscript Culture," pp. 1–10.

that comprise a medieval manuscript, replacing the highly visual folio opening with what Paul Saenger and Michael Heinlen have called the "blackening of the page,"[2] a feature of the book that began in the later fifteenth century and is perhaps the strongest visual characteristic of the modern printed page. We must also set aside—at least at the beginning stages of analysis—the assumption that miniatures simply illustrated the literary text and recognize that they, like the other features of the decorated page, may serve more formal purposes intended to aid reading.[3] One of the scholars who has done the most to redirect our attention to the manuscript context of medieval literature, Ralph Hanna, is surely right about "the power of the codex to generate meaning" and the importance of considering "codicological aesthetics" in our own readings. Hanna notes that "medieval book-producers, in every case, had to devise a format in order to present a text, had to plan out a *mise en page,* an apparatus, a decorative system. These choices, again, provide particularly provocative 'readings.'"[4]

The value of studying the manuscript representation of a medieval literary text is exemplified by an analysis of the twenty illustrated manuscripts of John Gower's *Confessio Amantis,* which is primarily known to scholars in the two volumes of the Early English Text Society (EETS) edited by G. C. Macaulay at the turn of the twentieth century.[5] The edition has had a formative influence on critical understanding of Gower's poem, particularly its use of Latin and the relationship between its

[2] Paul Saenger and Michael Heinlen, "Incunable Description and Its Implications for the Analysis of Fifteenth-Century Reading Habits," in Sandra L. Hindman, ed., *Printing the Written Word: The Social History of Books, Circa 1450–1520* (Ithaca, N.Y.: Cornell University Press, 1991), p. 253.

[3] See my essay, "Text and Image in the Ellesmere Portraits of the Tale-Tellers," in Martin Stevens and Daniel Woodward, eds., *The Ellesmere Chaucer: Essays in Interpretation* (San Marino, Calif.: Huntington Library, 1995), pp. 143–70. It questions the commonplace approach to the famous portraits introducing the tales in the Ellesmere Chaucer, which critics often treat as realistic depictions of the pilgrims as described in the General Prologue; it argues, instead, that the paintings, like other feature's of the manuscript's *ordinatio,* are better understood as markers to aid reading.

[4] Ralph Hanna III, "Producing Manuscripts and Editions," in A. J. Minnis and Charlotte Brewer, eds., *Crux and Controversy in Middle English Textual Criticism* (Cambridge: D. S. Brewer, 1992), p. 129.

[5] G. C. Macaulay, ed., *John Gower's English Works,* 2 vols., Early English Text Society [hereafter EETS], e.s., 81 and 82 (1900–1901; rpt. London: Oxford University Press, 1957). The English poem is cited parenthetically by book and line numbers; the Latin verses are cited by book and chapter, given in roman numerals; the Latin prose commentary and Macaulay's introduction are cited by volume and page numbers.

Latin elements and its English octosyllabic couplets. Macaulay postulated three recensions of the *Confessio,* which are distinguished by changes in the poem's dedication, epilogue, and some tales. The first, which includes a dedication to Richard II in the Prologue, is available in three stages of revision: unrevised, intermediate, and revised. The second recension adds and rearranges some passages in the tales and eliminates the praise of Richard in the epilogue, replacing it with a prayer for the state of England. The third recension keeps the revised epilogue and revises the preface so that the poem is written "for Engelondes sake" rather than being dedicated to Richard.[6] Although Macaulay's view that the poem's three recensions are authorial has been challenged, the classification of textual recensions remains a useful organizational tool that I will follow, with some modifications, in discussing the illustrated manuscripts.[7]

Almost universally acknowledged to be a careful and reliable edition of the poetic text, the EETS edition is based on Bodleian Library Fairfax MS 3, which Macaulay argued represents Gower's final "intention" for the *Confessio Amantis.* Of the forty-nine manuscripts (forty-one known to Macaulay), it contains the best text of the third and final recension of the poem, beginning as a revised manuscript of the first recension, but passing "from one group into another partly by erasure and partly by

---

[6] For the three recensions, see Macaulay, ed., ibid., 1:cxxvii–cxxxviii; and John H. Fisher, *John Gower: Moral Philosopher and Friend of Chaucer* (New York: New York University Press, 1964), pp. 116–27.

[7] For a critique of Macaulay's recensions, see three essays by Peter Nicholson: "The Dedications of Gower's *Confessio Amantis,*" *Mediaevalia* 10 (1984): 159–80; "Gower's Revisions in the *Confessio Amantis,*" *ChauR* 19 (1984): 123–43; and "Poet and Scribe in the Manuscripts of Gower's *Confessio Amantis,*" in Derek Pearsall, ed., *Manuscripts and Texts: Editorial Problems in Later Middle English Literature* (Cambridge: D. S. Brewer, 1987), pp. 130–42. My argument is concerned primarily with decorative rather than textual traditions, but it adds weight to Nicholson's critique of the recensions; their authorial status, however, is not an issue in the fifteenth-century reception of the poem, since each manuscript, no matter which recension it inscribes, claims Gower's authorship. Thus, until Macaulay's widely accepted typology is modified or replaced by the publication of the *Catalogue of Manuscripts of the Works of John Gower,* edited by Jeremy Griffiths, Kate Harris, and Derek Pearsall, it remains a handy shorthand for scholarly discussion. In adopting this tactic, I agree with James Simpson, who—although acknowledging Nicholson's view that "the three revisions of the first recension are not authorial" and that "many aspects of the revision of the second and third recensions" cannot with certainty be ascribed to Gower—maintains the value of Macaulay's three recensions. See Simpson, *Sciences and the Self in Medieval Poetry: Alan of Lille's Anticlaudianus and John Gower's* Confessio amantis (Cambridge: Cambridge University Press, 1995), pp. 293–94, n. 21.

substitution of leaves, apparently made under the direction of the author."[8] Macaulay's focus on Fairfax 3 for the establishment of his critical edition is not, therefore, at issue. Whether or not one agrees with Derek Pearsall that Fairfax was the authoritative exemplar, one of the "carefully proof-read copies of his major poems" that Gower kept "so that corrections and revisions could be entered under his scrupulous supervision,"[9] Macaulay's focus on Fairfax is appropriate for the study of the *text* of the *Confessio Amantis.* It is, however, problematic for the study of the medieval *reception* of Gower's poem, because it gives prominence to only one way in which the text was inscribed, laid out, rubricated, decorated, and illustrated in fifteenth-century manuscripts, the means by which the poem was received. As we will see below, by following Fairfax 3, the edition masks the complexity of the manuscript presentation of the text and thus the ways in which the manuscripts presented Gower as *auctor* and the variety of ways in which Gower was received by his contemporaries and later-fifteenth-century readers. As Eric H. Reiter states, "The history of medieval reading demands that we turn from texts to books, or more precisely, that we look at books not as carriers of texts, but as artifacts of the reading process."[10]

This essay examines illustrated manuscripts of the *Confessio Amantis* as "artifacts of the reading process," by directing attention from the poem's text to the books in which the poem was inscribed. Rather than privileging one textual recension or one manuscript tradition, I examine

---

[8] Macaulay, *Gower's English Works,* 1:cxxx. Fisher agrees that Gower intended Fairfax 3 to be "the final official version" (*John Gower,* p. 127), and Nicholson acknowledges that the manuscript's "alterations can only have been made under carefully prepared instructions which are again most easily attributed to the poet" ("Gower's Revisions," p. 136). For descriptions of the manuscripts, see Macaulay, ibid., 1:cxxxviii–clxviii, and Fisher, ibid., pp. 303–9.

[9] Pearsall, "The Gower Tradition," in A. J. Minnis, ed., *Gower's* Confessio Amantis: *Responses and Reassessments* (Cambridge: D. S. Brewer, 1983), p. 182. Fisher develops Macaulay's view that Gower supervised the copying of his manuscripts, possibly in his own scriptorium at the Priory of St. Mary Overeys in Southwark; see *John Gower,* pp. 59–60, 303–9. The existence of a personal scriptorium has been questioned by Malcolm B. Parkes, who studies the revision and correction of four manuscripts of the *Vox Clamantis* as well as Fairfax 3. Although agreeing that Fairfax was originally a first-recension manuscript revised during the poet's lifetime, Parkes finds no evidence Gower supervised the revisions. See "Patterns of Scribal Activity and Revisions of the Text in Early Copies of Works by John Gower," in Richard Beadle and A. J. Piper, eds., *New Science Out of Old Books: Studies in Manuscripts and Early Printed Books in Honour of A. I. Doyle* (Aldershot, Hants.: Scolar Press, 1995), pp. 81–121.

[10] Eric H. Reiter, "The Reader as Author of the User-Produced Manuscript: Reading and Rewriting Popular Latin Theology in the Late Middle Ages," *Viator* 27 (1996): 154.

the variety of ways in which Gower's poem was available during the fifteenth century to suggest some ways in which it was read in a manuscript culture. The essay begins by discussing the scholarly understanding of Gower's Latin, primarily based upon Macaulay's edition, and investigating the representation of Latin in the design of illustrated manuscripts of the *Confessio Amantis*. These opening sections will show that, in matters of design, manuscripts of the three textual recensions may be classified into two large groups. The essay then analyzes the treatment of two miniatures that are most often painted in illustrated manuscripts of the *Confessio,* again categorizing the manuscripts into two groups. In the next two sections, these conclusions regarding the *mise en page* of the illustrated manuscripts are developed to suggest how Gower may have expected his poem to be received—publicly, perhaps at court—and two other ways in which it was probably read during the fifteenth century: as a collection of love stories and as a latinate protohumanist text. The conclusion expands and tests these suggestions by examining two unique later manuscripts that include large cycles of miniatures. The essay thus explores "codicological aesthetics"—particularly the relationship of Latin to the design and illustration of manuscripts—to understand how fifteenth-century manuscripts encouraged different readings of the *Confessio Amantis* and different representations of Gower as *auctor.*

Latin in the *Confessio Amantis*

In an influential essay published in 1989, Derek Pearsall outlines four categories of Latin in the *Confessio.*[11] Two of these have received the most critical comment. The first, the unrhymed elegiac verses, Macaulay prints in italic type, indenting every other line, setting them in the text column at the beginning of the various subsections of the poem's Prologue and eight books, and assigning them small roman numerals.[12] The manuscripts similarly inscribe them in the text column, usually introducing them with one-line initials and sometimes writing them in

---

[11] Derek Pearsall, "Gower's Latin in the *Confessio Amantis,*" in A. J. Minnis, ed., *Latin and Vernacular: Studies in Late-Medieval Texts and Manuscripts* (Cambridge: D. S. Brewer, 1989), pp. 13–25.

[12] Precedent for numbering the verses is found in St. Catherine's College, Cambridge, MS 7, where a later hand has numbered them in the margin. The manuscripts do not indent the Latin verses and sometimes run them together as prose.

black, sometimes in red ink. There are sixty-eight sets of verses, usually four to six lines each, making a total of 390 lines of Latin.[13] The verses, as Pearsall notes, "are highly 'poetic,' and relate to the English in some way as the metres of Boethius to the prose, as if the English, that is, were prose." Distinguishing between the "literariness" of the Latin and the "literalness" of the English, Pearsall also contrasts the "literary, textual, conceptual, abstracting" features of the Latin and the "literal, quasi-oral, affective, concrete" of the English.[14] Robert F. Yeager similarly emphasizes the contrast between the Latin verses and Gower's English plain style, which he understands as appropriate for the poet's attempt to achieve a "middel weie" (Prol. 17), to "wryte a bok betwen the tweie / Somwhat of lust, somwhat of lore" (Prol. 18–19). To Yeager, the Latin verses were intended to serve as a "counterpoint" to the simpler style of Gower's English, to give "elegance, and solidity, to English verse," since "Gower equated Latin with high style and important utterance."[15]

The second Latin element is the prose commentary, which was almost certainly written by Gower.[16] Macaulay sets it in small roman type, placing the various passages of prose, ranging from just a few words to rather lengthy summaries, in the margins of the page. The placement and decoration of the Latin prose within illustrated manuscripts and the implications of the resulting *mise en page* of various manuscript traditions are central concerns of this essay, to which I will return below. Here I note only that the commentary serves several functions: to introduce new

---

[13] These have been translated by Siân Echard and Claire Fanger, *The Latin Verses in the* Confessio Amantis: *An Annotated Translation* (East Lansing, Mich.: Colleagues Press, 1991). In the preface, A. G. Rigg surveys the place of Latin in England in the later fourteenth century and notes that all the Latin verses—except for VIII.iv and the envoy—are unrhymed elegiac couplets.

[14] Pearsall, "Gower's Latin," pp. 13, 19. Pearsall comments on the difficulty of the Latin verses, noting that he once "was tempted to believe that Gower's Latin was not merely difficult to understand but not meant to be understood" (p. 17). Their difficulty is acknowledged by Echard and Fanger, *Latin Verses,* p. xxvi.

[15] R. F. Yeager, "'Oure englisshe' and Everyone's Latin: The *Fasciculus Morum* and Gower's *Confessio Amantis," SoAR* 46 (1981): 50.

[16] Jeremy Griffiths raises the possibility Gower did not write the commentary; see "'Confessio Amantis': The Poem and Its Pictures," in Minnis, ed., *Gower's* Confessio Amantis, pp. 174–75. Pearsall, Yeager, and most other scholars, however, assume Gower's authorship. Tim William Machan, in "Thomas Berthelette and Gower's *Confessio," SAC* 18 (1996): 143–66, summarizes the scholarly consensus: "[I]t is widely considered today that Gower himself must have written the glosses" (p. 164). Although I agree that the poet composed the commentary, as we will see below, many manuscripts delete it.

topics, summarize tales, explain functions of the frame and narratives, and identify sources. Thus, in critical discussions the Latin prose passages are referred to by a variety of terms, such as glosses, summaries, marginalia, and headnotes, as well as commentaries.[17] Although recognizing these various terms and functions, for convenience and to avoid confusion I refer to the poem's accompanying Latin prose consistently as commentary.

Critics have attributed a variety of purposes to the Latin commentary. To Pearsall, "the Latin commentaries are not means to the understanding of the English poem but instructions on how to read it according to the conventions of a specific code of reading," so that, along with the verses, they serve "as a fixative" for the "precarious, slippery, fluid" English.[18] To Rita Copeland, they are a crucial component of the scholastic nature of the *Confessio Amantis:* "The exegetical system dominates at all levels and junctures of this text. Prologues frame the text, marginal commentary interpolates the text, and the conventions of *ordinatio* give the text its structural underpinnings."[19] To Winthrop Wetherbee their "interplay" with the English poem becomes "in many respects a substitute for the traditional Boethian dialogue. The marginalia oscillate between the poles of authoritative commentary, which places Gower's narratives in a historical and religious economy, and a dogged, schoolmasterly moralism, pompous and at times ludicrously irrelevant in its attempts to engage the subtleties of the vernacular text."[20]

The other two categories of Latin that Pearsall discusses have received less critical attention. The third category includes the speaker markers

---

[17] A point made by Siân Echard in "With Carmen's Help: Latin Authorities in the *Confessio Amantis,*" *Studies in Philology* 95 (1998): 1-40. I thank Echard for showing me her essay before its publication and for her help on the present essay. Although we both stress the importance of studying the *Confessio* within its manuscript context, Echard does not discuss the miniatures, their relationship to the Latin, and their role in Gower's reception. As will be evident below, I agree with her view that specific manuscripts "produce, through their representation of the bilingual text, significantly different 'readings' of the poem" (p. 2).

[18] Pearsall, "Gower's Latin," pp. 24, 18.

[19] Rita Copeland, *Rhetoric, Hermeneutics, and Translation in the Middle Ages: Academic Traditions and Vernacular Texts* (Cambridge: Cambridge University Press, 1991), pp. 202–20; the quotation is from p. 203.

[20] Winthrop Wetherbee, "Latin Structure and Vernacular Space: Gower, Chaucer and the Boethian Tradition," in R. F. Yeager, ed., *Chaucer and Gower: Difference, Mutuality, Exchange* (Victoria, B.C.: English Literary Studies, University of Victoria, 1991), pp. 9–10.

that help identify the Lover and Genius as speakers in the dialogue that constitutes the unifying narrative frame of the poem.[21] Primarily identifying "Confessor" and "Amans," the markers are occasionally the two-word phrases "Confessio Amantis," "Opponit Confessor," or "Respondet Amans." Macaulay also sets the speaker markers in small roman type and in the margins, so that they appear to be a version of the prose commentary.[22] The speaker markers should be distinguished from the commentary as a type of Latin, however. Their function, for example, differs from the commentary since they identify speakers in the English frame rather than summarize tales or explain functions of narrative technique or poetic voice. Their purpose is to aid the eye as it scans the page in identifying the name of a new speaker within the English poem. That they are written in Latin rather than in English also distinguishes them from the narrative, making them a discrete feature of the Latin apparatus.

This function is highlighted by the manuscripts, which generally place the speaker markers in the margins even when the prose commentary is placed within the columns of the English text.[23] In decoration, the manuscripts often link a speaker marker to the corresponding English line where the identified speaker's dialogue begins, a relationship that is sometimes signaled by an alternating color scheme of paraphs and one-line initials. For example, Bodleian Library MS Bodley 902, fol. 61r (Fig. 1), inscribes in its left margin six such speaker markers set off by paraphs in alternating blue and gold, with similarly alternating color penwork. The corresponding English lines spoken by Amans and Confessor are also highlighted by one-line initials, whose colors alternate blue and gold in a vertical pattern as the eye moves down the text col-

---

[21] On the function and frequency of the speaker markers, see Siân Echard, "Dialogues and Monologues: Manuscript Representations of the Conversation of the *Confessio Amantis,*" forthcoming in a volume in honor of Derek Pearsall, ed. A. J. Minnis. Echard notes that the speaker markers "are much more likely than any other part of the Latin framework to vary significantly from manuscript to manuscript." Again I thank Echard for her kindness in showing me her essay before publication.

[22] Pearsall, "Gower's Latin," also includes in this category the occasional marginal glosses citing authorities and explaining allusions, but their function and their placement in manuscripts link them with the Latin prose commentary.

[23] The markers are sometimes placed at the end of the English line of dialogue. Echard ("Dialogues and Monologues") notes that of the forty-six manuscripts she has examined, fourteen place the speaker markers at the end of the English line and twenty-five place them in the margins. Other manuscripts mix their placement, and three center the speaker markers within the text column.

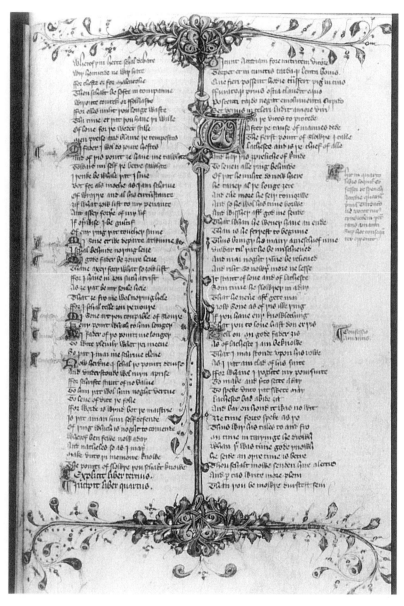

Fig. 1. Oxford, Bodleian Library, MS Bodley 902, fol. 61r; published by permission of the Bodleian Library, Oxford.

umn. These initials also alternate in a horizontal pattern with the colors of the paraphs identifying the speakers in the margins. On the other hand, the prose commentary inscribed in the right margin is not linked to a specific English line. None of these decorative markings are noted by Macaulay, although he does indent the English verses to mark changes in speakers.

The fourth category of Latin is what Pearsall calls Gower's "final packaging of the text,"[24] a rather elaborate Latin apparatus that concludes most manuscripts of the *Confessio.* It has received some attention because scholars have studied the changes in the Latin colophon to reconstruct Gower's developing political loyalties.[25] The apparatus includes a six-line Latin verse explicit that dedicates the poem to Henry of Lancaster, a prose rubric that introduces four lines of Latin verse praising Gower as a poet, and a lengthy colophon in four paragraphs describing Gower's three major poems. Another Latin poem comparing Gower favorably to Virgil is included in Fairfax 3, which, as will be discussed below, probably represents Gower's final arrangement of these matters. Regarding the laudatory Latin poems of this concluding apparatus, Pearsall states: "Whether offered to him, solicited, or composed by Gower himself, these poems represent the English poet in an extraordinary light, not merely kissing the steps on which the classical poets stand, which is what Chaucer modestly advises his book of *Troilus* to do, but clambering up them."[26]

In addition to these four categories outlined by Pearsall, Gower manuscripts include a fifth category of Latin, comprising the more typical apparatus used in the design of the page to aid reading: rubrics—short functional texts, not necessarily written in red; running titles; and, in some manuscripts, tables of contents. Siân Echard describes the Latin of this category as "an indexing tool" that "may be part of the panoply of authority," but that is "also simply functional."[27] The manuscripts are quite consistent in this formal apparatus, identifying the beginnings and conclusions of the Prologue and eight books with incipits and ex-

[24] Pearsall, "Gower's Latin," p. 24.

[25] See Fisher, *John Gower,* pp. 88–91; Fisher prints the three versions of the colophon in appendix B, pp. 311–12.

[26] Pearsall, "Gower's Latin," p. 24. Macaulay, ed., *Gower's English Works,* 2:479, attributed these poems to Strode.

[27] Echard, "With Carmen's Help" (n. 17 above), p. 11.

plicits inscribed within the text columns, as can be seen in the lower left column of Bodley 902, fol. 61r (Fig. 1), where the Latin rubrics are written in a slightly larger hand and introduced by decorated rubrics. They also provide running titles in the upper margins that are highlighted by colored rubrics, usually "Liber" on the verso of an opening and, on the facing recto, the number of the book written out in Latin.[28] Macaulay treats this apparatus in various ways, setting rubrics, for example, in boldface, always separating the "explicit" of one book from the "incipit" of the following book, which in his edition always heads a new page after a blank space of seven lines.[29]

Thus, Pearsall's comment that the *Confessio* "comes 'cased' or 'boxed' in Latin" seems apt.[30] He believes that "The Latin material of the *Confessio* acts as it were to stabilise the English poem within the learned Latin tradition as a self-conscious but not self-indulgent relaxation from more serious labours."[31] Pearsall here develops the argument earlier set out by A. J. Minnis, who in his *Medieval Theory of Authorship* states that "the person who provided the Latin commentary was concerned to make sure that the implications of the English text should not be missed. He says, in the third person, what Gower could not have said with decorum in the first person, thereby making his would-be *auctor* an actual *auctor.*"[32] This third-person voice is evident, for example, when the commentary explains early in book 1 that the author takes on the fictional persona of Amans, just at that point when the "I" of the English poem

---

[28] Even in those manuscripts that lack running titles, provision was often made for them. St. Catherine's College, Cambridge, 7, for example, includes blue and gold paraphs in its top margin but not the titles. This deluxe manuscript is unusual in placing the confession miniature in the bottom margin of fol. 8v, which suggests that it may have been an afterthought.

[29] In addition, in all four margins of his edition Macaulay adds a distinctly modern apparatus not found in the manuscripts. In the top margins he sets running titles in capital letters on right-hand pages and the poem's title in capital letters on left-hand pages; the right margins include line numbers and boldface references to Reinhold Pauli's edition, Confessio Amantis *of John Gower,* 3 vols. (London, 1857); the outer margins affix a new set of Macaulay's own topical headings, placed in brackets; and the bottom margins provide a list of variant readings.

[30] Pearsall, "Gower's Latin," p. 18.

[31] Ibid., p. 24.

[32] A. J. Minnis, *Medieval Theory of Authorship: Scholastic Literary Attitudes in the Later Middle Ages,* 2d ed. (Philadelphia: University of Pennsylvania Press, 1988), pp. 188–89. Minnis later states that "the commentary is in such complete sympathy with the moral *intentio* professed in the poem that one is emboldened to believe that Gower himself provided it to accompany his 'modern English classic'" (p. 190).

identifies himself as one who suffers from the pangs of love.[33] Unlike Chaucer, who in *The Canterbury Tales* seems to encourage the conflation of poet and narrator, Gower emphasizes the distinction, using the commentary to ensure that his readers do not confuse him as *auctor* with the often obtuse Lover of the frame story. Yeager thus rightly notes that the commentary allows "Gower the poet to step outside the fictive drama unfolding around John Gower the Lover at confession, to mark directly the deliberate progress of the poem. Thus, we find the prose passages telling us not only the outline of the narratives, but also what we are to think about them."[34]

To Yeager, Gower's Latin and English establish three voices in the *Confessio*. The first is the fictive voice of the English frame story, involving Amans, Genius, and the many exempla related by Genius. The second is the impersonal poetic voice of the Latin verses, which demonstrated "to sophisticated audiences that their author John Gower can sing as well at the top as the bottom of the scale."[35] The third is the voice of the Latin prose commentary, which Yeager here refers to as marginal glosses. He sees this voice as an attempt "to limit polysemy and avoid misunderstanding by directing the act of comprehension through an expansion of the poetic text to include the margins of his page."[36] Yeager concludes by rightly emphasizing that Gower understood the ways in which the folio page worked as a sign, how "the page itself can embody the message, can become clearly a sign," and furthermore "that the text is, *must be,* an element actively making meaning, regardless of specific literary approach."[37]

I fully agree with Yeager's emphasis upon the page as *sign* and its importance in producing meaning. His sophisticated argument needs to be qualified in one important respect, however, because it assumes that the Latin prose commentary is always inscribed in the margins of the manuscript page. Yeager—like others who in recent years have fo-

---

[33] "Hic quasi in persona aliorum, quos amor alligat, fingens se auctor esse Amantem, varias eorum passiones variis huius libri distinccionibus per singula scribere proponit"; Macaulay, ed., *Gower's English Works,* 1:37, commentary adjacent 1.59.

[34] Yeager, " 'Oure englisshe,' " p. 47.

[35] Robert F. Yeager, "English, Latin, and the Text as 'Other': The Page as Sign in the Work of John Gower," *Text* 3 (1987): 251–67; rpt. in and cited from Stephanie Trigg, ed., *Medieval English Poetry* (New York: Longman, 1993), pp. 203–16; the quotation is from p. 211.

[36] Ibid., p. 213.

[37] Ibid., p. 214.

cused attention on Gower's Latin, including Copeland, Minnis, Pearsall, and Wetherbee[38]—here discusses the Latin of the *Confessio Amantis* primarily as it is represented in Macaulay's edition, with the prose commentary set in the margins, imitating the design of Fairfax 3.[39] The *mise en page* of Fairfax is evident on fol. 8r (Fig. 2), which encompasses the conclusion of the Prologue and beginning of book 1. It inscribes the Latin verse within the text column, here placed below the miniature on the right and introduced by a one-line initial "N". Passages of prose commentary, on the other hand, are placed in both the left and right margins and are not introduced by initials or paraphs. This folio also includes the formal Latin of the rubrics in the lower left column and the running titles in the upper margin, inscribing these and all other Latin in the same black ink used for the English poetry.

Such a design, however, represents only one way in which fifteenth-century manuscripts treated Gower's Latin. To understand the various ways in which Gower's text was received during the later Middle Ages, we need to look beyond Macaulay's edition and Fairfax 3 at the range of fifteenth-century manuscripts. Such analysis will show that, by discussing the Latin of the *Confessio* primarily as it is edited by Macaulay, scholars have tended to overemphasize the "marginal" nature of the prose commentary, whereas, in fact, the vast majority of illustrated manuscripts do not inscribe the Latin commentary in their margins but in their text columns, the space that Macaulay reserves for either the Latin or English verse.

The Treatment of Latin in the Three Recensions of the *Confessio*

The appendix of this essay lists the illustrated manuscripts of the *Confessio Amantis* according to Macaulay's typology of recensions and standard sigla. Within each category, manuscripts are ordered by date, which is often approximate. In its middle three columns the appendix

---

[38] Other recent studies treating the Latin commentary as "marginalia" include Robert F. Yeager, "Learning to Read in Tongues: Writing Poetry for a Trilingual Culture," in Yeager, ed., *Chaucer and Gower*, pp. 115–29; and Kurt Olsson, *John Gower and the Structures of Conversion: A Reading of the* Confessio Amantis (Cambridge: D. S. Brewer, 1992).

[39] Machan criticizes the layout of Macaulay's edition: "Though Macaulay is highly critical of Pauli and dismissive of Morley, he nonetheless and equally without explanation imitates the former's practice of marginalizing the glosses" ("Thomas Berthelette," p. 165). But Macaulay places the Latin commentary in the margins because he follows Fairfax 3; the problem is not the edition but relying only upon the edition.

Fig. 2.   Oxford, Bodleian Library, Fairfax 3, fol. 8r; published by permission of the Bodleian Library, Oxford.

notes the color ink used to inscribe the Latin verses; the color of the Latin prose commentary and its placement, whether in the text column or in the margin; and the color of ink used to inscribe the speaker markers and the more formal Latin apparatus such as running titles, rubrics, and the concluding Latin verses and colophon. These columns show that manuscripts using red for the Latin verse and commentary tend to use red for the remaining Latin apparatus. In its right two columns the appendix identifies the type and placement of the two standard miniatures usually painted in these manuscripts, a placement, as we shall see below, related to their treatment of Latin.

The appendix shows that the treatment of Latin varies according to the recension of the English text, a feature of these manuscripts that has not been noted in previous studies. Most manuscripts of the first recension place the Latin prose commentary within the text columns.[40] These manuscripts also highlight the Latin, the verse, the prose, and the speaker markers, as well as the more formal apparatus, by writing the Latin in red. This is evident in British Library MS Egerton 1991, whose text Macaulay describes as "probably the best of its class."[41] Although the color of fol. 7v, beautifully illuminated with half border, is lost in a black-and-white reproduction (Fig. 3), the placement of both the Latin verses and the prose commentary within the text column is clear. The Latin verse is written below the miniature showing the confession, with Amans kneeling before Genius, whereas the Latin prose commentary is written near the end of the right column between book 1, lines 208 and 209.[42] Both forms of Latin are emphasized by being given one-line blue

---

[40] On the *ordinatio* and copying of *Confessio* manuscripts, see A. I. Doyle and M. B. Parkes, "The Production of Copies of the *Canterbury Tales* and the *Confessio Amantis* in the Early Fifteenth Century," in *Medieval Scribes, Manuscripts, and Libraries: Essays Presented to N. R. Ker* (London: Scolar Press, 1978), pp. 163–210; rpt. in and cited from Parkes, *Scribes, Scripts and Readers: Studies in the Communication, Presentation and Dissemination of Medieval Texts* (London: Hambledon Press, 1991), pp. 201–48. Doyle and Parkes describe the placement of the Latin prose in the text column as "a more 'developed' stage" in the copying of the poem (p. 233). A. S. G. Edwards and Derek Pearsall, "The Manuscripts of the Major English Poetic Texts," in Jeremy Griffiths and Derek Pearsall, eds., *Book Production and Publishing in Britain, 1375–1475* (Cambridge: Cambridge University Press, 1989), attribute this shift in the treatment of Latin to "exigencies of economy and space" (p. 264). But this seems unlikely, since the size and lavish decoration of these manuscripts implies that economic considerations were not primary; if saving space had been a goal, furthermore, the Latin prose would have been kept in the margin.

[41] Macaulay, ed., *Gower's English Works,* 1:cxlviii.

[42] Ibid., 1:41, numbers the Latin verse (iii) and places the four lines in italics; the Latin prose is placed in the right margin adjacent to 1.209–16.

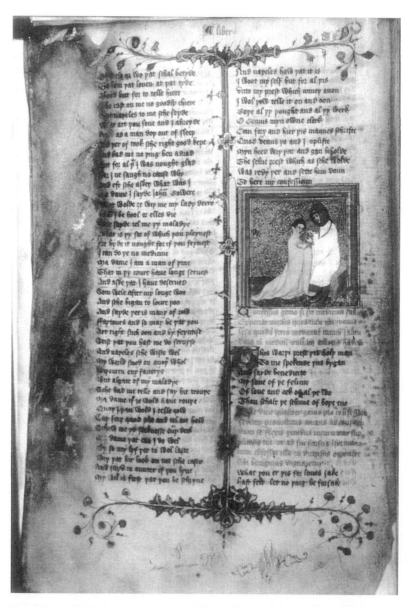

Fig. 3.   London, British Library, Egerton 1991, fol. 7v; published by permission of the British Library.

initials decorated with red penwork, and by being written in red. They are separated by six lines of English, written in black and introduced by a three-line initial "T" that is linked to the half border. Most of the unillustrated manuscripts of the first recension that have Latin elements similarly situate the Latin prose within the text columns and identify all Latin texts with red ink.[43]

Manuscripts of what Macaulay identifies as the revised first recension and the second recension are more complicated in their treatment of the Latin, so I will return to these below. Third-recension manuscripts, as we have seen with Fairfax 3, are more likely to place the Latin prose within the margin and to inscribe all Latin, including the verses, prose commentary, and scholarly apparatus, in a dark brown or black ink— that is, in the same color ink used for the English couplets. But third-recension manuscripts are not as uniform as manuscripts containing the unrevised or intermediate stages of the first recension. As is evident in the list of manuscripts given in the appendix, the three illustrated manuscripts of the third recension differ somewhat in their treatment of the Latin, a difference particularly noteworthy in the case of British Library, Harley 3869, a direct copy of Fairfax 3. This manuscript was written considerably later, perhaps as much as a half-century after Fairfax, and it represents one of the ways in which the later fifteenth century received Gower in deluxe manuscripts, with the Latin written in red and thereby emphasized, even though like Fairfax it continues to place the prose commentary in the margin. As can be seen on fol. 18r (Fig. 4), the manuscript seems extremely conscious of the distinction between the Latin prose and the verses, identifying them throughout with the rubric "versus," here inscribed below the right corner of the miniature's frame. This distinction between prose and verse sets Harley off from those first-recension manuscripts that also inscribe the Latin in red but tend to conflate the two forms of Latin, sometimes running them together within the text column. Harley, though, is unusual for later

---

[43] In addition to the illustrated manuscripts listed in the appendix, I have examined several unillustrated manuscripts of the *Confessio;* conclusions regarding manuscripts I have not seen are based on Macaulay's descriptions. The one unrevised first-recension manuscript that does not include the Latin commentary, Bodleian Library, Ashmole 35, still keeps the scholarly apparatus associated with the Latin by providing a commentary in English, which is inscribed in red ink. For a transcription of the English commentary, see Kate Harris, "Ownership and Readership: Studies in the Provenance of the Manuscripts of Gower's *Confessio Amantis*" (Ph.D. diss., University of York, 1993), appendix I.

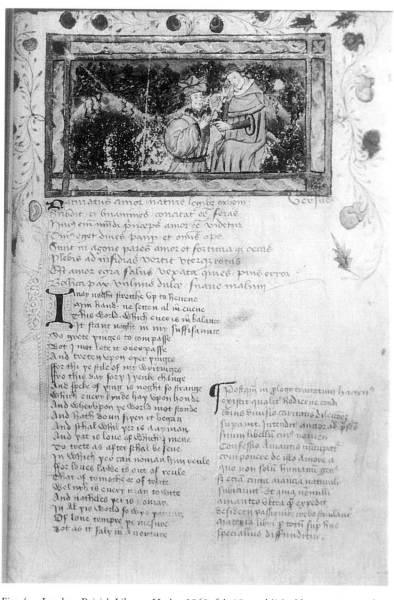

Fig. 4.   London, British Library, Harley 3869, fol. 18r; published by permission of the British Library.

third-recension manuscripts, which more often minimized the Latin apparatus of the *Confessio* and presented a more English Gower. Some manuscripts of this recension, for example, either omitted or abridged the Latin commentary.[44] In other words, the Latin third-person "voice" of Gower as *auctor* was lost in these manuscripts.

From the point of view of their *mise en page,* the revised first-recension and second-recension manuscripts are transitional and linked to either unrevised first- or third-recension manuscripts. Bodley 902 (Fig. 1), which typifies revised first-recension manuscripts, uses the same black ink for Latin as for English. Like Fairfax, which Macaulay and other editors believe began as a revised first-recension manuscript, these manuscripts usually place the Latin prose commentary in the margin.[45] But most unillustrated revised first-recension manuscripts drop the Latin commentary altogether.[46] In other words, just as is the case with many third-recension manuscripts, later revised first-recension manuscripts, which we would expect to place the Latin commentary in the margins, minimize the latinity of Gower's English poem.

John Fisher has questioned whether Macaulay's second recension really constitutes "a distinct version of the *Confessio,*" noting that it is "ill supported by the manuscripts."[47] Certainly, in terms of the *mise en page* of these manuscripts, they are transitional. As the list in the appendix shows, Huntington Library Ellesmere 26.A.17 (the "Stafford Manuscript") is related to Fairfax in its treatment of Latin. It is perhaps the earliest extant manuscript of the poem. As Fisher notes, it "ranks with

[44] For example, Geneva, Bibliotheca Bodmeriana, Bodmer 178, and Wadham College, Oxford, MS 13.

[45] Occasionally, both Bodley 902 and Cambridge University Library Mm.2.21 place the commentary in the text. Beginning with fol. 81v, they place the Latin verses, commentary, and rubrics in the margins; Macaulay, ed., *Gower's English Works,* 1:cxxxviii, thinks this was done to save space.

[46] Revised first-recension manuscripts that have no Latin at all include Manchester, Chetham's Library 6696, and Princeton University Library, Garret 136. See Kate Harris, "John Gower's *Confessio Amantis:* The Virtues of Bad Texts," in Derek Pearsall, ed., *Manuscripts and Readers in Fifteenth-Century England: The Literary Implications of Manuscript Study* (Cambridge: D. S. Brewer, 1983), pp. 27–40. Oxford, New College MS 326, has little Latin, although it keeps the Latin in the formal apparatus and adds occasional annotations (e.g., "Fabula," "Nota") in the margins. Some of the commentary has been inserted later in the margin of St. John's College, Cambridge, MS B.12; see Macaulay, ed., *Gower's English Works,* 1:cxxxix.

[47] Fisher, *John Gower,* p. 120. Nicholson finds "no certain evidence that the second recension preceded the third"; "Dedications," p. 179 n. 44.

the Fairfax in elegance and correctness" and may be the presentation copy Gower gave to Henry in the summer of 1393.[48] In my view, it provides the best evidence for the original *mise en page* of the poem. It inscribes the Latin verses in black within the text column and the Latin prose in black within the margins, and places a large miniature on fol. 1r at the beginning of the poem, above the opening Latin verses (Fig. 5), where it serves as an opening frontispiece.[49] It is clearly a transitional manuscript, however, lacking the "final packaging" that was later added to Fairfax and other manuscripts: it includes only the *Confessio Amantis* and no colophon, even though its last three folios are blank. Another illustrated second-recension manuscript, Princeton University Library, Taylor MS 5, is similar in its treatment of Latin.

The transitional nature of the second recension is also seen in the third illustrated manuscript of this group, Bodleian Library, Bodley 294, which in its treatment of Latin is related not to the third recension but to the unrevised and intermediate versions of the first recension. The Latin commentary is placed within the text column and the Latin is usually written in red.[50] However, this manuscript is not consistent in its treatment of Latin, using black ink for the Latin verses after fol. 63v, even when it usually continues to use red for the commentary. The manuscript is unusual in other ways as well. For example, perhaps to save space, the Latin commentary sometimes spills from the text column into the margin, and occasionally the Latin verses are run together so that they appear on the page as prose.[51] The unillustrated manuscripts

---

[48] Fisher, *John Gower*, p. 124. Macaulay thinks it "probable" that the manuscript "was prepared for presentation to a member of the house of Lancaster, probably either John of Gaunt or Henry" (*Gower's English Works*, 1:clii); even Nicholson ("Gower's Revisions") admits that perhaps "Gower had some part in its preparation" (p. 136). According to A. I. Doyle, "English Books In and Out of Court from Edward III to Henry VII," in S. J. Scattergood and J. W. Sherborne, eds., *English Court Culture in the Later Middle Ages* (London: Duckworth, 1983), pp. 169–70, the illumination in Huntington is similar to that of two books produced for Richard II.

[49] See Joel Fredell, "Reading the Dream Miniature in the *Confessio Amantis*," *M&H* n.s., 22 (1995): 72–76. The manuscript may have included a second miniature, but it is missing the folio for Prol. 1055–1.106.

[50] Echard, "With Carmen's Help" (n. 17 above), notes that in Bodley 294 "the Latin Gower supplants the English Gower," so that "both the narrative function of the English and the apparently explicating function of the Latin are undermined" (p. 25).

[51] See, for example, the Latin verses on fol. 1r, which are jammed between a two-line initial "T" and the rubric, set above a six-line initial "O" for the opening lines of the Prologue.

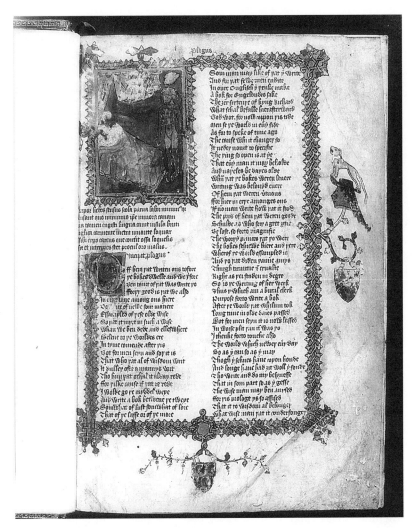

Fig. 5. San Marino, Calif., Huntington Library, Ellesmere 26.A.17, fol. 1r; published by permission of the Huntington Library.

of the second recension are similarly mixed in their treatment of the Latin: Sidney Sussex College, Cambridge, MS 63, and Nottingham University Library, Mi LM 8, usually place the Latin commentary in the text, but sometimes in the margin; British Library Additional 12043 places the Latin commentary in the margin until fol. 16r, then omits it altogether; and Trinity College R.3.2 sometimes places the Latin commentary in the margin and sometimes omits it. Thus, based on their disposition of the Latin, these second-recension manuscripts can be classified as transitional. Only Bodley 294 is generally like the unrevised and intermediate first-recension manuscripts. It is worth noting that it, like some first-recension manuscripts, was copied in part by Scribe D, who worked in London during the first two decades of the fifteenth century.[52]

Thus, although Macaulay outlined three recensions of the text of the *Confessio Amantis,* the illustrated manuscripts, based on their treatment of the Latin, may be categorized into two large groups, with minor variations. The first comprises those revised first-recension, second-recension, and third-recension manuscripts like Bodley 902 (Fig. 1), Huntington EL 26 A.17 (Fig. 5), and Fairfax 3 (Fig. 2) that place the Latin commentary in the margins and inscribe all Latin in the same color ink as the English, a *mise en page* that probably reflects Gower's own design for his poem. The second group comprises the unrevised and intermediate stages of the first recension, such as Egerton 1991 (Fig. 3), Columbia University Library, Plimpton 265 (Fig. 6), and Corpus Christi College, Oxford, MS 67 (Fig. 7), as well as the transitional second-recension manuscript, Bodley 294, which place the Latin commentary in the text column and inscribe all Latin in red. As we have seen, the unillustrated manuscripts of these various recensions tend to treat the Latin in a similar manner, although many manuscripts of the revised first recension, second recension, and third recension tend to minimize the role of Latin and, in some cases, even eliminate it altogether.

---

[52] See Doyle and Parkes, "Production of Copies." Of the illustrated first-recension manuscripts, Scribe D worked on Egerton 1991, Corpus Christi College 67, and Bodley 902.

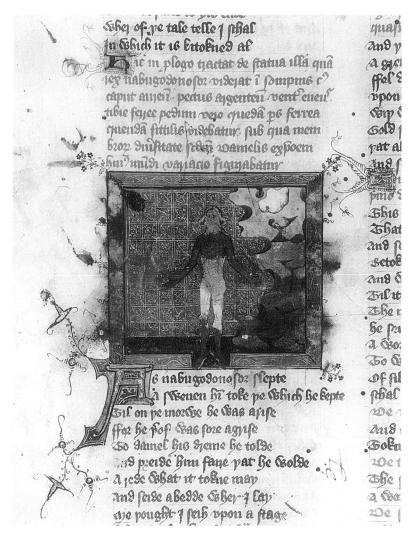

Fig. 6.   New York, Columbia University Library, Plimpton 265, fol. 1v; published by permission of Columbia University Library.

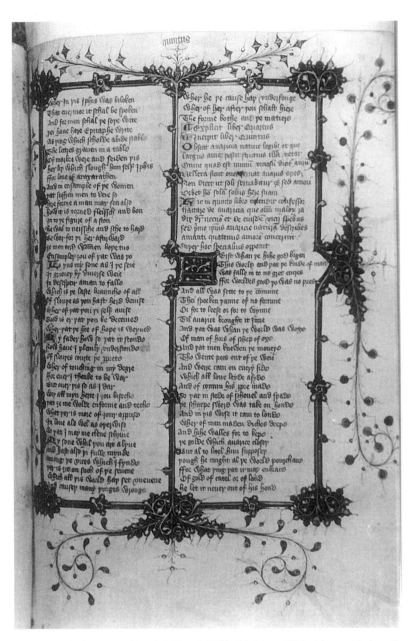

Fig. 7.   Oxford, Corpus Christi College, MS 67, fol. 93r; published by permission of Corpus Christi College, Oxford.

166

The Standard Miniatures in Illustrated Manuscripts

The iconography and placement of the miniatures similarly suggest that the manuscripts of Macaulay's three textual recensions may be categorized into two groups. Eighteen of the twenty illustrated manuscripts include either one or two illustrations representing the same general topics.[53] The two manuscripts with extensive cycles of miniatures will be considered in the conclusion of this essay. Until then, we will focus on the miniatures shared by most illustrated manuscripts and the relationship between these miniatures and the Latin in the *ordinatio* of these manuscripts.

The first miniature portrays the statue revealed in a dream to the Babylonian king, Nebuchadnezzar (Daniel 2), a huge image made of several metals that symbolized various kingdoms and empires throughout history. According to standard Christian exegesis, these historical empires culminated in Rome, and the toes of the statue represent the division of Rome into various states. The great stone that destroys the statue represents the ultimate destruction of earthly kingdoms by the second coming of Christ.[54] The statue, which seems to have fascinated Gower, symbolizes the history and divisions of worldly kingdoms as well as the ultimate power of God's eternal kingdom.[55] This miniature is of two types. Type one, as evident in Ellesmere 26.A.17, fol. 1r (Fig. 5), shows the Babylonian ruler in bed, dreaming. The statue of metals is placed either to the right of the bed or, as in Fairfax 3, fol. 1r, and Harley 3869, fol. 5r, in the foreground and to the right. This iconography is designated in the appendix list by the lowercase letter "n", which notes that Nebuchadnezzar is included in the scene. It must represent the original design of the miniature, since even manuscripts of the intermediate stage of the first recension, as well as revised first-recension, second-recension, and third-recension manuscripts, follow this iconog-

---

[53] Griffiths, "'Confessio Amantis,'" pp. 176–77, prints a table identifying the placement of the miniatures and noting blank spaces in manuscripts perhaps left for illustration.

[54] Standard exegesis follows Jerome; see *Jerome's Commentary on Daniel,* trans. Gleason L. Archer Jr. (Grand Rapids, Mich.: Baker Book House, 1958), pp. 30–33.

[55] Gower discusses Nebuchadnezzar's dream statue in *Vox Clamantis,* book 7. For its centrality to his poetry see Russell Peck, "John Gower and the Book of Daniel," in Robert F. Yeager, ed., *John Gower: Recent Readings* (Kalamazoo, Mich.: Medieval Institute Publications, 1989), pp. 159–87; and James M. Dean, *The World Grown Old in Later Medieval Literature* (Cambridge, Mass.: Medieval Academy of America, 1997), pp. 248–49, 253–59.

raphy.[56] This is true, for example, of Bodley 294, which otherwise in its *mise en page* resembles unrevised first-recension manuscripts.[57]

The second iconographic form of Nebuchadnezzar's dream deletes the Babylonian king and his bed, depicting the statue standing alone. This form, followed by Plimpton 265, fol. 1v (Fig. 6), is designated in the appendix list by the lowercase letter "s". About half of all extant miniatures depicting the dream follow this form. More significantly, all the unrevised first-recension manuscripts portray the statue standing alone, making this format a marker for these manuscripts that also highlight Gower's Latin. These miniatures also vary in size and placement within the manuscript. Third-recension manuscripts such as Fairfax 3 and Harley 3869, along with Huntington EL 26 A. 17 (Fig. 5)—which I have argued is in its *mise en page* like a third-recension manuscript—place large, eighteen-line miniatures depicting Nebuchadnezzar's dream at the beginning of the Prologue, where they serve as frontispieces for the entire poem. On the other hand, the first-recension manuscripts that portray the statue standing alone integrate miniatures of about half the size of the frontispiece-style pictures within the text of the poem, as can be seen in Plimpton 265 (Fig. 6). That this iconographic form and placement of the miniature developed relatively early in first-recension manuscripts is evident in Corpus Christi College 67, which is dated about 1405.[58] These smaller miniatures are now usually placed after the Latin prose commentary, written in red within the text column, which begins, "Hic in prologo tractat de Statua illa, quam Rex Nabugodonosor viderat in sompnis. . . ."[59] The English lines that begin to describe the

[56] Princeton University Library, Taylor MS 5, fol. 1r, is unusual for a second-recension manuscript in portraying the statue standing alone; it also does not include a confession scene, replacing it with what may be two portraits of the author, one painted within the frame of the dream miniature, the other within the initial "O" for the English opening of the Prologue. See Griffiths, "'Confessio Amantis,'" pl. 1, and Fredell, "Reading the Dream Miniature," fig. 6.

[57] Its miniatures—painted by Herman Scheerre, a German working in England, 1404–19—also link Bodley 294 to three unrevised first-recension manuscripts with miniatures by Scheerre or an artist associated with him: Corpus Christi College 67, Egerton 1991, and Royal 18.C.22. See Margaret Rickert, *Painting in Britain: The Middle Ages,* 2d ed. (Harmondsworth: Penguin, 1965), pp. 166–69; Gereth M. Spriggs, "Unnoticed Bodleian Manuscripts, Illuminated by Herman Scheerre and His School," *Bodleian Library Record* 7 (1964): 193–203; Doyle and Parkes, "Production of Copies," p. 234; and Kathleen L. Scott, *Later Gothic Manuscripts, 1390–1490,* Survey of Manuscripts Illuminated in the British Isles, vol. 6 (London: Harvey Miller, 1996), p. 2.86–88.

[58] See Scott, *Later Gothic Manuscripts,* 2:109–11.

[59] Macaulay, ed., *Gower's English Works,* 1:21, adjacent to Prol. 591–600.

dream, "As Nabugodonosor slepte, / A swevene him tok" (Prol. 595–96), usually follow. Moving the statue miniature from the large space used as a frontispiece at the beginning of the poem to the smaller space of the text column may also account for the elimination of Nebuchadnezzar from these scenes. Joel Fredell has argued that the move may have been politically motivated, but, as I will argue below, I think the shift in placement of the miniatures is better accounted for by a shift in reading practice.[60]

The second scene that most manuscripts illustrate is the Lover's confession to Genius. This scene, although it may vary in design, background, color, and even the age of the Lover, does not have the two distinct iconographic forms that distinguish the treatment of the dream miniature according to manuscript recension.[61] As the appendix shows, however, the placement of this miniature within the manuscripts does vary according to the particular recension of the text. First-recension manuscripts generally integrate the confession miniature into the text of the poem, usually placing it after the short English line "To hiere my confessioun" (1.202).[62] The Latin verses, beginning "Confessus Genio si sit medicina salutis" (I.iii), then follow, so that the confession miniature is framed by the English "confessioun" and the Latin "Confessus." The miniature in Egerton 1991 (Fig. 3) exemplifies the way the illustration is closely connected to the specific poetic content, its frame cleverly leading the eye from the final "n" of "confessioun" to the opening initial of the following Latin verse, "Confessus." The second descender of the "n" turns sharply to the right, first forming the upper line of the thin green frame that serves as an outer edge for the miniature, next demarcating the inner border of the right margin, and finally, gradually be-

---

[60] Fredell, "Reading the Dream Miniature," pp. 61–93. Although I do not find his arguments convincing, Fredell rightly directs attention to the manuscript reception of Gower's poem; he also prints the dream miniatures from eight manuscripts.

[61] The author portraits in the opening initials of Philadelphia, Rosenbach 1083/29, and Princeton University Library, Taylor MS 5, are a distinct tradition; see Griffiths, "'Confessio Amantis,'" pp. 163–66. For reproductions of all fourteen confession miniatures, see Thomas J. Garbáty, "A Description of the Confession Miniatures for Gower's *Confessio Amantis* with Special Reference to the Illustrator's Role as Reader and Critic," *Mediaevalia* 19 (1996): 319–43. See also John Burrow, "The Portrayal of Amans in 'Confessio Amantis,'" in Minnis, ed., *Gower's* Confessio Amantis, pp. 5–24.

[62] The exception is Royal 18.C.22, fol. 1r, which paints the confession in the initial "O" of Prol. 1. Griffiths, "'Confessio Amantis,'" thinks the picture filled "a space left by the scribe to correspond to that filled by the author pictures in the Rosenbach and Taylor manuscripts" (p. 166).

coming a light blue, joining with the dark blue initial "C" for "Confessus." The miniature is also linked by a thin line resembling a tendril to the half border that decorates this folio, the only time such decoration is found in this manuscript other than at the beginning of new books. In contrast, as the appendix shows, third-recension manuscripts such as Fairfax 3 (Fig. 2) and Harley 3869 (Fig. 4) place the confession miniature at the beginning of book 1, where once again they serve as a kind of frontispiece. These are, furthermore, significantly larger than the miniatures placed within the poetic text in first-recension manuscripts.

If Macaulay and the many scholars who follow him are right about the Fairfax manuscript, the topics and placement of these miniatures may represent Gower's final "intention" for the design and illustration of the *Confessio Amantis.* Unlike the miniatures placed within the text columns at those points where the poem discusses Nebuchadnezzar's dream and the Lover's confession, these frontispiece-like miniatures do not so much illustrate the poem as introduce and highlight its major concerns—with the macrocosm and microcosm, history and ethics, the world grown old and its effects on the individual "lover."[63] The placement of miniatures at the beginning of the Prologue, and therefore of the entire poem, and also at the beginning of book 1 also emphasizes the poet's two purposes in composing the *Confessio,* to write a book, as he says in his opening, "Somwhat of lust, somwhat of lore" (Prol. 19), purposes he repeats in his conclusion: "In englesch forto make a book / Which stant betwene ernest and game" (8.3108–9). The first purpose is to teach, particularly in terms of history, both past and present. This is the concern of the Prologue, which Minnis shows to be the poem's version of an academic extrinsic prologue; it is therefore introduced by the miniature depicting Nebuchadnezzar's dream with its statue representing the passing of kingdoms and the vicissitudes of world history. The second purpose is to entertain by relating a series of exemplary love stories. They begin in book 1 after the Lover's confession, which generates the storytelling. Book 1 is introduced by the poem's version of an academic intrinsic prologue and is visually similarly introduced by a miniature.[64]

---

[63] On these concerns see Dean, *World Grown Old,* pp. 260–63.
[64] On the poem's extrinsic and intrinsic prologues, see Minnis, *Medieval Theory of Authorship,* pp. 180–82; and Copeland, *Rhetoric, Hermeneutics,* pp. 214–16.

The Initial Reception of the *Confessio:* Gower as Public Poet

If Yeager is right that Gower "put much thought into the *look* of the page,"[65] then we should ask what the *mise en page* of the early illustrated manuscripts implies about Gower's expectations regarding the reception of his poem. The deluxe nature and the visual design of Fairfax 3 (Fig. 2) and Huntington EL 26 A. 17 (Fig. 5)—which was probably prepared as a presentation copy—suggest that Gower expected his poem to reach the highest levels of English society, perhaps to be received at court aurally during a public reading. As Joyce Coleman has persuasively argued in *Public Reading and the Reading Public in Late Medieval England and France,* aural reception was a typical way for a poem to be received at court and in other public gatherings in the later Middle Ages.[66] Aurality represents, in terms of the reception of a text, a "middel weie" (Prol. 17) between orality and literacy. Unlike orally composed poetry or poems originally written but performed from memory, aural poems were composed within the parameters of literacy and assumed all the expectations of bookish authority we associate with literacy. Dependent upon a written text, they were nevertheless performed, read at a public gathering, the way manuscript frontispieces show the public reading of a text before a court or other audiences.[67] Aural performance in no way assumes illiteracy on the part of the audience, only the importance of the literary text being read aloud for the public good or entertainment.

Although what follows is necessarily speculative, that Gower may have had such aspirations for his poem is suggested by his conception of the poet's role in society and supported by external, internal, and codicological evidence. Unfortunately, we know little about Gower's connection to the court during the early 1390s, the years in which he composed and revised the *Confessio Amantis.*[68] It is worth remembering, though,

---

[65] Yeager, "English, Latin, and the Text," p. 213.

[66] Joyce Coleman, *Public Reading and the Reading Public in Late Medieval England and France* (Cambridge: Cambridge University Press, 1996), esp. pp. 185–87.

[67] See Coleman, ibid., frontispiece and fig. 9. The opening miniature illustrating manuscripts of Guillaume de Deguileville's *Pèlerinage de la vie humaine* exemplifies the public reading of poetry; see Elizabeth Salter and Derek Pearsall, "Pictorial Illustration of Late Medieval Poetic Texts: The Role of the Frontispiece or Prefatory Picture," in Flemming G. Andersen et al., eds., *Medieval Iconography and Narrative: A Symposium* (Odense: Odense University Press, 1980), pp. 100–23, which reproduces several miniatures from Guillaume and other manuscripts.

[68] See John Scattergood, "Literary Culture at the Court of Richard II," in *Reading the Past: Essays on Medieval and Renaissance Literature* (Dublin: Four Courts Press, 1996), pp. 120–25.

that the poem was originally dedicated to Richard II and written "for king Richardes sake" (Prol. 24*) and then dedicated to the future Henry IV and written "for Engelondes sake" (Prol. 24). We know, furthermore, that in 1393 Henry Bolingbroke gave Gower a Lancastrian collar, perhaps to acknowledge the poem, and that the poet later became an important Lancastrian propagandist, a role commemorated by ten portraits of Gower "as prophet, preacher, and penitent" painted in a rich manuscript produced for John, the Duke of Bedford.[69] Public reading, furthermore, accords well with Gower's understanding of himself as a "public voice," to borrow David Lawton's term: a voice decrying contemporary events and the divisions within the kingdom, speaking to England for the common profit, and seeking the harmony once achieved by the mythical poet Arion (Prol. 1053–88).[70] Anne Middleton, who has traced Gower's centrality to the developing "public poetry" of the late fourteenth century, notes that by addressing a poem to the king, a poet does not narrow his audience but refers to "a public occasion," one in which "the king is not the main imagined audience, but an occasion for gathering and formulating what is on the common mind."[71]

Thus, although we have no record of the reading of the *Confessio Amantis* at court or in another public setting, it seems likely that Gower expected his poem to be received aurally, in a public reading. The poem, in fact, models such aural reception. It is filled with allusions to both hearing and reading, the ear being as important as the eye.[72] Repeatedly, the poem links reading to hearing, as when Amans states that "Min Ere with a good pitance / Is fedd of redinge of romance" (6.877–78). In her

[69] British Library, Additional MS 42131. See Sylvia Wright, "The Author Portraits in the Bedford Psalter-Hours: Gower, Chaucer and Hoccleve," *British Library Journal* 18 (1992): 190–201. For Gower's relationship to Henry, see Richard Firth Green, *Poets and Princepleasers: Literature and the English Court in the Late Middle Ages* (Toronto: University of Toronto Press, 1980), pp. 179–83.

[70] Lawton, "Dullness and the Fifteenth Century," *ELH* 54 (1987): 761–99. Lawton discusses later poets, but his analysis applies to Gower, whose concern with the state of England is most strikingly evident in *Vox Clamantis*. See also Russell Peck, *Kingship and Common Profit in Gower's* Confessio Amantis (Carbondale: Southern Illinois University Press, 1978); Elizabeth Porter, "Gower's Ethical Microcosm and Political Macrocosm," in Minnis, ed., *Gower's* Confessio Amantis, pp. 135–62; and R. F. Yeager, *John Gower's Poetic: The Search for a New Arion* (Rochester: D. S. Brewer, 1990).

[71] Anne Middleton, "The Idea of Public Poetry in the Reign of Richard II," *Speculum* 53 (1978): 107.

[72] This is confirmed by the entries under "Ere" and "Yhe" in J. D. Pickles and J. L. Dawson, eds., *A Concordance to John Gower's* Confessio Amantis (Wolfeboro, N.H.: D. S. Brewer, 1987), pp. 168–69, 753–54.

READING GOWER IN A MANUSCRIPT CULTURE

study of public reading, Coleman extensively details similar references throughout the *Confessio*. She also notes that the opening lines of the Prologue specify "most of the basic features of the aural-narrative constellation: written sources (lines 1–3), a writing author (lines 4–6) picking up the exempla (line 7) of his sources and presenting them in new form, to an audience conceived of as 'the worldes eere' (line 10)—a striking phrase that vividly asserts the perceived perpetuity of aurality."[73]

Significantly, Amans listens to all the stories told by Genius, stories that the Confessor repeatedly emphasizes come from books and that he calls on the Lover to hear carefully:

> And forto speke of this matiere
> Touchende love and his Supplant,
> A tale which is acordant
> Unto thin Ere I thenke enforme.
> Now herkne, for this is the forme. (2.2496–500)

The relationship between the two central figures in the frame story, in fact, exemplifies the relationship between the prelector—Coleman's term for the person performing the public reading[74]—and the audience, between the reader who has access to the book but speaks the exemplary stories and those who listen in order to learn while enjoying the stories. Thus, although listening to the reading, the audience is not necessarily passive. Like Amans in the poem, members of the audience may well ask questions or respond in other ways, perhaps even suggesting which sections of the poem should be read.

The likelihood of public reading is also supported by codicological evidence. The design of early versions of the revised first-recension, second-recension, and third-recension manuscripts—that is, of Bodley 902 (Fig. 1), Huntington EL 26.A.17 (Fig. 5), and Fairfax 3 (Fig. 2)— is best explained by the expectation of aural reception, for the *mise en page* of these manuscripts seems planned to aid public reading. For example, the Latin verses, written in the text columns of the manuscript, would be an important part of the public performance of the poem. They would serve various purposes depending on the sophistication of the

---

[73] Coleman, *Public Reading,* p. 186.
[74] Ibid., pp. 35–36.

audience and the extent to which its members understood Latin.[75] For some, the verses would be textual markers of the poem's smaller sections, and they would accomplish this purpose even for those members of the audience who might not understand the Latin, just as Latin serves as a marker of character for the popular audiences of the English mystery and morality plays.[76] For other members of the audience, the verses would point to thematic features of the following English text, and for yet others, they would set enigmatic clues or games.[77] The Latin verses are written within the text column and in the same color ink as the English lines, since, like the English, they are intended to be read aloud. They are distinguished from the English only by their smaller, one-line initials. Interestingly, in the Latin verses of the invocation Gower asks, "Let me . . . With Carmen's help, tell forth my English verse," which suggests that he understands the Latin, the language made possible by Carmen's gift of the alphabet, as an aid to his English.[78] He concludes the invocation by banishing "he who reads my verses ill," which critics usually understand to mean that he is banishing bad interpreters, but which may actually be a more literal reference to the public reading of the poem.

On the other hand, the Latin prose commentary in these early manuscripts is written in the margins because, as primarily a scholastic tool, it was not intended to be read aloud publicly. Instead, usually set off only by paraphs, the prose passages often provided brief summaries, helping the prelector move quickly from one section to another. They also provided short critical explanations, sometimes distinguishing the voices of the poem, sometimes explaining the purposes and moral les-

---

[75] Although the audience's knowledge of Latin would vary widely, Joyce Coleman ("Speaking in Glosses: The Aurality of Gower's Academic Apparatus," a paper read at the International Medieval Congress at Western Michigan University, May 8, 1997), cites evidence of Latin read aloud in schools and argues that the Latin verses would be performed. Yeager thinks "Gower would have had an audience able to mark, and understand, a language 'flagged' like this"; "Learning to Read in Tongues," p. 122.

[76] See my arguments in "'Englysch Laten' and 'Franch': Language as Sign of Evil in Medieval English Drama," in Alberto Ferreiro, ed., *The Devil, Heresy, and Witchcraft in the Middle Ages: Essays in Honor of Jeffrey B. Russell* (Leiden: Brill, 1998), pp. 305–26.

[77] In the introduction to their translation, Echard and Fanger state that "Unlike the glosses, the poems often seem to veil more than they make explicit; they frequently allude to ideas or situations that they do not explain; and in addition, they often involve subtle rhetorical flourishes, complex puns, and other kinds of wordplay" (*Latin Verses*, p. xxviii).

[78] For a translation and discussion of the invocation, see Echard and Fanger, ibid., pp. 2–3, who note that Gower also alludes to Carmen in 4.2637–39.

sons of its tales, and sometimes simply identifying *auctores*. The Latin prose, in other words, was not intended to be performed, but did aid public reading and any ensuing discussion of the poem by engaged members of the audience. The speaker markers, which are fully present in these manuscripts, would similarly have supported public reading.[79] They distinctly identify in the margins changes in the dialogue, which the prelector perhaps registered by a change in voice during performance.

Finally, the miniatures in Huntington and Fairfax also served a reading function similar to that of the Latin prose commentary, identifying the two major sections of the poem. Being quite large, the miniatures could be shown to the audience at the beginning of a reading—which may have been devoted only to the historical and political concerns of the Prologue—or, on different occasions, may have omitted the Prologue and begun with the frame focusing on Amans and the ensuing love stories. In any case, as we have seen, the miniatures introduce two major themes of the poem and are not intended to illustrate particular poetic passages. They are thus not placed within the poetic text where they would interrupt a public reading.

Gower as Author in Other Manuscript Traditions

If this hypothesis is plausible regarding the poet's aspirations for the *Confessio,* and if the early illustrated manuscripts were designed for public reading, what do those manuscripts with a rather different *mise en page* suggest about other ways in which the poem was received in the fifteenth century? Later manuscripts imply three forms of reception. The first, exemplified by Harley 3869, a copy of Fairfax 3, suggests that aural reception continued into the mid-fifteenth century. As we have seen (Fig. 4), Harley 3369 is particularly concerned with distinguishing the Latin verses from the prose commentary, a concern that fits public performance. Not surprisingly, it keeps its two miniatures as frontispieces introducing the Prologue and book 1. But this is rare for most fifteenth-

---

[79] Echard, "Dialogues and Monologues" (n. 21 above), n. 10, lists Bodley 902, Fairfax 3, and Huntington as manuscripts with a "high-frequency" use of speech markers. She notes that Huntington inscribes the markers "in the larger text hand, rather than in the smaller glossing hand," and that in these manuscripts the markers are "an extremely prominent constituent of the page."

century manuscripts, which usually present Gower as either an English love poet or a Latinate moral humanist to be read privately.

As we have seen, during the fifteenth century other third-recension as well as revised first- and second-recension manuscripts tended to minimize the Latin apparatus of Gower's poem. With the passing of public reading and in the more modest circumstances of merchant-class readers—who probably were less interested in the scholastic features of the prose commentary—manuscripts came to emphasize the English poem. The Latin aspects of the poem were reduced or omitted altogether, so that the *Confessio* was read as an essentially English collection of tales. For example, the abridged text in Manchester, Chetham's Library 6696, which has been dated to the 1530s, not only eliminates the Latin but also regularly drops passages from the frame story, thus emphasizing "the nature of the poem as a collection of stories."[80] These manuscripts present Gower as a collector and organizer of love stories, a Gower not unlike the poet encountered by our students in teaching editions.[81]

A third form of reception is implied by most fifteenth-century manuscripts, both illustrated and nonillustrated. They present the *Confessio* in a layout that suggests not only private reading but also silent study.[82] Most first-recension manuscripts, by far the largest category, move the Latin prose commentary from the margins into the text columns, so that it occupies the same space occupied by the Latin verses, which are sometimes written together as prose. Both forms of Latin, furthermore, are almost always written in red ink. In other words, the tripartite voices represented by the Latin verses, prose commentary, and English poetry became textualized into two major categories inscribed in distinct colors, English and Latin, the distinction between one kind of Latin and another being lost.

---

[80] Harris, "Virtues of Bad Texts," p. 29. For the manuscript's date see C. A. Luttrell, "Three North-West Midland Manuscripts," *Neophilologus* 42 (1958): 46. The six selections from the *Confessio Amantis* in the Findern Manuscript—an anthology focusing on love that includes poems by Chaucer, Hoccleve, and Lydgate—delete all Latin and present Gower as an English love poet. For a facsimile, see *The Findern Manuscript: Cambridge University Library MS. Ff.I.6,* with introduction by Richard Beadle and A. E. B. Owen (London: Scolar Press, 1977).

[81] See, for example, Russell A. Peck, ed., *Confessio Amantis,* Medieval Academy Reprints for Teaching, vol. 9 (1966; rpt. Cambridge, Mass.: Medieval Academy of America, 1980); this edition minimizes the Latin verses of the poem and deletes the Latin commentary altogether.

[82] For the growing importance of private reading and study, see Paul Saenger, "Silent Reading: Its Impact on Late Medieval Script and Society," *Viator* 13 (1982): 367–414.

The effect of this emphasis upon the Latin is evident in the *mise en page* of Corpus Christi 67, fol. 93r (Fig. 7), which comprises the end of the fourth and beginning of the fifth books of the *Confessio*. The three speaker markers that Fairfax places in the last twenty-five lines of book 4 are absent, although the three changes of dialogue are noted within the English text by three one-line initials in the left column. After the rubrics in the upper right margin comes the Latin verse that introduces book 5 and then the prose commentary that in Fairfax and in Macaulay does not appear until eight lines into the book. But in Corpus Christi the commentary precedes the opening of the fifth book, which begins with a four-line initial "F". The block of red script, enlarged by conflating the verse and prose, separates the Latin from the English and emphasizes the Latin, which remains an integral part of the reading process by being kept within the text column.

Gower is here presented as a highly Latinate poet, the "moral Gower" of tradition, and a scholarly protohumanist. The full Latin apparatus is now central to understanding his text. As Jeremy Griffiths notes, the Latin commentaries "come to dominate the page" and as a result become "a primary visual constituent of the page."[83] The Latin is to be read, probably silently and in the study, and thus both the prose and verses are brought together, whereas the Latin speaker markers, which I have suggested were designed to aid public reading, are minimized.[84] The movement of the miniatures in these manuscripts from the beginning of the Prologue and book 1 to the text columns similarly suggests a shift to silent reading and study. Rather than being introductory frontispieces to be shown during a public reading, the miniatures now illustrate the texts with which they are juxtaposed. They are now to be studied in terms of the Latin verse and prose commentary as well as of the English poetry.

That this shift from a poem to be read publicly to one to be studied privately happened early in the reception of the poem is apparent in Corpus Christi College 67, which is dated to within Gower's lifetime.

---

[83] Griffiths, "'Confessio Amantis,'" p. 174. To Griffiths, the placement of the Latin commentaries within the text columns "appears to distort their proper literary relationship to the English text."

[84] Echard, "Dialogues and Monologues" (n. 21 above), n. 11, lists Corpus Christi 67, along with Egerton 1991, St. Catherine's 7, Morgan M.125, and Bodley 294, as manuscripts with few or no speaker markers. These are all manuscripts that I argue were designed for private rather than public reading.

It suggests that, whatever Gower's intentions regarding the final form of his poem and its reception, manuscripts containing the very first version of the *Confessio* were in general circulation; and that "even before the poet's death the *Confessio,* like the *Canterbury Tales,* was already in the hands of the booksellers, who in their loosely organized way were responsible for the commercial production of a great many of the MSS of the poem that survive."[85] As is evident from the appendix, the poem in this original, unrevised form—with its dedication to Richard II— was widely available. It was probably being read privately by the "career diplomats, civil servants, officials and administrators who were attached to the court and the government,"[86] a coterie audience that Gower shared with Chaucer, whom Venus tells Gower to greet in an epilogue passage found only in first-recension manuscripts (8.2941*).[87] Although I have stressed a distinction between court and study, it is important to realize that the distinction between manuscripts designed for public aural reception and those designed for private study is based more on differing reading practices than on social position. These illustrated manuscripts emphasizing Latin are often quite lavish, and two of them were owned by later Lancastrian bibliophiles, John, Duke of Bedford, and Humphrey, Duke of Gloucester.[88]

Conclusion: Two Manuscripts with Large Cycles of Miniatures

Only two manuscripts of the *Confessio* include large cycles of miniatures that illustrate the tales as well as the statue in Nebuchadnezzar's dream and the Lover's confession. The first, New College, Oxford, MS 266

[85] Nicholson, "Gower's Revisions," p. 137.

[86] Scattergood, "Literary Culture at the Court of Richard II," p. 123.

[87] The exception is Nottingham University Library Mi LM 8, a second-recension manuscript retaining the allusion to Chaucer; for this manuscript, see Thorlac Turville-Petre, *Image and Text: Medieval Manuscripts at the University of Nottingham* (Nottingham: University of Nottingham Arts Centre, 1996), no. 2. Middleton, in "Idea of Public Poetry," suggests that in his final revisions Gower may have deleted the reference to Chaucer because "coterie references were out of place in a work now explicitly meant for the 'comune' at large" (p. 107).

[88] Pembroke College, Cambridge, 307, was owned by the Duke of Bedford; and Bodley 294 was owned by the Duke of Gloucester. In addition, an unillustrated first-recension manuscript copied by Scribe D (Christ Church, Oxford, 148) was probably commissioned for Thomas, Duke of Clarence. See Doyle and Parkes, "Production of Copies," pp. 246–47.

(Fig. 8), has nineteen miniatures extant from what were once at least thirty-two; their style associates them with the workshop of William Abell.[89] It includes a third-recension text that I have argued represents an English emphasis, with all Latin written in black and the Latin commentary placed in the margin. Unlike its contemporary third-recension manuscript, Harley 3869 (Fig. 4), it is designed for private reading rather than public performance and does not include the two frontispiece miniatures found in such manuscripts. However, unlike first-recension manuscripts, it does not emphasize the Latinate character of the poem either. Instead, it treats the *Confessio* primarily as an English collection of love stories to be read privately. It thus places all its miniatures within the English text of the poem and uses them to introduce the tales. Although the Latin verses remain, they are almost lost within the English poem; the Latin speaker markers are also minimized and the Latin running titles are dropped.

New College 266, moreover, tends to devalue the Latin commentary, as evident in its treatment of the miniature placed at the beginning of the tale of Midas (fol. 91r: Fig. 8), which typifies the *mise en page* of this manuscript. Here the miniature is set, as usual, within the English poem, between the reference to "þe clerk Ovide" and before the four-line initial "B" for Bachus (5.140–41). The miniature's frame is opened at the bottom, so that the picture flows into the English at the beginning of the tale. The Latin commentary, on the other hand, is written in a small hand, squeezed into the left and bottom margins, and distinguished from the English and the miniature. It is placed outside of the decorated frame on the left and is almost overcome by the floreated decoration in the bottom margin. The Latin prose now frames the English, its text functioning more as border decoration than commentary. Significantly, each line of English poetry is introduced by a capital marked by a red slash, the color other manuscripts associate with Latin. The English text and the love exempla are clearly privileged by this page design.

---

[89] For Abell, see J. J. G. Alexander, "William Abell 'lymnour' and 15th Century English Illumination," in Arthur Rosenauer and Gerold Weber, eds., *Kunsthistorische Forschungen: Otto Pächt zu seinem 70. Geburstag* (Salzburg: Residenz Verlag, 1972), pp. 166–72. Peter C. Braeger, "The Illustrations in New College MS. 266 for Gower's Conversion Tales," in Yeager, ed., *Gower: Recent Readings,* pp. 275–310, publishes seven miniatures. I cite the manuscript's amended foliation rather than the foliation cited by Macaulay, ed., *Gower's English Works,* 1:clx–clxi, which lists the miniatures.

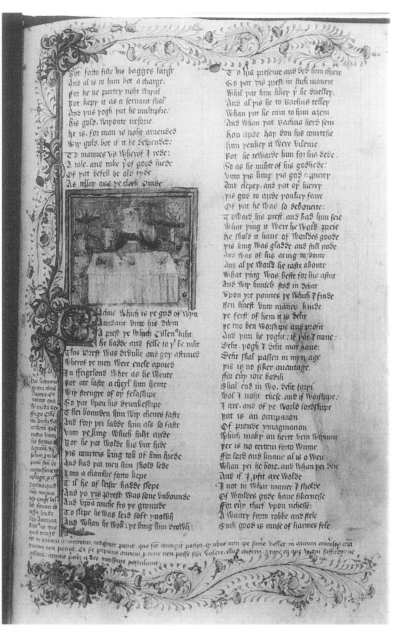

Fig. 8.   Oxford, New College, MS 266, fol. 91r; published by permission of the Warden and Fellows, New College, Oxford.

180

The other manuscript including a cycle of miniatures illustrating the tales is Pierpont Morgan Library M.126 (ca. 1470), a manuscript with Anglo-Flemish connections, which Martha Driver thinks was produced for Elizabeth Woodville, the book-collecting queen of Edward IV.[90] If my arguments regarding the manuscript traditions are correct, this intermediate-stage first-recension manuscript should emphasize the poem's Latin elements. In fact, it does so by providing a concluding tabula on fols. 207r–212r, an alphabetical index whose entries are often based on the Latin commentary rather than the English narrative.[91] Furthermore, it links its 106 miniatures to the Latin, which always precedes the pictures. Although they introduce the following English tales, the miniatures usually illustrate the preceding Latin passages, suggesting that they are to be studied in terms of the Latin. The Latin may be the elegiac verses or the prose commentaries, but it is always emphasized by being inscribed in red. The two forms of Latin are often combined and lengthy, as on fol. 26v (Fig. 9), which depicts the Tale of the Three Questions. The miniature seems to follow directly from the extensive Latin, since its frame is notched to fill the space remaining at the end of the Latin commentary. This is typical of the 77 miniatures introducing the exemplary tales.

The long cycle of miniatures in Morgan M.126 is unique in fully illustrating the entire poem and thus closely approximating the outline of the *Confessio* included in its Latin colophon. The miniatures visually portray all three elements of the poem that Gower there describes: first, "the prophecy of Daniel concerning the mutability of earthly kingdoms"; second, "those things by which King Alexander was trained, as much in his governing as in other things"; and third, "love and the promises of lovers, where the meanings of various chronicles and stories and also the writings of poets and philosophers are inserted for the sake of example."[92] The first and the third of these elements are the subject

---

[90] Martha Driver, "Printing the *Confessio Amantis:* Caxton's Edition in Context," in Robert F. Yeager, ed., *Revisioning Gower: New Essays* (Kalamazoo, Mich.: Medieval Institute Publications, forthcoming). I thank Driver for providing me with a copy of her essay before publication. For a description of M.126, see Scott, *Later Gothic Manuscripts,* 2:322–25. Patricia Eberle, "Miniatures as Evidence of Reading in a Manuscript of the *Confessio Amantis* (Pierpont Morgan MS M.126)," in Yeager, ed., *Gower: Recent Readings,* pp. 311–64, publishes eight miniatures. The manuscript originally included 108 miniatures.

[91] See Eberle, "Miniatures as Evidence of Reading," pp. 329–30. Harris, in "Ownership and Readership," edits the index on pp. 308–28.

[92] The translations are from Fisher, *John Gower,* p. 89; the colophon is edited by Macaulay, ed., *Gower's English Works,* 2:479–80.

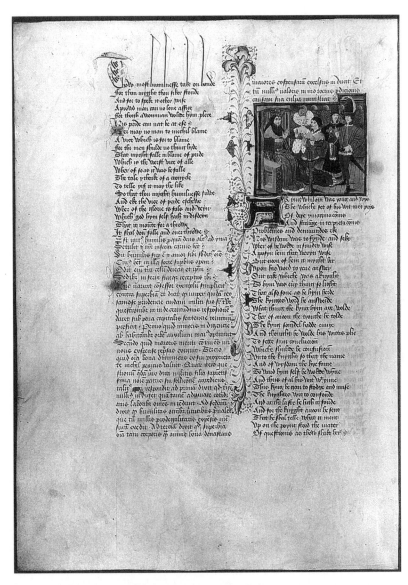

Fig. 9.   New York, Pierpont Morgan Library, M.126, fol. 26v; published by permission of the Pierpont Morgan Library.

of the two miniatures included in most illustrated manuscripts we have analyzed, but Morgan M.126 adds two other miniatures in the text to stress the poem's extrinsic and intrinsic prologues. In addition to Nebuchadnezzar's statue (fol. 4v), it portrays Arion's harping (fol. 7v); and in addition to the confession scene (fol. 9r), it pictures the poet meeting Venus and Cupid (fol. 8v), when Venus orders Amans to confess to her priest, Genius (1.139–47). Significantly, Morgan M.126 moves the confession miniature from its usual position in other manuscripts—linking English "confessioun" to Latin "Confessus"—and places it *after* the Latin verses, so that once again the miniature is tied directly to the Latin.

The third topic Gower mentions in his Latin colophon, "those things by which King Alexander was trained," has been treated as a digression from the poem's predominant theme of love. This is the subject of book 7, which Morgan M.126 alone emphasizes by including twenty-seven smaller miniatures representing the book's philosophical, astrological, and scientific teachings. Lesley Suzanne Lawton notes that these miniatures act as "an indexing system" for book 7, providing an "apparatus which intensifies its aspect as a manual of information."[93] In illustrating this most didactic section of the poem, its mirror for princes, this manuscript represents the culmination of the third, and most common, way the later fifteenth century received the "moral" Gower, one that emphasizes his latinity and bookishness and that understands him to be a scholarly protohumanist—a view of the poet that would continue in Renaissance printed editions.[94]

[93] Lesley Suzanne Lawton, "Text and Image in Late Mediaeval English Vernacular Manuscripts," 4 vols. (Ph.D. diss., University of York, 1982), 1:513.

[94] R. F. Yeager, "Ben Jonson's *English Grammar* and John Gower's Reception in the Seventeenth Century," in M. Teresa Tavormina and R. F. Yeager, eds., *The Endless Knot: Essays on Old and Middle English in Honor of Marie Borroff* (Rochester: D. S. Brewer, 1995), notes that Berthelette's 1532 edition, which sets the Latin verse and prose in the text column, "makes plain the integral nature of the Latin to the English poem, and highlights Gower's accomplishments as a learned poet" (p. 235). Machan states that in Berthelette's edition, "Gower's *Confessio* is conceptualized as an ethical and moral composition that will edify readers in the way humanist literary paradigms required" ("Thomas Berthelette," p. 148).

Appendix:
Illustrated Manuscripts of Gower's *Confessio Amantis*

Sigla[1]	Library Shelfmark / MS Date[2]	Latin Verses[3]	Latin Prose[4]	Latin Apparatus[5]	Nebuchadnezzar Statue Miniature[6]	Confession Miniature[7]
				First-Recension Unrevised Manuscripts		
C	Corpus Christi College, Oxford, MS 67, ca. 1405	red	red / text	a=red (−) / b=red	4v, after gloss (s)	9v, after 1.202
B₂	Bodleian Lib., Bodley 693, ca. 1410	red	red / text	a=red / b=red	4v, between Prol. 594 & gloss (s)	8v, in initial "T" for 1.203
E	British Lib. Egerton 1991, ca. 1410–15	red	red / text	a=red (−) / b=red	NO (Prol. lacks 1–134, 454–594)	7v, after 1.202
	Pierpont Morgan Lib. M.690, ca. 1410–15	red	red / text	a=red / b=red	4v, below gloss (bottom right) (s)	NO (lacks first 3 fols. of bk. 1)
	Pembroke College, Cambridge, MS 307, ca. 1410–25	red	red / text	a=red / b=red	4v, above gloss & Prol. 595 (s)	9r, after 1.202
R	British Lib. Royal 18.C.xxii, 1st q. 15th c.	red	red / text	a=red / b=red	4v, between gloss & Prol. 595 (s)	1r initial "O" to Prol. 1
L	Bodleian Lib., Laud Misc. 609, 1st q. 15th c.	red	red / text	a=red / b=red	5r, between gloss & Prol. 595 (s)	10r, after 1.202
	Columbia University Lib., Plimpton MS 265, 1st q. 15th c.	red	red / text	a=red / b=red	1v, between gloss & Prol. 595	NO
	Philadelphia Rosenbach Coll. 1083/29, 1st half 15th c.	red	red / text	a=red	3v, in initial to Prol. 595	NO (portrays author in initial to Prol. 1)

First-Recension Intermediate Manuscripts

First-Recension Intermediate Manuscripts						
Q	Pierpont Morgan Lib. M.125, ca. 1420	red	text	a=red (−) b=red	NO (Prol. lacks 1–341, 529–688)	3v, between verses I.iii & 1.203
Cath	St. Catharine's College, Cambridge, MS 7, ca. 1425–75	red	text	a=red (−) b= red & black	4v, between gloss & Prol. 595 (n)	8v, after verses I.iii (bottom margin)
	Pierpont Morgan Lib. M.126, ca. 1470	red	text	a=red b=black	4v, between gloss & Prol. 595 (n)	9r, between verses I.iii & 1.203
First-Recension Revised Manuscripts						
A	Bodleian Lib., Bodley 902, ca. 1405–08	black	margin & text	a=black (+) b=black	NO (begins Prol. 144)	8r, after 1.202 (bottom)
M	Cambridge University Lib., Mm.2.21, 1st half 15th c.	black	margin & text	a=black b=black	4r, between Prol. 578 & Prol. v verses (n)	8r, next to 1.202 (in right margin)
Second-Recension Manuscripts						
S	Huntington Lib. EL 26 A.17, late 14th c.	black	margin	a=black (+) b=black	1r, above opening of Prol. (n)	NO (lacks opening to bk. 1)
P_2	Princeton University Lib., Taylor MS 5, 1st q. 15th c.	black	margin	a=black b=black	1r, opening Prol. (s)	NO (portrays author in initial to Prol. 1)
B	Bodleian Lib., Bodley 294, ca. 1410–15	red (& black)	text	a=red (−) b=red	4v, between gloss & Prol. 595 (n)	9r, after 1.202

Sigla[1]	Library Shelfmark MS Date[2]	Latin Verses[3]	Latin Prose[4]	Latin Apparatus[5]	Nebuchadnezzar Statue Miniature[6]	Confession Miniature[7]
			Third-Recension Manuscripts			
F	Bodleian Lib., Fairfax 3, late 14th c.	black	black margin	a=black (+) b=black	2r, above opening of Prol. (n)	8r, above opening of bk. 1
H₂	British Lib., Harley 3869, ca. 1440–50	red	red margin	a=red b=red	5r, opening of Prol. (n)	18r, opening of bk. 1
N	New College, Oxford MS 266, ca. 1440–50	black	black margin	a=black b=black	NO	NO (lacks opening to bk. 1)

[1]Sigla, when available, are those used by Macaulay, *Gower's English Works*, 1:cxxxviii–clxvii.

[2]Dates in a general range are based on Albert E. Hartung, ed., *Manual of the Writings in Middle English*, (New Haven: Connecticut Academy of Arts and Sciences, 1967) 7: 2408; more specific dates are based on recent palaeographic and iconographic studies.

[3]Ink color of Latin elegiac verses. Illustrated manuscripts place verses at beginning of book sections/chapters, within text columns; A and M place them in margins beginning fol. 81v. Manuscripts sometimes run the verses together as prose.

[4]Color of ink used for Latin prose commentaries and their placement within the text columns or margins of the manuscripts; A and M usually place commentaries in margin, but sometimes in text columns.

[5]Color of ink used for a) speaker markers, usually placed in margin, even when the prose commentary is placed in the text columns; and b) color of other apparatus such as colophons, running titles, and rubrics. Not all manuscripts have all apparatus. Manuscripts with a high frequency of speaker markers are identified by the symbol "+"; those with a low frequency are identified by the symbol "−".

[6]Location of the miniature depicting the statue of Nebuchadnezzar's dream. If miniature is missing, specifies if the relevant text is missing. The symbol "n" specifies that the miniature depicts Nebuchadnezzar in bed dreaming of the statue; the symbol "s" specifies that the miniature only depicts the statue.

[7]Location of the miniature depicting the Lover's confession to Genius. If missing, specifies if relevant text is missing. Also identifies those manuscripts that have author portraits rather than confession miniatures.

"As just as is a squyre": The Politics of "Lewed Translacion" in Chaucer's *Summoner's Tale*

Fiona Somerset
University of Western Ontario

In solving the problem posed by Thomas's vernacular utterance, *The Summoner's Tale* makes use of information and techniques of argument drawn from what Middle English writers often call "clergie"; that is, the academic discourse employed chiefly by clerics with some university education.[1] That much has long been recognized: Pearcy's 1967 article on the tale explained quite thoroughly how calling the problem an "inpossible" and submitting it to demonstrative proof using natural science evokes the scholastic tradition of ingenious response to *insolubilia*—or what appear to be impossible or paradoxical statements—and especially the late-fourteenth-century fashion at Oxford, and at Merton in particular, for employing concepts from natural science in logical solutions.[2]

---

[1] All quotations from Chaucer are taken from the paperback edition of Larry D. Benson, gen. ed., *The Riverside Chaucer*, 3d ed. (Oxford: Oxford University Press, 1988); subsequent quotations from *The Summoner's Tale* will be identified by line number only. The title quotation comes from line 2090. Since most of the contemporary clerical material I will cite has never been published in any form or, if it has, is not widely available, I will give all quotations in the original Latin as well as in English. All translations are my own.

For a more extended discussion of attitudes to 'clergie', see my *Clerical Discourse and Lay Audience in Late Medieval England* (Cambridge U.P., 1998), especially the introduction, pp. 3–5, 10–16. I am grateful to Robert Hanning for his comments, and to Glending Olson for his continuing generous willingness to exchange writings and ideas on *The Summoner's Tale*. Thanks also to the Bodleian Library, to the library of Trinity College Dublin, and to the Durham University Library, for permission to quote from unpublished manuscripts in their possession.

[2] Roy J. Pearcy, "Chaucer's "An Inpossible" ("Summoner's Tale" III, 2231)," *N&Q*, n.s., 14 (1967): 322–25. On late-fourteenth-century argumentation, see further John E. Murdoch, "*Subtilitates Anglicanae* in Fourteenth-Century Paris: John of Mirecourt and Peter Ceffons," in Madeleine Pelner Cosman and Bruce Chandler, eds., *Machaut's World: Science and Art in the Fourteenth Century*, Annals of the New York Academy of Sciences,

STUDIES IN THE AGE OF CHAUCER

But what nobody has yet explained is why and how it matters that in this tale the conventions of clerical argument are not just translated into English, but expertly deployed by lay persons rather than clerics—especially when that "translation" in status from clerical to lay appears in conjunction with the Friar's failure, and the Squire's contrasting success, at gaining lay patronage.[3] While the methods by which the problem is posed and solved are thoroughly clerical, they are transferred to a lay setting, to lay speakers, and to lay adjudication. What needs to be examined is how the kinds of vernacular translation the tale enacts—of learned Latin material to English, of clerical capabilities to the laity, of money and power formerly given to the clergy to the laity—reflect contemporary controversy over just these sorts of loss of clerical prerogative.

Why is it feared that translation from Latin to English might entail loss of clerical prerogative, and even of church revenues? Scholars interested in investigating late-medieval English attitudes toward translation have commonly consulted the early fifteenth century's sweeping attempt to prohibit translations of every kind through legislation, Arundel's *Constitutions* implemented in 1409.[4] What sort of impact the *Constitutions* had upon vernacular translation and publication through the fifteenth century is very much open to debate. Regardless of their effects, however, one way to read the *Constitutions* is as a set of aspirations

---

vol. 314 (New York: New York Academy of Sciences, 1978), pp. 51–86; and Edith Dudley Sylla, "The Oxford Calculators," in Norman Kretzmann, Anthony Kenny, and Jan Pinborg, eds., *The Cambridge History of Later Medieval Philosophy* (Cambridge: Cambridge University Press, 1982; rpt. 1988), pp. 540–63.

[3] Larry Scanlon has explained that the tale stages a conflict between clerical and lay power, trenchantly dismissing the stale argument about whether the tale is theological or anticlerical: of course it is both; *Narrative, Authority, and Power: The Medieval Exemplum and the Chaucerian Tradition* (Cambridge: Cambridge University Press, 1994), pp. 160–75. However, as I show here, the politics of lay/clerical division in the tale can be further explained by reference to contemporary polemical writings and in the light of late-fourteenth-century topics of controversy.

[4] Recent discussions of the *Constitutions* sensitive to the ways they reflect contemporary attitudes to translation include Nicholas Watson, "Censorship and Cultural Change in Late-Medieval England: Vernacular Theology, the Oxford Translation Debate, and Arundel's Constitutions of 1409," *Speculum* 70 (1995): 822–64; Ralph Hanna III, "The Difficulty of Ricardian Prose Translation: The Case of the Lollards," *MLQ* 51 (1990): 319–40; and Anne Hudson, "Lollardy: The English Heresy?," *Studies in Church History* 18 (1982): 261–83, reprinted in Anne Hudson, *Lollards and Their Books,* (London: Hambledon Press, 1985), pp. 141–63. The *Constitutions* are printed in David Wilkins, ed., *Concilia Magnae Britanniae et Hiberniae,* 3 vols. (Oxford: Clarendon Press, 1964), 3:314–19, hereafter *Constitutiones.*

toward the preservation of clerical prerogative by means of the control of information, written into law by clerics for clerics: they are a repository of received opinion, and between their lines we can read what goes without saying when the clergy speak to each other about the laity. Thus, article 7 of the *Constitutions* speaks for concerns much broader and longer abiding than those of a small group of politically influential anti-Wycliffite clergy when, in justifying a prohibition against the production or distribution of any unsanctioned biblical translations or works containing portions of such translation, it asserts that such translation is dangerous. The reason given—on Jerome's authority—is that it is difficult to retain the same sense.[5] Yet why should the possibility of human error be so self-evidently dangerous that no further explanation need be provided for why new translations should be forbidden, all the more so when the source cited is the best–known medieval translator of the bible? Some answer can be found elsewhere among the *Constitutions*, where a wider–ranging set of prohibitions against any sort of "translation" of clerical learning to the laity is set out.

Three other articles of the *Constitutions* focus on "translation" more broadly defined. Article 3 requires that no one preach about the faults of the clergy to the laity, or vice versa.[6] Article 5 prohibits those teaching

[5] "Also, it is a dangerous matter, as Jerome attests, to translate the text of sacred scripture from one language to another. For in such translation the same precise sense is not easily retained; so much so that blessed Jerome, divinely inspired though he was, confessed that he often erred. Therefore we establish and ordain that no one henceforth should translate the text of sacred scripture into the English language, or any other language, on his own authority, whether in the form of a book, shorter written work, or treatise. Nor should anyone read any such book, writing, or treatise produced recently since the time of the said John Wyclif, or to be produced later, either in whole or in part, publicly or covertly, on pain of greater excommunication" ["Periculosa quoque res est, testante beato Jeronymo, textum sacrae scripturae de uno in aliud idioma transferre, eo quod in ipsis translationibus non de facili idem in omnibus sensus retinetur, prout idem beatus Jeronymus, etsi inspiratus fuisset, se in hoc saepius fatetur erasse; statuimus igitur et ordinamus, ut nemo deinceps aliquem textum sacrae scripturae auctoritate sua in linguam Anglicanam, vel aliam transferat, per viam libri, libelli, aut tractatus, nec legatur aliquis huiusmodi liber, libellus, aut tractatus jam noviter tempore dicti Johannis Wycliff, sive citra, compositus, aut inposterum componendus, in parte vel in toto, publice, vel occulte, sub maioris excommunicationis poena . . ."]; Wilkins, ed., *Constitutiones,* 3:317.

[6] "Furthermore, just as a good father sows wheat in land suited to it, so that it may bear more fruit, we wish and we order, that a preacher of the word of God coming in the manner written above, to preach to the clergy or people, should properly relate his subject to his audience, sowing his seed as is fitting for the audience. He should preach to the clergy about the vices that sprout amongst them, and to the laity about the sins generally practiced among them, and not the other way around" ["Insuper, sicut bonus paterfamilias triticum spargit in terram ad hoc dispositam, ut fructus plus afferat; volu-

boys engaged in the study of grammar or arts, or others at an elementary level of learning, from presenting theological material contrary to the church's determination, and particularly from allowing disputations about such material either publicly or privately.[7] And article 8 requires that no one state conclusions that sound as if they are contrary to Catholic truth or good morals, even if those conclusions can be defended by means of sophisticated argument using philosophical terminology.[8] The primary concern of article 3 is to prevent clerical matters' being pre-

---

mus et mandamus, ut praedicator verbi Dei veniens juxta formam superius annotatam, in praedicando clero sive populo, secundum materiam subjectam se honeste habeat, spargendo semen secundum convenientiam subiecti auditorii; clero praesertim praedicans de vitiis pullulantibus inter eos, et laicis de peccatis inter eos communiter usitatis, et non e contra"]; Wilkins, ed., *Constitutiones,* 3:316.

[7] "Likewise, because what a new vessel takes in seems well-tried, we establish and ordain that masters, or anyone teaching arts or grammar, instructing boys or others in primary subjects, should not include while instructing them any discussion about catholic faith, the sacrament of the altar, or the other sacraments, or any theological matter, that contradicts what the church has determined. Nor should there be anything about the exposition of sacred scripture, except the giving of a customary, established exposition of a text. Nor should they permit their students or disciples to dispute publicly or privately about catholic faith or the sacraments" ["Similiter, quia id quod capit nova testa inveterata sapit, statuimus et ordinamus, quod magistri sive quicunque docentes in artibus, aut grammatica, pueros, seu alios quoscunque in primitivis scientiis instruentes, de fide catholica, sacramento altaris, seu aliis sacramentis ecclesiae, aut materia aliqua theologica, contra determinata per ecclesiam, se nullatenus intromittant instruendo eosdem; nec de expositione sacrae scripturae, nisi in exponendo textum, prout antiquitus fieri consuevit; nec permittant scholares suos sive discipulos de fide catholica, seu sacramentis ecclesiae publice disputare etiam vel occulte"]; Wilkins, ed., *Constitutiones,* 3:317.

[8] "Furthermore, since the determiner of all things [i.e., God] cannot be determinately described by terms of human invention, either philosophical or otherwise, and blessed Augustine rather often recanted true conclusions, because they were offensive to the ears of the religious, we establish, and under the most particular witness of divine judgement we prohibit any person or persons of whatever degree, status, or condition, from asserting or proposing conclusions or propositions that sound adverse to catholic faith or good behaviour, beyond what is necessary for teaching in his own faculty, within the schools or outside them, in disputation or communication, with a prefatory protestation or without, even if they may be defended by some curiousity of words or terms. For as blessed Hugh says in his book *On the Sacraments,* 'Too often what is well said, is not well understood" ["Praeterea, cum terminis philosophicis sive alias humanitus adinventis concludi non poterit omnium terminator, beatusque Augustinus veras conclusiones, quia religiosorum aurium fuerant offensivae, saepius revocavit; statuimus, et sub obtestatione divini judicii specialissime inhibemus, ne quis, vel qui, cuiuscunque gradus, status, aut conditionis existat, conclusiones aut propositiones in fide catholica seu bonis moribus adverse sonantes, praeter necessariam doctrinam facultatis suae, in scholis, aut extra, disputando aut communicando, protestatione praemissa vel non praemissa, asserat vel proponat, etiamsi quadam verborum aut terminorum curiositate defendi possint: nam teste beato Hugone, de sacramentis, "Saepius quod bene dicitur, non bene intelligitur"]; Wilkins, ed., *Constitutiones,* 3:317.

sented to lay judgment, particularly perhaps where both clerics and lay-men are present—since otherwise the presentation of lay affairs to cler-ics would scarcely seem a concern. Most obviously, the article would prohibit anticlerical polemic before a lay audience; but it would also rule out political sermons addressing the three estates or the body politic as well as any address to a mixed audience. Articles 5 and 8, on the other hand, focus on lay argumentation: they aim to prevent the laity from being instructed in or allowed to engage in argument, most especially about matters that are within the exclusive province of clerical pro-nouncement. The eighth article seems especially concerned that laymen should not encounter (let alone learn to use) sophisticated clerical con-ventions of proof such as those used on *insolubilia*, by means of which apparently impossible statements may be shown to be logically sound.[9]

The uneasiness about potential lay judgment and argumentation that we find in the *Constitutions* also appears frequently in the work of polem-icists writing squarely within the "Age of Chaucer" in the 1380s and 1390s, and perhaps especially in the conservative posturings of anti-Wycliffites. For example, in his *Determinacio,* written probably in the late 1380s, Richard Maidstone accuses Ashwardby, who apparently has preached about theologically controversial matters to the laity, of a self-promoting offense against propriety:

These three assertions are errors, as it seems to me. Nor should my opponent be surprised that I say "errors." For he himself, while he was preaching before the people, where above all an example of charity ought to have been given, said that he did not care who, how many of, or how much such an honourable audience might be offended or made angry by his words. Who therefore should take account of the anger of the one who cared nothing for offending such an honourable audience, while nonetheless doing more than he himself did? I ask how far he should be offended or surprised, while he strives so much to aggran-dize himself before the laity in the mother tongue, that I on the contrary labour to defend myself in the schools before clerics in the Latin tongue.

[Isti 3 asserciones sunt tres errores vt michi videtur. Nec miretur doctor meus quod dicam errores. Ipse enim dum predicaret ad populum, vbi potissimum exemplum caritatis debuit ostendisse, dixit se non curare qui, quot, vel quanti de tam venerabili auditorio ex suis verbis offenderentur aut essent irati. quis

---

[9] On *insolubilia,* see n. 2.

igitur ponderaret iram suam, qui tam venerabilis auditorii pro nichilo quasi reputauit offensam tamen plus faciendo quam fecit ipse? rogo quatinus non offendatur nec miretur, ex quo conatur se tantum magnificare coram laicis in lingua materna, quod ego e contrario nitar me defendere in scolis et coram clericis in lingua latina.][10]

Ashwardby has preached to the people in a way that fails to show an example of charity; even saying that he does not care who, how many, or how much the members of his so-respectable audience are offended or made angry by his words. By this means he has sought to aggrandize himself before the laity in the maternal tongue. In contrast, Maidstone promises that he will defend himself with all proper decorum; that is, in Latin in the schools before clerics.

A similar ostentatious commitment to the normal conventions of clerical audience, and the corresponding implication that any violation of them is a self-promoting offense against charity, appears in William Rymington's *Dialogus inter catholica veritas et heretica depravitas.* Writing a reply to Wyclif's rebuttal of his *XLIV Conclusiones* in the mid-1380s, Rymington claims Wyclif had spread his pernicious doctrine in an inflammatory manner, such that it persists among his disciples even now, after his death. Rymington's more temperately disseminated dialogue will allow the holy mother church to judge the truth:

Nonetheless because this doctor is dead, yet his pestiferous teaching persists in various writings and in certain of his disciples unknown to me, I have decided that it is better for now, as concerns the business of censuring him and defending myself, to write a dialogue staged between the interlocutors Catholic Truth and Heretical Depravity. In this way holy mother church, or the congregation of catholic clerics, to whose judgement I always humbly submit myself, for my part unswervingly defending catholic truth, will be able to judge between us and put an end to the dispute. For then the christian faithful will be able to inspect [the truth] here, so that they will not be infected by erroneous or heretical teachings.

[Quia tamen doctor iste mortuus est, et eius doctrina pestifera in variis scriptis et in quibusdam ignotis mihi suis discipulis perseuerat, melius pro nunc in hac materia iudicaui super sua reprehencione et mea defensione inter veritatem

[10] Valerie Edden, "The Debate Between Richard Maidstone and the Lollard Ashwardby (ca. 1390)," *Carmelus* 34 (1987): 113–34, 122–23; on the dating, see 114–15.

catholicam et prauitatem hereticam velud inter colloquentes aliquos dialogare, vt iudicare possit inter nos et contentionem dirimere sancta mater ecclesia, seu congregacio cleri catholici, cuius iudicio semper humiliter me submitto, indubitanter vendicans veritatem catholicam pro parte mea quia hic inspicere poterunt christiani fideles ne per doctrinas erroneas seu hereticas inficiantur.]

Rymington submits himself to the "congregation of catholic clerics," but directs the Christian faithful not to assess his Latin dialogue for themselves (though they would probably not be capable of reading it unaided even if they were granted access to it) but to study the arguments of Catholic Truth so as not to become infected with heresy.[11]

All these writers implicitly appeal to a common model of what "proper" lay/clerical interaction would consist in: it posits 1) that the clergy and laity are entirely distinct and have their own separate spheres, 2) that each can be viewed as a seamless, consistent, unified whole, 3) that clerical governance, administration, judgment, and so on should be reserved to the clergy alone, and, crucially, 4) that the Latin literacy, competence in argumentation, and information the clergy have as a consequence of the kind of education they receive are equally their own particular reserved province. Needless to say, in reality relations between clergy and nobility are a lot more tangled and complicated than this model might lead us to believe, but the model does ideological work, for polemicists of many stripes; it can be exploited, and disrupted, to different ends.

From the examples given so far, the reader will already have noticed that one of the most important arenas in which this model does its work is the polemic dialogue involving the laity. There are several extant examples of this sort of dialogue in English or another vernacular, and an extensive Latin tradition lies behind them as well; they are instances of a distinctive and usually highly self-conscious genre that has not been much discussed—largely because it is mainly historians interested in political theory (and not much interested in the format of the works in which they find it) who have read polemical Latin prose dialogues.

Polemic dialogues involving the laity function as a testing ground wherein normal expectations of lay/clerical interaction can be questioned and renegotiated; this kind of "unconventional" questioning had

---

[11] William Rymington, *Dialogus inter catholica veritas et heretica depravitas* (Oxford, Bodleian Library MS Bodl. 158 fols. 188–97, fol. 188).

itself become a literary convention. In some such dialogues a lay audience witnesses and is invited to judge an argument staged before them between educated clerics. Many dialogues of this type are embedded within chronicles, where typically the type of lay audience in question would be explained, the dialogue reported in direct discourse, and the audience's reaction recounted.[12] Other dialogues of this type include the poetic twelfth-century dialogue *De presbytero et logico,* which includes within the fictional setting of the dialogue a lay audience that threatens the loser with violence; and dialogues written on behalf of the policies of, dedicated to, and submitted to the judgment of a member of the nobility, as for example Ockham's mid–fourteenth–century *Dialogus,* or the early–fifteenth–century Wycliffite *Dialogue between a Secular and a Friar.*[13] In other polemic dialogues involving the laity, the participants themselves are of contrasting status: one is a lay person, usually a member of the gentry or nobility, and the other an ecclesiastic, generally a clerk. As well as Trevisa's preface to the *Polychronicon,* the *Dialogue between a Lord and a Clerk,* examples include the late-thirteenth-century *Dialogus inter militem et clericem* that Trevisa would translate, and the Wycliffite *Dialogue between a Clerk and a Knight.*[14]

I have written at length elsewhere about Trevisa's *Dialogue between a Lord and a Clerk,* which he wrote ca. 1387 as a preface to his translation of the *Polychronicon,* and his translation and updating, probably in the 1380s to 1390s, of the *Dialogus inter militem et clericem* written by an

[12] Although many other examples might be mentioned, see for example the several dialogues embedded in the *Continuatio Eulogii,* in F. S. Haydon, ed., *Eulogium Historiarum,* 3 vols., Rolls Series, vols. 10–12 (London, 1858–63), 3:333–421 and 389–94; and my discussion focusing on one dialogue in particular in *Clerical Discourse,* ch. 5, pp. 148–53.

[13] See "De Presbytero et Logico," in Thomas Wright, ed., *The Latin Poems Commonly Attributed to Walter Mapes,* Camden Society, vol. 16 (London: J. B. Nichols & Son, 1841), pp. 251–57; William of Ockham, *Opera Politica,* ed. Jürgen Miethke (Darmstadt, 1992); Trinity College Dublin 244 fols. 212v–219.

[14] Trevisa's *Dialogue between a Lord and a Clerk* is published in Ronald Waldron, "Trevisa's Original Prefaces on Translation: A Critical Edition," in Edward Donald Kennedy, Ronald Waldron, and Joseph S. Wittig, eds., *Medieval English Studies Presented to George Kane* (Woodbridge, Suffolk: D. S. Brewer 1988), pp. 285–99. Trevisa's translation of the *Dialogus inter militem et clericem* appears in Aaron J. Perry, ed., *Dialogus inter Militem et Clericem, Richard fitzRalph's Sermon: 'Defensio Curatorum' and Methodius: 'þe Bygynnyng of þe World and þe Ende of Worldes' by John Trevisa, vicar of Berkeley,* Early English Text Society [EETS], o.s., 167 (London, 1925). The Wycliffite *Dialogue between a Clerk and a Knight* appears in Durham University Library Cosin v. iii. 6. Subsequent references will be made parenthetically in the text by page and line number.

anonymous supporter of Philip the Fair in around 1297.[15] Here I will concentrate mainly on the Wycliffite dialogues the *Dialogue between a Secular and a Friar* and *Dialogue between a Clerk and a Knight,* which I am in the process of editing.[16] But because the Trevisan dialogues are important nonheretical precursors to the sort of debate mounted in the Wycliffite dialogues and elsewhere, and because they are so closely bound up with issues of late-medieval English translation, I will first allow these two dialogues to introduce the genre.

Trevisa's *Dialogue between a Lord and a Clerk* will serve to show the sort of ideological work that disrupting the "proper" model of lay/clerical interaction can do. Trevisa's justification of "Englysch translacion" in this dialogue is spoken in the person of a Lord who demonstrates clerical capacity by showing a high level of ability in argument of a specifically clerical sort; but also allies his own interests and concerns with those of the lowest level of the laity. It is the Lord in Trevisa's *Dialogue* rather than the Clerk who makes extensive use of the terminology and techniques characteristic of academic argumentation: He introduces what looks as though it will be a confession of limited literacy with the technical term "Y denye" (290/56); he skilfully uses a scholastic distinction on the senses of "need" to explain in what sense it is true that all men "need" to know the chronicles (291/65–81); and he uses a syllogistic argument to show that because preaching in English is good and needful, so is translation into English (292/146–293/153). However, the Lord also asserts common cause with the laity as a whole, including even the poorest and least educated. In contrast to the Clerk's stodgy, conventional objections against his proposal that he should translate the *Polychronicon,* the Lord exhibits a detailed practical knowledge about the wider audience English translation might reach and the various constraints that prevent the ready spread of information to that audience. In the course of his sensitive explanation of the various impediments those who might want or need to read may face ("oþer maner bysynes . . . elde . . . defaute of wyt . . . defaute of katel oþer of frendes to vynde ham to scole . . ." (291/65–68)) and of hitches in the mediation process whereby the clerically educated should inform the uneducated ("þe lewed man wot

[15] See my *Clerical Discourse,* ch. 3, pp. 62–100. My discussion here will include many of the same examples used in the book.
[16] The two dialogues will appear in the volume *Four Wycliffite Dialogues,* to be published by EETS.

no3t what a scholde axe. . . . noþer wot comunlych of whom a scholde axe. Also no3t al men þat vnderstondeþ Latyn habbeþ such bokes . . . also som konneþ no3t and some wol no3t and som mowe no3t a whyle" (291/84–87)), it becomes apparent that the poor, the stupid, the old, and those without leisure—the whole of the lay population, it seems— all belong to the potential audience he projects for an English translation. In a sense, then, the Lord seems to espouse the clerical model by placing himself amidst an undifferentiated lay audience. But at the same time, his manner of doing so disrupts the model: he usurps clerical capacities in argument to make his point; and indeed, the role he takes up with respect to the lower laity is a quasi-pastoral one of the sort that would normally belong to a cleric. The Lord exploits the kind of solidarity the conventional model of clerical/lay interaction would advocate, but in a way that usurps clerical prerogative: his solidarity consists in pastoral activity rather than lumpen passivity.

The dialogue Trevisa translated, the *Dialogus inter militem et clericem,* illustrates affiliations between the Latin tradition of polemic dialogue and its English and other vernacular adaptations. The *Dialogus* became the focus of a great deal of interest in the late fourteenth and early fifteenth centuries, in France as well as England. The French *Somnium viridarii,* produced in the 1370s, is a massive extension and expansion of it; and a translation into French of the *Somnium viridarii, Le songe du vergier,* was produced in the same decade. Along with Trevisa's translation, several fifteenth-century English manuscripts testify to continuing interest in the Latin version in England—while not ruling out, of course, that the Latin version may have been popular in England earlier as well.

How did Trevisa alter this dialogue to provide a closer fit to the political concerns of late-fourteenth-century England? Briefly, Trevisa finds his material most unpalatable at the point where the Latin dialogue distinguishes between Christ's earthly and heavenly powers—largely, as I explain elsewhere, because he is unable to massage the distinction into a hard and fast separation between secular temporal and sacred ecclesiastical powers.[17] At that point, Trevisa interpolates a long note which, when it finally abandons its attempt to interpret the distinction, issues the most explicit directive of the reader's attention that Trevisa provides anywhere in his works: "But how hit euer be of þe distinccioun þat is

[17] See my *Clerical Discourse,* ch. 3, pp. 82–7.

196

made bitwene þe clerk & þe kny3t, of þe tyme of Cristes manhed & of þe
tyme of his my3t, power, and maieste," Trevisa recommends, "take hede
how þei spekiþ eiþer to oþer." If we do just that—pay heed to the style
of speech and kind of argumentation that the Clerk and Knight each
use on each other—we can see that their respective styles contrast with
their conventional roles, and that Trevisa has even heightened the contrast.

The kind of reversal effected in the *Dialogus*—where the layman argues using clerical information, and the cleric is unable to oppose him
effectively—had become intensely controversial in the milieu into
which Trevisa was translating the dialogue. Especially interesting to
late-medieval vernacular readers, as we saw in Trevisa's own dialogue,
was the conferral of *pastoral* characteristics on the laity. In this dialogue,
yet greater claims are made for a lay pastoral role, and that role is extended to cover questions of legal jurisdiction and rule. Trevisa's alterations add to the effect, as I explain in detail elsewhere—for example,
by extending the transferred use of "sauacion" to the point where it covers even defense of the realm.[18]

Two Wycliffite dialogues written close to when Chaucer wrote *The
Summoner's Tale,* when as a consequence of the Wycliffite controversy the
issue of translation of capacities from "clergie" to "lewed" was at its most
heated, provide an especially useful comparison with the dynamics of
lay/clerical interaction in *The Summoner's Tale.*[19]

The *Dialogue between a Secular and a Friar* presents itself as the written
record of a disputation held before the Duke of Gloucester. The written
account is addressed to the duke and submitted to his judgment (fols.
212v–213):

[18] See my *Imaginary Publics,* ch. 3, pp. 91–93.
[19] Chaucer is thought to have written *The Summoner's Tale* between approximately
1392 and 1395. (See Larry D. Benson's guide to the dating of Chaucer's works, *The
Riverside Chaucer,* p. xxv.) The *Dialogue between a Secular and a Friar* may probably be dated
before 1397 on the basis of its dedication and envoy, which state that it is the written
record of a dialogue staged before "Lord Glowcestre," probably referring to Thomas of
Woodstock (d. 1397). The *Dialogue between a Clerk and a Knight* contains no such precise
indications, although Anne Hudson has noted that the Clerk shows no surprise at the
Knight's knowledge of scripture, so that a date of composition before the implementa-
tion of Arundel's *Constitutiones* in 1409 may seem more likely; see Anne Hudson, "A
Lollard Quaternion," *RES,* n.s., 22 (1971): 451–65, reprinted in Hudson, *Lollards and
Their Books,* 193–200; quote from p. 195. Further details will appear in my introduction
to *Four Wycliffite Dialogues,* and descriptions appear in Hudson, "A Lollard Quaternion."

Moost worschipfulleste and gentilleste lord duke of Glowcestre, ȝoure seruaunt sendiþ ȝou disputusun writen þat was bifore ȝow bytwixe a frere and a seculer ȝoure clerk, preiynge of boþe sidis to chese and apreue þe trewþe. For as seyeþ oure bileue, "ouere alle þing vencuscheþ þe truþe." And as seiþ Aristotle acordynge wiþ oure bileue, "tweyn beynge frendis it is holy to be for honour þe / f. 213/ trewþe." þerfore to ȝou lord þat herde þe disputusun be ȝeue þe fyle, to rubbe aweye þe rust in eiþir partye.

And the dialogue's envoy indicates obliquely what that judgment is meant to be: it asks the duke to "fulfillen in dede þe trewþe," or bring about a fulfillment of truth through action. After the Secular's repeated comments that it is "untruthful" for members of religious orders to have possessions, it is clear enough what the writer is recommending.

This dialogue consists of a series of propositions by the Friar, each thoroughly refuted in turn by the Secular. Seven exchanges deal with sin and the commandments, one (inserted after the first on the commandments) with temporal possessions of friars, and six (beginning after the seventh question on sin) with voluntary mendicancy. The topics involve arcane scholastic material even where the Secular is not inveighing against the friars, and several of the exchanges are stated and solved in the form of an insoluble proposition. Involving as it does extensive biblical translation, criticism of the clergy to a lay audience, disputation on matters of faith, and use of sophisticated terminology and methods, we might imagine that this dialogue is just the sort of publication that the *Constitutions* would aim to prevent. This "translation" of scholastic material found nowhere else in English into the domain of lay judgment carries along with it the threat of clerical disendowment, even if some of the material translated seems quite innocuous.

The *Dialogue between a Clerk and a Knight* takes this threat a step further. Through a lengthy negotiation of the Clerk and Knight's contract of interaction, and a sustained contestation of their proper respective "lewed" and "clergial" roles—on one level as arguers, and on another, in their argument over jurisdiction and ownership—this dialogue pursues the consequences of the focus on interchange we found in Trevisa's translation. More than that, it enacts the possibilities of intellectual (and, consequently, juridical and monetary) disendowment that the Secular/Friar dialogue, in submitting itself to lay judgment, hopefully holds out.

As usual in dialogues between laymen and clerics, both the Knight and the Clerk begin by approving a definite separation of clerical and lay capacities and roles. In keeping with the conventional model of lay/clerical interaction, the Clerk at the outset attempts to assert that he holds the same pastoral relation to all laymen, whatever their status. Despite the fact that he implicitly tailors his address (as indeed all clerical writers surreptitiously do) to the precise status among the laity of his interlocutor—calling him "ser kniȝt" and worrying about being overcome by his "maistrie"—the Clerk's initial speech still places all members of the laity together in one class, and subordinates that class to all of "holi chirche," from the pope through bishops to ordinary parish clergy. The Clerk starchily disapproves of any "lewed" attempt to "mell" with the clergy (fol. 6):

I haue grete wonder, he said, þat þe kinge and som of his counseil and of his kniȝtes and oþer men of þe temperalte þat schuld be gouerned bi holi chirche, as bi þe pope and bi bihsschopes and bi þe clergy, melleþ þaim of men of holi chirch and of þair godes in mani maners aȝaynes goddes lawe and aȝaines holi chirch. For þer ne schuld no man melle o þe pope ne o þe clergi. For þai bene abouen alle men bi power ȝeuen to þaim bi Godd himself, als holi writt bereþ wittnes and þe law canone also.

"Melling," of course, can mean "speaking" as well as "mixing" or "meddling"; and for the Clerk they come to the same thing: for the Knight to speak about the clergy, even worse to argue like a cleric, is in itself to meddle with matters reserved to the clergy.

Although the Knight too pronounces his disapproval of "melling" so as to condemn clerical "melling" in secular governance, he spends most of his time doing it: he repeatedly evokes, exploits, and then breaks with conventional patterns of lay/clerical interaction. He conjoins himself to the rest of the laity, but on each occasion in a way that also lets him stand apart from them. He acknowledges his position among the lay persons of whose "melling" the Clerk disapproves by—ostensibly humbly—asking the Clerk to instruct him about the doubts lay people share (fol. 6):

þou spekes of a mater þat clerkes han oft moued amonge þe comone pupel, and þe pepel haþ oft bene and es in a were and in dout þerof. And I miself haue oft wondrid þat þe pope and þe clergi haþe taken vpon hem to supplant þe kinge þat es lorde of his land, and all daie bene about more and more to abrege and lessen his power and his lordschip, which as me þink schuld no man o þis half God haue to done wiþ ne mell him þerof. Naþeles, bicause þat I am a litil lettrid and understonde somdele holi writt, I drede me þat I miȝt trist to mich to myne own witt in þis matere and so offend and gilt to God. And þou ert a man of holi chirch, a preste, and semes a clerk connynge of clergi: I wold gladlich lerne of þe.

But at the same time, the instruction he is requesting is not available to the general run of the laity who, as Trevisa's Lord pointed out, do not know what they should ask, nor of whom. Similarly, the Knight validates lay criticism of the clergy on the model of the advice given to Balaam by his ass. But this example implies not universal lay authorization, but special authority conferred by grace on those singled out by God's special favor. Again, the Knight labels himself a lay questioner when asking the Clerk to respond patiently, as clerics normally do not when confronted by lay questioners; but once more, his request asserts his special privilege. And when the Knight criticizes the Clerk for engaging in the usual clerical attempt to preserve lay ignorance, he does so in a way that shows that this general ignorance is one he does not share.

In addition to announcing his solidarity with the "lewed" while also stressing his superiority to them, this Knight distances himself yet further from the negative connotations of lewedness by transferring them to clerics. When deciding whether the Clerk is a fit instructor for him at the beginning of their exchange, he counteracts the Clerk's attempt to endow all clerics alike with superior authority by separating learned from unlearned clerics and pronouncing himself willing to be advised only by the learned (fol. 6):

Bot it es oft sene þat moni prestes and clerkes þat beth gretelich auaunsid gone wele araied and wele fororrid, as þou dos, þat bene no connynge men of clergie ne of resoune. And þerfor, ser, I prai þe tell me what degre of scole þou has, þat I mow knowe wheþer þou be abil of connynge to teche me in þis matere þat I am in dout.

The Knight grudgingly allows the Clerk's membership among the "abil of connynge" (fols. 6r–v):

I am wele paied, for I hope to be wele taȝt bi þe of þat matere þat we haue /f. 6v/ spoken of. Neuerþeles, I had hopid þat þou haddest bene a maistere o diuinite

connynge of Goddes lawe, for þan þou woldist haue said þe soþe and bene noȝt
so fauorabil to þe pope as I suppose þou wolt be now, for þou art a doctor of his
lawe. Naþeles, tell me and teche me als wele als þou canst. . . .

But if the Clerk is not unlearned, then as far as the Knight is concerned
he can only hold the view he has and make the arguments he makes out
of hypocritical duplicity. He is even worse than a "lewed" unlearned
cleric who is merely ignorant. He is a hypocrite, and even "lewed" in
the sense that he gives a bad argument: he asserts a kind of trust in
God that (as the Knight notes) is normally used by unlearned laymen or
priests, but that in the Clerk's mouth can only be hypocritical (fol. 19):

Ow, ser clerk, now I se wele þat þou art at þi wittes ende. For be þin own wordes
it semeþ þat þou ne canst no resoune ne skill for to defend þi cause. Bot riȝt als
Iak Roker or a lewd preste answereþ, riȝt so dostow. For it es þe maner of all
sich lewde iauels when þai ne conne no forþer, þan þai concluden all þair mater
wiþ "God leue it wele be and God ȝeue grace to make a gode ende." And all
sich wordes semen holinesse when ȝe mene moste venyme in ȝoure hert.

Of course the Knight also repeatedly places his trust in God. But he is
not subject to the same criticism (according to the dialogue's own logic,
at any rate) because his trust is simple and genuine—the quality he does
wholeheartedly share with even the most uneducated among the laity.

In *The Summoner's Tale,* where clerical capacities are transferred to a lay
arena by means of vernacular translation, we see Maidstone's, Rymington's, and Arundel's worst nightmare enacted, as a series of responses
voiced by lay persons of differing statuses frustrate, then finally over-
turn, the friar's attempt to treat all members of the laity as if they were
in the same subordinate pastoral position with respect to him. Normally
in clerical discourse, as we have seen, a cleric who uses the convenient
fiction of lay uniformity needs covertly to accompany it with a quite
carefully modulated address to the particular status of his lay interlocutor. Friar John, however, seems blind to the status of the layman he aims
to instruct. When he first asserts the universal superiority in understanding of clerics to laymen regardless of status, he backs up his claim
with an argument based on clerical poverty (*SumT* 1871–75):

> . . . moore we seen of Cristes secree thynges,
> Than burel folk, although they weren kynges.
> We lyve in poverte and in abstinence,
> And burell folk in richesse and despence
> Of mete and drynke, and in hir foul delit.

The argument might be effective if it were voiced by a less obviously prosperous friar, especially if he were addressing nobles, lords, or at minimum prosperous gentry. But here the friar is speaking to the village smallholder Thomas. For someone of Thomas' status—and probably for any other reasonably skeptical lay listener—it is clear that the way of life the friar criticizes is not that of his interlocutor, but his own.

Indeed, Friar John's pastoral advice seems uneasily to gravitate toward addressing a layman of much the same status and position that he himself occupies; the ideal he holds up mirrors the one he claims (yet conspicuously fails) to achieve. When advising Thomas about anger—the very vice he himself is about to succumb to—Friar John makes use of exempla from the advice-to-princes tradition. It might seem incongruous enough already that a friar should be advising a churl using examples about the anger of kings. Yet, advice-to-princes was commonly read by those aspiring to virtuous gentility: the king's rule of self, household, and realm were all thought to work on analogous principles, so that any layman could model whatever governance is expected of him on the same temperate ideal that advice manuals recommend to kings.[20] However, the friar's exemplum-based advice in the end turns out not to be directed to kings or princes even on the overt level.

The morals of the friar's two exempla apply not to the angry kings upon whom they would more typically focus, but—jarringly—to those in the service of those kings who are subject to their wrath. Already Friar John's opening precept has turned in a surprising direction: ". . .

---

[20] For a summary of the debate and a balanced bibliography, see the recent assessment of scholarly views on the late-medieval English audience for advice-to-princes literature in Judith Ferster, *Fictions of Advice: The Literature and Politics of Counsel in Late Medieval England* (Philadelphia: University of Pennsylvania Press, 1996), pp. 178–85. On the rhetoric of linked realms of governance in advice-to-princes literature, and more particularly in attempts to advise Richard II during his reign, see *Clerical Discourse*, ch. 3 p. 75 and n. 23. For a different interpretation of the relationship during Richard's reign (and more broadly) between advice-to-princes literature, contemporary political writing, and political activity, see Ferster, *Fictions of Advice,* pp. 176–78 (in summary), as well as pp. 67–88 (for a political survey), pp. 89–107 (on Chaucer's *Melibee* and the reign of Richard II), pp. 108–59 (on Gower, Hoccleve, Richard's deposition, Henry IV, and Henry V).

Thomas, yet eft-soones I charge thee, / Be war from Ire that in thy bo-
som slepeth" (lines 1992–93) sounds like the beginning of advice to
Thomas about curbing his own anger, but instead, bizarrely, leads to the
warning that Thomas should beware of his wife's anger in case she might
murder him (lines 1996–2009). Similarly, when he moves from the
household to what Scanlon has labeled the "public exemplum," that is,
the exemplum focusing on matters of state,[21] Friar John's first exemplum
seems initially to focus on an angry ruler: "It is greet harm and certes
greet pitee / To sette an irous man in heigh degree" (lines 2015–16).
But the story quickly turns to the three knights deputed to carry out
their lord's commands, who are summarily executed for their efforts to
exercise their own judgment in response to changed circumstance (lines
2017–42). Friar John's second story (lines 2043–73) incorporates the
would-be advisor to the prince into the story as well: although the
drunken ruler "Irous Cambises" is again the starting point, it is the virtuous "lord of his meynee" who attempts to counsel him to temperance
whose son Cambises kills, and who is the subject of the story's moral
(lines 2074–78):

> Beth war, therefore, with lordes how ye pleye.
> Singeth *Placebo* and "I shal if I kan,"
> But if it be unto a povre man.
> To a povre man men sholde his vices telle,
> But nat to a lord, thogh he sholde go to helle.

Friar John repeatedly slips out of advising Thomas about how to manage
his own ire, and into showing him how to be a loyal servant and word-
mincing court flatterer mindful of the power and potentially erratic
temperament of his lord. This advice has scant usefulness for a smallholder intent on managing his own farm, unconcerned with household
politics and lacking any ambitions for court patronage; it applies much
more directly to the friar himself, or else to a layman of similar status
aiming to attain the same sort of relationship with his lord.

In uncomfortably direct proximity to these explanations of how advisors to princes should judiciously bend the truth, Friar John next assures
Thomas that he himself is an advisor of objectively perfect rectitude:

---

[21] Scanlon describes the characteristics of the public exemplum much more fully, distinguishing it from the sermon exemplum in the process, in *Narrative, Authority, and
Power*, pp. 81–87.

"Thou shalt me fynde as just as is a squyre," or measuring square, he assures him.[22] The advice-giving role Friar John claims to fulfill here places him in uneasy tension with the mode of behavior he himself has suggested. Already, on its face, Friar John's claim to rectitude conflicts with the word-mincing, flattering advisory mode he has recommended to Thomas. But the blatant pun makes it even worse: the friar is also comparing himself to a *squire,* a lay person of just the status that his advice on court conduct covertly addresses—and just the status in the lord or king's household that the friar himself aspires to.

The vernacular eruption with which Thomas responds to this speech rudely shatters the friar's model of clerical superiority, and precipitates his request for justice from his lay lord—during which despite the lord's pretense of deference to his confessor, the friar nonetheless finds himself in just the same sort of subservient position as any lay petitioner. The friar puts himself forward as a generic representative, unproblematically equivalent to any other, of a unified and harmonious ecclesiastical hierarchy.[23] The injury done to him is a wrong done to his order as a whole, and more than that, to the whole church (lines 2190–93):

> "Sire," quod this frere, "an odious meschief
> This day bityd is to myn ordre and me,
> And so, *per consequens,* to ech degre
> Of hooly chirche—God amende it soone!"

Yet once he has presented his case, the friar finds himself subject to a series of lay determinations that progressively accomplish a vernacular translation in the fullest possible sense: stage by stage they define his response as "lewed" while endowing the "lewed" churl's utterance with clerical authority.

---

[22] See line 2090 and note.

[23] Valuable work has been done on the antifraternal material employed in the squire's reply: see Penn R. Szittya, *The Antifraternal Tradition in Medieval Literature* (Princeton, N.J.: Princeton University Press, 1986), pp. 232–46, for a thorough treatment and summary of previous scholarship. I focus here on the logic of the friar's claims, which rather than being narrowly profraternal mount a defense based on his status as a member (and therefore representative) of the church. On the broadening of the debate in the later fourteenth century such that arguments previously applied for or against some particular religious group were directed instead at corrupt church members with little regard to their precise status, see Wendy Scase, *"Piers Plowman" and the New Anti-clericalism* (Cambridge: Cambridge University Press, 1989), especially the introduction, pp. 1–14.

My reading of the mechanics of this layward progression, and my interpretation of its end result, are my main point of difference with Scanlon's reading of this tale. In my view it is not enough to view the lower-status lay persons in the lord's service as straightforward exponents or instruments of his power.[24] Instead, it is important to see how the stable, harmonious lay hierarchy that in the end dismisses the friar is something the tale has to *achieve*. It must do so in opposition to a powerful clerical ideology (however ineptly it has been expressed by the friar) of universal lay subservience to the whole of the clerical hierarchy; and by means of a usurpation of clerical authority that supersedes class division. A succession of lay speakers each contributes to forging what becomes a lay unanimity, voiced in clerical terms, that drowns out the friar.

First to respond, the lady and lord begin by dismissing the churl Thomas. But whereas the lady does so quite summarily, in a way that puts the friar in the wrong only to the extent of highlighting the excessiveness of his anger (lines 2202–9), the lord's response has the effect of translating Thomas's insult into a scholastic problem (lines 2218–37):

> "How hadde this cherl ymaginacioun
> To shewe swich a probleme to the frere?
> Nevere erst er now herde I of swich mateere.
> I trowe the devel putte it in his mynde.
> In ars-metrike shal ther no man fynde,
> Biforn this day, of swich a question.
> Who sholde make a demonstracion
> That every man sholde have yliche his part
> As of the soun or savour of a fart?
> O nyce, proude cherl, I shrewe his face!
> Lo sires," quod the lord, "with harde grace!
> Who evere herde of swich a thyng er now?
> To every man ylike? Tel me how.
> It is an inpossible; it may nat be.
> Ey, nyce cherl, God lete him nevere thee!
> The rumblynge of a fart, and every soun,

---

[24] While Scanlon does note that the Squire's comic advantage in presenting a solution to the problem Thomas has posed "results as much from his own social position as his superior wit" (*Narrative, Authority, and Power*, p. 173), for Scanlon all there is to say about the Squire's social position is that he is a layman: the lord's household speaks through different mouths, but with one voice.

Nis but of eir reverberacioun,
And evere it wasteth litel and litel awey.
Ther is no man kan deemen, by my fey,
If that it were departed equally."

The lord has no greater respect for Thomas than the lady, but he is fascinated by the apparent insolubility of the problem itself. Even more so, tellingly, he is fascinated that it was a *churl*—a person of nonclerical status and, even more surprisingly, among the laity a person of low social status—who was able to pose the intriguing problem of how Friar John can fulfill his promise to distribute Thomas's donation equally among his convent. His response affirms both his own distance from Thomas in the lay hierarchy, and the conventional attitude that only clerics have the necessary knowledge to pose, solve, or adjudicate problems: he accentuates class distinctions rather than forging new alliances.[25]

This lay judgment of the tale's central lay/clerical interchange has half-accomplished a vernacular translation (in the extended sense): the lord's curiosity about Thomas's answer has at least turned it into a problem posed in terms of the lord's knowledge of natural science, even if it has not yet brought any respect for the "cherl" Thomas. The tale's next interjection, the squire's clerical but at the same time courtly solution, carries the translation further. By subjecting Thomas's utterance in the form of the problem posed by the lord to a scientifically informed solution couched in the sort of witty, courteous form best judged to please his lord, the squire validates the scholastic interest the lord has found in it (lines 2246–50, 2253–86). But he also reclaims it, and its utterer, as worthy of favorable judgment in the lay court; he transforms its insult into elegantly amusing vulgarity, and the churl who has posed it into a

[25] Many critics have noted that the lady and lord distance themselves socially from Thomas. Lee Patterson intriguingly points out that the Lord's ideological difficulties with Thomas's problem begin before its apparent insolubility, in bafflement at the mere notion of equal division: twice the Lord's expostulation begins at the notion that "every man yliche" should have a part; Lee Patterson, *Chaucer and the Subject of History* (London: Routledge, 1991), pp. 320–21. If this is indeed one focus of the Lord's objection, his bewilderment at a theory of social organization that could be either an alternative secular arrangement, or the terms of a cloistered institutional religious rule, seems appropriate. I pursue the Lord's concern with division in a different direction in my forthcoming paper on Eucharistic blasphemy in the *Summoner's Tale* and elsewhere. Glending Olson is as far as I know the only other scholar to have noticed the Eucharistic implications of the Lord's version of this problem of division.

thinker deserving of the respect due to anyone who can pose a question worthy of close attention.

Finally, the harmonious secular unanimity forged by the squire's jocular anticlericalism accomplishes a further lay judgment that has the effect of transferring clerical authority entirely to its lay challengers (lines 2287–92):

> The lord, the lady, and ech man, save the frere,
> Seyde that Jankyn spak, in this matere,
> As wel as Euclide dide or Ptholomee.
> Touchynge the cherl, they seyde, subtiltee
> And heigh wit made hym speken as he spak;
> He nys no fool, ne no demonyak.

The lord's household—lord, lady, and everyone else present with the exception of the friar—draws on the scholastic mathematical authorities Euclid and Ptolemy to validate the squire as a *clerical* speaker, and even goes so far as to transform the churl Thomas into a subtly *clerical* thinker.

Of course, an element of farce has crept in by this point. But it has the effect, I think, not so much of doing any damage to the lay unanimity that the progressive translation and appropriation of clerical prerogative have accomplished here, as of lampooning, in company with the terminology and techniques in which it is normally couched, the position of clerical authority. However radical they may be, Wycliffites always take "clergie" very seriously: in this one sense, it can be said that Chaucer has "translated" clerical authority even further than they— right off the edge.

The End of *The Summoner's Tale* and the Uses of Pentecost

Glending Olson
Cleveland State University

P erhaps the most fruitful decade in the academic appreciation
of *The Summoner's Tale* came during 1965–74, when some of the techniques of iconographic exegesis were applied to the poem's opening and
closing images and their implications linked to a tale revealed as rich
in biblical allusion. Chaucer's depiction of the unintentionally self-
revealing Friar John had long been admired, but the coherence of the
work and its wicked use of religious imagery had never before been so
clear. I take it that conventional critical wisdom still endorses the view
of the tale that emerged out of those studies: it is a shrewdly conceived
piece of antifraternal satire based in part on lines of attack that can be
traced back to William of St. Amour; the opening image of the friars
swarming out of the devil's ass parodies the Maria Misericordia; the closing image of a convent of friars kneeling around a cartwheel to receive
equal distribution of a fart parodies the descent of the Holy Spirit on
the apostles at Pentecost; and a number of verbal and thematic links tie
these images to the speech and behavior of the Friar. The tale's ending
in particular is adumbrated throughout in the portrayal of John's hypocritical claims to live the apostolic life and in wordplay where second
meanings are notably visceral or anal: "grope" (line 1817 vs. 2141,
2148; cf. *GP* 644), "*cor meum eructavit*" (line 1934), "ferthyng . . . parted
in twelve" (line 1967), "ars-metrike" (line 2222).[1] The Squire's proposed
solution to the problem of dividing Thomas's fart is thus poetically just,
bestowing on the Friar and his brothers a wind that conveys earthly

---

[1] All Chaucer quotations are from Larry D. Benson, gen. ed., *The Riverside Chaucer,* 3d
ed. (Boston: Houghton Mifflin, 1987).

contempt rather than the spiritual blessings sent as in a great wind by the Holy Spirit, gifts and powers the friars claim yet betray.[2]

I want to challenge none of this conventional wisdom. I seek rather to supplement it, recontextualize it, looking both more broadly and more narrowly at the question of Chaucer's parody of Pentecost at the end of the tale: broadly in that I will explore a wider range of presentations of Pentecost in the later Middle Ages than the visual images thus far adduced; narrowly in that I will suggest a more precise historical dimension to the parody than that argued by criticism stressing only Chaucer's place within exclusively iconographic or exegetical traditions. Newer forms of historical inquiry have helped us to think about such traditions, and other aspects of religious expression, not as independent conveyors of predetermined meaning but as sites of various and often contested meanings, differentially perceived depending on one's social or cultural circumstances.[3] This investigation attempts to suggest some of the varied practices and meanings that may have developed around Pentecost

[2] John V. Fleming, "The Antifraternalism of the *Summoner's Tale*," *JEGP* 65 (1966): 688–700; Bernard S. Levy, "Biblical Parody in the *Summoner's Tale*," *TSL* 11 (1966): 45–60; Fleming, "The Summoner's Prologue: An Iconographic Adjustment," *ChauR* 2 (1967): 95–107; Alan Levitan, "The Parody of Pentecost in Chaucer's *Summoner's Tale*," *UTQ* 40 (1971): 236–46; Penn R. Szittya, "The Friar as False Apostle: Antifraternal Exegesis and the *Summoner's Tale*," *SP* 71 (1974): 19–46, subsequently incorporated into *The Antifraternal Tradition in Medieval Literature* (Princeton, N.J.: Princeton University Press, 1986), pp. 231–46. For more recent work in this vein, see Paul A. Olson, *The Canterbury Tales and the Good Society* (Princeton, N.J.: Princeton University Press, 1986), pp. 214–34, and Jay Ruud, "'My Spirit Hath His Fostryng in the Bible': The Summoner's Tale and the Holy Spirit," in Susanna Greer Fein, David Raybin, and Peter C. Braeger, eds., *Rebels and Rivals: The Contestive Spirit in the* Canterbury Tales (Kalamazoo, Mich.: Medieval Institute Publications, 1991), pp. 125–48.

[3] Among many studies of this sort see Miri Rubin, *Corpus Christi: The Eucharist in Late Medieval Culture* (Cambridge: Cambridge University Press, 1991); Sarah Beckwith, *Christ's Body: Identity, Culture and Society in Late Medieval Writings* (London and New York: Routledge, 1993); David Aers and Lynn Staley, *The Powers of the Holy: Religion, Politics, and Gender in Late Medieval English Culture* (University Park: Pennsylvania State University Press, 1996); and several of the essays in Barbara A. Hanawalt and David Wallace, eds., *Bodies and Disciplines: Intersections of Literature and History in Fifteenth-Century England* (Minneapolis: University of Minnesota Press, 1996), among them Paul Strohm's afterword, which informs my use of the term "practice." For comparable rethinking of medieval antifraternal material in response to Szittya's approach, see Wendy Scase, Piers Plowman *and the New Anticlericalism* (Cambridge: Cambridge University Press, 1989), who argues for a historically distinct antifraternalism in Langland influenced principally by Archbishop FitzRalph; and for *The Summoner's Tale* specifically, Larry Scanlon, *Narrative, Authority, and Power: The Medieval Exemplum and the Chaucerian Tradition* (Cambridge: Cambridge University Press, 1994), pp. 160–75, who stresses the institutional, ecclesiological force of the satire and parody; see also Alan Fletcher's study cited below, n. 71.

in Chaucer's time and hence would have affected response to his evocation of it. It includes the following: a reaffirmation, after considering some recently proposed alternatives, of the final image of *The Summoner's Tale* as a parody of Pentecost; consideration of the possible influence on Chaucer of other parodies of Pentecost and of its appropriation in secular contexts; expansion of the idea of "sources" of the parody to include stagings of Pentecost in liturgical or dramatic settings; and finally a refocusing of attention to the implications of the parody in the 1390s, at a time when Lollard criticism of the misuse of images and of appeals to the sensory raised significant questions about the material representation of spiritual events. I hope that what emerges is a view of the tale no less appreciative of its brilliant parody but more alert to some of the cultural contexts, popular as well as learned, in which that parody was enmeshed and out of which its historical meanings—some of them beyond the strictly antifraternal—took shape.

I

When a critical idea is really persuasive it becomes a "discovery," and for some time that has seemed to be the status of Levitan's insight concerning the ending of *The Summoner's Tale*. Calling attention to the depiction of Pentecost in some examples of medieval art, he argued that Jankin's envisaged solution to Thomas's challenge to divide his "gift" equally among a convent of friars—twelve men around a cartwheel (and one beneath it), on their knees, below the buttocks of Thomas, receiving his fart through the spokes—parodies the descent of the Holy Spirit as in a mighty wind upon the twelve apostles on the day of Pentecost (Acts 2:1–4). His argument makes the final scene closely related to what has gone before, a humiliation appropriate to fraudulent fraternal claims to be living the apostolic life. As far as I know, only recently have serious challenges to or hesitations concerning Levitan's argument appeared. V. A. Kolve carefully advances the possibility that Jankin's proposal might have been influenced by a different image, the Wheel of False Religion discussed and depicted in some manuscripts of the *De rota verae et falsae religionis* of Hugh of Folieto. While not denying the Pentecostal resonance of Thomas's fart, he is "unconvinced" by Levitan's claim that the cartwheel used to solve the problem of dividing it is related to medieval artistic treatments of Pentecost:

211

Those pictures depict tongues of flame, not the great wind; the text they illustrate . . . has nothing to say of wheels or rotundity; and the standard iconography of the Pentecost . . . presents the apostles frontally (or only slightly turned toward each other), with Mary at their center, in a straight row, a semi-circle, or an inverted "U"; flames *descend* from the Holy Ghost above, either as flames or in abstract lines more reminiscent of a tent than of a wheel.

At best, he points out, there are a few illustrations of the descent where the positioning of the apostles relative to the rays emanating from the Holy Spirit makes it appear that they are at the circumference of a wheel with spokes; but no actual wheel is ever depicted, and these cases constitute a "marginal tradition, completely overshadowed by the traditional iconography."[4] In contrast, the Wheel of False Religion is, like Jankin's mechanism for solution, a wheel, and its parts are explicated in Hugh's text: the spokes, for example, are carnal impulses, the hub tolerance of vices by the abbot (pp. 282–83)—a "fit" appropriate to a poem satirizing spiritual failures.

It is possible that Chaucer was influenced by the Wheel of False Religion. It is also possible, as has recently been argued, that he was influenced by medieval wheel-shaped diagrams of winds (normally numbered twelve: four major and eight minor). Once the imaginative leap was made to associate the wind of Pentecost with Thomas's wind, Jankin's working out of the distribution might well have been prompted by scientific rather than (or in addition to) theological or moral images, particularly given the logical language in which the lord of the village articulates the "probleme" (line 2219).[5] Possibly too there were jokes or

---

[4] "Chaucer's Wheel of False Religion: Theology and Obscenity in The Summoner's Tale," in Robert A. Taylor et al., eds., *The Centre and its Compass: Studies in Medieval Literature in Honor of Professor John Leyerle* (Kalamazoo: Western Michigan University, 1993), pp. 265–96; citation from p. 289. Helen Cooper questions whether either the Wheel of False Religion or a wheel-like Pentecost image was of much currency in Chaucer's England; see *Oxford Guides to Chaucer:* The Canterbury Tales, 2d ed. (Oxford: Oxford University Press, 1996), p. 178.

[5] Phillip Pulsiano, "The Twelve-Spoked Wheel of the *Summoner's Tale*," ChauR 29 (1995): 382–89, and Robert Hasenfratz, "The Science of Flatulence: Possible Sources for the *Summoner's Tale*," ChauR 30 (1996): 241–61, both with illustrations. Pulsiano treats the possibility as providing "an additional layer of meaning" to the religious parody (p. 382); Hasenfratz thinks it provides a "better" explanation for the "atmosphere and significance of Jankin's solution" in light of the academic/scientific tone of the final scene (p. 243). This tone is thoroughly explored in Timothy D. O'Brien, "'Ars-Metrick': Science, Satire, and Chaucer's Summoner," *Mosaic* 23 (1990): 1–22, though I do not think his reading ultimately integrates academic and religious implications as fully as it might. Scientific and religious discourses in regard to the Pentecostal wind are briefly fused in the sermon on Pentecost by the Franciscan Anthony of Padua. He links the

riddles in circulation that proposed the wheel solution to the challenge of dividing a fart, as one might infer from a brief post-Chaucerian *demande*.[6] But I do not think that any or all of these conceivable sources for Jankin's wheel make it less likely that the final image of *The Summoner's Tale* parodies Pentecost. For that connection, as Szittya argued most persuasively, is urged by details in the story itself: the Friar makes apostolic claims, and the Squire's solution includes apostolic and Pentecostal associations in its allusion to the number of friars in John's convent (twelve and one leader), its envisaging of John placed directly below the fart to receive the "firste fruyt," and its view that he deserves such special placement because of his "prechyng" earlier in the day (lines 2275–86).[7] It is urged too by the most obvious polemical context within which the tale was written and first read: Wycliffite criticism of the friars, as we will see, constantly draws invidious comparisons between their behavior and that of Jesus and his apostles. Given both the literary and social contexts, a group of twelve friars kneeling around a cartwheel to receive a foul wind must surely evoke the windlike descent of the Holy Spirit. Thomas's "bely stif and toght" (line 2267) may further the analogy, as the burlesque bodily equivalent of the references to fullness and repletion that occur in Acts 2:1–4 and that loom large in the medieval imagining of the meaning of Pentecost.[8]

---

wind of Acts 2:2 with the four winds from which the spirit comes in Ezech. 37:9, names the four major winds on earth, and then offers two spiritual interpretations of them; *Sermones Dominicales et Festivi,* ed. Beniamino Costa, Leonardo Frasson, and Ioanne Luisetto, vol. 1 (Padua: Messaggero, 1979), p. 371. Is it possible that some such mixture of natural science and allegorizing as in this fraternal sermon is one of the targets of Chaucer's complex parodic scene?

[6] Richard Firth Green, "A Possible Source for Chaucer's Summoner's Tale," *ELN* 24, no. 4 (1987): 24–27.

[7] Szittya, *Antifraternal Tradition,* pp. 236–46. On the first fruit and its evocation of the Jewish Pentecost feast, see pp. 234–35; the reference may also suggest the fruits and gifts of the Holy Spirit, which were often associated with the descent at Pentecost; see Roy Peter Clark, "Wit and Witsunday in Chaucer's *Summoner's Tale,*" *AnM* 17 (1976): 48–57; citation from pp. 49–50. On charges of fraternal abuse of preaching, the "chief apostolic function," see Szittya, ibid., pp. 210–12. In medieval commentary on Acts 2, identification of the symbolic significance of the wind and the tongues of fire varies; either can be seen as a token of apostolic preaching or the power to communicate Christian knowledge. For a Lollard reading that connects the wind with the apostles' speaking, see the reference cited in n. 73 below.

[8] Acts 2:2: "et factus est repente de caelo sonus, tanquam advenientis spiritus vehementis et *replevit* totam domum"; Acts 2:4: "et *repleti* sunt omnes Spiritu sancto, et coeperunt loqui variis linguis, prout Spiritus sanctus dabat eloqui illis" (my italics); *Biblia Sacra iuxta Vulgatam Clementinam nova editio,* 7th ed. (Madrid: Biblioteca de autores cristianos, 1985). In the Sarum Use, the Office of the Mass on Pentecost Day begins with Wisdom 1:7: "Spiritus Domini replevit orbem terrarum"; J. Wickham Legg, ed., *The Sarum Missal* (Oxford: Clarendon Press, 1916; rpt., 1969), p. 161. A sermon on Pente-

Kolve's description of the usual appearance of the descent of the Spirit in medieval art is accurate, but that need not mean that Jankin's solution is unrelated to such images. For the most important idea parodied in Chaucer's scene is present in almost all the artistic examples: the emanation of the Holy Spirit from a single central point down and outward to the gathered apostles. In a great many cases that sending forth is depicted as twelve rays or lines, each going out to one recipient. Such an attempt to render visually the filling of the apostles with the Spirit could easily have suggested Jankin's twelve part distribution system, for while the rays often do look more like lines or tent-poles than wheel-spokes, it is not hard to imagine them as spoke-like if the vertical space between the Spirit and the apostles were compressed and the grouping given more firmly circular structure.[9] The purpose of the cartwheel, a conduit of insult rather than grace, is to distribute one fart among a group of pseudoapostles. Punishment will drop down on John from a central external source and radiate centrifugally to his brethren. Neither the Wheel of False Religion nor the wheel of the twelve winds involves exactly those vectors. Though either idea/image could have contributed to a complex of meanings in Chaucer's scene, neither seems as relevant to it, in terms of the action and allusions of the tale, as the standard representation of the descent of the Spirit in medieval art.

True, there is no "cartwheel" in Acts 2. But given the familiarity of wheels in medieval representations, diagrams, and literary motifs—not

---

cost by Pseudo-Augustine envisages the apostles as vessels filled by the Spirit and bubbling over: "Coeperunt vasa eorum vinum bulliendo ructare [cf. the pun in *SumT* 1934], et linguis omnium gentium resonare" (Sermo 186.2, *PL* 39, col. 2094). The *Glossa ordinaria* picks up on this image, beginning its comments on 2:4 by saying, "Ecce signum plenitudinis: plenum vas erumpit" (*PL* 114, col. 430). The *Legenda aurea* speaks extensively about this fullness, including some very earthly comparisons that would foster imaginative connection between spiritual and bodily repletion. One sign of fullness is that "no more can be taken in," as "when a man has eaten his fill"; Jacobus de Voragine, *The Golden Legend,* trans. William Granger Ryan, 2 vols. (Princeton, N.J.: Princeton University Press, 1993), 1:303–4.

[9] As Kolve points out, the most convenient place to see a large number of such pictures is Gertrud Schiller, *Ikonographie der christlichen Kunst,* vol. 4, pt. 1 (Gütersloh: Gerd Mohn, 1981), pp. 11–33 and plates 1–76. Schiller discusses various traditions of presentation. It is worth noting that one of these includes portrayal of a risen Christ (sometimes a Father and Son) above the apostles, with the rays of the Holy Spirit extending either from the mouth of a dove just below the figure(s) or directly from beneath the figure(s)— see pp. 27–30 and the relevant plates. Also significant is the fact that Mary is often included with the apostles in the Pentecost scene and frequently given a central place (pp. 24–25). Jankin's configuration of twelve friars in a circle with John in the center would seem to correspond most closely with illustrations in this tradition (e.g., pls. 17, 34, 40; and for Mary centered with representations of the Son or Son and Father above, pls. 33, 62–65).

to mention the tale's own rhyming association a hundred lines earlier of Thomas's "fart" and a horse-drawn "cart" (lines 2149–50)—it does not seem that Chaucer's use of one here necessarily demands distinct icono-graphic inspiration. Levitan suggested that a further possible source for the scene is the twelve-souled wheels (whose spokesmen are friars) in cantos 10–14 of Dante's *Paradiso*. And there is a wheel evoked in a bibli-cal passage close to Acts 2, at least in those medieval bibles that came with the *Glossa ordinaria*. Just before the ascension, in Acts 1:8, Jesus speaks to the apostles and predicts Pentecost and its consequences: "But you shall receive the power of the Holy Ghost coming upon you, and you shall be witnesses unto me in Jerusalem, and in all Judea and Sama-ria, and even to the uttermost part of the earth." The *Glossa* notes both the literal and spiritual significance of Jerusalem as central point and the promised movement from there to the ends of the earth. That jour-ney outward was made by the apostles preaching God's word, "through whom, like spokes of a wheel from the center of the earth where He has worked our salvation, spiritual grace and wholesome instruction have flowed out through the whole world." This is the most precise image I know of the apostles as spokes dispersing Christianity from centerpoint to circumference, but other allusions to the apostolic spreading of the Christian faith involve a similar conceptualization of the significance of Pentecost.[10] There is also another wheel in medieval art that sometimes appears not very distant from illustrations of Pentecost. For both chro-

---

[10] ". . . per quos quasi rotae radios de medio terrae ubi salutem operatus est, gratia spiritualis et salutaris doctrina per totum orbem defluxit" (*PL* 114, cols. 427–28). Else-where the apostles are compared to light radiating from the sun, and in a Pseudo-Augustine sermon on Pentecost specifically to twelve rays of light: "universum mundum tanquam duodecim solis radii ac totidem lampades veritatis illuminent" (Sermo 182.2, in *PL* 39, col. 2088). Since Latin *radius* can mean either "ray" or "spoke," the former meaning could easily suggest the latter in contexts where the rays are given a precise number and central source. Anthony of Padua, citing Ezech. 1:20 ("Spiritus vitae erat in rotis"), refers to the apostles as "rotae volubiles . . . Dei Filium per totum mundum deferentes" (*Sermones*, pp. 367–68). Even images of division and radiation outward that do not mention wheels or rays explicitly allow the inference, as in the *Speculum Sacerdo-tale:* "And the apostles fulfilled with the Holy Goste diuidyd hem a-sonderly by alle the world," thus fulfilling Psalms 18:5, "þe sownde of hem passeþ in-to yche londe and countres, and here wordes in-to alle costes of the world"; Edward H. Weatherly, ed., *Speculum Sacerdotale,* Early English Text Society [EETS], o.s., 200 (London, 1936), p. 160. Such ways of expressing the events of Acts may have had some influence on allegori-zations of *rota* in medieval *distinctiones* that specify one of its meanings as preachers or the world receiving preaching; see *Allegoriae in Sacram Scripturam, PL* 112, col. 1041: "Per *rotam* praedicatores . . . quod sancti praedicatores divino sunt amore inflammati"; also a *distinctiones* of William de Montibus, British Library MS Royal 8.G.2, fol. 69: "rota mundi id est vox predicandis christi in orbe terre."

nological and thematic reasons Christ's ascension was often shown close to treatments of the descent of the Spirit; one of the prefigurations of the ascension, frequently illustrated with it, was the raising of Elijah to heaven in a fiery chariot (4 Kings 2:11; "currus igneus"). Illustrations of this event often include a chariot with a very prominent wheel. Since Chaucer mentions Elijah twice in *The Summoner's Tale* (lines 1890–93, 2116–18), it is not inconceivable, though I would hardly call it probable, that the cartwheel solution developed out of an association of visual images of Elijah's ascent and the Spirit's descent.[11]

In short, there could have been many prompts to the invention of Jankin's wheel. Whatever may have led Chaucer to it, no medieval artistic representation of any wheel thus far discovered works very well by itself as a correlative to the Squire's idea, because his solution depends on something from outside and above the wheel traveling through it to a set of recipients. The wheel is only part of the narrative scenario Jankin conjures, which also includes a kneeling convent of friars, the posterior of a churl, and a sending out of smell and sound. And that image, given the evidence within Chaucer's text and the reasonable closeness of visual depictions of the descent of the Spirit, certainly seems to be a parody of Pentecost.

---

[11] The possibility of associating these two images would have been strengthened by the fact that another event involving Elijah is depicted in some sources as one of the types of Pentecost (3 Kings 18:36–38, where God sends fire down on Elijah's sacrifice). On the friars' use of Elijah, see Robert A. Koch, "Elijah the Prophet, Founder of the Carmelite Order," *Speculum* 34 (1959): 547–60; and for the relevance of his typological meanings to Chaucer, see Ian Lancashire, "Moses, Elijah and the Back Parts of God: Satiric Scatology in Chaucer's *Summoner's Tale,*" *Mosaic* 14, no. 3 (1981): 17–30. The image of Elijah's chariot as a type of the ascension appears in reasonably close proximity to Pentecost scenes in the *Biblia pauperum,* for which see Koch, ibid., figs. 2 and 3 (from a fifteenth-century blockbook); in the *Speculum humanae salvationis,* for which see Avril Henry, ed., *The Mirour of Mans Saluacioun* (Philadelphia: University of Pennsylvania Press, 1987), pp. 170–75; and at the top of the east window of the corona of the cathedral in Canterbury, for which see Madeline Harrison Caviness, *The Early Stained Glass of Canterbury Cathedral* (Princeton, N.J.: Princeton University Press, 1977), fig. 137, discussed pp. 75–77; for the program of the window, appendix fig. 20 (pp. 174–75). The association is less close in a program of illustrations for Joinville's *Credo,* since the organization is by the articles of the Creed rather than Christian history; Lionel J. Friedman, *Text and Iconography for Joinville's* Credo (Cambridge, Mass.: Mediaeval Academy of America, 1958), pp. 72–73, 76–77, and pls. 15–16 and 19–20. Elijah also appears as a type of St. Francis in Bonaventure's biography, which tells of Francis's spirit once appearing to his brothers as a fiery chariot ("currus igneus") and so leading them to realize that he was an "alter Elias." See Richard K. Emmerson and Ronald B. Herzman, *The Apocalyptic Imagination in Medieval Literature* (Philadelphia: University of Pennsylvania Press, 1992), pp. 66–67.

II

Critical discussion of Jankin's imagined solution, including my own above, has tended thus far to construct a context involving almost exclusively representations of Pentecost in medieval art, other images that might also fit Chaucer's text, and the biblical account in Acts 2 and its medieval interpretations. Yet Pentecost in the Middle Ages was not just something to be found in a picture or in a commentary. Access to it was not solely through texts. It was an event given public representation and celebrated as a major Christian feast day, and like any important cultural phenomenon it became a locus for various interests, some of which appropriated its details and meanings. Chaucer's parody has usually and tacitly been treated as a unique invention; yet among the possible sources of inspiration for it are earlier imitations and parodies of Pentecost, some of which he was in all likelihood acquainted with. Two of these—in the lore of Antichrist and in Dante—can be readily documented and have meanings consistent with the satirical attack in Chaucer. There may well have been others, in both learned and popular contexts, though the evidence here is much more circumstantial.

Part of the "biography" of Antichrist that developed in the course of the Middle Ages includes discussion of how he will persuade people to follow him.[12] In an influential contribution to this story, written in the middle of the tenth century, Adso of Montier-en-Der says that Antichrist will produce many "miracula," among them bringing fire down from heaven (this marvel is taken directly from Apoc. 13:13) and making the dead to rise, so that the faithful will be led to think that he may be Christ returning at the end of the world. Such miracles constitute one of three means by which Antichrist will elevate himself above the faithful: he will offer money to win over believers, instill fear in those whom money does not corrupt, and if neither of these tactics works, try to seduce his audience with "signis et miraculis." Anyone still unpersuaded will be tortured and killed.[13] Later discussions expand on this

---

[12] For a full treatment of the subject see Richard Kenneth Emmerson, *Antichrist in the Middle Ages* (Seattle: University of Washington Press, 1981).

[13] *Adso Dervensis De Ortu et tempore Antichristi,* ed. D. Verhelst, CCCM 45 (Turnhout: Brepols, 1976), pp. 24–25/67–85. These ideas, drawn from earlier descriptions of Antichrist, remain more or less intact in all the versions of Adso printed by Verhelst; some expanded versions make clear that such deceptive miracles are "mendacia" produced "per magicam artem et fantasiam" (p. 45/80–83; similarly pp. 70/92–94, 100/74–76, 121/93–96).

material and discuss examples of Antichrist's deceptive *imitatio Christi*. In late-fourteenth-century England the most accessible vernacular treatment of this set of strategic parodies was *The Prick of Conscience,* a didactic poem written midcentury that survives in more manuscripts than any other Middle English work in verse and that had enough popularity and authority to inspire a Latin translation later in the century. *The Prick* says that Antichrist will attack the faithful in four ways: through "fals prechyng," "fals miracles shewyng," "large gyftes," and finally "drede of turmentis griefe." [14] In discussing Antichrist's false miracles, it gives pride of place to what amounts to a fake Pentecost achieved through magic:

> He sal do fire fra þe heven don com,
> And þat sal be noght bot an ille spirit,
> þat out of þe ayre sal com doun tite,
> And omang his disciples don light,
> And with sere tunges til þam spek ryght,
> Als dyd til þe apostels þe haly gast
> And þat sal be in mens sight mast,
> For þa þat his disciples sal be cald
> Sal þam avant, and þam self hald
> Better of lif and to God mare dere,
> þan ever war Cristes appostels here.[15]

Antichrist's phony Pentecost is not mentioned in all medieval discussions of his deceptions, but it seems to be fairly well established, and it

[14] *The Pricke of Conscience,* ed. Richard Morris (Berlin: A. Asher, 1863), p. 117, lines 4257–60. On the poem and its distribution throughout late-medieval England, see Robert E. Lewis and Angus McIntosh, *A Descriptive Guide to the Manuscripts of the* Prick of Conscience, Medium Ævum Monographs, n.s., 12 (Oxford, Society for the Study of Mediaeval Languages and Literature, 1982). The authors say (p. 13) that Chaucer might have known *The Prick,* citing the parallels mentioned in Kate O. Petersen's *The Sources of the Parson's Tale* (Boston: Ginn, 1901). Few of these seem distinctive; in his notes to *The Parson's Tale* in *The Riverside Chaucer,* Siegfried Wenzel mentions parallels between the works in just two places (lines 253–54 and 1076–80), neither unique.

[15] Lines 4290–300. Here, and throughout its treatment of Antichrist, *The Prick* is indebted to Hugh Ripelin of Strassburg's *Compendium theologicae veritatis* 7.9: "malignum spiritum faciet super eos descendere, ut loquantur variis linguis. Spiritus enim malignus descendet in eos in conspectu hominum, sicut Spiritus sanctus descendit in Apostolos Christi. Unde jactabunt se esse meliores Apostolis Christi, qui Spiritum acceperunt in conclavi." The *Compendium* was attributed to various authors, including Albertus Magnus, and is printed in Auguste Borgnet's edition of Albert's *Opera omnia,* vol. 34 (Paris: Vivès, 1895); this passage is on p. 242.

is among those staged in the Chester Antichrist pageant.[16] Chester is the only one of the four more-or-less complete surviving cycles to have an Antichrist play, and the text is of course late. However, the Lollard *Tretise of Miraclis Pleyinge,* which dates from the late fourteenth or early fifteenth century, establishes that there were earlier enactments of this subject in England,[17] so that performance of a parodic Pentecost as part of a staging of the story of Antichrist could well have been contemporaneous with Chaucer.

Antichrist's parodic Pentecost can also be found in medieval art, where the depictions, like those of the true Pentecost, are suggestive enough of an emanation downward upon receivers to be a plausible prompt for the imaginative play of the Summoner's final scene. A series of eight illustrations of Apocalypse 13 in the *Bible moralisée* (British Library MS Harley 1527, fol. 136v) shows Antichrist's imitations of Christ's death, resurrection, ascension, and sending of the Holy Spirit. The roundel illustrating this last act includes the two-horned beast, the seven-headed beast, and rays of fire falling on the heads of followers from a mask above, a precise visualization of Apoc. 13:13 ("ignem faceret de caelo descendere in terram in conspectu hominum"). Directly below it is a traditional Pentecost scene, with rays of fire leading out of the mouth of a dove onto the apostles.[18]

The suitability of this portion of the medieval lore of Antichrist to Chaucer's designs in *The Summoner's Tale* becomes clearer when we consider his immediate social context. Identification of Antichrist, Emmerson points out, proceeded throughout the Middle Ages in two different ways. The "historical" or exegetical Antichrist was that being (man or monster) who would lead the forces of evil against Christendom in the last stage of the sixth age of history. But there was also a more generalized Antichrist, what Emmerson calls a "polemical" Antichrist, or rather

[16] See Emmerson, *Antichrist in the Middle Ages,* pp. 132–33, 183, and 284–85 n. 54, and p. 234 below. Szittya, *Antifraternal Tradition,* p. 246, discusses the parodic tradition briefly in connection with *The Summoner's Tale.*

[17] Clifford Davidson, ed., *A Tretise of Miraclis Pleyinge* (Kalamazoo, Mich.: Medieval Institute Publications, 1993), pp. 101–2, lines 294–99; the tract criticizes people who justify playing "a pley of Anticrist" or of Judgment Day on the grounds that someone might convert as a result of seeing it.

[18] See Emmerson, *Antichrist in the Middle Ages,* p. 133 and pl. 2, and for another illustration and fuller discussion, Emmerson and Herzman, *Apocalyptic Imagination,* pp. 16–18 and notes. For a later illustration of the pseudo-Pentecost, see Emmerson, *Antichrist in the Middle Ages,* pl. 9, where tongues of fire descend from a spiny demonic figure.

Antichrists: the name could be applied variously to heretics, Jews, or other people seen as opposing the church.[19] Within this polemical tradition, *mutatis mutandis,* lies the Wycliffite branding of the Pope, the friars, and other contemporary clergy as Antichrists. Of course, as Penn R. Szittya has shown, earlier antifraternal material had also incorporated eschatological motifs and thus already made associations between the friars and Antichrist, applying details from the exegetical Antichrist to their target.[20] While it seems to me that there is nothing distinctly apocalyptic about the end of *The Summoner's Tale,* Lollard readiness to call friars Antichrists must have created a discursive environment particularly hospitable to the assimilation of topoi from that tradition into antifraternal thinking, or to the inference of Antichrist in depictions of friars' behavior that bore a resemblance to his attitudes and actions.

In such a cultural climate, a text like *The Prick of Conscience*—overtly neither antifraternal nor Lollard—could easily have been read in a more tendentious way.[21] In delineating how Antichrist will secure power through "fals preching," the poem says that he will send his spokesmen throughout the world. They will "preche undir fals colour" that Christ's law is "not bot errour." They will prevent people from "expound[ing] haly writ / . . . to right undirstandyng" and instead "comend" and "defend" their leader's law. All this will lead Christians into the "errour" of believing that Christ's law will not save them (lines 4261–82). A similar description of the "deceyuabel persuasion" of Antichrist's preachers, based like *The Prick's* on the *Compendium theologicae veritatis,* appears in the entry on Antichrist in the Middle English translation of the Lollard encyclopedia known as the *Rosarium.*[22] To this depiction of how Antichrist leads people into misbelief, Wycliffite controversy in the 1380s

---

[19] Emmerson, *Antichrist in the Middle Ages,* pp. 62–73.

[20] Szittya, *Antifraternal Tradition,* passim; see also Scase, Piers Plowman *and the New Anticlericalism,* pp. 112–19.

[21] In this regard it is worth noting that four manuscripts of *The Prick* contain interpolations that include anticlerical material that is possibly Lollard or at least, as Hope Emily Allen said, "Lollardist." The additions would seem to testify to a perceived compatibility between at least some of the poem's ideas and later-fourteenth-century reformist sentiment. See Lewis and McIntosh, *A Descriptive Guide,* pp. 6–7, and Allen, *Writings Ascribed to Richard Rolle, Hermit of Hampole, and Materials for His Biography* (1927; rpt., New York: Kraus, 1966), pp. 387–94.

[22] Christina von Nolcken, ed., *The Middle English Translation of the Rosarium Theologie* (Heidelberg: Carl Winter, 1979), p. 60. See von Nolcken's note, p. 108, on the frequent use by Lollards of the *Compendium's* description of Antichrist's four strategies.

and 1390s brought implications and applications that were doubtless uncontemplated by the author of the *Prick of Conscience,* let alone the thirteenth-century Dominican Hugh of Strassburg. Antichrist's combination of erroneous preaching and authoritarian hermeneutics seems not very distant from the methods of Friar John, whose "sermon" earlier in the day is "[n]at al after the text of hooly writ" but rather according to a "glose" that will turn people's charity into profit for his own convent (*SumT,* 1789–96). Reformist criticism of such self-interested preaching and biblical interpretation is well known, and in a sense all of the third fragment of *The Canterbury Tales* engages it: first the Wife of Bath's questioning of clerical readings of various Bible passages,[23] then the Friar's easy turning of an exemplum into the kind of engaging storytelling that substituted entertainment and personal interests for strict attention to God's word, and finally the Summoner's more explicit assault on just such preaching and hypocrisy as a desecration of the original gift of tongues. The Lollard attack on clerical hegemony in preaching and interpretation was more blatant: "anticrist wolde quenche & owtlawe holy writt & make alle men dampnyd."[24]

Lollard antifraternal critique appeals often in a general way to the idea of Antichrist in order to stigmatize people and practices considered corrupt. Wyclif himself could use Antichrist simply according to what the name implies, as one "qui est Cristo contrarius in vita et doctrina."[25] In this tract he characterizes the Pope as Antichrist by listing twelve ways in which he is opposite to Christ: wealthy rather than poor, proud rather than humble, etc. He does not use the idea that the Pope/Antichrist deliberately imitates Christ for purposes of deception. But Lollardy could invoke such lore, even if the parallel drawn is metaphorical: "Freris also schewen and wittenessen in homself Anticristis miraclis," just as Lazarus and others raised by Christ "shewiden and wittenessiden Cristes miraclis." Lazarus was "verely" raised; false friars "feynen hom deede" to sin and pride but in fact are "reysid by Anticristis doying" to pride, avarice, and toleration of evil. They are dead to charity, raised to

---

[23] See Alcuin Blamires, "The Wife of Bath and Lollardy," *MÆ* 58 (1989): 224–42.

[24] *Speculum de Antichristo,* in F. D. Matthew, ed., *The English Works of Wyclif Hitherto Unprinted,* EETS, o.s., 74 (London, 1880), p. 109.

[25] *De Christo et suo adversario Antichristo,* c. 11, in Rudolf Buddensieg, ed., *John Wyclif's Polemical Works in Latin,* 2 vols. (London: Wyclif Society, 1883), 2:680. This simple etymological definition, followed by a list of differences between Christ and Antichrist, is commonplace and can be found at the beginning of Adso's *De Ortu,* p. 22.

sin—this is "Anticristis myracle."[26] If fraternal hypocrisy can be seen as evidence of one of the deceptions of Antichrist, then so might the friars' arrogant impiety. *The Prick of Conscience* says that Antichrist's followers, having received the "miracle" of the pseudo-Pentecost, will consider themselves "better of lif" and dearer to God than even the apostles; the Lollard tract just cited, conceivably allowing effect to imply cause, says that "freris falsely enhansen homself abofe Crist and his apostils."[27] The Summoner's Friar does not go quite so far, but he does assert a purity of fraternal behavior parallel to that of Christ and the apostles and as a result a superior acceptability to God (1869–84, 1904–14). In sum, important characteristics of Friar John—preaching untrue to the biblical text, hypocrisy, spiritual pride—are features that appear in the literature of both antifraternalism and Antichrist. Given the intertwinings of these discourses in contemporary religious controversy, the idea that Antichrist staged a false Pentecost could well have played a role in Chaucer's conception of the antifraternal mock-Pentecost that concludes *The Summoner's Tale*. In text, picture, or even performance he could have encountered the representation of a descent of fire on a group of evil believers, a replaying of Pentecost that ultimately serves to show how different its creator and recipients are from the Holy Spirit and the apostles; and in contemporaneous Lollard thought he would have found precedent for appealing to such false claims as a strategy of antifraternal criticism.

In Dante he would have found imagery from Acts 2 applied in a manner much closer to his own: not an effort at exact imitation like Antichrist's, but an evocation through selected details that adds depth to the satiric condemnation of cupidinous clergy. In *Inferno* 19, in which the pilgrim meets a pope punished for simony, all the clerical sinners are embedded upside down in holes in rock. Only their feet and calves are visible, and their feet are on fire:

> Le piante erano a tutti accese intrambe. . . .
> Qual suole il fiammeggiar de le cose unte
>   muoversi pur su per la strema buccia,
>   tal era lì dai calcagni a le punte.[28]

[26] Thomas Arnold, ed., *Select English Works of John Wyclif,* 3 vols. (Oxford: Clarendon Press, 1871), 3:399. Similarly, *Of Clerks Possessioners,* c. 10, in Matthew, ed., *English Works,* p. 123.

[27] Arnold, ed., *Select English Works,* 3:396.

[28] Lines 25–30. "They all had both their soles on fire. . . . As flame on oily things is wont to move only on their outer surface, so it did there, from the heels to the toes";

A number of critics read this detail as an ironic reference to the tongues of fire at Pentecost.[29] Simonists turn spiritual authority upside down by allowing it to become a matter of financial negotiation. Part of their *contrapasso* is to be "pursed" eternally in a pocket of stone that reminds them of their "pursing" of money (line 72); the fire, on the bottom of their feet rather than on their heads, causes their legs to writhe and is plausibly read as a painful reminder of their having inverted the holy purposes of the tongues of flame at Pentecost. Seeing an allusion to the descent of the Spirit here is encouraged by Dante's inclusion of other references to the Acts of the Apostles in this canto: Simon Magus is invoked in the very first line—his effort to buy the apostolic power whereby the Holy Spirit is given (Acts 8:14–24) looks back to the earlier episode in Acts 2 in which the apostles were the recipients. Later, in his chastizing of Pope Nicholas, Dante cites as an example of the apostolic separation of worldly from spiritual considerations the choosing of Matthias as the twelfth disciple to replace Judas (*Inf.* 19.94–96; cf. Acts 1:15–26). The failure of simonists to follow apostolic behavior is thus explicit in the canto and strengthens the likelihood of readers perceiving an allusion to Pentecost in the infernal flames on papal feet. And what resonance this canto would have had when read in England in a context of Wycliffite condemnation of simony, views on papal legitimacy, and regret over the Donation of Constantine. Here Chaucer would have found a feature of Pentecost used for literary goals much like those of *The Summoner's Tale*, in which the descent of the Spirit is evoked in a context both parodic and retributive to emphasize how men of the church have betrayed its meaning.[30]

---

text and translation in *The Divine Comedy: Inferno: Text and Commentary*, trans. and comm. Charles S. Singleton (Princeton, N.J.: Princeton University Press, 1980).

[29] E.g., Reginald French, "Simony and Pentecost," *Annual Report of the Dante Society* 82 (1964): 3–17; Joan Ferrante, "The Relation of Speech to Sin in the *Inferno*," *Dante Studies* 87 (1969): 33–46, esp. 40–41; Ronald B. Herzman and William A. Stephany, "'O miseri seguaci': Sacramental Inversion in *Inferno* XIX," *Dante Studies* 94 (1978): 39–65, esp. 40–41; Emmerson and Herzman, *Apocalyptic Imagination*, pp. 135–37.

[30] The explicit citation of Dante in *The Friar's Tale* and near-certain allusions in the Summoner's make the influence of the *Inferno* strongly felt in these linked stories; on how Chaucer works with it, see Richard Neuse, *Chaucer's Dante: Allegory and Epic Theater in* The Canterbury Tales (Berkeley: University of California Press, 1991), pp. 201–20. It is possible too that Chaucer would have sensed echoes of the Pentecostal tongues of fire in other cantos of the *Inferno*, particularly in the rain of fire in 14–15 and in the flame-speakers Ulysses and Guido da Montefeltro in 26–27. André Pézard argued for Pentecostal echoes in these and other instances in Dante where fiery punishment seems to be associated with distinctly intellectual or spiritual sins that abuse the gifts of the Holy Spirit; *Dante sous la pluie de feu* (Paris: J. Vrin, 1950), pp. 283–93. David Wallace observes some important parallels between *The Friar's Tale* and *Inferno* 27 in *Chaucerian*

But not all medieval parody was so morally directed. One other source of parodic Pentecosts—though here the evidence is circumstantial only—could well have been popular revelry. As a holiday period within the cycle of the church year, Pentecost was almost always, along with Easter, second only to Christmas in length: English lists of church feast-days generally designate Whitsunday and the following three days as holidays on which no one (with occasional exceptions) is to work.[31] Usually none of the other feasts involves more than a single day. Pentecost was not only a major Christian time of celebration but, as a moveable feast occurring between May 10 and June 13, the only point in the church calendar that entailed three or four feast days in a row during a period when the weather was likely to be pretty good. It was a Christian holiday at a time of the year that witnessed a good deal of festive May behavior, at least some of which appears to have become attached to it. It seems reasonable to think that its popularity as a choice for the playing of Christian plays, evidence of which will be cited later, had in part something to do with the usual sorts of negotiations that evolved over centuries between church celebrations and various forms of non-Christian entertainment and recreation.[32]

In some places at some times these different kinds of play at Pentecost intersected, either by accident or design. In 1338 in Wells, statutes promulgated by Walter de Lincoln, dean of the cathedral, prohibit vicars from participating in "ludos theatrales" during the Christmas holidays. This has a familiar ring. But in a later section the statutes not only condemn clerical play at that time but also censure "ludi theatrales" inside

---

Polity: Absolutist Lineages and Associational Forms in England and Italy (Stanford, Calif.: Stanford University Press, 1997), pp. 139–41.

[31] C. R. Cheney, "Rules for the Observance of Feast-Days in Medieval England," *Bulletin of the Institute of Historical Research* 34 (1961): 117–47, rpt. in Cheney, *The English Church and Its Laws 12th–14th Centuries* (London: Variorum Reprints, 1982). Of the fifteen lists printed here from the thirteenth and fourteenth centuries, eight—including the important 1362 legislation covering the province of Canterbury—establish both Easter and Pentecost as four-day holidays (i.e., Sunday plus the following three days); five indicate Easter and Pentecost are to be three-day holiday periods; two make the Easter holiday four days long and Pentecost three.

[32] See E. K. Chambers, *The Mediaeval Stage,* 2 vols. (London: Oxford University Press, 1903; rpt. 1967), 1:114, 141, 172–78; 2:94, 138; Charles Read Baskerville, "Dramatic Aspects of Medieval Folk Festivals in England," *SP* 17 (1920): 48–50. On the interpenetration of secular and sacred festivity within the ritual year in England, and on the methodological issues involved in determining what actually took place, see the first two chapters in Ronald Hutton, *The Rise and Fall of Merry England* (Oxford: Oxford University Press, 1994). He notes that May festivities constituted a "season" and that May-games might take place at any time from May 1 through June (p. 28).

the church made by the laity during Pentecost week and at other holiday times. The playing is characterized as mockery ("ludibria") that includes obscene gestures, and the threatened punishment is excommunication unless the dean and chapter judge that the perpetrators have made adequate satisfaction.[33] Pronouncements like this are notorious for their tantalizing vagueness; certainly one would not want to take Walter's criticisms as necessarily based on close personal observation, particularly since their wording echoes that of a statute from an earlier dean, which in turn echoes a passage from Innocent III that could be found in canon law.[34] Still, the specificity of Walter's notice of playing by the laity during Pentecost week, which is not part of the criticism of Christmas irreverence by his predecessor or by Innocent, certainly indicates that *something* was going on at that time that the dean didn't like, and it seems to be a kind of festive play that he associates with other holiday mockery. We know that much of that—whether the almost always sanctioned Boy Bishop or the almost always frowned-upon Feast of Fools—could take the form of imitation or parody of church ritual and hierarchy.

Nearly two centuries later, and more provocative, is a text from Norwich concerning performance at Pentecost. In 1527 the Guild of St. Luke appealed to city officials to legislate that other guilds share responsibility for the production of a Whitsun procession by having each one finance a pageant in it. The petition includes a description of what the Guild had been undertaking by itself:

. . . of long tyme paste the sayd Gilde of Saynt Luke yerly till nowe haue ben vsed to be kept and holden withyn the Citie aforesaid the Mondaye in Pentecoste Weke, at which daye and the daye next folowyng many and diuers disgisinges and pageauntes as well of the liff and marterdams of diuers and many hooly sayntes as also many other lyght and feyned figures and pictures of other persones and bestes, the sight of which disgisinges and pageauntes, as well yerly

---

[33] ". . . infra septimanam Pentecostes & etiam in alijs festiuitatibus fiant a laicis ludi theatrales in ecclesia"; James Stokes and Robert J. Alexander, eds., *Records of Early English Drama {REED}: Somerset Including Bath,* 2 vols. (Toronto: University of Toronto Press, 1996), 1:236–39 at 239; trans. Abigail Ann Young, 2:830–33.

[34] In *REED: Somerset* compare the passages in Walter's chapters 3 (1:236–37) and 26 (1:238–39) with the one from John de Godeley's earlier statutes (1:236). Both echo, and parts of Walter's chapter 26 quote directly from, the condemnation by Innocent III of performances in church of "ludi . . . theatrales" that include "monstra larvarum" introduced "ad ludiorum spectacula" and "debacchationes obscenas." For a recent text and translation of Innocent, see Lawrence Clopper, "*Communitas:* The Play of Saints in Late Medieval and Tudor England," *Mediaevalia* 18 (1995 for 1992): 82.

on the said Monday in Pentecost Weke in tyme of procession than goyng aboute a grete circuitt of the said Citie, as yerly the Tuysday in the same weke seruyng of the lord named the Lord of Mysrule at Tomland within the same Citie, have ben and yet is . . . covetid specially by the people of the countré. . . . [35]

JoAnna Dutka has provided the most illuminating discussion of the so-cial context and many of the details of the Guild's request, which the city of Norwich agreed to.[36] She points out that Norwich also had a fair at Pentecost, held at Tombland, an area near the cathedral, and on Pentecost Tuesday a civic procession. The Guild's contribution to the "Lord of Mysrule at Tomland," then, is quite possibly connected with the fair and this second procession rather than with a continuation of the Monday procession. Still, the combination of sacred and secular cele-bration here seems thickly intertwined. The text (at least if we follow a likely path through its syntactic forest) indicates that "disgisinges and pageauntes" occurred on both Monday and Tuesday and implies that on both days the content included serious treatment of saints as well as representations of "lyght and feyned" material. The Monday-Tuesday distinction seems to be mainly one of venue. It is not known for how many years such activity had been going on at Pentecost—Dutka thinks that probably Norwich staged religious plays on Corpus Christi day during the fifteenth century and then shifted them, perhaps as late as 1524, to Pentecost. If the Guild had been presenting Whitsun pageants only since then, its reference in 1527 to having done so "of long tyme paste" seems rather exaggerated. However far back Norwich's Pentecost celebrations went, and whatever their exact nature, the juxtaposition of procession and fair, martyrdom and levity, saints' pageants and Lord of Misrule, suggests something of the breadth of performative expression that the Whitsun holidays could accommodate.

And this appears to have been the cultural situation in Exeter at a date closer to Chaucer. The Receivers' Account Rolls indicate a payment

[35] Norman Davis, ed., *Non-Cycle Plays and Fragments,* EETS, s.s., 1 (London: Oxford University Press, 1970), p. xxvii.
[36] JoAnna Dutka, "Mystery Plays at Norwich: Their Formation and Development," *Leeds Studies in English,* n.s., 10 (1978): 107–20. See also her "The Lost Dramatic Cycle of Norwich and the Grocer's Play of the Fall of Man," *RES,* n.s., 35 (1984): 1–13. The problem for historians of the drama, which need not be resolved here in order to see the complexity of the Pentecost festivities in Norwich, is whether the pageants described by the Guild in the 1527 petition are biblical plays of the sort mentioned in other Norwich documents. For a view different from Dutka's, see Alan Nelson, *The Medieval English Stage* (Chicago: University of Chicago Press, 1974), pp. 119–37.

to minstrels for performance on Wednesday of Pentecost week in 1369, "when the men of the city displayed (their) arms before the earl of Devon."[37] This indication of a civic riding surfaces again and often in the early fifteenth century: payments to city pipers for a riding on Whit Monday in 1410 (p. 81), and similar Whitsuntide payments in 1412–13 (pp. 81–82). We learn from the Mayor's Court Roll—perhaps only because the disaffection of one citizen caused production problems—that in 1414 Exeter officials decided "for the greater convenience and honour" of the city to move the Corpus Christi play to the Tuesday of Pentecost week (pp. 357–58). Perhaps part of the motive for the change lay in the more extended holiday period at Whitsuntide: the Sunday services followed by a civic procession on Monday and then plays on Tuesday would make an attractive package for visitors. Since this is the only reference to a Corpus Christi play in Exeter, the success of the move cannot be determined. But the Pentecost holidays continued to be festive—in 1419 there were payments for bringing in the May and for playing before it (p. 86), and in 1443 for similar activities on Pentecost Monday, with added costs for linen to make an elephant (p. 97). By 1457 both the May and the elephant needed repair (p. 99). All this suggests that Whitsuntide in Exeter involved a lively combination of religious, civic, and traditional folk entertainment. May-games at Pentecost: to what extent and in what ways might the forms and images of the Christian service have become mixed with maypoles and round dances?[38]

The Pentecost holidays were a popular choice for all sorts of "playing" in England, from the cycle drama to processions (both religious and civic) to secular games to church ales, as a few examples will indicate.[39] A performance in honor of St. William of York, produced by the vicars

---

[37] *Records of Early English Drama: Devon,* ed. John M. Wasson (Toronto: University of Toronto Press, 1986), p. 72; trans. Abigail Ann Young, p. 347. Subsequent parenthetical references are to page numbers of this edition.

[38] On the early history of the maypole, for which there is little hard evidence before the fifteenth century, see Hutton, *Rise and Fall,* pp. 30 and 56–57, and Caroline Balderston Parry, "'The Maypole is Up, Now Give Me the Cup . . . ,'" *REED Newsletter* 11.1 (1986): 7–10. Unfortunately this essay is not well documented, and the quotation attributed to Chaucer on p. 8 is really from *The Chaunce of the Dice;* cf. *MED* s.v. *shaft(e* n. (2), 2(e). Hutton, p. 56, dates *The Chaunce* improbably early given its allusions to characters in *The Canterbury Tales.*

[39] For a longer inventory, see "Whitsunday" and "Whitsuntide" in the index to Ian Lancashire, *Dramatic Texts and Records of Britain: A Chronological Topography to 1558* (Toronto: University of Toronto Press, 1984), and the indexes to the various volumes published thus far in the REED series.

choral of York Minster, seems to have been presented throughout the fourteenth century during Whitsun week.[40] In 1505 a play about St. Christian was staged in Coventry at Pentecost, a "magnum ludum" memorable enough that more than two decades later witnesses could attest to a man's birth date because it came around the time of the play.[41] Whitsuntide was also a popular (though not the exclusive) time for performance in and around New Romney, Kent, during the fifteenth and sixteenth centuries.[42] In Salisbury, records from the same period indicate special parish-organized dancing days (at least in part for fund-raising purposes) during that week as well as a fair.[43] In 1446 the bailiff's accounts in Shrewsbury list expenses for wine associated with a "lusum" outside the town walls on two days of Whitsun week. Elsewhere in Shropshire, in 1637, court proceedings were brought against a man for "vnlawfully rearing and setting a summer Powle vpon the ffeast day of Pentecost last past."[44] Earlier in the seventeenth century, a man involved in a violent fracas on Pentecost Monday put the fighting in the context of the innocent "mirth musique and dansing" that had been taking place on "those holy daies tyme out of mynde."[45] These late examples, coming from a quite different social context, suggest the persistence of traditions of community revelry during the Pentecost holidays.

Pentecost was also subject to aristocratic secular appropriation, and the resulting mix of piety and self-regard would certainly have allowed for ironic notice. Chrétien de Troyes could open *Yvain* with a witty couplet about just such a combination of worldly expense and religious occasion: King Arthur, he says, held a magnificent court "a cele feste qui tant coste, / qu'an doit clamer la Pantecoste."[46] Geoffrey of Monmouth had established that Pentecost was the time of one of Arthur's most im-

---

[40] Nigel K. Tringham, "The Whitsuntide Commemoration of St. William of York: A Note," *REED Newsletter* 14.2 (1989): 10–12.

[41] *Records of Early English Drama: Coventry,* ed. R. W. Ingram (Toronto: University of Toronto Press, 1981), pp. 100, 127–28.

[42] William Tydeman, *The Theatre in the Middle Ages* (Cambridge: Cambridge University Press, 1978), pp. 204–5, 216, 241.

[43] Audrey Douglas, "'Owre Thanssynge Day': Parish Dance and Procession in Salisbury," *Folk Music Journal* 6 (1994): 600–16.

[44] *Records of Early English Drama: Shropshire,* ed. J. Alan B. Somerset, 2 vols. (Toronto: University of Toronto Press, 1994), 1:134, 56.

[45] *Records of Early English Drama: Herefordshire. Worcestershire,* ed. David N. Klausner (Toronto: University of Toronto Press, 1990), p. 74. On the ideological dimensions of holiday play in this period, see Leah S. Marcus, *The Politics of Mirth* (Chicago: University of Chicago Press, 1986).

[46] *Le Chevalier au lion (Yvain),* ed. Mario Roques, CFMA (Paris: Champion, 1965), lines 5–6.

portant feasts, and subsequent treatments of the story follow him on the date and expand on the celebrations. Whitsun becomes the customary day for the convening of the Round Table and plays an important symbolic role in romances where it is the occasion of a vision of the Holy Grail.[47] Hence for those nobles seeking to attach their lives to Arthurian tradition, the choice of Pentecost for festivities would have been natural, and this was the date that Edward III selected for his Round Table.[48] Pentecost was a favorite time for knighting ceremonies, no doubt due to realization of the religious and political value of conducting them on the day that God bestowed the Spirit on an elect group of men. There were a number in the thirteenth century; in 1306 Edward I knighted his son on that day at the famous Feast of the Swans; and a few years later Philip the Fair chose it as the beginning of a spectacular weeklong festival to celebrate the knighting of his three sons.[49] Pentecost seems as well to have been a popular time for tournaments: a thirteenth-century continental formulary letter illustrating how to invite a knight to a tournament places the event at Whitsun, presumably because the holiday was a recognized date for such festivities. In the fifteenth century, a celebration on Pentecost sponsored by the ever-partying Juan II of Castile included jousting in which the King appeared as God and his knights as the apostles.[50] The Order of the Holy Spirit, a chivalric organ-

[47] Baskerville, 50, and Szittya, *Antifraternal Tradition,* p. 238. St. Francis reportedly referred to his brothers as knights of the Round Table, but the Franciscans' choice of Pentecost for meetings of their general chapter obviously did not depend on Arthurian intermediaries. See Szittya, ibid., pp. 236–38. For a reading of the significance of Pentecost in Malory, see John F. Plummer, "*Tunc se Coeperunt non Intelligere:* The Image of Language in Malory's Last Books," in James W. Spisak, ed., *Studies in Malory* (Kalamazoo, Mich.: Medieval Institute Publications, 1985), pp. 153–71.

[48] Juliet Vale, *Edward III and Chivalry* (Woodbridge, Suffolk: Boydell Press, 1982), pp. 67–68. It is not clear whether this event ever took place; Pentecost does not otherwise appear often as a date for tournaments in Edward's reign, though the occasions of many cannot be fixed very precisely; see Vale's list, pp. 172–74.

[49] Elizabeth A. R. Brown and Nancy Freeman Regalado, "*La grant feste:* Philip the Fair's Celebration of the Knighting of His Sons in Paris at Pentecost of 1313," in Barbara A. Hanawalt and Kathryn L. Reyerson, eds., *City and Spectacle in Medieval Europe* (Minneapolis: University of Minnesota Press, 1994), pp. 56–86. A lot of the public entertainment at Philip's feast included tableaux of both religious and secular material, with some scenes involving Reynard the Fox probably serving as bourgeois counterpoint to aristocratic interests. See further Regalado, "Staging the *Roman de Renart:* Medieval Theater and the Diffusion of Political Concerns into Popular Culture," *Mediaevalia* 18 (1995 for 1992): 111–42. She cautions against reading the multiple voicings of the Paris celebration simply in terms of authority and carnivalesque subversion.

[50] Richard Barber and Juliet Barker, *Tournaments: Jousts, Chivalry and Pageants in the Middle Ages* (New York: Weidenfeld & Nicolson, 1989), pp. 136–37, 98–99; not all the chronicle accounts mention the religious costuming: see p. 218 n. 65.

ization founded in 1352 by Louis of Taranto, King of Naples and Sicily, was to meet every Pentecost, but not solely for devotional purposes: its members were to bring with them written accounts of their experiences during the previous year, the best of which would be copied into a Book of Adventures. The illuminated manuscript containing the statutes of the Order includes a scene featuring Louis enthroned, above him the familiar Pentecost iconography of a dove dispensing the grace of the Holy Spirit.[51] Self-identification with the apostles was not restricted to friars, apparently, and must have prompted comparable cynicism among the disenchanted.

Truly a range of play and ceremony at Pentecost. How much of it, if any, was precisely parodic is impossible to say, but there is reason to think that some of the celebration during the Pentecost holidays might have taken shape in directly imitative ways, given the medieval capacity for sporting with other liturgical or religious forms and practices.[52] Distinct from performance or revelry occasioned by the holiday itself, parodic treatment of the descent of the Spirit could have been part of satiric or comic reworkings of biblical texts or concepts, as in a version of the drunkard's mass that chooses a nearby passage, Acts 4:32–37, on which to base its "epistle" reading.[53] A thirteenth-century poem from

[51] Laura Kendrick, "The *Canterbury Tales* in the Context of Contemporary Vernacular Translations and Compilations," in Martin Stevens and Daniel Woodward, eds., *The Ellesmere Chaucer: Essays in Interpretation* (San Marino, Calif.: Huntington Library, 1997), pp. 281–84; for the picture of Louis, p. 282, fig. 55.

[52] On clerical parody of religious texts and ceremonies, such as drinkers' masses and encomiums on mock saints, see Martha Bayless, *Parody in the Middle Ages: The Latin Tradition* (Ann Arbor: University of Michigan Press, 1996). Chambers, *Mediaeval Stage,* 1:274–371, provides still the fullest documentation for the Feast of Fools and the Boy Bishop. On the early evidence for the *sermon joyeux,* see Jelle Koopmans and Paul Verhuyck, "Quelques sources et parallèles des sermons joyeux français des XVe et XVIe siècles," *Neophilologus* 70 (1986): 168–84. The authors establish some linkage between parody sermons and ritual festivity; Bayless finds no evidence of such linkage in the material she discusses and edits. One example of popular play with religious forms in England is the Order of Brothelingham. Known only through Bishop John de Grandisson's complaint in 1348, it seems to be a rare English analogue to the abbeys of misrule in France. It featured a mock-abbot in monastic costume and some sort of ceremony with followers worshipping ("adorantes") him to the sound of a trumpet, then turned into a money-raising venture. See *REED: Devon,* pp. 9–10, trans. pp. 322–23, and note p. 439.

[53] The parody invokes the entire book of Acts initially by referring to itself as "Lectio actuum potatorum" and beginning with the phrase "In diebus illis," which echoes the start of Acts 1:15. It visualizes the drunkards' communal poverty in light of the apostles': "In diebus illis multitudo potatorum erat in taberna, quorum corpora nuda, tunicae autem nullae, nec omnium illorum quicunque assidebant, suum aliquid esse dicebant, sed erant illis communia"; Bayless, p. 338 (trans. p. 342). Cf. Acts 4:32: "Multitudinis autem credentium erat cor unum, et anima una: nec quisquam eorum

Arras imagines an establishment of abbeys of fools, one each for men and women of the town, and the treatment appears to be playing with Whitsun themes.[54] At the least, it seems fair to say that the literary uses of Pentecost—in texts as varied as the Arras insult-poem, *The Prick of Conscience,* and *The Divine Comedy*—and the variety of performative activity on Pentecost—from irreverent *ludi theatrales* to knighting ceremonies to biblical pageants—would have invited recognition that Pentecost was not just an event but also a sign, something invoked for ends other than itself, ends involving motives or purposes not always directly aligned with its historical meaning or traditional religious significance. Such awareness not only creates a climate for parodic invention but complicates assumptions about exactly what point of view is to guide understanding of the purpose of such invention.

III

Is it possible even that aspects of the formal observation of Pentecost, in Chaucer's eyes, invited parody or became in some sense self-parodic? Much of what follows involves evidence that substantially postdates

---

quae possidebat, aliquid suum esse dicebat, sed erant illis omnia communia." The rest of the reading is less close verbally. There is a great deal of *mouvance* in the texts of drunkards' masses; for versions of this passage in related manuscripts, see Paul Lehmann, *Die Parodie im Mittelalter,* 2d ed. (Stuttgart: Anton Hiersemann, 1963), p. 236, and for its incorporation into the gamblers' mass in the *Carmina burana,* p. 248. I think there is a distinctly antifraternal evocation of John 20:22 and perhaps also of Acts 2:2 in Gower's ironic mention of the divine *spiritus* when he describes the rather heavier breathing of friars: "Spiritus vt domini, sic frater spirat vbique, / Et venit ad lectum quando maritus abest"; *Vox clamantis* 4.18, lines 835–36, in *The Complete Works of John Gower,* ed. G. C. Macaulay, vol. 4 (Oxford: Clarendon Press, 1902), p. 189. For a similar use of biblical parody (though not of Pentecost) in a satiric narrative, see Roy J. Pearcy, "Realism and Religious Parody in the Fabliaux: Watriquet de Couvin's 'Les Trois Dames de Paris,'" *Revue belge de philologie et d'histoire* 50 (1972): 744–54.

[54] The "carité" of St. Oison names about a dozen men foolish enough to be members; two of them are so eager to be mayor of the group that the only way to decide the issue is to draw lots (cf. Acts 1:23–26); their regular yearly meeting, in a rhyme that echoes Chrètien's, is held "devant Pentecouste" because that is the time when fat ganders "plus couste." Throughout the poem the disputatiousness and competitiveness of the Arras citizens contrasts implicitly with the standard image of the peacefulness of the apostles sitting and praying at Pentecost; their "carités [confraternity/charity] detrie" (line 52) in more ways than one. See Roger Berger, ed., *Littérature et société arrageoises au XIIIe siècle: Les chansons et dits artésiens* (Arras: Commission Départementale des Monuments Historiques du Pas-de-Calais, 1981), pp. 184–89. See further Joseph A. Dane, "Parody and Satire in the Literature of Thirteenth-Century Arras, Part II," *SP* 81 (1984): 119–44.

Chaucer, but I think it deserves a hearing for what it can suggest about late-fourteenth-century practice. If Chaucer's understanding of Pentecost included experiences beyond the textual, then among the sources of the end of *The Summoner's Tale* must surely lie his own encounters with its representations. If in his time they were at all like what we can document more fully for the fifteenth and sixteenth centuries, there is good reason to believe that on Pentecost he witnessed physical displays in church of the descent of the Holy Spirit and that outside church he could have seen somewhat similar stagings of this event in vernacular religious drama or other public performance.

Three of the four surviving Middle English cycles have Pentecost pageants. The only one that does not, Towneley, is missing twelve leaves at the point in the manuscript where a play on that subject is quite likely to have appeared.[55] A list of pageants in the Norwich cycle, from which only the Grocers' Play survives, indicates that for at least some time a play on "The Holy Gost" was its final episode.[56] E. K. Chambers inferred from a story in the *Hundred Merry Tales* that in the sixteenth century the Coventry cycle must have included a Pentecost play that, like the surviving Chester pageant, incorporated material on the creation of the Apostles' Creed. The jest concerns a priest who explained the twelve articles of the Creed to his congregation and added that if they wanted more "suffycyent auctoryte" on this topic they could see all twelve "playd" in the Coventry Corpus Christi play. Alexandra F. Johnston, partly on the basis of this story, goes a step beyond Chambers to argue that the Coventry plays might have formed a sequence based on the Creed rather than on biblical history.[57] If so, the pageants would probably have enacted the traditional myth of origins of the Creed as the

[55] Martin Stevens, "The Missing Parts of the Towneley Cycle," *Speculum* 45 (1970): 254–65. Stevens argues, on the basis of Towneley's affinities with the York cycle, that the missing material was probably three Mary plays and possibly also a Pentecost pageant. He argues that the excision was deliberate Reformation suppression of the material on Mary. In that regard, the York Pentecost is the only one of the three surviving pageants to include Mary among the apostles; before the descent of the Spirit her confidence contrasts with some of the apostles' fears, and after it she is the first to speak on its significance. If the Towneley texts were close to York's at this point, the Reformation censoring plausibly argued by Stevens would have wanted to delete a "Marian" treatment of Pentecost as well as the immediately following pageants on her death, appearance to Thomas, and assumption and coronation.

[56] Davis, ed., *Non-Cycle Plays and Fragments*, pp. xxix–xxx.

[57] Chambers, *Mediaeval Stage*, 2:358, 423; Alexandra F. Johnston, "What if No Texts Survived? External Evidence for Early English Drama," in Marianne G. Briscoe and John C. Coldewey, eds., *Contexts for Early English Drama* (Bloomington: Indiana University Press, 1989), p. 11.

product of inspiration from the descent of the Holy Spirit. In short, Pentecost seems to have been a popular topic for representation in English vernacular stagings of Christian history.

Chester's is the most extensive surviving Pentecost text, perhaps appropriately so since the fullest manuscripts of the cycle all date from a period when performance of the plays had shifted from Corpus Christi day to Whitsuntide and expanded to a three-day sequence.[58] What can we gather about the representation of Pentecost in the pageant? After the apostles discuss Christ's promise to send the Holy Ghost to them, they kneel in prayer and sing *Veni, creator spiritus.* "[I]n heaven" (152+ SD) the Son speaks to the Father, who promises that "my Ghooste to them shall appere" (164) and that "when my Ghoost ys them upon" (212) the apostles will be infused with steadfastness and power. The stage direction makes clear that the descent is to be represented visually:

Then God shall send out the Holy Spirit in the form of fire, and as it is sent, two angels shall sing the antiphon "Accipie Spiritum Sanctum. . . ." And as they sing they shall throw fire upon the apostles. And when this is done, the (first) angel in Heaven shall speak.[59]

The apostles indicate that they can "see" the Holy Ghost on them (256, 264), and the pageant then moves into their articulation of the various articles of the Creed, after which they agree to depart and preach the faith. It is reasonable to think that performance of this text would have included both upper and lower playing places, with some form of physical manifestation of the fire sent down from one level to the other. At the moment of reception the apostles are kneeling, and while a circular arrangement is not hinted at, it would be one possible configuration.

The N-town Proclamation for its Pentecost pageant intimates a visually explicit representation, noting that the Holy Spirit appeared to the gathered apostles "ful veruently / With brennyng fere thyrlyng here brest, / Procedyng from hevyn trone" (lines 496–98). The pageant itself,

---

[58] References are to line numbers and stage directions in R. M. Lumiansky and David Mills, eds., *The Chester Mystery Cycle,* 2 vols., EETS, s.s., 3 (London: Oxford University Press, 1974), 1:378–95. A brief summary of the history of the cycle is in David Mills, ed., *The Chester Mystery Cycle. A New Edition with Modernised Spelling* (East Lansing, Mich.: Colleagues Press, 1992), pp. xiii–xvi.

[59] Line 238+SD: "Tunc Deus emittet Spiritum Sanctum in spetie ignis, et in mittendo cantent duo angeli antiphonam 'Accipie Spiritum Sanctum. . . .' Et cantando projecient ignem super apostolos. Finitoque Angelus in caelo dicat." Mills, ed., *Chester Mystery Cycle,* p. 367; and see his remarks on the staging, pp. 357–58.

while very brief, implies something similar. The initial stage direction indicates that the apostles are to be kneeling and that the Holy Spirit is to descend on them.[60] Their spoken reactions, which mention being filled with a sweetness impossible to describe (lines 7–8), give less intimation of a physical manifestation of the Spirit than do those of the Chester apostles, but some such stage effect is not inconsistent with the text, and the sweetness, as we will see below, could be communicated physically through incense. Like the N-town pageant, the text of the York Pentecost neither urges nor prohibits a descent made visible to the audience. There the apostles and Mary await the coming of the Spirit. The only stage direction indicates that an angel then sings the Pentecost hymn *Veni, creator spiritus,* after which Mary says that the "high hali gaste" has now come to the apostles (lines 105–6), and Peter speaks of the Spirit's coming as a sudden light bright as the sun (lines 111, 115–16).[61] This brightness might or might not have been an actual stage effect; certainly nothing as distributive as the scene in Chester is implied.

The Chester pageant of Antichrist no doubt entailed a representation of his phony Pentecost. Speaking to four kings, Antichrist promises that he will "fulfill Whollye Wrytte" through his death and resurrection (line 113), after which "will I sitt in greate renowne / and my ghooste send to you downe / in forme of fyre full soone" (lines 130–32). He then manufactures these events, upon his ascension says, "I will nowe send my holye ghooste" (line 193), and according to the stage direction does so: "Tunc emittet spiritum. . . ." Each king remarks, "This holye ghoost is in me pight" (line 198, and see note 2:338). Since the central concern of this section of the play is Antichrist's own persuasively "staged" *imitatio Christi,* his version would most likely reproduce the representation of the descent of the Spirit in the Pentecost pageant, which as we have seen consists of fire being thrown down.

Could an enactment of Pentecost (or Antichrist's parody of it) have been among the factors contributing to Chaucer's image of that event in the "eyen of his mynde"?[62] The English examples certainly indicate vis-

---

[60] Stephen Spector, ed., *The N-town Play,* 2 vols., EETS, s.s., 11 (Oxford: Oxford University Press, 1991), 1:385: *"Apostoli dicant genuflectentes; Spiritus Sanctus descendat super eos, et cetera."*

[61] Richard Beadle, ed., *The York Plays* (London: Edward Arnold, 1982), pp. 380–85.

[62] *MLT* 552, cited and discussed in the context of the medieval linkage of image, memory, and thought by V. A. Kolve, *Chaucer and the Imagery of Narrative* (Stanford, Calif.: Stanford University Press, 1984), p. 20.

ual effects in some cases, and sound effects are known to have been a part of continental productions of Pentecost pageants.[63] Recent scholarship on the cycle drama has emphasized the lateness of the existing manuscripts and how risky it is to read these texts "backward" as indicative of earlier performance or even of the concept of a cycle drama in the fourteenth century. Still, there seems little doubt that some versions of a biblical drama existed in Chaucer's time, and his allusions to it both help delineate what did exist and reveal his responsiveness to the form.[64] He could well have viewed stagings of Pentecost that attempted to represent, with greater or lesser success, the mighty wind and the tongues of fire mentioned in Acts 2. And these stagings might have been within the church as well as outside it.

Of late date but large suggestiveness is William Lambarde's recollection in the sixteenth century of seeing as a child a Pentecost service in St. Paul's Cathedral, London, "wheare the comynge downe of the *Holy Gost* was set forthe by a white Pigion, that was let to fly out of a Hole" in the roof, from which also descended "a longe Censer . . . breathynge out over the whole Churche and Companie a most pleasant Perfume."[65] The stink from Thomas's hole that would descend on the friars is the antithesis of the sweet smell that descended from a hole above in St. Paul's. Whether it was prompted in part by Chaucer's memory of a similar practice at Pentecost is, obviously, sheer conjecture—but not unwarranted conjecture. Comparable spectacle at St. Paul's during Whitsun-

---

[63] Peter Meredith and John E. Tailby, eds., *The Staging of Religious Drama in Europe in the Later Middle Ages: Texts and Documents in English Translation* (Kalamazoo, Mich.: Medieval Institute Publications, 1983), pp. 148–49, 158. I thank Clifford Davidson for this and other references.

[64] Alexandra F. Johnston, "Chaucer's Records of Early English Drama," *REED Newsletter* 13, no. 2 (1988): 13–20. On more general artistic affinities between *The Canterbury Tales* and the drama, see John M. Ganim, *Chaucerian Theatricality* (Princeton, N.J.: Princeton University Press, 1990), pp. 31–55. For tantalizing but very general indications of what might have been available to Chaucer, see two passages in L. C. Hector and Barbara F. Harvey, eds. and trans., *The Westminster Chronicle* (Oxford: Clarendon Press, 1982), pp. 94, 476: in August 1384, the clerks of London presented at Skinners Well a "ludum valde sumptuosum" lasting five days; in July 1391, they created a "ludum satis curiosum," this one four days long, "in quo tam Vetus quam Novum Testamentum oculariter ludendo monstrabant." For other evidence on the London cycle, see Lancashire, *Dramatic Texts,* p. 113. The York plays date from at least 1376 in some form, and the *Ordo Paginarum* of 1415 establishes that by that date one of the pageants involved "Maria duo angeli xj apostoli & spiritus sanctus descendens super eos & iiij^or Iudei admirantes"; *Records of Early English Drama: York,* ed. Alexandra F. Johnston and Margaret Dorrell, 2 vols. (Toronto: University of Toronto Press, 1979), 1:23.

[65] Cited in Chambers, *Mediaeval Stage,* 2:66; also in Atchley, Young, and Wickham, notes 66 and 68 below.

tide—in this case an angel descending from above with a censer—can be documented from the earlier fifteenth century, including a performance witnessed by Henry V after he returned from Agincourt. The *Liber Albus,* compiled in 1419, indicates that similar ceremonies were a longstanding custom. It describes in some detail impressive processions on the Monday, Tuesday, and Wednesday of Pentecost week, in which the mayor of London and other dignitaries marched to St. Paul's, starting from a different church in the city on each day, entered the cathedral's west door, and, after being censed from above by an angel, proceeded to the altar. Censing seems to have been popular in English churches on Whitsunday from the thirteenth century on, particularly at the singing of *Veni, creator spiritus.*[66] An account book from Lincoln Cathedral indicates payment in 1395–96 for "repair of ropes and other items required for a dove and an angel on the feast of Pentecost."[67] Karl Young notes that there was not much "impersonation and drama" in the liturgical handling of Pentecost, but at the same time he describes the various ways in which the descent of the Spirit was materially represented in churches throughout Europe in the Middle Ages—the dropping down of flowers, herbs, wafers, wads of tow set afire, or real or fabricated doves. In the sixteenth century a church in Halle featured the lowering of a circle of candles around a dove.[68] Young may have been disappointed in the failure of Pentecost to yield liturgical plays of the sort that were generated around the nativity and the resurrection, but perhaps there was less felt need for "impersonation and drama" when such striking representations of the central event of Pentecost, the de-

[66] E. G. C. F. Atchley, *A History of the Use of Incense in Divine Worship* (London: Longmans, Green, 1909), pp. 300–305; Clifford Davidson, "Heaven's Fragrance," in Davidson, ed., *The Iconography of Heaven* (Kalamazoo, Mich.: Medieval Institute Publications, 1994), pp. 118–19. The source of the information on what Henry saw is a short passage from Thomas Elmham's Latin verse life: "Pluribus ornatis solemnibus organa cantant, / Angelus a celso turificando venit"; Atchley, ibid., p. 304. *Liber Albus* in H. T. Riley, ed., *Munimenta Gildhallae Londoniensis,* Rolls Series 12 (London, 1859), 1:29–30 (". . . angelo desuper misso thurificante"). On the suppression of Pentecost effects at St. Paul's in the sixteenth century, see Eamon Duffy, *The Stripping of the Altars* (New Haven, Conn.: Yale University Press, 1992), pp. 459–60.

[67] Nelson, *Medieval English Stage,* p. 101: "Item soluti J. Tetford pro reparacione cordarum & aliorum necessariorum pro columba & angelo in festo Pentecostali, ixd."

[68] Karl Young, *The Drama of the Medieval Church,* 2 vols. (Oxford: Clarendon Press, 1933; rpt., 1967), 1:489–91; see also Glynne Wickham, *Early English Stages 1300 to 1660. Volume Three: Plays and Their Makers to 1576* (New York: Columbia University Press, 1981), pp. 30–31. In addition, Young prints some sixteenth-century anti-Catholic material that includes attacks on the visual and aural representations of Pentecost; see 2:531, 537–38.

scent of the Spirit, could be achieved simply with props. There is no evidence for Pentecost stagings in England as elaborate as the outdoor performance in Vicenza in 1379, which according to a chronicle account included large, brightly colored representations of doves descending on a cord, along with sound effects, to signify the coming of the Holy Spirit.[69] But England appears to have shared with Italy and France at least some of the celebratory and dramatizing impulses that attached themselves to the holiday.[70] Chaucer, I assume, attended Pentecost services, and he certainly knew of stagings of biblical history. The exact nature of these performative Pentecosts may not be documented, but there is good reason to believe that they would have provided him with material representations of the descent of the Holy Spirit, experiences that perhaps helped lead, in one way or another, to his creation of a perverse Pentecost as a comic punishment for pseudoapostles—and possibly also as a vehicle for criticism of certain church practices.

IV

The central import of the final scene of *The Summoner's Tale* is antifraternal—to show through parody that friars have debased Christian apostolic ideals. But the scene is rich in implication beyond this immediate satiric goal. Pentecost in Chaucer's experience was a complex cultural practice, one whose images and ideas allowed, as we have seen, for enactment or appropriation in possibly quite disparate ways. Some of those ways were manifesting themselves in England in the late 1380s and 1390s in Lollard controversy, or, more accurately, in the varied attitudes toward a variety of religious and social issues that can be roughly categorized at either pole as orthodox and Lollard. Any effort at thinking about

---

[69] Alessandro D'Ancona, *Origini del teatro italiano,* 2d ed., vol. 1 (Turin: Ermanno Loescher, 1891), pp. 98–100.

[70] In Italy there are records of early-thirteenth-century entertainments near Padua on Pentecost, which later in the century took on religious dimensions, and of dramatic *representationes* in Cividale at the turn of the fourteenth century, which included a Pentecost play within a limited biblical sequence, played on three days beginning at Pentecost; see D'Ancona, *Origini del teatro* 1:88–91, and also for the Cividale accounts, Chambers, *Mediaeval Stage,* 2:77–78. For clerical processions at Pentecost in two French towns, see Margit Sahlin, *Etudes sur la carole médiévale* (Uppsala: Almqvist & Wiksells, 1940), pp. 150–51; one, at Chalon-sur-Saône, was clearly mimetic, involving a circle dance around a dome of some sort in the courtyard of the cloister while singing responses from the Pentecost service. For larger lay processions at Echternach, Luxembourg, and Liège on Pentecost Tuesday, see Sahlin, ibid., pp. 160–63.

the historical meanings of the end of *The Summoner's Tale* needs to acknowledge that context.[71]

One of the story's implications within that perspective has been argued previously: Roy Peter Clark contends that the parody of Pentecost alludes to "the controversy surrounding the translation of the Bible into English," an important issue for Wycliffites opposed to orthodox control of access to and interpretation of the divine word. Clark cites a Lollard argument that the gift of tongues at Pentecost proves that God wanted his word communicated in "al maner langagis to teche the puple Goddis lawe therby."[72] Clerical insistence on Latin, in this tract imputed specifically to friars, violates the purpose of the descent of the Spirit. Thus, Friar John's proprietary use of the Bible works against the apostolic gift of tongues, and the "soun" of Thomas's fart (lines 2151, 2226, 2233, 2273) points to fraternal refusal to understand the "sownd" from heaven signifying that the "apostlis hadden grace of God to speke his wordis."[73] Texts from the first decade of the fifteenth century, not cited by Clark,

[71] The resurgence of interest in Wyclif and Lollardy and the demonstration of the extensive production and circulation of Lollard materials in the late fourteenth century have led to a new interest in Chaucer's relationship to the ideas and the controversies. The central work on the movement, Anne Hudson's *The Premature Reformation* (Oxford: Clarendon Press, 1988), deals with Chaucer in a chapter on "The Context of Vernacular Wycliffism," pp. 390–445, and stresses that at that time there could be "open" expression of opinion on a variety of concerns without immediate pigeonholing as "pro- or anti-Wycliffite" (p. 398). Among many specific studies that wrestle with the question of Lollard influence on *The Canterbury Tales,* or Chaucer's response to issues generated by Lollard critique, see Blamires, "The Wife of Bath and Lollardy" (n. 23 above); Alan Fletcher, "The Preaching of the Pardoner," *SAC* 11 (1989): 15–35; Lynn Staley's chapter on Chaucer in Aers and Staley, *The Powers of the Holy* (n. 3 above), esp. pp. 194–217; Paul Strohm, "Chaucer's Lollard Joke: History and the Textual Unconscious," *SAC* 17 (1995): 23–42. In "The Summoner and the Abominable Anatomy of Antichrist," *SAC* 18 (1996): 91–117, Fletcher argues persuasively that one of the details in the Summoner's *Prologue* (the association of friars specifically with the "tayl" of the devil) is Lollard-inflected and that certain antifraternal themes in the narrative were of particular currency due to Lollard polemic.

[72] Clark, "Wit and Witsunday," pp. 48 and 51, quoting *De officio pastorali,* in Matthew, ed., *English Works,* pp. 429–30; the other important Lollard invocation of Pentecost occurs in a defense of translating the Bible into English; Clark, ibid., p. 52. We know that in the latter portion of the fourteenth century, advocating the Englishing of the Bible was not a uniquely Lollard position, but once Wycliffism became attached to the cause, even before the issuing of Arundel's Constitutions in 1409, the controversy seems to have become more charged. See Anne Hudson, "The Debate on Bible Translation, Oxford 1401" and "Lollardy: The English Heresy?" in *Lollards and Their Books* (London: Hambledon Press, 1985), pp. 67–84, 141–63; on 152 she cites other Lollard material invoking the apostles' use of many languages.

[73] From the sermon for Pentecost in the Lollard sermon cycle; Anne Hudson, ed., *English Wycliffite Sermons,* vol. 1 (Oxford: Clarendon Press, 1983), p. 598.

establish further the politicizing of Pentecost in debate on Bible translation: if for the Lollards it is a story about universal access, for establishment friars it is a story about hierarchical selectivity in distributing
knowledge. The Franciscan William Butler, completely opposed to vernacularization, observes that Christ's law was not presented in a written
form at Pentecost; the Holy Spirit brought it directly into the hearts of
the apostles, and they converted others "per linguas eorum." God wants
the laity to hear Christian doctrine through authorized speakers, not
read it independently. The Dominican Thomas Palmer, taking a somewhat less absolute position, grants that with the gift of tongues the
apostles preached to everyone, but only what was necessary for salvation;
that which is more "curiosa" and "ardua" in Scripture, or that which
might lead into error, is not appropriate for anyone except clerics.[74]

Of course, arguing that only certain biblical passages need to be available in the vernacular entails prior interpretive distinctions between
what is necessary to the faith and what is not. But who can guarantee
the correctness of judgment or the purity of motive in a cleric with the
power to make those distinctions? *The Summoner's Tale* exposes Friar
John's abuse of such power when he describes his sermon earlier in the
day: it avoided what is "hard" in "hooly writ" and presented instead his
own "glose," a procedure he justifies by noting briefly that the "lettre
sleeth."[75] Given the polemical use of Pentecost in debate on translating
the Bible, and given Chaucer's antifraternal context, the parodic replacement of the Spirit's gift of communicative power with a base, meaningless sound seems to convey criticism of any position that would endorse
Friar John's access to God's word but not that of Thomas or his wife.
Such a reading of the final scene would be consistent with Chaucer's
career-long commitment to writing in English and with his defense of

---

[74] Margaret Deanesly, *The Lollard Bible* (Cambridge: Cambridge University Press,
1920; rpt., 1966), pp. 409–10 for Butler, p. 436 for Palmer, who says that the apostles
"in omni lingua praedicaverunt omnibus quae erant eis necessaria saluti." On these texts,
see Hudson's articles cited in n. 72; she is not certain of Palmer's authorship of the
second.

[75] *SumT* 1789–96. A Lollard tract on how to read and study the Bible says, "be not
to moche aferid of obiectiouns of enemyes seyynge that *the lettere sleeth*," and it goes on
to explain what Paul means by that phrase; Deanesly, ibid., pp. 452–53. On the play
with letter and spirit in *The Summoner's Tale*, see, in addition to many of the works cited
in n. 2 above, Neuse, *Chaucer's Dante*, pp. 212–20, and John A. Alford, "Scriptural Testament in *The Canterbury Tales*: The Letter Takes its Revenge," in David Lyle Jeffrey, ed.,
Chaucer and Scriptural Tradition (Ottawa: University of Ottawa Press, 1984), pp.
197–203.

translation in the Prologue to the *Astrolabe,* which reasons in much the
same way as the Lollard and other texts that defend translating the Bible
into English.[76]

I think the parody also invites, by its audacious fusion of the spiritual
and the scatological, reflection on the act of representing Pentecost itself. So might any representation, it has been argued; but I focus here
on a historicized reflection arising out of the particular circumstances of
the 1390s. One of the most prominent of the Lollard ideas circulating
then was its criticism of images, usually centered on sculpted or painted
likenesses of the cross or the saints. Often the attack on images was
linked with attack on pilgrimages—going to a shrine in order to worship a relic or a statue of a saint. Lollards argued in part that people
confused the representation and the reality, that they prayed idolatrously
to the image rather than to what it stood for. Orthodox defenders argued
that people did not (usually) make such confusions, that images merely
helped prompt reflection on a person or event (the crucifixion, say), and
that reflection prompted devotion.[77] A related Lollard concern was that
some images, traditionally endorsed as books for the unlettered, would
mislead in one way or another in matters of belief or understanding.
One means of error is the historically untrue representation of events
like the crucifixion in ways that suggest the cross was adorned or Christ
lavishly dressed. Similarly decorated "ymagis of pore apostlis of Crist"
falsely intimate that they lived in a wealthy and self-indulgent manner—the exact "contrarie" of how they really lived—and thus wrongly
"counfort men in wordly pride and vanyte."[78] Even more serious doctrinally was the representation of abstract or spiritual realities as visible
forms, the sort of anthropomorphizing that Chaucer's Friar indulges in
when he describes how fraternal prayers shoot right up to "Goddes eres
two" (line 1941). Lollardy cited as the chief example of this mistake the

[76] See Ralph Hanna III's valuable essay, "The Difficulty of Ricardian Prose Translation: The Case of the Lollards," *MLQ* 51 (1990): 319–40, and my chapter on Chaucer
in David Wallace, ed., *The Cambridge History of Medieval English Literature* (Cambridge:
Cambridge University Press, 1999), pp. 580–84.

[77] On the debate, see W. R. Jones, "Lollards and Images: The Defense of Religious
Art in Later Medieval England," *Journal of the History of Ideas* 34 (1973): 27–50; Margaret
Aston, "Lollards and Images," in *Lollards and Reformers: Images And Literacy in Late Medi-
eval England* (London: Hambledon Press, 1984), pp. 135–92; Hudson, *Premature Refor-
mation,* pp. 301–9 and passim. Aston delineates the varied positions possible within
Lollardy on this point.

[78] Anne Hudson, ed., *Selections from English Wycliffite Writings* (Cambridge: Cambridge
University Press, 1978), p. 84.

depiction of the Trinity as a bearded old man, a young Christ on or with a cross, and a dove.[79] This criticism would certainly apply to late-medieval visualizations of Pentecost—whether in an illuminated manuscript, in church, or in a dramatic performance—where the Holy Spirit was often depicted as a dove or where material extraneous to the details of Acts 2 was inserted.

The problem of representing Pentecost would have been a particularly interesting one given the nature of the controversy. On the one hand, there is no dove mentioned in Acts 2 (in contrast to Luke 3) and so any such depiction would be historically misleading if it were taken to indicate the presence of the Spirit in the form of a dove at the event. But Pentecost is one of those instances in the Bible where divinity expresses itself through material signs, in this case a sound like that of wind and tongues as of fire, and so it could be used as part of a defense of images, an example of God's own recognition of the propriety of trying to communicate invisible meanings through perceptible means. But in that case, critics of images could say, tongues of fire should be represented by tongues of fire, not by the rays or lines that appear in pictures nor by anything that might be thrown down from the top of a church or the upper stage of a pageant wagon. Where in a manuscript illumination of Pentecost that depicts both a dove and a somewhat verisimilar distribution of flame does the symbolic stop and the mimetic start? Where is the dividing line in an illumination that depicts a dove, rays, and then tongues of flame?[80] A Lollardist critique of pictures like these would not seem to be simply a result of naive literalism, a failure to understand the nature of images; it would point rather to inaccuracies and inconsistencies within the representations themselves. Further, even if the possibility

---

[79] Aston, "Lollards and Images," pp. 139, 165; Hudson, *Selections,* p. 83, also p. 153 n. to line 97; von Nolcken, *Middle English Translation,* pp. 99–100. The eighth of the twelve Lollard conclusions promulgated in 1395 mentions the "ymage usuel of Trinite" as the most "abhominable" example of how images induce error in belief. In response, Roger Dymmok points out that in the Bible the persons of the Trinity sometimes appear in various visible forms, citing the example in Luke 3:22, where the Holy Spirit descends upon Christ at his baptism in the form of a dove. The dove is thus an appropriate image for the Holy Spirit, in his view, and any misunderstanding that the Spirit *is* a dove is the responsibility of the person making the inference, not of the representation itself; H. S. Cronin, ed., *Liber contra XII errores et hereses Lollardorum* (London: Wyclif Society, 1922), pp. 180, 199–200.

[80] For the first case, see Schiller (n. 9 above), pls. 30–31 (both of English provenance), and her comments, p. 22; for the second, pl. 72, Andrea da Firenze's fresco in the Spanish Chapel of Santa Maria Novella, completed in the 1360s, before Chaucer's visit to Florence.

of misinterpretation ought not foreclose expression (otherwise, as Dymmok pointed out, misinterpretation of the Bible would mean that the Bible should be suppressed), one can still wonder about the wisdom of certain kinds of representation that might be more likely to prompt misinterpretation than others or to generate a sense of awkward disjunction between immediate visual effect and intended meaning. Suppose Chaucer, acquaintance of more than one Lollard knight, did witness doves flying around a church on Pentecost, or a large censer swinging down from the roof. Suppose he saw a Whitsun pageant in which the descent of the Spirit was manifested by the strewing of scraps of red material or rose petals. What *would* his reaction have been?

The issue extends beyond the question of images per se to a related and more general set of Lollard concerns about the prevalence of material phenomena in the expression of religious belief. Wyclif was bothered not only by what he saw as people's responses to sculpted or painted images but also by their tendency to

indulge the senses: the sight, in costly spectacles of church ornaments; the hearing, with bells, organs, and new ways of telling the hours of the day by marvellous striking of bells; and sensuous objects are provided by which all the senses are moved in irreligious ways.[81]

The description of the material church in the *Lanterne of Lizt* speaks out against all forms of adornment in churches, citing and translating Jerome, who says that "boordis. lanterns. sencers. pannes. cuppis" and other precious objects may have been appropriate to the temple in the old dispensation, but not to the church under Christ. No one today should take pride in stone or wood, glass or plaster, "chalise booke or vestment" or any other ornament.[82] Lollard criticism of excess in ornamentation does not usually treat in much detail the problem of excess in the performance of church services, but there are enough general remarks to indicate disapproval of appeals to the senses in liturgical practices as well as in possessions, usually in the form of hostility to overly subtle music, especially when it gets in the way of understanding the meaning of words. One Lollard sermon condemns not only expensive

---

[81] From *De mandatis divinis;* trans. Aston, p. 139.

[82] Lilian M. Swinburn, ed., *The Lanterne of Lizt,* EETS, o.s., 151 (London: 1947), pp. 37, 41. On the idea of the material church, see Hudson, *Premature Reformation,* pp. 318–21, and for other Lollard criticism of ornamentation, pp. 321–22.

churches and their "ournementis" but also churches that feature a "multitude of syngeris and gay chaunteris," the "heerynge of manye masses," and other similar "signes of hoolinesse." [83]

If magnificent censers are a needless waste of money, what about the act of censing itself? Is it one of those "signes of hoolinesse" that Wycliffite critique would judge as hypocritical and evasive of the serious business of spreading true Christian belief? Dymmok, defending against Lollard censure of making offerings to saints' bones (a corollary in the *Twelve Conclusions* to the criticism of images), mentions censing as an appropriate activity because it is a sign of honor to divinity. Apparently he felt that the attack on images and offerings to relics in the *Conclusions* included implicitly an attack on other sensory appeals involved in devotional masses. A 1389 description of how a Lollard celebrated Mass, which notes his omission of certain prayers, may indicate his opposition to censing, and a later list of questions to be asked of people suspected of Lollardy includes one on the licitness of "thurificaciones" among other church practices. [84] If we look for censing in Chaucer, we find it dramatized only once: for Absolon, "sensynge" of the parish wives appears to be a kind of foreplay (*MilT* 3339–43); for Chaucer's readers, the placing of that liturgical activity in the hands of a singing, dancing, Herod-impersonating parish clerk may suggest that its contribution to worship is similarly stagey. Since some Pentecost services seem to have involved a particularly spectacular display of censing, and since censing appears to have been for some reformists evidence that the church preferred outward show to inward reflection, the repugnant odor of Thomas's fart would be a quite precise inversion of contemporary practice. Chaucer's emphasis on the distribution of the odor—each "nose" to the spoke or nave (lines 2263–66) in order to receive the "savour" (line 2226), the "stynk" (line 2274), the "smel" (line 2284)—has at least as plausible a referent in the late-medieval performance of Pentecost as in its evocation of the sweet smell of the holocausts at the Jewish Pentecost feast. [85]

The complex social meanings of Pentecost make judgments about the

---

[83] Gloria Cigman, ed., *Lollard Sermons,* EETS, o.s., 294 (Oxford, 1989), p. 42.

[84] Dymmok (n. 79 above), p. 196; Hudson, *Lollards and their Books,* p. 117.

[85] On which see Szittya, *Antifraternal Tradition,* p. 234. Parody of censing seems to have been an element in continental celebrations of the Feast of Fools; see Chambers 1.286–87 (censing with pudding and sausage at Beauvais), 289 (censing "preposterе" at St. Omer), 294 (censing with the foul-smelling smoke of old shoe leather, according to the University of Paris Faculty of Theology in 1445), 317–18 (a seventeenth-century Antibes reference to blowing the ashes out of censers, sometimes on people's heads).

effects of Chaucer's invocation of it difficult. I think that some of the implications of his parody take its antifraternal critique in directions related specifically to contemporary debate on the vernacular, on church display, and on how best to communicate that which lies beyond the sensory, and that in some of these areas they suggest solidarity with voices critical of orthodox thinking and practice. How much of the parody might even move past such specific targets to a broader criticism of the institutionalized church itself? How much might be seen as a kind of (possibly festive) irreverence or mockery?[86] One of the uses of Pentecost was to reinforce the authority of the church—the event designates that on earth God directly inspired Peter and the other chosen apostles to communicate his message, and Peter (in the orthodox if not the Wycliffite reading of Matthew 16:18) is the rock on which clerical and especially papal authority is built.[87] If the Whitsun holidays also generated their share of mockery of authority, then Chaucer's parody at some level of meaning could be seen as a participant in such subversion, at whatever level of serious social challenge this kind of literary misrule might achieve. At the very least, the final scene of *The Summoner's Tale* reminds us that the meaning of authoritative images is not controllable. Further, acknowledging its possible debts to popular play would link the end of the story more closely to its narrator, whose garland and shield of bread point to his own associations with the carnivalesque.[88] The iconographic parodies and biblical learning in the tale have usually been imputed to Chaucer rather than to the Summoner, who has small Latin indeed. Tale-teller appropriateness has been explored chiefly at the

---

[86] For a reading of the tale in this way, see James Andreas, "'Newe Science' from 'Olde Bokes': A Bakhtinian Approach to the *Summoner's Tale*," *ChauR* 25 (1990): 138–51. On the diversity of critical opinion as to the psychological or social functions of parodic inversion, see Bayless, pp. 177–212.

[87] On the institutional and hierarchical emphases of depictions of Pentecost in Italy in the quarter-century after the plague, see Millard Meiss, *Painting in Florence and Siena after the Black Death* (Princeton, N.J.: Princeton University Press, 1951; rpt., 1978), pp. 32–34 and figs. 39–41; on similar emphases in the window of Canterbury cathedral, Caviness, *Early Stained Glass* (n. 11 above), p. 118.

[88] The Summoner as a festive figure is discussed in Andreas, "'Newe Science,'" pp. 142–44, and particularly in reference to these images, in Jon Cook, "Carnival and *The Canterbury Tales*: 'Only Equals May Laugh,'" in David Aers, ed., *Medieval Literature: Criticism, Ideology, and History* (New York: St. Martin's Press, 1986), p. 180. With his "fyrreed cherubynnes face" (*GP* 624), he literally *embodies* religious parody from the start. Fletcher, "The Summoner," pp. 113–17, notes how voicing the tale through the Summoner and the presence of parody result in "surpluses of meaning" that are hardly Lollard in spirit.

occupational level of his quarrel with the Friar or at the moral and psychological levels of his irritability, coarseness, and corruption. But the
parody of Pentecost need not be seen as somehow "beyond" the Summoner. He would not have had to consult the *Ikonographie der christlichen
Kunst* to have his nasty but inventive mind stimulated; images of Pentecost would pervade the literary world he inhabits, as they did his author's—in missals and prayerbooks, in stained glass, in church services,
on scaffolds, in processions, and possibly in holiday play.

We know from the final scene between the Pardoner and the Host
that Chaucer at his most vulgar is often Chaucer at his most provocative
and in many respects his most serious. The closing episode of *The Summoner's Tale* seems to me no less rich, and I certainly do not claim to
have addressed all of it here. It has interesting social and ecclesiological
implications that have only recently come under scrutiny.[89] The emphasis on dividing what is indivisible and the academic language in which
the problem is couched respond in a complex way, Fiona Somerset and
I believe, to the eucharistic controversy. But the central image of the
end of the tale remains its parody of Pentecost, and that, as I have tried
to show, has a plurality of associations and implications that extend and
complicate its antifraternalism. If art emerges out of a society's "collective dynamic circulation of pleasures, anxieties, and interests," [90] we can
come to understand the final scene of *The Summoner's Tale* better the more
we know of the social and religious interests served by Pentecost in
Chaucer's time. In turn, his parody must have functioned not only as a
comment on but as a contribution to some of those interests. It must
have furthered certain of the multiple and even contested meanings of
what Acts 2 narrates, the descent of the Holy Spirit on a group of people
congregated in a Christian peace and unity not readily apparent in late-
fourteenth-century England.

[89] Linda Georgianna, "Lords, Churls, and Friars: The Return to Social Order in the
Summoner's Tale," in *Rebels and Rivals* (n. 2 above), pp. 149–72; Lee Patterson, *Chaucer
and the Subject of History* (Madison: University of Wisconsin Press, 1991), pp. 317–21,
which should be read in the context of his larger argument on how Chaucer deals with
"political protest," pp. 244–321; Scanlon, *Narrative, Authority, and Power,* pp. 170–75;
Wallace, *Chaucerian Polity,* pp. 145–52.
[90] Stephen Greenblatt, *Shakespearian Negotiations* (Berkeley: University of California
Press, 1988), p. 12.

Eulogies and Usurpations: Hoccleve and Chaucer Revisited

Ethan Knapp
Ohio State University

The search for descent is not the erecting of foundations: on the contrary, it disturbs what was previously considered immobile; it fragments what was thought unified; it shows the heterogeneity of what was imagined consistent with itself.

—Michel Foucault, "Nietzsche, Genealogy, History"

There is perhaps no ideology so central to the institution of literary history as that of filial piety. Despite recent debate over the content and function of literary canons, and despite theoretical critiques of organic, continuous historical models, the implicit frame within which we read and teach is still grounded in the last resort upon notions of sources and influence thoroughly genealogical at their core.[1] It is, indeed, hard to imagine a form of literary history that would not be genealogical. Could we imagine the field of literature other than as a succession of texts arrayed in time, locked together as a category by the influence of the earlier over the later, and given meaning by the dynamic interrelations among them? In the assumed parthenogenesis of this

---

[1] The earliest and most influential critique of this model has come through feminist arguments that characterized the idea of literary canons as exclusionary devices. This critique has gained additional momentum from the skepticism toward organic, teleological models of history widespread in poststructuralist thought. Influential examples of these critiques would include Michel Foucault's "What is an Author?," in Donald F. Bouchard and Sherry Simon, eds. and trans., *Michel Foucault: Language, Counter-Memory, Practice* (Ithaca, N.Y.: Cornell University Press, 1977), pp. 113–38; and, in the field of medieval studies, R. Howard Bloch, *Etymologies and Genealogies* (Chicago: University of Chicago Press, 1983), and Louise Fradenburg, "'Voice, Memorial': Loss and Reparation in Chaucer's Poetry," *Exemplaria* 2 (1990): 169–202.

247

tradition, the metaphor of paternity, the relation of fathers and sons, has always been central.[2]

This metaphor has been nowhere more influential than in representations of early-fifteenth-century English verse. The old label for this poetry, "Chaucerian," has always served, to a greater degree than most such nominative constructions, as a dynastic marker, suggesting that poets like Hoccleve and Lydgate were important chiefly for their custodianship as heirs.[3] Consequently, a sense of their poetry as "servile imitation" has always marked the reception of this verse, and its defining characteristics have been read largely as repetitions of or deviations from the models established by Chaucer.[4] It was the authority of the Chaucerian example that established the terms under which Ricardian vernacular experiments were consolidated and formed into a relatively unitary tradition. As A. C. Spearing has suggested, "[T]he fatherhood of Chaucer was in effect the constitutive idea of the English poetic tradition."[5] More recent studies of fifteenth-century verse have returned frequently to this genealogical motif. The most recent, and most ambitious, treatment of this period, Seth Lerer's *Chaucer and His Readers*, has made this genealog-

[2] A. C. Spearing nicely suggests the ubiquity of this metaphor among poets: "There is ample precedent for seeing the authority of the literary precursor over his successors as analogous to the authority of the father over his sons. Lucretius refers to Epicurus as father; Horace and Propertius both refer to Ennius as father; Cicero calls Isocrates the father of eloquence and Herodotus the father of history; and so on. . . . Descent and inheritance from father to son provide a basic explanatory model for literary history, and the model retains its power, for example in Harold Bloom's conception of the tensely Oedipal relation of son to father as characterizing the whole of English poetic history from Milton to the present"; Spearing, *From Medieval to Renaissance in English Poetry* (Cambridge: Cambridge University Press, 1985), p. 92.
[3] As Caroline Spurgeon wrote of Lydgate and Hoccleve: "So great and wholehearted was the admiration and devotion given to Chaucer by these two men, his friends and followers, that we cannot doubt they would have been the first to acknowledge it fitting that the principal value of their writings to us—five centuries later—lies in their references to their 'maister Chaucer'"; Spurgeon, *Five Hundred Years of Chaucer Criticism and Allusion, 1357–1900* (Cambridge: Cambridge University Press, 1925), 1:xiv. Hoccleve's first modern editor, F. J. Furnivall, spoke in similar terms, describing Hoccleve as a "weak, sensitive, look-on-the-worst-side kind of man," who made up for his faults chiefly through "his genuine admiration for Chaucer"; F. J. Furnivall and I. Gollancz, eds., *Hoccleve's Works: The Minor Poems*, Early English Text Society [EETS], e.s., 61 (London, 1892; revised by A. I. Doyle and Jerome Mitchell, 1970), p. xxxviii.
[4] The phrase "servile imitation" comes from H. S. Bennett, but similar judgments could be drawn from any number of handbooks of literary history; Bennett, *Chaucer and the Fifteenth Century* (New York: Oxford University Press, 1947; reissued 1954), p. 126. David Lawton has offered a powerful challenge to the usual reading of the self-confessed "dullness" of this age in "Dullness and the Fifteenth Century," *ELH* 54 (1987): 761–99.
[5] Spearing, *Medieval to Renaissance*, p. 92.

ical metaphor central to the period's vision of itself, suggesting that paternity was one of the key metaphors to structure both poetic identity and practice in the early fifteenth century.[6]

One difficulty, however, in discussing the impact of this metaphor in the early fifteenth century is the fact that it was actually used by only one poet, Thomas Hoccleve. Although Dryden's influence has made the title commonplace, and although there is certainly some continuity between the image of Father Chaucer and the ubiquitous confessions of inadequacy in the poetry of Lydgate and others in the period, the only references to Chaucer as father per se come from three eulogistic passages in Hoccleve's *Regement of Princes*.[7] This essay will thus consider the place of paternity in the fifteenth century by offering a reevaluation of the encomia for Chaucer in Hoccleve's *Regement*. These passages have always been read as one of the earliest appreciations of Chaucer's genius and of Hoccleve's modesty in the face of the Chaucerian example. My argument will be that, along with this praise of Chaucer, these passages present a strategy for poetic usurpation. In these passages we see Hoccleve both lay claim to an inherited poetic authority and also interrogate the notions of origins and authority that underwrite the idea of generational succession.

I will make this case in three stages. First, I will offer an analysis of the operation of "doubling" in the *Regement,* arguing that Hoccleve's verse is marked by a persistent recursivity, a tendency to cycle obsessively through a given set of conceptual terms. Second, I will turn to the eulogistic passages in the *Regement* and to the accompanying Chaucer portrait in order to demonstrate a pattern of instability within Hoccleve's metaphors of generational succession. Last, I will turn to the familiar history of Prince Henry's conflict with his father, Henry IV, in 1410–12

---

[6] "As children to the father, apprentices to the master, or aspirants before the laureate, those who would read and write after the poet share in the shadows of the secondary. It is the purpose of this book to understand the quality of post-Chaucerian writing in these terms"; Seth Lerer, *Chaucer and his Readers: Imagining the Author in Late-Medieval England* (Princeton, N.J.: Princeton University Press, 1993), p. 3.

[7] The rhetoric of poets like Lydgate might even be said to avoid suggestions of a specifically parental sponsorship. As Lee Patterson has commented: "Chaucer represents not a clean break from a rejected past but instead a transformation of that which was given: 'Wyth al hys rethorykes swete' he '*amendede* our langage' (*Pilgrimage of the Life of Man,* 19774–76). He is not source but model, the master who can teach his pupils a technical lesson rather than the father from whom derives an intangible and so all the more indispensable aptitude"; *Chaucer and the Subject of History* (Madison: University of Wisconsin Press, 1991), p. 16.

and consider this episode as a model for Hoccleve's challenge to Chaucer's prerogative.

"Doubling"—Progression and Recursivity in the Regement

Hoccleve's eulogy and praise of "father Chaucer" is produced in three passages of his *Regement of Princes.* The first two of these passages occur in the Prologue to the work, a preface in the form of a complaint, which proceeds as a dialogue between Hoccleve and an impoverished Old Man. Hoccleve describes lying awake in a sleepless, thought-filled night, and then walking out into the fields, where he meets the unnamed Old Man. Hoccleve laments his poverty, the delay in the payment of his annuity, and his fears that his financial situation will only worsen with age. The Old Man responds by reminding Hoccleve of the virtues which may follow from poverty, but also suggests the more practical remedy of writing some work for Prince Henry, the future Henry V, in order to secure patronage and the regular disbursement of his annuity. After this long Prologue comes the *Regement* proper, a compendium of moral and political advice drawn from three sources: the pseudo-Aristotelian *Secreta secretorum;* Egidio Colonna's *De regimine principum;* and Jacobus de Cessolis's *Liber de ludo scacchorum.*[8]

The *Regement of Princes* as a whole is probably best read as a somewhat uneasy generic hybrid. It was not unprecedented to bring together a Mirror for Princes with autobiographical material; Christine de Pizan, whose work Hoccleve translated early in his career, had created a similar fusion in her *L'Avision.*[9] The *Regement,* however, seems to have struck readers from a very early date as a problematic combination of these two elements. The rubrication among surviving manuscripts varies, suggesting some confusion about the relation between the Prologue and the

[8] On the sources for the *Regement,* see William Matthews, "Thomas Hoccleve: Commentary and Bibliography," in A. E. Hartung, ed., *A Manual of Writings in Middle English: 1050–1500,* vol. 3 (New Haven, Conn.: Connecticut Academy of Arts and Sciences, 1972), pp. 749–50; Jerome Mitchell, *Thomas Hoccleve: A Study in Early Fifteenth-Century Poetic* (Urbana: University of Illinois Press, 1968), pp. 24–27; and Allen H. Gilbert, "Notes on the Influence of the Secretum Secretorum," *Speculum* 3 (1928): 84–98.

[9] See Rosalind Brown-Grant, "*L'Avision Christine:* Autobiographical Narrative or Mirror for the Prince," in Margaret Brabant and Jean-Bethke Elshtain, eds., *Politics, Gender and Genre: The Political Thought of Christine de Pizan* (Boulder, Colo.: Westview, 1992), pp. 95–111.

Regement proper. On some occasions scribes have labeled the whole 5,000 lines as "De Regimine Principum," but on other occasions this title is applied only to the last 3,000 lines.[10] Among modern readers, this division between the autobiographical prologue and the latter half of the poem has become a central interpretive crux. The bifurcation between autobiography and counsel has been read in a number of significant ways: as a representation of the typological relations between ethics and state policy; as a device for meditating on the Foucauldian relation between the body of the subject and that of the prince; as a reflection of the historical crisis in annuities and debt that connected petitioner and ruler; and as a focal point for the paradoxes invoked when the powerless offer counsel to the mighty.[11]

In the present context, this generic hybridity will help us understand Hocsleve's complex presentation of his debt to Chaucer, because it is the first sign of one of Hocsleve's basic techniques in this work, a persistent doubling of key images and concepts. This operation of doubling is crucial to Hocsleve's verse at both narrative and conceptual levels. In his narrative, for example, we might note that both the *Regement of Princes* and the *Series* are shaped by the same shift from an initial solitary complaint into a forced dialogue, with the Old Man in the case of the

<hr />

[10] D. C. Greetham, "Self-Referential Artifacts: Hocsleve's Persona as a Literary Device," *MP* 86 (1989): 245. Other important studies of the *Regement* manuscripts include A. S. G. Edwards and Derek Pearsall, "The Manuscripts of the Major English Poetical Texts," in Jeremy Griffiths and Derek Pearsall, eds., *Book Production and Publishing in Britain, 1375–1475* (Cambridge: Cambridge University Press, 1989), pp. 257–78; M. C. Seymour, "The Manuscripts of Hocsleve's *Regiment of Princes*," *Transactions of the Edinburgh Bibliographical Society* 4 (1974): 253–97; D. C. Greetham, "Challenges of Theory and Practice in the Editing of Hocsleve's *Regiment of Princes*," in Derek Pearsall, ed., *Manuscripts and Texts* (Cambridge: D. S. Brewer, 1987), pp. 60–86; and Charles Blyth, "Editing the Regiment of Princes," in Catherine Batt, ed., *Essays on Thomas Hocsleve* (London: Centre for Medieval and Renaissance Studies, Queen Mary and Westfield College, University of London, 1996), pp. 11–28.

[11] See Greetham, "Self-Referential Artifacts"; Anna Torti, "Specular Narrative: Hocsleve's *Regement of Princes*," in her *The Glass of Form: Mirroring Structures from Chaucer to Skelton* (Cambridge: D. S. Brewer, 1991), pp. 87–107; Judith Ferster, "A Mirror for the Prince of Wales: Hocsleve's *Regement of Princes*," in *Fictions of Advice: The Literature and Politics of Counsel in Late Medieval England* (Philadelphia: University of Pennsylvania Press, 1996), pp. 137–59; Antony Hasler, "Hocsleve's Unregimented Body," *Paragraph* 13 (1990): 164–83; and Larry Scanlon, "The King's Two Voices: Narrative and Power in Hocsleve's *Regement of Princes*," in Lee Patterson, ed., *Literary Practice and Social Change in Britain, 1380–1530* (Berkeley: University of California Press, 1990), pp. 216–47, material from which is reworked in Scanlon's *Narrative, Authority, and Power* (Cambridge: Cambridge University Press, 1994), pp. 299–322.

Regement and with the unnamed Friend in the *Series*. James Simpson has commented on this structural similarity, suggesting that it allows Hoccleve's verse to move from private complaint into successively more public forms of address.[12] In addition to this sense of progression, there is also, however, a marked recursivity to Hoccleve's verse: a sense that generic shifts such as that from the complaint to the dialogue, shifts that might suggest some progression or resolution of the complaint, actually insist upon the nagging presence of the same difficulties through all the changes of generic presentation and form.

For an example, we might take the most basic of Hoccleve's objects in the *Regement,* the melancholy, semi-allegorical "Thought" with which he is afflicted. The *Regement* begins (Prol. 1–21):

> Mvsynge vpon the restles bisynesse
> Which that this troubly world hath ay on honde,
> That othir thyng than fruyt of byttirnesse
> Ne yeldeth nought, as I can vndirstonde,
> At Chestre ynnë, right fast be the stronde,
> As I lay in my bed vp-on a nyght,
> Thought me bereft of sleep with force and myght.
>
> And many a day and nyght that wykked hyne
> Haddë beforn vexid my poorë goost
> So grevously, that of anguysh and pyne
> No richere man was nougher in no coost;
> This dar I seyn, may no wight make his boost
> That he with thought was bettir than I aqveynted,
> For to the deth it wel nigh hath me feynted.
>
> Bysily in my mynde I gan revolue
> The welthe onsure of everye creature,
> How lightly that ffortune it can dissolue,
> Whan that hir lyst that it no lenger dure;
> And of the brotylnesse of hyre nature,

[12] James Simpson, "Nobody's Man: Thomas Hoccleve's *Regement of Princes,*" in Julia Boffey and Pamela King, eds., *London and Europe in the Late Middle Ages* (London: Centre for Medieval and Renaissance Studies, Queen Mary and Westfield College, University of London, 1995), p. 167.

My tremlyng hert so gretë gastnesse hadde,
That my spiritis were of my lyfë sadde.[13]

Unlike many traditional depictions of melancholy as a passive and le-
thargic state, Hoccleve presents his "thought" as a jittery, hyperactive
thing. Hoccleve also multiplies this thought, doubling and redoubling
it, so that his inner life is here presented through no less than four separate figures: "thought" most prominently, but also "my poore goost,"
"my tremlyng hert," and "my spiritis." Each of these elements pursues
its own activity, activities that are not at all coordinated. Thought, part
native participant and part foreign interloper, wrestles with the poor
ghost, in a prolonged bout—"to the deth it wel nigh hath me feynted."
Meanwhile the trembling heart and spirits look on fearfully. And, in
addition to the participants in this scene, there is the speaking "I" who
narrates. For a bedridden scene, it is a busy one.

It is also a scene that establishes the conceptual importance of this
doubling. In part it does so through the simple refusal of progression in
favor of recursivity, of dividing the aspects of consciousness into numerous avatars, not in order to resolve Hoccleve's anxiety but rather to stage
a self-examination in obsessive detail.[14] The figure he chooses to evoke
his own cogitation here—"Bysily in my mynde I gan revolue"—is, after
all, the very opposite of any progression. In addition to this, however,
the operation of doubling is particularly significant in the *Regement* because it undermines the apparent Boethian framework of the poem, and
with this framework the image of the wise Old Man as counselor, an
image easily connected to the presentation of paternity in the poem. On
its surface, the Prologue to the *Regement* seems neatly modeled on the
dialogic progression and consolatory ethic of Boethius's *Consolation of
Philosophy*. Many readers have taken it as a fairly straightforward adaptation of the *Consolation*, a story in which an initially resistant Hoccleve is

---

[13] F. J. Furnivall, ed., *The Regement of Princes*, vol. 3 of *Hoccleve's Works*, EETS, e.s., 72
(London: Kegan Paul, Trench, Trübner and Co., 1897). Further references will be drawn
from this edition.
[14] Lee Patterson has also drawn attention to the resonances between Hoccleve's complex depictions of interiority and the deployment of a Boethian language of "doubleness"; Patterson, "Bother Hoccleve!" (paper presented at the Thirty-Second International Congress on Medieval Studies, Kalamazoo, Mich., May 1997). Catherine Batt also
calls attention to the significant ubiquity of Hoccleve's "doubleness" in her insightful
introduction to *Essays on Thomas Hoccleve*, p. 3.

brought around by the Old Man's goodwill and pious sentiments until
he is able to admit that his sufferings are exaggerated and liable to be
mended through faith and careful appeal to literary patronage.[15] But the
striking point about the relationship between Hoccleve and the Old
Man is the extent to which Hoccleve refuses any of the proffered consola-
tions. The ground for this refusal is established in their initial encounter
(Prol. 131–40):

> He sterte vp to me, & seyde, "scleepys þou, man?
> Awake!" & gan me schakë wonder faste,
> And with a sigh I answerde attë laste.
>
> "A! who is þer?" "I," quod þis oldë greye,
> "Am heer," & he me toldë the manere
> How he spak to me, as ye herd me seye;
> "O man," quoþ I, "for cristës louë dere,
> If þat þou wolt aght done at my preyere,
> As go þi way, talkë to me no more,
> þi wordës al annoyen me ful sore. . . .

The imperative "scleepys þou, man? / Awake!" in the mouth of the Old
Man, and the description of "þis oldë greye" are clearly meant to establish him as a paternal figure of wise counsel, the masculine equivalent
to Lady Philosophy. But where the prisoner in Boethius's *Consolation* had
a generally willing, if initially somewhat petulant, attitude, Hoccleve
wants nothing to do with this Old Man. And when the Old Man does
finally cajole Hoccleve into dialogue, his resistance continues through
an insistence that his complaint arises from two separate sources—on
the one hand, poverty; and on the other hand, thought. Thus, the self-
division that Hoccleve establishes in the opening stanzas through the
process of doubling reestablishes itself within the Boethian narrative as a
doubling of the causes of his distress. This dual cause sets up the primary
rhythm of the dialogue that then follows. Whenever the Old Man offers

---

[15] Stephen Kohl provides a concise expression of this position: "In the course of this
debate, the old beggar, with his philosophy, succeeds in defeating melancholy Thought
and thus saves 'Hoccleve' from the contagion of Despair and spiritual death" ("More
Than Virtues and Vices; Self-Analysis in Hoccleve's Autobiographies," *Fifteenth Century
Studies* 14 [1988]: 119–20). See also Stephen Medcalf, "Inner and Outer," in his *The
Later Middle Ages* (New York: Holmes and Meier, 1981), pp. 135–38. James Simpson has
offered a very interesting anti-Boethian reading of the *Regement* in his "Nobody's Man."

to resolve Hoccleve's complaint concerning his annuity, Hoccleve responds that his problem really lies in thought, and whenever the Old Man addresses the problem of thought, Hoccleve turns again to money. By creating this rupture on the level of causality within the complaint, Hoccleve is able to produce a complaint that endlessly defers consolation, which circles back recursively through the same twin problems and never allows the consolatory dialogue to resolve itself into the monologic text of counsel.[16]

Tropes of Paternity

It is within the context of this deferred consolation that Hoccleve pauses to eulogize Chaucer. These eulogistic passages are usually read either as simply a spontaneous outpouring of Hoccleve's admiration for his predecessor or, especially in relation to the portrait of Chaucer that accompanies the last passage, as part of Hoccleve's bid to establish himself as the heir to a legitimate tradition of vernacular *auctoritas*.[17] These three encomia are spaced at wide intervals in the *Regement,* but they are tied together by a consistent metaphoric and functional pattern. Each of the three passages praises Chaucer through the key terms of "father" and "master." Similarly, each passage occurs at a moment in which the invocation of Chaucer—specifically, the elegiac invocation of his inheritable genius—serves to make a claim for Hoccleve's credentials for writing to the prince. There are thus a series of issues that will be important in determining the strategic use of metaphors of paternity in each of these passages: 1) the stability of these key metaphors; 2) the manipulation of elegy and its associated thematics of inheritance and lineage; and 3) the precise circulation of authority between Hoccleve and the absent figure of Chaucer. In these encomia, we will see that Hoccleve uses these terms to construct a figure of vernacular authority from whom to trace his own descent, but also that he does so in such a way as to throw the status of fatherhood and mastery into question.

---

[16] For a reading of Boethius's *Consolation* as a text that moves from the monologue of complaint, to the dialogue of pedagogical dialectic, to the final monologic voice of philosophy itself, see Seth Lerer, *Boethius and Dialogue: Literary Method in the Consolation of Philosophy* (Princeton, N.J.: Princeton University Press, 1985), p. 6.

[17] Alan T. Gaylord, for example, stresses Hoccleve's construction of Chaucer as an image of wisdom and authority in his "Portrait of a Poet," in Martin Stevens and Daniel Woodward, eds., *The Ellesmere Chaucer: Essays in Interpretation* (San Marino, Calif.: Huntington Library, 1995), pp. 121–42.

The first of these passages occurs at a moment in the Prologue when the Old Man is trying to persuade Hoccleve to write a treatise for Prince Henry. Hoccleve confesses his fear that he is inadequate to such a task and is led to the memory of Chaucer, a master rhetorician, capable of writing even for a prince.[18] This praise of Chaucer as a master of the aureate tradition also serves to suggest the potential dignity of an English vernacular poetry, dignity to which Hoccleve might have access as Chaucer's apprentice and immediate successor (lines 1954–67):

> With hert as tremblyng as þe leef of aspe,
> ffadir, syn ye me redë to do so,
> Of my symple conceyt wole I the claspe
> Vndo, and lat it at his largë go.
> But weylaway! so is myn hertë wo,
> That þe honour of englyssh tonge is deed,
> Of which I wont was han consail and reed.

> O, maister deere, and fadir reuerent!
> Mi maister Chaucer, flour of eloquence,
> Mirour of fructuous entendëment,
> O, vniuersel fadir in science!
> Allas! þat þou thyn excellent prudence,
> In þi bed mortel mightist naght by-qwethe;
> What eiled deth? allas! whi wolde he sle the?

Reading the eulogistic stanzas alone, as they are usually presented, the passage does indeed seem a straightforward, and moving, memorialization of Chaucer. However, taken in the context of the Prologue, and his relationship with that other father, the Old Man, the elegies for Chaucer must also be understood as a potential disruption of Hoccleve's poetic project. The problem here is one of genre, and is reflected in the differing relations between Hoccleve and the two fathers in this passage. Hoccleve's first father is the Old Man, whose counsel encourages him to unlock his "symple conceyt" and write something for the prince. But no sooner is this project announced than he thinks of another father, the absent Chaucer. With the thought of Chaucer, the idea of a book for the

---

[18] Jerome Mitchell emphasizes Hoccleve's enthusiasm for Chaucer's aureate rhetoric in his "Hoccleve's Tribute to Chaucer," in A. Esch, ed., *Chaucer und seine Zeit: Symposium für Walter F. Schirmer* (Tübingen: Max Niemeyer, 1968), pp. 275–83.

prince is set aside, and Hoccleve begins again to lament his losses. In other words, the memory of Chaucer functions here just as the threat of poverty had at the poem's outset. It creates a temptation to return endlessly to the complaint, a genre always understood in Hoccleve's work to be in conflict with exteriorized public discourse. The presence of two fathers in these stanzas is a refiguration of Hoccleve's chronic trouble, self-division and doubleness. The Old Man gives him fatherly advice and a solution for his poverty in writing; but just as he is about to avail himself of this advice, another father appears as a source of grief and precipitates him into the elegiac mode, or, in essence, back to the complaint with which he began the poem.

This passage then continues by deepening the consideration of death, and the bereavement he, and the whole land, face without Chaucer (lines 1968–81):

> O deth! þou didest naght harme singuleer,
> In slaghtere of him; but al þis land it smertith;
> But nathëlees, yit hast þou no power
> His namë sle; his hy vertu astertith
> Vnslayn fro þe, which ay vs lyfly hertyth,
> With bookës of his ornat endytyng,
> That is to al þis land enlumynyng.

> Hast þou nat eeke my maister Gower slayn,
> Whos vertu I am insufficient
> For to descreyue? I wote wel in certayn,
> ffor to sleen al þis world þou hasst yment;
> But syn our lorde Crist was obedient
> To þe, in feith I can no ferther seye;
> His creäturës mosten þe obeye.

As he considers death, the magnitude of the loss grows, and so too does the list of fathers. As Charles Blythe has pointed out, though most readings of these eulogies have focused on Chaucer, there is, in fact, a second master, given nearly equal time to Chaucer—John Gower.[19] But though Hoccleve uses this multiplication to stress the universal power of death, he also allows it to bring out a potential source of compensation: the

[19] Charles Blyth, "Thomas Hoccleve's Other Master," *Mediaevalia* 16 (1993): 349–59.

virtue that survives both poets, and the "name" and works that survive Chaucer and "enlumine" the land. Literary production is here both a guarantor of immortality and an inheritance. As Hoccleve's elegy develops, then, it shifts in its use of Chaucer from a simple elegy that would threaten the progression of the poem into a use of Chaucer as an authorizing point of origin for vernacular literature. The elegy would then function to reinforce both Hoccleve's own legitimacy in writing for the prince and also the trajectory suggested by the Old Man—that he should leave behind the lament and turn to writing for the prince because even death is defeated by the fame of literary works. The two fathers seem to fall into accord.

However, this accord is disrupted by the stanza immediately following this eulogy for Chaucer and Gower, a stanza usually not reproduced in discussions of the eulogies (lines 1982–86):

> . . . ffadir, ye may lawhe at my lewdë speche.
> If þat þow list; I am no thyng fourmeel;
> My yongë konyng may no hyer reche,
> Mi wit is also slipir as an eel;
> But how I speke, algate I menë weel.

Laughter is a remarkable conclusion to Hoccleve's elegy. It interrupts the fictional reverie in which Hoccleve had meditated on the significance of the paternal Chaucer, reinserting the alternative, and far less comforting, image of the Old Man. In its narrative movement, it is an exact replication of that moment so common in Hoccleve's verse in which he indicates the limitations of monologic genres such as the complaint and the elegy by staging the interruptions of dialogue and the social world. And here the interruption is explicitly connected to a pair of binary conflicts directly relevant to the present investigation: youth vs. age, and knowledge vs. lewdness. Scanning back over the five stanzas that make up the first eulogy, we can also see that Hoccleve deploys the term "fadir" with careful symmetry. It is used twice in reference to the Old Man, once at the beginning and once at the conclusion of this reverie, and once in the center for Chaucer. Thus, the appeal to Chaucer's memory is carefully framed by the alternative paternity of this Old Man. What is the effect of this *emboitement?* I would suggest that the framing serves first to establish the metaphor of paternity as a metaphor linked to a traditional image of counsel, a wise old man; but then to corrupt

this image by splitting the father into two, one urging a forward movement into writing and the other causing Hoccleve to fall back into the
recursive gestures of mourning. Moreover, certain details in the presentation of the Old Man serve to complicate the notion of paternity.
Though the Old Man offers himself as a figure of wise counsel, he is also
an embodiment of exactly the future Hoccleve tells us he fears in his
thoughtful night. He is penniless and seems unable to counsel Hoccleve
effectively on how to avoid such poverty. And with the final, mocking
laughter of this passage, Hoccleve suggests a deep conflict between
"yongë konyng" whose "wit is also slipir as an eel" and the paternal
authority that would "lawhe at my lewdë speche." This passage, then,
leaves us with a question: Are we meant to assume here the traditional
ascription of wisdom to old age, or is there an alternative claim to be
made for "yongë konyng"?

The second eulogy is quite similar, and again leans heavily on the
keywords "maister" and "fadir" in its invocation of Chaucer (lines
2073–93):

> Simple is my goost, and scars my letterure,
> Vnto your excellencë for to write
> Myn inward loue, and yit in auenture
> Wyle I me puttë, thogh I can but lyte.
> Mi derë maistir—god his soulë quyte!—
> And fadir, Chaucer, fayn wolde han me taght;
> But I was dul, and lerned lite or naght.

> Allas! my worthi maister honorable,
> This landës verray tresor and richesse,
> Deth, by thi deth, hath harme irreparable
> Vnto vs doon; hir vengeable duresse
> Despoilèd hath þis land of þe swetnesse
> Of rethorik; for vn-to Tullius
> Was neuer man so lyk a-mongës vs.

> Also, who was hiër in philosophie
> To Aristotle, in our tonge, but thow?
> The steppës of virgile in poesie
> Thow filwedist eeke, men wot wel y-now.
> That combre-world, þat þe, my maistir, slow,

> Wold I slayn were! deth was to hastyf
> To renne on þe, and reue the thi lyf.

The opening of the second eulogy is a perfect example of the dullness motif, analyzed so powerfully by David Lawton.[20] This eulogy comes as the second half of a parenthetical address to Prince Henry. Hoccleve uses this passage about Chaucer to shift gracefully from his own obeisance to the prince to a similar humility in the face of Chaucer. This parallel between the prince and Hoccleve has the dual effect of emphasizing Hoccleve's humility in front of masters both political and poetical while also claiming a great dignity for the idea of vernacular poetry, by placing Chaucer at a level with the prince as "this landës verray tresor." In its rhetorical function, this passage is very like the first eulogistic sequence. It begins with a confessional doubt about Hoccleve's capacity to write such a commission, then turns to Chaucer as an absent figure of mastery, and then to a meditation on the power of death, and the villainy of death in taking Chaucer.

There are, however, two significant variations in this second eulogistic passage. The first is that in this passage Hoccleve's thoughts of death turn to thoughts of self-destruction. To a certain extent, this is just a convention of the pseudo-Boethian language Hoccleve uses in his complaints, but there is also a sense in which this thought of suicide must affect our understanding of these eulogies. In order to represent vernacular poetry, and his own efforts, with adequate significance to stand before the prince, Hoccleve creates a poetic genealogy through which he might derive poetic virtue from the paternal figure of Chaucer. And in order to establish his own legitimacy as Chaucer's true heir, Hoccleve presents a highly dramatized display of mourning. This dramatization is reminiscent of Peter Sacks's argument that elegiac lyric develops out of the necessity of heirs to press their claims to inheritance by memorializing their grief. (The one who grieves is the one with a right to inherit.)[21] When played out fully, however, and in the context of poetic inheritance, the inheritor may be locked into a paradox. If the grief is real, why should the mourner write anything but elegy; and why should he live?

---

[20] Lawton, "Dullness and the Fifteenth Century."

[21] Peter Sacks, *The English Elegy: Studies in the Genre from Spenser to Yeats* (Baltimore, Md.: Johns Hopkins University Press, 1985).

Hoccleve's response to this paradox is to castigate the universal mastery of death (lines 2094–2107):

> Deth hath but smal consideracïoun
> Vnto þe vertuous, I haue espied,
> No more, as shewith þe probacïoun,
> Than to a vicious maistir losel tried;
> A-mong an heep, euery man is maistried;
> With hire, as wel þe porre as is þe riche;
> lered and lewde eeke standen al y-liche.

> She myghte han taried hir vengeance awhile,
> Til that sum man had egal to thè be.
> Nay, lat be þat! sche knew wel þat þis yle
> May neuer man forth bryngë lyk to the,
> And hir officë needës do mot she;
> God bad hir so, I truste as for thi beste;
> O maister, maister, god þi soule reste!

As we saw the key metaphor of "fadir" destabilized in the first passage by the operation of doubling, so here we see the same process affecting the term "maister." As we follow the term through this passage, it moves from a description of Chaucer meant to invoke the conditions of apprenticeship to the figure of the "vicious maister losel" (line 2097), the arch-traitor—some figure like Oldcastle, who is tried and condemned and demonstrates death's arbitrary nature by joining Chaucer as another of his victims. This pairing seems to raise no contradictions in the usage, as the "vicious losel" is a master in a sense diametrically opposed to Chaucer, and so is meant to confirm Chaucer's virtue through the harsh contrast. The "vicious losel maister" serves as a foil to Chaucer, emphasizing the vital poetic legacy to be drawn from Chaucer through a contrast with the illegitimate and corrupting influence of the losel (and, of course, opposing also the viciousness of the losel to Chaucer's implicit benignity). The stability of this neat contrast is lost, however, when we continue on to the third master in this passage: "A-mong an heep, euery man is maistried; / With hire" (lines 2098–99). Death, it turns out, is also a master (though, interestingly, a feminine one). The reference to the mastery of death corrupts this metaphor: death is much more like

261

Chaucer as a master than like the vicious losel, for death, like Chaucer, has power over the whole land equally.

Moreover, this sense that the meaning of "mastery" has become corrupt is confirmed by the return to Chaucer in the final stanza of this passage. After describing death's universal mastery, Hoccleve returns to suggest, as he had earlier (lines 2092–93), that death might have waited before taking Chaucer. But here he adds the surprising qualification that death might have waited "Til that sum man had egal to the be." In other words, the virtue of Chaucer, who was so markedly without peer in the opening stanzas of the eulogy (except for Aristotle and Cicero!), has now become contingent, and takes its place in a temporal order in which death should properly mean that his successor has arrived. Hoccleve immediately follows this assertion with "Nay, lat be þat!" (line 2103). This sort of interruption is quite common in verse like the "Male Regle," where Hoccleve is always pulling himself back from rambling interruption, but it breaks the tone in this elegiac passage and can only be read as a symptom of the scandalous implication of the previous line. The next line and a half then go on to directly contradict the implication that Chaucer is but one in a series by asserting that "þis yle / May neuer man forth brynge lyke to the" (lines 2103–4). The eulogy concludes with another reference to Chaucer's mastery—"O maister, maister, god þi soule reste!"—but mastery no longer means what it did before, and the stuttering repetition of the term in this line cannot reattach itself to Chaucer's virtue after its association with death and the losel.

In these first two eulogies we see fatherhood and mastery put into question through two processes. First, there is a persistent doubling of these metaphoric categories, which serves to undermine their simple reference to Chaucer. In addition, especially in this second passage, issues of death, inheritance, and authority begin to collide in such a way as to create a tension between the desire to praise Chaucer as a precedent without equal and the need to assert both his structural role as one in a series and the necessity of his death as necessary preconditions of Hoccleve's own inherited authority. The paradox of aggressivity hidden within the elegy is as old as the elegy itself, and is a paradox of which Chaucer had been well aware.[22] I want to turn now to the third of the

---

[22] A. C. Spearing makes a similar point, commenting on the relationship between Chaucer's Clerk and Petrarch: "'He is now deed and nayled in his cheste (iv 29): the death is much to be regretted and we shall all die in our turn, but how reassuring those nails are that keep Petrarch in his coffin!" (Medieval to Renaissance, p. 103).

three eulogistic passages, and to the accompanying portrait, in order to
explore further the place of a certain aggression in these eulogies.

The third eulogistic passage has received more critical commentary
than the first two, largely because it is accompanied in three of the *Regement* manuscripts by a marginal portrait of Chaucer.[23] The text in the
third eulogy refers explicitly to an accompanying image, so Hoccleve
most likely meant a portrait to be included in all copies of the poem
(the page containing the eulogistic stanzas and, most likely, the portrait,
has been cut out of MS Arundel 38). The most important of these portraits is that found in British Library MS Harley 4866, which I will
discuss below. The image shows Chaucer holding a rosary in his left
hand, with his right hand pointing to the text in which he is described.
The portrait is remarkable for its lifelike attention to detail. It is, of
course, impossible to determine whether or not the illustration presents
the actual image of Chaucer, but its detail gives an impression of verisimilitude, and the language of the eulogy itself suggests an attempt to
present the actual likeness (lines 4978–98):

> The firstë fyndere of our faire langáge
> Hath seyde in caas sembláble & othir moo,
> So hyly wel, þat it is my dotáge
> ffor to expresse or touche any of thoo.
> Alasse my fadir fro þe worlde is goo—
> My worthi maister Chaucer, hym I mene
> Be þou aduóket for hym, heuenes quene!
>
> As þou wel knowest, o blissid virgyne,
> Wyth louyng hert and hye deuocïoun
> In þyn honour he wroot ful many a lyne;
> O now þine helpe & þi promocïoun,

---

[23] British Library MS Harley 4866; British Library MS Royal 17.D.vi; and MS Rosenbach 1083/10. For a description and reproduction of these images, see Derek Pearsall,
The Life of Geoffrey Chaucer: A Critical Biography (Oxford: Blackwell, 1992), pp. 288–90.
For additional discussions of this portrait, see Jeanne Krochalis, "Hoccleve's Chaucer
Portrait," *ChauR* 21 (1986): 234–45; Jerome Mitchell, *Thomas Hoccleve*, pp. 110–15;
David R. Carlson, "Thomas Hoccleve and the Chaucer Portrait," *HLQ* 54 (1991): 283–300; A. S. G. Edwards, "The Chaucer Portraits in the Harley and Rosenbach Manuscripts," in Peter Beal and Jeremy Griffiths, eds., *English Manuscript Studies, 1100–1700*,
vol. 4 (London: British Library, 1993), pp. 268–71; Alan Gaylord, "Portrait of a Poet";
and M. C. Seymour, "Manuscript Portraits of Chaucer and Hoccleve," *Burlington Magazine* 124 (1982): 618–23.

To god þi sonë make a mocïoun,
How he þi seruaunt was, maydén marie,
And lat his louë floure and fructifie.

Al-þogh his lyfe be queynt, þe résemblaunce
Of hym haþ in me so fressh lyflynesse,
þat, to putte othir men in rémembraunce
Of his persóne, I haue heere his lyknesse
Do makë, to þis ende in sothfastnesse,
þat þei þat haue of hym lest þought & mynde,
By þis peynturë may ageyn hym fynde.

The portrait of Chaucer that accompanies these verses in the Harley
MS is one of the earliest we have, and is probably based on an exemplar
shared with the famous Ellesmere portrait.[24] It is also something of a
landmark in the history of illumination for the simple reason that it
claims to be an attempt to present a realistic, mimetic image of Chaucer.
Lifelike portraiture, the attempt to model faces not on symbolic or idealized features but on realistic detail, was not a regular feature of manuscript illumination in this period. Such portraiture tended to represent
individuality by means not of particular physiognomy but rather
through the presence of symbolic objects, clothing, or heraldic devices.
For instance, in the illumination found in the Arundel MS showing
Hoccleve presenting his book to Prince Henry, the faces of the two men
are indistinguishable. The men are distinguished by their clothing, and
by their relative position (and even physical size) within the frame.[25]
But this period also saw the beginnings of major changes in such strategies of representation.

Jeanne Krochalis has singled out the memorial effigy as a likely precedent for Hoccleve's innovative decision to provide a lifelike, and not

---

[24] Pearsall, *Life of Geoffrey Chaucer*, pp. 288–89.

[25] This image is reproduced as the frontispiece to Mitchell's *Thomas Hoccleve*. Krochalis
("Hoccleve's Chaucer Portrait," p. 237) maintains that the faces are indistinguishable,
and from my own examination of the reproduction, I would agree. For a differing opinion, see Gervase Matthew's detailed description of the presentation portrait, in which
he asserts that it is intended as an individualized picture of the two men; *The Court of
Richard II* (London: John Murray, 1968), pp. 203–4. For the relative backwardness of
English illumination, especially with regard to early Dutch naturalism, see J. J. G. Alexander, "Painting and Manuscript Illumination for Royal Patrons in the Later Middle
Ages," in V. J. Scattergood and J. W. Sherborne, eds., *English Court Culture in the Later
Middle Ages* (London: Gerald Duckworth and Co., 1983), pp. 141–62.

simply iconographically charged, image of Chaucer. This fact, and the fact that the two stanzas that directly follow the portrait and eulogy constitute an attack on Lollard doctrines denying the usefulness of images of the saints, lead her to suggest that in inserting a portrait of Chaucer, Hoccleve seems to be asserting a parallel between the meditation on the images of saints and meditation on the images of poets.[26] We can add to this claim the fact that the memorial passage occurs within a section of the *Regement of Princes* that lays out Hoccleve's claim for the place of poets as necessary counselors to royalty, a section that is highly reminiscent of one of Hoccleve's sources, the *Secreta secretorum*. The mythical origins of the *Secreta* were, of course, a series of letters written by Aristotle to his young pupil Alexander the Great while the latter was off on campaign in the East and so unavailable for firsthand edification. In the history of English vernacular poetry, Hoccleve's work is one of the first to assume a position from which it could advise a prince, and in Hoccleve's own life the composition of this text seems to have been a bid to assume the role of poetic adviser to the court, a figure who would combine the classical virtues of Cicero and Aristotle (as the second eulogy suggested Chaucer had done). The memorial is thus inserted into the *Regement* at this moment both in order to establish a particular interpretation of Chaucer (poet as advisor to princes) and, further, to attach Chaucer's prestige to Hoccleve's own claim on this position. In essence, Hoccleve praises the man, but does it in order to establish an office, now vacated by Chaucer's death, which he might claim to inherit.

The language of the eulogy continues to develop these thematic points. The passage opens and closes with what is a very evocative word in this context: "find." "Find" contains an important internal contradiction, for it can refer either to the discovery of a preexistent object or to the establishment of something without precedent[27] (a historically residual meaning retained in its wandering past tense "found," as in "to

---

[26] "But to put a poet's image in a church is to equate him with saints—which Hoccleve's text comes close to doing—and, by implication, with kings, in dignity and importance, both in this world and the next"; Krochalis, "Hoccleve's Chaucer Portrait," p. 240. James McGregor makes a similar point in "The Iconography of Chaucer in Hoccleve's De Regimine Principum and in the Troilus Frontispiece," *ChauR* 11 (1976): 338–50. The wider origins of the author portrait per se lie in Italy, with commemorations of Dante and Petrarch. See Sylvia Wright, "The Author Portraits in the Bedford Psalter-Hours: Gower, Chaucer and Hoccleve," *British Library Journal* 18 (1992): 190.

[27] These meanings are attested in other Middle English usage. See Hans Kurath and Sherman M. Kuhn, eds., *Middle English Dictionary* [hereafter *MED*] (Ann Arbor: University of Michigan Press, 1956), 3:568–73.

found a city"). This ambiguity is particularly significant to our discussion because it is the action of finding that is at the root of Chaucer's figurative paternity. In what sense is Chaucer the "finder" of the language? On one level this is a simple reference to Chaucer's creation of a high style—the "fair langage"—out of the raw materiel of English vernacular. But are we to take him as the founder of something that had never before existed, or did he "find" it in the sense of drawing attention to something already there? The modification "first" only increases the suspicion that Chaucer's originary status is not so secure, for it introduces an element of repetition into a rhetoric of foundations. If the founder is only the first in a series of such, how can we consider him to be a source in the strict sense? The use of "find" at the end of the passage (line 4798) is equally problematic. Hoccleve says that he has had an image made to remind his readers of Chaucer's features, to let them "find" his face again. But as Hoccleve knew well, many of his readers would never have seen Chaucer or any picture of him. So again, the word "find" refers to some operation midway between repetition and original creation. This is a fundamental ambiguity, or, perhaps, an ambiguity in the status of the fundamental.

I would go further and suggest that there may even be a measure of antagonism contained within these ambiguities. This third memorial passage comes as another interruption to the *Regement,* one ostensibly motivated by Hoccleve's recognition that he is wasting labor in writing advice to the prince concerning counselors. After all, Chaucer has already written on the subject and done so with far more skill than he could claim. This is, in itself, in itself an example of the highly conventional topos of humility. However, the wording of Hoccleve's self-denigration is, again, functionally ambiguous. He suggests his inferiority to Chaucer through the language of reverence for age (the "maister" here invoking the gravity of an elder counselor or teacher, like Aristotle) and the familial hierarchy of father and son, but the term with which he sums up his inadequacy is "dotage," a word which then as now meant foolishness in the context of advanced age.[28] This term reactivates the chain of associations Hoccleve has built through the series of eulogies, raising again the question of whether age is to be associated reflexively with wisdom. He confesses his inadequacy in relation to Chaucer, but chooses a word fraught with implications that age brings no wisdom.

[28] *MED,* 2:1244.

The portrait of Chaucer in the *Regement* provides a visual representation of this antigenealogical impulse. Alan Gaylord has recently described this image in the context of the *Regement*'s thematization of
youth and age, of counsel, and of the literature of "prudence," concluding that the presentation of Chaucer via "the iconography of wise old
men" assists Hoccleve in claiming Chaucer as the "patron and godfather
of the book Hoccleve will compile." [29] Much of the iconographical detail
does indeed bear out such associations. The portrait represents Chaucer
as a bearded older man, in a costume that might well be associated with
the "maister" of the eulogistic descriptions. The left hand holds rosary
beads while the right hand points from the right hand margin toward
the last stanza of the eulogy, directing the reader's attention toward
Hoccleve's text.

But this gesturing hand also suggests another reading, a recontextualization of the wise old man presented in the image. In later portraits
Chaucer is uniformly shown pointing to himself, or to a pen-case worn
on his chest as a metonymic sign of his occupation and source of his
fame. In the *Regement* portraits, however, the gesturing hand points away
from Chaucer's body and toward the text, specifically toward that portion of the text which directs the reader to look into the margin at the
illustration. The portrait would then direct the reader back to the text,
and then the text back to the portrait, ad infinitum. In other words,
the relation of image to text does not establish Chaucer as an authority
underlying Hoccleve's text, but rather creates a circuit of authority, in
which Chaucer's authority supports that of the text but is also itself created by the text. Michael Camille's recent work on marginalia in *Images
on the Edge* has uncovered numerous examples of such interplay between
text and image, both situations in which images reinforce texts and in
which marginal illuminations comment satirically. [30] The portrait of
Chaucer in the Harley MS should be read as part of this tradition. The
text and image do not relate to each other satirically, but their mutual
dependence suggests that authority is not a legacy to be inherited, but
a circuit running from the present through the past.

One might be tempted to dismiss this reading with the suggestion
that relations between text and margin play mirroring games with such

---

[29] Alan Gaylord, "Portrait of a Poet," pp. 126–29.
[30] Michael Camille, *Images on the Edge: The Margins of Medieval Art* (Cambridge: Harvard University Press, 1992), esp. pp. 20–22.

frequency as to make them commonplace, and less than helpful in ana-lyzing the poetic project of any single author. However, I think we are justified in placing some interpretive pressure on the arrangement of Hoccleve's text and marginalia, for the simple reason that of all English medieval poets, he was one to whom we may attribute the greatest per-sonal control over the exact appearance of his texts. He was by profession a scribe; he is unique in the number of autograph manuscripts to have survived; and he seems to have exercised considerable personal control over the production of manuscripts of his work.[31] If we take seriously the relation between margin and text, we are confronted with a number of paradoxes. First, although Chaucer is still playing the role of the fa-ther whose authority Hoccleve wants to attach to his own work, the father is now consigned to a literally marginal position. In addition, this circularity demonstrates the inadequacy of the language of either adoration or Oedipal insurrection in describing Hoccleve's relation to father Chaucer. For neither the text nor the picture may be said to pro-vide a founding authority for the other. Without the picture, the text is incomplete, and without the text, the pointing hand makes no sense.

This portrait provides an ideal metaphor for Hoccleve's relationship to Chaucer. Given the usual accuracy of autobiographical elements in Hoccleve's work, his professed reverence and grief for Chaucer were most likely quite sincere and significant. Equally significant was Chaucer's crucial role as the informal laureate of English vernacular poetry, the predecessor whose prominence might legitimate Hoccleve's own efforts. But at the same time, Hoccleve was well enough aware of the circular nature of such legitimation as to produce a current of resistance to simple expressions of filial devotion. The portrait is thus commissioned, but placed in the margin.

Fathers and Sons, 1410–12

I have been arguing for a degree of instability in the key metaphoric categories that Hoccleve uses to praise Chaucer as father, master, and wise Old Man. I'd like to conclude by suggesting that the grounds for this instability may be found not simply in the inevitable polyvocality of metaphor, but also in the particular historical context in which this

[31] John M. Bowers, "Hoccleve's Huntington Holographs: The First 'Collected Poems' in English," *Fifteenth-Century Studies* 15 (1989): 27–51.

poem was composed. The *Regement* was written between the years 1410 and 1412, the very years in which the ailing Henry IV, still trying to consolidate the rule gained by the usurpation of Richard II's throne, was faced by a strong challenge for power from his eldest son, the future Henry V.[32] The prince is a constant presence in the *Regement*, appearing as both patron of the work and potential guarantor of Hoccleve's future. From his position in the Privy Seal, Hoccleve could not have been unaware of the conflict between prince and king. How, then, might this historical incident color Hoccleve's treatment of the metaphoric constellation of age, wisdom, and paternity?

The exact maneuverings of these years are obscure in the contemporary chronicles, perhaps because of a need to keep the future king's name spotless, but what facts we do know indicate that the prince was perceived at the time to be encroaching on his father's prerogative.[33] Indeed, the prince's independent activity in these years was so aggressive that many historians argue that he assumed all but formal control of the government, and the accusation was even heard among his enemies that the prince wanted nothing short of his father's abdication.[34] The tension between Henry IV and the prince was an open secret in these years, a

[32] The *Regement* can be clearly dated to between 1410 and 1413, the *terminus ad quem* provided by habitual reference to Henry (who became king in March 1413) as "my lord the Prince," and a *terminus a quo* provided by reference to the burning of the Lollard John Badby Smithfield on March 1, 1410. M. C. Seymour and John Burrow both think the poem may have been completed in late 1411, Seymour because the records of Hoccleve's annuities seem to indicate a dry spell in 1411 that would match the specific complaints of the Prologue, and Burrow because the presentation of such a poem might have been especially appropriate while the prince was governing the Council. My own argument will connect language in the *Regement* to documents from as late as June 1412, but is not meant to reflect a belief that the *Regement* was necessarily completed after 1411, as such language was likely current throughout the years from 1410 onward; Burrow, *Thomas Hoccleve*, Authors of the Middle Ages, no. 4 (Aldershot, Hants: Variorum, 1994), p. 18; and Seymour, *Selections from Hoccleve* (Oxford: Clarendon Press, 1981), pp. 114–15.

[33] Peter McNiven describes the relevant chronicle accounts as "so brief and apparently so selective that much of the material which they include makes little sense until it is collated with the gleanings from other sources," and goes on to suggest that "[i]t may be that one of the reasons for the erratic coverage of the period by the chroniclers, most of whom were favourably disposed towards Prince Henry, is that a full and objective account would have proved difficult to reconcile with his unblemished image as king"; "Prince Henry and the Political Crisis of 1412," *History* 65 (1980): 1.

[34] For the events of these years, see K. B. McFarlane, "Father and Son," in *Lancastrian Kings and Lollard Knights* (Oxford: Clarendon Press, 1972), pp. 102–13; Christopher Allmand, *Henry V* (Berkeley: University of California Press, 1992), pp. 39–58; and especially McNiven, "Prince Henry and the Political Crisis of 1412," pp. 9–16, where a strong case is made for attributing Prince Henry's actions to his fear that a conspiracy existed at court to disinherit him in favor of his brother Thomas.

tension so potentially volatile as to produce rumors that the prince might resort to an armed rising in support of his aims.[35] The most pressing moment of this crisis passed in November of 1411 when the king recovered his health and removed the prince and his allies from their positions of power on the King's Council, but conflict between the king and prince seems to have simmered on until the king formally declared his son's loyalty in October of 1412.[36]

Several recent arguments have connected the composition of the *Regement* to the political intrigue of these years. G. L. Harris, for example, has tied the production of works like Hoccleve's *Regement* and Lydgate's *Troy Book* to a sense of optimism among the prince's followers created by the well-publicized reforming spirit of the Council under the prince's direction.[37] Derek Pearsall, on the other hand, connects the *Regement* to the darker anxieties of the moment.[38] In Pearsall's reading, the crucial issue lies in Prince Henry's desire after these tense years to represent himself as a sound ruler who would be open to wise counsel. The sponsorship of the first English "Mirror for Princes" provided the prince with an opportunity to make a public declaration that he was not only willing to listen to such counsel but would actively seek it out, a declaration that he was "content enough to play Alexander to Hoccleve's Aristotle."[39] Pearsall is very careful not to suggest that the prince actually

[35] McNiven points out that the letter from the prince that has been preserved in *St. Albans Chronicle* admits that very serious allegations had been pressed against him, and suggests further that these allegations were so serious that not only disinheritance but charges of treason may have been leveled against the prince; "Prince Henry and the Political Crisis of 1412," p. 13.

[36] McFarlane, "Father and Son," p. 112.

[37] "The date of these compositions was important. Lydgate records that the *Troy Book* was commissioned on 31 October 1412. The *Regement*, completed in 1411, was probably commenced two years earlier. These two years were precisely those in which the prince, at the head of a council of his own choosing and virtually without reference to his father, was carrying through a programme of 'bone governance' to which he had pledged himself in the parliament of January 1410. . . . The prince's brief period of rule thus furnished a solid expectation of an effective and reinvigorated kingship very different from the pious hope which Gower had expressed in Richard II's youth"; G. L. Harris, *King Henry V: The Practice of Kingship* (Oxford: Oxford University Press, 1985), p. 9.

[38] Derek Pearsall, "Hoccleve's *Regement of Princes*: The Poetics of Royal Self-Representation," *Speculum* 69 (1994): 386–410. For arguments concerning the representation of dynastic succession in another important Lancastrian advocate—Lydgate—see Alan Ambrisco and Paul Strohm, "Succession and Sovereignty in Lydgate's Prologue to *The Troy Book*," *ChauR* 30 (1995): 40–57, and Lee Patterson, "Making Identities in Fifteenth-Century England," in Jeffrey N. Cox and Larry J. Reynolds, eds., *New Historical Literary Study* (Princeton, N.J.: Princeton University Press, 1993), pp. 69–107.

[39] Pearsall, "Hoccleve's *Regement*," p. 389. Pearsall also points out that the chancellor's text for the opening of Henry V's first parliament as king was "*Ante omnem actem consilium stabile*" ["Steadfast counsel before all action"].

"commissioned" the piece (and Hoccleve is equally circumspect in avoiding that implication), but, as he explains, there is a string of circumstantial reasons to think of this poem as a propaganda effort for the prince. Prince Henry had ability and interest in the use of propaganda; a learned clerk in the Privy Seal was a convenient channel for the importation of a French technique of propaganda; and the luxurious presentation copies of this well-distributed manuscript, which were far too expensive for Hoccleve to have funded, found their way into the hands of important men who were prospective allies of the prince.[40]

The *Regement of Princes* was only one of several documents generated by the prince in the years 1410–13 to assert his loyalty to his father and his worthiness for kingship.[41] Another such document is the signet letter that Prince Henry sent to his father in June of 1412, and which he claimed to have circulated widely. This letter is a response to his exclusion from power following his removal from the Council in 1411. It addresses both the claims that he had been interfering with his father's policies in Aquitaine and the assertions that he was dangerously disloyal.[42] The prince contests these charges, offering his own complicated version of his exclusion from the campaigns in Aquitaine, and the counteraccusation that his enemies have planted suspicions against him in order to disturb the line of succession. He then concludes the letter by protesting the "great love," "great fidelity," and "filial humility" he felt toward his father.[43] The conflict between the prince and king in the years 1410–12 was understood by both participants and onlookers to be a trial of generational succession, in which a highly competent prince demonstrated little patience in waiting for his aging and ill father to vacate the throne. If one were to draw a history of the concept of paternity, especially in its connections to authority and inheritance, the public discourse of the early fifteenth century would provide one of the most complex chapters.

The representation of paternity in the *Regement* is also part of this his-

---

[40] Pearsall, "Hoccleve's *Regement*," pp. 393–94.

[41] Antonia Gransden discusses Henry's lifelong concern for effective propaganda in *Historical Writing in England II, c. 1307 to the Early Sixteenth Century* (Ithaca, N.Y.: Cornell University Press, 1982), pp. 197–219.

[42] V. H. Galbraith, *The St. Albans Chronicle, 1406–1420* (Oxford: Clarendon Press, 1937), pp. 66–67. This letter is also discussed in McFarlane, "Father and Son," pp. 109–10, and forms the basis of much of McNiven's argument in "Prince Henry and the Political Crisis of 1412," pp. 7–8.

[43] The prince's letter reads: "tantus amor, tanta fidelitas et tanta subiectio quantas concipere novit aut valet humilitas filialis"; Galbraith, *St. Albans Chronicle*, pp. 66–67.

tory. The eulogies for Chaucer, with their ambiguous representation of the role of paternity and the dynamics of inheritance, make up part of a work dedicated to Prince Henry in those very years in which he publicly encroached on his father's prerogative. As Harris has suggested, many subjects viewed the prince's careful fiscal governance during 1410–11 as a welcome sign of future competence after the chronic fiscal problems of Henry IV's reign.[44] If there was ever a moment in which we should not assume an idealized connection between age and good counsel, or paternity and wisdom, it was this moment. Moreover, we should not lose sight of the fact that the *Regement* was dedicated to the prince, and quite possibly written on his direct commission, in the years of his struggle with his father. In writing propaganda for the prince, Hoccleve was not just writing for Lancastrian interests. He was also stepping into a potentially dangerous feud within the Lancastrian house itself, a feud between father and son, at a moment at which notions of paternity, inheritence, and counsel could not be used simply and innocently.

This reading of Hoccleve's eulogies for Chaucer is meant not only to suggest the function of an important ideological concept in Hoccleve but also to draw an implicit portrait of Hoccleve himself, and to suggest a certain way of reading his texts. In leaning very heavily on the metaphoric construction of paternity in these eulogies, I am suggesting a greater level of ironic play, or polyvocality, in Hoccleve's texts than is often assumed. This is justified in part by the complex traditions surrounding the idea of paternity, and in part by the crises around authority and paternity in the years of the *Regement*'s composition. But in conclusion, I would also like to suggest that the profound ambivalence I have tried to register here should be more central to our sense of Hoccleve's poetry. Hoccleve has always, quite rightly, been set in opposition to Chaucer as the less subtle metrist, the one less interested in the construction of fictional worlds, and the one more prosaic and colloquial in his vocabulary.[45] This seems beyond debate. But along with these descriptions has gone an implicit judgment about tone, and hence about our reading practices. Chaucer, especially in our post-Donaldson readings, has become a poet of linguistic play and of ironic skepticism. Hoccleve, on the other hand, is still often read as a poet destined for illustrative

---

[44] See above, n. 37.

[45] See John Burrow, "*Hoccleve and Chaucer,*" in Ruth Morse and Barry Windeatt, eds., *Chaucer Traditions: Studies in Honour of Derek Brewer* (Cambridge: Cambridge University Press, 1990), pp. 54–61.

historical footnotes. However, as we've seen in Hoccleve's very complex depiction of his debt to Chaucer, he is a poet better read with an eye toward irony and even aggression than toward moral idealism and documentary reportage. The final irony here may be that for all his skepticism and play with the concept of inheritance, what we see in these passages is a Hoccleve whose wariness about authority and paternal figures makes him, in these issues at least, a true son of Chaucerian wit.

"Oure Fadres Olde and Modres": Gender, Heresy, and Hoccleve's Literary Politics

Ruth Nissé
University of Nebraska

I n a poem written for the occasion of Henry V's first passage from Southampton to Harfleur in 1415, Thomas Hoccleve accuses the Lollards of having robbed Sir John Oldcastle, with "sly colored arguments," of both his class and sex:

> þat he is overcharged with the lode
> Which yee han leid on his gode old knighthode,
> That "now 'a wrecchid knyght' men calle may.
> The lak of faith hath qwenchid his manhode."
> ("The Remonstrance against Oldcastle," lines 284–87)[1]

Oldcastle, "þat were a manly knight" (line 9), has been feminized, which here means that he has been led to presume too much of his "wit" by adherence to a heresy that involves improper thought or argument by laypeople—bailiffs and reeves as well, but especially by women. At least part of the current excitement about Hoccleve derives from the explosion of interest in his closely related main anxieties: vernacular theology and women readers. The most often quoted lines, in recent years, from

I presented earlier drafts of this article to the New Chaucer Society conference, Los Angeles, 1996, and to the Medieval and Renaissance Studies Group at the University of Nebraska–Lincoln. I would like to thank Paul Olson, Larry Scanlon, Paul Strohm, and Jennifer Summit for their valuable comments and suggestions for revision.

[1] All citations of this poem are from M. C. Seymour, ed., *Selections from Hoccleve* (Oxford: Clarendon Press, 1981), pp. 61–74; the rubric of Hoccleve's holograph, MS Huntington Library HM 111 (written between 1422–26), reads, "Ceste feust faicte au temps que le Roy Henri le Vt (que Dieu pardoint) feust a Hampton sur son primer passage vers Harflete."

Hoccleve's so-called "Address to Oldcastle" are from his attack on Lollard women (lines 145–49):

> Some wommen eeke, thogh hir wit be thynne
> Wole argumentes make in holy writ!
> Lewde calates! sittith doun and spynne,
> And kakle of sumwhat elles, for your wit
> Is al to feeble to despute of it!

The question that interests me in this article is, what does this "women's wit" have to do with Henry V's expedition to France?

Richard Firth Green has characterized the "Address" as propaganda intended for an audience at home during the war, a warning to other potential converts to Lollardy from the nobility.[2] Moreover, as the poem's exhortations for Oldcastle's quick repentence imply, Henry's offer to pardon him for his role in the Lollard revolt the year before was still good.[3] Hoccleve's poem interestingly shows that at this historical moment, Oldcastle, as he pondered the king's offer, was still in the process of becoming the figure most fully represented at the opening of the *Gesta Henrici Quinti* (1416–17). Here, the arch-heretic and traitor who, sent by God to prove the king's merit "in the furnace of tribulation," steadfastly refuses all of Henry's attempts to dissuade him from his Wycliffite beliefs.[4] Paul Strohm has shown that this fictive Oldcastle, "a Lollard leader who [would] embody the whole mixture of menace and fallibility, seductiveness and unreliability, suggested by the revolt" was a creation of Lancastrian propaganda following the 1414 rout at St. Giles's fields, at which Sir John was not even present.[5] In the *Gesta*, indeed, Oldcastle has become Henry's inheritance from his father, a grotesque parody of Henry IV and everything that was amiss during his reign—

[2] Richard Firth Green, *Poets and Princepleasers: Literature and the English Court in the Late Middle Ages* (Toronto: University of Toronto Press, 1980), pp. 183–86.
[3] Reginald Sharpe, ed., *Calendar of Letter-Books of the City of London,* Letter Book I (London: Corporation of the City of London, 1909), p. 133.
[4] *Gesta Henrici Quinti,* ed. and trans. Frank Taylor and John Roskell (Oxford: Clarendon Press, 1975), p. 3.
[5] Paul Strohm, "Sir John Oldcastle: Another Ill-Framed Knight," *The William Matthews Lectures,* Birkbeck College (London, 1997), p. 7.

continual civil war, anticlericalism, financial chaos, and, of course, his illegitimate claim to the throne:[6]

This enemy and subverter of the church, nature had indeed first made humble in rank. Then, slaughtering and pillaging the Welsh secured his promotion to knighthood, and, later still, flattering fortune called him through marriage to be Lord Cobham. And then, last of all, swollen with the lust to dominate, he desired, great as he was to be made greater, rich as he was to be made richer, and though but a subject, to become a ruler.[7]

None of the Lancastrian accounts of the period really suggest an explanation for why Hoccleve not only constructs the fiction of Oldcastle's "good old knighthood" as opposed to the *Gesta*'s account of his dubious recent "promotion" in Henry IV's civil wars, but also writes of its loss in such feverishly gendered terms. Susan Jeffords's fascinating examination of representations of the Vietnam War in the 1980s, *The Remasculinization of America,* provides a surprisingly helpful if loose analogy to Hoccleve's own imagination of war "at home." For Jeffords, an array of images of Vietnam in novels, movies, and memoirs (ranging from Nixon's apologetics to Rambo) has "restaged" the war in terms of gender, the most radical opposition amid the cultural and political confusion. Gender relations at home have become the "matrix" through which the war is reinterpreted to restore a "lost" manhood in American culture; and responsibility for the "loss" in Vietnam itself is inextricably bound up with the women's movement and a "feminized" government.[8] Much like the eighties' revisionary authors that Jeffords considers, Hoccleve is much less interested in the practical goals of England's past and future wars than in the cultural meanings of war within the frame of a national "recovery."

In both his best-known poem, *The Regement of Princes,* and the "Ad-

---

[6] On the anticlericalism of Henry IV's retainers, see Peter McNiven, *Heresy and Politics in the Reign of Henry IV: The Burning of John Badby* (Woodbridge: Boydell, 1987), pp. 73–78. See also the Franciscan *Continuatio Eulogium Historiarum,* for accounts of Henry's execution of rebellious friars and of the Archbishop of York, Richard Scrope; Frank Haydon, ed., *Eulogium Historiarum,* Rolls Series, vol. 3 (London: Longmans, 1858), pp. 333–421.

[7] *Gesta Henrici Quinti,* p. 11.

[8] Susan Jeffords, *The Remasculinization of America: Gender and the Vietnam War* (Bloomington: Indiana University Press, 1989).

dress to Oldcastle," Hoccleve grounds England's recovery from the reign of Henry IV in a revival of chivalry that encompasses a rigidly gendered literary model as well as a social ideal of war against unbelievers or heretics. In response to the threat of Lollardy to turn "good old knights" into unorthodox vernacular exegetes, Hoccleve not only seeks to portray his "father" Chaucer as a champion of orthodoxy, but formulates an idea of Chaucerian reading as a kind of chivalric practice that directly counters the feminine Lollard program of translation and interpretation.

Regimenting Wit

Questions of national identity are, of course, foremost in Hoccleve's own poetic constructions of an ideology of war and knightly governance in *The Regement of Princes,* probably written in 1412 at the height of Prince Henry's struggle with his father over the king's abandonment of the Burgundian alliance for the Armagnac side in the French civil war.[9] As in Jeffords's analysis, the nation is constituted not by an opposition between factions or the parties of war and peace, but instead a war of genders—in Hoccleve's work, principally an opposition between a nostalgic military masculinity and a disruptive feminine "wit." Toward the end of the poem, Hoccleve praises Henry for exemplifying an ideal knighthood that will, when he is finally king, keep "wit" in its proper place, in the service of battle (lines 3963–67):

> O worthy Prince! I trust in ȝour manhode,
> Medlid wiþ prudence and discrecioun
> That ȝe shal make many a kniȝtly rode
> And þe pride of our foos thristen adoun
> Manhode and witt conqueren by renoun.[10]

Wit, for Hoccleve, is not only the reason essential to wise rule but also the kind of potentially unruly thought that must itself be governed:

[9] The dating of *The Regement of Princes* is a source of much debate: Derek Pearsall argues for a date of early 1411, since Hoccleve's annuity was finally paid that year; "Hoccleve's *Regiment of Princes:* The Poetics of Royal Self-Representation," *Speculum* 69 (1994): 386–410. For arguments in support of a 1412 date, see David Lawton, "Dullness and the Fifteenth Century," *ELH* 54 (1987): 761–99; and more recently, Judith Ferster, *Fictions of Advice: The Literature and Politics of Counsel in Late Medieval England* (Philadelphia: University of Pennsylvania Press, 1996), pp. 137–59.

[10] Frederick Furnivall, ed., *The Regement of Princes,* vol. 3 of *Hoccleve's Works,* Early English Text Society [EETS], e.s., 72 (London, 1897).

"Whan reuled wit and manly hardinesse / Ben knitte to-gidre, as yok of mariage / Ther floweth of victorie the swetnesse (lines 3991–93)." As Hoccleve characterizes the current reign of Henry IV, an unruled wit rules manhood.

From the first line of the *Regement,* Hoccleve is metaphorically besieged—or ravished—by thought (lines 1–7):

> Musing upon the restless business
> Which that this troubly world hath ay on hand
> That othir thing than fruit of bitterness
> Ne yeldith nought, as I can understand.
> At Chestre inne, right fast by the stronde
> As I lay in my bed upon a nyght
> Thought me bereft of sleep with force and myght.

For the rest of the *Regement,* Hoccleve treats "thought"—his own and others'—as a symptom of an ineffectual and hence explicitly feminized political situation. Beginning with this sharp focus on the psychology of the subject rather than the prince whose moral and political formation is the ostensible topic of the poem, Hoccleve presents his deeply tormented inner condition as a kind of psychic index of the English nation.[11] As a subjectivity entirely formed by, and responsive to, political events, the poet's psyche is governed by two catastrophic national losses: the fall of Richard II, and hence all "estaaat royal" (line 23), in the Prologue, and the death of his "father" Chaucer in the *Regement* itself. As Larry Scanlon points out, the form of the *Regement,* a "Mirror of Princes" addressed to the future Henry V, "can be seen as a direct attempt to secure Lancastrian rule"; however, Hoccleve recognizes the Lancastrians' need for new terms of authority as much as time-honored traditions.[12] In both parts of the poem, Hoccleve negotiates a breakdown in the logic of paternity, seeking ultimately to repair the damage to England's masculine order with the new idea of literary authority exemplified by his relationship to Prince Henry.

Recently, James Simpson has aptly characterized Hoccleve's dialogue

---

[11] For a fascinating reading of the subtle exchanges of power, bodily and psychic, between subject and prince in the *Regement,* see Anthony Hasler, "Hoccleve's Unregimented Body," *Paragraph* 13 (1990): 164–83.

[12] Larry Scanlon, "The King's Two Voices: Narrative and Power in Hoceleve's *Regement of Princes*" in Lee Patterson, ed., *Literary Practice and Social Change in Britain, 1380–1530* (Berkeley: University of California Press, 1990), pp. 216–47.

with the beggar in the Prologue of the *Regement* as "Boethian and thera-
peutic"—a consolation and a talking cure—but also an extended consideration of the political dangers of transforming thought into speech.[13]
By drawing an initial comparison between himself and the Lollard John
Badby, recently burnt at Smithfield, Hoccleve especially suggests the
danger of writing in English in the years immediately following the
issuing of Arundel's *Constitutions* in 1409. As Nicholas Watson has argued, Hoccleve walks a thin tightrope by using vernacular writing even
to defend orthodoxy, since the Constitutions' seventh article, forbidding
anyone to "translate any text of Holy Scripture into English or any other
language *on his own authority*" (my emphasis) inevitably put all English
texts that considered doctrinal issues under suspicion of heresy.[14] Several
critics, moreover, have recently described at length how the opponents
of biblical translation in the academic debate that preceded the *Constitutions* (ca. 1400) drew such intense polemical focus to the figure of the
reading and preaching woman as the embodiment of misinterpretation,
that all vernacular theology came to be understood in hermeneutic
terms as essentially feminine.[15] In both the *Regement* and the "Address
to Oldcastle," Hoccleve transforms this newly invigorated antifeminist
discourse into a language of national politics; he effectively uses the contemporary suppression of Lollardy and the *lingua materna* to construct a
masculine, knightly paradigm of translation that, as I will discuss in
greater detail below, finally recalls the common French and English chivalric literary culture of the thirteenth century.

In the *Regement,* vernacular public poetry, written from sheer eco-

---

[13] James Simpson, "Nobody's Man: Thomas Hoccleve's *Regiment of Princes,*" in Julia
Boffey and Pamela King, eds., *London and Europe in the Late Middle Ages* (London: Westfield Publications in Medieval Studies, 1996), pp. 149–80.

[14] Nicholas Watson, "Censorship and Cultural Change in Late-Medieval England:
Vernacular Theology, the Oxford Translation Debate, and Arundel's Constitutions of
1409," *Speculum* 70 (1995): 821–64. For the text of the seventh constitution, see David
Wilkins, *Concilia Magnae Britanniae et Hiberniae,* vol. 3 (London, 1737), p. 317; for a
translation, see John Foxe, *Acts and Monuments,* ed. G. Townsend, vol. 3 (London, 1843–
49), p. 245.

[15] This is, as Watson points out, especially clear in Richard Ullerston's 1401 *determi-
natio* in defense of translation, which emphasizes the clerical opposition's fear of women
(*muliericulae*) teaching men; "Censorship," p. 843. See also Ralph Hanna III, "The Difficulty of Ricardian Prose Translation: The Case of the Lollards," *MLQ* 51 (1990): 319–40.
For a reading that focuses on the problem of "feminine hermeneutics," see Rita Copeland, "Why Women Can't Read: Medieval Hermeneutics, Statutory Law and the Lollard
Heresy Trials," in Susan Heinzelman and Zipporah Wiseman, eds., *Representing Women:
Law, Literature and Feminism* (Durham, N.C.: Duke University Press, 1994), pp. 253–86.

nomic necessity, is the only alternative to a dangerously excessive interiority. The beggar who prompts Hoccleve into talking is the consummate public man who "wele telle al and more" (line 259) for money; his inner life and his livelihood are one and the same. He advises Hoccleve to "bewar of þoght, for it is perillous / . . . His violence is ful outrageous" (lines 267–69) and to follow his own professional example of profitable speech rather than risk Badby's heresy: "som man, for *lak of occupatioun* / museth further than his wit may strecche" (lines 281–82; my emphasis). Without disavowing the depths of his sickness, Hoccleve must nevertheless declare its symptoms free of theological content: "Of our feith wol I not despute at all" (line 379). If Lollardy is the potential extreme of Hoccleve's own gloomy "wit," immediately caused by the nonpayment of his annuity, the beggar explains that orthodoxy is his real paternal inheritance (lines 354–57):

> As holy chirche us byt, let us be-leve;
> But we þer-to obeye, it schal us greve
> Importably; lat us do as she byt,
> Oure goede fadres olde han folwyd it.

This said to absolve themselves further of feminizing heretical "thought" in their English dialogue, the beggar and Hoccleve together deliver a harsh complaint on the reign of Henry IV precisely in terms of the failure of inheritance and masculinity.

In the account of Henry IV's first parliament in 1399, it is the king himself who is the remasculinizing savior of England. Immediately preceding the text of the "Record and Process" of Richard's "renunciation," Archbishop Arundel lauds the new ruler:

The archbishop confirmed that the honorable kingdom of England, which is the most abundant "corner of riches" in all the world, had been for a long time led, ruled and governed by children and the counsel of widows; by which the said realm had been almost at the point of destruction, and very sorrowfully would have been thrown into great desolation and trouble, if God almighty in his great grace and mercy had not sent a wise and discreet man to govern the kingdom. . . .

[le Ercevesq avoit monstre, Qe cest honorable Roialme d'Engleterre, q'est le pluis habundant Angle de Richesse parmy tout le monde, avoit estee par longe temps mesnez, reulez, & governez par Enfantz, & conseil des Vesves; par ont mesme le Roialme feust en point de perdition, & d'avoir este mys a tres grande desolation & mescheif tres doulourousement, s'il ne feusse que Dieu tout-puissante de sa grand grace et mercy avoit mys un Homme sachant & discret pur Governance de mesme le Roialme. . . .][16]

In the *Regement,* however, it becomes apparent that the formerly "wise and discreet man" has clearly misgoverned England with the same "wast & destruction" as the widows and children.[17] For the beggar, the economic disarray of England under Henry IV is exemplified by lavish fashions that obscure not only the estates but the sexes. He asserts, in vocabulary typical of complaints on the decline of chivalry, that if a lord were attacked in the street, his retainer would be helpless with his "out-rageous" £20 sleeves: "He may nat him availle. / In swych a cas he nys but a woman; / He may nat stand him in steed of a man" (lines 468–69).[18] Addressing the lords themselves, he warns (lines 480–83):

> Yeve unto your men hir pars
> That so doon, and aqwente hem bet with Mars,
> God of bataile; he loveth non array
> That hurteth manhode at preef or assay.

England's social ills are due, then, to an collapse of knightly ideals, an effeminate abandonment of war. To evoke the old style, when men dressed like men, the beggar turns to "of Lancaster duk John": "I never sy a lord that cowde hym gye / Bet like his estat; Al knightly prowesse / Was to him girt" (lines 516–18). His nostalgia for John of Gaunt, how-ever, underscores all the more his son's failure as king to follow in his manly footsteps: "O England! stande up-ryght on thy feet!" (line 537), the beggar concludes.

Hoccleve picks up the complaint in much the same nostalgic vein, attributing his "woful mourning" (line 795) to his inability to collect

---

[16] *Rotuli Parliamentorum,* vol. 3 (London, 1783), p. 415. All translations are my own, unless otherwise noted.

[17] For a reading of the *Regement*'s harsh assessment of Henry IV's financial policies, see Ferster, *Fictions of Advice,* pp. 142–50.

[18] These observations are, of course, not original to the beggar: for a similarly gen-dered attack on English fashions, see the *Eulogium Historiarum*'s account of 1362 (vol. 3, pp. 230–31). On contemporary French ideas on the role of style in chivalric reform, see *The Book of Chivalry of Geoffroi de Charny,* ed. and trans. Richard W. Kaeuper and Elspeth Kennedy (Philadelphia: University of Pennsylvania Press), pp. 55–56 and 195.

his annuity of twenty marks and comparing himself, in his impending poverty and with body literally broken by twenty-four years of office work, to the "old men of armes" (line 890), veterans of the French wars from Edward III's and John of Gaunt's time (lines 878–81):

> Now al forgete is þe manly labour
> þorgh which ful ofte þey hire foos afferde
> Now be þo worþi men bet with þe yerde
> Of nede, allas!

Hoccleve's own situation as a Privy Seal clerk, "ful sore / in evere veyne and place of his body" (lines 1025–26) and haunted by "thought," is typical of a larger devaluing of "manly" service in an age where war has lost its force of national unity and identity.

Hoccleve acknowledges that payment for his work has none of the certainty of inheritance—"servyse, I wot wel, is non heritage" (line 841); but in the *Regement* as a whole, it is clearly heritage that is no longer heritage. The beggar's practical advice to Hoccleve, which generates the poem itself, is to pass over the king and appeal to Prince Henry to pay the debt instead, a move that casts some ambiguity on his acclaim of the prince as "no man bet *next* his father our lord lige" (line 1835; my emphasis).[19] The symbolic fragility of the Lancastrian line had become public in the political crisis of 1411–12, when Henry IV dismissed the prince and his supporters from the Council, and then, reversing the prince's policy toward the warring French factions, appointed his son Thomas to lead his expedition in support of the Armagnacs.[20] In his "open letter" to his father, declaring his full loyalty, the prince claims that "creators of schism" who wanted "to disturb the line of sucession" had accused him of planning a coup to usurp the throne.[21] By, as Simpson puts it, "quietly sidelining" the king in his address to the prince, Hoc-

---

[19] On Hoccleve's clear slights to Henry IV, see Lawton, "Dullness and the Fifteenth Century," pp. 776–77.

[20] On the power struggle between Henry IV and the prince, see Peter McNiven, "Prince Henry and the English Political Crisis of 1412," *History* 65 (1980): 1–16. See also Christopher Allmand, *Henry V* (Berkeley: University of California Press, 1992), pp. 39–58.

[21] *The St. Albans Chronicle 1406–1420,* ed. V. H. Galbraith (Oxford: Clarendon Press, 1937), p. 66: ". . . quidam iniquitatis filii, dissencionum alumpni, fautores scismatis, seminatores ire et discordiarum causatores qui consuetudinario quodam usu regie securitatis invidentes stabili fundamento ac serpentina calliditate quadam successionis sue seriem impetere cupientes." See also McNiven, "Prince Henry," pp. 7–8.

cleve confirms the collapse of the very ideas of genealogy that Henry IV had himself once so assiduously deployed to support the Lancastrian title to the throne, the "prototypical propaganda machine" of dubious claims that Strohm has catalogued.[22] Writing in this vacuum of royal authority, the poet signals the need for a novel strategy of legitimation—the fictional genealogy of Chaucerianism.[23]

As soon as Hoccleve demurs from the beggar's suggestion that he write an appeal to Henry in Latin or French, he reveals both his own name and his more significant identity as one "acquainted with Chaucer" (line 1867). Hoccleve's relationship with Chaucer defines his role as an exclusively vernacular author, despite his work at the Privy Seal. The beggar insists: "Althogh þou seye that þou in latyn, / Ne in frenssh nowther, canst but smal endite, / In englyssh tonge canst þou wel afyn" (lines 1870–72). Chaucerianism, as a self-consciously literary idiom and ideology, becomes Hoccleve's vehicle for the "remasculinization" of England. As Derek Pearsall has written, "Chaucer was clearly important in the establishment of this narrative of nationhood: his already established reputation made him eminently well-suited to serve as the father of English poetry."[24] Hoccleve, however, almost entirely obscures Chaucer's actual works with the elusive subject of his acquaintance, an abstract concept of the Ricardian poet's new Lancastrian cultural role. The idea of the "Chaucerian" text as a lost ideal recalls the earlier, chivalric England of John of Gaunt and becomes a means of overthrowing the androgynous excesses of the current king's reign by defining the terms of a continuous history of vernacular literature and the relationship between poet and power.

As his introductory address to Prince Henry makes clear, far more important than which work of advice Hoccleve translates is *how* he conceives of the acts of translation and offering advice. After all, he assures the prince he has already read all three of his Latin sources, Giles of Rome's *De regimine principum,* the *Secretum secretorum,* and Jacobus de Cessolis's *Ludo de scachorum.* Hoccleve's ideology of translation here is close

---

[22] Simpson, "Nobody's Man," p. 174. Paul Strohm, "Saving the Appearances: Chaucer's 'Purse' and the Fabrication of the Lancastrian Claim," in *Hochon's Arrow* (Princeton, N.J.: Princeton University Press, 1992), pp. 75–94.

[23] Larry Scanlon reads Hoccleve's "canonization" of Chaucer as a strategy to secure Lancanstrian legitimacy: "Hoccleve's celebration of the nascent English tradition embodied in Chaucer and the political authority embodied in Henry are the twin faces of the same moral vision" ("The King's Two Voices," p. 242).

[24] Pearsall, "Poetics of Royal Self-Representation," pp. 398.

to the constellation of ideas in John Trevisa's *Dialogus Inter Dominum et Clericum* that Ralph Hanna identifies with the "magnate culture" of Trevisa's patron, Thomas Berkeley.[25] According to Trevisa's Dominus, Higden's *Polychronicon* should be translated:

forthey Ich cunne speke and rede and understone Latyn þer ys moche Latyn in theus bokes of cronyks that Y can noȝt understonde, noþer þou wiþoute studyinge and avysement and lokyng of other bokes. Also þey hyt were noȝt neodful vor me hyt is neodful vor oþere men that understondwþ so Latyn.[26]

This is translation in the service of aristocratic privilege; as Hanna recounts, Trevisa produced for Berkeley "a complete analysis of the created world (Bartholomeus Anglicus's *De Proprietatibus Rerum*), a complete depiction of human activity (*Polychronicon*) and a model for the exercise of control over the world (*De Regimine Principum*)."[27] Within the *Dialogus*'s frame of aristocratic nationalism, the problem of female readership never even arises. Dominus's defense of translation does come close to Lollard anticlerical polemic, especially when he enumerates the translations of the Bible already made from Latin into French and English: "Also holy writ was translated out of Gru into Latyn and þanne out of Latyn ynto Frensch. þanne what hath Englysch trespased that hyt myȝt noȝt be translated into Englysch?" (line 292).[28] As Hanna argues, though, Dominus's desire is more for encyclopedic knowledge than "holy writ," for information that will strengthen his and other lords' power.[29] For Hoc-

[25] Ralph Hanna III, "Sir Thomas Berkeley and His Patronage," *Speculum* 64 (1989): 878–916.

[26] Ronald Waldron, ed., "Trevisa's Original Prefaces on Translation: A Critical Edition," in Edward Kennedy, Ronald Waldron, and Joseph Wittig, eds., *Medieval Studies Presented to George Kane* (Woodbridge: Boydell, 1988), pp. 290–91.

[27] Hanna, "Sir Thomas Berkeley," p. 898. On the various models of English translation in the fourteenth and fifteenth centuries, see Rita Copeland, *Rhetoric, Hermeneutics, and Translation in the Middle Ages: Academic Traditions and Vernacular Texts* (Cambridge University Press, 1991), pp. 221–29.

[28] The General Prologue to the Wycliffite Bible makes a similar case: "Also Frenshe men, Beemers, and Britons han the bible . . . translated in here modir langage; whi shulden not English men have the same in here modir langage, I can not wite, no but for falsnesse and negligence of clerkis"; J. Forshall and F. Madden, eds., *The Holy Bible . . . Made from the Latin Vulgate by John Wycliffe and His Followers*, vol. 1 (Oxford, 1850), p. 59. Richard Ullerston, in his orthodox defense of translation, also cites a long list of historical precedents, many of which are also included in the Lollard tract derived from his work; see Watson, "Censorship," pp. 844–45, and Curt Bühler, "A Lollard Tract: On Translating the Bible into English," *MAE* 7, no. 3 (1938): 167–83.

[29] Hanna, "Sir Thomas Berkeley," pp. 896–99.

cleve, writing a crucial decade later, the challenge is precisely to define such aristocratic English literature, including Chaucer's writing, as absolutely distinct from the Lollards' idea of vernacularity.[30] As he explains to his patron, the purpose of the *Regement's* exemplary "stories" is actually to protect him from thought should he find himself in the same sleepless condition as the poet (lines 2138–42):[31]

> Yf that you list of stories to take hede,
> Somewhat it may profite, by your leve:
> At hardest, when þat ye ben in chambre at eve,
> They ben goode to drive forth the nyght;
> They shaull not harme, yf þey ben herd a-right.

As in Trevisa's *Dialogus,* English is "harmless," despite potential clerical objections; it is the most intimate and best understood idiom of counsel, the antidote to, rather than the source of, Lollard theological musings.

By representing his "dere maister" Chaucer's death as a mirror of the ravages of war, Hoccleve at once recalls the blow to "estaat royal" in the opening stanzas of the poem and points to his and the prince's common project of English recovery (lines 2080–86):

> Allas! My worthy maister honorable
> This landes very treasure and richesse,
> Deth, by thi deth, hath harme irreparable
> Unto us doon: hir vengeable duresse
> Despoiled hath þis land of þe sweetnesse
> Of rhetorik; for un-to Tullius
> Was never man so lyk amonges us.

If the prince's future (or perhaps even present) task will be to replace the dead-end, effeminate reigns of both Richard II *and* Henry IV, Hoccleve's will be to write in English in a land bereft of rhetoric, to define himself as the heir to a literature that can be safely defined only by analogy to a secular, nontheological classical tradition: Chaucer was, he explains, the English Aristotle and Virgil as well as Cicero. Yet if in Chaucer's time

---

[30] On the prince's "preemptive strike" to claim English for his own governmental uses, as opposed to theology, see Pearsall, "Poetics of Royal Self-Representation," p. 408.
[31] See Simpson, "Nobody's Man," p. 180.

English had what Scanlon calls "traditional authority," it had since undergone radical change.[32] As Hoccleve laments, it is not just Chaucer but the "English tongue" that has died: "But weilaway so is my herte wo, / That þe honour of the englyssh tonge is deed, / Of which I wont was han consail and reed" (lines 1958–60). The vernacular has become identified with heresy and subject to censorship; its authority has been lost to the kind of theological "despute" that Hoccleve refuses. As representatives of what English literature will henceforth mean, both Hoccleve and the prince are committed to a concept of legitimacy understood as a fiction of tradition, a restoration of knightly "honor" strangely based at the same time on a new level of theoretical abstraction and a renunciation of new "thought."

In the poem's single most famous passage, explaining Chaucer's portrait toward the end of the *Regement,* Hoccleve sets forth the relation between "the firste finder of our fair langage" (line 4978) and thought. As Pearsall notes, Hoccleve prefaces the portrait by characterizing Chaucer as a devotional poet of perfect orthodoxy who "wroote ful many a lyne" to the Virgin Mary (line 4987). Chaucer's picture, moreover, is a quasi-religious image, which Hoccleve includes so "þat þey þat have of him lost thought and mind / By this peynture may ageyn him fynde (lines 4997–98)."[33] Pearsall argues that this formulation is close to Walter Hilton's and others' orthodox defenses of the value of images against Lollard iconoclasm.[34] Hoccleve, however, adds a unusual epistemological twist to the doctrine of image and prototype circulating in such contemporary arguments, focusing on the consequences not just of seeing but also of *not seeing* images: "Where oft unsyte of hem causith restreyntes of thoughtes good" (lines 5002–3). In other words, not seeing Chaucer for what he truly was could lead to bad thoughts, which here clearly encompass the poet's own melancholy, as well as Lollardy, and worse. Beyond the fixed, directed devotion suggested by a saint's image, Chaucer's portrait functions here as a kind of thought-police, a regimenting of the possibilities of English writing into either orthodox devotional poetry or a secular and nationalist "Chaucerian" literature. It is, in effect, an internal censorship of English poetry as imaginatively restrictive as the *Constitutions.* The image, much like Hoccleve's poem

[32] Scanlon, "The King's Two Voices," p. 241.
[33] Pearsall, "Poetics of Royal Self-Representation," pp. 401–3.
[34] Ibid., pp. 405–6.

as a whole, in a sense *replaces* Chaucer's own writing with a politicized memory of the poet and his reception; it erases heresy or rebellion by definition from what Prince Henry and the English knightly class could conceivably "see" or "fynde" in Chaucer's works.

The *Regement,* as Hoccleve ideologically frames it, a translation of works *already known* to the prince, becomes the "Chaucerian" and "Lancastrian" work par excellence, using English neither to offer new ideas nor to inspire them at high levels of rule. In this assessment of the psychic nation under the rule of Henry IV—a condition plagued by loss and doubt like the poet himself in the Prologue—it is the portrait of *Hoccleve's* "father" and "master," and pointedly not the prince's father, that curtails the kind of dangerous "thought" that could turn the mother tongue into an idiom for a theology of the lower estates and women.

It is only with the license of Chaucer's portrait that Hoccleve adopts an ironic "Chaucerian" voice to deliver the *Regement's* final advice, controversial only in its unwillingness to endorse any faction: a call for an end to all civil wars, followed by a plea for peace with France urging Henry to marry Princess Catherine, the youngest daughter of Charles IV.[35] Avoiding any mention of both Henry IV's new policies toward France or the prince's temporarily thwarted military ambitions, Hoccleve constructs an elaborate facetious argument in favor of women's advice and women's sovereignty that draws on both *The Tale of Melibee* and *The Wife of Bath's Prologue* and *Tale.*[36] Praising women's geometrically perfect "cercly shape" (line 5127) against the patristic antifeminist image of Eve as a "crooked rib," Hoccleve maintains that husbands should obey their wives in order to secure peace: "Thogh a woman hir housbonde contrarie / In his oppynoun erroneous, / Shul men for þat deme her his adversarie?" (lines 5188–90). In a more somber tone, Hoccleve

---

[35] Negotiations for a truce between England and France had involved a proposed match between the Prince of Wales and one of the French princesses since 1406, and Catherine was suggested in 1408; however, in both the years immediately before and after he became king, Henry V also flirted with marriage to one of the daughters of John, Duke of Burgundy in order to shore up their alliance. See Allmand, *Henry V,* pp. 47–50; J. Hamilton Wylie, *History of England under Henry the Fourth,* vol. 3 (London: Longmans, 1896), pp. 44 and 100, and vol. 4 (1898), pp. 31–65. For an outspoken objection to marriage between Henry V and Princess Catherine from the Armagnac side in 1414, see J. H. Wylie, "Memorandum Concerning a Proposed Marriage between Henry V and Catherine of France in 1414," *EHR* 29 (1914): 322–23.

[36] Catherine Batt, "Hoccleve and . . . Feminism? Negotiating Meaning in *The Regiment of Princes,*" in Batt, ed., *Essays on Thomas Hoccleve* (Turnhout: Brepols, 1996), pp. 55–84.

also reveals the proper courtly role of women as figures who represent the desire for peace, like Princess Catherine and St. Bridget, but only within a national rhetoric that continues to pursue the aims of war: English rule in France and a "crusade" against heresy. As Catherine Batt interprets the confusing register of this section, it is here that the poet most shrewdly thematizes his own precarious position as an advice-giver during a time of political crisis: by echoing the voices of both his literary father and his fictional female advisors, Hoccleve underscores the continually shifting position of the writer with regard to power in the post–Chaucerian state. The figure of Chaucer thus represents the subversive end of reintroducing an abstract "feminine" language into the exclusively masculine "political arena" in order to show how power determines meaning. Hoccleve's Chaucerian allusions, however, raise the issue of women's sovereignty not to end the poem with a "multiplicity" of interpretations but to introduce the ultimate problematic topic of "my mateere of werre inward" (line 5286), civil strife in both France and England.[37]

Hoccleve's Chaucerian fiction of a "rule of women" in fact conveniently stands in for the misgovernance of England by Henry IV. Having decried Adam's obedience to Eve as a Lollard-sounding "pees inordinat . . . as thus, whan to his soget a prelate obeyeth" (lines 5090–93), Hoccleve worries:

> If þat þis come into the audience
> Of women, I am sure I shal be shent:
> ffor that I touch of swich obedience,
> Many a browe shal on me be bent;
> Thei wille wayten been equipollent,
> And sumwhat more unto hir husbondis
> And sum men seyn swich usage in þis lond is. (lines 5104–9)

With this final line echoing the beggar's attack on androgynous styles earlier in the *Regement,* Hoccleve again elaborates his vision of the prince's rule as a break with his father's policies. For a translation— however free—of *De regimine principum,* a work so pointedly directed to men, to "come into the audience of women" illustrates Hoccleve's larger sense of political "usage" in 1412. This scenario, which imagines Prince

[37] Ibid., p. 81.

Henry's immediate disempowerment as a feminized vernacular misreading of the standard works of counsel, sets up Hoccleve's call for peace as a final contrast between the current political situation and a future era of unity. To this end, Hoccleve devotes considerable space to the French civil war as a mirror of England (lines 5303–6):

> O! nowe adayes is noon enemye
> Lyke oon þat is to othir of bloode nye;
> Beth ware! correct it! lest men of yow seye,
> "lo! whilom this was ffraunce of hye nobley!"[38]

Henry IV's reign, like France under the helpless Charles le Fol, is characterized by "the ryot þat haþ ben with-in þis lande / Among our-self, many a wyntres space" (lines 5216–17), including the division between the king and the prince. By contrast, Henry V's reign and marriage will unite the two nations, fulfilling the divine revelation of Christ to St. Bridget (lines 5388–90):

> "I am pees verray; þere I wole abide
> Where as pees is; non oþer wole I do
> Of ffraunce and Engelond þe kynges two
> If þei wole have pees, pees perpetuel
> Thei schul han"; thus hir book seiþ woot I wel.

With this turn to visionary authority, Hoccleve anticipates much of Henry V's future pious propaganda by affirming that, unlike his father, he is the legitimate heir to the *English* throne as well as the French.[39]

Having forcefully condemned war among "cristen princes," Hoccleve further looks ahead to the "Address to Oldcastle" by shifting the focus of battle to heresy in the last lines of the poem (lines 5433–6):

> Upon þe mescreantys to make werre,
> And hem unto the feith of crist to brynge,

---

[38] Although there is no evidence that Hoccleve would have known the text, this entire section of the *Regement* is remarkably similar in tone to Christine de Pizan's "Lamentacion sur les maux de la guerre civile," written in 1410. See Josette Wisman, ed., *The Epistle of the Prison of Human Life with An Epistle to the Queen of France and Lament on the Evils of the Civil War* (New York: Garland, 1984), pp. 84–95.

[39] On the trope of Henry as God's elect in Lancastrian writing, see Strohm, "Sir John Oldcastle," pp. 8–9.

Good were; therynne may ye no thyng erre,
That were a meritorye werrying.[40]

Ending where he began, with an echo of the Lollard Badby—whom the prince, "thristynge sore his savacioun," (line 298) had unsuccessfully tried to convert—Hoccleve signals both his own "cure," his new political identity as a Chaucerian author, and his ideological program for the future king. The remasculinization of England will be achieved by war, not with France but with "thought."

Oldcastle's Books

By 1415, Hoccleve had abandoned his call for peace in favor of an ostensible celebration of the cultural goals of Henry V's war. In an article on Hoccleve's near-contemporary John Lydgate, Lee Patterson has shown how Henry's rhetoric of national identity during the war created the contradictions at the core of what became after Charles IV's death the "dual monarchy":

On the one hand it had insisted on English integrity versus French duplicity, presenting England as politically unified and ethically coherent while France was riven by internal divisions and corrupted by duplicity. Yet on the other hand, it had also claimed that the war was undertaken to heal the rift between the fraternal nations England and France, to bring back to unity—to oneness and integrity—two crowns that were in truth part of a single whole.[41]

For Hoccleve, this idea of unity is an occasion, like the *Regement,* to reinvent "good old knighthood," a reactionary French and English chivalric ideology, as a force to oppose the Lollards. His chivalry is, however, more concerned with books than with actual battle, a theory of interpretation grounded in the culture of war.

[40] While these lines have usually been taken as a call for a crusade to the Holy Land, the language closely mirrors Hoccleve's other attacks on the Lollards as "foos of Christ," including of course the "Address to Oldcastle" and the "Ballads to Henry V and the Knights of the Garter," in *Hoccleve's Works: The Minor Poems,* ed. Frederick Furnivall and I. Gollancz, EETS, 1892; rev. by Jerome Mitchell and A. I. Doyle (New York: Oxford University Press, 1970), pp. 41–43.

[41] Lee Patterson, "Making Identities in Fifteenth-Century England: Henry V and John Lydgate," in Jeffrey Cox and Larry Reynolds, eds., *New Historical Literary Study* (Princeton, N.J.: Princeton University Press, 1993), p. 89.

In the "Address to Oldcastle," the poem composed for the outset of
Henry V's French expedition, the feminizing of thought implicit in the
Regement becomes the open theme of a polemic on "wit" and war. Here,
Oldcastle the soldier takes Hoccleve's place as the representative Lancas-
trian subject, seduced by Lollard "thought." Since his escape from the
Tower in 1413, after his condemnation for heresy, Oldcastle had been in
hiding, inspiring narratives that emphasized his military leadership of
the Lollard "forces" even after the 1414 rebellion.[42]

As in the Prologue of the *Regement,* Hoccleve imagines orthodox faith
as an English birthright (lines 153–58):

> Oure fadres old and modres lyved wel
> And tagthe hir children as hemself taght were
> Of holy chirche, and axid nat a del
> Why stant this word here and why this word there?
> Why spak God thus and seith thus elles where?
> Why did he this wise and might han do thus?

Neither Oldcastle's parents nor Hoccleve's nor King Henry's were theologians or, more to the point, textual critics. This crisis of inheritance
and obedience in their own generation, featuring mothers—tongues
untied—as exegetes, is the result of Lollard ideas of translation. Likewise, neither a Lancastrian military leader *nor* a court poet should treat
the Bible as a text for open discussion, as do the Lollard women with
their "thin wit" and "arguments." Hoccleve goes on to link orthodoxy
to the lineal basis of the nobility (lines 161–78):

> If land to thee be falle of heritage,
> Which þat thy father held in reste & pees
> With title just and trewe all his age,
> And his fadir before him brygelees
> And his and his & so foorth doutelees
> I am ful suer who so wolde it thee reve

[42] The most bizarre story that Walsingham recounts, in order to emphasize Oldcastle's
renewed threat to England since the king's departure for Harfleur, claims that his
hiding-place discovered in 1415 was found to hold, besides arms and money, "a banner
. . . on which he had had painted the chalice and the host in the form of bread as if the
sacrament could be celebrated there." This and other banners painted with "the cross
with the scourges, lance and nails" were meant "to seduce the common people." *St. Albans Chronicle,* p. 89.

Thow woldest thee deffende and put in prees
Thy right thow woldest nat, thy thankes, leve.
Right so where as our goode fadres olde
Possessid were, & hadden the seisyne
Peisible of Crystes feith, & no man wolde
Impugne hir right; it sit us to enclyne
Ther-to. Let us no ferthere ymagyne
But as that they dide! Occupie our right
And in our hertes fully determyne
Our title good & keep it with our might
Who so hath right and nat wole it deffende
It is no manhode, it is cowardyse.

The "right" to refuse thought and interpretation is Oldcastle's inheritance, his "manhood" even, stolen by a feminine heresy that still holds some sway in the kingdom only recently inherited by Henry V. Indeed, like the French "land," this faith is a title to be maintained by force: the occasion of the poem has become the metaphor for the war "at home."

By comparing the war with France to the war against heresy as defenses of England's traditional realms, Hoccleve of course echoes the new king's own propaganda efforts directed at internal and external enemies.[43] The practical effects of this line of argument are particularly evident in a text like the letter sent to the king in France by the mayor and aldermen of London in 1415, announcing the sentencing of John Cleydon to be burned as a relapsed heretic:

Forasmuch as the King of all might and the Lord of Heaven, who of late graciously taught your hands to fight; and has guided your feet to the battle, has

---

[43] In describing the inherited right of faith, Hoccleve echoes the rhetoric of Chancellor Henry Beaufort from Henry V's third parliament, held at Westminster in 1414: "And so the chancellor, by command of the king, pronounced the summons to the said Parliament, declaring from the outset how our very sovereign lord the king desires above all that good and honest policy be made towards his enemies abroad, and beyond that how he would strengthen himself in order to recover the inheritance and right of his crown now outside the kingdom, which had long been kept and wrongfully witheld since the time of his progenitors and predecessors, the kings of England"; ["Et puis mesme le Chanceller, del commandement le Roy, pronuncia la cause del somons du dit Parlement, declarant a commencement comment nostre tres soverain Sr le Roi desire soverainment le bone et discrete governace estre fait vers ses Enemys dehors, & outre ceo coment luy afforcera pur recoverer de l'enheritance & droit de sa corone, esteant hors du Roialme, quell ad estee longement retreit & torcenousment detenu es temps de ses progenitours & predecessours Rois d'Engleterre"] (*Rotuli Parliamentorum,* 4: 34).

now, during your absence, placed in our hands certain persons who not only were enemies of Him and of your dignity, but also, in so far as they might be, were subverters of the whole of your realm; men commonly known as "Lollards."[44]

Read in this local political context, the passage of the "Address" on the "title just" of faith makes it readily apparent why *this* poem—singularly uninterested in France and its politics—is in fact Hoccleve's manifesto on the new king's military strategy. For Hoccleve, the real war is actually over Oldcastle and an abstract "manhood," a war about reading that concerns the English forces far more than the French territories.

Following the idea of the secular, traditional "Chaucerian" literature that he constructs in the *Regement,* Hoccleve in the "Address" further recuperates this patrilineal vernacular, imagining gender as politically constituted through forms of textual reception. In what is perhaps the most peculiar passage in the poem, Hoccleve warns Oldcastle to abandon the Bible in favor of more masculine vernacular texts (lines 193–200):

> Bewar Oldcastle & for Crystes sake
> Clymbe no more in holy writ so hie!
> Rede the story of Lancelot de lake,
> Or Vegece the aart of Chivalrie,
> The seege of Troie or Thebes thee applie
> To thyng þat may to thordre of knight longe!

With this succinct reading-list, Hoccleve presents Oldcastle with the cultural unity of France and England as an alternative to heresy. These are, at once, the great French vernacular courtly works of the twelfth and thirteenth centuries, including the prose *Lancelot,* Jean de Meun's translation of Vegetius's *De re militari,* Benoit de Ste.-Maure's *Roman de Troie* and the *Roman de Thèbes,* and also works recently produced in En-

---

[44] H. T. Riley, ed. and trans., *Memorials of London and London Life in the Thirteenth, Fourteenth, and Fifteenth Centuries, 1276–1419* (London, 1868), p. 617; Sharpe, ed., *Calendar of Letter Books,* Letter Book I, pp. 140–41. For more on Cleydon and his trial, see Anne Hudson, *The Premature Reformation: Wycliffite Texts and Lollard History* (New York: Oxford University Press, 1988), pp. 211–14.

glish. Oldcastle can recover his heritage or "order of knighthood" by means of this series of translations, which both gestures toward Chaucer's *Troilus* and *Knight's Tale* and deftly reduces them to studies of siege technique alongside the new English version of Vegetius.[45] This latter work epitomizes Hoccleve's ideal of a text without "thought." A blunt how-to manual for winning a war with the Roman army, Vegetius's late-fourth-century text is hopelessly out of date technically, but oft-translated and impeccably traditional. John Walton introduces Vegetius in his 1408 translation, "the whiche tretys techith holliche of knighthood and of chivalrye": it is about war in its essence, drawn even by its author from "olde writeris."[46] The translation serves to create a historical line between an idealized age of chivalry and fifteenth-century English military goals. Like Oldcastle's knightly orthodoxy, a title ideally passed down unchanged by his male line, Hoccleve's list of books focuses on a similarly static "genealogy" of war.

Hoccleve treats war itself as an ideology of interpretation, a lens with which Oldcastle's class should read vernacular literature. Far more striking than his idea of Lancelot's "story" as a substitute for biblical exegesis, though, is Hoccleve's extension of the notion of chivalric reading to a historical-romance canon of the Old Testament. He admonishes Oldcastle (lines 201–8):

> If thee list thyng rede of auctoritee,
> To these stories sit it thee to goon:
> To Judicum, Regum, and Iosue,
> To Judith & to Paralipomenon
> And Machabe & as siker as stoon,
> If þat thee list in hem bayte thyn ye,
> More autentike thing shalt thow fynde noon,
> Ne more pertinent to Chivalrie.

[45] Although Hoccleve figures Oldcastle as a representative aristocratic vernacular reader, the historical Oldcastle was literate in Latin; see Hudson, *The Premature Reformation*, pp. 116–17.

[46] Geoffery Lester, ed., *The Earliest English Translation of Vegetius'* De Re Militari (Heidelberg: Carl Winter Universitätsverlag, 1988), pp. 47–48. Vegetius is also the source for the final section of Giles of Rome's *De regimine principum*, on "chevalrye." See *The Governance of Kings and Princes: John Trevisa's Middle English Translation of the* De Regimine Principum *of Aegidius Romanus*, ed. David Fowler, Charles Briggs, and Paul Remley (New York: Garland, 1997), pp. 393–439. See also J. Wisman, "*L'Epitoma Rei Militaris* de Végèce et sa Fortune au Moyen Age," *Le Moyen Age* 85 (1979): 13–31.

Again, Hoccleve recalls French chivalric culture, specifically the thirteenth-century vernacular versions of these particular books of the Old Testament made during the later Crusades, as well as the voluminous literature on the "Nine Worthies."[47] In a sense, Hoccleve's implication that the Bible should be available in English as well as French is in line with both Trevisa's and the Lollards' "nationalist" cultural arguments for translation; however, the Bible he envisions is effectively censored by its own theory of reception. Rather than condemn biblical translation outright, Hoccleve gestures toward Oldcastle as a vernacular reader who, instead of usurping the feminized role of a priest as the knight's "soules norice" (line 212), should adopt a chivalric ideology shaped by a narrowly limited access to scripture and exegesis. In this knightly idea of translation, so different from the Lollards', the military virtues of *Maccabees* lend biblical "auctoritee" to those in *Lancelot* and other works of chivalry.[48]

Given Hoccleve's demonstration of his familiarity with the vocabulary of Lollard polemic, which he answers point by point in the second half of the "Address," he clearly intends this lopsided canon as a rejoinder to the Wycliffite politics of vernacular exegesis. The General Prologue to the Wycliffite Bible envisions a society based on open access to doctrine: "cristen men and wymmen olde and yonge shulden study fast in the newe testament, for it is ful of autorite, and opyn to undirstondyng of simple men as to the poyntis that be moost nedeful to salvacioun."[49] In the subsequent summary and discussion of the Old Testament and apocrypha, the Wycliffite author illustrates how these texts, traditionally the doctrinal basis of discussions of good and bad rule, should specifically be used for the "edification" of aristocratic English readers.[50]

---

[47] On French translations of the bible, see C. A. Robson, "Vernacular Scriptures in France," in G. W. H. Lampe, ed., *The Cambridge History of the Bible*, vol. 2 (Cambridge: Cambridge University Press, 1969), pp. 436–52. On the chivalric mythology of Old Testament military leaders and the "nine worthies" (*neuf preux*)—Joshua, David, Judas Maccabeus, Hector, Alexander, Julius Caesar, Arthur, Charlemagne, and Godfrey de Bouillon—see Maurice Keen, *Chivalry* (New Haven, Conn.: Yale University Press, 1984), pp. 119–24.

[48] On the influence of the Lancelot romances on later chivalric ideology and, specifically, on a handbook of chivalry that summarizes much of the tradition, see *The Book of Chivalry of Geoffroi de Charny*, pp. 18–28; for Charny's account of Judas Maccabeus as the most perfect knight, see p. 163.

[49] Forshall and Madden, eds., *Holy Bible*, 1:2.

[50] In a contemporary example of political exegesis of the Old Testament, Richard Ullerston includes citations from precisely these historical books, together with the New Testament and numerous patristic authorities, in *his* Aristotelian advice-tract for Prince Henry, *De Officio Militari* (c. 1408–9), MS Trinity College Cambridge, B.15.23.

Paralpominon 1–2, for example, becomes the Prologue's basis for a lengthy polemic on the duty of lords to protect their subjects from the corrupt clergy:

. . . for here thei mown se, hou sore Gode punschide yvele kingis, that lyveden yvele and drowen the peple to idolatrie, either other gret synnes . . . summe cristene lordis in name and hethene in condiscouns defoulen the sentuarie of God, and bryngin in symonient clerkis, ful of covetise, eresie, and ypocrisie, and malice, to stoppe Goddis lawe, that it be not knowen and kept, and frely preched.[51]

Judith, while an semiapocryphal book, without full authority, "natheles . . . comendeth chastitie and abstinence, penaunce, and wideuhood." Furthermore, the text provides a stern, if misogynistic, warning to lords:

Of this proces proude werriours schulden drede God, that made proud Olofernes to be slayn of a womman, and a his greet oost to be scaterid and distroied; and cristen men schilden be comfourtid greetly, for to have ful trist in God and in his helpe, that so myghtily delyverede his puple fro so greet an enemy."[52]

In the structure of the General Prologue, these Old Testament narratives are most important for a tropological or moral exegesis that uses Scripture to dictate knightly conduct within the Lollards' sweeping reformist politics. The role of the "cristen lords" in these polemical passages is to defend the open study of Scripture and the authority of all lay readers against an oppressive church. The Lollards, echoing Wyclif's own realist position on biblical truth, further draw an absolute distinction between the authority of Scripture and the "fablis" of literary texts: the apocalyptic *Opus Arduum,* for example, rails against current "pseudopreachers" who preach "histories of Hector, Troy, Achilles and other such pagans as if they were the most sacred history of the gospels."[53]

In his response to the Lollard exegetes, also addressed to Oldcastle as a "Christian knight," Hoccleve advocates a kind of radically literal, anti-

---

[51] Forshall and Madden, eds., *Holy Bible,* 1:30.

[52] Ibid., 1:36.

[53] *Opus Arduum,* MS Brno Mk 28, fol. 182rb, quoted in Curtis Bostick, *The Antichrist and the Lollards: Apocalypticism in Late Medieval and Reformation England* (Leiden: Brill, 1998) p. 110. For another example, see Thomas Arnold, ed., *Select English Works of John Wyclif,* vol. 3 (London, 1871), p. 147: "thei schulden not preche cronyclis of tho world, as tho batel of Troye, ne othir nyse fablis." See also Hudson, *Premature Reformation,* p. 270.

interpretive model of reading as chivalric practice. He transfers the authority of the Gospels to the edifying Old Testament "stories" themselves, casting them as essentially a more authentic account of history than the romances of Thebes or Troy. In Hoccleve's account, moreover, the exegetical possibilities of these historical books are limited to their relevance to "chivalry." For a reader like Oldcastle, they are divorced from their allegorical relation to the New Testament or to Christian ethics; like the other books on the list, they above all provide insight into the conduct of war.[54] Like Chaucer's image in the *Regement,* this version of the Bible imposes a strict internal censorship on its imagined aristocratic readers; they can no more find heretical ideas in *Judges* or *Maccabees* than in *The Canterbury Tales* or Vegetius. It seems especially fitting that *Judith*—with its national heroine, sometimes figured as a type of female Judas Maccabeus, one of the nine "heroines"—would serve as Hoccleve's answer to the Lollard threat of the reading and disputing woman: the female armed leader herself becomes an image of the "remasculinized" knight, rescued from the female priests.[55] If the Bible is to be translated into English, it must be as history understood as "story," literature in the service of knighthood.

Hoccleve's efforts to "remasculinize" the Lancastrian knight, to reconstruct Oldcastle's lost "manhood" from a textual basis, make the vernacular theology associated with the Lollard "lewed calates" the central problem of national identity. For Hoccleve, the gendered war of representations over English writing is of equal importance to the recovery of the English nation's lost glory as Henry V's invasion of France. When, at the end of the "Address," Hoccleve reminds Oldcastle of the king's "laboure in armes" (line 501) overseas, he laments (lines 505–7):

> Sum tyme was no knightly turn no where,
> Ne no manhood showed in no wyse,
> But Oldcastel wolde, his thankes, be there.

---

[54] Hoccleve's ideological position is in keeping with the king's subsequent exegetical propaganda: on the parliamentary speeches on themes of Old Testament rule by Henry V's chancellors, Henry Beaufort and Thomas Langley, in support of the French war, see *Rotuli Parliamentorum,* v. 4, pp. 62, 70, 106 ["*Confortamini, viriliter agite, & gloriosi eritis*" (1 Maccabees 2:64)], 116, 123, and Allmand, *Henry V,* pp. 408–9.

[55] On the figure of Judith, see, for example, Christine de Pizan's *Ditié de Jehanne d'Arc,* ed. Angus Kennedy and Kenneth Varity, Medium Aevum Monographs, n.s., 9 (Oxford: Society for the Study of Mediaeval Language and Literature, 1977). See also Keen, *Chivalry,* p. 121.

In this final plea, Hoccleve connects his literary ideal to his sense of the moment. If King Henry embodies Hoccleve's hopes for a Lancastrian England restored to masculine order through texts and images, it is Oldcastle, the Lancastrian knight-reader, who must be there—not only in France but in the "real" arena of masculine identity, Hoccleve's chivalric or Chaucerian library.

Poems by Chaucer in John Harpur's Psalter

Thorlac Turville-Petre
University of Nottingham

One of the treasures of Nottingham University Library is the Rushall Psalter (Nottingham University Library, MS Me LM1), actually a chained Book of Hours with a liturgical Psalter. This large (380 × 260 mm) and handsomely illuminated volume from the mid-fifteenth century is of particular interest because it contains copies of two short poems by Chaucer, *Truth* and *Gentilesse,* as well as verse by Lydgate. The volume was overlooked and reported as "lost" for a considerable time,[1] but in 1969 Norman Davis rescued it from the neglect into which it had fallen, giving a brief account of the history of the book and transcribing its text of *Gentilesse,* together with the other verses on the same page (fol. 20r).[2] Some years later, in 1975, A. I. Doyle and George B.

---

[1] The *Index of Middle English Verse* of 1943 does not list the Nottingham text of either *Truth* (no. 809) or *Gentilesse* (no. 3348), though it accurately records "This present book" (3637). In 1965 the *Supplement to the Index* added the Nottingham copy of *Truth,* but not *Gentilesse.* In Rossell Hope Robbins, ed., *Secular Lyrics of the Fourteenth and Fifteenth Centuries* (Oxford: 1952), the note to "This present book" (no. 94) reports that "The present owner and location of the MS are not known" (repeated in the reprint of 1968), and the text of the poem is taken from J. W. Clark, *Cambridge Antiquarian Society Proceedings* 11 (1905): 76–77. As a prime example of confusion piled upon confusion, *A Linguistic Atlas of Late Mediaeval English* lists as a source a Church Book from Rushall, Norfolk [*sic*], "present whereabouts unknown," referring to "Transcripts, from a partly modernised version, in possession of *MED.*" I am grateful to Douglas Moffat for sending me copies of these transcripts, which turn out to be an inaccurate copy by P. Laithwaite of a transcript by "Dr. Willimore" [*sic*] of the prose history of Rushall, Staffordshire, in the Rushall Psalter. Curiously, Laithwaite does not give a reference for his source, Frederic W. Willmore, *Records of Rushall* (Walsall: 1892).

[2] Norman Davis, "Chaucer's *Gentilesse:* A Forgotten Manuscript, with Some Proverbs," *RES* n.s., 20 (1969): 43–50.

Pace gave a short description of the manuscript and transcribed its copy of *Truth,* with an analysis of its textual relationships.[3]

Doyle and Pace gave an account of the contents of the volume, but this begged perhaps the most interesting question. Why were Chaucer's poems copied into a volume of Latin devotions in the first place? Furthermore—and this may be thought odder still—what sort of Book of Hours and Psalter is this that begins with the mundane advice "For helthe of body couere for colde þin heed. / Ete no raw mete take goode hede therto"—that is to say, with the text of Lydgate's *Dietary?* It is often the case that such questions, though intriguing, can never be answered satisfactorily because we have such imperfect knowledge of the history of the manuscript and the motives of its compiler. We may not even be able to tell, for example, whether quires of different origins were bound up by a librarian some centuries later. Even if we know that the present contents are integral to the original conception of the volume, it is often useless to inquire about the stages in which different items were copied, and even less fruitful to speculate on the purposes of scribes and owners in assembling the contents of the volume. A commonplace book can indeed reveal information about the range of interests of those who owned it, but we must always bear in mind that the heterogeneity of its contents may be as much a reflection of the random way in which copies came to hand as of any design on the part of its owners.

We are on much firmer ground with the Rushall Psalter. For one thing, the volume has remained in the hands of the same family, so we can trace its history quite clearly back through the generations to its first owner.[4] For another thing, information provided in the volume itself, backed up with the historical records, discloses a considerable amount about the motives behind its compilation. From this it is safe to conclude that, however heterogeneous its contents seem at first glance, this is a planned volume that reflects the interests, preoccupations indeed, of one John Harpur, whose descendant, Sir Charles Buchanan, arranged for the manuscript to be taken into the care of Nottingham University in 1951.

John Harpur came into the lordship of Rushall in south Staffordshire in 1429 on the death of his father-in-law, William Grobbere of Rushall.

---

[3] A. I. Doyle and George B. Pace, "Further Texts of Chaucer's Minor Poems," *Studies in Bibliography* 28 (1975): 45–57.

[4] There is an account of Rushall, the family, and the Psalter in Willmore, *Records of Rushall.*

One of the English texts in the manuscript is a prose account of the descent of the manor of Rushall from the time of the Conquest, which relates that "in kynge Henries dayes the syxthe, Alianore, doghtir & heyr to the seyd William of Russhale at the age of xv ʒeer was weddid to John Harpur. And *with*inne two ʒeer aftir deyde þe seyde William of Russhale."[5] Harpur quickly became a man of considerable significance in Staffordshire society, sitting as justice of the peace from 1430 until his death, tirelessly acting on commissions to raise money and troops for war, commissions of oyer and terminer, inquisitions, and other duties of local importance.[6] He also set about improving his estate, building a new church that was consecrated on St. Wulfstan's Day (January 19) 1440, according to the entry in the Calendar of his Psalter. A license of that year was granted at the request of John and Eleanor to allow them to settle lands on a perpetual chaplain and his successors, the first of whom was named as William Ball.[7] It was perhaps Ball himself who penned notes in the Calendar preceding the Hours that recorded the death of William of Rushall in 1429 (fol. 14r) and of his wife a year later (fol. 16r), and no doubt his successor John Ayliff who noted Ball's death in 1455 (fol. 14v). Some years later John Harpur's own death is recorded: "Here on 3rd July 1464 died John Harpur esquire, lord of Rushall, between the seventh and eighth hour after noon, on whose soul may God have mercy" (fol. 17r).[8]

A poem facing the first page of the Hours records that the volume, chained to its place in the church or house, was bought by John Harpur

[5] The text is inaccurately printed in Stebbing Shaw, *History & Antiquities of Staffordshire* (1807), 2: 62–64.

[6] *Calendar of Patent Rolls, 1429–1436,* e.g. pp. 127 (commission to raise a loan for war), 523 (commission of array), 624 (justice of the peace); *CPR 1436–1441,* e.g., pp. 84, 268 (commissions of oyer and terminer), 472 (justice of the peace); *CPR 1441–1446,* e.g., pp. 92 (commission to raise a loan for war), 478 (justice of the peace); *CPR 1446–1452,* e.g., pp. 140 (commission of inquisition), 190 (commission *de walliis et fossatis*), 299 (commission to raise a loan for war), 595 (justice of the peace); *CPR 1452–1461,* e.g., pp. 403 (commission of array), 442 (commission of inquisition), 677 (justice of the peace); *CPR 1461–1467,* e.g., pp. 191 (appointment as auditor of the king's ministers), 572 (justice of the peace).

[7] *CPR 1436–1441,* p. 396. For a list of the lands settled on Ball in 1443, see *CPR 1441–1446,* p. 175.

[8] "Hac iija die Julij & anno domini millesimo ccccmo lxmo iiijto obijt Joh'es harpur Armig' ac dominus de Ruyssheale int' horam septimam et octauam post nonam cuius anime propicietur deus Amen." This epitaph to John Harpur was formerly also inscribed in the Franciscan friary at Lichfield, Staffordshire, but it was destroyed in 1545. See A. R. Martin, *Franciscan Architecture in England,* British Society of Franciscan Studies, vol. 18 (Manchester: 1937), p. 171.

to commemorate the establishment of his new church. Examination of the quiring, made possible at the time of the rebinding in 1993, makes clear that at the outset the volume began conventionally enough with the Hours of the Virgin, ending with a blank verso (fols. 21r–78v); continuing at the beginning of a new quire with the Psalter (fols. 79r–187r); followed by the Litany of Saints, ending with a blank verso (fols. 187v–192v); and concluding with "Originalia Doctorum," quotations from Bernard, Augustine, Jerome, and others (fols. 193r–195v). Harpur's shield was painted into the space left for it at the foot of the magnificent first page of the Hours, and another copy of the shield was added, less comfortably, to the design of the first page of the Psalms (fol. 79r), which also has the miniature of King David as a harper—standard enough, but presumably the pun did not go unnoticed.[9] Perhaps it was commissioned in London, for rich illumination in the current metropolitan style decorates the volume, with whole- or three-quarter-page illuminated frames with fine leafwork and bell-shaped flowers, and seventeen flourished capitals. At the front was added a separate quire of six leaves containing a Sarum calendar (fols. 14r–19v), which has an original entry specifically for the chapel at Rushall. A leaf was inserted between the Calendar and the Hours (fol. 20) so that when the book was opened, the grand first page of the Hours, with its floriated initial and frame and the Harpur shield, would be displayed on the right-hand side; and on the left, the reader standing even some distance away would be able to read the English poem recording Harpur's ownership: a poem in three stanzas that fills the page with lines of very large and elegant textura written in ink of blue, crimson, black, and red.

The specific references in this poem to Harpur's stipulations for the safekeeping of the book attached to its place by its chain suggest that the volume was at Rushall by this time, and the dialect forms of the poem give additional support to this supposition.[10] Not long—if at

---

[9] Doyle and Pace suggest that the second portion of the volume (following the Hours) may have been adapted for Harpur's use ("Further Texts," pp. 45–46). Certainly the shield on fol. 79r is an addition to the original design.

[10] Although Doyle and Pace imply that the spellings are London, there are indications that the dialect of the scribe was West Midlands rather than London; e.g., strong ppl. *-on* line 23, *bondon,* (see *Linguistic Atlas of Late Mediaeval English* [*LALME*], dot map 664); *urthely* (line 10) as a spelling of "earthly" (dot map 738). The ending of the pres 3 sg. is *-eth,* line 12, *begynneth* (dot map 646), and so also is the pl. ending, line 13, *doth* (dot map 654); "them" is *hem,* line 7 (dot map 40); "gave" is *yafe,* line 15 (dot map 425); "much" is *moche,* line 9 (dot map 103).

all—afterward, a further quire was added at the front,[11] the contents of which are all in English and written in an expert textura. The first text in the volume is Lydgate's *Dietary,* followed by his *Kings of England* (fols. 1v–2v), which begins with William the Conqueror and ends with Henry VI; this text accompanies the *Dietary* in no fewer than thirteen other manuscripts, twice elsewhere following and three times immediately preceding the *Dietary.*[12] A space was left at the foot of the first column of fol. 2v, presumably for the addition of future kings, and three stanzas taken from Lydgate's *Fall of Princes* (from book 3, lines 372–78, 533–39, 554–60) begin at the top of the second column. The unique prose history of Rushall starts on the next leaf (fols. 3r–5Ar); like the *Kings,* this begins at the time of the Conqueror and ends in the reign of Henry VI with John Harpur's marriage and the deaths of his parents-in-law.[13] This completes the quire, and in fact the last lines of the history are on a stub that has been bound into a later quire of miscellaneous sheets of parchment of various sizes and qualities (fols. 5A–13B), some blank, others containing later notes of the family at Rushall continuing into the seventeenth century, together with advice on "howe to live well" and "howe to dye well" in a sixteenth-century hand (fol. 12r).

With the manuscript now presumably chained in its place, someone in the household took the opportunity to add a few more items.[14] In the space left below Lydgate's *Kings of England* (on fol. 2v) has been written Chaucer's poem *Truth,* and at the foot of the second column is added the stanza entitled "A Balade for dysceyuors," beginning "Dysceyt dysceyvyth," which is extracted from Lydgate's *Fall of Princes* (bk. 4, lines 4432–38) but often occurs on its own.[15] It was possibly the same scribe writing in a much less formal script who turned to the back of the leaf

[11] These are now preceded by two modern endleaves from the 1993 rebinding, followed by a blank quire of four, probably from the seventeenth-century rebinding.

[12] For details, see Albert E. Hartung, ed., *A Manual of the Writings in Middle English,* (New Haven: Connecticut Academy of Arts and Sciences, 1980), 6: 1827, 2092–94.

[13] The detailed local knowledge implies an author from the West Midlands. Although the scribal forms are not markedly regional, note the following, which are at least consistent with a West Midlands scribe: *doghtir* (*LALME,* dot map 720, mainly Midlands); forms of "give," *зeue, gyue* infin., *gaf* pa.t.sg., *gauen* pa.t.pl. (dot maps 424–27); 3 sg. pres. *-ith* (dot map 646 and *LALME,* 4:109); weak pa.t. *-ide,* ppl. *-id* (dot map 659); strong ppl. *-on* (dot map 664); *hem,* "them" (dot map 40); *here* and *there,* "their" (dot maps 51–52); *land* and *lond* (dot maps 936–37).

[14] Doyle and Pace describe this as "a versatile amateur hand, perhaps of one of the clergy or family" ("Further Texts," p. 47). The scribe uses the form *wull* for "will" (sg.), which is mainly found in the West Midlands (*LALME,* 4:44).

[15] Index 674; see Robbins, ed., *Secular Lyrics,* no. 107.

on which the ownership poem had been written (fol. 20r)—which was still invitingly virgin—and there wrote Chaucer's *Gentilesse*, together with a collection of proverbial sayings, two in Latin, and headed the whole page "Lerne or be lewde."[16] This hand is very similar to that of some of the additions in the Calendar, and therefore is perhaps that of Harpur's chaplain William Ball. Among the proverbs, another hand has written four lines on "Sapiens."

How can one account for this strange mélange of English poetry and prose within a grand volume of Latin devotions? The key to understanding its motivation is provided by John Harpur's ownership poem, in itself a most unusual piece of writing. Marks of ownership are common enough, of course, and some extend to simple rhymes of this type:

> John Twychener ys boke.
> he that stellys thys booke
> he shall be hangid apon a hoke,
> that wyll macke ys necke to brake
> and that wyll macke ys neck awrye.[17]

John Harpur's poem is, however, a far more elaborate and sophisticated affair, indeed a piece of considerable literary quality, presenting and subtly resolving a paradox; a poem composed by an obviously professional poet in three eight-line stanzas in the most fashionable "aureate" style, rhyming on only three sounds throughout, and written out by a scribe in a very formal script to complement the page it faces. It speaks of the Psalter attached to its place by a chain, where it will remain forever, passed on from heir to heir. It warns anyone who attempts to remove it that he will bring upon himself the curse of Christ, God the Father, and Mary, but pronounces a blessing on anyone who repairs the book when it starts to fall apart:

---

[16] The contents of the page are printed by Davis, "Chaucer's *Gentilesse*," pp. 46–50. The language is decidedly West Midland: e.g., *bodon*, ppl. of *beden*, "offer" (dot map 664); "though" spellings *thawh* and *thawe* (dot maps 195, 205); the rare ending of the weak ppl. *enherytode* (dot map 660), which *LALME* records as the major form only in a document in the Walsall Cartulary (LP. 301, Staffs, *LALME*, 3:461). Doyle and Pace say that the additions on fol. 2v are in a hand "competent enough to make arguable an identification with the scribe of f. 20" ("Further Texts," p. 47), but of course the writing is a different style.

[17] Quoted in Robbins, ed., *Secular Lyrics*, p. 256.

This present book legeble in scripture,
Here in this place thus tacched with a cheyn,
Purposed of entent for to endure
And here perpetuelli stylle to remeyne
Fro eyre to eyre; wherfore appone peyn
Of Cryst is curs, of Fadres & of Moderes,
Non of hem hens atempt it to dereyne
Whille ani leef may goodeli hange with oder.

But for as moche that noo thyng may endure
That urthely ys, alwey, y trowe, certeyn,
When so euer thys book here aftyr in scripture
Eyder in koueryng begynneth fause ayeyn,
All tho therto that diligence doth or peyn
Hit to reforme, be they on or other,
Haue they the pardon that Criste yafe Magdaleyn,
With daili blessyng of Fader and of Moder.

Gret reson wolde that euery creature,
Meued of corage on hit to rede or seyn,
Shuld hym remembre in prayer, that so sure
Bothe preest and place and bokes lust ordeyn
At his gret cost, John Harpur, noght to leyn;
Wherfor in speciall his eires, wyth alle oder,
Ar hyly bondon to pray the souereyn
Lord of all lordes present hym to hys Moder.

The first stanza of this poem directs attention to a physical object, indeed this very object that the reader is now looking at, "here," "present," "in this place." The sense of the book as physical object is powerfully confirmed by the chain that attaches it permanently to its fixed spot, perhaps in the church at Rushall. The book will always be present to the reader of the poem, "here perpetuelli stylle to remeyne," and the reader is warned of the moral duty to ensure the book's permanence, with Christ's curse as a punishment for anyone who would remove it. The book represents certainty and stability, not only in the present, here and now, but "to endure" for evermore.

The second stanza begins with a troubling paradox that directly contradicts the "to endure" of line 3, for "noo thyng may endure." From the stability of the eternal present of the first stanza, the reader is moved to the discomforting insecurity of the future, where the only certainty is mutability with the inevitability of loss and decay. The resolution of this paradox is the healing power of repair and renewal, a constant process, so that when the book once again begins to deteriorate ("fause ayeyn"[18]) it will be necessary to reconstitute ("reforme") it. To avoid a loss that is irreparable, there is a constant need to be vigilant.

In this way the second stanza resolves the paradox of a perpetually present earthly object, establishing the endurance of the book even more securely. The third stanza reveals what the book stands for or, more precisely, what it speaks of: that is to say, the lord John Harpur and his family. Indeed, references to family run through the poem, beginning in the first stanza (line 5) with the notion of the family as an institution renewing itself through time as it proceeds "fro eyre to eyre," and continuing with the model of the Holy Family in the second (line 16). In the third stanza, the concept of the family is brought to the forefront. Harpur's heirs will always have present to them the evidence of their debt to him, "this present book" that will speak to them of their obligation to ensure that Christ will *present* him to his Mother. Harpur's considerable financial outlay is directed to the single purpose of stabilizing the future for his family. In line 20, the mention of "preest and place and bokes" reminds his successors that they owe to him the establishment of a family priest, protecting for all time their moral and spiritual interests; that it was Harpur who built the place in which they now read his psalter, and more generally the estate that his wealth and good husbandry set on firm foundations; and that he commissioned the books that will speak to them of him.

This is a poem that is deeply aware of time, contrasting the certainty of the present moment with the fragility of the future in which the example of the past will need to be recalled and reenacted. Its central image of the book, so physically there in front of them, represents the family as it now is to the family that is to come, holding up a model to guide Harpur's successors through constant renewal to a future as secure as the future can ever be.

We might think of a psalter as a devotional book, which in one sense,

---

[18] The verb *fause* usually has the sense "be false." The sense required here, "be defective," "fail," is recorded only in the thirteenth century, in Laʒamon's *Brut* and *Ancrene Wisse* (*MED falsen* 6[b]).

of course, it is. But the size and magnificence of this book tell us at a glance that this is not an object that proclaims the triviality of worldly goods. It is far more secular in its concerns. It speaks of status, power, and stability in the face of change and decay. As it rested chained to its lectern in Rushall, open at the first page of the Hours, it displayed the significance of John Harpur and his family to the world. Harpur's good sense in his provisions for his memorial has been confirmed by time. Though there is now no place to chain the book—for Rushall is now swallowed up within Walsall, and Harpur's church was replaced in the nineteenth century, and only traces of the gatehouse of the medieval house remain[19]—even so the book survives in its glory, repaired as he asked that it should be, to speak over five hundred years later of John Harpur.

Once we understand the particular significance that the Psalter had for Harpur, the choice of contents in the volume becomes clearer. The first of these, *The Dietary,* is John Lydgate's most popular poem in terms of surviving manuscript copies. Its popularity was due to the great range of practical advice it gave, for it is about much more than eating. The word *diet* could carry a broader sense, "way of living, course of life,"[20] and the emphasis of the poem is as much upon general good behavior as on diet. Lydgate gives tips on the importance of living within one's means, behaving generously to the poor, and (no doubt of particular appeal to Harpur) running a smooth household at peace with itself. So the fourth verse warns of the danger of allowing tittle-tattle, telling the family to hold troublemakers in contempt, to permit no quarreling in the household, and to live at peace with its neighbors. Underlying all Lydgate's advice is the need to practice moderation, to avoid too much food, too much drink, too many late nights: "Ryche with litil, content wiþ suffisaunce" (line 14).

[19] See N. J. Baker, "The Gatehouse of Rushall Hall, Staffs: A Survey and Excavation," *Transactions of the South Staffordshire Archaeological and Historical Society* 23 (1983 for 1981–2): 79–88. This is followed by an appendix by J. W. Whiston, "The Rushall Psalter," pp. 89–91.

[20] *MED diete* 2, though *MED* does not recognize this sense of *dietarie.* The Rushall copy of Lydgate's poem follows the order of Bodley MS Rawlinson C.86, printed in Robbins, ed., *Secular Lyrics,* no. 78, without the eight additional stanzas on food and drink in BL MS Lansdowne 699, as printed in *The Minor Poems of John Lydgate,* ed. Henry Noble MacCracken, Early English Text Society, vol. 192 (1934), pp. 703–7, and by Carl F. Bühler, "Lydgate's *Rules of Health* in MS. Lansdowne 699," *Medium Ævum* 3 (1934): 51–56. For a full edition based on BL MS Sloane 3534, see Max Förster, "Kleinere mittelenglische texte," *Anglia* 42 (1918): 176–92.

Lydgate's *Kings of England,* which follows, is another text without literary qualities but that provides plenty of information with its thumbnail sketches of fifteen monarchs.[21] Though so often accompanying the *Dietary,* it needs also to be taken in relation to the two items that were copied after it in the volume. The three stanzas taken from Lydgate's *Fall of Princes*—that huge compendium written for Humphrey, duke of Gloucester, brother of Henry V, to show rulers examples from the past that illustrate the instability of power in the world of Fortune—state respectively that subjects will withdraw their support from princes who are niggardly, that God places no value on power and high estate, and that a wise ruler exercises moderation in all his decisions. The lines stress the fragility of worldly achievement and add a moral dimension to the bare list of English kings. Furthermore, the *Kings of England* provides the national framework for the local story recounted by the prose history of Rushall. The sources for this history, which is reliable enough insofar as it can be checked, are evidently local and estate records backed by family tradition. Beginning with William's defeat of Harold, it continues: "In þese dayes as wel bifore þe seyd conquest & *in* tyme of þe conquest & aftir, ther dwellide a squyer at Russhale þat was lord of þe same lordshipe, the whiche was callid Neel of Russhale, in latinis verbis Nigellus de Russhale, whos auncestre & progenitour com *in* to this lande *with* þe Saxon Conquerour þat broghte *with* him the langage of Englisshe" (fol. 3r), and goes on to give generally brief accounts of the succeeding generations at Rushall. Sometimes the source is quoted: "a dede of the foundacion of the priorie of Duddeley," "as þe book of domusday in þe kyngis tresorie makith mencion." Each generation placed its mark on the estate, which is constantly in need of repair and renewal: "And þe same Geffrey Ive pullide doun an olde halle at Russhale & sette up a newe halle" (fol. 4v). As the history approaches John Harpur's own time, there is a little more personal detail. It relates that Eleanor Harpur's brother James "wente to gramer scole a Lutterworthe and þere deyde at xiiij ȝeer age" (fol. 5Ar). But even this sad detail serves its purpose, because it explains how it happened that Eleanor inherited the manor.

The additions of Chaucer's *Truth* and the "balade for dysceyuors" on fol. 2v, and of the proverbs together with Chaucer's *Gentilesse* on fol. 20r,

---

[21] The text from Bodley MS Rawlinson C.48 is printed in Rossell Hope Robbins, ed., *Historical Poems of the Fourteenth and Fifteenth Centuries* (New York:), no. 1.

are of a piece with the other English contents of the book. The title given to *Truth* is the usual one, "Le bon councell de Chawcer." Like the verses from the *Fall of Princes* that it accompanies, it offers moral counsel. We should note in this respect that it lacks the playful envoy to Vache so familiar from our *Riverside Chaucer* but absent in all but one of its thirty manuscripts and early prints.[22] As it stands in this volume, the poem consists of a series of well-turned admonitions reflecting on our restless world and suggesting a wise attitude to that instability where every rise is followed by a fall "For horede hathe hate, and clymyng tykylnes" (line 3). It is addressed to those tempted by ambitions to be in with the crowd at court (line 1), those who want to set the world to rights (line 8), and those who want to control others (line 13). Put all such ambitions aside: accept what you are (line 2), don't struggle for what you can't get (line 17), be happy with what you're given. Both *Truth* and the *Fall* verses urge the reader to be satisfied with his lot: in *Truth*, "Grete rest stant in litell besynes" and "Stryve not as doth a crokke wyth þe walle"; in the *Fall*, "Grettire richesse is found in suffi-caunce / Than in the floodis of superfluite."

On fol. 20r the proverbial and admonitory nature of *Gentilesse*—"The firste stokke, fader of gentilnesse, / What man that cleymeth gentyll for to be / Muste felowe hys tras"—is foregrounded by the heading to the page, "Lerne or be lewde."[23] *Gentilesse* reflects on the standard proposition that noble behavior is not the preserve of the gentleman; that miter, crown, and diadem cannot confer true nobility. The theme is reinforced by the short texts that immediately follow, proverbs about *gentilesse*—four English lines, six lines in Latin. Other proverbs on wisdom, virtue, honor, and good husbandry offer further reflections that might be particularly designed for the edification of children, such as

> Whoso in youthe no vertu vseth,
> In age al honour hym refuseth.

---

[22] For details, see George B. Pace and Alfred David, eds., *The Minor Poems*, pt. 1, vol. 5 of *A Variorum Edition of the Works of Geoffrey Chaucer* (Norman: University of Oklahoma Press, 1982), pp. 49–65; and Ralph Hanna III, "Authorial Versions, Rolling Revision, Scribal Error? Or, the Truth about *Truth*," *SAC* 10 (1988): 23–40.

[23] The textual tradition of *Gentilesse* is analyzed by Pace and David, eds., *Minor Poems*, pp. 67–76.

and

> Yong wyse, sone ryche.
> Grace groweth after gou*er*naunce.
> Who that wole be holy helful & ryche
> Go betyme to hys bed & ryse erlyche.

Below this is a series of maxims on the running of the household, ending "Thus shal gode houshold gou*er*nede be." This page consists of a series of commonplaces for family use. There is need for a family to act prudently if it is to survive in a world characterized by loss:

> Sapiens to man sayth in hys yowthe
> To travayle in trewthe tyme hyt ys
> To gete the ryches yff thou kouthe
> In age to reste and lyve therewyth.

It is clear that Chaucer's two poems find their place in the Psalter not as monuments of English literature collected by an enthusiast, but as texts of practical wisdom, offering useful guidance on a sensible approach to living—in short, as moral precepts. It is appropriate that the very last English proverb copied on fol. 20r is "Yowthe may age ou*er* renne bote not ouerrede," a saying found also in that repository of proverbial lore, *The Knight's Tale* (*CT* 2449). To look to Chaucer as a moral guide is a perfectly sensible reading, but it is not a twentieth-century one.

For John Harpur, the Psalter speaks of piety (to some extent), but more importantly of the interrelated concepts of status, place, and continuity. Harpur acquired his status when his wife inherited the estate, and in order to secure that position he built the church and established a perpetual chaplain. The English texts express his anxiety that a position easily won can be easily lost; his awareness of the need for caution, for wise governance, and for constant vigilance to repair what has decayed; and his determination to create something that will stand firm and speak for all time. All of these anxieties and reassurances are expressed in his book, which is itself the guarantee that his name and achievements will live on through future generations. He recognized, as did many owners who kept their family notes in Books of Hours, that the revered texts ensured the survival of the book. To spend lavishly on a

Psalter is not extravagant but praiseworthy, notwithstanding the precept on fol. 20r: "Qui plus expendit then his plought may tylle in a twelmough, Non admiretur thawe he borwe a loof at his neyburgh." A valuable devotional book will be looked after as a treasure that is appropriately chained safely in the church. In this way the book becomes a wonderfully secure repository for the story that Harpur really wants to tell, about the estate he acquired, about his wealth that allowed him "at his great cost" to establish his position and his family—a story that will be passed down with the book "from heir to heir." [24]

---

[24] Succeeding generations of the family regarded the book in the same light as Harpur did. In 1671 Edward Leigh left in his will "the olde booke with a leather cover and a chaine (mentioning our several ancestors, living at Rushall Hall from the Conquest)" to his eldest son, Henry, to "continue to the familie in successive generations"; Whiston, "The Rushall Psalter," p. 90.

Contents of Nottingham University Library, MS Me LM1

Lydgate, *Dietary* (1r–v)
Lydgate, *Kings of England* (1v–2v)
Lydgate, 3 stanzas from *Fall of Princes* (2v)
Chaucer, *Truth* (2v)
Additional stanza from *Fall of Princes* (2v)
Prose history of Rushall (3r–5Ar)
Later family notes in various hands (5Av–8r)
8v–11v blank
"Howe to live well"; "Howe to dye well" (12r)
13Ar–13Br blank
Notes on land temp. Hen VII (13Bv)
Calendar (14r–19v)
Chaucer's *Gentilesse.* Proverbs. In another hand: "Sapiens" (20r)
"This present book" (20v)
Hours of the Virgin (21r–78r)
78v blank
Psalter (79r–187r)
Litany of the Saints (187v–192r)
192v blank
"Originalia Doctorum" (193r–195v)
There are family jottings throughout, including a fifteenth-century
memorandum of William Harpur on the last folio (195v).

REVIEWS

F. R. P. AKEHURST and STEPHANIE CAIN VAN D'ELDEN, eds. *The Stranger in Medieval Society.* Medieval Cultures, vol. 12. Minneapolis: University of Minnesota Press, 1997. Pp. xii, 149. $44.95 cloth, $17.95 paper.

This slim but engaging volume of essays is a selection of papers delivered at the University of Minnesota Center for Medieval Studies' 1994 conference on "The Stranger in Medieval Society." The book's title is rather broader than its actual scope. Readers searching for essays on the "marginal" or the "alienated" will not find them here; the collection's conception of "the stranger" limits itself to "those persons who have their own community and culture, and who come into a new environment. They are within the law, they tend not to be parasites, and they may be very beneficial in their new milieu" (p. vii). A search for essays about the earlier centuries of the medieval period will prove futile as well; the work included here deals exclusively with topics drawn from the twelfth to fifteenth centuries. And although the collection's authors hail from the fields of both history and literature, the majority of the essays concern themselves with notions of the stranger in late medieval French, German, and English literature.

The first three essays employ historical approaches. Kathryn Reyerson's "The Merchants of the Mediterranean: Merchants as Strangers" is a careful examination of the problems met by western European merchants in their attempts to develop markets in Muslim areas of the Mediterranean basin, and the strategies employed by these merchants to "[acquire] sufficient cultural baggage and language skills to gain the subtlety of approach necessary to do business on a high level." The focus on merchants-as-strangers continues in William Phillips's "Voluntary Strangers: European Merchants and Missionaries in Asia during the Late Middle Ages." Phillips discusses the opportunities opened to Western traders and missionaries—including Marco Polo—by the *Pax Mongolica* of the thirteenth and early fourteenth centuries. Again, Phillips focuses on how their success in opening markets depended upon losing "their status as complete strangers and assimilating to some degree into their host country" (p. 21). As he points out, this was not easily done, especially given a sometimes insuperable language barrier. William Jordan's "Home Again: The Jews in the Kingdom of France, 1315–1322" examines the status of medieval Jews as strangers. Set in the context of Louis X's 1315 "trial" readmission of the French Jews after their expulsion from France by this father in 1306, Jordan's essay shows how, even though this should have been a "homecoming of sorts," the returning Jews were perceived as strangers: "They were aliens in law. They were sojourners . . . owing to the impermanence of their expected residence. They were enemies because of their economic role in the years 1315–1322" (p. 28). Such perceptions led to much persecution of the Jewish settlers and the eventual failure of King Louis's experiment.

The selections that will be of most interest to Chaucerians are Derek Pearsall's "Strangers in Late-Fourteenth-Century London" and Susan Crane's "Knights in Disguise: Identity and Incognito in Fourteenth-Century Chivalry." In his essay, Pearsall discusses how late-fourteenth-century Londoners used the word "straunge" and what its connotations and associations were. Citing examples drawn mostly from Chaucer and Langland, Pearsall demonstrates that the word designated not only people from other countries but also those "not of one's own social group," and "not one of the family" (p. 47). These meanings were deployed to differentiate "native" Londoners from recent provincial transplants as well as the foreign merchants and workers who inhabited the city. According to Pearsall, such usage reflects a "verbal architecture of xenophobia" (p. 48) that finds its ultimate expression in the Londoner's slaughter of Flemish cloth workers during the 1381 revolt. Citing Chaucer's "brutally trivializing reference" to the event in *The Nun's Priest's Tale,* Pearsall suggests that Chaucer "allows his poetry to here become associated with an unthinking dehumanization of a whole group of 'straungers'" (p. 59). Crane's essay examines the ubiquitous phenomenon of the disguised knight in late medieval literature. Drawing on examples from both history and literature, she suggests that disguise is used by the knight not to alienate himself from the chivalric community, but rather to invite a closer inspection that will garner renown and thus "establish or revise the perception of others concerning the disguised knight's merits" (p. 70). Crane makes this point by setting forth her own model of medieval chivalric subjectivity, positing that it "derives from, rather than precedes, public judgment" (p. 65). Crane explores how this form of chivalric identity is instituted in Edward III's use of disguise and foundation of chivalric orders, as well as how such attempts to establish chivalric identity can go awry, as in the case of Sir Gawain in *Sir Gawain and the Green Knight.*

Edward Haymes's "The Sexual Stranger: The Sexual Quest in Wolfram's *Parzival*" cleaves only tenuously to the volume's definition of "stranger," taking as its focus the romance motif of the quest, and how it "is almost always associated with the quest for sexual union with the sexual stranger" (p. 80). This, he suggests, is particularly the case in Wolfram's *Parzival,* which differs from its source in making the sexual natures of Gawan and Parzival explicit and thus emphasizing the role of their love interests as sexual strangers "to be sought and leaned about" (p. 90). Maria Dobozy's "Creating Credibility and Truth through Performance: Kelin's Encomium" discusses the outsider status of the *Spruchdichter,* or poet-minstrels, of medieval Germany. Dobozy shows how in the case of Kelin, this problematic status is exploited as part of his performance, employing a strategy that allows him and other *Spruchdichter* to play the role of medieval "spin doctors."

William Calin's "The Stranger and the Problematics of the Epic of Revolt: *Renaut de Montauban*" discusses the differences between that *chanson de geste* and the more canonical *Chanson de Roland.* Calin emphasizes how *Roland* "depicts a relatively unproblematic universe [in which] the hero embodies the values of the community" (p. 105), whereas *Renaut*'s hero is a stranger whose realistic epic interrogates both medieval social formations and its characters' psychological impulses. Finally, Janet Solberg's "'Who Was That Masked Man?': Disguise and Deception in Medieval and Renaissance Comic Literature" examines three trickster tales in which a cross-dressing stranger uses his disguise to gain access to—and eventually engage in sex with—otherwise unattainable women. Solberg suggests that these tales of masked strangers reveal an anxiety about the inability of powerful patriarchal figures to control female sexuality, as well as a corresponding uneasiness about the validity of language's signifying power.

Though some of the collection's pieces are only marginally connected to the idea of the stranger, especially as this notion is delimited in the book's preface, this is nevertheless an interesting, entertaining, and provocative book, and well worth the time spent reading it.

RICHARD FEHRENBACHER
University of Idaho

THOMAS H. BESTUL, *Texts of the Passion: Latin Devotional Literature and Medieval Society.* Philadelphia: University of Pennsylvania Press, 1996. Pp. viii, 264. $39.95.

The Christocentric nature of late medieval devotion has drawn increasing attention from both literary critics and historians. As evident in the work of Sarah Beckwith, Miri Rubin, and Caroline Walker Bynum, the study of Christ's body has allowed scholars to examine the materialism of medieval spirituality. Thomas Bestul joins these scholars with a comprehensive and insightful account of Christ's Passion in Latin devotional texts written between the eleventh and fifteenth centuries. His study could be broadly characterized as recuperative. It recuperates Latin devotional texts from critical neglect, and it returns them to the historical context from which they claim to be exempt, from "the ideals of transcendence embodied in the texts, their proclaimed intention to remove the reader from the temporal, the historical, and above all the material" (p. 20).

The introductory chapter lays the theoretical groundwork for this "cultural contextualization." Drawing on New Historicist views of texts as "products of social processes" (p. 20) and current debates about canon formation, Bestul wants to complicate "background/foreground" and "transmitter/receptor" models for the relationship between Latin and vernacular texts. The texts he has chosen occupy a middle ground between Latin scholastic texts (whose language they share) and vernacular texts of devotion (whose popularity they share). His view of all popular devotional texts as participants in a multilingual and multilayered conversation about devotion certainly provides grounds for further inquiry, particularly as it relates to the translation debates of late-fourteenth- and early-fifteenth-century England. His second chapter offers a helpful survey of the Latin narratives of the Passion: he begins with Gospel accounts and traces the tradition through to the fifteenth century. As he states in his introduction, such a survey can suggest an unproblematic linear evolution; however, the survey helps to illustrate the popularity and the continuity of the Latin devotional treatises. The survey is supplemented with a bibliography of these texts in appendix 2.

After thus outlining the defining characteristics of the Latin devotional tradition, Bestul turns to an analysis of the changes made between the eleventh and fifteenth centuries in the representation of Jews, women, and the tortured Christ. Although Bestul argues that these changes reveal the "inevitable impress of history upon the text" (p. 24), he does not inform the reader whether these are the only changes, or only the ones that he finds most interesting. Chapter 3 examines the texts' increasing anti-Judaism, "the evolving consciousness among Christians . . . that the Jew was the other, a threat to the well being and purity of the social order" (p. 79). He characterizes this anti-Judaism as a "semiology of the concrete" in which Jews were rendered completely physical, often described as animals or in terms of bodily functions. In tracing the historical context for this semiology, Bestul begins with the broader picture—ecclesiastical decrees and literary texts contemporary with the accounts. He then turns to the texts' more particular context, their authors and the communities in which they lived and worked. His discussion includes Ekbert of Schönau's *Stimulus amoris* (late twelfth century), the *Vitis mystica* of Bonaventura (late thirteenth century), John of Pecham's *Philomena* (mid- to late thirteenth century), and Ludolphus of Saxony's *Vita Christi* (mid- to late fourteenth century). His analysis of Ekbert is representative of his approach: "Ekbert used his learning, his command of history, his rhetorical and literary skill, not exclusively, but frequently, in the creation of the categories of otherness" (p. 82). In arguing for the authors' role in creating these categories, Bestul follows R. I. Moore's thesis (in *Formation of a Persecuting Society* [1987]) that we should understand persecution not as a natural part of medieval society but as a process encouraged and established by institutions.

In his fourth chapter, Bestul discusses representations of the Virgin Mary in the Passion sequences. After surveying the critical debate over the position of women in medieval texts, he cautions against critics' tendencies to view devotional texts as either "uniformly misogynous" or as "emancipatory and transgressive" (pp. 116, 117). His persuasive reading of the lamentations of the Virgin, the "Quis dabit," shows the Virgin to be increasingly the product of a masculine imagination, a "male fascination with a woman tormented, passive, and frequently . . . literally immobilized by suffering" (p. 123). Bestul focuses primarily on the "Meditacio Bernardi de lamentacione beate virginis" (written by Logier de Ocedio in the early thirteenth century and attributed to Bernard), which he translates in appendix 1. For Bestul, Mary's sorrow threatens male control by establishing a counterclaim to Jesus' body, but her sorrow is ultimately recuperated as sign of her passivity. He suggests that

the lament "might have functioned as a potent antidote to male appre-
hensions that were likely to have been raised by the literature of women's
visionary experience" (p. 136).

The final chapter analyzes the devotional tradition's growing emphasis on Jesus' physical suffering. Bestul reads these details historically (as
evidence of the authors' knowledge of judicial torture) and not stylis-
tically (the increasing formal realism of medieval texts). Drawing on
Elaine Scarry's study *The Body in Pain,* he argues that the authors of these
narratives were troubled by the inexpressibility of pain. In order to create a language for Christ's pain, the authors turned to the language of
judicial torture: ". . . the detailed punishments of Christ well illustrate
the workings out of a fully developed state mechanism for the prosecu-
tion of an undesirable and dangerous outcast" (p. 157). Here Bestul is
more interested in depictions of physical torment as manifestations of
"extreme materialization" (p. 163) in the later Middle Ages than in the
close textual analysis he has offered in the previous chapters. For Bestul
the consequences of this "extreme materialization" are dire: depictions
of torture desensitize readers and, like movies in our own culture, portray violence as an acceptable part of human experience.

Bestul's focus on the marginal actors, the Jews and the women, works
against the texts' own focus on "the overwhelmingly detailed accounts
of the suffering of Christ" and the effect of this focus—"isolating the
body of Christ for clinical attention, separating it in these narratives
from a social context of which it had traditionally always been a part"
(p. 163). Moreover, in placing these texts in dialogue with contemporary
theory, he works against another form of isolation—the marginalization
of Latin texts in the study of medieval literature.

KATHERINE LITTLE
Vassar College

ALCUIN BLAMIRES. *The Case for Women in Medieval Culture.* Oxford:
Clarendon Press, 1997. Pp. viii, 279. $24.95.

If a reader finishes *The Case for Women In Medieval Culture* bemused by
the medieval fascination with woman-as-subject and fascinated by the

complicated relationship between rhetoric, gender, and social reality, that is not the fault of this intelligent and interesting book. Having provided a useful collection of documents in his earlier anthology, *Woman Defamed and Woman Defended,* Alcuin Blamires here turns to a generic and thematic analysis of a relatively neglected corpus of texts that constitute what he defines as "the case for women." Apparently generated by the more familiar "case against women," the defense is, according to Blamires, a quasi-judicial argument designed to present the feminine gender as socially valuable and morally virtuous. Although obviously many different kinds of works incorporate positive representations of women, his book concentrates on what he calls the "formal" case, characterized by certain topoi which he discusses in detail in five of his eight chapters. Typically, a defense as he defines it will interrogate the psychology and character of those who slander women; call into question the validity of slanderous generalization as an intellectual tool; remind readers of the crucial role of women as mothers and domestic partners; refer back to women's notable roles in secular and religious history, with, of course, particular reference to the Virgin; and compare (unfavorably) male and female morality.

The scope of the study is deliberately restricted, not treating ancillary texts such as catalogues and encomia, avoiding courtly matter, and giving very little historical or cultural context for individual texts and authors. It begins with Marbod of Rennes, the earliest example Blamires could find, and ends for practical reasons with Christine de Pisan, clearly not the last to write in this tradition. (Virginia Woolf's *A Room Of One's Own,* with its viciously witty portraits of misogynist dons and resurrected history of Shakespeare's sister, fits his model rather neatly.) Even with these limitations, the book surveys a sufficiently wide range of material to suggest its value for those studying medieval and early modern culture, and I am probably not the only one to start thinking about possible ramifications as I read. It certainly makes clear the extent to which Chaucer and Christine are not unique in their representations of the "problem" of women, as too many critics claim.

I would like to have known a bit more about where and how he found his particular choices, since his parameters for inclusion are inevitably somewhat arbitrary and many of the examples are difficult to find. The kind of archival work a book like this represents is often undervalued, even though we know that manuscripts, for example, can be an effective guide to intention and audience. Are there a lot more "defenses" lying unedited, like Christine's *City of Ladies,* which remained essentially unavailable in French or English until fairly recently?

His first example, Marbod's "De muliere bona" seems already fully formed, and may indicate the prior existence of the genre. "De muliere" is paired with a poem about bad women, and like many of the works dealt with in the study seems to be primarily a rhetorical exercise, designed to show off the author's skill in manipulating language and logic. Similar to Helen Solterer's *The Master and Minerva* (1995), this study once more demonstrates the complex but pervasive link between rhetorical and social mastery. Embedded even in the defense in a clerical and intellectual culture that continues to recirculate and rework some very old ideas, medieval writing often seems like the Nun's Priest, compelled over and over again to demonstrate masculine superiority. On the other hand, as the discussion of Abelard and Christine shows, medieval thinkers were sometimes freer in their approach to authorities, e.g., Augustine, than we sometimes credit them with being; and whether or not one is interested in "women," Blamires has made a significant contribution to our sense of how medieval writers manipulated and renewed their intellectual heritage: the "case for women" was a "prime instrument for demystifying literary authority and for penetrating the subjectivity of discourse" (p. 241).

If misogynist compositions generated the defense, modern feminist scholarship clearly generated both the audience and the theoretical framework for this book. The author's use of this scholarship is very thorough and sensible, if not groundbreaking, and his notes and bibliography enable a student to trace the development of critical thinking on medieval women and women's issues. In order to avoid the anachronistic application of contemporary concepts, he labels his material "profeminine," a term that emphasizes the socially constructed notions of gender implicit in criteria of praise or blame. In fact, I would argue that he is too careful to distinguish between medieval and modern notions of "liberation," pointing out over and over how ultimately limiting the models presented are for women. I think most of us recognize that the case will inevitably have arisen out of the values and demands of its own culture, and that rather than identifying stereotypes it would be more productive at this point to understand why and in what instances particular ideas were foregrounded, and how individuals within particular cultural locations used them.

In his penultimate chapter, a more extended look at Christine, Chaucer, and Abelard, Blamires's immersion in the debate and his commitment to feminism leads him to some unexpected findings—unexpected at least to those of us accustomed to detaching literary from moral judgments. He admires Abelard for "his sweeping historical vision . . . his characteristically defiant interpretive moves, and above all [for] championing feminine *auctoritas*" (p. 207). Christine he judges to have produced "the most powerful profeminine work of the Middle Ages" (p. 219). Chaucer, on the other hand, he finds evasive, so fascinated with the possibilities of irony and the complexities of voice that he is incapable of "giving women serious *auctoritas*" (p. 208). What is personally crucial to Abelard, who wrote his defense of women in order to provide Heloise and her nuns with an authorizing tradition, and to Christine as a woman, thus appears, in the *Legend* at least, to be merely another intellectual and rhetorical game for Chaucer.

ARLYN DIAMOND
University of Massachusetts

DAVID BURNLEY. *Courtliness and Literature in Medieval England,* Longman Medieval and Renaissance Library, London and New York: Longman Press, 1998. Pp. xiii, 241. $54.95 cloth, $25.31 paper.

The Longman Medieval and Renaissance Library Series publishes books that introduce a general audience of students and readers interested in things medieval to a general topic, through coverage broad and various. In his study, David Burnley announces the vast provenance he envisions for courtliness in medieval life and literature—finding it reflective of "all aspects of approved behaviour"—and delimits his ambitious goal: to trace "some of the themes [of courtliness] which surface and submerge, separate and re-combine during the four hundred and fifty years of the later middle ages" (pp. ix, xi). The book's chapters treat courtliness in relation to its emergence, values, and qualities, and its concerns with aesthetics, personal beauty, individuality, language, courtly love, and religion. Although the chapters could stand alone—indeed, a number are developed from previously published materials—they gain a richness from the interplay among them: later chapters offer expansions and modifications, provide counter-examples, and draw subtle distinctions. A methodical exploration of complex issues in related social and linguistic registers, this study offers a sophisticated interaction one would not expect of such a broadly conceived study.

Burnley describes the method through which he reconstructs the values of the medieval period as "essentially one of calling to witness relevant passages from texts written in Middle English or Anglo-Norman" (p. x). He provides the "breadth and variety of coverage" deemed essential by his editors as he works through texts civic, philosophical, legal, and literary (to offer only the most obvious categories), and, unsurprisingly, he calls the usual expert witnesses: Chaucer, Gower, the *Gawain*-poet, and Langland. However, equally central are lesser-read medieval texts. As the hundred-odd primary sources suggest, Burnley's interpretive techniques address influences, sources, redactions, and manuscript transmission, but at base, his interpretations rest on "the informal lexical analysis of words which seem to be of key importance to the concepts with which [he] is concerned" (p. x).

He begins by tracing the evolution of the concept of knighthood from the Bayeux tapestry, and finds the "threshold of courtly society" to have emerged around the millennium, when concerns with "self-possession, insight, tact, and eloquence" delineated the "beginnings of that self-regard from which social theory grows" (p. 19). He then maps the expansion and mystification of the concept of courtliness, first lexically in its increasing abstraction, and then by reference to a literature that defines, promulgates, and valorizes courtly social behavior, before circling around and discussing the invention of foundational myths of courtliness. He argues that such a courtly aesthetic value system depends on the belief that external courtliness arises from an inner worth and nobility, and sees this medieval essentialism as an appeal to a self-awareness that allows readers to connect their individual emotional experiences to "contemporary theorizing about the nature of the refined soul and its emotional susceptibility" (p. 79). This inwardness he finds linked to "the increased emphasis on affectivity found in religion after the eleventh century, which derived from Patristic teachings on charity, and which found literary expression in the religious lyric" (p. 80).

Several chapters examine the complex relationship between courtly and Christian values, at times combative and at times consonant. The *Ancrene Wisse*—which boasts the first use of the term *courtesie*—proves a rich and early example, offering a fully developed courtly metaphor of the church and her people: the "image of the attack by the devil on a soul is already allegorized as the siege of a lady (the soul) in a castle of earth (the body)" (p. 185). Burnley considers the meanings and provenances of the central concepts of courtliness as they occur in lexical clusters—i.e., *pite, mesure,* and *largesce;* or *grace, mercy,* and *pitee*—to explore further the intimate connection between courtly sustaining myths and Christian values.

Regarding courtly language use, Burnley investigates texts that address a middle group between nobles and churls, such as the *Secretum Secretorum,* and discusses the noble anxiety that such language and behavior might be appropriated by those *not* to the manners born. He notes that by the closing decades of the fourteenth century, those in the wealthy merchant class were adept at adopting the values of both royal and provincial courts and applying them within their own world. Middle English, according to Burnley, marks such linguistic duplicity with a subtle distinction between two phrases describing courtly linguistic prowess—*curteis speche* and *faire speche*—and concludes that *"faire speche* carries implication of illusion or deception" (p. 115). The courtly insistence that *"Fine amor* is the product of the *fin cuer*—the quality of the heart determines the quality of the love"—is perhaps motivated by the fear of appropriation.

Finding courtly literature more difficult to define than courtliness itself, Burnley is content to characterize it, declaring that only in Chaucer can one find "court poetry written in the courtly mode, and with courtly sympathies" (p. 141). His detailed examination of courtly love begins with Gaston Paris's "courtly love" and Andreas Capellanus's *fin amor,* and though it covers well-trodden ground, Burnley brings to it a fresh view derived from his detailed exploration of the semantic breadth of related terms. Through a series of systematic, local readings, he dissects the lexical contexts of such terms, situating them both within their specific texts and in their relationship to other discourses on love and friendship.

Burnley finds that the Church's objections to courtliness center on the fear that leisure and luxury might lead to an eclipse of moral values by aesthetic ones, and that "sensuous self-gratification might supplant intellectual direction" (p. 178). He sees the Church's condemnation as "a fundamental theme of social re-orientation in the fourteenth century," and credits it with bringing about "a steady change in the conceptions of courtliness" (p. 182). Tracing attitudes toward extravagance and exclusivity through time, he delineates how the Church and the state prevailed against the courtly community.

Arguing that in the later Middle Ages such criticisms of courtliness, especially of its lavish ostentation, broaden beyond the pulpit, Burnley concludes that the resultant perspective "saw courtliness as combining a valuable refinement of behaviour with a morality based on religious teaching, free from the abstractions of theology, but accompanied by a healthy appreciation of the values of economics and politics" (p. 205). As courtliness adapted to the requirements first of religion and then of an urban society, *courtesie* was supplanted by *honeste, reverence,* and *regard* in a process he terms the democratization of courtliness.

Burnley's prose is clear and his scholarly apparatus and bibliography helpful, if not as complete as those of the earlier articles upon which he draws. The shortcomings of this book are those typical of texts written for the general audience: oversimplification here, too little theorizing there, not enough evidence in between. Nevertheless, his arguments are interesting and accessible to the advanced-student reader, while the rich lexical analysis and breadth of sources he employs spark in the specialized reader both memory and desire. In sum, I would apply to Burnley's book his own laudatory description of Chaucer: "His borrowings of ideas are . . . drawn from the bran-tub of medieval doctrine, and his handling of love is eclectic" (p. 168).

MARK ADDISON AMOS
Southern Illinois University at Carbondale

JEFFREY JEROME COHEN and BONNIE WHEELER, eds. *Becoming Male in the Middle Ages.* New York and London: Garland, 1997. Pp. xx, 387. $68.00.

The seventeen essays in *Becoming Male in the Middle Ages,* framed by Jeffrey Jerome Cohen and Bonnie Wheeler's "Becoming and Unbecoming" and Michael Uebel's "On Becoming-Male," share a strong, largely unified thesis. Gesturing toward existentialist modes of "becoming," but less toward a processual understanding of cultural relations that might be identified as materialist, the collection examines the "ways in which masculinity is written on the body, through the body, and by the mind into culture" (p. xiii). Time and again, *Becoming Male* examines medieval culture using the premises of postmodern analyses of gender as relational, multivalent, and oppositional. Unsurprisingly, then, the collection as a whole draws heavily on the work of such familiar figures as Judith Butler, Michel Foucault, and Eve Sedgwick. To capture, however fleetingly, the processual nature of becoming-male (as Uebel puts it) is to read medieval culture as a map traversed by multiple discourses of the body. Desire, discipline, transgression, transformation, and the fluidity of sexualities and genders are key themes in this "alchemical" project of becoming male. The magic of alchemy (emphasized by D. Vance Smith in "Body Doubles: Producing the Masculine *Corpus*," as well as by Cohen and Wheeler) turns matter into the gold of a maleness shot through with "impurity and phantasmatic 'refinement'" (p. xi).

Becoming Male in the Middle Ages tends to stress the impurities of the process rather than the desire for gold, although R. James Goldstein ("Normative Heterosexuality in History and Theory: The Case of Sir David Lindsay of the Mount") tracks Lindsay's anxious emphasis on normative masculine heterosexuality throughout his writing on kingship and court life, and David Townsend's fascinating "Ironic Intertextuality and the Reader's Resistance to Heroic Masculinity in the *Waltharius*" traces the ways in which a resisting male reader might evade the illusory gold of hypermasculine heroism. For Smith, the male body, "bound up in artifice" (p. 16) and abstracted from its matter, signifies in idealized discourses of production—labor, currency, medicine—each of which undermines the natural ease with which man becomes a homology for world. Uebel ("On Becoming-Male") pushes such homologies further in search of the moment(s) when the "private," presocialized body emerges. Uebel's move into the body (into corporeality), however minimally examined and however unexamined his use of the notorious terms "public" and "private," offers a fitting conclusion to the collection's emphasis on "becoming" with a new project—that of the body within.

Others essays are less concerned with corporeality than with the many discursive processes that elicit maleness. Allen J. Frantzen continues his work on the Anglo-Saxon penitentials with an essay on the sex acts of children: "Where the Boys Are: Children and Sex in the Anglo-Saxon Penitentials" offers a compelling account of how the sexuality of the boy is constructed on that of the adult man. Already a "man," the boy disciplined by the penitentials is thus becoming "male." Ruth Mazo Karras uses the evidence of the universities, itself a rarely considered resource for the history of gender and sexuality, in "Sharing Wine, Women, and Song: Masculine Identity Formation in the Medieval European Universities," to demonstrate how these single-sex, univocal institutions of learning inculcate "mature" models of maleness, not simply with frequent misogynous curricular materials but also with such strikingly familiar extracurricular rituals as drinking, feasting, fighting, and gambling.

The disciplining of eros, evident in Karras's account of the relation between prostitution and the universities and Frantzen's account of childhood sexuality, is also evident in two other essays. "Erotic Discipline . . . or 'Tee Hee, I Like My Boys to Be Girls': Inventing with the Body in Chaucer's *Miller's Tale*," by Glenn Burger, rethinks the disorganization of gender, sex, and sexuality of bodies in *The Miller's Tale* to argue that "proper" masculinity is that which is received violently. The tale, however, by traversing fantasies of the feminine ultimately closed down by the narrative "constructs an alternative *masochistic* trajectory of desire: back toward a (humiliating) acknowledgment of the bodily, toward persuasion rather than instruction, contract rather than demonstration" (p. 254, his emphasis). Fantasies of the feminine (this time of the divine) are also at work in Elliot R. Wolfson's "Eunuchs Who Keep the Sabbath: Becoming Male and the Ascetic Ideal in Thirteenth-Century Jewish Mysticism." Wolfson examines the role of abstinence in the construction of masculinity in the mystic fraternities associated with the *Zohar* in late-thirteenth-century Castile. Sublimation of heterosexual desire permits the reintegration of the feminine into the masculine—a desire that fulfils "the homoerotic bonding of the mystic to the male body of God" (p. 169). The Christian heresy of Judaism, allied to that of Islam, and its implications for gender "disturbance" (p. 21) in Christian works is the subject of Steven F. Kruger's "Becoming Christian, Becoming Male?" Kruger examines representations of Jewish and Muslim men in Christian texts as carnal, feminized, and infantilized, together with the masculinization of Jewish women, to address the question of the maleness of the Christian.

If to become a Christian is to become male, in other medieval texts to become human is to reconfigure maleness. Leslie Dunton-Downer's "Wolf Man" makes the point economically in a reading of Marie de France's *Bisclavret,* arguing that the werewolf figure, with its traditional associations of masculine violence, is refashioned by Marie into a figure whose humanity is part of the process of becoming male. Cohen's "Gowther Among the Dogs: Becoming Inhuman c. 1400" has a similar trajectory. The monstrous hero of *Sir Gowther,* read as a pre-oedipal figure who solves the riddle of his paternity, is both domesticated and transformed in the process of the romance, becoming *inter alia* a dog, a hero, and a saint. For Cohen, *Sir Gowther* "teaches that bodies, genders, and identities have no limits other than the illusory 'final,' 'stable' selves that culture manufactures and sanctifies and that never in the end constrain" (p. 239). Three essays on Abelard rethink the apparent constraints of one particular male body. For Martin Irvine, "Abelard and (Re)Writing the Male Body: Castration, Identity, and Remasculinization," Abelard's castration ushered in a lengthy process of remasculinization, while for Wheeler ("Origenary Fantasies: Abelard's Castration and Confession"), both Abelard and Heloise collaborate in essentializing his masculinity. Yves Ferroul offers a different, bold perspective, as his title indicates: "Abelard's Blissful Castration."

Many of these essays, then, examine processes of resignification, although Robert S. Sturges ("The Pardoner, Veiled and Unveiled") gets right to the point in his essay on another putative castrate whose "masculinity is *only* a role, never achieved but only assumed" (p. 267, his emphasis). Sturges's point is borne out more generally in Ad Putter's essay on cross-dressing, "Transvestite Knights in Medieval Life and Literature," while the relation between performativity and performance is surveyed both by Garrett P. J. Epp ("The Vicious Guise: Effeminacy, Sodomy, and *Mankind*") and Claire Sponsler ("Outlaw Masculinities: Drag, Blackface, and Late Medieval Laboring-Class Festivities"). Sponsler's treatment of the gender implications of such neglected practices as drag and blackface is unique in the collection for its emphasis on the relation between class and maleness. Indeed, Sponsler's essay serves as a salutary reminder that this collection, richly diverse as it is in culturally specific examples of the project of "becoming male," is nonetheless driven by a unified and largely uncontested agenda about maleness and masculinity. Paradoxically, the book's emphasis on multivalence, oppositions, and fluidity results in a striking uniformity about the ways in which medieval men came to be.

CLARE A. LEES
University of Oregon

HELEN COOPER and SALLY MAPSTONE, eds. *The Long Fifteenth Century: Essays for Douglas Gray.* Oxford: Clarendon Press, 1997. Pp. xi, 362. $85.00.

In their preface to *The Long Fifteenth Century,* the editors offer the plan for the book they have produced to mark the retirement of Douglas Gray, one of the most learned, humane, and genial literary scholars to teach at Oxford in the last thirty years. It is, they note, "a collection of essays to accompany one of [Gray's] most significant contributions to medieval studies, *The Oxford Book of Late Medieval Verse and Prose* (1985) . . . a period that for him . . . extends well into the sixteenth century (p. v)." Hence, *The Long Fifteenth Century* embodies Gray's vision, and its contents (as a glance at the bibliography of Gray's writings, carefully prepared by Joerg O. Fichte, illustrates) reflect Gray's own published interests. The book presents, in roughly chronological order, essays by Gray's former students and Oxford colleagues on Lydgate and Chaucer, Hoccleve and his French predecessors, the *Kingis Quair,* "Jon the Blynde Awdelay," *The Wars of Alexander,* ballads, morality plays, Henryson, *Mum and the Sothsegger,* Skelton's *Bowge of Court* and his *Replycacion,* Elyot's *Pasquil the Playne,* John Bale as a literary/historical critic and two generic/ theoretical pieces, on "Frames and Narrators in Chaucerian Poetry" and "Civil Strife and Father-Killing in the Prose Romances." The range of subject in this collection is remarkable, and designedly achieved.

In her *Introduction* to the volume, Helen Cooper makes the point that Gray's *Oxford Book* was the most influential of a small handful of books that in the early 1980s began the reappraisal of then scarcely studied fifteenth-century literature. Now a decade later that "obscure" century is receiving significant scholarly attention. To carry forward Gray's groundbreaking achievement, "to help to change the way the [fifteenth century] is perceived," is, Cooper asserts, the mission and the challenge of this collection. And happily, the promise of such breadth is fulfilled by the accomplishment and richness of the essays the editors have chosen to include.

In keeping with their commitment to bring forth the writers of the fifteenth century afresh, Cooper and Mapstone allot the first four places in their collection to essays that help sharpen distinctions between Chaucer and some of his "followers." In "'Dysemol daies and fatal houres': Lydgate's *Destruction of Thebes* and Chaucer's *Knight's Tale,*" which opens the book, James Simpson carefully prunes away the chestnut foliage of cliché—so oft repeated, so listlessly unexamined—that takes Lydgate's poem as a botched extension of the opening Canterbury tale. "Lydgate's poem known as the *Siege of Thebes*," Simpson writes, "is in every respect a much darker, more saturnine work than has been commonly allowed. The strongest manuscript tradition, endorsed by Lydgate from within the work, calls it the *Destruction of Thebes*, and destruction is indeed its subject. In this it may well answer to the period of its composition, which in my view is after the death of Henry V" (p. 15). The number of strong claims made here in a few sentences is striking—a new, "darker" interpretation, a fresh consideration of the manuscripts, the suggestion of a more accurate name and a better date of composition for a well-known work—and Simpson's historicized reading of Chaucer and Lydgate justifies his claims by essay's end.

I quote Simpson at length here because in every way his opening lines epitomize the assertive originality of opinion and careful, transformative argumentation found throughout *The Long Fifteenth Century*. It is high time, as John Burrow points out, that Hoccleve's poetry was closely compared to the French poets he undoubtedly read, as well as to Chaucer. Here his essay, "Hoccleve and the Middle French Poets," points the way by placing Hoccleve's *Series*, the *Male Regle*, and even (in passing) the *Regiment of Princes* in the context of the *dits* of Machaut and Froissart and the work and career of Deschamps. Similarly, by foregrounding what the historical record has to tell us of the political and the personal James I, Sally Mapstone rereads the *Kingis Quair* in ways quite new and equally unsettling to any who would cling to the comfortable-as-carpet-slippers view of the poem as a Chaucerian fiction done up in Highland plaid. And again, in Helen Phillips's hands, the familiar category "Chaucerian poetry," insofar as it represents a tradition of "courtly" verse descended from the *dits amoureux*, receives redefinition and redirection. Her essay, "Frames and Narrators in Chaucerian Poetry," at once affirms the "centrality of Chaucer for composition in these genres in England and Scotland" (p. 71) while at the same time helping to make plain how our small store of remaining pieces by the likes of de Worde, Pynson, Scogan, and Roos illustrates a contemporary awareness of genre that includes Chaucer but also reaches beyond him to French sources read by the "minor" writers of the fifteenth century with a zeal and comprehension no less than Chaucer's own. Phillips's focus and conclusions thus second Burrow's, and vice versa.

Eric Stanley's contribution, "The Verse Forms of Jon the Blynde Awdelay," is as fine a piece of scholarship of its kind as can be found. It is an essay on a manuscript and a poet little known to most (one exception being Douglas Gray, to whose interest in MS Douce 302 and "Awdelay" Stanley attributes his own), unwavering in its scholarship and sound good sense, which will undoubtedly become the foundation for further discussions of both poet and manuscript. Stanley establishes the authorship of the collection (the poems are by Audelay, and possibly the book itself was his) and carefully positions it, and its author, within the *geist* of the fifteenth century.

Like Stanley, Peter Dronke follows Gray's lead to discuss a work but narrowly known, and succeeds in illustrating amply why it deserves greater attention. Dronke himself is obviously charmed with the anonymous English poet and his alliterative creation, finding in it an "Alexander of the great feats of outdoing . . . complimented by [an] Alexander of familiar human littleness" (p. 139), drawn in ecphrastically in "vivacious, humorous and pungeant language" and "fired" with "a sense of imaginative purpose" (p. 124). Very likely Gray would have concurred.

Helen Cooper's is a piece of a different color, and it takes nothing away from any of the fine essays in the collection to claim that hers stands out from the rest to the degree that its subject—patricide, incest, and the political nexus of desire and kingship—thrusts us beyond the boundaries of literary scholarship. Cooper's thesis is that the unsettled times of the waning Middle Ages drew forth from the writers of prose romance the mordant truth that even (or perhaps *especially*, Cooper suggests) the noblest of Camelot, those with the firmest commitments to the highest ideals of chivalry, can find themselves inexorably "betrayed by that ethos into an act of 'evill prowesse'" (p. 162). Hers is an essay unsuited to summary; rather, it is one to read in full and (like much of Gray's work) to think over carefully.

In "The Ballad and the Middle Ages," Richard Firth Green seeks to reverse what he sees as a trend of the last thirty years, to short-shrift the ballad. Addressing directly David C. Fowler's argument in his *Literary History of the Popular Ballad* (1968), that "a given ballad took the particular shape it has about the time that it was written down" (which effectively confines scholarly study of the ballad to but twenty-five of Child's collection and thereafter to the Percy Folio Manuscript, ca. 1650), Green stakes out his position clearly: "I want to challenge Fowler's conviction that it is fruitless to speculate about an oral tradition anterior to the earliest appearance of any given ballad in print, and hence that the medievalist has little to learn from the study of traditional ballads first copied down in more recent times" (p. 165). To do so, Green first demonstrates the significant antique features preserved in postmedieval copies, features that provide evidence of medieval ballad shapes. Then, in what most will find the more controversial half of the essay, Green concludes "by suggesting how study of the humble ballad can sometimes throw an interesting light on far more elevated works" (p. 183). He chooses as his example lines 1109–218 of *The Wife of Bath's Tale,* connecting the Hag's lengthy lecture on *gentillesse* with a tradition of the groom's credentials found in the ballad "King Henry" (Child 32) and "The Half Hitch," a ballad collected in Vermont.

Both Robert Easting and Malcolm Godden find little-known texts offering glimpses into "other"—albeit very different—worlds. In his essay "'Send thine heart into purgatory': Visionaries of the Other World," Easting describes four visions of purgatory from the fifteenth century, two by laymen (*The Vision of William of Stranton* and *The Vision of Edmund Leversedge*) "and two by Benedictines, a nun, *A Revelation of Purgatory to an unknown woman,* and a monk, *The Revelation to the Monk of Eynsham*" (p. 191). Godden's "other world" is mundane—a look behind the scenes of a performance of the morality play *Wisdom*—but no less riveting in its suggestion that the monks of Bury may have presented a *Wisdom* during the reign of Henry VI that included scantily clad dancing girls.

"'Abject odious': Feminine and Masculine in Henryson's *Testament of Cresseid*" is a strong piece of criticism, as profoundly disturbing as the painting *Les Amants Trepasses* by the fifteenth-century Swabian Master, which Felicity Riddy uses to focus her powerful argument. She positions Henryson's poem between the revulsion invoked by *Les Amants* ("They are revenants, walkers on the boundary; excluded, abominable, defiled" [p. 229]), van Eyck's silently troubling portrait of Giovanni and Giovanna Arnolfini, Julia Kristeva's *Powers of Horror,* and a late medieval mysogyny typified by Henryson, which demanded the foul end of Cresseid for Troilus's "humanitie" to show.

The following two essays, "'Spekyng for one's sustenance': The Rhetoric of Counsel in *Mum and the Sothsegger,* Skelton's *Bowge of Court,* and Elyot's *Pasquil the Playne,*" by Helen Barr and Kate Ward-Perkins, and "Justification by Faith: Skelton's *Replycacion,*" by Vincent Gillespie, seek to illuminate and define literary form in terms of contents thrust upon writers by the politics of the final decade of the fifteenth century and the first thirty years of the sixteenth. As one might expect in those troublous times, Skelton in particular found challenge and purpose rhyming advice to his king, and defining the role of a humanist poet in a period grown darker and ever more scornful of classical wisdom.

The final essay in the collection is "*Visio Baleii:* An Early Literary Historian," by Anne Hudson, in which she makes a compelling case for understanding John Bale as the first true literary critic to discuss English letters. In a collection arranged chronologically according to subject, Hudson's effort would have come at the end of *The Long Fifteenth Century* in any case; but how fortuitous that it should be so. Hudson's brief study of Bale as bibliographer reveals how much there is in Bale's catalogues (beyond the fiercely Protestant bias) to teach us. Hudson concludes, after weighing Bale's lists and commentary on Chaucer, Gower, Lydgate, Pecock, Hilton, Douglas, and others, "It would perhaps be fanciful to suggest that Bale's work had more wide-ranging effects: that it focused literary study on the historical development of named writers, to the diminution of interest either in form or in works regardless of authorship, and that consequently only in very recent times have major areas of fifteenth century writing (areas such as lyrics, plays, and much religious prose) been reclaimed as legitimate areas of study" (p. 328). With an elegant trope, and characteristic insight, Hudson places Douglas Gray in line with Bale, but a step ahead, noting that it is Gray who most recently has been responsible for changing a direction in literary study set, as Hudson shows here, by Bale, to include the anonymous works Bale had apparently disdained.

Certainly, then, in its diversity of subject and the contribution it makes to our understanding of the late literature of medieval England, *The Long Fifteenth Century* is true to its intentions: It is a portrait in letters of Douglas Gray, a scholar to whom so many owe so much.

ROBERT F. YEAGER
University of North Carolina

Catherine S. Cox, *Gender and Language in Chaucer.* Gainesville: University of Florida Press, 1997. Pp. x, 196. $49.95.

Despite a plethora of intelligent guides, the maze of text and gender in Chaucer's work has yielded few clear pathways and even fewer satisfying destinations. We are often led in one direction by the author's erudition and by his vocation as translator and in quite another by the extraordinary modernity (or so it seems to us) of the gendered—that is, human—relationships he creates as a *makyr* of vernacular poetry. In *Gender and Language in Chaucer,* Catherine Cox sets out to explore the maze by delineating the roles text and gender play in the construction of subjectivity and in the articulation of a metapoetics through a variety of Chaucer's texts. She identifies as particular concerns the "en/gendering" of a text's internal epistemologies and the self-reflexive nature of much of Chaucer's poetic (p. 5). More broadly, Cox argues that in medieval texts,

> Medieval Woman is not only the carnal or only the passive, or submissive, or whatever; complex and multiple, often contradictory and paradoxical, Woman is representative textually not only of the carnal . . . but also of the potential multiplicity of meaning that gives rise to the polysemy necessary for language to transcend literal constraints. Woman may be understood to represent not only the body of the text . . . but also its figurative capacity to generate and articulate meaning; Woman corresponds to both form and process. (p. 12)

Cox argues that Chaucer exploits these representational potentialities through "complex and reflexive tropes" that point to the role of the "feminine" in epistemology and hermeneutics (p. 12).

Cox also sees the feminine in Chaucer as enabling a violation of the decorums inherited from the very canonical texts the author relies upon as sources:

> . . . the feminine *translatio* inscribes the capacity of signification to challenge—or violate—proper decorum in order that multiple senses (*poly/seme*) obtain. The feminine *signa,* as improper, are frequently articulated in conjunction with sexual metaphors since the unlimited sense of the epistemological feminine is, in effect, promiscuous (*pro/miscere,* mixed, confused, indiscriminate), for *signa translata* resist constraint and challenge masculine insistence on ordered decorum. (p. 13)

Cox has read widely in both postmodern theory (with a particular debt acknowledged to Carolyn Dinshaw) and in patristic literature. Bringing these two discourses to bear on Chaucer's poetry yields some intriguing analyses of the "inextricable coincidence of flesh and text" (p. 120). However, this reader found herself longing for a clearer articulation of those conclusions.

Although there is not space here to work through each chapter of *Gender and Language in Chaucer,* a brief discussion of chapters on the Wife of Bath, *Troilus and Criseyde,* and the *Retraction* will point to the volume's strengths and weaknesses. After the introduction, Cox begins, appropriately enough, with a study of the Wife as glossator, arguing, as others have done before, that the erotic play of language takes precedence for the Wife over the sexual act itself—that the text is sexualized just as much as it textualizes sex (p. 26). Cox emphasizes the issue of control over bodily and textual fertility, arguing that in her perpetuation of the patriarchal binary, virginity/promiscuity, and in her insistence on private, internal discourse, the Wife is, ironically, "revirginizing" language even as her own polysemous language resists that control. This concern with the codification of virginity and its textual permutations resurfaces in chapter 3 as Cox argues that the tales of suffering virgins, in *The Legend of Good Women, The Physician's Tale, The Second Nun's Tale,* and elsewhere, are also tales of virgin texts: that is, texts circumscribed, constrained, and barren (pp. 63–64).

Cox's reading of the Wife is nuanced and complex. She does not succumb to the simplistic notion that the fecundity of the Wife's *Prologue* and the portrayal of feminine power in the *Tale* render them feminist texts. In this reading, usurpation and transference are crucial to the Wife's appropriation of language for pleasure and public display, and yet she is understood as finally privatizing language herself as she engages patriarchal discourse in a contest for authority (p. 35). Cox argues that in the Wife's *Prologue,* autoeroticism, glossing, and privatization generate a "quasi-feminist" sexual rhetoric that is, in the end, promiscuous and without satisfaction or efficacy.

In the chapter on *Troilus and Criseyde,* Cox again directs our attention to the woman as embodiment of the "slydyng" text, manipulated and inscribed upon by men. Much of this chapter is marked by Cox's passionate advocacy of Criseyde, a brief that enables her to trace the fault lines in the decorum of *fin' amors,* but which also leads her into the mimetic fallacy and certain anachronistic moves. Thus, she finds Criseyde's desertion of Troilus "less than tragic" and "relatively trivial" (p. 46). This characterization of what is presented in the poem as an incomprehensible, and ultimately fatal, violation of trust undermines her analysis of the interplay between text and gender in that she resists understanding the text's complicity in a thoroughly gendered betrayal. She rightly points out that there is humor in the poem's melodrama (p. 47), but it may be a mistake to allow a deflation of the rhetoric of book 4 to trivialize the price Troilus pays for literalizing the *fin' amors* code. Nevertheless, Cox is perceptive in finding that, in its "explication of literary decorums and their artifice, the text . . . exposes their insufficiency in the face of situational and contextual shifts" (p. 49).

The analysis of *Troilus and Criseyde* highlights what is at once a strength and a flaw in this book. Cox successfully mirrors the modern reader's discomfort and perplexity in the face of medieval gender and religious codes. The univocality of the ballades, the melodrama and hyperbolic rhetoric of *fin' amors,* the cumulative misery of suffering virgins and virtuous wives, and the final, seemingly dissonant, *Retraction* all come under brave and extended scrutiny here. However, the reluctance to see Chaucer as a man for his age as well as for all ages can simplify and dismiss precisely those texts that offer us the greatest moral and intellectual challenges. One further example will have to suffice. Cox finds in the Manciple's clearly insincere retraction of his attack on the Cook (*ManP* 81) a clue to the puzzle of Chaucer's *Retraction.* Recognizing "profound differences" between them, she still characterizes both as using "renunciation as a narrative and rhetorical technique." Dismissing the *Retraction* and, by implication, *The Parson's Tale,* as marked by "theological heavy-handedness," Cox argues that in the *Retraction* the poet "feigns regret" for his secular works in order to prompt us to imagine "a kind of world where codes of silence, like those posited in the *Manciple's Tale,* the *Parson's Tale,* and the *Retraction,* have been successfully implemented . . . where joylessness and rigidity are celebrated as part of God's grace and where the sole purpose of existence is to pray grimly for salvation" (p. 109). In its characterization of the Parson's Christianity, this may strike us as simplistic; in its dismissal of some of Chaucer's thornier texts, it seems a bit like wishful thinking. Gower is not the only moralist the fourteenth century has to offer us, and in his accolade to "moral Gower" Geoffrey Chaucer may, through characteristic sleight of hand and text, be diverting our attention from the ethical dilemmas that lie at the center of his own textual maze.

Gender and Language in Chaucer fruitfully examines the struggle with orthodoxy, sometimes playful, sometimes deadly serious, that marks much of Chaucer's work. Catherine Cox traces the chaotic trail of Chaucer's "subversive erotics" (p. 132) through a diverse collection of texts, and argues, often successfully, that the poet refuses essentialist constructions of gender (p. 131). This is an important project, passionately undertaken, but compromised by the occasional anachronistic reading and a weakness for convolution and neologism.

SEALY GILLES
Long Island University

JOSEPH A. DANE. *Who Is Buried in Chaucer's Tomb?: Studies in the Reception of Chaucer's Book.* East Lansing: Michigan State University Press, 1998. Pp. ix, 309.

The study of Chaucer developed largely independently of the study of the rest of Middle English, and over a much longer period, so today the Chaucerian edifice towers over everything else in Middle English. Joseph Dane's book questions the security of the foundations on which this edifice is constructed; it interrogates the history of the reception of Chaucer and attacks some of the foundational assumptions and inherited wisdom on which the modern study of Chaucer rests. Dane sees Chaucer studies as enshrining various myths that, as the rather arch interrogative title of the book suggests, he wants to debunk. It's the kind of title that would usually send the professional medievalist running, with its hint that it ought to be on the shelf with the books about the true Arthur's grave or the secrets of the grail. The actual book, of course, conflicts entirely with this image, being in every other way framed as a respectable scholarly work, while the discussion of Chaucer's tomb turns out to be a highly erudite and often amusing analysis of the various things that are, were, or have been said to be on Chaucer's tomb (rather than in it).

This play with readerly expectations is no doubt deliberate, because one of Dane's principal concerns here is the material realizations of texts in books, specifically, the material realizations of what he calls the Chaucer book. These "are to be distinguished from Chaucer's text[, which] is reproducible exactly. . . .. The Chaucer book, by contrast, is never reproducible exactly, whether it is considered a manuscript, a printed book, or a group of book-copies of either kind" (p. 1). This is, then, a material history of Chaucerian reception, concerned not solely with what has been said about Chaucer but with the physical forms in which Chaucer has been presented and what they might have meant at different times.

With ten chapters, introduction, and conclusion, this is a solid work. It follows Chaucerian reception roughly chronologically, moving from the discussion of the tomb to a consideration of Thynne's 1532 edition, then to other blackletter Chaucers, before diverting into a discussion of Usk's (once "Chaucer's") *Testament of Love,* which takes us from Foxe's construction of Chaucer as a Wycliffite via the *Testament,* to the nineteenth century and W. W. Skeat's and Henry Bradley's solutions to the acrostic in this text and the attribution to Usk. Dane then addresses the eighteenth century, first looking at the vicissitudes of what he expresses as "[Chaucer's] *Retraction*" and then the reception of eighteenth-century editors. The final four chapters are more concerned with issues that have arisen in twentieth-century criticism and literary history: Jean Destrez's booklet theory and its possible impact on Chaucerian texts; notions of the Chaucerian persona in American Chaucer criticism from Kittredge onwards; internal and external evidence used in Chaucer editions; scribes as critics.

The most valuable and refreshing thing about the book is Dane's concern to give us a history of discontinuities and simultaneously to dispose of the smoothly coherent narrative generations of Chaucerians have constructed for their subject. He does this without explicit recourse to such prior models for this kind of approach as Hans Aarsleff's notion of a history of error, or Michel Foucault's various theorizings of discontinuity. Instead, he works from the richly ideological raw material of Chaucerian reception itself, bringing to it a deep skepticism about received ideas.

There are moments when a more explicitly theorized approach would have been valuable. The substitution of skepticism for methodology can produce blind spots, usually through some literal-minded readings. Discussing the notion of Chaucer's presentation of himself as naive, Dane questions whether—given Chaucer's survival of the vicissitudes of the late fourteenth century—Chaucer's "feigned naiveté" could have provoked admiration from his audience at the same time as it was "an extremely effective facade" (p. 167). Did Chaucer's employers, Dane asks, "forking over their daily tuns of wine," fail to see the poet's "charlatanry" (p. 167)? Given current opinion about Chaucer's audience, there is no reason why the answer cannot be yes, those employers *did* fail to see through the Chaucerian facade. Few critics (and surely not the skeptical Dane) still believe that that daily wine was handed over for poetic services rendered; the picture presented here of politically hoodwinked princes is not backed up by any evidence that Chaucer's employers were much concerned with what he did after packing up the customs house for the day.

Elsewhere, Dane is concerned with what he calls the myth of Thomas Tyrwhitt's greatness. Making this interesting case, he argues that the most reviled of all Chaucer editions, Urry's of 1721, was the more radical and groundbreaking edition. This may be true (and in fact it is convincingly argued) but what then to do with Tyrwhitt? Is it enough simply ro topple the broken idol? Isn't there work to be done in understanding why the myth was constructed in the first place? Dane thinks that what marked Tyrwhitt out was the way he redefined the Chaucerian canon, excluding texts instead of adding them, as had been done up to and including Urry's edition. But he does not make enough of the fact that what the nineteenth-century scholars appreciated about Tyrwhitt was the way in which he compared a large body of manuscripts—an achievement not emulated until Skeat in the 1890s (and perhaps not even then: Eleanor Hammond in 1908 did not believe that Skeat had paid as much attention to the manuscripts as Tyrwhitt had done). Certainly, what Tyrwhitt did should not entitle him to secular sainthood; but the fact that no one else did what he did for more than a century after surely suggests his work was part of a paradigm shift or rupture in forms of knowledge. This requires more than a skeptical dismissal.

This skepticism is, however, often a great strength of the book. There are, broadly, two ways of historicizing the study of English literature. One is to do it in a celebratory way, the other to expose its various ideological investments. In recent years the second has become the norm, but many medievalists are resistant to studies that expose their subject's dirty laundry. Dane's account of Chaucerian reception will provoke many disagreements, at the very least because it ranges over so much material, but it is to be welcomed as a revisionary account of why it is that Chaucerians study what they do.

DAVID MATTHEWS
University of Newcastle, NSW

James Dean. *The World Grown Old in Later Medieval Literature.* Medieval Academy Books, no. 101. Cambridge, Mass.: The Medieval Academy of America, 1997. Pp. xi, 379. $50.00.

This is a large and ambitious book underpinned by a wealth of citation, both primary and secondary. Its aim is "to demonstrate the significance of the medieval idea of the world grown old . . . to the structures and themes of late-medieval literature" (p. 1). This is not, it must be said, a new idea. The implications of the medieval formulation of the concept of the ages of man has been fruitfully explored recently by John Burrow, Mary Dove, and Elizabeth Sears, among others. Dean, however, seeks to give it a more specific focus through an examination of its representation in the literary culture of fourteenth-century Europe. After several introductory chapters (amounting to over a third of the book), there are individual examinations of this subject in Jean de Meun, Dante, Langland, Gower, and Chaucer.

The underlying preoccupation of this book is, then, with the exploration of various forms of retrospection associated with an idealized past, which are juxtaposed against aspects of contemporary decline. Dean's basic argument is that such preoccupations are recurrent and significant in the works of a number of major poets. This assumption raises some obvious questions. The chief of these is, to what extent is it definable in ways that suggest it draws, across time and culture, on a common store of shared concerns that make it a readily identifiable formulation?

Dean seems to acknowledge this problem implicitly in his long opening chapter, "A Morphology of Subtopics De Senectute Mundi" (pp. 37–111), in which he attempts to define the various categories or "topics" (his term) that he sees as encompassing his subject: historical-doctrinal, apologetics, moral, scientific, and literary. Most of these categories are themselves subdivided, occasionally with further subdivisions. There are obvious dangers in such enumeration of complex material, some of which are represented in the discussion of "the eternity of the world" (pp. 89–94), which swiftly traverses philosophical terrain from Plato and Aristotle to Duns Scotus, Avicenna, Aquinas, Henry of Ghent, Grosseteste, and Bernardus Silvestris. Such scope leads inevitably to a degree of compression that leaves some of these matters seeming to be unclearly related to the chapters on particular authors that follow, which are concerned primarily with literary topics. The impressive erudition Dean presents throughout (the bibliography runs to over thirty pages) often seems unfocused in this chapter. There seems to be a quality of inert encyclopedism to much of his documentation, a sense at times of straining to get everything in in ways that make it difficult to be sure what may be relevant to the argument because it is not clear what the argument is. Thus, to take a single instance, the brief discussion of hunting (pp. 154–64) contains examinations of its relationship to the figure of Jupiter, its place among "the seven mechanical sciences" (p. 156), the relationship between man and animals as a metaphor for seduction, the importance of Thebes and the issue of private property. At such times, the weight of citation and engagement with secondary criticism deflects the development of a clearly focused thesis. Footnotes sometimes aim for a kind of exhaustiveness that is simply exhausting.

Such lack of focus is linked to a general lack of literary analysis. Dean's conclusion about *Piers Plowman,* for example, is that it "should be regarded as more of a spiritualized historical narrative in a tradition of clerical reform and the world grown old and less of a political treatise in a tradition of social realism" (p. 231). This is to create spurious distinctions. I am not sure modern critics have thought of the poem as a "political *treatise*," but it is hard to see how "historical narrative" and "clerical reform" can be considered without a sense of their political implications. Or why "the world grown old" is necessary to Langland's historical and spiritual explorations.

The final chapter, on Chaucer (or, as Dean puts it "the late fourteenth-century English poet and member of Richard II's faction at court" [271]—a curious mixture of the banal and the tendentious), is often reductive in its summaries ("She admires Jankyn's legs and feet as she carries her fourth husband's bier to the grave. She claims to love Jankyn best of all her husbands" [285]). The discussion in this chapter rarely rises above the level of paraphrase and plot summary.

Indeed, the problem with Dean's formulations is that it becomes quite quickly fairly hard to distinguish his approach from any other kind of social, political, or historical complaint. Any form of criticism can be seen as a deviation from an imagined norm established in the past. A vision of a "debased" (p. 200) modern world is a version of social (or other) criticism too generalized to be at all distinctive. Dean's concerns are too diffuse to be generally illuminating and seem often to be explored by skirting round the periphery of a work rather than offering any very central insights.

A. S. G. EDWARDS
Girton College, Cambridge

342

SHEILA DELANY. *Impolitic Bodies: Poetry, Saints, and Society in Fifteenth-Century England. The Work of Osbern Bokenham* (New York and Oxford: Oxford University Press, 1998). vii, 236 $45.00 cloth, $19.95 paper.

Osbern Bokenham, a fifteenth-century Augustinian friar at Clare Priory, Suffolk, is identified as the author of two works: a collection of thirteen lives of female saints known by the editorial title *Legends of Holy Women* and a translation of a portion of Ranulf Higden's *Polychronicon* entitled *Mappula Angliae;* he is also the likely author of a genealogical poem describing the historical patronage of Clare Priory and a translation of a portion of Claudian's *De consulatu Stilichonis.* In *Impolitic Bodies,* Sheila Delany argues that Bokenham's writing, particularly the legendary of female saints, can enhance our understanding of a wide range of issues, including "Chaucer's work and Chaucer reception, gender studies, late-medieval European cultural history, the development of hagiography, and English political life" (p. 4). Delany demonstrates Bokenham's relevance to these topics largely through situating the author's life and work within a series of highly detailed contexts, ranging from East Anglian patronage networks and fifteenth-century political theory to late medieval representations of the breast and recent feminist debates on sexuality and violence. This proliferation of contexts suggests the value of Bokenham's work for scholars of literary history and late medieval politics, as well as for historians and theorists of gender and power.

Delany's first three chapters include biographical detail and much information about the education of Augustinian friars, late-medieval ecclesiastical politics, the regional history of East Anglia, and local power structures in the town of Clare. Delany notes that the development of lay piety and the important role of women, especially as addressees of devotional writing, meant that the "time was ripe" (p. 29) for Bokenham's legendary, the first collection of lives of female saints written in English. However, she argues, it was neither the tradition of English devotional writing nor Latin and Anglo-Norman legendaries that served as the primary model for Bokenham's work, but rather Chaucer's *Legend of Good Women.* Delany identifies a series of parallelisms between the two works: Bokenham's Saint Margaret is a reconstruction of Chaucer's daisy, or marguerite; Saint Anne and Alceste are each related to the god of love and their lives include some association with hell; Christine and Cleopatra are each associated with three officials, a snakebite, and a scene at sea; Dido and Faith each die on a bed, and so forth. But, as Delany

343

admits, some of the similarities are minor (the stories of Lucrece and Dorothy each include a detail about the woman's feet [p. 41]), or are so generalizable as to be unremarkable (Hypermnestra and Cecelia are "young brides with a secret" [p. 42]), and the correspondence does not extend to the last three lives of Bokenham's legendary, although, Delany improbably suggests, this "could correspond to a lost portion of Chaucer's *Legend*" (p. 43). A further problem lies in Delany's decision to single out Chaucer as Bokenham's most significant predecessor. Although Bokenham mentions Chaucer throughout the legendary, it is always in the context of a formulaic triumvirate—"Gower, Chaucer, Lydgate"—representing an emergent English literary tradition. It is Bokenham's development of an ongoing dialogue with a collective literary tradition that gives a surer sense of the legendary's order and coherence. This broader relationship to courtly culture is the subject of Delany's discussion of Bokenham's Augustinianism; she argues that the legendary is an "Augustinian polemic against the abuse of rhetoric and of classical culture by the courtly classicizing trend in recent English poetry" (p. 70), an attempt to "cleanse hagiography of its courtly ironic and its bureaucratic accretions to return to the fundamentals of faith" (p. 65).

The middle third of the book is a conceptual unit, in which Delany argues that Bokenham deliberately organized his legendary in the image of a body. Delany claims that "Bokenham deliberately produced a somaticized text; that is, he meant his text to be seen as a body, specifically a female body, at first fragmented but finally reassembled" (p. 78). It is true that the legendary is full of fragmented bodies and isolated body parts, but one of the interesting features of the virgin martyr vitae in general is the lack of bodily reincorporation the saints experience. Indeed, as Bokenham's account of the translation of Margaret's body reveals, the saint's body may continue to be dismembered after her death. Hence, perhaps, it is not surprising that Delany's attempt to identify a reintegrated, whole body in the legendary on the basis of the existence of two feet, one in the Life of Saint Margaret and the other in the legendary's concluding Life of Saint Elizabeth of Hungary, is unconvincing. This, however, does not detract from the value of the wealth of detail regarding historical and literary contexts and antecedents for Bokenham's representations of the bodies of the virgin martyrs that Delany brings together here.

In the last part of the book, Delany moves her argument into the arena of mid-fifteenth-century partisan politics. Based on the heavily Yorkist patronage of the legendary, its "distinctive representational strategies"

(p. 129), and the larger context of works generally attributed to Boken-ham, Delany argues convincingly for the legendary's Yorkist agenda. Delany's discussion of female succession in English political life during the fourteenth and fifteenth centuries demonstrates the political impli-cations of Bokenham's decision to write an all-female legendary: in as-serting the virtue and power of women, Bokenham gave important sup-port to the Yorkist claim to the throne, which passed through Phillipa, the daughter of Lionel of Clarence. Delany's careful and thorough docu-mentation of the legendary's relationship to mid-fifteenth-century po-litical history is the strongest part of the book, demonstrating the dynas-tic implications of late medieval representations of female bodies and speech.

Delany's concluding discussion of the implications of Bokenham's strategic representations of powerful holy women beyond the context of the exigencies of Yorkist propaganda reveals the challenges that the religious culture of the late Middle Ages poses to modern critics. For instance, Delany argues that Bokenham's legendary opposes the misogy-nist attacks on woman's nature by Lancastrian political theorists such as John Fortescue: "To choose to compile an all-female hagiography was the first step in the statement of a complex and forward-looking social vision" (p. 157). But the question of intentionality is vague here: this "social vision"—a "protofeminist" (p. 197) vision of women produc-tively engaged in the public sphere—is not Bokenham's vision; his leg-endary appropriates feminine piety for the Yorkist cause. If it is true that "rehabilitating the body is rehabilitating women" (p. 183), it remains unclear whether the lives of virgin martyrs, with their scenes of brutal dismemberment, can be understood as a means of rehabilitating the body. If they do so, it is likely through their association with Christ's redemptive suffering (though Delany argues that "Bokenham does not offer Jesus crucified as his chosen image of redemption but, rather, Jesus incarnated" [p. 183]). Further, the relationship between such corporeal power and the kind of political empowerment Delany advocates is, she ruefully concludes, indirect and often elusive. Nonetheless, Delany's book considers these issues in a complex and suggestive fashion, and will likely serve as the foundation for more work on this contradictory and fascinating writer.

CARROLL HILLES
Union College

LAURENCE DE LOOZE. *Pseudo-Autobiography in the Fourteenth Century: Juan Ruiz, Guillaume de Machaut, Jean Froissart, and Geoffrey Chaucer.* Gainesville: University of Florida Press, 1997. Pp. xi + 211. $49.95.

Autobiography has been investigated by literary theorists, but strangely enough, little attention has been paid to medieval texts; when it has, it has hardly ever extended beyond the scope of a specific text. Following Philippe Lejeune's assumption of a "pacte autobiographique," Paul Zumthor could argue that both the concept of a personal "I" and that of a clear distinction between history/truth and fiction were alien to the Middle Ages, and he overtly questioned the very existence of medieval autobiography ("Autobiographie au Moyen Age?"). But the Middle Ages are not a monolithic era, and the late thirteenth century was marked by a shift in mentality. A number of issues were reconsidered, among them the modes of reading. What de Looze calls a pan-European phenomenon (I would reduce the geographical span to "West-European," especially since he limits his demonstration to Spain, France, and England) has been favored by similar reexaminations. Typically, the terms *auctor/actor/autor* underwent significant changes and became associated with *auctoritas* ("authority") and Greek *authentin* ("authenticity"), and the author's actual life and personal experience gave weight to the events of the text, particularly in vernacular literature. The contemporary rise of single-author codices pertains to the same logic; more and more narratives cast the poet as protagonist. The author's status had utterly changed; because of the presence of a group of semiprofessional poets supported by grand patrons, the poet/patron relationship could easily become an element of the narrative. At the same time, the social and political crises of the time marked a turning point in Western culture. The ravages of the plague and of endless wars, the birth of new social classes, not to mention the overt Schism and "heretic" movements, threatened the traditional order and gave birth to a "crisis of truth." The presence of two popes, the disturbing debates over the legitimacy of the English kings reactivated the thirteenth-century theory of two truths (one could believe one thing as a philosopher and another as a theologian). Although the latter theory had been condemned, its denial of monologic truth was revived by Ockhamism. What Jacqueline Cerquiglini has called a "crisis of signs" (universals were mental constructs; the only true signs stood directly for actual experiences in the real world) had considerable implications on the writing process. Fictional truth could not be true; in literature there was no real difference between truth and lie, and the two could easily be inverted. It is not astonishing, then, that authors such as Guillaume de Machaut, Juan Ruiz, Jean Froissart, and Geoffrey Chaucer should use a number of equivocal signs, neither is it astonishing that the Liar's Paradox should have been so central to their work (Machaut claimed that "nothing was true except the lie") or that today's truth should become tomorrow's error (the decision of the *Jugement Behaingne* is refuted as unjust in the *Jugement Navarre,* and, I would add, *The Legend of Good Women* recants Chaucer's earlier defamation of women in *Troilus & Criseyde*).

There also arose a general scrutiny of generic classification. Being constructs of the mind, generic categories had to be unstable and relative. As Hans Robert Jauss has maintained, pure, stereotypical works became atrophied; great examples of a genre were generically mixed and upset the reader's expectations. Some of them lend themselves to a double reading, each based on different generic conventions; the level of fictionality of an autobiographical narrative is particularly controversial, especially since it involves highly complex issues such as authorial intentions and sincerity. De Looze proposes a reader-oriented typology of autobiographical writing and delineates four major categories—autobiography, autobiographical fiction, autobiographical pseudo-fiction, and pseudo-autobiography: "Autobiography implies a *perception* of nominal identity between the author and the 'I' of the narrative and a reading of the first-person narrative as sincere" (p. 27). The reader does not suspend disbelief and opts for a theory of simple mimesis. While "autobiographical fiction, by contrast [. . .] is read as disjoining the identity of the author from that of the protagonist or narrator" (p. 29), and is accompanied by a suspension of disbelief, "autobiographical pseudo-fiction results in the reader's refusal to engage in a suspension of disbelief, since what might be read as fiction [. . .] is doggedly referred back to autobiography" (p. 30). The pseudo-autobiography works in the opposite direction: "[A]lthough seen as proffering an identity between author and narrator [. . .], [it] nevertheless contests a purely autobiographical reading by calling into question the possibility that the (implied) author can know himself or history correctly" (p. 30).

I would argue that the period also engaged its audience in a new process of response to literature. Drawing on recent research (e.g., Richard Firth Green and Anne Middleton), Lillian M. Bisson [*Chaucer and the*

Late Medieval World, New York, 1998] observes that "the ironic, detached stance of late medieval poets encouraged a shift from 'a literature of performance' to 'a literature of participation' that draws the audience into conversation about issues raised in the poem [. . .]. This highly interactive relationship between the poet-performer and his attending audience supports the recent critical emphasis on a community of readers'/auditors' rôle in creating the text's meaning" (p. 25). I would also add that, simultaneously, the gradual shift from listeners to readers allowed Chaucer, for instance, to construct a heterogenous audience subtly mixing his fictional and real-life "implied readership." This approach to fourteenth-century literature is strangely similar to today's reader-response criticism, i.e., considering the production of meaning within the reading process. Connections between medieval and modern texts, and between sociohistorical data and contemporary theoretical debates, do indeed pervade de Looze's study. He illustrates, for instance, what he really means by pseudo-autobiography with a discussion of a recent and concrete shift toward this category. After publishing autobiographical sketches, Mary McCarthy wanted to redress a number of errors that she had discovered. She gathered the texts in *Memories of a Catholic Girlhood* (New York, 1981) with corrective analyses, discussing the errors from within the work. In the second version, while she preserved her nominal identity, McCarthy no longer claimed to have participated in all her protagonist's experiences. The readers are confronted with self-contradictions, with an endless Derridean *différance,* and any discourse becomes suspect.

De Looze's volume was initially prompted by his discovery of how divergent the responses to a number of late-medieval authors had always been. After the first chapter's detailed account of his theory, he examines the latter's implications for our understanding of the four authors. Space does not allow me to dwell on each chapter, but readers will want to know that after declaring that "major narratives by Chaucer flirt with an autobiographical dimension to a greater or lesser extent" (p. 133), the author explores the pseudo-autobiographical dimension of *The Canterbury Tales* in the nineteen-page chapter devoted to Chaucer. Needless to say, since the theoretical approach was delineated on the basis of contradictory readings and double-edged truths, the analyses of chapters 2 (Juan Ruiz), 3 (Guillaume Machaut), 4 (Jean Froissart), and 5 (Geoffrey Chaucer) emphasize these features and provide stimulating reading to all of us who do not want to interpret the four authors as monologic. The last chapter, "Modern Readers/Medieval Texts" (pp. 148–57), is slightly disappointing, probably because its title made us expect more than what is actually just a rather repetitive conclusion.

My own conclusion highlights the importance of this interdisciplinary contribution. It also congratulates the author and the editor for the correctness of the French quotations, names, etc., and even the reliability in their use of French accents. There are, however, a few slight errors or inconsistencies. Names starting with a first de/De are difficult to spell and to classify alphabetically. Those of Dutch/Flemish origin should in general be spelled with a capital D and appear under D, but since there are different practices, I would not object to a different system. Let me simply say that we find De Man, Paul, in the index, versus de Man, Paul, in the bibliography (yet under the letter D); Bruyne, Edgar de, in the index and bibliography (under the letter B) versus Bruyne in the text (his actual name is De Bruyne). Anthime Fourrier's book should read *L'Humanisme médiéval dans les littératures romanes du XIIe au XIVe siècle,* and not *médiévale* (twice on p. 193). On p. 189, Terence Scully's edition ought to read *"Le Court d'Amours" de Mahieu le Poirier et la "Suite Anonyme de la Court d'Amours."* Let me also suggest the addition of Bakhtin (cf. p. 182) to the index; and, to the bibliography, an edition (or translation) of Gerald of Wales's *De rebus a se gestis*—"a crucial text" (p. 168). It is often a bit mean to pinpoint such small details; given the exceptional neatness of the presentation, I hope that this very short list will rather show that it has almost reached editorial perfection.

JULIETTE DOR
Université de Liège

CAROLINE D. ECKHARDT, ed. Castleford's Chronicle *or* The Boke of Brut, vols. 1 (introduction and books 1 to 6) and 2 (books 7 to 12), Early English Text Society [EETS], o.s., 305 and 306. Oxford: Oxford University Press, 1996. Pp. xvi and vii, 1065. $125.00.

Castleford's Chronicle, as it is usually called (from the name written at the top of the opening folio, although this is not necessarily the name of the author), is "a long verse chronicle, written in a Northern English dialect" and surviving in a single copy (from the fifteenth-century) in the

Niedersächsische Staats-und Universitätsbibliothek in Göttingen (vol. 1, p. xi). It belongs to "a broad family of medieval texts, widely distributed in Latin and French versions as well as in English, that recount the traditional history of the British Isles, attributing the early settlement of Britain to Brutus, a descendant of Aeneas" (1:xii). The text "follows the general contents of the other vernacular 'Brut' chronicles . . . but it does not agree with any of them exactly" (1:xiii). It includes, for example, "a strange version of the Norman Conquest in which Harold is said to marry William's sister Elaine" (1:xi), and appears to conflate Geoffrey, Duke of Brittany (son of Henry II), with his illegitimate half-brother, Geoffrey, Archbishop of York (1:xiii). After a prologue explaining why Britain was originally named Albion, it "presents a series of legendary rulers—including Brutus, Lear, and Arthur—who reflect the construction of early British history established some two centuries earlier by Geoffrey of Monmouth's *Historia regum Britanniae* . . . then proceeds through the period of the Saxon and Norman conquests and continues into more recent times, closing with the events of the year 1327" (1:xii). The text ends "perhaps incomplete, with the deposition of Edward II and his imprisonment in Berkeley Castle," but makes no mention of his death (1:xiii).

Excerpts from *Castleford's Chronicle* have been published before, but Eckhardt's edition (completing the work begun by Angus McIntosh in 1938 and continued by Frank Behre) gives us for the first time a printed text of the whole thing. The two volumes so far published contain the complete text (nearly 39,500 lines, in short rhyming couplets) preceded by a brief introduction; volume 3 will include the main editorial matter, "a description of the manuscript, an overview of previous work on *Castleford's Chronicle,* a discussion of the sources of the chronicle and of its date and authorship, explanatory notes, an index of names, a glossary, and a bibliography."

The text is conservative, with "relatively few editorial insertions, deletions, or corrections" (1:xvi). In accordance with current EETS policy (except for diplomatic editions), abbreviations have been silently expanded, capitalization and word-division have been modernized, and punctuation has been supplied—never an easy matter with Old and Middle English texts, especially in passages where (as not infrequently in fifteenth-century texts) "the meaning can be understood only approximately" or "the syntax resists analysis" (1:xv). One might quibble about some decisions—if *onsoght* (line 7208), *ouerwyn* (line 9425), *ouergas* (line

11225), and *outegate* (line 10899) are treated as one word, should not *thorowe soght* (line 2637), *out wyne* (line 2108), *ouer passe* (line 9415), and *outh tane* (line 10874) be treated similarly?—but these are minor matters, of interest (perhaps) only to lexicographers and fellow editors: they do not detract from the reader-friendliness of the text, with its rubricated headings from the manuscript printed in boldface type, line numbers in the right margin, and textual notes appearing unobtrusively at the foot of the page.

Apart from the intrinsic interest of the subject matter and the similarities and differences between this and other "Brut" chronicles, *Castleford's Chronicle* is of particular interest for its language. More than one scribe was involved in the production of the manuscript, and Eckhardt promises in volume 3 "a detailed discussion of the number of scribes represented" (1:xiv). Since the *Middle English Dictionary* has used only those extracts that have previously been published, it is not surprising that the complete text contains words, spellings, and usages only rarely recorded elsewhere, or not previously recorded at all. There is, for example, no record in *MED* of *amages* or *emages,* both of which appear frequently here as forms of *among(es).* The "bipen" with which Corineus kills many of his enemies (lines 2705, 2731) is a fearsome weapon, but it does not appear in *MED.* The verb *spreven* 'to plunder' is well attested in *MED,* but there is no record of the corresponding noun *spreve,* as in the decision of Carause and his followers, after their despoliation of Britain: "Oþer contres þe godes to reue, / And so to lif þase daies of spreue" (line 9625). The "tuppes" of line 791, made of "togh tre, well schod wyth yryn," are evidently battering rams, adding a second example to the single instance of *tup(pe)* in this sense recorded in *MED;* and the "cosinesse(s)" of lines 8986 and 9330 add further examples to *MED*'s two instances of *cosines,* "female relative." But these are just a few of the more obvious examples: the full extent of such riches will not be apparent until the publication of volume 3. May that be soon!

T. L. BURTON
University of Adelaide

351

JOAN M. FERRANTE. *To the Glory of Her Sex: Women's Roles in the Composition of Medieval Texts.* Bloomington and Indianapolis: Indiana University Press, 1997. Pp. xii, 295. $39.95 cloth, $19.95 paper.

At the end of this book, Joan Ferrante laments women's loss of "their proper place in political, religious, and literary history" (p. 213), enlisting the present volume in the "restoration" of that place. But this work can be more fittingly termed the unveiling of a monument, one based on the last twenty years' excavation and assemblage of medieval women's writings and literary roles. Defining its scope broadly in the subtitle, this study sketches a "tradition," though not a self-conscious one, of female literary activity from the fourth to the fourteenth century. By so doing, this work helps ensure that the tradition of scholarship on medieval women writers of which it is part will be far more self-conscious, and less prone to loss, than the earlier tradition it outlines.

Ferrante's book emerges from her research into the surprisingly rich field of medieval women's letters, a genesis that enables Ferrante to contextualize her survey within an awareness of the issues raised by women in epistolary venues. The promised companion volume on medieval women's letters will no doubt enable Ferrante's readers as well to view the accomplishments of medieval women as writers and patrons of writing against the backdrop of negotiation, diatribe, and support she alludes to in the letters. The aim of the present volume, then, is to explore women's shaping of medieval writings, whether as writers themselves or as patrons, instigators, or recipients of texts written by men. The roles surveyed range from "collaboration" (chapters 2–4, women as instigators or patrons of men's writing on women) to "control" (chapters 5–6, women as authors writing on women); the writers, from Jerome to Christine de Pisan; the areas of writing, from religious to historical, courtly, and visionary.

Sometimes generalizing from a few works, but always drawing on the tremendous depth and breadth of her research, Ferrante argues for significant distinctions across genres and times between works produced by and for women and those produced by and for men (or for general audiences).

Religious works written by or for women, beginning with the oft-cited letters of Jerome, demonstrate respect for women as serious thinkers, and often insist on identifying their first audience as female, writing as if to underscore the significance of the lack of "sexual discrimination"

(p. 66) in their responses to queries put to them by women. Women from Eustochium to Heloise are analyzed as instigators or collaborators in the religious works written to or for them by men like Alcuin, or Peter Damian. According to Ferrante, whatever their hypothetical or principled objections to women in positions of power, the male writers she discusses, clerical and secular, by and large deal respectfully with their female audiences or patrons. Likewise, in contrast to male-commissioned histories, those written by or for women are more "alert to . . . women in history and . . . [provide them] models to follow and avoid" (p. 72), pay more attention to women in power, emphasize family ties (especially maternal), and admire "active women, both in the public sphere and in the patronage of letters" (p. 106). For example, in the outburst of history-writing that surrounds the Norman conquest of England, Ferrante singles out for their political support of the women who requested them the two works commissioned by the English queens Emma and Edith (p. 90), and notes the unusually close attention paid to women's actions and simply to naming women in the *Gesta regum anglorum* written by William of Malmesbury at the request of queen Matilda (later presented to her daughter Empress Matilda). Similarly, women who commissioned romances may have had political as well as literary motives. In highlighting "the lady in command or the damsel in distress" (p. 107), romances by or for men are more likely to feature women who need rescue, whereas romances by or for women more often feature "the lady in command," heroines who are well educated, powerful, the heirs and rulers of their land, women "with powers like the poet's to manipulate characters and events" (p. 120). Eleanor of Aquitaine and Marie de Champagne are centerpieces of the chapter on courtly literature, and Chretien de Troyes comes in for special treatment for his "open rebellion against his patron" (p. 120). Two lesser-known romances from the latter half of the thirteenth century, *Escanor* and *Cleomades,* in contrast, celebrate either women with extraordinary powers, or women who are "models of loyalty, courtesy, and wisdom . . . and work together and within a male world" (p. 132).

Most markedly differing from their male counterparts' writings are those of "visionary" writers like Hildegarde of Bingen, Elizabeth of Schonau, Hrotsvit of Gandersheim, Clemence of Barking, Marie de France, and Christine de Pisan. These are women representing women, whether in secular or religious writing, in which misogynistic representations of women are debunked and destroyed, whether implicitly or explicitly. Adding to the considerable bibliography that has accumulated around the works of these women over the last two decades, Ferrante subjects to scrutiny their representations of women as writers and as models for other women, noting how, for example, "Hildegarde's prestige made it easier for Elisabeth to make her messages public" (p. 140), or how Hildegarde's "contradictory" "self-effacement and self-assurance" (p. 158) is subtly transformed by its reflection in other paradoxical representations of women ("As Hildegarde frequently says, the Virgin Mary was impregnated with Christ without the help of a man, that is, through God woman can do what man cannot" [p. 159]). She notes that all of these women writers had male as well as female audiences (p. 176), but focuses on what their works would have said about women to the women in their audience. Hrotsvit "allow[s] her female characters to take on and make fools of the emperor and his court [in *Pafnutius*]" (p. 183); Clemence "may be commenting on women who are worshipped (in courtly lyrics?) but not allowed a voice" (p. 187). The works of the trobairitz show that "women are very aware of the hypocrisy of male rhetoric" (p. 190). Marie de France, whose *Lais* Ferrante has translated (with Robert Hanning), is credited with "a lai that allows the female world of love and sisterhood to conquer definitively the male world of violence and betrayal" (p. 202). And, like Ferrante herself, we might say, "Christine [de Pisan] had faith in women's ability to accomplish great things."

GAIL BERKELEY SHERMAN
Reed College

JAMES L. GILLESPIE, ed. *The Age of Richard II.* New York: St. Martin's Press, 1997. Pp. viii, 256. $55.00.

This volume, based on the work of the Society of the White Heart, presents eleven essays on diverse aspects of the reign of Richard II and on later medieval English history generally. The concentration is on politics as a "lens through which we can bring the late medieval kaleidoscope into focus without unduly narrowing our range of vision" (p. 2).

James L. Gillespie, editor of the volume (and sometime president of the Society), also contributed two essays with linked themes. "Richard II:

Chivalry and Kingship" stresses connections between royalty and the chivalric ethos and marshals evidence for Richard's personal involvement with chivalry. "Richard II: King of Battles?" concedes Richard's costly failure to create a martial reputation, but (while noting significant evidence of military capacity) argues that the king never sorted out the difference between the royal image of dispenser of justice and the pragmatic use of force. G. H. Martin studies "Narrative Sources for the Reign of Richard II" and suggests that their value increases even as archival investigations proliferate, since they can tell what people thought and supposed, supplementing what record evidence shows they did. A chapter by Nigel Saul, "Richard II, York, and the Evidence of the King's Itinerary," contests John Harvey's assertion that Richard II considered the city of York a possible alternative capital to London. Richard's rule was largely based on southern England, and careful sifting of evidence shows that his visits to York were shorter and less frequent than supposed. A. K. Hardy, "Haxey's Case, 1397: The Petition and its Presenter Reconsidered," argues that the presenter of this controversial petition for household reform was a royal clerk acting not for aristocratic political interests but for administrative reform that would benefit gentry and royal clerks of his circle.

Several essays expand this core of studies of Ricardian politics, either by subject matter or chronology. In "Politics, Procedure and the 'Non-Minority' of Edward III: Some Comparisons," Frank L. Wiswall III compares the position of Edward III in 1326–30 with the minorities of Henry III and Richard II, arguing that his greater age at coronation better prepared him to take and exercise personal power. Doris Fletcher traces "The Lancastrian Collar of Esses: Its Origins and Transformations Down the Centuries." Apparently already a royal emblem (although the meaning of the SS device itself remains uncertain) in the youth of John of Gaunt, the collar was worn by some mayors but was more often given to nobles, and to some commoners (as a reward for battlefield feats), before becoming restricted by the seventeenth century to judges and officials. In "The Oxford Trial of 1400: Royal Politics and the County Gentry," John Leland finds Henry IV securing his shaky régime by trying conspirators before jurors of the same social and political background—knights, squires, and some even more obscure men; though they bowed pragmatically to the new king's reign, they win points from Leland by rendering one symbolic verdict of *non culpabilis*.

Wendy R. Childs, "Anglo-Portuguese Relations in the Fourteenth

Century," finds a "mini-boom" in trade between England and Portugal during Richard's reign, encouraged by political ties, especially as the significant Anglo-Gascon trade inversely suffered from political tensions.

Two final essays consider issues of health care. J. M. Theilmann examines "The Regulation of Public Health in Late Medieval England." The picture is not encouraging: only the market seems to have governed health issues; the crown largely passed on any regulation to local authorities and to physicians, surgeons, barber surgeons, and apothecaries— all of whom may have been more interested in protecting their career interests than patients' health. David K. Maxfield examines one particular institution for the poor in "St. Anthony's Hospital, London: A Pardoner-Supported Alien Priory, 1219–1461." By the fourteenth century, the hospital, which cared for a dozen old men, had itself become rich and lasted until the Reformation; it could have been supported by Chaucer's pardoner.

The range of topics is matched by that among the scholars contributing, some newcomers joining well-established academics. James Gillespie is to be commended for editing the collection, of interest to scholars in a number of fields. One wonders why a good scholar has found it necessary to be, as he describes himself, in "exile from American academia" (p. 5).

RICHARD W. KAEUPER
University of Rochester

THOMAS HAHN and ALAN LUPACK, eds. *Retelling Tales: Essays in Honor of Russell Peck.* Woodbridge, Suffolk: D. S. Brewer, 1997. Pp. vi, 359. $71.00.

This collection of seventeen essays honors Russell Peck and recognizes his long association with the University of Rochester. The theme of the volume is described in its title, *Retelling Tales*—a theme that proves to be an apt one for organizing the diverse contributions, which reflect the broad scholarly and teaching interests of the honorand. Naturally the emphasis falls on Middle English literature, but also included are essays on medievalism and the Cinderella legend.

The volume begins propitiously with Derek Brewer's wide-ranging exploration of various aspects of the phenomenon of narrative retelling. Topics such as truth verification, repetition and variation, intertextuality, and inconsistency are briefly discussed in general, yet very suggestive, terms. The essay raises critical issues rather than arriving at conclusions, as it opens the discussion of the many theoretical and critical questions that are raised by the act of reworking already known material in both oral and literate cultures.

Theresa Coletti's substantial examination of the different versions of the traditional story of Herod as it appears in medieval mystery plays supports her thesis that the variants are the result of a conscious understanding by the authors of the plays of the narrative's capacity to articulate contemporary social and political concerns.

Alfred David contributes a graceful discussion of Chaucer's different Adams in *The Monk's Tale, The Nun's Priest's Tale,* and elsewhere. The result is a series of insightful readings of several tales, especially *The Pardoner's Tale,* where David calls attention to the sexual associations of the verb "struggle," used to describe the plan to murder the youngest brother. John Fleming's essay on the Wife of Bath's exegetical strategies begins with the useful reminder that *The Canterbury Tales* is not, properly speaking, a collection of tales, but a collection of retellings of tales. This distinction is used to good effect to expound the significance of the Wife's literal-minded retelling of the Midas story, which articulates what Fleming sees as the major theme of the Wife's *Prologue,* "the chasm separating surface and substance, letter and spirit" (p. 89).

Thomas Hahn compares different versions of the tale of the Loathly Lady, which forms the basis of *The Wife of Bath's Tale.* Hahn shows, in a complex argument, that Chaucer's retelling, narrated by a woman, reflects a particular kind of historically determined female consciousness, one that reinforces for a bourgeois audience the ideals of heterosexual desire.

Ronald Herzman's essay on Christine de Pizan's *Book of the City of Ladies* examines the role of Virgil and the Bible in shaping Christine's work, inventively comparing Christine's nuanced engagement with Dante's encounter with these two paramount authorities.

Sarah Higley's diffuse account of tales involving artificial humans, or parts of humans (mainly heads), begins in ancient Egypt and moves through Albertus Magnus, Robert Grosseteste, Paracelsus, Thomas Edison, and beyond. This informal and entertaining essay is clearly a preliminary exploration of a very large topic.

David Jeffrey returns us to the Middle Ages with a carefully focused study of the Wycliffite retelling of the story of Susannah, suggesting that with its emphasis on abuse of civil authority and ultimate justice, it became a highly pertinent exemplum for faithful Wycliffites in the time of their persecution.

Richard Kaeuper's brief essay on Mark Twain's depiction of chivalry in *A Connecticut Yankee in King Arthur's Court* states some rather obvious points about Twain's views of the Middle Ages and chivalry in particular, but has more interesting things to say about Twain's seeming consciousness of the folly of both medieval and modern tendencies to romanticize violence.

The Arthurian theme is continued in Anne Laskaya's comparative analysis of the idea of manhood in Thomas Chestre's *Sir Launfal*. She concludes that Chestre's retelling, compared to the earlier version of Marie de France, for example, suppresses the more overt homosexual elements in the story, possibly reflecting the increasing homophobia of later medieval culture.

With Alan Lupack's essay on American writer Elizabeth Stuart Phelps (1844–1911), little known today but enormously popular in her own time, we return to the theme of medievalism. Phelps's transplantation of the Arthurian stories to the grimy milieu of the working-class nineteenth century is best regarded as a curiosity—her engagement with the medieval past hardly results in a deeper understanding of her own time.

Monica McAlpine presents a fascinating account of the successive iterations of the story of the Burghers of Calais, from Froissart to Rodin. She notes that from the first the story has had a close connection with the visual arts. The various representations have emphasized different aspects of the episode, determined by the immediate social and political context. The obscurity of the story at the present time leads to the conclusion that the story is "part of a cultural canon that is past" (p. 254).

The contribution by Charles A. Owen deals with Chaucer's Manciple and his *Tale,* a matter that has engaged the recent attention of several Chaucer scholars. In Owen's reading, the *Tale* is substantially transformed by the dominating voice of the mother's monologue, which contributes to the moral deficiencies of the *Tale*'s conclusion.

Eve Salisbury gives us an overview of versions of the male Cinderella story, including among these the romances *King Horn* and *Havelok the Dane,* the Horatio Alger stories, and the 1960 Jerry Lewis film *Cinderfella.* Salisbury remarks on the potential of these male retellings to challenge conventional gender roles even as they function, like other fairy tales, as instruments of acculturation.

Lynn Staley analyzes the fifteenth-century MS Huntington 140 as a cultural text, situated in a particular moment of history. The Huntington anthology, which includes Chaucer's *Clerk's Tale* with works by Lydgate and others, in effect recontextualizes that tale to reflect political concerns about tyranny and wise rule that were especially prominent in the time of the War of the Roses.

James Wimsatt recuperates Malory's often underappreciated tale of Tristram by showing how Malory's alterations of his source connect it to the central themes of the *Morte D'Arthur*. The main achievement of *Sir Tristram*, Wimsatt demonstrates, is to emphasize multiple perspectives on moral values and human conduct, thus establishing a complex and enriched view of human experience.

The final essay, by R. F. Yeager, deals with Gower's *Confessio amantis*, a work especially important in Russell Peck's scholarly career. Yeager shows that Gower's transformation of a fable of Avianus made it suitable to the Christian moral context of the *Confessio* by replacing the cynicism of Avianus with an emphasis on the possibility of individual change and growth.

These brief summaries cannot convey the subtlety and complexity of many of the essays in this collection. Students of the Middle Ages will find much here to command their attention. Thomas Hahn and Alan Lupack have produced a worthy tribute to the many-faceted career of an exemplary scholar and teacher. Finally, a word of praise is due the introductory essay by Thomas Hahn. After reading it, one knows why Russell Peck continues to inspire admiration and affection in so many.

THOMAS H. BESTUL
University of Illinois at Chicago

ANNE HUDSON, ed. *Selections from English Wycliffite Writings*. Medieval Academy Reprints for Teaching 38. Toronto: University of Toronto Press, 1997. Pp. xii, 235. $16.95.

When this volume first appeared in 1978, reviewers thought it would inspire further research into the political and social forces represented by John Wyclif (d. 1384) and his followers, the Wycliffites or Lollards. They seem to have been right. Certainly, there have been several important books and articles dealing with just such matters since that date, and the success of the recently formed Lollard Society suggests there will soon be many more. Hudson's selections have also been frequently featured in this research: her text of the *Twelve Conclusions* in papers marking the sixth-hundredth anniversary of the nailing of the Conclusions to the doors of Westminster Hall in 1395, for example, and her text of the 1430 *Confession* of Hawisia Moone in some recent papers concerned with women's history. Yet just as teachers were increasingly wanting to use Hudson's volume in their courses, Cambridge University Press let it go out of print. As one of those who particularly asked Medieval Academy Reprints for Teaching to include it in their series, therefore, I am delighted to announce its reappearance.

Users of the earlier volume already know how judiciously it draws from the writings we can reasonably describe as Wycliffite or Lollard (terms Hudson uses interchangeably), and how skillfully it makes its selections accessible even to nonspecialists. It provides a clear impression not only of what the Lollards thought was involved in preaching the Word, but also of their assorted polemical views and the energy with which they prepared a surprisingly wide variety of vernacular texts. It completely supersedes our only similar volume, Herbert E. Winn's *Wyclif: Select English Writings* (Oxford: Oxford University Press, 1929; rpt., New York: AMS Press, 1976).

For the most part, the present version of the volume represents a photographic reproduction of its predecessor (although it has also acquired a more interesting cover). This has the advantage that we can use either version without adjusting page references and the like. But it has also meant that Hudson has been unable to take account of recent writing on the Lollards even when, as so often, this was her own. She has expanded the volume's select bibliography by about a page. But all she has otherwise changed is a two-line note about a *Seynt Sithe* whom she originally took to be Osyth but whom she now thinks was Zita of Lucca (p. 182). To get the most out of the volume, therefore, readers should also use some of the additional works she lists in its present bibliography including, most notably, her own *Premature Reformation: Wycliffite Texts and Lollard History* (Oxford: Clarendon Press, 1988).

Hudson has acquainted us with a wide range of texts that the Wycliffites wrote in English. Let us hope she will soon do the same for some of the texts they wrote in Latin.

CHRISTINA VON NOLCKEN
University of Chicago

STEVEN JUSTICE and KATHRYN KERBY-FULTON, eds. *Written Work: Langland, Labor and Authorship.* Middle Ages Series. Philadelphia: University of Pennsylvania Press, 1997. Pp. ix, 347. $45.00.

The essays in this exciting volume all situate Langland historically. All take their cue from the poet's own most sustained yet enigmatic representation of himself, the so-called autobiographical passage, or the author's "apologia," C-text passus 5, lines 1–104, in which Will is interrogated about his life by Reason and Conscience. Collectively these essays offer us rich new possibilities for conceptualizing the poet as social and historical agent. The volume should advance *Piers* criticism irrevocably (I would hope) beyond attempts to mine this passus for biographical facts, or, at the opposite extreme of the critical spectrum, to read it formalistically, as inwardly but not outwardly referential. The most exciting contributions are aware that the creator of *Piers Plowman* was beset by the problem of articulating a new authorial identity commensurate with and able to legitimate the challenging agenda of his writing. The richest readings show that the negotiations in the poet's self-portrayals are also legible in and through their dialogue with the textual and compositional histories of the poem.

Steven Justice's introduction shows how each of the contributions moves beyond the formalist critical approaches that pull "writing free from contingency." He illustrates the problems associated with formalist approaches to *Piers* by discussing a problem associated with the B-text manuscripts, the variant readings in passus 15 of the B-text that may offer evidence for two alternative authorial textual traditions. Kane and Donaldson, Justice proposes, cannot recognize this possibility because it is at odds with their formalist editorial assumption that there is only one authorially sanctioned B-version of the poem.

An edition of the C-text *apologia* and a parallel modern-English verse

translation, both by Derek Pearsall, serve as a second preface to the essays, but also as the first reading of the text: some of the interpretative
problems silently addressed in Pearsall's translation (e.g., the meanings
of the words *lollare* and *lyeth*) are reopened in the essays. The London
location of the C.5 passage gives Pearsall the opportunity in an essay
called "Langland's London" to explore relationships between the poet's
figurative language and his rural and urban environments. He argues
that while Langland gives London "vivid and localised expression," he
thinks about the ideal society in agrarian terms (pp. 185–86).

Two essays consider Langland's persona in relation to religious discourses. Ralph Hanna, in "Will's Work," proposes that Langland uses
eremitic discourse for Will's self-depiction to critique the less sophisticated minstrel stance adopted by earlier alliterative poets. Of all of the
contributors, Hanna is the least keen to argue for the historical implications of his material, making no "particular claims about any specifiable
history external to *Piers* itself" (p. 24). Lawrence M. Clopper, in "Langland's Persona: An Anatomy of the Mendicant Orders," by contrast, interprets the persona as a composite construct of "Francis's two callings,
mendicant and hermit" (p. 173), which would have been particularly
meaningful for Franciscan readers and would have served to call the order to reform.

Kathryn Kerby-Fulton's own contribution, "Langland and the Bibliographic Ego," is one of two extremely long pieces in the volume. Her
attempt to understand Langland's self-representation in C.5 is richly
layered and suggestive. She recognizes the need to develop new theoretical and historical frames of reference to understand medieval authorial
self-representation. She insists on the importance of understanding the
modes of publication available for politically sensitive writings in medieval culture and is productively alert to the possible impact that audience response may have had on the continuing composition of the poem.
She sometimes seems, however, less alert than she might be to the difficulties of using textual criticism to establish the poem's composition
history. She proposes that Langland deliberately chose to base his C-text
revisions on a corrupt B-version manuscript because it was this text that
had been in circulation. This is ingenious, but the basic premise requires
some discussion, at least, in the light of Charlotte Brewer's recent proposal that the "C-reviser's corrupt B-text" may be an artifact of the modern editorial process. But if this proposal and the many other suggestions in this essay inspire further discussion—as they should—then

Kerby-Fulton will have achieved her purpose of engaging "other scholars in these problems" (p. 74).

The volume closes with the second monumental piece (well over 100
pages): Anne Middleton's "Acts of Vagrancy: The C Version 'Autobiography' and the Statute of 1388." This essay is written throughout with
Middleton's characteristic energy and engagement; it demands equal in-
put from its reader, and it repays the effort. Other essays depart from or
arrive at, or notice in passing, the C.5 *apologia;* Middleton focuses her
formidable intellectual energies on interrogating the meanings of the
passage, considering the passage's chronological, structural, and narrative placings, asking "why here?" and "why now?" (p. 277). She sees
the composition and interpolation of the *apologia* as Langland's final and
fullest authorial intervention in his work and in his world, arguing that
parallels between the passage and the 1388 Statute of Laborers help to
situate the passage both in the poet's own career (it was probably his
final work) and in contemporary social history. Langland prefers to have
the king's justices Reason and Conscience attempt to represent Will as
a vagrant worker—what they, and Will, call a *loller*—than that an ecclesiastical court should attempt to represent him as a heretic.

Middleton asks why Langland should risk having his own status interrogated in these terms. On the evidence of two examples—the applications of the word *loller* to Chaucer's Parson and to Margery Kempe—
Middleton offers an answer: by 1388 *loller* could mean not only "idler"
and "heretic" but also one who practices "religion out of place"; in this
sense the word imputes merely social transgression, not doctrinal error.
But arguably her two examples show only what contemporaries
claimed—that the term might be mistakenly applied to people who
were not (by their own lights, at least) heretics. In any case, this posited
third sense still raises the specter of the heretical loller, and so applying
it to Will would still have been risky. I suggest that there is a simpler
answer: because of external circumstances, Langland had little choice.
Middleton is open to Scase's proposals that a version of the *distinctio* on
lollers interpolated in C-text passus 9 had already circulated before the
composition of C-text passus 5 and that this material is referred to in
C.5 (pp. 276, 314–315). She does not, however, appear to consider the
related suggestion that in C.5 Langland was engaging with the *reception*
of the *distinctio,* with hostile responses to his identifications of *lollers* that
rebounded as an attack on himself as its author. If this is so, then Langland would have had little choice: he could *only* have responded by artic-

ulating (or representing the articulation of) a self-defense that engaged once more in the battle over the meaning and application of the word *loller.*

The essays in this volume are not only different in approach to the material and to the matter of historical contingency; they also have (I infer) different composition histories with respect to the compilation as a whole. This appears to have presented the editors with problems that are not completely resolved. Some of the footnotes give cross-references where there are overlaps or coincidences of subject, but one cannot but suspect that these are in some cases inserted by the editors, when the passages so annotated show no awareness of the arguments or material in the essay to which the reader is referred (e.g., the cross-references to Middleton's essay, p. 181 n. 53 and p. 204 n. 18).

In still bearing the marks of its compositional history, this volume, as in much else, mimics its subject: it may not be completely harmonized editorially, but it is by turns engaging, thought-provoking, frustrating, and brilliant. It is an important and timely intervention in Langland studies that also has much to offer to any scholar interested in late medieval cultural and literary history.

WENDY SCASE
University of Hull

KARMA LOCHRIE, PEGGY MCCRACKEN, and JAMES A. SCHULTZ, eds. *Constructing Medieval Sexuality.* Medieval Cultures, vol. 11. Minneapolis: University of Minnesota Press, 1997. Pp. xviii, 205. $17.95 (cloth); $18.95 (paper).

This volume takes as its point of departure the "constructedness" of heterosexuality, and offers a set of essays, noteworthy for their novelty, imagination, and solid scholarly grounding, that collectively expose the instability of categories of gender in the Middle Ages. Marked by an unusual degree of cohesion in its subject matter, the volume is also interdisciplinary in the very best senses of the term, engaging scholars from history, philosophy, art history, and also from French, German, and English literature. If there is a single ethical demand voiced in this volume, it is that we interrogate the premises that have discursively naturalized heterosexuality, both in the Middle Ages and today. The collection could be aptly titled "Queering Medieval Sexuality."

One of the fundamental questions posed in this volume is the status of sexualities before "homosexuality" and "heterosexuality" were understood as fundamental categories of selfhood. Mark Jordan and Joan Cadden both address this question in narrowly situated historicolinguistic studies that examine commentaries on sodomy. In "Homosexuality, Luxuria, and Textual Abuse," Mark Jordan argues, in a brilliant tour de force, that the understanding of sodomy as a specifically sexual form of deviance can be located in Thomas's misreading, and hence "textual abuse," of Augustine. Discursive uncertainty around the issue of sodomy in the Middle Ages can be traced to the location of its pleasures outside of the economy of sexuality; disrupting natural teleology, the pleasures of sodomy have no rhetorical grounding in a lexicon of bodily experiences, and hence sodomy often is described as the "sin that has no name."

Also examining a commentary on sodomy, Joan Cadden's essay, "Sciences/Silences: The Nature and Languages of 'Sodomy' in Peter of Abano's Problemata Commentary," argues that this early-fourteenth-century commentary on Aristotle does suggest that homosexuals had a "conceptual existence" in premodern times, even though the commentary offers no serious analogue to the modern term "homosexuality" (p. 51). Of particular interest in Cadden's essay is Peter's anatomical explanation that a disorder of blocked spermatic pathways, or pores, accounts for the pleasure that some men find in anal penetration; while Peter's commentary medicalizes anal pleasures, it also acknowledges that these pleasures can become an acquired habit.

Several essays in the volume interrogate the fixity of heterosexuality, examining the ways that modern critics as well as medieval artists reify heterosexual norms even as that very practice points to the existence of unexamined or queer desire. In "Conversion and Medieval Sexual, Religious, and Racial Categories," Stephen Kruger reviews the literature on homologies between racial, religious, and sexual otherness, looking at overlapping susceptibility to conversion in these categories. In spite of the fact that Jews were generally deemed convertible by the Church, Kruger detects anxieties about the completeness of Jewish conversion, particularly when it came to marriages, and argues for a "queer residue" (p. 176) in this sexualized surplus.

In an essay marked with her customary rhetorical "jouissance" Louise Fradenburg explores homologies between *fin amors* and the medieval

STUDIES IN THE AGE OF CHAUCER

ethic of charity, both of which establish a fantasy of rescue through obstacles and tropes of absence that fix heterosexual categories. In "Love of
Thy Neighbor," a reading of Chaucer's *Legend of Good Women,* Fradenburg
argues that the lady in chivalric fictions exists as a phantasm of otherness
for a masculine subject. If chivalric romance generates an ethical rescue,
it comes at the cost of polymorphous pleasures: "[T]he folly of honor is
not its sacrifice of the good but rather its sacrifice of jouissance" (p. 154).
Also inviting us to question heteronormative readings of medieval texts
and images (although in far simpler terms), Karma Lochrie argues that
women's spirituality has been "rigidly heterosexualized" in studies of
female mysticism, most notably by Caroline Walker Bynum. In "Mystical Acts, Queer Tendencies," Lochrie points in particular to Christ's
wound, the vulnus/vulva, and asks, "[W]hat does it signify when a female mystic desires and adores the feminized body of Christ?" This is
an excellent question; what is regrettable is that Lochrie does not answer
it, but uses her essay as a platform for raising a set of questions. The last
essay in the volume, Lochrie's is the only one to address lesbian desire.
This indeterminacy in the volume's single study of lesbianism leaves
female same-sex desire in the Middle Ages as a dark continent still: what
do women want?

In "Manuscript Illumination and the Art of Copulation," art historian
Michael Camille also directs us to consider how visual images of sexed
bodies were read in the Middle Ages. With particular attention to Aldo-
brandino of Siena's *Regime du Corps,* a thirteenth-century self-help guide,
Camille argues that pictures of copulating couples in premodern illustration are ideological constructs that depict normative (and heteronormative) sexuality, and that also present women's bodies as inherently
inferior. The essay gives us a visual tour (peep show?) of positions of
copulation, and ends, rather like Lochrie's essay, with a topic for further
research: a split, in medieval representation, that places woman as text
on the side of "peinture" and man, as pen/is and stylus, on the side of
the word.

Two of my favorite essays in the volume are remarkably complemen-
tary studies of costume in medieval romance. In "Bodies That Don't
Matter: Heterosexuality before Heterosexuality in Gottfried's Tristan,"
James A. Schultz shows how costume makes gender legible in Gottfried.
"Morphologically indistinguishable" (p. 95) in a blurring of attributes
that is foreign to twentieth-century descriptive practices, male and female bodies in Gottfried can be told apart by costume, which also de-

fines them in terms of class. In the French Lancelot cycles, E. Jane Burns argues, clothing also "supersedes anatomy as the prime indicator of gender identity" (p. 113); but the very play with costume in courtly romances also exposes the fragility of fixed gender categories. Burns's essay also applies contemporary gender theory to a historically situated and perceptive close reading of medieval texts.

If the collection can be said to have a flagship essay, it would likely be its opening piece, Dyan Elliott's "Pollution, Illusion and Masculine Disarray: Nocturnal Emissions and the Sexuality of the Clergy." Arguing that nocturnal emissions, which were connected with menstruation, gave medieval ascetics a "sensitive gauge for clocking the relative success or failure of disciplinary efforts to gain mastery over the body," Elliott tracks the discourse from patristic texts through Gerson. This highly readable and skillful work of original historical scholarship ends in the fascinating observation that the obsession with pollution in late medieval clerical manuals mirrors the concomitant emphasis on eucharistic ritual. Both articulate a similar "masculine disarray," Elliott speculates, that can be read in the overdetermined status of forms of "manhandling," where the "unalloyed masculine ascendency" of clerical ritual in late medieval culture bespeaks anxieties about the very fixity of gender.

Constructing Medieval Sexuality is an excellent essay collection with much that will be useful to students, both undergraduate and graduate. It should be essential reading for medieval scholars from all disciplines interested in queer theory and gender studies.

SARAH STANBURY
College of the Holy Cross

MARY RHINELANDER MCCARL, ed. *The Plowman's Tale: The c. 1532 and 1606 Editions of a Spurious Canterbury Tale.* Renaissance Imagination Series. New York: Garland Publishing, 1997. Pp. 318. $72.00.

This combined edition of two early printed editions of *The Plowman's Tale* gives readers a chance to reconsider this tale in a Renaissance context, while somewhat slighting its more than 200-year role as a *Canterbury Tale.* I particularly enjoyed reading the 1606 edition, which differs from the 1533 edition principally in that the later recension has extensive explanatory notes and glosses by Antony Wotton, a Puritan clergyman. The earlier edition, inexplicably dated 1533 in McCarl's text and 1532 in the title, has its own notes in Latin, most of which quote the Latin Vulgate. Both sets of side notes are printed in McCarl's edition at the bottom of the page of the text; the proximity of the side notes to the text is the most exciting thing about the volume. This edition grew out of McCarl's research on sixteenth-century printed books, and it exists in the underexplored territory of the influence of the Middle Ages on the Renaissance, and how the Renaissance shaped our view of the Middle Ages. Part of the series *The Renaissance Imagination: Important Literary and Theatrical Texts from the Late Middle Ages through the Seventeenth Century,* edited by Stephen Orgel, the edition presumably aims to help make such connections.

This edition is only available in expensive cloth, so it is clearly not intended for teaching, and in any case there is a serviceable teaching edition in James M. Dean's *Six Ecclesiastical Satires* put out by the Consortium for the Teaching of the Middle Ages (TEAMS). I therefore assume that this edition is intended for scholars of both the Renaissance and the Middle Ages who would like easy access to a sixteenth- and a seventeenth-century version of the poem. The extensive introduction and glossary often seem aimed more at students than at scholars, but that may be due to McCarl's varied audiences. For example, most medieval scholars probably will not need her interesting introductory information about Lollardry, but perhaps some Renaissance scholars would find it useful.

McCarl chooses to edit two different texts of the poem without regularizing spelling or collating texts. She does not mention any emendations, but also does not explain her editing choices. There are some benefits to such diplomatic editions, but I wonder what the benefits are for publication of *The Plowman's Tale* and why these two recensions are chosen.

Each of these versions of the poem was published as an independent text rather than as part of *The Canterbury Tales,* as it also was printed from 1542 until 1778. McCarl's primary interest seems to be in the independent editions of the sixteenth and early seventeenth centuries, since she explains why she does not print the independent edition of 1548, though not why she excludes editions that were printed with Chaucer's *Works,* nor what the differences might be between the independent versions and the ones in Chaucer's *Works*. This choice of two independent editions, each printed with contemporary side notes, positions the poem as part of early Protestant and then Puritan reading lists rather than as a long medieval poem or as a viable part of the Chaucer canon. The possibility that Spenser read *The Plowman's Tale* as a *Canterbury Tale* and referred to it in *The Shepheardes Calender* seems especially interesting to McCarl, for example.

Sixteenth- and seventeenth-century medieval reading lists are of interest to medieval scholars—I still want to argue that Spenser also read *Piers Plowman*—as are long fourteenth-century Lollard poems. This edition could prove useful to medievalists who are interested in studying fourteenth-century anticlerical writing or those interested in studying the formation of medievalism in the Renaissance. The one available manuscript of *The Plowman's Tale* probably dates from the late fifteenth century at the earliest, so this 1533 edition could be helpful to medievalists who want to see the earliest printed version of the *Tale,* which draws on a different manuscript than the one extant. *The Plowman's Tale* is not part of the *Piers Plowman* tradition, since it does not refer directly to *Piers Plowman,* but it does refer to other poems in that tradition, and its Renaissance readers had no difficulty including it in both a plowman tradition and Chaucer's *Works.* Contemporary critics are beginning to draw connections between the Chaucerian and plowman texts; Renaissance uses of *The Plowman's Tale* can help us analyze what assumptions first connected and later severed those traditions. When I began studying medieval literature I felt that Chaucer's England and Langland's England must have been on separate islands. Had I been given a copy of *The Plowman's Tale* at the time, I would have located it in Langland's England, despite its apparent lack of familiarity with *Piers Plowman.* Connections between Chaucer and Langland are just one facet of an examination of the shaping of a medieval canon that privileges and separates Chaucer from other late medieval authors and that neatly separates orthodox from Lollard writings. Both of these simplistic approaches to categorizing medieval texts are increasingly rejected; more receptive readings of what we know as Chaucerian apocrypha can help medievalists continue to break down those categories. We can gain a new perspective on that canon shaping by reading *The Plowman's Tale* and looking at its uses by Renaissance scholars—marked in part by the side notes in these two editions.

Yet this volume has many limitations. The discordance between the title and the text in dating the earlier edition of *The Plowman's Tale* is unfortunately a sign of the care that has been taking in copyediting the entire volume, which has several typographical and grammar errors. The page layout is also messy and difficult to find one's way around, with unnecessary spaces between paragraphs, too little distinction between footnotes and text, misleading page headers, and insufficiently marked section titles. These limitations are all the fault of the press and should not be acceptable in such an expensive book.

The introduction could use a revision for better organization; for example, it needs a clear, brief statement about the manuscript and publication history of *The Plowman's Tale.* The fifteenth- or sixteenth-century manuscript of the *Tale,* now held at Texas, is referred to but not identified in the acknowledgements, and when brought up again in the introduction is even less clearly identified; the reader is apparently expected to remember those helpful Texas librarians cited in the acknowledgements in order to begin to locate the manuscript. There are two sections called "Contents of the Poem"; they do not build on each other and neither is very clear.

I do not often wish for more interpretation from the editor when I use an edition, but in this case I do wish that I could hear more from McCarl on why she juxtaposed these two early editions, and what importance she thinks the poem and its publications had in shaping Renaissance ideas about the Middle Ages and then on later medievalisms. Very little has been written on *The Plowman's Tale,* and few people have spent as much time working with it as McCarl no doubt has; I hope she has the resources and time to write more about this poem. I also hope that more scholars are drawn to read *The Plowman's Tale* and to analyze the connections it draws on and creates between a variety of textual traditions, yet I am afraid that this edition, despite its fascinating sixteenth- and seventeenth-century notes, may not yet be sufficient incentive.

KARI KALVE
Earlham College

ROSEMARIE P. MCGERR. *Chaucer's Open Books: Resistance to Closure in Medieval Discourse.* Gainesville: University Press of Florida, 1998. Pp. x, 210. $49.95.

Few of us these days are likely to quarrel with the proposition that Chaucer's poems offer challenges to interpretation rather than pat conclusions. Rosemarie McGerr's contribution to reading Chaucer's openness is her steady insistence on placing the poems in dialogue with medieval (rather than modern or postmodern) discourses on the issue of closure. This strategy has the advantage of including many medieval voices, interesting in themselves, in the discussion of Chaucer's poetics.

There are, of course, many ways to evade closure and many kinds of closure to evade. The introductory chapter canvasses a good many of them and concludes that, although strong closure was always advised in the rhetorical treatises, medieval writers found various playful ways to keep their texts open. Although it is probably true that rhetorical theory places more stress on closure than poets deliver in practice, much of the quoted argument for closure could be interpreted as a broader call for self-consciousness about rhetorical or artistic effects. Once established as the rhetoricians' desideratum, "closure" in *Chaucer's Open Books* is used to suggest the assertion of unmodified truths, which is probably not the experienced sense of the endings of many, perhaps most, medieval texts. The blurred distinction between poetic closure for "greatest impact on the audience" (p. 24) and the closure of great human dilemmas (like God's view of human love) ends up claiming openness of one sort or another for most of the valued texts of the era. It would take a more detailed argument than that presented here, for example, to show that *Roland* is deliberately unclosed because it ends with Charlemagne's lament when Gabriel commands his return to the battlefield. None the less, McGerr's discussions of so many evasions of closure in French and English texts nicely undermines a still-prevalent popular assumption that a formidable hegemony banished playfulness from medieval writing.

In historicizing the issue of closure, McGerr places *Book of the Duchess* in the tradition of the *demande d'amour* as well as that of the dream vision and *House of Fame* in the circular structure of the rondeau. The two poems exhibit different kinds and degrees of openness: for if the goal and conclusion of the *Duchess* is the "moment of recognition and sympathy" (p. 54) between the dreamer and the Black Knight, there is certainly a stronger evocation of that in "hyt ys routhe," the ending of the hunt, and the waking from the dream than in the ellipses ending the *House of Fame*. *Parliament of Fowles* is discussed in terms of the sung ballades of Machaut, the effect of polyphony producing something like Bakhtin's effect of the dialogic, the inconclusive debate seen as a deliberate statement about life and a deliberate refusal of parliamentary adjudication. If the particular insight offered by the *Parliament* is that "human beings live in a state of incompleteness," then the poem's inconclusive ending has in fact made that point quite nicely. As Sartre said, not deciding is itself a decision.

In discussing *Troilus and Criseyde*, McGerr uses Geoffrey of Vinsauf's *Poetria nova* to evoke the double vantage point from which the reader watches the unfolding narrative—that of Providence (since the end is known) and that of the lovers. Her lucid commentary on the passages in which the characters and narrator specify (or mystify) terms like *mene, ende,* and *entencione* demonstrates how insistently the poem has interrogated the meaning(s) of human love, and ultimately of meaning itself. The "piling on" of devices of closure cannot successfully "end" the poem by reframing its pagan setting in Christian theology. *The Legend of Good Women* similarly encourages readers to interpret for themselves by promising closed and exemplary legends in the Prologue and then providing the variety of differently situated stories the collection actually contains.

McGerr sees the *Retraction* at the end of *The Canterbury Tales* as both alluding to and interrogating Augustine's *Retractiones*. This tactic historicizes the controversy over the *Retraction*, illuminating its three-part structure, but I'm not sure it leads as directly as claimed to the conclusion that the *Retraction* offers one more voice to the various voices asserting ethical priorities in the tales themselves. Augustine's subject is not "the value of literature" but the value of writing, and therefore confronts Chaucer's musings over the value of fiction less obviously than suggested here. That *The Canterbury Tales* considered as a whole "weans us away from more traditional concepts of literary closure" (p. 152) is surely true, and a closer reading of the tales McGerr mentions would further strengthen that general point. But if the text offers "reading lessons," we ought to hear more about the specific lessons learned than just the advice to be open-minded and patient enough to wait for the end.

Chaucer's Open Books demonstrates broad learning about medieval texts and offers some good insights into the ways in which closure was insisted upon in the abstract and yet denied through the playful subver-

sion of the formal devices which should have insured it. McGerr's historicizing tactics, though, must sometimes rely on insights from critics
like Eco and Bakhtin, suggesting that our own history also be evoked
when we attempt to historicize Chaucer. The book would have proved
still more valuable, therefore, if it had not blurred relevant questions we
are now pondering about the means, ends, and intentions of literary
texts. Chief among these is whether McGerr is arguing for *indeterminacy*
or *ambiguity,* since the terms are used interchangeably throughout. If, for
example, *The Canterbury Tales,* including the *Retraction,* offer a "reading
lesson," then its various ambiguities lead to that insight, which might
be called its conclusion. If, on the other hand, it is impossible to tell
where the textual argument about the ethics of reading and writing
comes to rest, *The Canterbury Tales* is an indeterminate text and its evasion of closure are far more telling.

Peggy A. Knapp
Carnegie-Mellon University

Stephen G. Nichols and Siegfried Wenzel, eds. *The Whole Book:
Cultural Perspectives on the Medieval Miscellany.* Recentiores: Later
Latin Texts and Contexts. Ann Arbor: University of Michigan
Press, 1996. Pp. viii, 188. $37.50.

There has been a considerable growth of interest on the part of medieval
literary scholars during the last thirty years in the manuscripts of the
texts they study. This interest has not, as in the more distant past, focused exclusively on the capacity of individual manuscripts to furnish
an authentic or reliable witness of a text, but has extended to all aspects
of text production and reception. Some of the most fruitful manuscripts
for the study of these broader aspects of literary culture are those that
consist of compilations of a miscellaneous or apparently miscellaneous
nature. Many questions of genre, of the relationship between texts, of
textual status and integrity, of the very nature of what constitutes a text,
can be profitably reexamined, and in a more appropriately historical way,
in the context of such codices. It was therefore a good idea for the University of Pennsylvania and Johns Hopkins University to call a colloquium of scholars in 1993 to discuss "the nature and usefulness of the
concept 'miscellany,'" as the editors explain in their introduction. The

present volume is a compilation of the papers presented at the conference, and is in that sense an example of the phenomenon—or a symptom of the condition—that it describes.

For there is a specter that haunts miscellany-scholarship, in the form of the ever-present danger of attributing literary and cultural significance to aspects of compilation practice that may have most to do with the practical necessities of text production and the availability of exemplars. Most scholars are reluctant to rest content with mere observation and description: conclusions must be drawn and theses proposed, if only to demonstrate the worthwhileness of the scholarly engagement. Miscellanies will be promoted to anthologies (quite a different category of compilation), organized according to ascertainable principles of judgment; or they may be seen as compilations that have been put together on such unusual principles that no one has hitherto detected them. It can become an exciting new game, with rules waiting to be made or no rules at all, and no necessary premise but the assumption that the compiler knew what he was doing—and maybe not even that.

It is a great virtue of the present volume that the essays in it are by scholars experienced in their different fields, not likely to fall into jejune enthusiasms for finding significances where there are none. But in the absence of consistent arguments for hidden significance such as I have characterized, the volume is bound to lack coherence of the kind one usually looks for. Scholars will report this, and they will report that, and it was very nice of Michigan to publish their findings. I find it quite touching that the editors can claim that the "chapters" of their book "yield a certain and firm methodological or heuristic consensus" (p. 6). Brave words—but a scrutiny of the preceding paragraph will suggest that the consensus was that there are lots of differences between different manuscripts and lots of questions to be asked. I have no debate at all with this conclusion, but it is not quite what it is claimed to be.

The individual essays, if we can now abandon the pretense that they are "chapters" of a "book," are of generally high quality, and they range widely. I shall not have much to say about the discussion by Georg N. Knauer of a late Latin miscellany that furnishes a missing link in the history of the pseudo-Homeric *Batrachomyomachia;* the essay has little to do with the rest of the volume, though it might help to explain the volume's presence in the series. Siegfried Wenzel's "Sermon Collections and Their Taxonomy" is a useful survey by an experienced scholar, but it is really about "sermon-miscellanies," not "miscellanies." All the manuscripts discussed, ranging from noncyclic sermon collections, through "sermon-diaries," to collections of sermons and related texts, are united by their common genre and common interest in providing materials for the preacher. There is nothing that specially needs explaining. Ralph Hanna deals with a manuscript that does need explaining, Winchester College MS 33, and he does manage to educe a principle of selection, a theme of divine mercifulness (p. 46), though he recognizes more clearly than anyone how such a selection procedure might coexist with "happenstance acquisition" (p. 47). He thinks the element of randomness is inevitable in a period when there was "no single literary canon" for the vernacular and when "exemplar poverty" may have been the principal motive for writing down pieces in collections. Hanna deserves credit for having at least tried to find a historical explanation for miscellaneity in the conditions of vernacularity, and his argument works well for Winchester 33 and some other manuscripts containing religious and devotional writing. But it does not work well with the anthologies of Chauceriana that are quite common in the fifteenth century and that give evidence of quite well established principles of canonical selection and reasonable access to exemplars. It is, oddly enough, one such manuscript (MS Arch. Selden B.24) that provides the subject-matter for the essay by A. S. G. Edwards. For him, the Selden MS is an example of the "durability" of the "Chaucerian *compilatio*" (p. 58). Even in its Scots poems it responds to "the imperatives of established Chaucerian compilation" (p. 61).

Julia Boffey returns to the question of "anthologies or miscellanies?" in her meticulous examination of the minor Lydgate poems in BL MS Harley 116 and Cambridge University Library MS Hh.4.12. The very meticulousness of her examination means that she can draw no conclusions, and she ends, rather plaintively, with the question with which she began: "How is one to tell where an anthology, a miscellany, or even simply a compilation begins and ends?" Stephen Nichols, on the other hand, declares himself to be "looking for principles of order" in a French lyric compilation (Morgan MS 819), and it is he who comes nearest to overstraining one's credulity. "Dissimilarity" of texts is claimed here to be the principle on which the reading program of the manuscript is organized (p. 83)—the heterogeneous dialectic of the one and the many (p. 95). The manuscript, in which both spiritual and secular poems are present, speaks of the coexistence of the spiritual and the sensual in a world ruled by restraint and self-governance. There are echoes of the aesthetics of D. W. Robertson here, of criteria for determining meaningfulness so comprehensive that nothing could possibly be irrelevant.

The last three essays have little to do with the "miscellany." Sylvia Huot describes BN MS fr.24429 as a manuscript carefully designed for the meditative reading and instruction of a queen. It is a devotional anthology, and its purposes and the reasons for the choice of texts are perfectly clear. It is not a "miscellany" at all, and Huot nowhere mentions the word. E. Ann Matter returns to the idea that what may appear a "miscellaneous" collection may have "an internal logic that takes some effort to understand" (p. 145). The logic that she finds in Carolingian manuscripts containing Alcuin's *De fide*—already, it must be said, highly specialized compilations and not miscellanies—is that of the schoolbook, and behind that she discerns, accurately communicated, the intentions of the author. Her argument is brief, to the point, and authoritative: it has important consequences for the modern publication of Alcuin's writings and for the understanding of the politics of Carolingian theology. Barbara Shailor, similarly, thinks that on closer examination "miscellaneous" manuscripts may not be as miscellaneous as they first appear (p. 153). She examines four Beinecke manuscripts, the first three of which are in Latin: they demonstrate not so much the idea of a hidden internal logic as the truth of Hanna's proposition concerning the essentially vernacular nature of miscellaneity. For no scholar of the truly miscellaneous would recognize these three manuscripts as miscellanies. The first is a monastic anthology of Bernardiana, the second a Benedictine almanac and reference-collection, and the third a straightforward commonplace-book. The fourth manuscript is a compilation in English of useful information for a fifteenth-century member of the English gentry. It is as near to a miscellany as Shailor gets, but its miscellaneousness is pretty systematic.

Some judiciously brief and wry "Retractations" by James J. O'Donnell put a poststructural gloss on the matter. "The failures to classify . . . are implicit criticisms of our ability to classify" (p. 169). "They repeatedly derail the readers' expectations" (p. 172). So there you are: you began the book expecting to learn something, but you end by knowing less than you thought you did. Fortunately, O'Donnell's is not an accurate description of the book.

DEREK PEARSALL
Harvard University

Monica Brzezinski Potkay and Regula Meyer Evitt. *Minding the Body: Women and Literature in the Middle Ages, 800–1500.* New York: Twayne, 1997. Pp. xii, 238. $33.00.

This study focuses on textual representations of and literary production by women across a broad range of medieval languages and genres. The book's title articulates its organizing principle: what pulls together analyses of these potentially disparate materials is the idea of "minding the body," a trope that the authors invoke simultaneously to convey and disrupt the familiar medieval identification of women with body and men with mind. The essays in this book track the various ways that the body is "minded" in medieval texts about and by women: as unruly feminine carnality, as generator of life, as suffering and salvific flesh, as constituent of human society itself. The authors target their book primarily for nonspecialists but also express the hope that "something here will interest . . . medievalist colleagues" (p. 9). Both types of readers are likely to find this book ever intelligent and alternately useful, provocative, and at times frustrating, because its ambitions for coverage do not consistently complement the sophistication of several of its arguments.

Minding the Body concentrates on medieval English literature but also pays significant attention to important texts in Latin, French, and Provençal. Its introduction and conclusion frame nine chapters, which focus on religious constructions of female authorship, Anglo-Saxon poetry, Provençal love poetry and Marian lyrics, romance, the lais of Marie de France, English biblical drama, dream visions, Chaucer, and mystical texts by women. The book also includes a fourteen-hundred-year chronology of literary events and a bibliography.

Potkay and Evitt apply a commensurately broad sense of historical and cultural context to their wide-ranging literary analyses, invoking "literary and artistic conventions; religious and philosophical traditions; psychological needs; economic, ecclesiastic, political, and other social institutions; and cultural practice" to elucidate medieval textual representations of women and the feminine. Despite male dominance of the social forces constructing medieval femininity, they generally conclude that "women did not always passively conform to manufactured images but might remodel, resist, or even reject them" (p. 10). Individual chapters arrive at this conclusion through engaging arguments that draw upon relevant historical and cultural materials to inform selective readings of literary texts.

Given the scope and complexity of the issues this book seeks to address, some of these chapters are admirably lucid models of condensation. For example, chapter 1, "Body and Soul: Religious Constructions of Female Authorship," examines linkages between classical and Christian misogyny and antifeminism and the self-conceptions expressed by medieval women authors. Writers such as Hrotsvitha, Heloise, Hildegard of Bingen, and Christine de Pizan are able to challenge the culture's monolithic "disparagement of the feminine" (p. 22) by manipulating metaphoric constructions of textuality (e.g., as body and fabric) and the symbolic potential of dominant culture discourses that gendered *ratio* and *anima* as feminine. Chapter 3, "Mirror and Window: The Courtly Lady in Provençal Love Poetry and English Marian Hymns," provides a useful overview of *fin'amor* as a social and poetic ideology that underwrites the fundamental narcissism of troubadour poetry; it then argues that this narcissism is powerfully critiqued in the poems of the trobairitz and implicitly reversed by certain Middle English Marian lyrics, which transform the "visual climax" (p. 61) of troubadour lyric narcissism through a kind of looking, filtered by the Virgin Mary, that is transparent, communal, and redemptive.

Other chapters advance arguments that are more obliquely formulated and hence more difficult to summarize. Chapter 6, "Body Broken, Body Whole: Eucharistic Devotion, Fabliaux, and the Feminine Impulse of the Corpus Christi Drama," establishes the tension between fragmentation and wholeness in medieval ideologies of Corpus Christi as a governing trope for exploring gender relationships and women's roles in English cycle plays. Contending that Corpus Christi drama and the fabliaux "regularly make woman's body or the feminized male bodily sites of inquiry and dramatic fiction making" (p. 112), this chapter examines the ways in which the drama's feminine bodies stand in for the fragmentation and wholeness of the Christian social body, which is fissured in the image of a feminized, crucified Christ and recuperated in the healing and salvific body of the Virgin Mary. Though not quite as multilayered or as densely argued, chapter 7, "Chaucer, Rape, and the Poetic Powers of Ventriloquism," similarly addresses an ambitious variety of texts to demonstrate that Chaucer wrote "narratives that hinge on rape" to critique the traditional "metaphoric equation of deceptive language with female infidelity" (p. 140). Building on Gavin Douglas's characterization in *Eneados* of Chaucer as "all womanis frend," the chapter examines Chaucer's double identification of the poetic personality with both genders (p. 142) in a discussion that ranges across the 1380 document that released Chaucer from the accusation of rape; legal rhetoric of rape in fourteenth-century England; "Adam Scriveyn"; the *Legend of Philomela* in *The Legend of Good Women;* and *The Wife of Bath's Tale.* Representations of women in Chaucer's poetry, this chapter asserts, were deeply influenced by the poet's rape accusation.

These summaries of selected chapters should suggest how and why this book may merit the attention of both nonspecialists and medievalists. Portions of this book can furnish an aid to first-time teachers (nonspecialist or medievalist) of the many texts it considers that are regularly used in the undergraduate classroom. I came away from my reading with new ideas about how I might juxtapose in different ways those texts that I teach frequently, and how I might incorporate into my teaching medieval texts that I've never taught before. Other parts of this book provide challenging arguments that scholars will want to interrogate. To note just one example, I think that the chapter on Corpus Christi plays urges the link between cycle drama and Eucharist too strenuously; however much the implications of eucharistic symbolism may resonate in this drama, the theological and festive dimensions of Corpus Christi are not uniformly relevant to the auspices and structures of the English cycle plays. On the whole, though, in *Minding the Body* Potkay and Evitt have assembled an impressive group of essays whose thematic focus on gender and the body provides a very usable guide to the fundamental issues at stake in a wide range of important medieval texts.

THERESA COLETTI
University of Maryland

P. R. ROBINSON and RIVKAH ZIM, eds. *Of the Making of Books: Medieval Manuscripts, Their Scribes and Readers. Essays Presented to M. B. Parkes.* Aldershot, U.K.: Scolar Press, 1997. Pp. xiii, 324. $68.95.

It is a tribute to the influence of Malcolm Parkes that this festschrift, gathered to mark his retirement, should serve almost as an interim report on British manuscript studies. With the exception of two fine essays on the history of the idea of authorship by A. J. Minnis and David Ganz, each contribution is based on a meticulous examination of a carefully selected sample of manuscripts. The essays describe the state of the discipline, including its isolation (for good or ill) from the more hectic pace of literary criticism and its suspicion of easy generalization. Outsiders may admire the elegance and clarity of the demonstrations and the sheer labor behind them, while wishing in some cases that the broader historical implications of the work had been more fully explored.

Some of the essays round out work that has been ongoing for some time. A. I. Doyle returns to an old friend, the troublesome Carthusian Stephen Dodesham, to offer the most recent list of works he copied, some twenty-three or twenty-four volumes. Helmut Gneuss examines BL MS Cotton Tiberius A.3, a mid-eleventh-century collection of ninety-one items, many of them associated with the Benedictine reform movement, including the earliest copy of a full Marian office in England. Gneuss reviews all the evidence and establishes the widely accepted provenance, Christ Church, Canterbury, as a near certainty. Jeane Krochalis adds five manuscripts to Neil Ker's list of those that belonged to Kirkstall Abbey.

Other essays set out hypotheses that will need to be tested in years to come. The great increase in the number of patristic texts in England from the late eleventh century on has often been attributed to the efforts of Norman reformers anxious to expand the holdings of libraries that they considered backwards. Teresa Webber argues that this view is in part a misconception, based on misleading comparisons to Carolingian collections. She shows that the English often had to seek much further than Normandy for their exemplars and traces the outline of a broader Continental connection, noting, for example, that English copies of Augustine's *Confessions* appear to have been based on Flemish exemplars.

In some cases the manuscripts yield remarkably full accounts of human lives. Richard Beadle examines the work of Geoffrey Spirleng (c. 1426–94), an estate servant for Sir John Fastolf and later a civic and gild official in Norwich, who with the help of his son made a copy of *The Canterbury Tales,* Glasgow University Library MS U.1.1. Beadle sketches the career of this occasionally overzealous "gentleman bureaucrat," examining various signed records that allow us to distinguish Spirleng's hand from that of his son, a point on which Manly and Rickert had remained discreetly vague. What makes Spirleng of such interest is that his exemplar also survives, CUL Mm.2.5, giving us a rare opportunity to assess the patterns of scribal variation. Beadle shows that Spirleng made numerous minor corrections independently. This scribal independence is not especially surprising—why should an intelligent copyist not correct obvious errors? But it does play havoc with one of the principles of traditional recension, scribal deterioration.

Often these studies turn up complex cultural artifacts that fall outside traditional disciplinary boundaries. A particularly striking instance is a portable tabula, or table, with five images of the Virgin accompanied by Latin verses, which was intended for the new Lady Chapel at York Minster ordered by Archbishop John Thoresby. The table does not survive and may never have actually been completed. Vincent Gillespie, who edits the description for the first time, examines the unusually elaborate symbolism of the York table, places it in the context of dramatic activity and popular devotion in York, and traces its debt to the thirteenth-century Cistercian *Pictor in carmine,* one of the fullest English accounts of the use of images as books for the laity. The York table might indeed be described as a form of hypertext, as Gillespie suggests, an analogy others might wish to pursue further. Jeanne Krochalis explores the rich combination of legendary and historical material in a twelfth-century collection from Kirkstall Abbey, BL Titus A.19, which includes the Pseudo-Turpin, the *Pilgrim's Guide* to Compostela, the legend of Amis and Amile, and various accounts of the history and burial of Arthur. Krochalis locates a major source for the Arthurian material in the *Magna Tabula* at Glastonbury, a large box with six pages on the abbey's history displayed for pilgrims. Peter Lucas examines the development of type fonts for printing Old English under the direction of Archbishop Mathew Parker. While Parker advocated archaizing hands for copying Old English from manuscripts so that antiquity might be "counterfeited," the fonts designed under his supervision are actually quite close to humanist ones. To explain why this should be so, Lucas examines some sixty-one Anglo-Saxon manuscripts that Parker might have used.

Several of the essays suggest general patterns in book production and circulation. P. R. Robinson discusses the work of an anonymous twelfth-century nun from St. Mary's Abbey, Winchester, the Nunnaminster, and concludes that it is impossible to determine the gender of medieval copyists from their handwriting. In particular, the hand of this anonymous scriptrix does not support the hypothesis, advanced by some, that the handwriting of nuns tends to be more conservative than that of their male contemporaries. Jean Vezin provides a list of references to leaflets kept in loose parchment folders, referred to variously as *codicelli, libelli, quaderni,* or *quaterniones,* and shows that they were common, even in princely libraries. The prevalence of such *quaderni* permitted several scribes to work simultaneously after dividing up the sections of their exemplar. Jean Preston shows how a late-twelfth-century Cistercian collection of works by Bernard, Bede, and Augustine was preserved by neighboring Catholic families after the Dissolution.

Finally, two essays contribute to current investigation of medieval categories of authorship. A. J. Minnis explores the discourses of authority, asking how a medieval theologian might regard the question of whether an immoral man, or by implication any human, can tell a moral tale, while David Ganz shows how autograph letters were valued for their intimacy or authenticity and seen as reflections of the writer's character.

Andrew Taylor
University of Saskatchewan

M. C. Seymour. *A Catalogue of Chaucer Manuscripts: Volume II,* The Canterbury Tales. Aldershot, U.K., and Brookfield, Vt.: Scolar Press, 1997. Pp. x, 270. $89.95.

To date, there has been a dearth of adequate descriptions of the manuscripts of *The Canterbury Tales,* despite many previous treatments. The manuscripts could be better described than they were by J. M. Manly and E. Rickert in their 1940 edition of *The Canterbury Tales,* partly because study of late medieval English manuscripts has advanced considerably since they completed their work. Malcolm Parkes has provided standardized descriptions for English bookhands. He and Ian Doyle have demonstrated the significance of the *ordinatio* of manuscripts, for which we need detailed information, e.g., on textual division. Kathleen L. Scott's work on illuminated manuscripts, *Later Gothic Manuscripts 1390–1490* (1996), too recent for Seymour to have used, provides standardized nomenclature for manuscript decoration. Although W. McCormick, with J. Heseltine, usefully include manuscript rubrics in their 1933 work, scholars interested in *ordinatio* need more information.

Seymour seems to be offering an improved catalogue, yet from the beginning of his book, he encourages users to be wary. He excuses himself from providing even minimally adequate bibliography, commenting that much of the scholarship reads like "the minutes of a convention of arthritic Hungarian jugglers." Instead, he recommends the bibliography in the CD-ROM *Wife of Bath's Tale* (1996), produced by The Canterbury Tales Project, edited N. Blake and P. Robinson, appreciatively noting D. W. Mosser's descriptions of manuscripts provided there. Seymour never signals where or why he supports or differs from other scholars. Apparently he expects us to trust his judgment and share his opinions, and he is opinionated, as his "Introduction" shows.

Some features of Seymour's *Catalogue* will annoy those who must use it. The subtitle of volume 2 indicates that it includes all manuscripts containing *The Canterbury Tales,* but it does not. The seventeen manuscripts containing extracts from *The Canterbury Tales* are treated in volume 1, pp. 131–54, although eight manuscripts containing smaller fragments complete volume 2, pp. 246–55. Moreover, although identifying manuscripts of the *Tales* by their Manly-Rickert sigils has become standard notation through their continuing use in the Variorum Chaucer and The Canterbury Tales Project, Seymour does not use the sigils and is inconsistent in supplying information for cross-referencing. When he first lists the MSS, pp. 3–6 he supplies "(ex Devonshire)," i.e., Ds[1], for Takamiya MS 24, but not "(ex Sion College)," Si, for Takamiya MS 22.[1]

To describe manuscripts, Seymour follows a template for each entry, consisting of physical description, watermarks (if applicable), collation, contents (corresponds to McCormick), sequence, decoration, rubrics, glosses (if applicable), scribe, history, and address of owner (for smaller and private collections). He is more concise than Manly-Rickert not only because he omits their speculative hypotheses but also because he makes definite decisions where they report variation, ambiguities, special features, even uncertainty, or because he conflates their more specific observations or applies them more broadly than is warranted.

To test Seymour's work, I consulted several British Library manuscripts, of which MS Additional 25718 (Ad[2]) may serve as a primary,

---

[1] Changes in ownership of other manuscripts listed in Manly-Rickert are as follows: Phillipps MSS 8136 and 8137 (Ph[2] and Ph[3]) are now Fondation Bodmer MS 48 (Cologny, Geneva) and Rosenbach Foundation MS 1084/1 (Philadelphia). Phillipps 6750 (Ph[1]) is now University of Texas pre–1700 MS 46 (Austin); Phillipps 8299 (Ph[4]) is now Huntington Library MS HM 140 part 1 (San Marino). The Helmingham MS (He) is now Princeton University, Firestone Library MS 100. The Merthyr fragment (Me) is now National Library of Wales MS 21972D (Aberystwyth).

though not in itself an important, example (it does not contain *The Wife of Bath's Prologue,* so Mosser's description is not easily available). A supervisor in the Students Room described this manuscript to me as a "typical nineteenth-century British Museum repair to make a tatty manuscript presentable," but Seymour offers no hint of the manuscript's condition, its most interesting feature for students. Manly-Rickert (who mistyped the manuscript number as 25178) are more informative: "Vellum (coarse), occasionally patched, with writing carrying over the patch (cf. ff. 28, 29)." Despite all the repairs, there are still rips in the vellum among fols. 14–22. Without explanation, Seymour dates Ad^2 "1400–25 late" (pp. 99 *and* 9) earlier than Manly-Rickert's date of "1430–50." They agree that all hands (i.e., scribes) use a SW Midlands dialect, with Seymour identifying the hands as *anglicana formata,* and they agree that fols. 41–47 are the work of Hand 2 and fols. 1–40 the work of Hand 1, but they disagree in allocating fols. 48–88 between Hands 1 and 3. Seymour improbably, given the visual evidence, allocates by quires, while Manly-Rickert reasonably confess some doubt that Hand 3 implies a different scribe from Hand 1, though they distinguish better than Seymour the different look of the hand(s).

Neither Manly-Rickert nor Seymour offer acceptable accounts of the decoration, but Seymour's is more seriously misleading. Manly-Rickert's claim that the decorative penwork varies with the hands is not credible; it appears to be the work of one hand, as Seymour suggests, though the cruder penwork on fols. 82–83 might be excepted. Erroneously, Seymour applies to "all fragments until f. 74" Manly-Rickert's claim about *The Clerk's Tale,* fols. 64–79, that penwork-decorated initials with champs mark major textual divisions. Seymour does not define "major textual divisions," nor does he anywhere give full and accurate details of the decoration.

Seymour's description of Addition 25718 yields several errors, one so inconsistent with surrounding data that a copyeditor should have queried it; namely, the report twice that *The Shipman's Tale* begins on fol. 72 (it begins on fol. 80), when parts of *The Clerk's Tale* are described, immediately before, as beginning on fols. 73v and 76. The penwork-decorated *N* that Seymour claims for fol. 72 does not exist there or on the correct fol. 80, the beginning of quire 10: there is only an ordinary brown-ink *N*. Comparing the phantom decorated *N* to the decorated *I* that begins quire 7, fol. 41, both midtext and midsentence, i.e., at no major textual division, Seymour concludes: "[T]hese unusually placed capitals suggest that the ms. was decorated after leaves had been lost" (p. 99). His conclusion is vitiated by the error on which it is based.

Other errors or inconsistencies riddle Seymour's description. He describes *The Clerk's Tale* as "unspaced stanzas, marked by parafs," without noting the inconsistency with which the program is carried out, and without noting a similar (inconsistent) program for *The Man of Law's Tale.* The boxed rubrics Seymour describes as "flamboyantly decorated" do not clearly belong to a later hand; they occur on fols. 32, 47 (not 41); and they involve calligraphic work with faces in profile on the ends of the boxes (see Scott, 1.61, noting such profile faces to be characteristic of fifteenth-century MSS; they also occur in the ascenders common in BL MS Lansdowne 851). Under glosses, Seymour reports "none, apart from *auctor* names in red f. 86"; but there are several abbreviated Latin glosses, partly trimmed off, for *The Pardoner's Tale.*

Inconsistent reporting of glosses also affects Lansdowne 851: there Seymour reports glosses for *The Man of Law's Tale* under "Contents" (mystifyingly, he also reports "8 after 301"), but denies their existence under "Glosses." He also misses two small glosses for *The Knight's Tale,* fols. 15v and 26—and perhaps more.

Getting details wrong cannot be deemed unimportant in a catalogue. High levels of error; faulty reasoning, often on the basis of error; and inconsistency destroy confidence in Seymour's catalogue. Any library or scholar who has not paid for this *Catalogue* should invest instead in Manly-Rickert, the CD-ROM *Wife of Bath's Prologue,* or Scott, and wait for more complete publication of Mosser's work.

CHARLOTTE C. MORSE
Virginia Commonwealth University

CLAIRE SPONSLER. *Drama and Resistance: Bodies, Goods, and Theatricality in Late Medieval England.* Medieval Cultures, vol. 10. Minneapolis and London: University of Minnesota Press, 1997. Pp. xvii, 209. $54.95 cloth, $21.95 paper.

In Claire Sponsler's *Drama and Resistance: Bodies, Goods, and Theatricality in Late Medieval England,* Michel Foucault's axiom "Where there is power, there is resistance" is both credo and organizing principle. By asking searching questions about how the readers, viewers, and listeners of late-medieval official culture appropriated and transformed "disciplining" discourses through theatrical performance, *Drama and Resistance* finally brings medieval drama scholarship into full, knowing dialogue with influential postmodern theorists of power, material culture, and spectatorship. But though Sponsler frequently invokes the cultural insights of Foucault, Bakhtin, and Elias, she is also the very model of resistance here, boldly critiquing both those theorists' formulations about spontaneous eruptions of peasant carnival and their facile constructions of a simple, devout medieval world docilely lying in wait for the self-fashioning, reforming, and civilizing impulses of the Early Modern. The late-medieval performance history Claire Sponsler is interested in telling in this book is one in which "within the licensed space of the theater, official scripts for living could be rewritten—no matter how fleetingly or contingently—to explore alternate possibilities of action and being" (p. xv).

The book's structure is a point/counterpoint of power and defiance. Chapters 1, 3, and 5 scrutinize late-medieval disciplinary discourses of sumptuary laws, conduct literature, and books of hours; chapters 2, 4, and 6 counter these with studies of the social and gender disguisings of the Robin Hood plays and ballads, the flamboyant unruliness of Vices in the morality plays, and the spectacular transgressions of the Corpus Christi pageants. In every case, Sponsler evades the easy conclusions such a dialectic might invite, exploring instead in arguments of considerable complexity and subtlety the nuanced minglings of compliance and subversion in late-medieval theatrical performances.

Throughout this book, Sponsler unabashedly uses the present as an instructing lens on the past. Chapter 1, on medieval sumptuary laws, for example, begins with an extended exemplary anecdote about a bandana worn by an Mashpee Indian in a tribal court case in Massachusetts in 1976, an anecdote that Sponsler deftly weaves into an argument about the crucial role of garments in the constructing of self and community identity. Her study of the ways that medieval clothing regulations served the purposes of political order undergirds her claim in the second chapter that late-medieval Robin Hood disguisings had "the effect of calling categorizing systems of all kinds—social, economic, sexual—into question" (p. 36). Given the paucity of surviving medieval dramatic texts, such an argument requires her to link scant fragments of Robin Hood plays (only one of them actually medieval) with medieval archival evidence for Robin Hood games and Morris dancers—and especially with Robin Hood ballads of doubtful date. Although this chapter on Robin Hood performances is, thus, necessarily the most speculative, it is written with such skill and tact that Sponsler makes a persuasive case for a medieval gender-bending and class-challenging Robin of misrule who was very different from the "gentleman outlaw" of sixteenth- and seventeenth-century Arcadian fantasy.

In chapter 3, "Conduct Books and Good Governance," Sponsler's central purpose is to show that "Despite the assumptions of Elias, Bakhtin, and Foucault about medieval bodies," "long before the sixteenth century, the 'civilizing' work of bodily discipline was already well under way" (p. 53). In numerous treatises regulating proper behavior for women and children as well as codes of conduct for self-fashioning males, both medieval private and social identities were constructed and bodies were duly disciplined—but usually with the full desire and compliance of their social-climbing readers. Unlike prose conduct literature, Sponsler claims, late medieval morality plays were not only a theater of discipline but a theater of subversion, mischievously complicating the audience's response by their flamboyantly misbehaving Vice characters who literally steal the show. In medieval morality plays it is the outrageous Vices who are the best roles, if not the best role models; indeed, the disapproving sixteenth-century Puritan Philip Stubbes might well have been right to object that theater always taught the unwary spectator "to playe the vice" (p. 75).

In chapter 4, "Mischievous Governance: The Unruly Bodies of Morality Plays," Sponsler offers useful and compelling readings of the misrule of the disgruntled laborer in *Mankind,* of the reckless youth in *Interlude of Youth,* and the defiant female in the Dutch dramatic dialogue *Mary of Nemmegen.* (Sponsler justifies using a Dutch text to cope with the lacuna in English morality play texts about unruly women by arguing that there is an analogous extant English prose version that may have been a "reading version of the enacted play," but which is anyway a text of "distinctly dramatic flavor" [p. 96]). She views all of these morality plays as double-voiced; on the one hand, they existed for "ritually exorcizing antisocial tendencies" (p. 102) among their spectators, but on the other, those spectators, much like the spectators assumed by contemporary cinema theory, would have had "shifting and conflicting identification" (p. 103) with the antisocial characters in ways that actually destabilized and resisted reintegration into the social order.

In perhaps the most provocative chapter of a very provocative book, "Devoted Bodies: Books of Hours and the Self-Consuming Subject," Sponsler considers the discipline and resistance of books of hours. In the family coats of arms, name inscriptions, and portraits illuminated in the pages of luxurious books of hours, "the act of devotion," Sponsler writes, "comes to involve self-worship as well, creating thereby a spectacular subjectivity in which the self is made the object of intense scrutiny" (p. 107). Sponsler explores here the "complexly interwoven dynamics of voyeurism, identification, and reification that shaped the presentation of the devout subject for scopic consumption" (p. 123). Human bodies of pious owners painted within comfortably furnished domestic spaces become commodified subjects placed in real estate—even as the intrusive figures of patron saints looming over them "bring with them a reminder of the ultimate dissolution of the things of the material world" (p. 132), and even as perspective is exploited in fifteenth-century books of hours to destabilize rather than provide meditative focus. The windows framing city or landscape views, for example, are liminal rather than containing; they distract the meditating eye and simultaneously reveal both enclosed and open space, the private and the public. Thus, owner-portraits in these devotional books are less images for pious identification and meditative discipline than images uneasily performing "an interplay between the themes of permanence and loss, materiality and disembodiment" (p. 134).

Much of this same liminality exists in the enfleshed images on Corpus Christi stages and pageant wagons in which "the acts of spectatorship and participation were blurred" (p. 151). The transgressive drama of the mystery plays, Sponsler argues, is at once communal and intensely private; it both affirms and interrogates "the notion of orderly social harmony" (p. 138). In the performed violence of the torn body of Christ this theater tempts sadistic delight, eroticizes Christ's "feminized bleeding" (p. 152), shatters the myth of social order, and defies the guild's "commodification" of Christian culture. Although this final chapter on "Violated Bodies" in the Corpus Christi pageants ends by asserting that in the contested territory of theater, the play is "sometimes resisting, sometimes capitulating to authority" (p. 161), Sponsler is perhaps unnecessarily vague about what kinds of political resistance or capitulation religious drama may have responded to or encouraged. The documented archival evidence of quarrels and violence that followed the slapstick of the York Mason's play of the Funeral of the Virgin Mary (p. 157), for example, almost certainly had much more to do in this North Country performance with the fact that the unruly laughter was at the expense of a character with the Scots name of Fergus than with the general "disruptive dramatic energy" (p. 152) that Sponsler analyzes in this chapter.

But how do we know? Sponsler's book asks, finally (p. 161), and makes us ask ourselves. Some readers of this book will object to the sleight of hand with which Claire Sponsler produces texts when the English fifteenth-century dramatic texts do not exist; some will object that her claims for the transgressions of medieval Robin Hood performances seem more inspired by Katarina Witt's cross-dressed, ice-skating Robin Hood in her 1994 Winter Olympics comeback than by anything a medieval document or play fragment told her. But this is a book to be reckoned with, a study of late medieval drama that boldly goes where no such book has gone before and that mediates with the authority of a traveler's guide between our own obsessive cultural questions and a distant late medieval theater. *Drama and Resistance* attempts to do no less than write the unwritten, and the intelligence and astuteness of this book will impress even the most skeptical reader. "To look for moments of resistance within late medieval culture, as I have done," Claire Sponsler writes in her afterword, ". . . inevitably reveals as much about the searcher as it does about the practices found and scrutinized" (p. 161). What this book surely reveals is a very perceptive searcher indeed.

GAIL MCMURRAY GIBSON
Davidson College

JANE TAYLOR and LESLEY SMITH, eds. *Women and the Book: Assessing the Visual Evidence.* The British Library Studies in Medieval Culture. Toronto: University of Toronto Press, 1997. Pp. 287. $75.00 cloth; $29.95 paper.

The purpose of this collection of essays is to examine visual images from the Middle Ages—primarily manuscript illuminations, but also misericord carvings and occasionally other media—in an effort to approach medieval conceptualizations of women and, in particular, of the relationship of women to books. As the editors point out, one cannot simply assess visual images without taking into account various factors surrounding both the origins and the destinations of the objects in question: for whom they were made, by whom, about whom, and for what purpose. Thus, the essays address a wide range of materials, including books authored by women, designed and executed by women, commissioned by women, owned by women, used by women, or simply containing representations of women. This diversity of approach is fruitful and allows the questions of the use and meaning of images, and their implications for gender constructions, to be considered from many different perspectives.

The essays themselves are somewhat uneven, but overall the volume includes much that is interesting and informative. Lesley Smith's essay poses the provocative question of why medieval manuscripts, despite the plethora of images depicting women reading or handling books, include so very few images of women writing. While her essay provides no real answer—perhaps none can be given—it does call attention to an interesting iconographic problem as well as identifying a small but fascinating series of representations of female scribes and authors. Sandra Hindman in turn examines two illuminated manuscripts of the *Fables* attributed to Marie de France, suggesting that the juxtaposition of author portraits and miniatures illustrating the opening and closing fables respectively serves to highlight the role of the female author. Some of Hindman's arguments might be questioned; she argues, for example, that Marie as a female author is treated differently from male authors such as Chrétien de Troyes or Benoit de Sainte-Maure, for whom no author portraits exist. But the portraits of Marie exist in manuscripts of the *Fables,* not in those of the *Lais* that may or may not have been written by the same author; and manuscripts of the *Fables* would be more appropriately compared with those of didactic texts such as other *Ysopet* collections or bestiaries—which often do feature author portraits—than with courtly romance. Hindman's examples are nonetheless informative and her essay forms a useful counterpart to Susan Ward's study in this volume of the celebrated manuscript Bibl. de l'Arsenal 3142, which includes an illustrated text of the *Fables.*

Several essays devoted to manuscripts made or owned by women offer informative and stimulating analyses of specific books, libraries, or scriptoria. The studies by Judith Oliver, Marie-Luise Ehrenschwendtner, and Kate Lowe focus on the activities of nuns in making and collecting books, while Richard Gameson, Anne Stanton, Anne Sutton, and Livia Visser-Fuchs offer detailed studies of books known to have been owned by aristocratic women. These essays offer a wealth of ideas concerning both the design and the use of books by women artists, scribes, and readers. Oliver, for example, discusses the possible influence of embroidery on the stylistic features of illuminations executed by nuns, while Stanton examines the themes of good and bad government, marital fidelity or infidelity, and motherhood in the Queen Mary Psalter in light of its probable connection to Queen Isabella of England, wife of Edward II and mother of Edward III. Sutton and Visser-Fuchs in their collaborative essay, in turn, focus on a fifteenth-century book of hours possibly made for Queen Elizabeth Woodward, wife of Edward IV, situating it in the context of the cult of Guardian Angels popular at the time. The essays by Stanton, Sutton, and Visser-Fuchs, together with Gameson's analysis of the Gospels of Queen Margaret of Scotland, make an interesting comparative study of the differing extents to which books might or might not reflect the gender, ideological preoccupations, or personal experiences of their owners. As such they serve very well to highlight the difficulties inherent in iconographic studies that aim to uncover the identities and interests of owners or readers, as well as the important insights that careful and judicious analysis can nonetheless lead to.

Other essays in the collection address various issues in the study of books and images. Wendy Armstead's study of women with books in misericord carvings, while less specifically focused on the depictions of women per se, is a fascinating exercise in the Bakhtinian reading of misericord imagery. Martha Driver identifies various problems encountered in the reading of visual images, such as the need to distinguish between "realistic" and "allegorical" imagery. Flora Lewis offers an interesting if somewhat unfocused survey of depictions of Christ's wound and its possible implications for female readers, who presumably reacted to the vaginal associations implicit in such images in a way quite different from male readers. Sandra Penketh, finally, provides a general overview of books of hours and the role models that they offered to female readers.

Though admirably wide-ranging in content, the volume is thematically coherent and offers an informative survey of a field in which there is currently much interest. It will be of use both to students and to specialists in diverse areas of medieval studies.

SYLVIA HUOT
Pembroke College, Cambridge

PAUL BEEKMAN TAYLOR. *Chaucer Translator.* Lanham, N.Y., and Oxford: University Press of America, 1998. Pp. v, 209. $51.00 (cloth); $31.00 (paper).

At the end of his introductory chapter, Taylor recognizes the limitations of his approach to Chaucer's translation: he does not "address the manifold complexities of Chaucer's *idea* of translation," or the theoretical implications of literacy, writing, and vernacularization discussed by others, "such as Rita Copeland, Brian Stock and Alistair Minnis" (p. 13). Rather, he restricts his tasks to placing Chaucer's translations "within a broad context of the literary history of ideas," and to tracing the implications of the "manner in which his 'appropriation' of earlier texts infuses his poetry with fresh meaning" (pp. 13–14). The reader is thus amply warned that despite its title, this book does not engage in the critical investigation of translation familiar to medievalists over the past decade, and that its approach is not new. Taylor's primary references for translation theory are classic but very dated observations by George Steiner and W. H. Auden, and his attention to recent Chaucer criticism is so scant that the effects are sometimes astonishing. He states in his preface, for example, that a major stumbling block to his discussion of Chaucer's method is C. S. Lewis's 1958 suggestion that Chaucer clung to medieval attitudes and renounced the direction of Boccaccio's Renaissance thought (pp. iii–iv)—Taylor gives not even a hint of recognition here that in the forty years since *The Allegory of Love,* scholarship has reconsidered Chaucer's relationship with his Italian contemporaries. It must also be noted that eight of the book's twelve chapters rework material from articles published in various journals between 1979 and 1997, and attempts to underscore their coherence are sporadic.

Despite the limitations of this book's scope and theoretical approach, some details of its individual studies deserve attention. Taylor accurately describes his method in one sentence in the preface: "In the chapters that follow, I identify a number of recycled linguistic elements which bring fresh meaning to [Chaucer's] story" (p. ii). The book's method of identifying sources and then analyzing the implications of their use in a new context accords with the current trend in both source studies and in some areas of translation studies. So, for instance, Taylor's second chapter, "Genesis and Apocalypsis: Zephirus and The Canon's Yeoman's Breath," carefully documents the biblical and literary underpinnings of Zephirus's breath and the earth's *licour* as found in the *Prologue* to *The*

Canterbury Tales, and then traces their implications for other references to breath and odor throughout the tales. The next four chapters, which similarly analyze some of the many passages in *The Canterbury Tales* focused on speech, offer informative genealogies and suggest provocative juxtapositions. Taylor is most comfortable, however, with the patristic methods that developed in the sixties, and his attempts to rejuvenate or camouflage them are unsuccessful. His interjection of Jameson's observations on parody between Kaske's and Kolve's interpretations of *The Miller's Tale,* for instance, is superficial (pp. 42–43 and notes), and his application of the rubric of translation is so broad and inconsistent that it loses cogency. In chapter 3 we learn that "[t]he Knight had translated the ideological programme of Theseus and his Athens into Ricardian England, and the Miller's jesting anecdote translates the world of Scripture and Scriptural exegesis into his own social experience"; in the next paragraph we find that "the Miller collaborates with Chaucer the reporter to translate terms from the fictive reality of pilgrimage context into the fictive fable of his performance" (pp. 40–41). Later in the chapter, "one thing in light is translatable by darkness into another" (pp. 43–44).

Taylor states in his preface that chapters 2 through 6 "reveal Chaucer confronting the implications of Nominalism and Realism to translation" (p. ii); it would be more accurate to say that their common interest is in proving Chaucer a realist, a conclusion largely based—after some worthwhile explorations of Chaucer's attention to both nominalism and realism—on the Parson's critique of the Pardoner's and the Manciple's performances. The remaining chapters ostensibly demonstrate Chaucer's modernity, in the sense that he contemporized or reinvented his borrowings from old texts. As with the previous chapters, Taylor's strength is in the pursuit of detail, and his studies do illustrate the complexity of Chaucer's interaction with "olde bokes." The sections on Chaucer's reference to the eye of the lynx in *Boece* (chapter 9), his translations of his names Geoffrey and Malin throughout his works (chapter 11), and his recontextualization of Petrarch's "In vita di Madonna Laura" in *Troilus and Criseyde* (chapter 12) provide rewarding glimpses of Chaucer's poetics. These chapters are weakest, however, when Taylor attempts to superimpose upon them discussions of translation that are sometimes awkward and sometimes platitudinous.

Finally, *Chaucer Translator* lacks good editing, and its superficial flaws point toward its more fundamental problems. Typographical errors are frequent enough to be disconcerting, as are the inconsistent practices for providing translations and the unacknowledged repetition of both material and references throughout its chapters. Such inconsistencies accurately indicate that this book, despite the merits of its detail, is a stitching together of previous work under the fashionable rubric of translation, rather than a concerted study of Chaucer as a translator.

KATHLEEN DAVIS
Bucknell University

ANDRÉ VAUCHEZ. *Sainthood in the Later Middle Ages,* trans. Jean Birrell, with a foreword by Richard Kieckhefer. Cambridge: Cambridge University Press, 1997. Pp. xxviii, 645, 43 plates, 34 tables, 3 maps. $95.00.

This publication is a complete, elegant, and most welcome translation of the revised edition (1988) of Vauchez's classic, *La sainteté en occident aux derniers siècles du moyen âge, d'après les procès de canonization et les documents hagiographiques* (Rome: Ecole Française, 1981). Vauchez's book, which has also been translated into Italian, is one of the regrettably small number of studies that not only draws on scholarship in most of the major relevant languages (especially French, Italian, German, and English) but has gained a worldwide academic readership, providing a basic reference point for all scholars of hagiography for the last two decades. Like its two predecessors—*La spiritualité du moyen âge occidental: VIIIe–XIIe siècles* (1975), and *Religion et société dans l'occident médiéval* (1980)—and like *Les laïcs au moyen âge: Pratiques et expériences religieuses* (1987), Vauchez's next book—*Sainthood in the Middle Ages* is a rich mix of archival work and carefully considered synthetic analysis, written with a flair for language and a hopeful, but far from naive, understanding of medieval ecclesiastical politics. All this brief review can do is to explain what is and is not here, and suggest some of its uses to scholars of Middle English.

Despite its overgeneralized English title, what Vauchez's book is not is a consideration of all aspects of sainthood and sanctity in later medieval culture. There is little about the saints medieval people spent most of their time venerating: the early Christian apostles, martyrs, and confessors, whose feasts were long-established events in the liturgical year, and whose lives and usually violent deaths are the subject of the vast majority of medieval hagiographic writings. This is, rather, a study of how medieval people came to be venerated as saints themselves or decided to venerate one another, how the Church (especially the papacy) tried to regulate and channel these decisions, and how sainthood was defined and imagined in both the official and the popular mind. Book 1 describes from various angles the growth (from the eleventh century on) of the idea that moderns could truly be considered as saints and of the canonization process itself, the thirteenth-century heyday of processes and canonizations, and the decline in canonizations in the fourteenth and early fifteenth centuries (apart from an upsurge during the Great Schism), as the length and expense of processes grew, and as the papacy redefined formal sainthood in more and more explicitly political terms. Book 2, building on an earlier discussion of the increasing number of figures venerated as saints despite their failure to achieve canonization (chapter 5), provides typologies of three kinds of sainthood, "popular," "local," and "official," focusing (in the hundred-page chapter 12) on how the criteria for official sainthood changed between 1100 and 1400, especially in favor of members of the mendicant orders, mystical women religious, and the laity. (Chapter 11, pp. 249–84, previews this discussion with a long series of charts and maps, which usefully distinguish canonization processes by various criteria, including date, geographical origin, and profession). Book 3 describes the relative importance given to pre- and posthumous miracles, personal virtues, and career achievements in popular and official attitudes to sanctity, and how these, too, both evolved and became increasingly dichotomized in the centuries after 1100. Finally, two appendices provide editions of documents connected with the canonization of Thomas Cantilupe (the bishop of Hereford who died in 1282 on his way to Rome to plead against his excommunication by archbishop John Peckham), while a lengthy list of sources and bibliography (to 1987; pp. 559–621) offers North American readers an invaluable point of access to a century of European scholarship on matters relating to hagiography and the papacy. All this makes for a bulky book, which few will have time to read in its entirety. Yet nearly twenty years after it was first published, this witty and perceptive analysis still offers not simply a view of the topic that must be taken into account by anyone interested in medieval church history, but also a colossal amount of information that cannot be got anywhere else.

Many different strands of the book's argument are worth careful discussion, but here I can point to only two. The first has to do with how England measured up to other parts of Europe in its promotion of saints and its attitude to specific types of sanctity. England, Scotland, and Ireland accounted for almost twenty percent of canonization processes between 1198 and 1431 (table 24, p. 270), slightly less than France (20.4%) and much less than Italy (31%), but much more than the German and Scandinavian countries (9.5% and 9.9%) or the whole of Eastern Europe (5.6%). Relatively well organized both ecclesiastically and politically, and with a reputation for orthodoxy and loyalty to the papacy, the English church was especially good at promoting bishops as saints, and unrivaled at bringing processes to a successful conclusion: nearly a third of all actual canonizations between 1198 and 1431 were of English saints (table 25a, p. 274, where the figures actually include one Welsh, one Scottish, and one Irish canonization). On the other hand, official English interest in rewarding ecclesiastical administrators with the Church's ultimate accolade was balanced by a relative indifference to sanctifying laypeople or others with mystical leanings: while a few such received unofficial veneration (thus, an unofficial office survives in honor of Richard Rolle), only one Welsh layman, Caradoc (d. 1124), was briefly examined as a candidate for sainthood, and only one member of the laity from the whole of the British Isles was actually canonized, Queen Margaret of Scotland (died 1044, canonized 1250). These figures and Vauchez's accompanying discussion tell us much about the priorities of the English ecclesiastical establishment over several centuries, and about the low prestige accorded mystical experience and other kinds of lay-identified devotion. They provide a fascinating context, for example, for the careers of the two late-medieval Englishmen most identified with women visionaries, the Augustinian hermit William Flete and the Norwich Benedictine, cardinal Adam Easton, both of whom found their spiritual destinies in Italy, not England, as associates, respectively, of Catherine of Siena and (posthumously) Bridget of Sweden. They even help explain why the best year of Margery Kempe's life was probably her year of voluntary poverty in Rome.

The other strand particularly relevant to readers of this journal has to do with Vauchez's balanced analysis of the relation between official and popular attitudes to sanctity, especially his insistence on an intermediary category of the "local"—often equated with a given diocese, its bishop, priests, and powerful laypeople—and his sensitivity to the mutual interdependence of popular devotion and official promotion in even the most highly politicized canonization processes. By the fifteenth century a majority of modern saints venerated in even the larger urban centres of Europe by the most well established religious orders had not been canonized, so expensive and unpromising had the process become. Although Vauchez interprets this as a failure on the Church's part to reconcile the official, the local, and the popular, even these local cults could only work if the laity as well as the bishop and his minions wanted them to work. Further research on individual local cults by scholars such as Aviad Kleinberg has somewhat complicated this picture, and its overly generalized definition of the "popular." However, like Eamon Duffy's work on late-medieval English devotion, Vauchez's study stands as a challenge to the binaries that literary scholars (including myself) have sometimes assumed in analyzing medieval religious culture, and makes provocative reading for this reason alone.

NICHOLAS WATSON
University of Western Ontario

DAVID WALLACE. *Chaucerian Polity: Absolutist Lineages and Associational Forms in England and Italy. Figurae:* Reading Medieval Culture series. Stanford, Conn.: Stanford University Press, 1997. Pp. xix, 555. $55.00.

At the turn of the present decade, a number of influential Chaucer studies, appearing in quick succession, wrought important changes in the way Americans, at least, understand and teach the poet. Carolyn Dinshaw's *Chaucer's Sexual Poetic* (1989), Paul Strohm's *Social Chaucer* (1989), H. Marshall Leicester Jr.'s *The Disenchanted Self* (1990), and Lee Patterson's *Chaucer and the Subject of History* (1991) brought gender and psychoanalytic theory, deconstruction, and Ricardian social, political, economic, and institutional history to bear on the Chaucerian corpus in deeply enlightening (and to some, deeply unsettling) ways.

David Wallace's *Chaucerian Polity* now takes its place in this elite group of Chaucerian blockbusters. Its major contribution is to contextualize Chaucer doubly as a political poet: more immediately in the context of Ricardian England, but (and this is Wallace's special claim to our attention and gratitude) more broadly within the orbit of the politics of *trecento* northern Italy, and thus of the Italian humanism (not just the poetic production) of Petrarch and Boccaccio, which reflects the confrontations and crises at the center of *trecento* political theory and practice.

Wallace starts from the major political fact of trecento Italian politics: the struggle for mastery of northern Italy between Florence and Milan, a struggle with profound implications for the subsequent history of western Europe. "Florence typically celebrated its own sense of republican *libertas* by developing . . . an associational ideology, suggesting that all inhabitants of the city-state share equal footing on a lateral plane." By contrast, for "northern Italian despotisms of the late Trecento[,] [t]he chief ideological vector . . . is vertical, one-way, and downward descending," and "generates ideological forms that, like their associational counterparts, are reproduced at both local and national levels" (p. 2).

In other words, the political struggle conditions the perspectives of the first generation of humanist writers and specifically provides the basic contrast between Petrarch, whose writings reflect his association with the Visconti and other despotic *signori,* and Boccaccio, who worked and wrote for a Florentine commune governed, between 1343 and 1378, by an often uneasy coalition of disparate economic and social groups.

Chaucer, both by his firsthand observation of Florence (1373) and Lombardy (1378), and by his reading of Petrarch and Boccaccio, understood the issues at stake in the struggle between the two types of polity. In addition, "Chaucer's experience in seeking to establish and stabilize a distinctive poetics" is complicated by the "complex and conflicted" nature of "his own political positioning . . . at the intersection of royal, magnate, and mercantile worlds," and his exposure to "a dizzying succession of polities, from the broadest-based associational model (peasant uprising) to the narrowest form of hierarchy (the tyranny of Richard II)." Accordingly, "he functions within both associational and hierarchic forms; in responding to the exceptional complexity of fourteenth-century English polity he is at once the poet of Florence and Lombardy" (p. 64), engaged in "testing . . . the structures (substructures and anti-structures) of associational governance" (p. 81), with *The Canterbury Tales' General Prologue* and *The Clerk's Tale* representing respectively "the political axes of Chaucerian fiction; his other fictions may be plotted within their vertical and horizontal planes" (pp. 2–3).

After considering the innovatively associational polity of *The General*

Prologue (chapter 2) and its relationship to the English parish guild (chapter 3, where Wallace builds on the 1985 study of Carl Lindahl, *Earnest Game*), *Chaucerian Polity* surveys Chaucer's political fictions in two groups of chapters. The first, more loosely organized sequence (chapters 4–7) explores the impact of, and resistance to, associational forms or impulses in state-making, rural, urban, legal, commercial, and religious contexts within *The Canterbury Tales* (and, by way of comparison and contrast, the *Decameron*).

In the second, more unified (and innovative) sequence of chapters, Wallace analyzes tales designed, he argues, to portray the excesses of despotic male behavior and consider the possibilities of restraining such behavior by means of "the most powerful and distinctive aspect—or tool or weapon—of Chaucerian polity . . . [:] wifely eloquence" (p. 5). Chapters 8 and 9 pair *The Tale of Melibee* and *The Manciple's Tale* as contrasting examples of households in which wives can and cannot, respectively, control angry men and prevent male violence. Linking the two chapters is Wallace's useful and effective analysis of how the writings of Albertano of Brescia (whose importance for Chaucer studies William Askins has tirelessly promoted for over a decade) underlie both tales. Chapter 10, on the Clerk's and Merchant's tales (and an expansion of Wallace's well-known 1990 essay), shows Chaucer responding directly to the fabled excesses of "tyrantez of Lombardye," and (with a self-conscious vernacularity that recalls Boccaccio) placing under scrutiny the Latinate, despot-friendly humanism of Petrarch.

In a long, fascinating last chapter, Wallace analyzes the "F Prologue" of *The Legend of Good Women* as a fictive record of Chaucer's connection with Anne of Bohemia, Richard II's queen, who is frequently depicted in contemporaneous texts as an intercessor for those who had become objects of his royal wrath. Arguing with verve, and supported as always by capacious documentation, Wallace suggests "various ways in which Chaucer's court-based writings might have served, meshed, or intersected with Bohemian interests" at Richard's court" (p. 362). (Wallace's argument should be compared with the somewhat different conclusions drawn about Chaucer and Anne by Andrew Taylor in *SAC* 19 [1997].)

In perhaps its single most novel and provocative argument, *Chaucerian Polity* contends that Chaucer adapts the "sixth of six" authorial topos—through which ambitious medieval European poets (e.g., Dante in *Inferno* 4) insert themselves into the company of illustrious *auctores*—to suggest that he may, after all, be the Wife of Bath's sought-after sixth husband! He thereby acknowledges his dependence, as a vernacular poet, on what the Wife represents within the pilgrim compaignye: ". . . knowledge of the body; wifely eloquence; dealing in *textus; felaweshipe,* pilgrimage, and 'wandryng by the weye,'" and commits himself "to exemplifying the social and political efficacy of wifely eloquence—within associational groupings [and] within mercantile, magnate, royal, and despotic households" (p. 82). One awaits with interest the response of feminist scholars to this Wallace-arranged marriage of Geoffrey and Alisoun.

Space limitations prevent more than the merest mention of *Chaucerian Polity*'s polemic against the traditional binary of "medieval" and "Renaissance" and its "new historicist" perpetuators, or its astute demonstrations of how the political absolutism established in England by Henry VIII prevented the Elizabethans (including Shakespeare) from understanding the associational dimensions of Chaucer's poetical polity.

Even given the length of *Chaucerian Polity,* there are a few places where I would have liked Wallace to expand his argument in order to further his reader's understanding of the complexities of Chaucer's (or Boccaccio's) mediation of political ideologies through narrative fictions. One example must suffice: in discussing *The Manciple's Tale,* Wallace notes that "the poet and the wife, within the household, would appear to be natural allies: each practices a rhetorical art to please, and not enrage, a lord and master. In the *Melibee,* wifely eloquence saves private and public society; in the *Prologue* to the *Legend of Good Women,* it saves the poet Chaucer. How, then, might the masculine poet reciprocate by helping the wife? The *Manciple's Tale* provides a short and chilling answer . . . [;] a wife is betrayed within her own household by one she might have looked to as an ally" (pp. 250–51). What are we to make of this betrayal within the overall context of Chaucer's associational preferences and imaginings? Wallace does not suggest an answer.

But for all the insightful and richly documented answers it does offer, *Chaucerian Polity* deserves the acclaim it is sure to earn from Chaucerians well into the new century.

R. W. HANNING
Columbia University

KAREN A. WINSTEAD. *Virgin Martyrs: Legends of Sainthood in Late Medieval England.* Ithaca and London: Cornell University Press, 1997. Pp. x, 201.

The popular and often lurid female saints' lives of medieval England have long deserved a book-length treatment. In her lucid, meticulously researched study, Kate Winstead situates the lives of virgin martyrs written in England between 1200 and 1450 within their historical and cultural contexts. Given the broad historical range of the book, this project poses multiple pitfalls, which Winstead gracefully avoids. While encompassing in scope, her study—a wonderfully balanced engagement with scholarship, primary texts, and visual representations— is nonetheless attuned to the specifics of each period and alert to the paradoxes and ambiguities of each individual text. Winstead's study is impressive not only for its usefulness as a source for future studies, but also for its intelligent assessment of the implications of these works for the medieval reader, whether male or female.

Winstead explores the lives of virgin martyrs produced in three periods, the early Middle English period, the high Middle Ages, and the post-Chaucerian age. Beginning with a careful summary of the "generic" Latin saint's life as the model for most of the lives produced by English hagiographers, Winstead argues that the enduring appeal of these lives lies, first, in their usefulness for the clergy's exposition of the boundary between the clergy (allied with saints) and the laity; second, with the appeal of representations of sexual violence; and third, with the ability of these lives to reiterate the central belief of Christianity that even the weakest of those embodied in the flesh, women, can triumph over the desires of the body. Central to the argument and methodology of the book as a whole is Winstead's thesis that, like the Eucharist (a symbol that has received so much important and provocative critical attention recently in work by critics such as Caroline Bynum, Miri Rubin, and Sarah Beckwith), these saints' lives act as particularly flexible cultural symbols, able to encompass both the tenets and the contradictions of a given period's cultural, economic, political and social concerns.

Winstead traces the development of representations of saints from the devotional figures of the earlier periods to the defiant, disorderly heroines of the fourteenth century and finally to the quelling of that disorderliness in the fifteenth-century's creation of decorous female heroines. The lives that appear in England from 1100 to 1250, she argues, are primarily monastic productions intended for male and female readers alike and ultimately serve monastic needs as models of faith and devotion, emphasizing the triumph of those who defy secular pressures to leave the religious life. After 1250, when English culture begins to feel the effects of the 1215 Fourth Lateran Council, these saints' lives, to Winstead, begin to contend with the clergy's anxiety about an educated lay public. Winstead turns her attention to the North and South East Legendaries and the female saints' lives written by Geoffrey Chaucer and Matthew Paris. The North East Legendary, a collection intended for the private lay reader, she persuasively shows, especially reflects lay concerns over estates, property and possessions. In their portrayal of saints even more egregiously active in their defiance of the state than in the earlier lives yet miraculously untouched by suffering, these later female saints become "emblems of ecclesiastical prerogative." As such, she concludes, these women embody clerical rather than feminine power, a claim at once provocative and contestable. It is not always entirely clear in Winstead's argument, especially in her discussion of the lay hagiographies of Chaucer and Paris, to whom the defiance of the female saint is directed, and whose needs are served in the representation of such defiance. Winstead argues that these late hagiographers, whether clerical or lay, also express their ambivalence toward the subversive potential of such representations of female defiance. This ambivalence springs, Winstead argues, from the rapid social changes in the position of women in this period. Winstead here makes particularly effective use of the recent proliferation of historical studies of medieval English women in work by historians such as Judith Bennett, Ruth Karras, and P. J. P. Goldberg.

By the fifteenth century, as concerns for Lollardy grew, the hagiographers of virgin martyrs writing from 1400 to 1450, serving the needs of a growing middle-class readership aspiring to the mores of those of higher status, Winstead shows, shift their representations of women as defiant, rebellious, and physically aggressive to images of women as decorous gentlewomen, mirrors of courtesy, refinement, and eloquence. She illustrates this new focus on saints as models of decorum in the saints' lives of two East Anglian hagiographers, John Lydgate and Osbert Bokenham. Particularly striking is Winstead's demonstration of Lydgate's transformation of the pugnacious, physically and verbally aggressive St. Margaret into a meek, passive innocent. One question raised by these lives' return to earlier devotional models of women is the different function self-abnegation serves for the religious or the lay reader. Winstead concludes her study with a chapter on "the politics of reading" in which she compares two lives of St. Katherine: one an anonymous early-fifteenth-century life written at the height of Henry V's triumphs that celebrates contemplation as an aspect of successful politics; and the other, John Capgrave's, written c. 1445 during the less-optimistic age of Henry VI, in which ambivalence about female lay literacy particularly comes to the fore.

Given Winstead's primary focus on the intersection of saints' lives with the concerns and interests of secular lay audiences, her argument is necessarily strongest in her consideration of later texts where information about date, authorship, provenance, and historical context is much more readily available. Her demonstration of the political anxieties about contemplative learning in Capgrave's Life of St. Katherine as opposed to the valorization of learning that appears in the version written under the reign of Henry V is wholly convincing. Her discussion of early Middle English lives, however, does not go much further than the analyses of earlier critics, although her discussion is an admirable summary of those views. Fragmentary evidence admittedly makes it more difficult to assess the valence of these lives as either critiques of or tools of the Church; nonetheless, Winstead characterizes these lives as generally uniform in their monastic devotional emphases. Perhaps her interest in the secular rather than the religious led her to overlook the tensions and contradictions present in the religious system itself even before these conflicts were manifested in the form of Lollardy. One might have wished to hear more of Winstead's voice in this section and less repetition (sometimes not fully acknowledged as such) of arguments already made by previous critics. It would also have been useful if she had engaged more directly with the vexing topic of the role of sexual violence directed toward women who speak out in these early works. Other than Timea Szell, no critic has yet to fully address this topic. Winstead makes occasional observations throughout her study about the role of sexual violence in the saints' lives, but her general point that the violence simply enhances a saint's triumph over the vicissitudes of the flesh does not seem sufficient. Similarly, Winstead brings up the interesting issue, first raised by Jocelyn Wogan-Browne, of the saints' lives' representation of female resistance to secular marriage as topically responsive to debates about marriage. Given Winstead's later concerns with topical issues, one would have expected her to develop her argument more here. Nonetheless, Winstead's thorough and consistently measured analysis of a large body of primary and secondary material makes this chapter and, indeed, the book as a whole an indispensable resource for future scholars interested in this fertile subject.

ELIZABETH ROBERTSON
University of Colorado at Boulder

BOOKS RECEIVED

Allmand, Christopher, ed. *The New Cambridge Medieval History, Vol. 7. c. 1415–1500.* Cambridge: Cambridge University Press, 1998. Pp. xxi, 1048. $95.00.

Altmann, Barbara K. *The Love Debate Poems of Christine de Pizan.* Gainesville: University Press of Florida, 1998. Pp. 294. $49.95.

Bisson, Lillian M. *Chaucer and the Late Medieval World.* New York: St. Martin's Press, 1998. Pp. x, 294. $45.00.

Brothers, Thomas. *Chromatic Beauty in the Late Medieval Chanson: An Interpretation of Manuscript Accidentals.* Cambridge: Cambridge University Press, 1997. Pp. xiii, 226. $64.00.

Clopper, Lawrence M. *"Songes of Rechelesnesse": Langland and the Fransiscans.* Ann Arbor: University of Michigan Press, 1998. Pp. ix, 368. $52.50.

Cowan, Alexander. *Urban Europe, 1500 1700.* London: Arnold, 1998. Pp. xi, 229. $70.00 cloth, $19.95 paper.

Cox, Catherine S. *Gender and Language in Chaucer.* Gainesville: University Press of Florida, 1997. Pp. x, 196. $49.95.

Davenport, W. A. *Chaucer and His English Contemporaries.* New York: St. Martin's Press, 1998. Pp. x. 245. $55.00 cloth, $19.95 paper.

Daniell, Christopher. *Death and Burial in Medieval England 1066–1550.* London and New York: Routledge, 1997. Pp. ix, 242. $24.99 paper.

Dyas, Dee. *Images of Faith in English Literature: An Introduction.* London and New York: Longman, 1997. Pp. x, 332. $59.93 cloth, $23.44 paper.

Echard, Siân. *Arthurian Narrative in the Latin Tradition.* Cambridge: Cambridge University Press, 1998. Pp. ix. 256. $69.95.

Edwards, Robert R., ed. *John Lydgate, Troy Book: Selections.* Kalamazoo: Medieval Institute Publications at Western Michigan University, 1998. Pp. ix, 430. $20.00 paper.

Ellis, Steve. *Geoffrey Chaucer.* Plymouth: Northcote House, 1996. Pp. 80. $19.95 paper.

Fein, Susanna Greer, ed. *Moral Love Songs and Laments.* Kalamazoo: Medieval Institute Publications at Western Michigan University, 1998. Pp. 400. $20.00 paper.

Hebron, Malcolm. *The Medieval Siege: Theme and Image in Middle English Romance.* New York: Oxford University Press, 1997. Pp. xi, 191. $58.00.

Kindrick, Robert L., ed. *The Poems of Robert Henryson.* Kalamazoo: Medieval Institute Publications at Western Michigan University, 1997. Pp. 313. N.p.

Mills, David. *Recycling the Cycle: The City of Chester and Its Whitsun Plays.* Toronto: University of Toronto Press, 1998. Pp. x, 281. $55.00.

Newman, Barbara. *Sister of Wisdom: St. Hildegard's Theology of the Feminine.* 1987. Reprint, with new preface, bibliography, and discography. Berkeley and Los Angeles: University of California Press, 1998. Pp. xxii, 305. $14.95 paper.

———, ed. *Voice of the Living Light: Hildegard of Bingen and Her World.* Berkeley: University of California Press, 1998. Pp. ix, 278. $48.00 cloth, $19.95 paper.

Norri, Juhani. *Names of Body Parts in English 1400–1550.* Saarijärvi: Academia Scientiarum Fennica, 1998. Pp. 470. N.p.

O'Keefe, Katherine O'Brien, ed. *Reading Old English Texts.* Cambridge:

Cambridge University Press, 1997. Pp. 231. $59.95 cloth, $18.95 paper.

Phillips, Helen, and Nick Havely, eds. *Chaucer's Dream Poetry*. London and New York: Longman 1997. Pp. 438. $28.95 paper.

Roberts, Anna, ed. *Violence against Women in Medieval Texts*. Gainesville: University Press of Florida, 1998. Pp. 254. $49.95.

Rosenberg, Samuel N., Margaret Switten, and Gérard Le Vot, eds. *Songs of the Troubadours and Trouvères: An Anthology of Poems and Melodies*. New York and London: Garland, 1998. Pp. 378. $85.00.

Scase, Wendy, Rita Copeland, and David Lawton, eds. *New Medieval Literatures* vol. 1. Clarendon Press: Oxford, 1997. Pp. vi, 278. $70.00.

Solomon, Michael. *The Literature of Misogyny in Medieval Spain: The "Arcipreste de Talavera" and the "Spill."* Cambridge: Cambridge University Press, 1997. Pp. 221. $54.95.

Stone, Gregory. *The Ethics of Nature in the Middle Ages: On Boccaccio's Poetaphysics*. New York: St. Martin's Press, 1998. Pp. 250. $45.00.

Talbot, C. II., ed. and trans. *The Life of Christina of Markyate: A Twelfth-Century Recluse*. Oxford: Oxford University Press, 1959. Reprint. Toronto and Buffalo: University of Toronto Press, in association with the Medieval Academy of America, 1998. Pp. ix, 204. $14.95 paper.

Tomasch, Sylvia, and Sealy Gilles, eds. *Text and Territory: Geographical Imagination in the European Middle Ages*. Philadelphia: University of Pennsylvania Press, 1998. Pp. 330. $45.00 cloth, $19.95 paper.

Woodhouse, John, ed. *Dante and Governance*. Oxford: Clarendon Press, 1997. Pp. 179. $55.00.

An Annotated Chaucer Bibliography
1997

Compiled and edited by Mark Allen and Bege K. Bowers

Regular contributors:

Dansby Evans, *Atlanta, Georgia*
Bruce W. Hozeski, *Ball State University* (Indiana)
George Nicholas, *Benedictine College* (Kansas)
Martha S. Waller, *Butler University* (Indiana)
Marilyn Sutton, *California State University at Dominguez Hills*
Larry L. Bronson, *Central Michigan University*
Glending Olson, *Cleveland State University* (Ohio)
Jesús Luis Serrano Reyes (*Córdoba*)
Winthrop Wetherbee, *Cornell University* (New York)
Elizabeth Dobbs, *Grinnell College* (Iowa)
Brian A. Shaw, *London, Ontario*
Masatoshi Kawasaki, *Komazawa University* (Tokyo, Japan)
William Schipper, *Memorial University* (Newfoundland, Canada)
Daniel J. Pinti, *New Mexico State University*
Erik Kooper, *Rijksuniversiteit te Utrecht*
Amy Goodwin, *Randolph-Macon College* (Virginia)
Cindy L. Vitto, *Rowan College of New Jersey*
Richard H. Osberg, *Santa Clara University* (California)
Margaret Connolly, *University College, Cork* (Ireland)
Juliette Dor, *Université de Liège* (Belgium)
Mary Flowers Braswell and Elaine Whitaker, *University of Alabama at Birmingham*
Denise Stodola, *University of Missouri–Columbia*
Cynthia Gravlee, *University of Montevallo* (Alabama)
Gregory M. Sadlek, *University of Nebraska at Omaha*
Cynthia Ho, *University of North Carolina, Asheville*
Richard J. Utz, *Universität Tübingen* (Tübingen, Germany)

Thomas Hahn, *University of Rochester* (New York)
Rebecca Beal, *University of Scranton* (Pennsylvania)
Valerie Allen, *University of South Florida*
Stanley R. Hauer, *University of Southern Mississippi*
Mark Allen, Gail Jones, and Connie Sabo-Risley, *University of Texas at San Antonio*
Andrew Lynch, *University of Western Australia*
Joyce T. Lionarons, *Ursinus College* (Pennsylvania)
John M. Crafton, *West Georgia College*
Robert Correale, *Wright State University* (Ohio)
Bege K. Bowers, *Youngstown State University* (Ohio)

Ad hoc contributions were made by the following: Eileen Krueger (*University of Texas at San Antonio*); Paule Mertens-Fonck (*Liège, Belgium*); Juliet Sloger (*University of Rochester*); Paul R. Thomas (*Brigham Young University*); and Arturo Vasquez II (*University of Texas at San Antonio*).

The bibliographers acknowledge with gratitude the MLA typesimulation provided by the Center for Bibliographical Services of the Modern Language Association; postage from the University of Texas at San Antonio Division of English, Classics, and Philosophy; and assistance from the library staff, especially Susan McCray, at the University of Texas at San Antonio.

This bibliography continues the bibliographies published since 1975 in previous volumes of *Studies in the Age of Chaucer*. Bibliographic information up to 1975 can be found in Eleanor P. Hammond, *Chaucer: A Bibliographic Manual* (1908; reprint, New York: Peter Smith, 1933); D. D. Griffith, *Bibliography of Chaucer, 1908–53* (Seattle: University of Washington Press, 1955); William R. Crawford, *Bibliography of Chaucer, 1954–63* (Seattle: University of Washington Press, 1967); and Lorrayne Y. Baird, *Bibliography of Chaucer, 1964–73* (Boston: G. K. Hall, 1977). See also Lorrayne Y. Baird-Lange and Hildegard Schnuttgen, *Bibliography of Chaucer, 1974–1985* (Hamden, Conn.: Shoe String Press, 1988).

Additions and corrections to this bibliography should be sent to Mark Allen, Bibliographic Division, New Chaucer Society, Division of English, Classics, Philosophy, and Communication, University of Texas at San Antonio 78249–0643 (Fax: 210–458–5366; E-mail: MALLEN@ LONESTAR.JPL.UTSA.EDU). An electronic version of this bibliography (1975–97) is available via the New Chaucer Society Web page (via http://ncs.rutgers.edu) or via TELNET connection (UTSAIBM.UTSA.

EDU; type "library" at the applications prompt, "cho chau" at the request for a database, and "stop" to exit the database). Authors are urged to send annotations for articles, reviews, and books that have been or might be overlooked.

Classifications

Abbreviations of Chaucer's Works

ABC	An ABC
Adam	Adam Scriveyn
Anel	Anelida and Arcite
Astr	A Treatise on the Astrolabe
Bal Compl	A Balade of Complaint
BD	The Book of the Duchess
Bo	Boece
Buk	The Envoy to Bukton
CkT, CkP, Rv–CkL	The Cook's Tale, The Cook's Prologue, Reeve–Cook Link
ClT, ClP, Cl–MerL	The Clerk's Tale, The Clerk's Prologue, Clerk–Merchant Link
Compl d'Am	Complaynt d'Amours
CT	The Canterbury Tales
CYT, CYP	The Canon's Yeoman's Tale, The Canon's Yeoman's Prologue
Equat	The Equatorie of the Planetis
For	Fortune
Form Age	The Former Age
FranT, FranP	The Franklin's Tale, The Franklin's Prologue
FrT, FrP, Fr–SumL	The Friar's Tale, The Friar's Prologue, Friar–Summoner Link
Gent	Gentilesse
GP	The General Prologue
HF	The House of Fame
KnT, Kn–MilL	The Knight's Tale, Knight–Miller Link
Lady	A Complaint to His Lady
LGW, LGWP	The Legend of Good Women, The Legend of Good Women Prologue
ManT, ManP	The Manciple's Tale, The Manciple's Prologue
Mars	The Complaint of Mars
Mel, Mel–MkL	The Tale of Melibee, Melibee–Monk Link
MercB	Merciles Beaute

MerT, MerE–SqH	*The Merchant's Tale, Merchant Endlink–Squire Headlink*
MilT, MilP, Mil–RvL	*The Miller's Tale, The Miller's Prologue, Miller–Reeve Link*
MkT, MkP, Mk–NPL	*The Monk's Tale, The Monk's Prologue, Monk–Nun's Priest Link*
MLT, MLH, MLP, MLE	*The Man of Law's Tale, Man of Law Headlink, The Man of Law's Prologue, Man of Law Endlink*
NPT, NPP, NPE	*The Nun's Priest's Tale, The Nun's Priest's Prologue, Nun's Priest's Endlink*
PardT, PardP	*The Pardoner's Tale, The Pardoner's Prologue*
ParsT, ParsP	*The Parson's Tale, The Parson's Prologue*
PF	*The Parliament of Fowls*
PhyT, Phy–PardL	*The Physician's Tale, Physician–Pardoner Link*
Pity	*The Complaint unto Pity*
Prov	*Proverbs*
PrT, PrP, Pr–ThL	*The Prioress's Tale, The Prioress's Prologue, Prioress–Thopas Link*
Purse	*The Complaint of Chaucer to His Purse*
Ret	*Chaucer's Retraction {Retractation}*
Rom	*The Romaunt of the Rose*
Ros	*To Rosemounde*
RvT, RvP	*The Reeve's Tale, The Reeve's Prologue*
Scog	*The Envoy to Scogan*
ShT, Sh–PrL	*The Shipman's Tale, Shipman–Prioress Link*
SNT, SNP, SN–CYL	*The Second Nun's Tale, The Second Nun's Prologue, Second Nun–Canon's Yeoman Link*
SqT, SqH, Sq–FranL	*The Squire's Tale, Squire Headlink, Squire–Franklin Link*
Sted	*Lak of Stedfastnesse*
SumT, SumP	*The Summoner's Tale, The Summoner's Prologue*
TC	*Troilus and Criseyde*

Th, Th–MelL	*The Tale of Sir Thopas, Sir Thopas–Melibee Link*
Truth	*Truth*
Ven	*The Complaint of Venus*
WBT, WBP, WB–FrL	*The Wife of Bath's Tale, The Wife of Bath's Prologue, Wife of Bath–Friar Link*
Wom Nob	*Womanly Noblesse*
Wom Unc	*Against Women Unconstant*

Periodical Abbreviations

Æstel	*Æstel* (Seattle, Wash.)
Anglia	*Anglia: Zeitschrift für Englische Philologie*
Anglistik	*Anglistik: Mitteilungen des Verbandes deutscher Anglisten*
Archiv	*Archiv für das Studium der Neueren Sprachen und Literaturen*
BWVACET	*Bulletin of the West Virginia Association of College English Teachers*
Chaucer Yearbook	*Chaucer Yearbook: A Journal of Late Medieval Studies*
ChauR	*Chaucer Review*
CL	*Comparative Literature* (Eugene, Ore.)
CLAJ	*College Language Association Journal*
CLS	*Comparative Literature Studies*
ComH	*Computers and the Humanities*
DAI	*Dissertation Abstracts International*
Disputatio	*Disputatio: An International Transdisciplinary Journal of the Late Middle Ages*
ÉA	*Études Anglaises: Grand-Bretagne, États-Unis*
EHR	*English Historical Review*
ELH	*ELH*
ELN	*English Language Notes*
EMS	*English Manuscript Studies, 1100–1700*
Envoi	*Envoi: A Review Journal of Medieval Literature*
ES	*English Studies*
ESC	*English Studies in Canada*
Exemplaria	*Exemplaria: A Journal of Theory in Medieval and Renaissance Studies*
Expl	*Explicator*
FCS	*Fifteenth-Century Studies*
Florilegium	*Florilegium: Carleton University Papers on Late Antiquity and the Middle Ages*
FMLS	*Forum for Modern Language Studies*
JEGP	*Journal of English and Germanic Philology*
JFR	*Journal of Folklore Research* (Bloomington, Ind.)
JMEMS	*Journal of Medieval and Early Modern Studies*

L&LC	*Literary and Linguistic Computing: Journal of the Association for Literary and Linguistic Computing*
Library	*The Library: The Transactions of the Bibliographical Society*
MÆ	*Medium Ævum*
Mediaevistik	*Mediaevistik: Internationale Zeitschrift für Interdisziplinäire Mittelalterforschung*
MedPers	*Medieval Perspectives*
MFN	*Medieval Feminist Newsletter*
MLR	*The Modern Language Review*
MP	*Modern Philology: A Journal Devoted to Research in Medieval and Modern Literature*
N&Q	*Notes and Queries*
Neophil	*Neophilologus* (Dordrecht, Netherlands)
NLH	*New Literary History: A Journal of Theory and Interpretation*
NM	*Neuphilologische Mitteilungen: Bulletin of the Modern Language Society*
OT	*Oral Tradition*
PBA	*Proceedings of the British Academy*
PMLA	*Publications of the Modern Language Association of America*
ProverbiumY	*Proverbium: Yearbook of International Proverb Scholarship* (Burlington, Vt.)
R&L	*Religion and Literature* (Notre Dame, Ind.)
Renascence	*Renascence: Essays on Value in Literature*
RES	*Review of English Studies*
RMR	*Rocky Mountain Review of Language and Literature*
SAC	*Studies in the Age of Chaucer*
SAP	*Studia Anglica Posnaniensia: An International Review of English*
SELIM	*SELIM: Journal of the Spanish Society for Medieval English Language and Literature*
SIcon	*Studies in Iconography*
SiM	*Studies in Medievalism*
SMART	*Studies in Medieval and Renaissance Teaching*
Soundings	*Soundings: An Interdisciplinary Journal*
SP	*Studies in Philology*
Speculum	*Speculum: A Journal of Medieval Studies*
SSEng	*Sydney Studies in English*
Style	*Style* (DeKalb, Ill.)

Text   *Text: Transactions of the Society for Textual Scholarship*
TLS   *Times Literary Supplement* (London, England)
YLS   *The Yearbook of Langland Studies*

Bibliographical Citations and Annotations

Bibliographies, Reports, and Reference

1. Allen, Mark, and Bege K. Bowers. "An Annotated Chaucer Bibliography, 1995." *SAC* 19 (1997): 353–447. Continuation of *SAC* annual annotated bibliography (since 1975); based on 1995 *MLA Bibliography* listings, contributions from an international bibliographic team, and independent research. A total of 397 items, including reviews.

2. Boswell, Jackson Campbell, and Sylvia Wallace Holton. "References to Chaucer's Literary Reputation." *ChauR* 31 (1997): 291–316. Assembles references to Chaucer's character and literary reputation recorded in English books 1475–1640, the dates of the *Short Title Catalogue.* Entries include author, title, publisher, and *STC* and University Microfilm (UMD) numbers and establish the context for fifty citings.

3. Burton, T. L., and Rosemary Greentree, eds., with annotations by David Biggs, Rosemary Greentree, Hugh McGivern, David Matthews, Greg Murrie, and Dallas Simpson. *Chaucer's* Miller's, Reeve's, *and* Cook's Tales. The Chaucer Bibliographies, no. 5. Toronto, Buffalo, and London: University of Toronto Press, 1997. xxxvi, 287 pp. A complete annotated bibliography of scholarly and critical treatments of *MilT, RvT,* and *CkT* from 1900 through 1992, subdivided into the following categories: editions, translations, and modernizations (52 items); sources and analogues (36 items); linguistic and lexicographical items (105 items); the tellers as characters (62 items); treatments of the three *Tales* together (200 items); and each of the individual *Tales* (*MilT*—195 items, *RvT*—73 items, *CkT*—30 items). The entries in each category are arranged by date of publication. Includes an index and an introduction that summarizes trends in criticism decade by decade.

4. Seymour, M. C. *A Catalogue of Chaucer Manuscripts: Volume II,* The Canterbury Tales. Aldershot, Hants: Scolar Press, 1997. x, 270 pp. Describes fifty-six manuscripts of *CT,* providing detailed contents and collations, plus briefer comments on binding, decoration, glosses, rubrics, scribes, and provenance. Follows Manly and Rickert's classifications of the manuscripts and records the order of the tales in the manuscripts as they relate to these classifications. Presents the descriptions alphabetically by city of location and includes descriptions of nine "Smaller Frag-

ments," a list of "Other Recorded Manuscripts" (now lost), an index of "Former Owners and Inscribed Names," and addenda and corrigenda for Seymour's *Volume I* (non-*CT* manuscripts; *SAC* 19 [1997], no. 7). The twenty-eight-page introduction summarizes classification issues, comments on the relative chronology and affiliations of the seven earliest manuscripts, and considers questions of Chaucer's revisions and later interpolations.

Recordings and Films

5.   *The Miller's Tale.* NCS Readings, no. 11. Provo, Utah: Chaucer Studio, 1996. Audiocassette; 85 min. Dir. and ed. Paul R. Thomas. Recorded at radio station KRCW, Santa Monica College, during the Tenth International Congress of the New Chaucer Society. Side one: dramatized reading of *MilT* from the Hengwrt manuscript; side two: solo reading from Ellesmere. Readers include Alan T. Gaylord, Paul R. Thomas, William A. Stephany, Richard Firth Green, Thomas L. Burton, Christine Herold, Michael A. Calabrese, D. Thomas Hanks Jr., Nicholas R. Havely, Winthrop Wetherbee, and Peter G. Beidler (side one); Alan T. Gaylord (side two).

6.   *The Reeve's Tale.* NCS Readings, no. 12. Provo, Utah: Chaucer Studio, 1996. Audiocassette; 30 min. Dir. Thomas L. Burton; ed. Paul R. Thomas. Recorded at radio station KRCW, Santa Monica College, during the Tenth International Congress of the New Chaucer Society. Readers include Alan T. Gaylord, Richard Firth Green, Nicholas R. Havely, William A. Stephany, Paul R. Thomas, Peter G. Beidler, Mary Hamel, and Susan Yager.

7.   Schwartz, Barth David. *Pasolini Requiem.* New York: Pantheon, 1992. x, 785 pp. Includes an account of the making and reception of Pier Paolo Pasolini's films *The Decameron* (1971) and *Canterbury Tales* (1972). In the latter, Pasolini plays Chaucer and includes seven *Tales: MerT, FrT, CkT, MilT, WBP, RvT,* and *SumT.*

8.   *The Shipman's Tale.* NCS Readings, no. 13. Provo, Utah: Chaucer Studio, 1996. Audiocassette; 27 min. Recorded at radio station KRCW, Santa Monica College, during the Tenth International Congress of the New Chaucer Society. Readers include Nicholas R. Havely, Mary Hamel, Winthrop Wetherbee, and Peter G. Beidler.

See also no. 53.

Chaucer's Life

See nos. 54, 102, 142, 166, 254, 272, 278.

Facsimiles, Editions, and Translations

9. Boffey, Julia, and A. S. G. Edwards, introd., with an appendix by B. C. Barker-Benfield. *The Works of Geoffrey Chaucer and the* Kingis Quair: *A Facsimile of Bodleian Library, Oxford, MS Arch. Selden. B. 24.* Cambridge: D. S. Brewer, 1997. viii, 61 pp., 231 folio leaves. Includes *TC, Truth, Mars, Ven, PF, LGW,* several pieces of Chaucerian apocrypha, and works by Lydgate, Hoccleve, James I, and anonymous authors (twenty-five works total). Eight color plates complement the sepia-tone facsimile, photographed in 1994 during a conservation effort. The introduction and appendix include a complete codicological description of the manuscript (ca. 1489), its provenance, binding, restorations, and so forth.

10. Carlson, David R. "Woodcut Illustrations of the *Canterbury Tales,* 1483–1602." *Library,* ser. 6, 19 (1997): 25–67. Traces the history of two related series of woodcuts. The first, cut for Caxton's 1483 edition, apparently derives from miniatures in the manuscript now known as the Oxford Fragments (Ox^1 and Ox^2). The second series was copied from Caxton for Pynson's 1492 edition. Both series were used in later editions. Appendices describe the editions and provide tables indicating placements of individual woodcuts.

11. Dane, Joseph A. *Who Is Buried in Chaucer's Tomb? Studies in the Reception of Chaucer's Book.* East Lansing: Michigan State University, 1998. x, 309 pp. Eleven studies on the publishing history of Chaucer's works attempt to correct misinformation and misconceptions about the nature of book production, extant editions and issues of Chaucer's works, and the reliability of bibliographical descriptions. Discussion ranges from the inscription on Chaucer's tomb (a reprint of *SAC* 18 [1996], no. 45) to modern arguments among Chaucerians about the relations between criticism and scholarship. Recurring topics include canon formation and apocrypha, the influence of technology on print and reception, bibliographical evidence, the eccentricities of key Chaucerians, the relations between textuality and individual books, and the historical separation of professional "Chaucerianism" from the popular reception of Chaucer.

12. Donaghey, Brian. "William Thynne's Collected Edition of Chaucer: Some Bibliographical Considerations." In John Scattergood and Julia Boffey, eds. *Texts and Their Contexts: Papers from the Early Book Society* (*SAC* 21 [1999], no. 143), pp. 150–64. Considers Thynne's 1532 collected edition of Chaucer's work, assessing the planning of the work, its physical makeup, and the technical processes of producing it. Printer Thomas Godfray took an active role in bringing the work into existence.

13. Haas, Renate. "The Old Wives' Tale and Dryden." In Marie-Françoise Alamichel and Derek Brewer, eds. *The Middle Ages After the Middle Ages in the English-Speaking World* (*SAC* 21 [1999], no. 78), pp. 91–101. Recognizing parallels between *WBT* and contemporary female practice, Dryden intensified the elements of faery and magic in his version of the *Tale*. In addition, he greatly reduced the lively presence of the Wife, producing a view of women and their emancipatory endeavors that is substantially more negative than Chaucer's.

14. Keyburn, Karen. "The Variorum on Chaucer's 'Second Nun's Tale.'" *DAI* 58 (1997): 861A. *SNT* as prepared for the *Variorum Chaucer,* based on the Hengwrt and Ellesmere manuscripts, with explanatory notes and critical commentary to 1994.

15. Phillips, Helen, and Nick Havely, eds. *Chaucer's Dream Poetry.* London and New York: Longman, 1997. xiv, 438 pp. Edits *BD, HF, PF,* and portions of *LGW* (G-version Prologue and Dido), providing an introduction, bottom-of-the-page glosses and commentary, selected source material, and textual notes for each poem, plus a bibliography, selective glossary, and comprehensive list of names for the entire volume. The general introduction comments on classical and medieval dream theories, the literary tradition of the dream vision, relations with the *Roman de la Rose,* and Chaucer's narrative techniques.

16. Robinson, Peter M. W. "Is There a Text in These Variants?" In Richard J. Finneran, ed. *The Literary Text in the Digital Age.* Ann Arbor: University of Michigan Press, 1996, pp. 99–115. Argues that electronic editions are both archival and interpretive, enabling users "to find the one text they seek" and recording data that reflect reception history and provide linguistic information. Cites examples from the electronic *WBP* (*SAC* 20 [1998], no. 11) to demonstrate how texts change as we view them in different ways and from different perspectives.

17. Wheatley, Edward. [Forum.] *PMLA* 112 (1997): 271–72. The treatment of Chaucer (often in translation) in cultural studies programs

tends to divest his verse of its poetic qualities as, for example, in the tournament in *KnT.*

See also nos. 43, 60, 267, 309.

Manuscripts and Textual Studies

18.   Beadle, Richard. "Geoffrey Spirleng (c. 1426–c. 1494): A Scribe of the *Canterbury Tales* in His Time." In P. R. Robinson and Rivkah Zim, eds. *Of the Making of Books: Medieval Manuscripts, Their Scribes and Readers. Essays Presented to M. B. Parkes* (*SAC* 21 [1999], no. 140), pp. 116–46. Describes Glasgow, University Library, Hunterian MS U.I.1 (Gl) and its relation to its exemplar—Cambridge University Library Mm.2.5 (Mm). Spirleng was the sole scribe for the portion of Gl that depends on Mm, and preliminary analysis of variations between the two manuscripts details his habits. Assesses *KnT* 1785–1805 and *PrT* 488–508.

19.   ———, and A. J. Piper, eds. *New Science out of Old Books: Studies in Manuscripts and Early Printed Books in Honour of A. I. Doyle.* Aldershot, Hants: Scolar Press, 1995. xii, 455 pp. Fifteen essays by various authors on topics in book production from the twelfth to the seventeenth centuries, including discussion of Gower manuscripts (M. B. Parkes), a Wyclif manuscript (Anne Hudson), Wynkyn de Worde (Lotte Hellinga), codicological terminology (Kathleen L. Scott), book division (George R. Keiser), and other issues related to Chaucer study. None of the essays focuses primarily on Chaucer or Chaucerian manuscripts, although several mention Chaucerian material. Includes a bibliography of Doyle's publications. See also no. 315.

20.   Blake, Norman F. "The Project's Lineation System." In Norman F. Blake and Peter Robinson, eds. *The* Canterbury Tales *Project Occasional Papers, Volume II* (*SAC* 21 [1999], no. 22), pp. 5–14. Describes a system of lineation for consistent citation of all materials relating to the textual history of *CT,* not only lines generally accepted as genuine but also all spurious and contested lines, including spurious tales. Explains the need for and principles of such lineation, providing a chart that clarifies relations with traditional systems of lineation and identifies base manuscripts for lines not found in Hengwrt.

21.   ———. "Language and Style in Additions to *The Canterbury*

Tales." In Jacek Fisiak, ed. *Studies in Middle English Linguistics* (*SAC* 21 [1999], no. 70), pp. 59–78. Fifteenth-century scribal additions and changes to manuscripts of *CT* indicate the "linguistic and stylistic prejudices and attitudes" of scribes and their audiences. Treats Hengwrt as a base text and explores how changes in Ellesmere, British Library Harley 7334, Bodley 686, and Cambridge University Library Dd.4.24 reflect a tendency to "correct" Chaucer's meter and increase his colloquialisms, not to make his diction more ornate.

22. ———, and Peter Robinson, eds. *The* Canterbury Tales *Project Occasional Papers, Volume II.* Office for Humanities Communications Publications, no. 9. London: King's College, Office for Humanities Communications, 1997. viii, 184 pp. Nine essays by various authors and a preface by the editors, all of which pertain to textual issues of *CT* or to the principles and practices of the *Canterbury Tales* Project. See nos. 20, 28, 29, 31, 32, 34, 37, 205, and 208.

23. Edwards, A. S. G. "John Shirley and the Emulation of Court Culture." In Evelyn Mullally and John Thompson, eds. *The Court and Cultural Discourse: Selected Papers from the Eighth Triennial Congress of the International Courtly Literature Society, The Queen's University of Belfast, 26 July–1 August 1995* (*SAC* 21 [1999], no. 131), pp. 309–17. John Shirley lived on the "fringes of the aristocracy," and aspects of the manuscripts he produced suggest that he desired to emulate courtliness in his book production.

24. Fredell, Joel. "Paraphs and Patterns: Two Early Forms of the *Canterbury Tales.*" *Early Book Society Newsletter* 3:2 (1998): [7–12]. Categorizes patterns of paragraphing in the "landmark" manuscripts of *CT* as "sparse" or "dense," arguing that the patterns emphasize the "florilegium qualities" of *CT* and focusing on uses of paraphs in *SqT.*

25. Hardman, Phillipa. "Interpreting the Incomplete Scheme of Illustration in Cambridge, Corpus Christi College MS 61." *EMS* 6 (1996): 52–69. Discusses the blanks left for illustration in Corpus Christi College MS 61, suggesting a possible strategy for prospective illustrations, including initials: the illustrations would have emphasized choice as an aspect of narrative structure. The illustrations might not have been completed for a number of reasons, or there might not have been a program for completion, but the section on *TC* seems to indicate one.

26. Hodapp, William F. "The Visual Presentation of Chaucer's *Troilus and Criseyde* in Three Fifteenth-Century Manuscripts." *Manuscripta* 38 (1994): 237–52. Of the sixteen extant manuscripts of *TC,* the organ-

ization of the Morgan, Corpus Christi, and St. John's shows the greatest concern for both readers and listeners of the fifteenth century.

27. Horobin, Simon. "Additional 35286 and the Order of the *Canterbury Tales.*" *ChauR* 31 (1997): 272–78. In determining Chaucer's plan for *CT,* too much attention has been placed on the Ellesmere and Hengwrt manuscripts at the expense of the other eighty-one manuscripts, where the order of the tales may differ. In Ad³ (British Library MS Additional 35286), *CkP* and *CkT* fall between *ManT* and *CYP; SNT,* between *SumT* and *ClP.* Such variations provide for alternate readings of various groups of tales.

28. ———. "Editorial Assumptions and the Manuscripts of *The Canterbury Tales.*" In Norman F. Blake and Peter Robinson, eds. *The* Canterbury Tales *Project Occasional Papers, Volume II (SAC* 21 [1999], no. 22), pp. 15–21. Demonstrates the dangers of over-reliance on Hengwrt, Ellesmere, or any limited number of privileged manuscripts in establishing the text of *CT,* arguing for attention to all available material. Uses Ad³ (British Library MS Additional 35286) to show (1) how its unique ordering of tales may preserve an early stage in Chaucer's composition process and (2) how two passages that Ad³ shares only with Ellesmere (*FranT* 1455–56, 1493–98) may preserve an authorial revision.

29. Mosser, Daniel W. "The Language, Hands, and Interaction of the Two Scribes of Egerton 2726 Chaucer Manuscript (En¹)." In Norman F. Blake and Peter Robinson, eds. *The* Canterbury Tales *Project Occasional Papers, Volume II (SAC* 21 [1999], no. 22), pp. 41–53. Examines characteristic features of the two similar scribal hands of *CT* manuscript En¹, correcting errors and emphases in Manly and Rickert's analysis (1940). The scribes appear initially to have divided their labors before Scribe 2 completed and corrected Scribe 1's portion as well as his own. The dialect is from near Colchester. The date is "the mid-to-late second quarter of the fifteenth century."

30. Partridge, Stephen. "A Newly Identified Manuscript by the Scribe of the New College *Canterbury Tales.*" *EMS* 6 (1996): 229–36. Handwriting, materials, decoration, and language indicate that the scribe of Oxford New College MS 314 also copied Bodleian Library MS Dugdale 45 (Hoccleve's *Regement of Princes*). Though not first-rate, MS 314 was executed by a paid scribe.

31. Pidd, Michael, and Estelle Stubbs. "From Medieval Manuscript to Electronic Text: A Transcriber's Tale." In Norman F. Blake and Peter Robinson, eds. *The* Canterbury Tales *Project Occasional Papers, Volume II*

(*SAC* 21 [1999], no. 22), pp. 55–59. Describes how the difficulties and decisions involved in transcribing manuscripts for the *Canterbury Tales* Project parallel fifteenth-century scribal practice.

32. Pidd, Michael, Estelle Stubbs, and Clare E. Thomson. "The Hengwrt *Canterbury Tales:* Inadmissible Evidence?" In Norman F. Blake and Peter Robinson, eds. *The* Canterbury Tales *Project Occasional Papers, Volume II* (*SAC* 21 [1999], no. 22), pp. 61–68. Describes how the marginal note "Stokes" in the Hengwrt manuscript of *CT* may have been erased in a conservation project in 1956, arguing that attention must be given to facsimiles and descriptions as well as to manuscripts. Explores the implications of the note to the provenance of the manuscript and announces the Hengwrt Project, which will compile and analyze the entire legacy of Hengwrt.

33. Pidd, Michael, Peter Robinson, Estelle Stubbs, and Clare E. Thomson. "Digital Imaging and the Manuscripts of *The Canterbury Tales.*" *L&LC* 12 (1997): 197–201. Argues that digital imaging of all available reproductions of *CT* manuscripts is necessary to make a pictorial history of the manuscripts. Reproductions of Hengwrt show changes over time.

34. Robinson, Peter. "Stemmatic Analysis of the Fifteenth-Century Witnesses to *The Wife of Bath's Prologue.*" In Norman F. Blake and Peter Robinson, eds. *The* Canterbury Tales *Project Occasional Papers, Volume II* (*SAC* 21 [1999], no. 22), pp. 69–132. Analyzes textual variants of *WBP*, using the data and computer analyses available on Robinson's *The Wife of Bath's Prologue on CD-ROM* (*SAC* 20 [1998], no. 11). Corroborates Manly and Rickert's A, B, C, and D groupings and their affiliations, suggests two more (E, F) that are affiliated, and identifies several independent lines of descent. Confirms the preeminence of Hengwrt and describes the implications of characteristic variants of each manuscript grouping. Clarifies the two exemplars of Ellesmere and describes in detail the source and transmission of the so-called added passages.

35. Robinson, Peter M. W. "Computer-assisted Stemmatic Analysis and 'Best-Text' Historical Editing." In Pieter van Reenan and Margot van Mulken, eds., with the assistance of Janet Dyk. *Studies in Stemmatology.* Amsterdam and Philadelphia: Benjamins, 1996, pp. 71–103. Describes the value of cladistic analysis in generating multiple, flexible stemmata for texts, arguing that stemmata are useful for indicating what can be used as a best text for editing, not for establishing the text itself. Analyzes variants in *Svipdagsmál* manuscripts and *WBP* manu-

scripts, focusing for the latter on spellings in Hengwrt, Ellesmere, Ha[4] (British Library Harley 7334), and Cp (Corpus Christi Oxford MS 198), manuscripts attributed to scribes "B" and "D."

36. Smith, Jeremy J. "Handmade Tales: The Implications of Linguistic Variation in Two Early Manuscripts of Chaucer's *Canterbury Tales*." In Jacek Fisiak, ed. *Studies in Middle English Linguistics* (*SAC* 21 [1999], no. 70), pp. 551–60. Although the Hengwrt and Ellesmere manuscripts were both copied by "Scribe B," their differences indicate how a variety of factors affect textual transmission.

37. Solopova, Elizabeth. "Chaucer's Metre and Scribal Editing in the Early Manuscripts of *The Canterbury Tales*." In Norman F. Blake and Peter Robinson, eds. *The* Canterbury Tales *Project Occasional Papers, Volume II* (*SAC* 21 [1999], no. 22), pp. 143–64. The metrical and stylistic habits reflected in the variants of *WBP* manuscripts Hengwrt, Ellesmere, Gg, Ha[4], Cp, and Dd indicate scribal rather than authorial origins. In comparison with Hengwrt, Ellesmere does not reflect a consistent effort to improve meter, but in the first half of *WBP* Ellesmere shares with Gg a relatively formal style. Ha[4] and Cp reflect consistent metrical revision; Dd, somewhat less consistent metrical revision.

38. Staley, Lynn. "Huntington 140: Chaucer, Lydgate, and the Politics of Retelling." In Thomas Hahn and Alan Lupack, eds. *Retelling Tales: Essays in Honor of Russell Peck* (*SAC* 21 [1999], no. 106), pp. 293–320. Manuscript environment (in the case of Huntington 140, the copying of *ClT* alongside several pious poems by Lydgate and circulation with a paraphrase of Job, the *Libelle of Englyshe Polycye,* and several edifying narratives), combined with the interests of specific readerships and larger political forces, may alter, complicate, or enrich the ways a particular poem is understood, both by its original audiences and by scholars.

See also nos. 4, 10, 16, 79, 140, 205, 208, 277.

Sources, Analogues, and Literary Relations

39. Cooper, Helen. "*Sources and Analogues of Chaucer's* Canterbury Tales: Reviewing the Work." *SAC* 19 (1997): 183–210. An advance first chapter of a proposed revision of Bryan and Dempster's *Sources and Analogues* (1941), in process under the editorship of Robert Correale and Mary Hamel. Cooper evaluates the relation of *CT* to other medieval storytelling collections, arguing that Boccaccio's *Decameron* was Chaucer's

model. The dialogic *CT* shares features with several medieval debate poems, especially the *Dialogue of Solomon and Marcolphus.* Its tale-telling competition owes a debt to *puys,* societies that held literary contests. Cooper distinguishes between *CT* and the tradition of tall-tales told about pilgrimages but notes evidence of historical pilgrims' amusing themselves with storytelling.

40.   Lázaro, Luis Alberto. "Some Speculations About Chaucer's Spanish Literary Sources." *SELIM* 5 (1996): 18–28. Surveys scholarship and evidence concerning Chaucer's familiarity with Spanish literature, arguing that critics have exaggerated the possible influence. It is "highly improbable" that Chaucer was directly influenced by medieval Spanish writers; similarities are better explained by the homogeneity of Western medieval tradition.

See also nos. 59, 85, 88, 155, 159, 170, 172, 174, 183, 185, 190, 196, 201, 203, 206, 207, 209, 211, 227, 235, 238, 243, 255, 260, 263, 270, 274, 276, 290, 296, 297, 299, 300, 305.

Chaucer's Influence and Later Allusion

41.   Baswell, Christopher. "*Troy Book:* How Lydgate Translates Chaucer into Latin." In Jeanette Beer, ed. *Translation Theory and Practice in the Middle Ages* (*SAC* 21 [1999], no. 83), pp. 215–37. By inserting elements of Chaucerian narrative and language and making direct references to Chaucer and *TC,* Lydgate replaces the Latin model of literary accomplishment with a vernacular model, thus translating Chaucer's English writing into the high social and political position originally occupied by Latin works such as Guido delle Colonne's *Historia destructionis Troiae,* Lydgate's chief source.

42.   Blythe, Hal, and Charlie Sweet. "O'Connor's 'A Good Man Is Hard to Find.'" *Expl* 55:1 (1996): 49–51. Argues that *CT* is a major source for O'Connor's story, evident in their shared motifs of pilgrimage and storytelling, the name Bailly/Bailey, and specific echoes of *PardT.*

43.   Brewer, Derek. "Modernising the Medieval: Eighteenth-Century Translations of Chaucer." In Marie-Françoise Alamichel and Derek Brewer, eds. *The Middle Ages after the Middle Ages in the English-Speaking World* (*SAC* 21 [1999], no. 78), pp. 103–20. Surveys the reception of Chaucer reflected in translations by Dryden, Samuel Johnson, Pope, and Wordsworth, viewing them as the beginning of modern criti-

cism, the modern idea of a national literature, modern textual criticism, and modern incomprehension of Chaucer's language. As understanding and enjoyment increased, poetic influence decreased.

44. Burrow, John. "Hoccleve and the Middle French Poets." In Helen Cooper and Sally Mapstone, eds. *The Long Fifteenth Century: Essays for Douglas Gray* (*SAC* 21 [1999], no. 95), pp. 35–49. Although Hoccleve's poetry is in many ways "at a further remove than Chaucer from French formal models," some features of his verse suggest a "closer affinity," especially the holograph manuscripts that can be seen as single-author "collected poems."

45. Gillespie, Vincent. "Justification by Faith: Skelton's *Replycacion*." In Helen Cooper and Sally Mapstone, eds. *The Long Fifteenth Century: Essays for Douglas Gray* (*SAC* 21 [1999], no. 95), pp. 273–311. One of the ways that Skelton sought to achieve a status as high as Chaucer's was to present himself as a combination of poet, priest, and prophet in *Replycacion*.

46. Kaylor, Noel Harold, Jr. "Interpolations in *The Boke of Coumfort of Bois*: A Late-Medieval Translation of Boethius's *Consolation of Philosophy*." *FCS* 23 (1997): 74–80. The translator of *The Boke of Coumfort* borrowed from Chaucer's *Bo* when translating Boethius, Christianizing and expanding both.

47. Lerer, Seth. "The Courtly Body and Late Medieval Literary Culture." In Dolores Warwick Frese and Katherine O'Brien O'Keeffe, eds. *The Book and the Body*. University of Notre Dame Ward-Phillips Lectures in English Language and Literature, no. 14. Notre Dame, Ind., and London: University of Notre Dame Press, 1997, pp. 78–115. Examines how Stephen Hawes's *Conforte de Louers* and *Pastime of Pleasure*, in selected allusions and references to *TC*, conflate the poet's identity and the act of reading. Reactions to the Hawesean poems in Humphrey Wallys's manuscript collection suggest that both Hawes's and Wallys's works serve as early modern paradigms of reading and subjectivity.

48. Mapstone, Sally. "Kingship and the *Kingis Quair*." In Helen Cooper and Sally Mapstone, eds. *The Long Fifteenth Century: Essays for Douglas Gray* (*SAC* 21 [1999], no. 95), pp. 51–69. The *Kingis Quair* is distinct from the "Chaucerian tradition" insofar as the former deals with public issues as well as personal ones. Its presentation of Boethian philosophy contrasts with that in *TC* and *KnT*, from which it "self-consciously draws."

49. Medcalf, Stephen. "The World and Heart of Thomas Usk." In

A. J. Minnis, Charlotte C. Morse, and Thorlac Turville-Petre, eds. *Essays on Ricardian Literature: In Honour of J. A. Burrow* (*SAC* 21 [1999], no. 129), pp. 222–51. Summarizes Usk's life and career. While assessing the fusion of various levels of meaning in *The Testament of Love,* Medcalf observes what Usk borrows from Chaucer (*HF* and *TC*) and Langland, as well as from Boethius and Anselm.

50. Phillips, Helen. "Frames and Narrators in Chaucerian Poetry." In Helen Cooper and Sally Mapstone, eds. *The Long Fifteenth Century: Essays for Douglas Gray* (*SAC* 21 [1999], no. 95), pp. 71–97. Attempts to define fifteenth-century "Chaucerian poetry," commenting on the historical use of the term and positing several thematic and formal features, especially the "meta-fictive and self-reflexive virtuosity" that results from various kinds of framing techniques.

51. Rossen, Janice. "Philip Larkin at Oxford: Chaucer, Langland, and Bruce Montgomery." *Journal of Modern Literature* 21 (1997–98): 295–310. Philip Larkin's undergraduate essays and notes, preserved among Bruce Montgomery's papers at the Bodleian Library, record his reactions to Chaucer (generally positive) and Langland (negative).

52. Rumble, Patrick. *Allegories of Contamination: Pier Paolo Pasolini's Trilogy of Life.* Toronto and Buffalo, N.Y.: University of Toronto Press, 1996. xxvi, 207 pp.; 20 b&w illus. The films *The Decameron, Canterbury Tales,* and *The Arabian Knights* make up Pasolini's *Trilogy,* here explored for how the films reflect understanding of the literary works from which they derive—in particular, how Pasolini's "Abiura," or recantation, recalls and parodies *Ret.*

53. Simpson, James. "'Dysemol Daies and Fatal Houres': Lydgate's *Destruction of Thebes* and Chaucer's *Knight's Tale.*" In Helen Cooper and Sally Mapstone, eds. *The Long Fifteenth Century: Essays for Douglas Gray* (*SAC* 21 [1999], no. 95), pp. 15–33. Reads Lydgate's *Destruction* as a Canterbury tale and a "pre-text" to *KnT.* Set historically before *KnT,* Lydgate's poem expands the boundaries of Chaucer's poem but "forecloses" its "limited possibilities for constructive human activity."

54. Stanley, E. G. "Chaucer at Woodstock: A Theme in English Verse of the Eighteenth Century." *RES,* n.s., 48 (1997): 157–67. Geoffrey Chaucer, traditionally thought to be an early resident of Woodstock, and John Churchill, first duke of Marlborough, are united by geography. Together, they represent English glory and are thus commemorated in minor verse of the eighteenth century, samples of which are included in

Stanley's article. Chaucer's residency at Woodstock, however, is mere pretense.

55. Torti, Anna. "Henryson Reading Chaucer: From *Troilus and Criseyde* to *The Testament of Cresseid*." In Margarita Giménez Bon and Vickie Olsen, eds. *Proceedings of the 9th International Conference of the Spanish Society for Medieval Language and Literature* (*SAC* 21 [1999], no. 104), pp. 346–65. Examines Henryson's treatment of Chaucer's story of Criseyde, focusing on Henryson's innovation and concern with artistic creativity, evident in his punishment of Cresseid with leprosy.

56. Utz, Richard J. "Inventing German(ic) Chaucer: Ideology and Philology in German Anglistics Before 1945." *SiM* 8 (1996): 5–26. Uses Will Héraucort's *Die Werwelt Chaucers* (1939) as the focal point for examining the interplay between philology and ideology in German Chaucer studies between 1848 and 1945. Germanic elements were exaggerated, and French influence was downplayed.

See also nos. 2, 113, 214, 290.

Style and Versification

57. Baker, David, ed. *Meter in English: A Critical Engagement.* Fayetteville: University of Arkansas Press, 1996. xxiv, 368 pp. A symposium on English poetic meter. Robert Wallace proposes ten rules for clarifying discussion of meter, and fourteen writers critique the validity and utility of the propositions; Wallace responds in a final essay. Recurring concerns include the variety of meters in English, degrees of stress, and the precision of metrical terminology. The essays include examples from Chaucer's works throughout.

58. Crépin, André. "Versification anglaise et histoire de la langue: Valeurs de 'e' en syllabe faiblement accentuée dans la poésie de Chaucer." In Guy Bourquin, ed. *Hier et aujourd'hui: Points de vue sur le moyen âge anglais* (*SAC* 21 [1999], no. 87), pp. 117–23. Examines diachronically the values of *e* in weakly stressed syllables, revealing the extent, causes, and consequences of phonetic and morphosyntactic changes: loss of syllables and inflectional endings, efforts to make spelling consistent, and shifts in verb paradigms.

59. Duffell, Martin J. "Chaucer, Gower, and the History of the Hendecasyllable." In C. B. McCully and J. J. Anderson, eds. *English His-*

torical Metrics (*SAC* 21 [1999], no. 126), pp. 210–18. Surveys the development and scholarship of hendecasyllabic meter, identifying the innovations whereby Chaucer produced the first English iambic pentameter and whereby Gower experimented with variable caesura in hendecasyllabic lines to produce Anglo-Norman iambic pentameter.

60. Duggan, Hoyt N. "Libertine Scribes and Maidenly Editors: Meditations on Textual Criticism and Metrics." In C. B. McCully and J. J. Anderson, eds. *English Historical Metrics* (*SAC* 21 [1999], no. 126), pp. 219–37. Comments on Dryden's and Tyrwhitt's views of Chaucer's meter as background to assessing editorial treatments of the meter of *Pearl.* Argues that editors need to emend the manuscript of *Pearl* more aggressively to minimize scribal interventions and clarify the metrical virtuosity of the poem.

61. Gutiérrez Arranz, José María. "The Precepts of Epistolary Discourse and Letters in Geoffrey Chaucer's *The Canterbury Tales.*" In Margarita Giménez Bon and Vickie Olsen, eds. *Proceedings of the 9th International Conference of the Spanish Society for Medieval Language and Literature* (*SAC* 21 [1999], no. 104), pp. 140–45. Examines "epistolary discourse" in *ClP, PrP, NPP, SqT,* and *PardP* in terms of style, using Isidore of Seville's recommendations about decorum.

62. Li, Xingzhong. "Chaucer's Meters." *DAI* 57 (1997): 3948A. Surveys the history of approaches to Chaucer's meter and critiques individual approaches. Proposes principles of Chaucer's tetrameter and pentameter, focusing on syntactic inversions and phrase boundaries. Chaucer's verse developed from rough tetrameter to regular pentameter to less regular pentameter.

63. Phillips, Betty S. "Chaucer's Voices." *CLAJ* 61 (1997): 93–103. Comparison of Romance vocabulary, direct discourse, the first person (singular or plural), finite verb forms, and other grammatical elements such as independent and dependent clauses in *KnT* and *WBT* shows that "Chaucer did indeed use the language of his narrators within their tales to enrich their characterization."

64. Standop, Ewald. "Wie Lautet der Erste Vers der *Canterbury Tales?*" *Anglistik* 8 (1997): 65–67. Assesses the meter of line 1 of *CT.*

65. Youmans, Gilbert. "Reconsidering Chaucer's Prosody." In C. B. McCully and J. J. Anderson, eds. *English Historical Metrics* (*SAC* 21 [1999], no. 126), pp. 185–209. Reexamines Halle and Keyser's three principles of the iambic line as applied to Chaucer's verse, arguing that the verse is better explained by a prototypical hierarchy of stresses than

by a pattern of alternating weak and strong stresses. Kiparsky's Mono-syllabic Word Constraint Principle better explains Chaucer's (and Shakespeare's and Milton's) inversions for meter than does Halle and Keyser's Stress Maximum Principle.

See also nos. 124, 268.

Language and Word Studies

66. Blake, N. F. "Chancery English and the Wife of Bath's Pro-logue." In Terttu Nevalainen and Leena Kahlas-Tarkka, eds. *To Explain the Present: Studies in the Changing English Language in Honour of Matti Ris-sanen* (*SAC* 21 [1999], no. 133), pp. 3–24. Computer-assisted analysis of forms of Chancery English in manuscripts of *WBP* indicates a drift toward standardization, most striking in the change from "swich" to "such." Yet, the pull to the Chancery Standard is not always clear.

67. Burnley, David. "Chaucer's Literary Terms." *Anglia* 114 (1996): 202–35. Explores Chaucer's literary self-consciousness by tabulating and analyzing his wide-ranging and complex variety of literary terms, including terms that describe the process of writing and the impact of literature, as well as terms of genre, rhetoric, and sources. Compares Chaucer's terms with those of Gower and Usk to find the "beginnings of English literary criticism."

68. Burnley, J. D. "'As Thise Clerkes Seyen': Exophoric Reference in Middle English and French Narrative." In Stewart Gregory and D. A. Trotter, eds. *De mot en mot: Aspects of Medieval Linguistics. Essays in Honour of William Rothwell.* Cardiff: University of Wales Press, with the Modern Humanities Research Association, 1997, pp. 1–15. The use of "thise" plus a noun (e.g., "thise clerkes," "thise men"), rarely found in Old En-glish, is "particularly common" in Chaucer and Gower; it probably de-veloped in early clerical discourse and, encouraged by some French par-allels, spread to colloquial use in London in the fourteenth century.

69. Dauby, Hélène. *Exercises avec leurs corrigés sur l'histoire de l'anglais.* AMAES, Hors Série, no. 3. Amiens and Paris: Association des Médié-vistes Anglicistes de l'Enseignement Supérieur, 1997. 146 pp. Two exercises deal with passages from *CT* (28–45 and 477–84).

70. Fisiak, Jacek, ed. *Studies in Middle English Linguistics.* Trends in Linguistics, Studies and Monographs, no. 103. Berlin and New York: Mouton de Gruyter, 1997. xii, 621 pp. Twenty-six essays by various

authors, exploring issues of syntax, lexicon, phonology, and morphology. Chaucerian materials are cited as data throughout, but for essays that pertain directly to Chaucer, see nos. 21, 36, 75, and 77.

71.   Green, Richard Firth. "Ricardian 'Trouthe': A Legal Perspective." In A. J. Minnis, Charlotte C. Morse, and Thorlac Turville-Petre, eds. *Essays on Ricardian Literature: In Honour of J. A. Burrow* (*SAC* 21 [1999], no. 129), pp. 179–202. Documents the medieval legal understanding of "trouthe" as an aspect of personal "oathworthiness" rather than of verifiability of facts; argues that this early sense obtains in *MLT* 630 even though it was fast becoming an archaic sense.

72.   Harris, Martha Janet. "Rhetoric and Reading in Late Medieval and Early Modern England: Lollardy, Plain Speech, and the Question of Literature." *DAI* 57 (1997): 4753A. Lollard insistence on plain speech brought about a split between plain and literary language that persisted into the sixteenth century. Harris considers the *Pearl* poet and the fifteenth-century reception of Chaucer.

73.   Louis, Cameron. "The Concept of the Proverb in Middle English." *ProverbiumY* 14 (1997): 173–85. The first English citations for the word "proverb" come from Chaucer's works, in which the word appears twenty-six times. Chaucer uses the word primarily in its modern and most common sense of "traditional folk sayings"; however, he also uses it with less common meanings in works such as *WBP* and *Buk*.

74.   Molencki, Rafał. "Albeit a Conjunction, Yet It Is a Clause: A Counterexample to the Unidirectionality Hypothesis?" *SAP* 31 (1997): 163–77. Traces the history of the phrase "al be it" from its late medieval "heyday" through its reduction to a single-word conjunction to its current status as a marker of "concessivity" or contradiction. Most medieval instances are cited from Chaucer.

75.   ———. "Concessive Clauses in Chaucer's Prose." In Jacek Fisiak, ed. *Studies in Middle English Linguistics* (*SAC* 21 [1999], no. 70), pp. 351–71. Anatomizes concessive clauses (those beginning with "yet," "although," "nevertheless," etc.), exploring their syntactic variety and semantic use. The subjunctive mood dominates, although instances of the indicative prefigure Modern English.

76.   Peitsara, Kirsti. "*Enough* and *Enow* in Middle English." In Terttu Nevalainen and Leena Kahlas-Tarkka, eds. *To Explain the Present: Studies in the Changing English Language in Honour of Matti Rissanen* (*SAC* 21 [1999], no. 133), pp. 163–83. Assesses the distribution of the two forms "enough" and "enow," using Chaucer's works in the database. In Chau-

cer, "enow" is generally a "poetic non-plural variant" useful for rhyme, while "inowe"/"ynowe" is the plural (with exceptions). Explores the historical conflation of the forms.

77. Taavitsainen, Irma. "Exclamations in Late Middle English." In Jacek Fisiak, ed. *Studies in Middle English Linguistics* (*SAC* 21 [1999], no. 70), pp. 573–607. Statistical analysis of Middle English exclamations in several literary modes and genres. Exclamations are a marker of fiction, and interjections are "particularly frequent" in Chaucer's works.

See also nos. 21, 36, 97, 98, 105, 133, 139, 148, 167, 184, 242, 246, 254, 264, 265, 292–94.

Background and General Criticism

78. Alamichel, Marie-Françoise, and Derek Brewer, eds. *The Middle Ages after the Middle Ages in the English-Speaking World.* Woodbridge, Suffolk: Boydell and Brewer, 1997. ix, 166 pp. Eleven essays study the influence and impact of the Middle Ages on Western life and culture from the sixteenth century to the present. The essays cover a wide range of topics—literature, stylistics, lexicography, art, the cinema, philosophy, history and myth-making, oral traditions, feminist issues—and reflect the enduring influence of the Middle Ages on European art and life. For the two essays that pertain to Chaucer, see nos. 13 and 43.

79. Alexander, Jonathan J. G. "Art History, Literary History, and the Study of Medieval Illuminated Manuscripts." *SIcon* 18 (1997): 51–66. Shifts within the related fields of art history, literary history, and the study of illuminated manuscripts have led to greater emphasis on interdisciplinary scholarship; Chaucer studies (particularly those concerning the Ellesmere manuscript) are a meeting ground for literary and art historians.

80. Allen, Elizabeth Gage. "'Let the Chaf be Stille': Exemplary Fictions in Late Medieval England." *DAI* 58 (1997): 1699A. Examines how late medieval changes in audience and breadth of subject transformed responses to exemplary literature, exploring *Livre du Chevalier de la Tour Landry,* Caxton's translation of it, and works of Gower, Chaucer (*PhyT, PardT,* and *TC*), and Henryson, plus Chaucerian apocrypha.

81. Andersen, Jennifer Lotte. "Structuring Images: Readers and Institutions in Late Medieval and Early Modern English Literature." *DAI* 57 (1997): 4747A. Though the printing press and the Reformation have

long been assumed to have altered radically the concepts of reader and writing, the persistence of the architectural trope in literature indicates that technology was less important than institutions. Andersen's study considers works by Chaucer (*HF*), Milton, Herbert, and Marvell.

82. Battles, Paul. "Chaucer and the Traditions of Dawn-Song." *ChauR* 31 (1997): 317–38. Chaucer draws on a variety of sources—Boccaccio, Ovid, French dawn-songs, popular dawn-song traditions, courtly dawn-songs, and (perhaps) popular poetry—for the dawn-songs in *RvT, MerT, Mars,* and *TC*. He uses these sources in a variety of idiosyncratic ways.

83. Beer, Jeanette, ed. *Translation Theory and Practice in the Middle Ages.* Studies in Medieval Culture, no. 38. Kalamazoo, Mich.: Medieval Institute, 1997. 282 pp. Includes two essays that pertain to Chaucer; see nos. 41 and 215.

84. Bitot, Michel, ed., with Roberta Mullini and Peter Happé. *Divers Toyes Mengled: Essays on Medieval and Renaissance Culture in Honour of André Lascombes.* Tours: Université François Rabelais, 1996. 425 pp. Twenty-eight essays by various authors addressing Chaucer, Langland, medieval drama (English, Spanish, and French), Malory, Thomas More, and Renaissance drama, especially Shakespeare. For the four essays that pertain to Chaucer, see nos. 153, 161, 214, and 305.

85. Blamires, Alcuin. *The Case for Women in Medieval Culture.* Oxford: Clarendon Press, 1977. viii, 279 pp. Documents a formal "profeminine"—though not "feminist"—tradition in medieval literature, exploring its origins and its sustaining arguments. Rooted in the apocryphal biblical book of Esdras, the tradition developed in the high Middle Ages in works such as Marbodus of Rennes's "De muliere bona," Peter Abelard's "Authority and Dignity of Nuns," *The Thrush and the Nightingale,* Albertano of Brescia's *Liber consolationis* (the source of *Mel*), and Jean Le Fèvre's *Livre de Leësce.* Blamires assesses *Mel, WBP, MerT,* and *LGW,* arguing that Chaucer—unlike Abelard, Christine de Pizan, and others—never presents a fully profeminine perspective. Instead, he either asserts female virtue without providing supporting evidence or playfully exploits it.

86. Bodi, Russell John. "Philological Applications of Play and Game Theory." *DAI* 58 (1997): 234A. Literary uses of play and game both subvert and reinforce social order while encouraging readers to become involved. Medieval works tend to relate chivalry and war to game

and play, while Platonism questions their value. Considers *TC* among works ranging from *Sir Gawain and the Green Knight* to works of Swift.

87.   Bourquin, Guy, ed. *Hier et aujourd'hui: Points de vue sur le moyen âge anglais*. Publications de l'Association des Médiévistes Anglicistes de l'Enseignement Supérieur, no. 21. Nancy: Association des Médiévistes Anglicistes de l'Enseignement Supérieur, 1997. For essays that pertain to Chaucer, see nos. 58 and 182.

88.   Brewer, Derek, ed. *Medieval Comic Tales*. 2d ed. Woodbridge, Suffolk; and Rochester, N.Y.: D. S. Brewer, 1996. xxxiv, 190 pp. An expanded revision of the 1973 edition, with one additional tale translated from French, three from Spanish, five from Middle English, three from German, six from Dutch (with three deleted), and one from Latin, for a total of eighty tales, songs, and anecdotes. The introduction appears for the first time, with frequent references to Chaucer and his fabliaux and other tales (not included). See also no. 319.

89.   Bruster, Douglas. [Forum.] *PMLA* 112 (1997): 438–39. Comments on David Shumway's "The Star System in Literary Studies" (*SAC* 21 [1999], no. 144), citing Manly and Rickert as Chicago "stars."

90.   Bullough, Vern L., and James A. Brundage, eds. *Handbook of Medieval Sexuality*. Garland Reference Library of the Humanities, no. 1696. New York and London: Garland, 1996. xviii, 441 pp. Eighteen essays by various authors, addressing topics such as confession, medicine, chaste marriage, contraception, homosexuality, lesbianism, cross-dressing, prostitution, castration, and various cultural studies: Jewish, Muslim, Eastern Orthodox, French, Norse, and English. For an essay that pertains to Chaucer, see no. 121. See also no. 322.

91.   Butterfield, Ardis. "French Culture and the Ricardian Court." In A. J. Minnis, Charlotte C. Morse, and Thorlac Turville-Petre, eds. *Essays on Ricardian Literature: In Honour of J. A. Burrow* (*SAC* 21 [1999], no. 129), pp. 82–120. Assesses aspects of the social and political exchange between France and England as background to their poetic exchange. Focuses on how lyric refrains (especially "Qui bien aimme," found in *PF* and elsewhere) were "common currency" between the two cultures and how Gower's *Cinquente Balades* reflects the intimate relations between English and French lyric traditions.

92.   Cohen, Jeffrey, and Bonnie Wheeler, eds. *Becoming Male in the Middle Ages*. The New Middle Ages, no. 4. New York and London: Garland, 1997. xx, 387 pp. Eighteen essays by various authors and an intro-

duction on topics ranging from Old English penitentials to Sir David Lindsey. For the two essays that pertain to Chaucer, see nos. 188 and 233.

93.   Coleman, Joyce. "On Beyond Ong: Taking the Paradox Out of 'Oral Literacy' (and 'Literate Orality')." In Hildegard L. C. Tristram, ed. *Medieval Insular Literature between the Oral and the Written II: Continuity of Transmission.* ScriptOralia, no. 97. Tübingen: Narr, 1997, pp. 155–76. Challenges the blunt opposition between orality and literacy, arguing from evidence in Chaucer and Langland that transitional terms are needed. Borrowing from the linguistic terms "exophoric" and "endophoric," Coleman argues that the Wife of Bath's knowledge of books can be described as "endophoric aurality" (hearing of books read); such terminology would also enable us to discuss Chaucer's audience more precisely.

94.   Cooke, Jessica. "Nice Young Girls and Wicked Old Witches: The 'Rightful Age' of Women in Middle English Literature." In Evelyn Mullally and John Thompson, eds. *The Court and Cultural Discourse: Selected Papers from the Eighth Triennial Congress of the International Courtly Literature Society, The Queen's University of Belfast, 26 July–1 August 1995* (*SAC* 21 [1999], no. 131), pp. 219–28. Examines references to the ages of women in *Sir Gawain and the Green Knight, WBT, MerT,* and *Rom* in an effort to understand how the ages of women were perceived.

95.   Cooper, Helen, and Sally Mapstone, eds. *The Long Fifteenth Century: Essays for Douglas Gray.* Oxford: Clarendon Press, 1997. xii, 362 pp. Fourteen essays by various authors on topics in English literature of the late fourteenth through the early sixteenth centuries. Includes an introduction and a bibliography of Gray's publications. For essays that pertain to Chaucer, see nos. 44, 45, 48, 50, 53, 113, and 202.

96.   Courtenay, William J. "The Dialectic of Divine Omnipotence in the Age of Chaucer." In Hugo Keiper, Richard J. Utz, and Christoph Bode, eds. *Nominalism and Literary Discourse: New Perspectives* (*SAC* 21 [1999], no. 120), pp. 111–21. Surveys the history and state of scholarship on a key concept of fourteenth-century nominalism—the dialectic of divine omnipotence—and its applications to Chaucerian and other Middle English texts. Warns that a view of the *potentia absoluta* as undermining the self-binding, covenantal relation of God to his established *ordo* can lead scholars astray.

97.   Cox, Catherine S. *Gender and Language in Chaucer.* Gainesville: University Press of Florida, 1997. xii, 196 pp. A study of "the intercon-

nectedness of gender, epistemology, and poetics in Chaucer's texts," focusing on "idioms of gender that attend narrative protocols of reflexivity and appropriation." Examines the linguistic, discursive, and sexual ambiguities of the Wife of Bath (chapter 1), as well as Criseyde's function as a metatextual, polysemous character (chapter 2). In *LGW, PhyT, SNT, MLT,* and *ClT,* the suffering of women manifests various cultural codes (chapter 3). *Wom Unc, Form Age, Sted, For, Gent, Ros,* and *Wom Nob* are narratives that "articulate gender categories in the absence of a fictive female" (chapter 4), while in *ManT* the mother is significantly absent (chapter 5). Sexually ambiguous, the Pardoner and the Summoner represent an equally ambiguous gendered poetic (chapter 6).

98.   Craun, Edwin D. *Lies, Slander, and Obscenity in Medieval English Literature: Pastoral Rhetoric and the Deviant Speaker.* Cambridge Studies in Medieval Literature, no. 31. Cambridge: Cambridge University Press, 1997. xiii, 255 pp. Draws from thirteenth-century pastoral literature (much of it in manuscript) that treats "Sins of the Tongue" to demonstrate how a pastoral "speech code" was "woven into late medieval [literary] texts." Chapters 1 and 2 distinguish in the pastoral literature certain "rhetorical paradigms," while chapters 3–6 identify and explore these paradigms in *Patience, Confessio Amantis, Piers Plowman,* and *CT.* Craun concludes that in *GP, ManP,* and *ManT* the Manciple "subverts the prudential strain in pastoral discourse, just as he practices deviant speech with impunity." In *ParsT,* however, the Parson restores order, "responding" to the Manciple with "conventional pastoral discourse on verbal sin" and "enact[ing] what he exhorts of others."

99.   Dahlberg, Mary Margaret. "'Now She Understood': Free Indirect Discourse and Its Effects." *DAI* 58 (1997): 155A. Free indirect discourse appears in *TC* and in works by Lyly and Gascoigne primarily for dramatic effects. Multiple voices in free indirect discourse may also mimic, distance, and achieve irony, as in many novels of the nineteenth and twentieth centuries.

100.   Dean, James M. *The World Grown Old in Later Medieval Literature.* Medieval Academy Books, no. 101. Cambridge, Mass.: Medieval Academy, 1997. xii, 379 pp. Surveys the *senectus mundi* topos in late medieval literature, particularly in Latin, French, and English literature, from Jean de Meun to Chaucer. Separate chapters address the topos, Middle English historical writing, Jean de Meun, Dante, *Piers Plowman,* Gower, and Chaucer. A recurring concern is the contrast between the depicted present and an ideal past. The discussion of Chaucer ("Chaucer

and the Decline of Virtue," pp. 271–313) concentrates on his moral lyrics and the depiction of marriage in *CT.* The lyrics are less ironic and evasive than is *CT,* but both reflect concern with the demise of "trouthe" and "gentilesse" and a "coarsening of human relationships."

101.   Dyas, Dee. *Images of Faith in English Literature, 700–1500: An Introduction.* London and New York: Longman, 1997. xii, 332 pp. An introduction to the influence of Christian thought and history on Old and Middle English literatures. A chapter on *Piers Plowman* and *CT* (pp. 101–38) surveys late-medieval ecclesiastical offices, the theology of salvation, penance and pilgrimage, and heresy, focusing on definition and clarification of terms. Also includes four chapters on Old English literature and one each on Middle English contemplative literature, religious lyrics, the works of the *Pearl* poet, and drama.

102.   Evitt, Regula Meyer. "Chaucer, Rape, and the Poetic Powers of Ventriloquism." Ch. 8 in Monica Brzezinski Potkay and Regula Meyer Evitt. *Minding the Body: Woman and Literature in the Middle Ages, 800–1500.* London: Twayne, 1997, pp. 139–65. Himself accused of rape, Chaucer could inhabit the "role of masculine agent" of the crime and that of the "feminized victim of accusation," reworking the traditional "metaphoric equation of deceptive language and female infidelity." In *Adam,* the narrator-author is "doubly gendered"; as text and textile, the story of Philomela in *LGW* is "doubly voiced." In *WBT,* the juxtaposition of rape and ventriloquism divides empathy for the victim and the "clement hope for the rapist's reform."

103.   Fisher, John H. "The New Humanism and Geoffrey Chaucer." *Soundings* 80 (1997): 23–39. Examines the evolution of the word "humanism" and explores Chaucer's artistic application of fourteenth-century nominalism as it relates to his fusion of medieval ideas of community, tradition, and the emerging figure of the individual. Treats *CT, KnT, MLT, SNT, PrT, TC, LGWP,* and *HF.*

104.   Giménez Bon, Margarita, and Vickie Olsen, eds. *Proceedings of the 9th International Conference of the Spanish Society for Medieval Language and Literature* [SELIM, 26–28 September 1996]. Vitoria-Gasteiz: Dpto. Filología Inglesa, 1997. 384 pp. Thirty-eight essays, including eight on Chaucer. For those that pertain to Chaucer, see nos. 55, 61, 175, 176, 178, 206, 232, and 272.

105.   Gray, Douglas. "'Pite for to Here—Pite for to Se': Some Scenes of Pathos in Late Medieval Literature." *PBA* 87 (1995): 67–99. Surveys the art and rhetoric of scenes of sorrow or pity in Chaucer,

Gower, Langland, Henryson, Malory, and others, arguing that Chaucer is "undoubtedly the master of the various modes of pathetic writing" in the period. Comments on scenes in *KnT, MLT, ClT, MkT, LGW,* and *TC.*

106. Hahn, Thomas, and Alan Lupack, eds. *Retelling Tales: Essays in Honor of Russell Peck.* Woodbridge, Suffolk; and Rochester, N.Y.: D. S. Brewer, 1997. vi, 359 pp. Includes five essays that pertain to Chaucer; see nos. 38, 163, 201, 203, and 258.

107. Hallisey, Joan F., and Mary-Anne Vetterling, eds. *Proceedings: Northeast Regional Meeting of the Conference on Christianity and Literature.* Weston, Mass.: Regis College, [1996]. iv, 137 pp. Twenty-three essays by various authors delivered at the *Northeast Regional Meeting of the Conference on Christianity and Literature* 10–12 October 1996, topics ranging from medieval to modern. For the two essays that pertain to Chaucer, see nos. 192 and 284.

108. Hamaguchi, Keiko. "Social Position of Women in Chaucer's England." In Masahiko Kanno, ed. *Medieval Heritage: Essays in Honour of Tadahiro Ikegami (SAC 21 [1999], no. 118),* pp. 269–82. The Black Plague resulted in economic advantages for townswomen and peasant women, enabling them to be active and powerful.

109. Honegger, Thomas. *From Phoenix to Chauntecleer: Medieval English Animal Poetry.* Schweizer Anglistische Arbeiten/Swiss Studies in English, no. 120. Tübingen, Basil: Francke, 1996. x, 288 pp. Assesses the "most important" poems about animals in English literature, ca. 700–1400 A.D., focusing on three traditions: *Physiologus;* bird debates; and beast fable and epic. Considers *PF* as a bird debate, describing how it transcends the allegorical limitations of that tradition. Discusses Chaucer's eclectic uses of all the traditions in *NPT* and his achievement of a powerfully original combination of comedy and morality. See also no. 336.

110. Horvath, Richard Paul. "The Romance of Authorship in Late Middle English Poetry." *DAI* 57 (1997): 3287A. Late-medieval English poets asserted their authorial identity in a commercial environment in various ways, including producing fascicles or pamphlets. Chaucer asserted his authorship through letters (*Scog, Buk,* and the letters in *TC*). Horvath also considers techniques of Lydgate and Hoccleve.

111. Hostetler, Margaret Mary. "Dwelling on Women: Reading the Spatial Discourses of Medieval Texts." *DAI* 57 (1997): 3011A. Applies spatial metaphors from contemporary feminist scholarship to medieval texts of various genres, including *Sir Gawain and the Green Knight,* Chrét-

ien's *Yvain, TC,* the *Life of Christina de Markyate,* the *Ancrene Wisse,* and the *Book of Margery Kempe.*

112. Howes, Laura L. *Chaucer's Gardens and the Language of Convention.* Gainesville: University Press of Florida, 1997. xi, 142 pp. Examines gardens in Chaucer's narratives as a means to show how literary and social conventions impose constraints and provide opportunities for the poet and characters alike to react to conventions. Surveys literary and historical gardens with which Chaucer was familiar, showing how medieval parks anticipate Renaissance formal gardens and how medieval gardens carry complex metaphorical, rhetorical, and cultural values, as well as implications for genre. In *BD* and *PF,* Chaucer adapts familiar garden topoi to escape their conventionality. In *TC,* gardens create the illusion of safety for the lovers, but like conventions of courtly love, the illusion betrays them. In *KnT, MerT,* and *FranT,* gardens manifest the efforts of men to control women and of women to break this control. As women escape control, so Chaucer escapes literary conventions.

113. Hudson, Anne. "*Visio Baleii:* An Early Literary Historian." In Helen Cooper and Sally Mapstone, eds. *The Long Fifteenth Century: Essays for Douglas Gray* (*SAC* 21 [1999], no. 95), pp. 313–29. Describes how John Bales sought to preserve English literary tradition by cataloging it in his *Scriptorum illustrium maioris Brytanniae . . . Catalogus* (1557 and 1559). Comments on Bales's treatment of Chaucer in the "longest entry concerning a medieval writer in the vernacular."

114. Hum, Sue. "Knowledge, Belief, and Lack of Agency: The Dreams of Geoffrey, Troilus, Criseyde, and Chauntecleer." *Style* 31 (1997): 500–522. Dreams in Chaucer function as authoritative texts within power structures. In *PF,* the systems represented by Affrycan and Nature protect authoritative knowledge and devalue individual experience. In *TC,* because knowledge and belief are interactive, the protagonists are complicit in their obedience to dreams, while Pandarus's subversive challenge finally reinforces dominant power. In *NPT,* Pertelote more overtly questions authoritative discourse.

115. Huth, Jennifer Mary. "'For I Have Tools to Truss': Women, Work, and Professionalism in Late Medieval Literature." *DAI* 58 (1997): 159A. Examines the rise of professionalism and women's efforts to achieve autonomy in fourteenth- and fifteenth-century England as represented in the mystery cycles, Chaucer's Wife of Bath, and Margery Kempe.

116. Jacobs, Nicholas. "Ricardian Romance? Critiques and Vindi-

cations." In A. J. Minnis, Charlotte C. Morse, and Thorlac Turville-Petre, eds. *Essays on Ricardian Literature: In Honour of J. A. Burrow* (*SAC* 21 [1999], no. 129), pp. 203–21. The romances of Chaucer and of the *Gawain* poet are similar in treating the genre as a decaying or decadent form. Chaucer treats the genre and its traditional themes lightly, at times parodically, while the *Gawain* poet seeks to redeem the genre and its ideals.

117. Justice, Steven, and Kathryn Kerby-Fulton, eds. *Written Work: Langland, Labor, and Authorship.* Philadelphia: University of Pennsylvania Press, 1997. x, 347 pp. Includes an introduction by Justice, five essays by various authors, and an edition and translation of the "autobiographical" passage in *Piers Plowman* (C-text, passus 5.1–104). All the essays take the passage as a point of departure, exploring the cultural and social conditions of authorship and literary self-representation in late medieval England. *Written Work* includes many references to Chaucer, especially to Chaucer's familiarity with Langland's work and the two authors' techniques of self-representation.

118. Kanno, Masahiko, ed. *Medieval Heritage: Essays in Honour of Tadahiro Ikegami* [*Chusei Eibungaku No Dento*]. Tokyo: Yushodo, 1997. x, 657 pp. Includes six essays that pertain to Chaucer; see nos. 108, 184, 185, 234, 246, and 294. In Japanese and English.

119. Keiper, Hugo. "A Literary 'Debate over Universals'? New Perspectives on the Relationships Between Nominalism, Realism, and Literary Discourse." In Hugo Keiper, Richard J. Utz, and Christoph Bode, eds. *Nominalism and Literary Discourse: New Perspectives* (*SAC* 21 [1999], no. 120), pp. 1–85. Reexamines the correspondences between literary nominalism and realism as competing paradigms and analyzes critical approaches to the literary debate on universals in late medieval (especially Chaucerian) and early modern literary studies.

120. Keiper, Hugo, Richard J. Utz, and Christoph Bode, eds. *Nominalism and Literary Discourse: New Perspectives.* Amsterdam and Atlanta: Rodopi, 1997. vi, 370 pp. Explores the correspondences between late medieval, early modern, and contemporary critical and literary nominalism. Includes five essays that pertain to Chaucer; see nos. 96, 119, 135, 179, and 303.

121. Lampe, David. "Sex Roles and the Role of Sex in Medieval English Literature." In Vern L. Bullough and James A. Brundage, eds. *Handbook of Medieval Sexuality* (*SAC* 21 [1999], no. 90), pp. 401–26. Surveys depictions of sexuality in Old and Middle English literature,

commenting on love and sex in Chaucer's works, especially in the fabliaux.

122. Lawlor, Jennifer L. "Representations of Exile in Early English
Literature, 1100–1500 A.D." *DAI* 57 (1997): 3012A. A cross-generic
study (excluding drama) of the effect of exile on such diverse characters
as the Christian or the secular hero, the lover, and the pilgrim. Discusses
works by Chaucer, Gower, and Langland.

123. Leicester, H. Marshall, Jr. "Chaucer Criticism in 1996: Report
to the Plenary Session of the New Chaucer Society, July 29, 1996." *Envoi*
6 (1997): 1–14. Traces the interdisciplinary character of Chaucer studies
generally, with specific interest in historicism and word-image relations.

124. Léon Sendra, Antonio R. *Ensayos Chauceriensis.* Grupo de In-
vestigación J. A., no. 5.075. Biblioteca de Estudios de Anglística, no.
18. Córdoba: Universidad de Córdoba, 1996. viii, 240 pp. Includes six
essays about Chaucer by León Sendra and a summary-introduction by
Jesús L. Serrano Reyes. The first essay proposes a sociolinguistic approach to Chaucer's works, based on the textual-linguistic theory of
M. A. K. Halliday, and the other essays apply some aspect of this approach. In *HF*, the relation between sign and style encourages the audience to reach beyond interpretation. Critical responses to Criseyde reflect how ambiguities in *TC* promote the reader's participation. In
PardT, ClT, WBT, and *FranT,* the personal topic of love engages the audience. Halliday's systemic-functional approach to style makes clear the
various levels of discourse and the particularly English features of *Th.*
Chaucer's references to Spain in *GP, MkT, PardT, HF,* and *Rom* capitalize
on common assumptions about Spain.

125. McCabe, John. "On Reading Chesterton's *Chaucer.*" *Renascence*
49:1 (1996): 79–87. G. K. Chesterton's *Chaucer* makes the "spacious-
ness" and capacity of Chaucer's writings available to twentieth-century
readers. Chesterton associated Chaucer's sanity and vitality with Aquinas, who shared with Chaucer orthodox medieval Christian views on sin,
freedom, and joy.

126. McCully, C. B., and J. J. Anderson, eds. *English Historical Metrics.* Cambridge and New York: Cambridge University Press, 1996. xii,
257 pp. Thirteen essays (plus an introduction) from the 1991 G. L.
Brook Symposium on Old and Middle English Metrics. For the three
essays that pertain to Chaucer, see nos. 59, 60, and 65.

127. Minnis, A. J. "The Author's Two Bodies? Authority and Falli-

bility in Late-Medieval Textual Theory." In P. R. Robinson and Rivkah Zim, eds. *Of the Making of Books: Medieval Manuscripts, Their Scribes and Readers. Essays Presented to M. B. Parkes* (SAC 21 [1999], no. 140), pp. 259–79. Explores the "complicated medieval matrix of ideas concerning the relationship between authority and fallibility," commenting on representations of the topic from Petrarch's depiction of Cicero to Chaucer's depiction of the Pardoner. As a preacher and an author, the Pardoner reflects late medieval questions about the authority of immoral clerics, questions confronted in Archbishop Arundel's efforts to eradicate Wycliffite opinion in 1409.

128. ————. "Looking for a Sign: The Quest for Nominalism in Chaucer and Langland." In A. J. Minnis, Charlotte C. Morse, and Thorlac Turville-Petre, eds. *Essays on Ricardian Literature: In Honour of J. A. Burrow* (SAC 21 [1999], no. 129), pp. 142–78. Belief in the salvation of virtuous pagans (the "*facere quod in est* principle") has been associated with nominalist thought. Minnis examines Chaucer's praise of Cambuyskan in *SqT* to argue that there is no real evidence of nominalist influence on the poet. Langland's treatment of Trajan is likewise not distinctly nominalistic.

129. ————, Charlotte C. Morse, and Thorlac Turville-Petre, eds. *Essays on Ricardian Literature: In Honour of J. A. Burrow.* Oxford: Clarendon Press, 1997. xvi, 358 pp. Sixteen essays by various authors on Anglo-French, Latin, and (especially) English literature produced during the reign of Richard II. Includes bibliography of Burrow's publications. For essays that pertain to Chaucer, see nos. 49, 71, 91, 116, 128, 130, 139, 173, 239, 270, and 302.

130. Morse, Charlotte C. "From 'Ricardian Poetry' to 'Ricardian Studies.'" In A. J. Minnis, Charlotte C. Morse, and Thorlac Turville-Petre, eds. *Essays on Ricardian Literature: In Honour of J. A. Burrow* (SAC 21 [1999], no. 129), pp. 316–44. Traces the history and reception of J. A. Burrow's term "Ricardian" as an alternative to "Age of Chaucer," considering its use and its future in light of the present critical climate.

131. Mullally, Evelyn, and John Thompson, eds. *The Court and Cultural Discourse: Selected Papers from the Eighth Triennial Congress of the International Courtly Literature Society, The Queen's University of Belfast, 26 July–1 August 1995.* Woodbridge, Suffolk; and Rochester, N.Y.: D. S. Brewer, 1997. x, 426 pp. Thirty-seven essays by various authors arranged under five headings: Contexts for Courtliness, Fashioning His-

tory and Romance, Negotiating a Courtly Voice, Texts and Readers, and Limits of Courtliness. For essays that pertain to Chaucer, see nos. 23 and 94.

132. Murray, Jacqueline, and Konrad Eisenbichler, eds. *Desire and Sexuality in the Premodern West.* Toronto; Buffalo, N.Y.; and London: University of Toronto Press, 1996. xxviii, 315 pp. Fifteen essays by various authors and an introduction on topics literary, historical, and social, all pertaining to sexuality in Europe before 1700. For three essays that pertain to Chaucer, see nos. 212, 222, and 281.

133. Nevalainen, Terttu, and Leena Kahlas-Tarkka, eds. *To Explain the Present: Studies in the Changing English Language in Honour of Matti Rissanen.* Mémoires de la Société Néophilologique de Helsinki, no. 52. Helsinki: Société Néophilologique, 1997. xx, 503 pp. Twenty-nine essays, by various authors, on English historical and developmental linguistics; includes a list of publications by Rissanen. For the two essays that pertain to Chaucer, see nos. 66 and 76.

134. Nilsen, Don L. F. *Humor in British Literature, From the Middle Ages to the Restoration: A Reference Guide.* Westport, Conn., and London: Greenwood, 1997. xxvi, 226 pp. Chronological description of humor in British literature, with individual discursive bibliographies on literary humor in the fourteenth through the seventeenth centuries and on individual writers in these periods. Surveys the criticism of humor in Chaucer's works (pp. 16–27).

135. Penn, Stephen. "Literary Nominalism and Medieval Sign Theory: Problems and Perspectives." In Hugo Keiper, Richard J. Utz, and Christoph Bode, eds. *Nominalism and Literary Discourse: New Perspectives* (*SAC* 21 [1999], no. 120), pp. 157–89. Nominalism and literature were never parts of a single, seamless discourse; influences between them are at best complex and indirect. Penn surveys research on literary nominalism in late-medieval (mostly Chaucerian) texts, arguing that sources other than nominalist philosophy better explain the ambiguities, linguistic playfulness, and similar symptoms of "nominalist" tendencies in late-medieval literature.

136. Pickering, O. S., ed. *Individuality and Achievement in Middle English Poetry.* Woodbridge, Suffolk; and Rochester, N.Y.: D. S. Brewer, 1997. xi, 227 pp. Twelve essays by different authors examine the achievements of frequently neglected works, exploring the quality of the poems, their relations to various traditions and genres, and their poetic methods. Brief references to *ABC, BD, GP, MilT,* and *RvT.*

137. Pollner, Clausdirk, Helmut Rohlfing, and Frank-Rutger Hausmann, eds. *Bright Is the Ring of Words: Festschrift für Horst Weinstock zum 65 Geburtstag.* Abhandlungen zur Sprache und Literatur, no. 85. Bonn: Romanistischer Verlag, 1996. iv, 372 pp. For two essays that pertain to Chaucer, see nos. 200 and 259.

138. Rasmussen, Mark David. "Feminist Chaucer? Some Implications for Teaching." *SMART* 5:1 (1997): 77–85. Argues that Jill Mann's approach to Chaucer's treatment of women is more helpful for classroom application than is Elaine Hansen's.

139. Rigg, A. G. "Anglo-Latin in the Ricardian Age." In A. J. Minnis, Charlotte C. Morse, and Thorlac Turville-Petre, eds. *Essays on Ricardian Literature: In Honour of J. A. Burrow* (*SAC* 21 [1999], no. 129), pp. 121–41. Explores how English displaced Latin as a literary language in the court of Richard II and assesses meter, Anglicization, and historical topics as common features of Anglo-Latin verse by Gower and John Berry.

140. Robinson, P. R., and Rivkah Zim, eds. *Of the Making of Books: Medieval Manuscripts, Their Scribes and Readers. Essays Presented to M. B. Parkes.* Aldershot, Hants: Scolar Press; Brookfield, Vt.: Ashgate, 1997. xiv, 324 pp. Twelve essays by various authors, a celebratory introduction of testimonials, and a bibliography of publications of M. B. Parkes. For the two essays that pertain to Chaucer, see nos. 18 and 127.

141. Roper, Gregory. "Cyberspace, Theory, and Power in the Classroom: A Non-Techie Guinea Pig Tries Out the World Wide Web in His Undergraduate Chaucer Class." *Æstel* 4 (1996): 117–41. Personal chronicle of problems in dealing with technology in teaching, including inadequate facilities, poor student preparation, and time-consuming searching and class preparation. Includes two appendices: a *Labyrinth* assignment and student responses.

142. Saul, Nigel. *Richard II.* New Haven and London: Yale University Press, 1997. xiv, 514 pp.; 28 b&w illus. A biography that assesses Richard II, the quality of his rule, and the events of his reign. Uses Shakespeare's play as a perceptive point of departure and argues that Richard's accomplishments and excesses resulted in large part from the fusion of "exercise of power" with a narcissistic "sense of being." References to Chaucer are few, concentrated in a section on the status of the arts in the court of Richard, who favored visual over verbal arts as a means of image-making. Chaucer had little or no royal patronage from Richard.

143.   Scattergood, John, and Julia Boffey, eds. *Texts and Their Contexts: Papers from the Early Book Society.* Dublin: Four Courts, 1997. 252 pp. Ten essays initially presented at the first three conferences of the Early Book Society: Durham, 1989; Trinity College, Dublin, 1991; and Sheffield, 1993. The essays consider texts and books produced between the late fourteenth and early sixteenth centuries, available to English readers. For the essay that pertains to Chaucer, see no. 12.

144.   Shumway, David R. "The Star System in Literary Studies." *PMLA* 112 (1997): 85–100. Contrasts the "star system" of contemporary critics (e.g., Derrida) with the previous paradigm of dominant but nonstellar scholars in Chaucer studies. George Lyman Kittredge, John M. Manly, and John Livingston Lowes serve as examples. See also no. 89.

145.   Sigal, Gale. *Erotic Dawn-Songs of the Middle Ages: Voicing the Lyric Lady.* Gainesville: University Press of Florida, 1996. xii, 241 pp. Examines the active role of women in medieval albas, or dawn-songs, as indications of women in society. Defines the lyric genre and its history, exploring its relations with courtly tradition, the fantasies reflected in the genre, and the sexual politics that underlie it. Considers, among other works, *FranT* and *TC*. See also no. 360.

146.   Smith, Susan L. *The Power of Women: A Topos in Medieval Art and Literature.* Philadelphia: University of Pennsylvania Press, 1995. xvii, 294 pp. Examines visual and verbal representations of the sexual power of women as "a topos of exemplification within the theory and practice of ancient and medieval rhetoric," especially as it developed in the twelfth through the fourteenth centuries. Focuses on representations of Virgil in the basket and the mounted Aristotle, with passim references to *TC* and *WBPT*. See also no. 362.

147.   Sparrow, Edward Harrison. "Man-Making and the Modernist Code Duello, 1898–1934." *DAI* 57 (1997): 3952A. The proof of masculinity by man-to-man combat continues to fascinate modern writers, though as early as Chaucer the duel had been perceived as inherently wrong.

148.   Taylor, Paul Beekman. "Chaucer's Strategies of Translation." *Chaucer Yearbook* 4 (1997): 1–19. Explores Chaucer's meanings for "translation" and related terms, using them to examine Chaucer's use of source material. Conjointure, verbal play, etymologizing, and transfer of meaning typify Chaucerian translation, exemplified in Troilus's complaint from Petrarch (*TC* 1.400–420) and emblematized in the magic ring and brass steed of *SqT*. Taylor also explores the point at which

Chaucer stops translating in *Rom*, the personification of sound in *HF*, and various instances of verbal play in *CT*.

149. Travis, Peter. "Chaucer's *Chronographiae*, the Confounded Reader, and Fourteenth-Century Measurements of Time." *Disputatio* 2 (1997): 1–34. Describes five medieval ways of looking at time (computistical, philosophical, mechanical, astrolabic, kalendric) and examines three Chaucerian passages that appear to indicate exact dates and time of day. Concludes that each passage presents an intentional *insolubilium* through which Chaucer forces readers to focus on the process of intellection.

150. Travis, Peter W. "Chaucer's Heliotropes and the Poetics of Metaphor." *Speculum* 72 (1997): 399–427. Discusses uses of solar metaphor in Chaucer by way of Ovid and Machaut, focusing on *LGWP* and *NPT*.

151. Utz, Richard J. "*Sic et Non:* Beobachtungen zu Funktion und Epistemologie des Sprichworts bei Geoffrey Chaucer." *Das Mittelalter* 2:2 (1997): 31–43. Fourteenth-century nominalist challenges to realism also challenged the universalizing truth of proverbs. Through his treatment of proverbs in *NPT, WBP,* and *TC,* Chaucer contrasts the *sic* of dominant realist discourse with the *non* of nominalist counterdiscourse, sometimes parodically.

152. Valentine, Virginia Walker. *Chaucer's Knight: A Man Ther Was.* Tampa, Fla.: Axelrod, 1994. x, 94 pp. Six critical essays by the author on topics ranging from Old English to modern literature. For those that pertain to Chaucer, see nos. 186 and 304.

153. Vial, Claire. "Images of Kings and Kingship: Chaucer, Malory, and the Representations of Royal Entries." In Michel Bitot, ed., with Roberta Mullini and Peter Happé. *Divers Toyes Mengled: Essays on Medieval and Renaissance Culture in Honour of André Lascombes (SAC* 21 [1999], no. 84), pp. 43–54. Chaucer's accounts of royal entries in *KnT, Anel, MLT,* and *LGWP* indicate how the confluence of historical records and literary practice influenced the idea of kingship in the late Middle Ages.

154. Wack, Mary. "Chaucer in the Secondary Schools: 'Electronic Chaucer.'" *SMART* 5:1 (1997): 63–68. Reports on pedagogical applications of digitized images and concordancing programs in the Chaucer classroom. The goal is to improve students' abilities to perform research and to read closely.

155. Wallace, David. *Chaucerian Polity: Absolutist Lineages and Associational Forms in England and Italy. Figurae:* Reading Medieval Culture.

Stanford, Calif.: Stanford University Press, 1997. xxii, 555 pp. Reads Chaucer's works (especially *CT*) as his responses to and imaginings of the politics of his age, politics he experienced at home, in his journeys to Italy, and in his readings of Italian literature—especially that of Petrarch and Boccaccio but also that of Dante and Albertano of Brescia. The "compagnye" of *GP* represents the "associational ideology" of early Florentine humanism, while the despotism of *KnT* reflects the absolutist tyranny of Visconti Lombardy, the seedbed of later patronizing humanism. Aligning Boccaccio with associational forms and Petrarch with despotic ones, Wallace shows how Chaucer responds to his predecessors as he depicts feminine or wifely eloquence as desirable in politics, especially in *Mel* and *LGWP* (F version) and, obversely, in *ManT.* Chaucer's fabliaux present tensions between the city and the country, while *MLT* explores mercantilism. *ClT* and *MerT* examine humanism vs. tyranny; *MkT* depicts the fate of despotism. Wallace provides much new historical context for the works of Petrarch, Boccaccio, and Chaucer and argues that Chaucer adumbrates Shakespeare's humanism, although in a form more feminist and communal and less despotic.

156. ———. "In Flaundres." *SAC* 19 (1997): 63–91. Biennial Chaucer Lecture, the New Chaucer Society, Tenth International Congress, 26–29 July 1996, University of California, Los Angeles. Summarizes the political, economic, and social aspects of late-medieval Flanders and evokes a sense of English attitudes toward them. Chaucer's references and allusions to Flanders and Flemings in *GP, Th, ShT, PardT,* and *CT* anticipate the more aggressively anti-Flemish rhetoric of the fifteenth-century *Libelle of Englysche Polycye.*

157. Wheeler, Jeffrey Matthew. "Palpable Fictions: Religious Relics, Populist Rhetoric, and the English Reformation." *DAI* 57 (1997): 3043A. Although false relics often figured in polemics, relics were popular through the early Reformation. Attitudes vary less than has been assumed among such writers as Guibert de Nogent, Lorenzo Valla, Wycliffe, Chaucer, Foxe, Latimer, Tyndale, and later Renaissance writers.

158. Wright, Will, and Steven Kaplan, eds. *The Image of Nature in Literature, the Media, and Society: Selected Papers, 1993 Conference, Society for the Interdisciplinary Study of Social Imagery, March 11–13, 1993, Colorado Springs, Colorado.* Pueblo, Colo.: Society for the Interdisciplinary Study of Social Imagery, [1993]. 367 pp. Fifty-seven essays on a variety of topics; for essays that pertain to Chaucer, see nos. 279 and 299.

454

159.   Zieman, Katherine. "Chaucer's *Voys.*" *Representations* 60 (1997): 70–91. Explores Chaucer's "literary voice" as a self-conscious reflection of late-fourteenth-century vernacularizing. Chaucer fuses discursive gestures to separate authorial and narratorial voices. In *MilT,* the fabliau resonates ironically with the science of music theory. With its allusions to Virgil's *Aeneid, HF* exemplifies vernacular poetics derived from classical literature.

See also nos. 202, 238, 298.

The Canterbury Tales—General

160.   Allen, Valerie, and Ares Axiotis, eds. *Chaucer.* New Casebooks. New York: St. Martin's, 1996. xi, 268 pp. Reprints fourteen essays originally published in the 1980s and 1990s, all pertaining to *CT* and characterized by their contemporary theoretical approaches. In the introduction, the editors survey critical approaches to Chaucer and provide suggestions for further reading in traditional criticism; structuralist-formalist approaches; criticism based on gender, psychoanalysis, and the body; deconstruction and language criticism; and historicist-political readings. The collection includes essays by Timothy D. O'Brien (*SumT*), Peter Goodall (fragment 1), Monica E. McAlpine (*PardT*), Brooke Bergan (*KnT*), Gerald Morgan (*FranT*), Sheila Delany (*ManT*), Carolyn Dinshaw (*PardT*), Barrie Ruth Straus (*WBPT*), R. Howard Bloch (*PhyT*), Stephen Knight (*GP*), Lee Patterson (*MilT*), Louise O. Fradenburg (*PrT*), James Andreas (*SumT*), and R. Allen Shoaf (*FranT*).

161.   Axton, Richard. "Chaucer and the Idea of the Theatrical Performance." In Michel Bitot, ed., with Roberta Mullini and Peter Happé. *Divers Toyes Mengled: Essays on Medieval and Renaissance Culture in Honour of André Lascombes (SAC 21 [1999], no. 84), pp. 83–100. Examines theatricality in Chaucer's work evidenced in spacial representations, the specialized behavior of performers, and the presence of an audience in *PrT, SNT,* and *MilT.* Some attention to *TC, HF, MkT, SqT,* and *FranT.*

162.   Barker, David Stephen. "On Adjudication and Narrative in the 'Canterbury Tales.'" *DAI* 58 (1997): 2199A. Law and its applications influence literary audiences, and Chaucer exploits the possibilities variously. In *KnT,* trial by combat fails to effect closure; Theseus must intervene. Melibee's final verdict acts similarly in *Mel.* In *SumT,* however, the closure is narrowly legalistic.

163. David, Alfred. "Chaucer's Adams." In Thomas Hahn and Alan Lupack, eds. *Retelling Tales: Essays in Honor of Russell Peck* (*SAC* 21 [1999], no. 106), pp. 61–72. A consideration of the four "Adams" in *CT* (*MkT, Mel, MerT, NPT*) clarifies Chaucer's continuously revised sense of the allusive potential of the biblical figure, as well as the changing, expansive meaning within the various *Tales*.

164. Fichte, Jörg O. "Konkurrierende und Kontrastierende Zeit-muster in Chaucers *Canterbury Tales*." In Trude Ehlert, ed. *Zeitkonzeptionen Zeiterfahrung Zeitmessung: Stationen ihres Wandels vom Mittelalter bis zur Moderne.* Paderborn: Ferdinand Schöningh, 1997, pp. 223–41. Assesses time and its relations with history and eschatology in *CT,* exploring how genre and variations in genre affect the depiction of time. Examines *KnT* and *Th* as romances, *SNT* and *MLT* as saints' lives, *PhyT* and *MkT* as exempla, and *ShT* as fabliau; also considers how *GP* and *ParsT* establish and transcend worldly time.

165. Gallacher, Patrick J. "Fairness and Generosity in *The Canterbury Tales*." *SMART* 5:1 (1997): 55–62. Considers relations among fairness, generosity, and justice as depicted in *MilT, ClT,* and *PardT,* discussing them as they might be presented to an audience of high school students.

166. Guidry, Marc S. "The Counsel Group: Rhetorical and Political Contexts of Court Counsel in 'The Canterbury Tales.'" *DAI* 58 (1997): 2224A. As diplomat, MP, and associate of important political figures, Chaucer understood the operation of government and its rhetoric, reflected in *Mel, MLT, ClT, KnT,* and *MerT.* Chaucer's themes of class and gender relate to the nature of counsel-taking.

167. Harding, Wendy. "The Function of Pity in Three Canterbury Tales." *ChauR* 32 (1997): 162–74. Chaucerian pathos derives from the rigidity of fourteenth-century social hierarchies. In *KnT,* pity brings the ruler and ruled closer together; *ClT* advocates Christ-like endurance and humility for the weak and God-like justice and mercy for the powerful. In *ParsT,* power and weakness, glory and humiliation are united in one paradoxical form.

168. Holsinger, Bruce Wood. "Music, Body, and Desire in Medieval Literature and Culture, 1150–1400: Hildegard of Bingen to Chaucer." *DAI* 57 (1997): 3928A. Patristic tradition regarded music as both carnal and spiritual, capable of evoking a gamut of emotions. Diatribes against musical innovation parallel those against unconventional sexual

practice. Holsinger considers musical imagery in *KnT, MilT, PrT,* and *PardT.*

169. Homan, Delmar C. "Chaucer, General Education, and 'Lasting' Popular Culture." *Kansas English* 82:4 (1997): 30–40. Advocates fusion of high art and popular culture in general-education curricula, commenting on the use of principles of group dynamics to analyze *CT.*

170. Lee, Dongchoon. "Chaucer as a Storyteller." *DAI* 58 (1997): 858A. Contrasts Chaucer's storytelling techniques in *KnT, MilT, PardT, WBT, MLT,* and *MerT* with those of their sources, contemporary writings, and folk traditions. Uses the approaches of Propp, Bal, Bakhtin, and Frye.

171. Moloney, Rowland. "Plod This Past Them." *{London} Times Education Supplement,* Mar. 1, 1996, Extra English Section, p. v. Lesson ideas for teaching *CT* to twelve-year-olds; mentions a prospective BBC animated version of *CT.*

172. Olivares Merino, Eugenio M. "El retrato de la sociedad medieval en *The Canterbury Tales* y el *Rimado de Palacio* de Pero de Ayala." In Juan Paredes, ed. *Medioevo y literatura, III: Actas del V Congreso de la Asociación Hispánica de Literatura Medieval (Granada, 27 septiembre–1 octubre 1993).* 4 vols. Granada, Nicaragua: University of Granada Press, 1995, pp. 491–97. Comments on Chaucer's description of Pedro I of Spain in *MkT* and on similarities between *CT* and de Ayala's *Rimado.*

173. Pearsall, Derek. "Pre-empting Closure in 'The Canterbury Tales': Old Endings, New Beginnings." In A. J. Minnis, Charlotte C. Morse, and Thorlac Turville-Petre, eds. *Essays on Ricardian Literature: In Honour of J. A. Burrow (SAC* 21 [1999], no. 129), pp. 23–38. Addresses issues of the order of *CT* and, following the discussion of Charles A. Owen, Jr. (1977), argues that *ParsT* was once intended to complete the work. However, Chaucer revised his plan when he "evolved a new and impossibly grandiose scheme for the *Tales.*"

174. Powell, Brian. "Las técnicas narrativas de Juan Ruiz y Geoffrey Chaucer." In María Isabel Toro Pascua, ed. *Actas del III Congreso de la Asociación Hispánica de Literatura Medieval (Salamanca, 3 al 6 de octubre de 1989), II.* 2 vols. Salamanca: Biblioteca Española del Siglo XV, Departamento de Literatura Española e Hispanoamericana, 1994, pp. 789–96. Compares narrative aspects of *CT* and Juan Ruiz's *Libro de buen amor,* especially their uses of irony and an author-narrator; also explores relations between the Prioress and Ruiz's Doña Garoça.

175. Ramírez Arlandi, Juan. "Reconsiderations on the Theme of Marriage in *The Canterbury Tales.*" In Margarita Giménez Bon and Vickie Olsen, eds. *Proceedings of the 9th International Conference of the Spanish Society for Medieval Language and Literature* (*SAC* 21 [1999], no. 104), pp. 247–52. Investigates varying presentations of marriage in the Marriage Group of *CT,* concluding that the "true idea of marriage is the result of combining the features that different characters exhibit."

176. Sola Buil, Ricardo J. "Parodic Elements and the Perception of Self in *The Canterbury Tales.*" In Margarita Giménez Bon and Vickie Olsen, eds. *Proceedings of the 9th International Conference of the Spanish Society for Medieval Language and Literature* (*SAC* 21 [1999], no. 104), pp. 338–45. Explores Chaucer's use of parody and manipulation of narrative tradition to develop realistic characters or "subjectivities" in *CT.*

177. Taylor, Paul Beekman. *Chaucer's Chain of Love.* Madison and Teaneck, N.J.: Fairleigh Dickinson University Press; London: Associated University Presses, 1996. 215 pp. Reads *CT* as Chaucer's effort to "see, speak and write" into fiction the bond of love that is to him an "ontological fact of creation." The road to Canterbury is a metaphor of salvation; the pilgrims and their *Tales* are links in the spiritual chain of love. Recurring concern with language both reflects Chaucer's anxieties about human ability to express the truth of love and celebrates human language and art as "a distant and riotous imitation of God's order." Taylor also considers the "chain of love" as metaphor and metonym in *PF, TC,* and *LGW.*

178. Vila de la Cruz, Mª Purificación. "Variables and Perspectives Between Men and Women in *The Canterbury Tales.*" In Margarita Giménez Bon and Vickie Olsen, eds. *Proceedings of the 9th International Conference of the Spanish Society for Medieval Language and Literature* (*SAC* 21 [1999], no. 104), pp. 375–84. Discusses the women in *CT* as emotional and intellectual reflections of male characters.

179. Watts, William H. "Chaucer's Clerks and the Value of Philosophy." In Hugo Keiper, Richard J. Utz, and Christoph Bode, eds. *Nominalism and Literary Discourse: New Perspectives* (*SAC* 21 [1999], no. 120), pp. 145–55. Discusses the problematic nature of relating late medieval nominalism to Chaucer's literary texts. Chaucer's representation of philosophizing clerks suggests that he took a dim view of such figures of contemporary life, whom he tended to portray as either devious or irrelevant.

See also nos. 4, 7, 18, 20–22, 24, 27–33, 39, 42, 61, 69, 97, 98, 100, 101, 103, 121, 124, 148, 155, 156, 225, 245, 259, 260.

CT—The General Prologue

See nos. 64, 98, 156, 160, 164, 180, 230, 233, 239, 245, 258.

CT—The Knight and His Tale

180. Bell, Adrian. "England and the Crusade of Nicropolis, 1396." *Medieval Life* 4 (1996): 18–22. Comments on the *GP* sketch of the Knight, Gower's "To King Henry the Fourth," and the Wilton Diptych as evidence of English support for Philippe de Mézières's promotion of the 1396 crusade against the Turks, perhaps evidence of English participation in the crusade.

181. Fradenburg, Louise O. "Sacrificial Desire in Chaucer's *Knight's Tale*." *JMEMS* 27 (1997): 47–75. The logic of sacrifice (in particular, the sacrifice of the subject, Arcite) that permeates *KnT* produces a *jouissance*, which the discourse of charity attempts to disguise.

182. Greenwood, M. K. Smolenska. "Pointlessness, Parody and Paradox in Chaucer's *The Knight's Tale*." In Guy Bourquin, ed. *Hier et aujourd'hui: Points de vue sur le moyen âge anglais* (*SAC* 21 [1999], no. 87), pp. 45–55. *KnT* creates puzzling effects. Chaucer's subversion of several issues (genre, nobility, love, wisdom) highlights their absurdity.

183. Jungman, Robert E. "Chaucer's *The Knight's Tale* 2681–82 and Juvenal's *Tenth Satire*." *Expl* 55:4 (1997): 190–92. Lines 2681–82 of *KnT* do not (as Wolfgang Rudat supposed) echo Virgil's *Aeneid* 4.569–79 but instead adapt Juvenal's *Tenth Satire* 72–73 to identify Emily with changeable fortune.

184. Kawasaki, Masatoshi. "'This Wordes Transmutacioun': The Meaning of *Loci* in *The Knight's Tale*." In Masahiko Kanno, ed. *Medieval Heritage: Essays in Honour of Tadahiro Ikegami* (*SAC* 21 [1999], no. 118), pp. 455–65 (in Japanese). Examines changes in the word *loci* in *KnT*, exploring the topography of "to and fro" and "up and doun."

185. Sudo, Jan. "A Note on Chaucer's *Knight's Tale* Compared with Boccaccio's *Teseida*." In Masahiko Kanno, ed. *Medieval Heritage: Essays in Honour of Tadahiro Ikegami* (*SAC* 21 [1999], no. 118), pp. 255–68. Un-

like *Teseida, KnT* lacks the formal invocations of the epic, perhaps as a result of Chaucer's fitting the story into the *CT* frame.

186.   Valentine, Virginia Walker. "Chaucer's Knight: A Man Ther Was." In Virginia Walker Valentine. *Chaucer's Knight: A Man Ther Was* (*SAC* 21 [1999], no. 152), pp. 1–23. Argues from evidence in *KnT* and *GP* that Chaucer presents not an idealized figure but a complex, realistic character. Valentine treats the narrative and rhetorical features of *KnT* and its relations with Boccaccio's *Teseida* as evidence of the Knight's character; she argues that the *GP* information must have been learned by the narrator from the Knight himself.

187.   Vaszily, Scott. "Fabliau Plotting Against Romance in Chaucer's *Knight's Tale.*" *Style* 31 (1997): 523–42. Pearcy's structural approach enables us to recognize the generic markers of fabliau in nonfabliau tales by identifying dupers, dupes, and misinterpretation of signs. Two episodes in *KnT* reflect fabliau structures: Arcite's reading of Palamon's declaration of love, and Saturn's reading of Arcite's prayer. These and other aspects of *KnT* question the idealizations of romance.

See also nos. 17, 18, 48, 53, 63, 103, 105, 112, 153, 160, 162, 164, 166–68, 170, 281.

CT—The Miller and His Tale

188.   Burger, Glenn. "Erotic Discipline . . . or 'Tee Hee, I Like My Boys to Be Girls': Inventing with the Body in Chaucer's *Miller's Tale.*" In Jeffrey Cohen and Bonnie Wheeler, eds. *Becoming Male in the Middle Ages* (*SAC* 21 [1999], no. 92), pp. 245–60. *MilT* reproduces the "sadism" of *KnT* in its assertion of heteronormativity but simultaneously resists this sadism. In the bedroom-window scene, gender is loosened and "queered," enabling readers to escape from the hegemony of masculinist and heterosexual perspectives.

189.   Mosher, Harold F., Jr. "Greimas, Bremond, and the *Miller's Tale.*" *Style* 31 (1997): 480–99. Applying A. J. Greimas's systems to *MilT* leaves Alison in the role of passive object. Claude Bremond's model discloses a more active Alison as she learns about seduction and dissimulation, which are overvalued in the world of *MilT*.

See also nos. 3, 5, 7, 159–61, 165, 168, 170, 179.

CT—The Reeve and His Tale

See nos. 3, 6, 7, 82, 179.

CT—The Cook and His Tale

See nos. 3, 7.

CT—The Man of Law and His Tale

190.   Allen, Elizabeth. "Chaucer Answers Gower: Constance and the Trouble with Reading." *ELH* 64 (1997): 627–55. Gower's *Confessio Amantis* presents Genius's tales as morally simple, although the incest stories stimulate readers to ask moral questions. In *MLT,* Chaucer represents his narrator as misreading Gower, affecting a simplistically moral stance and vehemently disavowing impropriety; the poet thereby shows the potential failure of Gower's techniques to elicit a moral response. Constance incites violence in others and through passive silence implies her lack of self-knowledge. Also discusses the dedication in Chaucer's *TC.*

191.   Astell, Ann W. "Chaucer's 'St. Anne Trinity': Devotion, Dynasty, Dogma, and Debate." *SP* 94 (1997): 395–416. Examines Chaucer's two brief but similar references to the "St. Anne Trinity," a portrayal of Mary, Jesus, and St. Anne in the cultural context of fourteenth-century England. Concludes that the references in *MLT* and *SNT* represent two sides of a complex debate between those who saw the legend of St. Anne as promoting the sacred nature of marriage and those who saw it as strong support for virginity.

192.   Burns, Nicholas. "Christian-Islamic Relations in Dante and Chaucer: Reflections on Recent Catholicism." In Joan F. Hallisey and Mary-Anne Vetterling, eds. *Proceedings: Northeast Regional Meeting of the Conference on Christianity and Literature* (*SAC* 21 [1999], no. 107), pp. 19–24. Unlike modern thinkers who pose Islam as an "Other" in opposition to Christianity, Dante and Chaucer depict the continuities of the two religions. In *Divine Comedy,* Dante disapproves of Islam but incorporates it into his cosmic scheme. In *MLT,* Chaucer presents Islam and Anglo-Saxon paganism as "paired marginalities," bridging the two in his use of the name "Alla."

193.   Dauby, Hélène. "Trahison dans le Conte de l'Homme de Loi

des *Canterbury Tales*." In Marcel Faure, ed. *Félonie, trahison, reniements au moyen âge. Actes du troisième colloque international de Montpellier Université Paul-Valéry, 24–26 novembre 1995.* Cahiers du CRISIMA (Centre de Recherche sur l'Imaginaire et la Société au Moyen Âge), no. 3. Montpellier: Publications de l'Université Paul-Valéry, 1997, pp. 432–39. Compares acts of treachery in the tales of Constance by Trivet, Gower, and Chaucer, showing that *MLT* has a feminist point of view and a religious stance. The liveliness of the debate scenes in *MLT* may result from the occupation of the teller.

194. Dugas, Don-John. "The Legitimization of Royal Power in Chaucer's *Man of Law's Tale*." *MP* 95 (1997): 27–43. Additions to *MLT* suggest Chaucer's concern with aristocratic power, particularly with *translatio imperii*. Considered in the "context of the second decade of Richard II's reign," *MLT* "subtly legitimizes kingly authority."

195. Goodman, Jennifer R. "Marriage and Conversion in Late Medieval Romance." In James Muldoon, ed. *Varieties of Religious Conversion in the Middle Ages.* Gainesville: University Press of Florida, 1997, pp. 115–28. Examines *MLT* as one of several historical and literary accounts of princesses who marry husbands of a different religion and either convert themselves or persuade their husbands to convert. In addition to Constance, Goodman considers accounts of Clovis and Clothilde, Ethelbert and Bertha, and Floripas, the Saracen princess, from Bagnyon's *Histoire de Charlemagne* (1470) and its Castilian translation (ca. 1500).

196. Shoaf, R. A. "'Noon Englissh Digne': Dante in Late Medieval England." In Theodore J. Cachey, Jr., ed. *Dante Now: Current Trends in Dante Studies.* Notre Dame, Ind.: University of Notre Dame Press, 1995, pp. 189–203. Arguing that Chaucer was more deeply influenced by Dante than is generally accepted, Shoaf demonstrates Chaucer's dependence on Dante in *MLT*.

197. Silar, Theodore I. "The *Man of Law*'s Custance: Administrator of Frankalmoign." *N&Q* 242 (1997): 306–9. Citing examples from feudal law and practice, Silar argues that *MLT* 168 has a specific legal sense and should be translated "[Custance's] hand, in which the right to grant estates in the feudal tenure of frankalmoign."

See also nos. 71, 103, 105, 153, 164, 166, 170, 210.

CT—The Wife of Bath and Her Tale

198.   Beer, Frances. "The Wife of Bath: Sexuality vs. Symbol." *Canadian Woman Studies* 3:2 (1981): 7–8. Commentary on the Wife of Bath as a vital character who reflects Chaucer's distaste for antifeminist categorization of women as saints or whores.

199.   Delasanta, Rodney. "Nominalism and the Wife of Bath." *Providence: Studies in Western Culture* 3 (1996): 285–310. Assesses the Wife of Bath's admissions of lying, her glossings of Scripture, and her sexual punning as "nominalistic discourse" underpinned by her preference for the empirical and experiential over the universal. Disagrees with feminist readings of *WBP* and argues that Chaucer satirizes the Wife.

200.   Erzgräber, Willi. "The Wife of Bath and Molly Bloom: Self-Portrait of Two Women." In Clausdirk Pollner, Helmut Rohlfing, and Frank-Rutger Hausmann, eds. *Bright Is the Ring of Words: Festschrift für Horst Weinstock zum 65 Geburtstag (SAC* 21 [1999], no. 137), pp. 75–82. Compares Molly Bloom's concluding monologue with *WBP,* assessing the two characters' views on sexuality and euphemism and their relations with their husbands.

201.   Fleming, John V. "Sacred and Secular Exegesis in the Wyf of Bath's Tale." In Thomas Hahn and Alan Lupack, eds. *Retelling Tales: Essays in Honor of Russell Peck (SAC* 21 [1999], no. 106), pp. 73–90. The sources for the Wife of Bath's performance as exegete—and the authorities she cites in her *Tale* (in particular Ovid, for the Midas story)—make clear that the underlying theme and conflict in *WBPT* concern "surface and substance, letter and spirit." Other interpretive starting points, such as realism or misogyny, operate as subsets of this dynamic.

202.   Green, Richard Firth. "The Ballad and the Middle Ages." In Helen Cooper and Sally Mapstone, eds. *The Long Fifteenth Century: Essays for Douglas Gray (SAC* 21 [1999], no. 95), pp. 163–84. Surveys ballad scholarship and argues that exploration of medieval ballads has value for broader study, suggesting, for example, that "King Henry" provides useful context for the gentility speech in *WBT.*

203.   Hahn, Thomas. "Old Wives' Tales and Masculine Intuition." In Thomas Hahn and Alan Lupack, eds. *Retelling Tales: Essays in Honor of Russell Peck (SAC* 21 [1999], no. 106), pp. 91–108. In drafting learned sources (Ovid, Boethius, Dante) onto the core of a popular story, *WBT* generates a form of romance with appeal for "serious" readers; the appeal of this genre rests not on marvels and adventure but on individual ful-

fillment through identification with the passion and compatibility of the heterosexual couple.

204. Henebry, Charles W. M. "Apprentice Janekyn/Clerk Jankyn: Discrete Phases in Chaucer's Developing Conception of the Wife of Bath." *ChauR* 32 (1997): 146–61. Working through *WBP* at various points in his writing career, Chaucer conceived of changing the character "Janekyn" to make him "Jankyn," the Wife's fifth husband. Thus, the character changes from an apprentice to a scholar boarding with the Wife to a scholar boarding with her "gossip." The Jankyn passages reveal alterations in Chaucer's initial conception.

205. Kennedy, Beverly. "Contradictory Responses to the Wife of Bath as Evidenced by Fifteenth-Century Manuscript Variants." In Norman F. Blake and Peter Robinson, eds. *The* Canterbury Tales *Project Occasional Papers, Volume II (SAC* 21 [1999], no. 22), pp. 23–39. Argues that two distinct scribal attitudes toward the Wife of Bath can be perceived: a misogynous scholarly response typical of one manuscript family, and a more sympathetic popular response typical of another. Considers evidence from *WBP*, including spurious links, glosses, minor variants, and the "two major variants"—the renumbering of the Wife's husbands and the so-called added passages.

206. Olivares Merino, Eugenio M. "The Wife of Bath and St. Paul's Teachings on Marriage: 'Th'apostel, Whan He Speketh of Maydenhede.'" In Margarita Giménez Bon and Vickie Olsen, eds. *Proceedings of the 9th International Conference of the Spanish Society for Medieval Language and Literature (SAC* 21 [1999], no. 104), pp. 222–29. Focuses on the presentation of polygamy, virginity, and sexuality in *WBT*, using St. Paul's teachings as background.

207. Smith, Warren S. "The Wife of Bath Debates Jerome." *ChauR* 32 (1997): 129–45. In *WBP*, the Wife takes not an extremist position on marriage but rather a centralist one, often adhering to the doctrine of Augustine. By burning Jankin's book and by according husbands bliss after she attains "mastery," Alisoun refutes the misogynistic diatribes and opts for reconciliation between the sexes.

208. Solopova, Elizabeth. "The Problem of Authorial Variants in the Wife of Bath's Prologue." In Norman F. Blake and Peter Robinson, eds. *The* Canterbury Tales *Project Occasional Papers, Volume II (SAC* 21 [1999], no. 22), pp. 133–42. Analyzes the manuscript variants of the so-called added passages of *WBP*, concluding that the passages were

composed by Chaucer and that they extend from a single exemplar, probably an unfinished authorial draft.

209.   Speed, Diane. "Quest and Question in *The Wife of Bath's Tale.*" *SSEng* 22 (1996): 3–14. Comparison of *WBT* with its analogues reveals Chaucer's manipulation of generic expectations to create a sequence of "evocations and subversions of romance optimism." The hero's conventional quest is supplanted by "a textual quest on the part of the reader."

210.   Thomas, Susanne Sara. "What the Man of Law Can't Say: The Buried Legal Argument of the *Wife of Bath's Prologue.*" *ChauR* 31 (1997): 256–71. In *WBP,* the Wife delivers not a sermon but a mock legal case. Her reasoning is typical of courtroom reasoning, and (like lawyers) she buries her argument in rhetoric. Her unwritten law of marriage triumphs over the written laws of St. Paul, thus aligning her with the "new order of things"—legal negotiation and interpretation.

See also nos. 7, 13, 16, 34, 35, 37, 63, 66, 73, 85, 93, 94, 97, 102, 115, 146, 151, 160, 170.

CT—The Friar and His Tale

211.   Brody, Saul Nathaniel. "The Fiend and the Summoner, Statius and Dante: A Possible Source for the *Friar's Tale.*" *ChauR* 32 (1997): 175–82. The questioning of the fiend by the Summoner in *FrT* echoes *Purgatorio* 25. Both humans (Dante and the Summoner) ask material questions of their superhuman guides; both guides direct the questions to the realm of the spiritual. The place of both humans in the afterlife depends on their ability to understand what they are being taught. Dante, however, ascends to Paradise; the Summoner descends into Hell.

212.   Brundage, James A. "Playing by the Rules: Sexual Behaviour and Legal Norm in Medieval Europe." In Jacqueline Murray and Konrad Eisenbichler, eds. *Desire and Sexuality in the Premodern West* (*SAC* 21 [1999], no. 132), pp. 23–41. Cites *FrT* as evidence that the archdeacon's court and its officers were "bitterly disliked," in turn evidence of the gap between legal norms of sexual behavior and actual practice in medieval Europe.

See also no. 7.

CT—The Summoner and His Tale

213.   Hanks, D. Thomas, Jr. "Chaucer's *Summoner's Tale* and 'the firste smel of fartes thre.'" *Chaucer Yearbook* 4 (1997): 33–43. *SumP* and various puns in *SumT* not only transform Friar John into a fart but also indicate that his prayers invert the Pentecostal wind and "suggest that his brethren share his odious nature."

214.   Roy, Bruno. "Le problème d'*ars-metrike* du *Summoner's Tale.*" In Michel Bitot, ed., with Roberta Mullini and Peter Happé. *Divers Toyes Mengled: Essays on Medieval and Renaissance Culture in Honour of André Lascombes* (*SAC* 21 [1999], no. 84), pp. 17–25. A late-fifteenth-century French riddle about the dividing of a fart cites Chaucer as the solution, evidence that *SumT* was known at the time in France.

See also nos. 7, 97, 160, 162.

CT—The Clerk and His Tale

215.   Astell, Ann. "Translating the Female." In Jeanette Beer, ed. *Translation Theory and Practice in the Middle Ages* (*SAC* 21 [1999], no. 83), pp. 59–69. The link of Griselda and Job in *ClT* recalls Saint Gregory's *Moralia in Job,* which "translates" Job as feminine. In casting Job as a female figure, Chaucer reveals the contradictions and misogyny of Gregory's exegesis.

216.   Delasanta, Rodney. "Nominalism and the *Clerk's Tale* Revisited." *ChauR* 31 (1997): 209–31. Chaucer intensifies the voluntarist diction found in sources of *ClT,* thus urging a reconsideration of the *Tale's* principal characters and of the will of God as it was understood in late-fourteenth-century England.

217.   Harding, Wendy. "The Dynamics of Law in the *Clerk's Tale.*" *Chaucer Yearbook* 4 (1997): 45–59. *ClT* is neither an affirmation of traditional hierarchies nor a critique of them, but rather an exploration of the ways individuals interact with social, marital, and spiritual authority. Michel de Certeau's notions of "intextuation" and "incarnation" help explain how *ClT* "represents the subject's continuing struggle for definition in a world where identity is not fixed but produced through interaction."

218.   Stanbury, Sarah. "Regimes of the Visual in Premodern England: Gaze, Body, and Chaucer's *Clerk's Tale.*" *NLH* 28 (1997): 261–89.

C/T is about visual investigation. Contemporary manuscript illumination, panel painting, and statuary are instructive for understanding Chaucer's representations of lines of sight framing the female body. Relying on complex tensions between an eroticized body and repression of its own eroticizing hints, *C/T* presents Griselda's body as inflected by doubled and contradictory codes governing how bodies, sacred and profane, can be seen and known.

See also nos. 38, 61, 105, 165–67, 179.

CT—The Merchant and His Tale

219. Cooke, Jessica. "Januarie and May in Chaucer's *Merchant's Tale.*" *ES* 78 (1997): 407–16. Medieval texts on the ages of humankind (such as *The Parlement of the Thre Ages*) indicate that January of *MerT* is not extremely old or about to die; he is at the transition between middle and old age. May is in an early stage of adulthood.

220. Kraman, Cynthia. "Communities of Otherness in Chaucer's *Merchant's Tale.*" In Diane Watt, ed. *Medieval Women in Communities.* Toronto and Buffalo, N.Y.: University of Toronto Press, 1997, pp. 138–54. In *MerT,* the marginal communities of females and Jews maintain ambiguous statuses, serve as subtext to the *Tale,* and assert the seductiveness of the suppressed. The ambiguity of the garden—exciting but exclusionary—is associated with female bodies and derives from the Jewish *Song of Songs.*

221. Rose, Christine. "Women's 'Pryvete,' May, and the Privy: Fissures in the Narrative Voice in the *Merchant's Tale, 1944–86.*" *Chaucer Yearbook* 4 (1997): 61–77. A feminist reading of *MerT* as a diptych in which sympathy for May as the victim of marital rape is replaced by response to her as a fabliau shrew. May's reading and disposal of Damyan's letter are a "fissure" that marks her transformation and reflects a "fear of the outbreak of the feminine," contained by fabliau conventions. May's literacy, her connections with the raped Proserpina, and rhetorical instability enable Chaucer to expose patriarchal discourse and to explore a poetics of gender difference.

222. Taylor, Andrew. "Reading the Dirty Bits." In Jacqueline Murray and Konrad Eisenbichler, eds. *Desire and Sexuality in the Premodern West* (*SAC* 21 [1999], no. 132), pp. 280–95. Cites E. Talbot Donaldson's appreciation of May in *MerT* as an example of "iconologia," sexualized

analysis or penetration of art or literature. Sexual titillation in reading is evident in medieval manuscripts and in modern responses to medieval works, perhaps helping us explore and understand a suppressed aspect of Western culture that is still with us.

See also nos. 7, 82, 85, 94, 112, 163, 166, 170.

CT—The Squire and His Tale

223. DiMarco, Vincent. "Supposed Satiric Pointers in Chaucer's *Squire's Tale.*" *ES* 78 (1997): 311–14. Replies to M. C. Seymour's identification of seven satiric loci in *SqT* (*SAC* 13 [1991], no. 153), arguing that Chaucer's manipulations of convention may be seen as innovation rather than parody.

224. Heffernan, Carol F. "Chaucer's *Squire's Tale:* The Poetics of Interlace or the 'Well of English Undefiled.'" *ChauR* 32 (1997): 32–45. *SqT* is Chaucer's one foray into the genre of "interlace" romance, where characters and episodes are treated, then dropped, and subsequently treated again. *SqT* is not a parody like *Th;* it is a different genre that Chaucer wanted to try. He did not complete *SqT* because his talents were not suited to this kind of writing.

225. Kamowski, William. "Trading the 'Knotte' for Loose Ends: The *Squire's Tale* and the Poetics of Chaucerian Fragments." *Style* 31 (1997): 391–412. An unfinished *Tale* that constantly calls attention to stories it is not telling, *SqT* epitomizes the poetics of Chaucer's fragments, including *CT* itself. Successful fragments prompt intensified reader response; they imply infinitude. Medieval cultural contexts (including manuscript production, open-ended genres such as the *demande,* and continuations) suggest contemporary appreciation of the fragment. *CT,* like *SqT,* may be intentionally incomplete.

See also nos. 24, 61, 128, 148, 161.

CT—The Franklin and His Tale

226. McGregor, Francine. "What of Dorigen? Agency and Ambivalence in the *Franklin's Tale.*" *ChauR* 31 (1997): 365–78. Although the initial description of the egalitarian marriage in *FranT* seems to open liberating possibilities for Dorigen, the ultimate concern is which man

is most "fre." Dorigen's actions and intentions have been lost in the insistence of Arveragus and Aurelius to view her in terms of male sacrifice.

227.   Taylor, Mark N. "Servant and Lord/Lady and Wife: The *Franklin's Tale* and Conjugal Love." *ChauR* 32 (1997): 64–81. Finds parallels between *FranT* and Chrétien de Troyes's *Eric and Enid* as both courtly texts and antiadulterous ones. Chaucer's contribution to the dialectic is the integration of *fin'amour* with Truth expressed as Christian virtue, defending courtly love against the tradition of adulterous love.

See also nos. 28, 112, 145, 160, 161.

CT—The Physician and His Tale

228.   Lee, Brian S. "Justice in the *Physician's Tale* and the *Pardoner's Tale:* A Dialogic View." *Chaucer Yearbook* 4 (1997): 21–32. A Bakhtinian approach to the juxtaposition of *PhyT* and *PardT*. In its aloof style and its paralleling of Apius and Virginius as figures of justice, *PhyT* is marked by a "tendency to monologue." *PardT* is dialogic in its comic replacement of justice with mercy.

229.   Pelling, Margaret. "The Women of the Family? Speculations Around Early Modern British Physicians." *Social History of Medicine* 8 (1995): 383–401. Comments on the appropriateness of *PhyT* to its teller, both in its classical learning and in its "gender-related ambivalences," also found among historical physicians.

See also nos. 80, 160, 164.

CT—The Pardoner and His Tale

230.   Cooper, Helen. "Literary and Symbolic Inspiration in the Pardoner's Prologue 1924." In Patrick Mileham, ed. *Harry Mileham, 1873–1957: A Catalogue. His Life and Works, with a Selection of Paintings, Designs, and Sketches.* Paisley: University of Paisley, 1995, pp. 45–47. Comments on Harry Mileham's painting of the Canterbury pilgrims, depicted in a tavern during the telling of *PardPT*. Mileham is sensitive to literary and historical detail, derived especially from *GP* and the Ellesmere illustrations. The painting reflects subtler implications in its similarities to depictions of the Marriage at Cana and, especially, of the Last Supper.

231.   Gerke, Robert S. "Avarice and Mercy in the *Pardoner's Tale*."

BWVACET 14 (1992): 23–33. In plot and dominant ideas, *PardT* reflects the opposition between avarice and mercy common in the medieval vices-virtues tradition. The avaricious Pardoner lacks mercy, and the recurring notion of voluntary poverty in *PardPT* can be linked with mercy in works such as the preaching handbook *Fasciculus morum*.

232. Lázaro, Luis Alberto. "Orality and the Satiric Tradition in *The Pardoner's Tale*." In Margarita Giménez Bon and Vickie Olsen, eds. *Proceedings of the 9th International Conference of the Spanish Society for Medieval Language and Literature* (*SAC* 21 [1999], no. 104), pp. 146–53. Discusses oral satiric performance in *PardPT,* focusing on medieval flytings, sermons, and "additive" oral structure.

233. Sturges, Robert S. "The Pardoner Veiled and Unveiled." In Jeffrey Cohen and Bonnie Wheeler, eds. *Becoming Male in the Middle Ages* (*SAC* 21 [1999], no. 92), pp. 261–77. Provides Freudian and Lacanian analysis of two references to veils in the *GP* sketch of the Pardoner and the Host's threat at the end of *PardT.* The Pardoner's vernicle signifies his collusion with masculinist equations of penis and word, while his other veil indicates that masculinity is "*only* a role, never achieved but only assumed."

See also nos. 42, 61, 80, 97, 127, 156, 160, 165, 168, 170, 228.

CT—The Shipman and His Tale

See nos. 8, 156, 164.

CT—The Prioress and Her Tale

234. Asakawa, Junko. "History and Society in *The Prioress's Tale*." In Masahiko Kanno, ed. *Medieval Heritage: Essays in Honour of Tadahiro Ikegami* (*SAC* 21 [1999], no. 118), pp. 467–79 (in Japanese). Assesses the place of *PrT* in fragment 7, exploring the social and historical background of the *Tale.*

235. González Fernández-Corugedo, Santiago. "A Marian Miracle in England and Spain: Alfonso X's *Cantigas de Santa María* nº 6 and Chaucer's *The Prioress' Tale*." In Luis Alberto Lázaro Lafuente, José Simón, and Ricardo Sola Buil, eds. *Medieval Studies: Proceedings of the IIIrd International Conference of the Spanish Society for Medieval English Language*

and Literature. Madrid: Universidad de Alcalá de Henares, 1994, pp. 151–75. Comparative analysis of *PrT* and its Spanish analogue reveals how the author of each uses different rhetoric to achieve different aims, although the two share a tendency to direct personal appeal.

236. Holsinger, Bruce. "Pedagogy, Violence, and the Subject of Music: Chaucer's *Prioress's Tale* and the Ideologies of 'Song.'" *New Medieval Literatures* 1 (1997): 157–92. Both *ManT* and *PrT* reflect the violence inherent in medieval teaching of music, especially evident in the role of tactile solmization—through the use of the Guidonian hand— in ecclesiastical tradition. In both, Chaucer suggests that music fuels the violence of the "narrative progression from pedagogy to martyrdom and massacre."

237. Lampert, Lisa Renee. "After Eden, out of Zion: Defining the Christian in Early English Literature." *DAI* 58 (1997): 450A. In patriarchal tradition, the Christian is defined as male and spiritual; the female, as Other, Hebrew, and carnal. Lampert traces tensions in the parallel between women and Jews from Bernard de Clairvaux to Shakespeare's Shylock, including medieval drama and *PrT.*

238. Lindahl, Carl. "Some Uses of Number." *JFR* 34 (1997): 263–73. Folklorists' recent interest in performance tends to neglect the chronological context of storytelling, for which now-maligned type and motif indexes remain useful. A change in pattern usually signals a change in meaning. For example, the ending of *PrT* is "singularly vicious" compared to the bulk of surviving analogues, suggesting the hypocrisy of the narrator, who has praised Mary's mercy.

239. Meale, Carol M. "Women's Pity and Women's Power: Chaucer's Prioress Reconsidered." In A. J. Minnis, Charlotte C. Morse, and Thorlac Turville-Petre, eds. *Essays on Ricardian Literature: In Honour of J. A. Burrow* (*SAC* 21 [1999], no. 129), pp. 39–60. Argues that Chaucer was familiar with the realities of female monastic existence but chose to create his *GP* sketch of the Prioress from literary satire. The spirituality of *PrT,* however, is particularly apt for females, and many discussions of the relation between the teller and the *Tale* ignore their discontinuities and seek chimerical unity.

240. Oliver, Kathleen M. "Singing Bread, Manna, and the Clergeon's 'Greyn.'" *ChauR* 31 (1997): 357–64. The "greyn" placed on the little child's tongue by the Virgin in *PrT* represents the Eucharistic Host, also known as "singing bread." "Greyn" means "particle," such as

that broken from the wafer. The viaticum possessed properties of restoration and health; one portion was reserved for the sick and dying to assure a passage into heaven.

241. Rambuss, Richard. "Devotion and Defilement: The Blessed Virgin Mary and the Corporeal Hagiographics of Chaucer's *Prioress's Tale.*" In Lori Hope Lefkovitz, ed. *Textual Bodies: Changing Boundaries of Literary Representation.* Albany: State University of New York Press, 1997, pp. 75–99. The Prioress's identification with the little clergeon of *PrT* and her elisions of history indicate a "desire for transcendence" rather than sentimentality. The presence of bodily violence and prurience in *PrT* accords well with some of the "corporealities" traditionally attributed to the Virgin Mary, situating the *Tale* firmly in the genre of miracles of the Virgin.

See also nos. 18, 61, 103, 160, 161, 168, 174.

CT—The Tale of Sir Thopas

See nos. 124, 156, 164, 224.

CT—The Tale of Melibee

242. Grace, Dominick M. "Chaucer's Little Treatises." *Florilegium* 14 (1995–96):157–70. Interpretations of "tretys" in *MelP* have assumed a single referent for both occurrences of the term. But here and elsewhere Chaucer challenges assumptions of consistency between word and meaning. In making the first use of "tretys" refer to *Mel* and the second to its source, Chaucer encourages readers to think of the relationship between word and meaning as a problem, not a given.

243. Keller, Kimberly. "Prudence's Pedagogy of the Oppressed." *NM* 98 (1997): 415–26. *Mel* resembles several other late-fourteenth-century retellings of this story as a proper model for wifely imitation. In using the form of the scholastic arts lecture, however, Prudence co-opts a masculine discursive style and its authoritative language, thereby offering female readers a potential route to empowerment.

244. Staley, Lynn. "Chaucer and the Postures of Sanctity." In David Aers and Lynn Staley. *The Powers of the Holy: Religion, Politics, and Gender in Late Medieval English Culture.* University Park: Pennsylvania State University Press, 1996, pp. 179–259. Revises, and reprints as one, the

following essays: "Inverse Counsel: Contexts for the *Melibee*" (*SAC* 14 [1992], no. 228) and "Chaucer's Tale of the Second Nun and the Strategies of Dissent" (*SAC* 16 [1994], no. 248).

See also nos. 85, 162, 163, 166.

CT—The Monk and His Tale

245. Mertens-Fonck, Paule. "Un chroniqueur liégeois sur la route de Canterbury." *Bulletin de la Société Royale Le Vieux-Liège* 13 (1997): 707–18. Argues that the *GP* portrait of the Monk evokes Jean le Bel, chronicler of Edward III, and suggests that *MkT* is a poetic chronicle. With the Knight and the Prioress, the Monk is evidence that contemporary personalities and events lie behind *CT*.

246. Tsuchiya, Tadayuki. "Chaucer's 'Reyn' and Somerset Maugham's *Rain*." In Masahiko Kanno, ed. *Medieval Heritage: Essays in Honour of Tadahiro Ikegami* (*SAC* 21 [1999], no. 118), pp. 481–92 (in Japanese). Examines the play on "reyn" (as rain, reign, and rein) in Chaucer, especially in *MkT*, comparing such play with that in Somerset Maugham's *Rain*.

See also nos. 105, 161, 163, 164, 172, 248, 297.

CT—The Nun's Priest and His Tale

247. Houwen, L. A. J. R. "Flattery and the Mermaid in Chaucer's *Nun's Priest's Tale*." In L. A. J. R. Houwen, ed. *Animals and the Symbolic in Mediaeval Art and Literature*. Mediaevalia Groningana, no. 20. Groningen: Egbert Forsten, 1997, pp. 77–92. Assesses references to mermaids' singing in medieval tradition to argue that Chaucer's reference (*NPT* 7.3270) suggests flattery and thereby anticipates Chaunticleer's fall.

248. Jensen, Emily. "'Winkers' and 'Janglers': Teller/Listener/Reader Response in the *Monk's Tale*, the Link, and the *Nun's Priest's Tale*." *ChauR* 32 (1997): 183–95. As a triad, *MkT*, *Mk-NPL*, and *NPT* present such a variety of motifs, themes, and nuances that one must be mindful of their multiplicity and not reduce their reading to a "hevy" tragedy or a performance of "sentence" alone, thus falling prey to the warning in

NPT: one must neither close one's eyes when they should be open nor open one's mouth when it should be shut.

249.   Kempton, Daniel. "The Nun's Priest's Festive Doctrine: 'Al That Writen Is.'" *Assays* 8 (1995): 101–18. *NPT* is a "mock-*summa*" that skeptically examines how authority is conveyed and parodies "didactic mechanisms." Mocking various kinds of rhetoric and discourse, the Nun's Priest also evokes a laughter of merriment that "laughs without laughing at someone," the merriment of the "play of words."

250.   Narkiss, Doron. "The Fox, the Cock, and the Priest: Chaucer's Escape from Fable." *ChauR* 32 (1997): 46–63. Chaucer's *NPT* tests the limits of the fable tradition. Containing two complete fables—one from the first half (ending with the cock's downfall and capture) and another from the second (don't open your mouth)—the *Tale* combines to form a third fable, with additional morals. The added length, and the diversity it affords, allows Chaucer to deepen his characterization and to add complexity.

251.   Warner, Lawrence. "Cain, Nimrod, and the Erotics of Wandering in Late-Medieval Narrative." *DAI* 58 (1997): 862A. In medieval literature, the sins of Cain and Nimrod acquired sexual overtones associated with wandering. Warner assesses in this light the *Alliterative Morte Arthure,* Dante, Abelard, Langland, and *NPT.*

252.   ———. "Woman Is Man's Babylon: Chaucer's 'Nembrot' and the Tyranny of Enclosure in the *Nun's Priest's Tale.*" *ChauR* 32 (1997): 82–107. *NPT* is a treatment of "wandering" in sexual, genealogical, and narrative senses, informing "its presentation and enactment of tyrannical enclosure."

See also nos. 61, 109, 114, 150, 151, 163.

CT—The Second Nun and Her Tale

253.   Raybin, David. "Chaucer's Creation and Recreation of the *Lyf of Seynt Cecile.*" *ChauR* 32 (1997): 196–212. The context of *CT* changes the meaning of *SNT.* Although *SNT* is a clear statement of the "right path," *ParsT* reminds us at the end that we cannot come close to following that path. Spiritual perfection is rare; for the rest of us, there are remedies for our sins.

254.   Weise, Judith A. "Chaucer's Tell-Tale Lexicon: Romancing Seinte Cecyle." *Style* 31 (1997): 440–79. Statistical analysis, based on

Mersand's still-valid assumption that Chaucer's romance vocabulary increased throughout his career, establishes different dates for the composition of different parts of *SNT*. The first part was probably written in the early 1380s, perhaps as oblique "avoidance behavior" in connection with the Cecilia de Chaumpaigne affair. The second part was written in the mid-1390s, when *SNT* was incorporated into *CT*.

See also nos. 14, 103, 161, 164, 191, 244.

CT—The Canon's Yeoman and His Tale

255.   Doyle, Charles Clay. "'He That Will Swear Will Lie': A Further Note." *ChauR* 32 (1997): 108–10. Peter Beidler asserted (*SAC* 19 [1997], no. 49) that a "shadow allusion" to *CYT* in "Rip Van Winkle" had gone unnoticed; in fact, scholars of seventeenth-century literature have recognized the allusion. Further, Chaucer's statement that one cannot trust someone who swears to be true until death is proverbial.

256.   Linden, Stanton J. *Darke Hierogliphicks: Alchemy in English Literature from Chaucer to the Restoration.* Lexington: University Press of Kentucky, 1996. x, 373 pp. Assesses literary references and allusions to alchemy as an aspect of the transition from the medieval to the modern age, focusing on works by Chaucer, Bacon, Jonson, Donne, Herbert, Henry Vaughan, Milton, and Samuel Butler but also considering a wide array of other works. The chapter on Chaucer (pp. 37–62) identifies the aspects of *CYPT* that became "persistent motifs" in later satires of alchemy. Stanton argues that *CYP* and *CYT* are unified as a warning against false alchemy; they merit recognition as the "beginning of the tradition of literary alchemy." See also no. 346.

257.   Patterson, Lee. "The Place of the Modern in the Late Middle Ages." In Lawrence Besserman, ed. *The Challenge of Periodization: Old Paradigms and New Perspectives* (*SAC* 20 [1998], no. 63), pp. 51–66. A revised, shortened version of Patterson's "Perpetual Motion: Alchemy and the Technology of the Self" (*SAC* 17 [1995], no. 218).

CT—The Manciple and His Tale

258.   Owen, Charles A. "Chaucer's Manciple: Voice and Genre." In Thomas Hahn and Alan Lupack, eds. *Retelling Tales: Essays in Honor of Russell Peck* (*SAC* 21 [1999], no. 106), pp. 259–74. The autobiographi-

cal character of Chaucer-the-pilgrim's reportage and of the individual *Tales* in *CT* intensifies the nuanced contradictions of the Manciple's portrait in *GP*, of the competing voices in the lengthy *ManP*, and of the Manciple's aggressiveness and lack of assurance in his *Tale*.

See also nos. 97, 98, 160, 236.

CT—The Parson and His Tale

259. Ridley, Florence H. "The *Canterbury Tales:* Questions and an Answer." In Clausdirk Pollner, Helmut Rohlfing, and Frank-Rutger Hausmann, eds. *Bright Is the Ring of Words: Festschrift für Horst Weinstock zum 65 Geburtstag* (*SAC* 21 [1999], no. 137), pp. 251–57. Briefly surveys the ways Chaucer leaves "gaps" in *CT*—omissions, repetitions, reversals, etc.—and suggests how *ParsT* provides a wholeness despite these gaps.

See also nos. 98, 164, 167, 173, 253, 262.

CT—Chaucer's Retraction

260. De Looze, Laurence. *Pseudo-Autobiography in the Fourteenth Century: Juan Ruiz, Guillaume de Machaut, Jean Froissart, and Geoffrey Chaucer.* Gainesville: University Press of Florida, 1997. xii, 211 pp. Defines a genre that "plays with questions of truth, authority, and the relationship between the life *in* a book and life *outside* a book," a genre that both asserts autobiographical verity and calls "into question the possibility that the (implied) author can know himself or his own story correctly." De Looze explores roots of the genre in Augustine, Boethius, Dante, and the *Roman de la Rose* and examines more particularly Ruiz's *El libro de buen amor,* various works by Machaut and Froissart, and *CT. Ret* plays a crucial role in compelling readers to wonder whether "to believe Chaucer about Chaucer."

261. Furrow, Melissa. "The Author and Damnation: Chaucer, Writing, and Penitence." *FMLS* 33 (1997): 244–57. Uses extracts from the Middle English *Mirrur,* the fourteenth-century translation of Robert de Gretham's thirteenth-century sermon collection, to explore the context and significance of *Ret.*

262. Pigg, Daniel F. "Figuring Subjectivity in *Piers Plowman C,* the

Parson's Tale, and *Retraction:* Authorial Insertion and Identity Poetics."
Style 31 (1997): 428–39. Like the fifth passus in the C-text of *Piers Plowman, ParsT* and *Ret* use confession as a means of inscribing the author's
identity within the poem. Langland's "autobiographical" passage—part
confession, part *apologia*—integrates his subjectivity into the poem as
the penitent is integrated into the Church. Similarly *Ret,* in the context
of *ParsT,* creates an identity for Chaucer through a negotiation of power
between author and institution.

    263.   Serrano Reyes, Jesús L. "Spanish Modesty in *The Canterbury
Tales:* Chaucer and Don Juan Manuel." *SELIM* 5 (1995): 29–45. Argues
that Chaucer's *Ret* was influenced by the prologue to Don Juan Manuel's
El Conde Lucanor, citing parallels not only in attitude and sentiment but
also in structure, syntax, and grammar. Uses discourse analysis to compare linguistic features.

See also nos. 52, 308.

Anelida and Arcite

See no. 153.

Boece

    264.   Koivisto-Alanko, Päivi. "The Vocabulary of Cognition in
Early English Translations of Boethius from Chaucer to Preston." *NM*
98 (1997): 397–414. An examination of "wit" and its near synonyms
provides a control for the study of terms of cognition. *Bo* discards native
words such as "understanding" and "knowing," in favor of Romance
words such as "intelligence" and "science." These latter terms take on
more specialized meanings in early modern English, so translators generally go back to the native, more general words passed over in *Bo.*

    265.   Rissanen, Matti. "In Search of *Happiness: Felicitas* and *Beatitudo*
in Early English Boethius Translations." *SAP* 31 (1997): 237–48. Compares *Bo* with the versions of "Alfred," Walton (1410), Colville (1556),
"I. T." (1609), and Preston (1695), tracing the assimilation of sophisticated Latin terminology into English discourse.

See also no. 46.

The Book of the Duchess

266. Park, Roswell, IV. "The Authority of the Dream: Geoffrey Chaucer's 'Book of the Duchess,' 'Parliament of Fowls,' and 'House of Fame.'" *DAI* 58 (1997): 160A. In his first three dream visions, Chaucer employed traditional form to transcend the genre, exploring poetic authority and ironic possibilities.

267. Phillips, Helen, ed. *The Book of the Duchess.* 2d rev. ed. Durham Medieval Texts, no. 3. Durham: Durham Medieval Texts, 1993. 224 pp. First published in 1982, this revised edition includes all original texts, notes, commentary, and analogues from Machaut and Froissart, as well as an updated bibliography and a brief comment on recent criticism (pp. 69–73).

See also nos. 15, 112.

The House of Fame

268. Arnovick, Leslie K. "'In Forme of Speche' Is Anxiety: Orality in Chaucer's *House of Fame.*" *OT* 11 (1996): 320–45. Chaucer's proverbs in *HF* point up the provocative tension between orality and literacy in the Middle Ages. Ultimately, however, the poem illustrates that Chaucer favors literacy.

269. Boenig, Robert. "The Fragmentation of Visionary Iconography in Chaucer's *House of Fame* and the *Cloisters Apocalypse.*" In Ann Hurley and Kate Greenspan, eds. *So Rich a Tapestry: The Sister Arts and Cultural Studies.* Lewisburg, Pa.: Bucknell University Press; London: Associated University Presses, 1995, pp. 181–99. Like the *Cloisters Apocalypse, HF* depicts the Day of Judgment. Both works "select, rearrange, and fragment" the biblical account of the apocalypse, reminding us that interpretation is necessary for sinners.

270. Havely, N. R. "Muses and Blacksmiths: Italian Trecento Poetics and the Reception of Dante in 'The House of Fame.'" In A. J. Minnis, Charlotte C. Morse, and Thorlac Turville-Petre, eds. *Essays on Ricardian Literature: In Honour of J. A. Burrow* (*SAC* 21 [1999], no. 129), pp. 61–81. The Dantean aspects of *HF,* especially its invocations, not only recall the *Divine Comedy* but also reflect contemporary Italian reception and performance of Dante's masterpiece.

271. Robeson, Lisa G. "Monuments of Time: Time and the Semiol-

ogy of Inscription in the Literature of the Later Middle Ages." *DAI* 58 (1997): 451A. Ancient writings, especially inscriptions in stone, impressed the medieval reader as the most reliable of records of past wisdom, even though they might be paradoxical or, eventually, disregarded. Considers *Queste del Saint Graal, HF,* and Malory.

272.   Serrano Reyes, Jesús L. " 'Els Castells Humans': An Architectural Element in *The House of Fame.*" In Margarita Giménez Bon and Vickie Olsen, eds. *Proceedings of the 9th International Conference of the Spanish Society for Medieval Language and Literature* (*SAC* 21 [1999], no. 104), pp. 326–37. Argues that Chaucer visited Catalonia sometime between 1365 and 1366. Exposure to the country's folklore results in Chaucer's description of folk "alle on an hepe" in *HF* (2149). Serrano Reyes provides contemporary pictures of this type of "human tower" to support his hypothesis.

273.   Terrell, Katherine. "Reallocation of Hermeneutic Authority in Chaucer's *House of Fame.*" *ChauR* 31 (1997): 279–90. The chaos in *HF* is partly the result of multiple interpretations of texts and massive disagreement among the characters. Geffrey may curse the individual who "misinterprets" his writing, but he is partly joking. Only those authors whose texts are unread can expect to have complete control over their art.

See also nos. 15, 49, 81, 103, 124, 148, 159, 161, 266.

The Legend of Good Women

274.   Burns, Maggie. "Classicizing and Medievalizing Chaucer: The Sources for Pyramus' Death-throes in the *Legend of Good Women.*" *Neophil* 81 (1997): 637–47. Argues that Chaucer drew on Ovid's *Metamorphoses* and the *Ovide moralisé* rather than on Geoffrey of Monmouth for his description of Pyramus's death in *LGW.*

275.   Fradenburg, Louise O. "The Love of Thy Neighbor." In Karma Lochrie, Peggy McCracken, and James A. Schultz, eds. *Constructing Medieval Sexuality.* Medieval Cultures, no. 11. Minneapolis and London: University of Minnesota Press, 1997, pp. 135–57. Lacanian analysis of *LGW* that considers the hope of redemption as a function of charity in Aquinas and in Freud's commentary on Daniel Paul Schreber. Though beautiful and concerned with love, *LGWP* promises but does not fulfill

the desires it creates, leaving the legends as enactments of the "failure of metamorphic promise."

276.   Harding, Wendy. "Trahison d'amour et trahison d'auteur: A propos du Troïle et Crisède et du Légendier des dames vertueuses de Chaucer." In Marcel Faure, ed. *Félonie, trahison, reniements au moyen âge. Actes du troisième colloque international de Montpellier Université Paul-Valéry, 24–26 novembre 1995.* Cahiers du CRISIMA (Centre de Recherche sur l'Imaginaire et la Société au Moyen Âge), no. 3. Montpellier: Publications de l'Université Paul-Valéry, 1997, pp. 441–52. In *LGW,* Chaucer reflects on his role as poet, his relation to past and present, and his responsibility to his readers, comically exploring how literature must betray its sources through the accusation that the dreamer betrays courtly values. *TC* and *LGW* reflect Chaucer's discovery of a new literary world in Boccaccio and a new treatment of source.

277.   Seymour, M. C. "Chaucer's Revision of the Prologue to *The Legend of Good Women.*" *MLR* 92 (1997): 832–41. Compares the original (F) version with the revised (G) version of *LGWP,* commenting on stages of transmission of G—from its composition to the extant manuscript Cambridge University Library Gg 4.27. Hypothesizes that Chaucer revised *LGWP* as a separate work after Henry IV's usurpation, imitating Gower's *Confessio Amantis* and motivated by political and aesthetic concerns.

278.   Taylor, Andrew. "Anne of Bohemia and the Making of Chaucer." *SAC* 19 (1997): 95–119. Reconsiders what role Anne may have had as a patron of Chaucer, examining her literary interests and political career and assessing the relation between these and the depiction of Alceste in *LGWP.* From Lydgate forward, the construction of Chaucer as "masculinized" master poet has obscured the possibility that Anne had an impact on Chaucer's career.

See also nos. 9, 15, 85, 97, 103, 105, 150, 153, 155, 177.

The Parliament of Fowls

279.   Hoffman, Donald L. "The Court of Nature and the Nature of Courts: An Inquiry into the Function of Natura in Chaucer's *Parliament of Fowls.*" In Will Wright and Steven Kaplan, eds. *The Image of Nature in Literature, the Media, and Society* (*SAC* 21 [1999], no. 158), pp. 61–67. Compares the depiction of social order in Aristotle's *Politics* with that

in *PF.* Chaucer's Natura is a figure of "communal order" who properly subordinates the drive for procreation to the need for social hierarchy.

280.   Kikuchi, Akio. "The Mythological Authorization of Kingship in Chaucer's *The Parliament of Fowls.*" *Shiron* 36 (1997): 1–15. Explores political implications of *PF,* commenting on the theme of common profit and on Chaucer's political situation. Examines the role of Nature as an advocate of hierarchy and a suppresser of rebellion.

281.   Straus, Barrie Ruth. "Freedom Through Renunciation? Women's Voices, Women's Bodies, and the Phallic Order." In Jacqueline Murray and Konrad Eisenbichler, eds. *Desire and Sexuality in the Premodern West* (*SAC* 21 [1999], no. 132), pp. 245–64. The formel eagle in *PF,* Emily in *KnT,* and Margery Kempe seek to delay or renounce sexual activity. The eagle's blush embodies her later request to delay a choice of mate; Emily's desire to remain unmarried is marked by her desire to reject the "physical effects of heterosexuality." In these works, as in Margery Kempe, female choice is constrained by masculine discourse.

282.   Watson, Nicholas. "Visions of Inclusion: Universal Salvation and Vernacular Theology in Pre-Reformation England." *JMEMS* 27 (1997): 145–87. The belief that all humanity will attain salvation occurs with surprising frequency in Middle English writings. Though influenced by Latin theology, the sentiment was generated primarily by English and Anglo-Norman vernacular culture. *PF* shows the limits of such universalism, as well as the potential power of the motif.

See also nos. 9, 15, 91, 109, 112, 114, 177, 266.

Troilus and Criseyde

283.   Andretta, Helen R. "Spirit, Psyche, and Self in *Troilus and Criseyde.*" In Joan F. Hallisey and Mary-Anne Vetterling, eds. *Proceedings: Northeast Regional Meeting of the Conference on Christianity and Literature* (*SAC* 21 [1999], no. 107), pp. 1–7. Considers Criseyde, Troilus, and Pandarus as figures of Spirit, Psyche, and Self, respectively, suggesting that the interactions among the three characters in *TC* depict a "false theology" that is made right in Troilus's translation.

284.   Andretta, Helen Ruth. *Chaucer's* Troilus and Criseyde: *A Poet's Response to Ockhamism.* Studies in the Humanities, no. 29. New York: Peter Lang, 1997. 201 pp. Surveys Ockhamism and Chaucer's exposure to it. Through both a "philosophical interpretation of character" and a

close analysis of images, words, and discourse, Andretta maintains Chaucer's allegiance to "manifest truths that are Boethian, traditionally scholastic, and therefore certain—a challenge to propositions that are Ockhamist, skeptical, and only probable." Considers the epilogue to *TC* as revealing "the entire poem's message: one must look up beyond this world, to behold real truth."

285. Bankert, Dabney Anderson. "The Poetics of Religious Conversion in Medieval English Literature." *DAI* 57 (1997): 4733A. Considers biblical, historical, traditional, and hagiographical accounts of conversion, exploring Chaucer's appropriation of them to psychologize courtly love or "*fin'amors* as a surrogate religion" in *TC*.

286. Bloomfield, Josephine. "Chaucer and the Polis: Piety and Desire in the *Troilus and Criseyde*." *MP* 94 (1997): 291–304. Although Chaucer's narrator is sympathetic to the hero of *TC*, Troilus's "stellification" contradicts our expectations because he values his own desires over the welfare of the polis. Chaucer's "political and moral judgment against Troilus's behavior" may reflect guarded criticism of the courts of Edward III and Richard II.

287. Camargo, Martin. "Where's the Brief? The Ars Dictaminis and the Reading/Writing Between the Lines." *Disputatio* 1 (1996): 1–17. Considers the letter as a means of spoken and written transmission and demonstrates how the most important elements and functions of the letter prescribed by the *artes dictaminis* were put to creative use in medieval literary texts such as the *Chanson de Roland* and *TC*.

288. Classen, Albrecht. "The Dangers and Promises of Reading, Two Medieval Viewpoints: Wolfram von Eschenbach and Geoffrey Chaucer." *MedPers* 11 (1996): 43–63. Summarizes the scholastic idea of the book and applies the concept of the written word (book) as "essential epistemological instrument" to Wolfram's *Titurel* fragments (ca. 1220) and to *TC*. Chaucer presents Troilus as a misreader of texts who only at the end of the romance—and tragically—learns to read accurately.

289. Fehrenbacher, Richard W. " 'Al That Which Chargeth Nought to Seye': The Theme of Incest in *Troilus and Criseyde*." *Exemplaria* 9 (1997): 341–69. Readers who refuse to recognize Pandarus's incestuous desire risk participating in the denial of such desire in patriarchal societies; they also risk colluding in society's invocation of the incest taboo, which underlies traffic in women.

290. Fichte, Joerg O. "Von der Historie zur Tragödie: Macht und Ohnmacht des Schicksals über Troilus und Cressida." In Walter Haug

and Burghart Wachinger, eds. *Fortuna.* Tübingen: Max Niemeyer, 1995, pp. 192–215. Surveys the theme of Fortune's influence in treatments of the story of Troilus and Criseyde from Boccaccio to Dryden, including *TC* and the versions of Henryson and Shakespeare.

291.   Goodman, Jennifer R. "Nature as Destiny in *Troilus and Criseyde*." *Style* 31 (1997): 413–27. Aristotelian natural philosophy, specifically the doctrines of natural place and natural motion, lie at the heart of the structure and meaning of *TC*. Troilus and Criseyde are bodies in motion toward their natural resting places; their natures—her slidingness and his steadfastness—are their destinies. The poem's Christian ending is appropriate to the ultimate destiny of human beings.

292.   Hanning, Robert W. "*Troilus and Criseyde*, 4.210: A New Conjecture." *Chaucer Yearbook* 4 (1997): 79–83. Reads "thus seyde here and howne" (*TC* 4.210) as "everyone agreed," a reading supported by reference to Henry Knighton's *Chronicle,* in which Howne's army ("Hownher") may have connoted wide consensus in popular tradition.

293.   Jimura, Akiyuki. "Chaucer's Description of Nature Through Adjectives in *Troilus and Criseyde*." In *English and English Teaching, Vol. 2: A Festschrift in Honour of Kiichiro Nakatani.* Hiroshima: Department of English, Faculty of School Education, Hiroshima University, 1997, pp. 57–69. In *TC,* descriptions of nature, including natural objects, plants, and animals, reflect the characters' emotions. When characters "act in harmony with nature," things go well; when they act against nature, they are destroyed by its "uncontrollable power."

294.   Kanno, Masahiko. "A Contextual Meaning of 'Penaunce' in *Troilus and Criseyde*." In Masahiko Kanno, ed. *Medieval Heritage: Essays in Honour of Tadahiro Ikegami* (*SAC* 21 [1999], no. 118), pp. 241–54. Whereas Boccaccio uses the straightforward word "tradimento" of Criseyde, Chaucer uses the roundabout phrase "hire hertes variaunce." In *TC,* "in gret penaunce" means both that "Criseyde was in great misery" and "Criseyde was in hell for her sins."

295.   Kelen, Sarah Ann. "'Clerkes, Poetes, and Historiographs': Chaucer, Langland, and the Literature of History." *DAI* 57 (1997): 3928A. Identified by Caxton as "historiographs," Chaucer and Langland write as historians and consider the meaning of writing history. In *TC,* Chaucer discusses sources and antiquity as marks of authority and hindrances to reading. The English literary canon is also a historical canon.

296.   Kellogg, Laura D. *Boccaccio's and Chaucer's Cressida.* Studies in the Humanities, no. 16. New York: Peter Lang, 1995. xi, 144 pp. As-

sesses Boccaccio's and Chaucer's attitudes toward their sources by examining the relations of their narrators with Cressida in *Filostrato* and *TC*. Cressida's legendary status as dishonest and inconstant had been established before Boccaccio and Chaucer were writing, but other antecedents are reflected in her character. Cressida's literary heritage owes much to female characterizations in Virgil and Ovid, as well as to Dante's readings of Virgil and Ovid, all of which provide compelling models for the Cressida of the High Middle Ages. See also no. 340.

297. Kelly, Henry Ansgar. *Chaucerian Tragedy.* Cambridge: D. S. Brewer, 1997. xi, 297 pp. Chaucer was the first to consider Boccaccio's stories tragedies. But unlike Boccaccio, who served a cautionary moralism and wished to stress retributive justice, Chaucer aimed primarily at sympathy and empathy, developing a generic theory that included all kinds of falls and misfortunes and that set him apart from writers who simply wrote ably on the theme of mutability or who had a keen sense of *lacrimae rerum*. With *TC,* Chaucer introduced the word "tragedy" into English, established its meaning for later generations, and wrote the first tragedy with any claims to greatness since the Greek tragedies.

298. Kolve, V. A. "God-Denying Fools and the Medieval 'Religion of Love.'" *SAC* 19 (1997): 3–59. Presidential Address, the New Chaucer Society, Tenth International Congress, 26–29 July 1996, University of California, Los Angeles. Documents the pictorial (25 b&w illus.) and intellectual traditions of the "fool . . . who says in his heart, There is no God," using the traditions as backdrop for analyzing *Folie de Tristan* and *TC*. In his love of Criseyde, Troilus is similar to the God-denying fool. In the tensions between Troilus's apotheosis and the Palinode of *TC,* Chaucer explores the limits of paganism and courtly passion, both of which lack Christian deity.

299. Quinn-Lang, Caitlin. "'The Augerye of Thise Fowles': Treacherous Birds in Chaucer's *Troilus and Criseyde.*" In Will Wright and Steven Kaplan, eds. *The Image of Nature in Literature, the Media, and Society* (*SAC* 21 [1999], no. 158), pp. 38–47. Examines the literary backgrounds of the birds in *TC* to argue that the birds "carry with them themes of treachery and unnatural and sorrowful love"; they help depict the "dubious nature of temporal love."

300. Ross, Valerie A. "Believing Cassandra: Intertextual Politics and the Interpretations of Dreams in *Troilus and Criseyde.*" *ChauR* 31 (1997): 339–56. Both Criseyde's dream in bk. 2 and Troilus's dream in

bk. 5 of *TC* are generally understood in terms that debase Criseyde. But Chaucer's intertextual construction of these dreams and his reconstruction of Cassandra and Criseyde from his sources indicate Chaucer's concern for a female audience.

301. ———. "Resisting Chaucerian Misogyny: Reinscribing Criseyde." *Æstel* 4 (1996): 29–56. Examines feminist and antifeminist readings of Criseyde, arguing that—like Chaucer, who appropriates his sources, and like his narrator, who constantly negotiates and repositions himself in relation to Lollius—Criseyde performs, mimes, and parodies gendered behavior and language, appropriating them for her own purposes.

302. Spearing, A. C. "A Ricardian 'I': The Narrator of 'Troilus and Criseyde.'" In A. J. Minnis, Charlotte C. Morse, and Thorlac Turville-Petre, eds. *Essays on Ricardian Literature: In Honour of J. A. Burrow* (*SAC* 21 [1999], no. 129), pp. 1–22. Surveys critical opinion about the narrator of *TC,* arguing that the narrator is not best regarded as unreliable, that it is difficult to separate narrator from author, and that it is unwise or impossible to construct a single stable narratorial persona from the poem.

303. Utz, Richard J. "'As Writ Myn Auctour Called Lollius': Divine and Authorial Omnipotence in Chaucer's *Troilus and Criseyde.*" In Hugo Keiper, Richard J. Utz, and Christoph Bode, eds. *Nominalism and Literary Discourse: New Perspectives* (*SAC* 21 [1999], no. 120), pp. 123–44. Surveys the critical history of "Lollius"—Chaucer's putative source for *TC*—and argues that the invention poses a poetic analogy to the absolute power of the nominalist God. By creating Lollius, Chaucer makes his general audience believe in the intuitive cognition of a nonexistent power. Informed readers such as Gower and Strode recognized the invention as a parodic indicator of poetic self-consciousness.

304. Valentine, Virginia Walker. "Apologia pro Criseyde: 'Of Harmes Two, the Lesse Is for to Chese.'" In Virginia Walker Valentine. *Chaucer's Knight: A Man Ther Was* (*SAC* 21 [1999], no. 152), pp. 25–33. Though there are elements of courtly love in *TC,* the poem does not evaluate Criseyde by courtly standards. Instead, it shows her choosing the "lesser harm" of being unfaithful rather than endangered.

See also nos. 9, 25, 26, 41, 47–49, 55, 80, 82, 86, 97, 99, 103, 105, 110–12, 114, 124, 145, 146, 148, 151, 161, 177, 190, 276.

Lyrics and Short Poems

See nos. 9, 91, 97, 100, 102, 306.

An ABC

305. Stevenson, Kay Gilliland. "Medieval Rereading and Rewriting: The Context of Chaucer's 'ABC.'" In Michel Bitot, ed., with Roberta Mullini and Peter Happé. *Divers Toyes Mengled: Essays on Medieval and Renaissance Culture in Honour of André Lascombes* (*SAC* 21 [1999], no. 84), pp. 27–42. Explores literary and historical contexts that complicate reception of *ABC,* including works by Jean de Meun, Guillaume de Deguileville, and John Lydgate. Chaucer's stand-alone translation initiates an immediacy with its audience that is not apparent in Deguileville's *Pèlerinage de la vie humaine* or Lydgate's *Pilgrimage of the Life of Man.*

Adam Scriveyn

See no. 102.

The Envoy to Bukton

See nos. 73, 110.

The Complaint of Mars

306. Van Dyke, Carolynn. "'To Whom Shul We Compleyn?' The Poetics of Agency in Chaucer's Complaints." *Style* 31 (1997): 370–90. Chaucer's complaints develop a "poetics of agency" as they explore questions of subjectivity and causation. His most sophisticated complaint, *Mars,* presents "incompatible forms of causation" but makes them congruent poetically, achieving a compassion that links subjectivity to the larger created world.

See also nos. 9, 82.

The Envoy to Scogan

See no. 110.

Chaucerian Apocrypha

307. Essaku, Joshua. "Chaucer's *Ghoast* and Gower's *Confessio Amantis.*" *N&Q* 242 (1997): 458–59. *Chaucer's Ghoast,* published in 1692, is a rendering of twelve stories from Gower; it has nothing to do with Chaucer.

308. Forni, Kathleen. "Did Usk's *Testament of Love* and *The Plowman's Tale* Ruin Chaucer's Early Reputation?" *NM* 98 (1997): 261–72. The attribution of *Testament of Love* and *The Plowman's Tale* to Chaucer seems to have had no unfavorable effect, though the acceptance of his authorship of *The Plowman's Tale* may have fueled the belief that *Ret* was a monkish forgery.

309. McCarl, Mary Rhinelander, ed. *The Plowman's Tale: The c. 1532 and 1606 Editions of a Spurious Canterbury Tale.* The Renaissance Imagination. New York and London: Garland, 1997. 318 pp. Prints two versions of *The Plowman's Tale* (ca. 1400)—the 1533 edition originally intended for publication in Francis Thynne's 1532 edition of Chaucer's *Works* but suppressed and the 1606 edition by Anthony Wotton, which includes more than five hundred notes. Includes original notes and glosses, additional explanatory notes, a glossary and index, and a sixty-five-page introduction exploring the textual history of the poem, its Lollard roots and Puritan response, and its relations with Chaucer's corpus.

See also nos. 9, 11, 80.

The Romaunt of the Rose

See nos. 94, 124, 148.

Book Reviews

310. Andrew, Malcolm, Charles Moorman, and Daniel J. Ransom, eds., with the assistance of Lynne Hunt Levy. *The General Prologue* (*SAC* 17 [1995], no. 11). Rev. N. F. Blake, *The* Canterbury Tales *Project Occa-*

sional Papers, Volume II (SAC 21 [1999], no. 22), pp. 165–68; Larry Scanlon, *Speculum* 72 (1997): 127–29.

311. Arn, Mary-Jo, ed. *"Fortunes stabilnes": Charles of Orléans's English Book of Love (SAC* 19 [1997], no. 76). Rev. Michael G. Hanly, *SAC* 19 (1997): 211–13.

312. Ashby, Cristina, Geoff Couldrey, Susan Dickson, et al., developers. *Chaucer: Life and Times CD-ROM (SAC* 19 [1997], no. 3). Rev. Craig A. Berry, *ComH* 30 (1996–97): 472–74.

313. Astell, Ann W. *Chaucer and the Universe of Learning (SAC* 20 [1998], no. 112). Rev. Thomas J. Farrell, *Envoi* 6 (1997): 147–52; Norm Klassen, *MÆ* 66 (1997): 329–31.

314. Baswell, Christopher. *Virgil in Medieval England: Figuring the* Aeneid *from the Twelfth Century to Chaucer (SAC* 19 [1997], no. 292). Rev. Charles Blyth, *Speculum* 72 (1997): 106–8; Theresa M. Krier, *SAC* 19 (1997): 216–19; Wendy Chapman Peek, *MFN* 24 (1997): 58–60; Kenneth J. Tille, *R&L* 29 (1997): 117–18.

315. Beadle, Richard, and A. J. Piper, eds. *New Science out of Old Books: Studies in Manuscripts and Early Printed Books in Honour of A. I. Doyle (SAC* 21 [1999], no. 19). Rev. Hoyt N. Duggan, *SAC* 19 (1997): 219–23; A. S. G. Edwards, *MÆ* 66 (1997): 308.

316. Beidler, Peter G., ed. *Geoffrey Chaucer:* The Wife of Bath *(SAC* 20 [1998], no. 165). Rev. John McLaughlin, *Envoi* 6 (1997): 30–33; Daniel F. Pigg, *SAC* 19 (1997): 224–25.

317. Boenig, Robert. *Chaucer and the Mystics:* The Canterbury Tales *and the Genre of Devotional Prose (SAC* 19 [1997], no. 136). Rev. Laurie Finke, *SAC* 19 (1997): 227–30.

318. Bowers, John M., ed. *The Canterbury Tales: Fifteenth-Century Continuations and Additions (SAC* 16 [1994], no. 6). Rev. N. F. Blake, *The* Canterbury Tales *Project Occasional Papers, Volume II (SAC* 21 [1999], no. 22), pp. 169–71.

319. Brewer, Derek, ed. *Medieval Comic Tales,* 2d ed. *(SAC* 21 [1999], no. 88). Rev. Melissa Furrow, *N&Q* 242 (1997): 378–79.

320. Bronfman, Judith. *Chaucer's* Clerk's Tale: *The Griselda Story Received, Rewritten, Illustrated (SAC* 18 [1996], no. 199). Rev. Joerg O. Fichte, *Anglia* 115 (1997): 397–400.

321. Brown, Peter. *Chaucer at Work: The Making of the* Canterbury Tales *(SAC* 18 [1996], no. 136). Rev. David Staines, *Speculum* 72 (1997): 119–20.

322. Bullough, Vern L., and James A. Brundage, eds. *Handbook of*

Medieval Sexuality (*SAC* 21 [1999], no. 90). Rev. Lawrence Warner, *SAC* 19 (1997): 230–32.

323. Coleman, Joyce. *Public Reading and the Reading Public in Late Medieval England and France* (*SAC* 20 [1998], no. 72). Rev. James J. Murphy, *MÆ* 66 (1997): 328–29.

324. Cowen, Janet, and George Kane, eds. *Geoffrey Chaucer: The Legend of Good Women* (*SAC* 19 [1997], no. 18). Rev. Peter Robinson, *The* Canterbury Tales *Project Occasional Papers, Volume II* (*SAC* 21 [1999], no. 22), pp. 171–79; M. C. Seymour, *MLR* 92 (1997): 690–91.

325. Crane, Susan. *Gender and Romance in Chaucer's* Canterbury Tales (*SAC* 18 [1996], no. 139). Rev. Catherine Batt, *MLR* 92 (1997): 168–69; Sheila Fisher, *MP* 95 (1997): 87–90.

326. Desmond, Marilynn. *Reading Dido: Gender, Textuality, and the Medieval* Aeneid (*SAC* 18 [1996], no. 82). Rev. Brigitte Buettner, *SIcon* 18 (1997): 221–24; Robert S. Sturges, *Chaucer Yearbook* 4 (1997): 103–7.

327. De Weever, Jacqueline. *Chaucer Name Dictionary: A Guide to Astrological, Biblical, Historical, Literary, and Mythological Names in the Works of Geoffrey Chaucer* (*SAC* 11 [1989], no. 77). Rev. David Raybin, *SAC* 19 (1997): 233–35.

328. Earp, Lawrence. *Guillaume de Machaut: A Guide to Research* (*SAC* 19 [1997], no. 4). Rev. Charles S. Heppleston, *MÆ* 66 (1997): 150–55.

329. Edwards, Robert R., ed. *Art and Context in Late Medieval English Narrative: Essays in Honor of Robert Worth Frank, Jr.* (*SAC* 18 [1996], no. 85). Rev. Ruth Morse, *YLS* 10 (1997): 191–94.

330. Evans, Ruth, and Lesley Johnson, eds. *Feminist Readings in Middle English Literature: The Wife of Bath and All Her Sect* (*SAC* 18 [1996], no. 86). Rev. Denise L. Despres, *CL* 49 (1997): 87–88; Jill Mann, *Archiv* 234 (1997): 142–45.

331. Fisher, John H. *The Emergence of Standard English* (*SAC* 20 [1998], no. 55). Rev. Thomas Cable, *SAC* 19 (1997): 241–44.

332. Gellrich, Jesse M. *Discourse and Dominion in the Fourteenth Century: Oral Contexts of Writing in Philosophy, Politics, and Poetry* (*SAC* 19 [1997], no. 168). Rev. Michael W. Twomey, *JEGP* 96 (1997): 253–56.

333. Grudin, Michaela Paasche. *Chaucer and the Politics of Discourse* (*SAC* 20 [1998], no. 84). Rev. D[onald] C. Baker, *ELN* 35:1 (1997): 70–71.

334. Havely, Nicholas R., ed. *Chaucer:* The House of Fame (*SAC* 19 [1997], no. 22). Rev. Janet M. Cohen, *N&Q* 242 (1997): 381–82.

335.   Heffernan, Carol Falvo. *The Melancholy Muse: Chaucer, Shakespeare, and Early Medicine* (*SAC* 19 [1997], no. 284). Rev. Lea T. Olsan, *SAC* 19 (1997): 253–54.

336.   Honegger, Thomas. *From Phoenix to Chauntecleer: Medieval English Animal Poetry* (*SAC* 21 [1999], no. 109). Rev. Richard Newhauser, *SAC* 19 (1997): 255–58; Dorothy Yamamoto, *MÆ* 66 (1997): 326–27.

337.   Justice, Steven. *Writing and Rebellion: England in 1381* (*SAC* 18 [1996], no. 95). Rev. Mark Amsler, *SAC* 19 (1997): 258–66; E. Kay Harris, *Chaucer Yearbook* 4 (1997): 145–49.

338.   Kanno, Masahiko. *Studies in Chaucer's Words: A Contextual and Semantic Approach* (*SAC* 20 [1998], no. 56). Rev. Leo Carruthers, *ÉA* 50 (1997): 470.

339.   Kay, Sarah, and Miri Rubin, eds. *Framing Medieval Bodies* (*SAC* 19 [1997], no. 239). Rev. Celeste Patton, *CLS* 34 (1997): 184–88.

340.   Kellogg, Laura D. *Boccaccio's and Chaucer's Cressida* (*SAC* 21 [1999], no. 296). Rev. Disa Gambera, *SAC* 19 (1997): 267–71.

341.   Kimmelman, Burt. *The Poetics of Authorship in the Later Middle Ages: The Emergence of the Modern Literary Persona* (*SAC* 20 [1998], no. 91). Rev. David Greetham, *Text* 10 (1997): 390–96.

342.   Klassen, Norman. *Chaucer on Love, Knowledge and Sight* (*SAC* 19 [1997], no. 103). Rev. Ebbe Klitgård, *ES* 78 (1997): 576–77.

343.   Kuczynski, Michael P. *Prophetic Song: The Psalms as Moral Discourse in Late Medieval England* (*SAC* 19 [1997], no. 104). Rev. Christina van Nolcken, *N&Q* 242 (1997): 112–23.

344.   Lambdin, Laura C., and Robert T. Lambdin, eds. *Chaucer's Pilgrims: An Historical Guide to the Pilgrims in* The Canterbury Tales (*SAC* 20 [1998], no. 118). Rev. Laura F. Hodges, *Chaucer Yearbook* 4 (1997): 166–71; Dolores Warwick Frese, *SAC* 19 (1997): 271–74.

345.   Laskaya, Anne. *Chaucer's Approach to Gender in the* Canterbury Tales (*SAC* 19 [1997], no. 149). Rev. Ebbe Klitgård, *ES* 78 (1997): 576–77; Nicola F. McDonald, *MÆ* 66 (1997): 139–40.

346.   Linden, Stanton J. *Darke Hierogliphicks: Alchemy in English Literature from Chaucer to the Restoration* (*SAC* 21 [1999], no. 256). Rev. Andrew Hadfield, *TLS,* May 23, 1997, p. 24.

347.   Machan, Tim William. *Textual Criticism and Middle English Texts* (*SAC* 18 [1996], no. 29). Rev. Hoyt Duggan, *Text* 10 (1997): 377–88; response from Machan, *Text* 10 (1997): 388–90.

348.   Minnis, A. J., ed. *Chaucer's* Boece *and the Medieval Tradition of*

Boethius (*SAC* 17 [1995], no. 220). Rev. Alfred David, *MLR* 92 (1997): 691–92.

349. ———, with V. J. Scattergood and J. J. Smith. *The Shorter Poems* (Oxford Guides to Chaucer) (*SAC* 19 [1997], no. 112). Rev. Robert W. Hanning, *SAC* 19 (1997): 275–79.

350. Myles, Robert. *Chaucerian Realism* (*SAC* 18 [1996], no. 111). Rev. Peter Brown, *MLR* 92 (1997): 169–70; Joerg O. Fichte, *Archiv* 234 (1997): 146–47; David Lyle Jeffrey, *ESC* 23 (1997): 480–83; Kritz Kemmler, *Anglia* 115 (1997): 396–97; Stephen Partridge, *Mediaevistik* 19 (1997): 586–88.

351. Newhauser, Richard G., and John A. Alford, eds. *Literature and Religion in the Later Middle Ages: Philological Studies in Honor of Siegfried Wenzel* (*SAC* 19 [1997], no. 114). Rev. M. Teresa Tavormina, *SAC* 19 (1997): 282–86.

352. Nicolaisen, W. F. H., ed. *Oral Tradition in the Middle Ages* (*SAC* 19 [1997], no. 115). Rev. Nancy Mason Bradbury, *SAC* 19 (1997): 286–88.

353. Pask, Kevin. *The Emergence of the English Author: Scripting the Life of the Poet in Early Modern England* (*SAC* 20 [1998], no. 4). Rev. H. R. Woudhuysen, *TLS*, June 27, 1997, p. 26.

354. Plummer, John F., III, ed. *The Summoner's Tale: A Variorum Edition of the Works of Geoffrey Chaucer* (*SAC* 19 [1997], no. 23). Rev. William Kamowski, *SAC* 19 (1997): 289–91.

355. Rand Schmidt, Kari Anne. *The Authorship of the* Equatorie of the Planetis (*SAC* 17 [1995], no. 233). Rev. E. G. Stanley, *N&Q* 242 (1997): 383–85.

356. Rex, Richard. *"The Sins of Madame Eglentyne" and Other Essays on Chaucer* (*SAC* 19 [1997], no. 118). Rev. Douglas Wurtele, *SAC* 19 (1997): 292–94.

357. Robinson, Peter, ed., with contributions from N. F. Blake, Daniel W. Mosser, Stephen Partridge, and Elizabeth Solopova. *The Wife of Bath's Prologue on CD-ROM* (*SAC* 20 [1998], no. 11). Rev. Michael Fraser, *Computers & Texts* 12 (1996): 21–23; Anne Hudson, *MÆ* 66 (1997): 332–34; Paul G. Remley, *Envoi* 6 (1997): 211–21.

358. Scanlon, Larry. *Narrative, Authority, and Power: The Medieval Exemplum and the Chaucerian Tradition* (*SAC* 18 [1996], no. 120). Rev. Gloria Cigman, *MLR* 92 (1997): 429–30; Paul Strohm, *MP* 95 (1997): 84–86.

359. Seymour, M. C. *A Catalogue of Chaucer Manuscripts, Volume 1: Works Before the* Canterbury Tales *(SAC* 19 [1997], no. 7). Rev. N. F. Blake, *ES* 78 (1997): 572–73; Alfred David, *Speculum* 72 (1997): 1216–18; A. S. G. Edwards, *RES,* n.s., 48 (1997): 82–84; Daniel J. Ransom, *SAC* 19 (1997): 299–302.

360. Sigal, Gail. *Erotic Dawn-Songs of the Middle Ages: Voicing the Lyric Lady (SAC* 21 [1999], no. 145). Rev. Marianne E. Kalinka, *JEGP* 96 (1997): 403–4; Theo Stemmler, *N&Q* 242 (1997): 538.

361. Singman, Jeffrey L., and Will McLean. *Daily Life in Chaucer's England (SAC* 19 [1997], no. 124). Rev. Lorraine Stock, *SAC* 19 (1997): 308–10.

362. Smith, Susan L. *The Power of Women: A Topos in Medieval Art and Literature (SAC* 21 [1999], no. 146). Rev. Bella Millett, *MÆ* 66 (1997): 307; Miri Rubin, *EHR* 112 (1997): 1251–52.

363. Spencer, H. Leith. *English Preaching in the Late Middle Ages (SAC* 17 [1995], no. 118). Rev. Thomas G. Duncan, *N&Q* 242 (1997): 254–56.

364. Stevens, Martin, and Daniel Woodward, eds. *The Ellesmere Chaucer: Essays in Interpretation (SAC* 19 [1997], no. 26). Rev. R. W. Hanning, *SIcon* 18 (1997): 258–64; A. A. MacDonald, *ES* 78 (1997): 573–75; Daniel J. Ransom, *JEGP* 96 (1997): 441–43; Peter Robinson, *SAC* 19 (1997): 315–19.

365. Tavormina, M. Teresa, and R. F. Yeager, eds. *The Endless Knot: Essays on Old and Middle English in Honor of Marie Borroff (SAC* 19 [1997], no. 128). Rev. David G. Allen, *Chaucer Yearbook* 4 (1997): 200–202; John H. Fisher, *SAC* 19 (1997): 322–24; Thorlac Turville-Petre, *N&Q* 242 (1997): 249–50.

366. Thompson, N. S. *Chaucer, Boccaccio, and the Debate of Love: A Comparative Study of* The Decameron *and* The Canterbury Tales *(SAC* 20 [1998], no. 128). Rev. Peter G. Beidler, *MÆ* 66 (1997): 331–32; John Usher, *TLS,* May 23, 1997, p. 25.

367. Tinkle, Theresa. *Medieval Venuses and Cupids: Sexuality, Hermeneutics, and English Poetry (SAC* 20 [1998], no. 111). Rev. Derek Brewer, *MÆ* 66 (1997): 303–4; Nicola F. McDonald, *N&Q* 242 (1997): 242.

368. Utz, Richard J., ed. *Literary Nominalism and the Theory of Rereading Late Medieval Texts: A New Research Paradigm (SAC* 19 [1997], no. 130). Rev. Rodney Delasanta, *SAC* 19 (1997): 328–32.

369. Weisl, Angela Jane. *Conquering the Reign of Femeny: Gender and*

Genre in Chaucer's Romance (*SAC* 19 [1997], no. 132). Rev. Jean E. Jost, *SAC* 19 (1997): 335–44; Nicola F. McDonald, *MÆ* 66 (1997): 139–40.

370.   Wilkins, Nigel. *Music in the Age of Chaucer, with Chaucer Songs* (*SAC* 19 [1997], no. 134). Rev. Christopher R. Wilson, *RES,* n.s., 48 (1997): 516–17.

371.   Wynne-Davies, Marion. *Woman and Arthurian Literature: Seizing the Sword* (*SAC* 20 [1998], no. 182). Rev. Bruce A. Beatie, *Chaucer Yearbook* 4 (1997): 213–17; Linda Marie Zaerr, *RMR* 51 (1997): 109–12.

Author Index—Bibliography

1998 CONGRESS PROGRAM

Friday, 17 July

2:30 p.m.—Welcome and business meeting
Presider: Mary Carruthers (*New York University*)

3:30 p.m.—Concurrent sessions
Carpe Florem: Chaucer and the *Roman de la Rose* (papers)
Organizer and presider: A. J. Minnis (*University of York*)
Alan Gaylord (*Dartmouth College*)
   "Ribald and Auctor: Jean de Meun as Chaucer's 'Model for a
   Literary Life'"
Maria Bullon-Fernandez (*Seattle University*)
   "'The Word Mai Worch Above Kinde': From Jean De Meun's to
   Gower's Pygmalion"
Rosalind Brown-Grant (*University of Leeds*)
   "Christine de Pizan as Reader of the *Rose*"

Textual Criticism and the Reception of Chaucer's Work (papers)
Organizer and presider: Tim W. Machan (*Marquette University*)
Miceal Vaughan (*University of Washington*)
   "Taking Back the *Retractions*"
Charlotte Brewer (*Hertford College, Oxford*)
   "Editing Chaucer in the Nineteenth Century"
Stephen Barney (*University of California–Irvine*)
   "The *Riverside Chaucer:* Textual Politics and the Via Media"

Chaucer and Public Order (papers)
Organizer: R. F. Green (*University of Western Ontario*)
Presider: David Wallace (*University of Pennsylvania*)
Wendy Allman (*Baylor University*)
   "Purveying Kingship: *The Knight's Tale*"
David Lampe (*Buffalo State College*)
   "Verses of Order, Visions of Disorder: Chaucer's Apocalyptic
   Lyrics"

Penn Szittya (*Georgetown University*)
"Illicit Conventicles and the Public Order: The Crisis of the 1380s"

Place and Space in *Troilus and Criseyde* (colloquium)
Organizer and presider: Peter Brown (*University of Kent at Canterbury*)
Kenneth A. Bleeth (*Connecticut College*)
"Space, History and Fiction Making in *Troilus and Criseyde*"
Sylvia Federico (*Washington State University, Tri-Cities*)
"'New Troy' as a Political Space"
John Ganim (*University of California at Riverside*)
"Chaucer *le Flaneur*"
Laura L. Howes (*University of Tennessee*)
"The *Troilus* Frontispiece as Aristocratic Pleasure-Ground"
Nicola McDonald (*St. John's College, Oxford*)
"Visualizing Troy: Place and Space in *Troilus and Criseyde* and Contemporary Manuscript Illumination"

Masculinities in *The Canterbury Tales* (colloquium)
Organizer and presider: Peter G. Beidler (*Lehigh University*)
Jonathan Watson (*Indiana University*)
"Toward a Masculine Poetics in Chaucer: Noah in *The Miller's Tale*"
Janet M. Jesmok (*University of Wisconsin–Milwaukee*)
"'Under Youre Yerde': Manly Disobedience in *The Clerk's Tale*"
Rebecca S. Beal (*University of Scranton*)
"Words and the Man: Masculinities in *The Franklin's Tale*"
Celia M. Lewis (*Baylor University*)
"Pilgrimage to Death: The Masculine World of *The Pardoner's Tale*"
John M. Hill (*U.S. Naval Academy*)
"A Chaucerian Calibration: Masculine Rectitude in *The Monk's Tale*"
Jean E. Jost (*Bradley University*)
"A Nun's-Eye View: Masculine Determination in *The Prioress's Tale*"

5:00 p.m.—Opening plenary lecture
Presider: Mary Carruthers (*New York University*)
Introduction: André Crépin (*Paris IV–Sorbonne*)
Address: Professor Emmanuel Le Roy Ladurie (*Collège de France*)
   "Linguistic Minorities in Peripheral Zones in the Late Middle
   Ages: The French Case"

Saturday, 18 July

9:00 a.m.—Concurrent sessions
Chaucer's Influence on His French Contemporaries (papers)
Organizer: Helen Phillips (*University of Nottingham*)
Presider: Jacqueline Cerquiglini-Toulet (*Paris IV–Sorbonne*)
Martha Driver (*Pace University*)
   "French Connections: Chaucer, Christine and their Readings of
   the *Rose*"
Julia Boffey (*Queen Mary and Westfield College, University of London*)
   "Evidence from Manuscripts"
Helen Phillips (*University of Nottingham*)
   "Chaucer and Oton de Graunson"

Anglo-French Relations and the Hundred Years' War (papers)
Organizer and presider: Ardis Butterfield (*University College, London*)
Philippe Contamine (*Paris IV–Sorbonne*)
   "Siege Poetry"
Andrew Wathey (*Royal Holloway and Bedford New College, London*)
   "Music and Poetry in the Hundred Years' War"
Lynn Staley (*Colgate University*)
   "Richard II and the Production of French Culture"

Chaucer and the Non-Christian World (papers)
Organizer: Brenda Schildgen (*University of California–Davis*)
Presider: John Ganim (*University of California–Riverside*)
Dolores W. Frese (*University of Notre Dame*)
   "The Trace of Bede's *History* in *The Man of Law's Tale:* A Case of
   Poetic Conversion"
Leonard Michael Koff (*University of California, Los Angeles*)
   "Who are the Christians in *The Prioress's Tale?*"

Suzanne Conklin Akbari (*University of Toronto*)
"'Straunge Nacioun': Chaucer's Orientalism and the Idea of Nation"

The House of Fame (papers)
Organizer: Jesús L. Serrano Reyes (*University of Còrdoba*)
Presider: Antonio R. León Sendra (*University of Còrdoba*)
Sylvia Rogers (*College of Notre Dame, Calif.*)
"Art as Illusion: Imaging Techniques in Chaucer's *House of Fame*"
Anne Worthington Prescott (*Pinole, Calif.*)
"The Aesthetics of Chaucer's *House of Fame:* 'Sound' as a Guide to Meaning"
Jesús L. Serrano Reyes (*University of Còrdoba*)
"More than a 'Clarion' from 'Cataloigne and Aragon' in *The House of Fame*"

Chaucer and Langland: Teaching the Dream Vision (colloquium)
Organizer and presider: Louise M. Bishop (*University of Oregon*)
Josephine Koster Tarvers (*Winthrop University*)
"'Why Don't Girls Have Dream Visions?' and Other Questions of Gender and the Dream Vision Genre"
Frank Grady (*University of Missouri–St. Louis*)
"'Exclusive of Chaucer': Curricular Animadversions"
Joan Baker (*Florida International University*)
"'Sir Dowel and the Green Knight': Dream(y) Visions in Passus 9 and *The Merchant's Tale*"
Kellie P. Robertson (*University of Southern Illinois*)
"Dreaming Dissent: Historicist Criticism in the Classroom"
Edward I. Condren (*University of California, Los Angeles*)
"From London to Yorkshire via Malvern: Three Kinds of Dream Vision in Chaucer, Langland, and the *Pearl* Poet"

11:00 a.m.—Concurrent sessions
Chaucer in a Francophone Culture (papers)
Organizer and presider: R. F. Yeager (*University of North Carolina at Asheville*)
Karla Taylor (*University of Michigan*)
"Puns and Doublets: Economy and Plenitude in *The Shipman's Tale* and *Melibee*"

Helen Maree Hickey (*University of Melbourne*)
"Thomas Hoccleve's French Collection: A Formula for Self-
Preservation"
Karen K. Jambeck (*Western Connecticut State University*)
"*The Nun's Priest's Tale* and the *Livre* of Marie de France"

Chaucer and Medieval Latin Literary Culture (papers)
Organizer: Winthrop Wetherbee (*Cornell University*)
Presider: Teresa Kennedy (*Mary Washington College*)
Betsy Bowden (*Rutgers–Camden*)
"*Melibee* and the Traditions of Latin Pedagogy"
Warren Ginsburg (*State University of New York–Albany*)
"Petrarch's Griselda Story and Chaucer's Relations to
Protohumanism in Italy"
Stephen Partridge (*University of British Columbia*)
"Apostrophe, Prayer and Other Forms of Address in Chaucer and
Boethius"
Krista Twu (*University of California–Irvine*)
"Raymond of Pennaforte and *The Parson's Tale*"

Chaucer and Christine de Pizan: Writing and Difference (papers)
Organizer and presider: Marilynn Desmond (*Binghamton University*)
Andrew Taylor (*University of Saskatchewan*)
"Harley 4431 and the Dangers of Writing"
Michel-André Bossy (*Brown University*)
"Searching for Proper Tales: Jean d'Angoulême as Fifteenth-
Century Reader of Chaucer and Christine"
Laurie Finke (*Kenyon College*)
"Christine and the Fifteenth-Century Chaucerians: The
Aesthetics of Emergent Nationalism"

Faith and Skepticism (colloquium)
Organizer: Elizabeth Robertson (*University of Colorado*)
Presiders: Elizabeth Robertson (*University of Colorado*) and David
Raybin (*Eastern Illinois University*)
Thomas Hahn (*University of Rochester*)
Sarah Stanbury (*College of the Holy Cross*)
Elizabeth Walsh (*University of San Diego*)
John Hirsh (*Georgetown University*)

505

Kate McKinley (*Campbell University*)
William Askins (*Community College of Philadelphia*)

The *Monk's Tale* (colloquium)
Organizer and presider: Jim Rhodes (*Southern Connecticut State University*)
Ann Astell (*Purdue University*)
Terry Jones (*London*)
H. A. Kelly (*University of California, Los Angeles*)
Stephen Knight (*University of Wales–Cardiff*)
Richard Neuse (*University of Rhode Island*)

4:00 p.m.—Special session
Large Chaucerian Projects
Organizer: John Burrow (*University of Bristol*)
Presider: Derek Pearsall (*Harvard University*)
Dan Ransom (*University of Oklahoma*), The Variorum Chaucer, The Chaucer Encyclopedia
(In the absence of Robert Correale, Derek Brewer of Boydell and Brewer (publishers) spoke of the plans to publish volume 1 of the revised *Sources and Analogues of the* Canterbury Tales.)

6:00 p.m.—Plenary session: Biennial Chaucer Lecture
Presider: Helen Cooper (*University College, Oxford*)
Address: Robert W. Hanning (*Columbia University*)
"'And countrefete the speche of every man / He koude, whan he sholde telle a tale': Toward a Lapsarian Poetic for *The Canterbury Tales*"

Sunday, 19 July

9:00 a.m.—Concurrent sessions
Parisian Intellectual Culture and Beyond: Conflicts and Legacies (papers)
Organizer: Rita Copeland (*University of Minnesota*)
Presider: Michael Hanly (*Washington State University*)
Rita Copeland (*University of Minnesota*)
"La Trahison des Clercs Médiévaux? Exporting Ambivalent Intellectual Identities"

Ian Wei (*University of Bristol*)
"Parisian Intellectuals Save the World"
Michael Camille (*University of Chicago*)
"Imagery and Pedagogy at the University of Paris"

Chaucer and His English Contemporaries (papers)
Organizer and presider: Larry Scanlon (*Rutgers University*)
George Economou (*University of Oklahoma*)
"Chaucer and Langland, a Fellowship of Makers"
Sheila Lindenbaum (*Indiana University*)
"Faction in the Archives: Activist Writers and Disinterested
Poets in Chaucer's London"
Christy Auston (*Washington University*)
"The Cosmological Sir: (Ab)Errant Narration in Mandeville's
Travels and *The Canterbury Tales*"

Representations of Death (papers)
Organizer: New Chaucer Society
Presider: Velma Bourgeois Richmond (*Holy Names College*)
R. James Goldstein (*Auburn University*)
"Chaucer, Suicide and the Agencies of Memory"
Rosemarie McGerr (*Indiana University*)
"Seeing Double: Dialogism in a Late Medieval Representation of
Death"
Sandra Pierson Prior (*Columbia University*)
"Virginity and Sacrifice in *The Physician's Tale*"

Chaucer and Manuscript Study (colloquium)
Organizer and presider: A. S. G. Edwards (*University of Victoria*)
John Thompson (*Queen's University, Belfast*)
"Anthologizing Chaucer in the Later Middle Ages"
Elizabeth Solopova (*The Canterbury Tales* Project; University of
Kentucky)
"The Alpha Tradition of *The Canterbury Tales*"
T. Prendergast (*College of Wooster*)
"Lansdowne 851 and the Construction of a 'Chaucerian' Text"
Paul Thomas (*Brigham Young University*)
"What Are You Doing with My Text? Scribes at Work on *The
Nun's Priest's Tale*"

Carol Meale (*University of Bristol*)
  "Family Ties? The Descent of Chaucer Manuscripts in the Fifteenth Century"

Feminism and Chaucer Studies (colloquium)
Organizer and presider: Felicity Riddy (*University of York*)
Sarah Kay (*University of Cambridge*)
Ruth Evans (*University of Wales, Cardiff*)
Kim Phillips (*University of Auckland*)
Sheila Delany (*Simon Fraser University*)

A Walk with Love and Death (1969 film by John Huston set in France during the Hundred Years' War)
Film showing: 9:00–10:30 a.m.
Colloquium: 10:30 a.m.–12:00 p.m.
Presider: Sandra Gorgievski (*University of Toulon*)
François de la Bretèque (*University of Montpellier*)
Kevin Harty (*La Salle University*)

11:00 a.m.—Concurrent sessions
Channel Crossings (papers)
Organizer: Wendy Harding (*University of Montpellier*)
Presider: Maria K. Greenwood (*Paris VII–Charles V*)
Michelle Wright (*University of Nottingham*)
  "Playing with Time in *Le Roman de la Rose, L'Orloge Amoureuse,* and *Le Joli Buisson de Jonece*"
Mary-Jo Arn (*Bloomsburg University*)
  "What's That Strange New Flower? Charles d'Orléans, Poète Anglais"
Jessica C. Brantley (*University of California, Los Angeles*)
  "The Fairfax 16 Miniature and Its Continental Inheritance"

Literary and Nonliterary Concepts of Time in *The Canterbury Tales* (papers)
Organizer and presider: Joerg Fichte (*University of Tübingen*)
Martin Camargo (*University of Missouri*)
  "Time as Rhetorical Topos in *The Canterbury Tales*"
Richard Utz (*University of Northern Iowa/University of Tübingen*)
  "Gendered *Tyme* in *The Canterbury Tales*"

Stefania d'Agata d'Ottavi (*Università di Siena*)
   "Metafictional Time in *The Knight's Tale*"

Norms Governing Speech in Chaucer's Narratives (papers)
Organizer and presider: Edwin Craun (*Washington and Lee University*)
Michael P. Kuczynski (*Tulane University*)
   "'Don't Blame Me': Metaethics in *The Canterbury Tales*"
David Lawton (*University of East Anglia*)
   "Debate, Voice and Impersonation in Chaucer's Narratives"
Derrick Pitard (*Slippery Rock University*)
   "Speech, 'Ordinatio,' and Authority in *The Canterbury Tales*"

Virgins Material, Mythical, and Metaphorical (colloquium)
Organizer: Kathryn Lynch (*Wellesley College*)
Presider: Kathleen Kelly (*Northeastern University*)
Bonnie Wheeler (*Southern Methodist University*)
   "Becoming a Virgin: Boys and Men in Chaucer"
John Bowers (*University of Nevada*)
   "Male Virgins, Richard II, and Chaucer's Poetry in the 1380s"
Kathryn Lynch (*Wellesley College*)
   "The Virgin Wife of Bath"
Derek Brewer (*Emmanuel College, Cambridge*)
   "Daughter's Virginity and Father's Honour in *The Physician's Tale*"
Michael Uebel (*University of Kentucky*)
   "Public Fantasy and the Logic of Sacrifice in *The Physician's Tale*"

Chaucer and Postcolonial Theory: Risks and Possibilities
   (colloquium)
Organizer and presider: Kathleen Davis (*Bucknell University*)
Kathleen Biddick (*University of Notre Dame*)
   "Dances with Elves: Chaucer's Blackface, Miscegenation, and
   Colonial Trauma in Chaucer Studies"
Carolyn Dinshaw (*University of California–Berkeley*)
   "Queer Relations: Postcoloniality, Postmodernism, Lesbian/Gay/
   Bisexual/Transgender Studies, Humanism, Medieval Studies, and
   Chaucer"
Arlyn Diamond (*University of Massachusetts–Amherst*)
   "Travelling Far in Hethenesse: Chaucer's Knight and the
   Contradiction of Crusading"

509

Patricia Clare Ingham (*Lehigh University*)
  "Old Days of Romance: Premodern History, Postcolonial Theory, and *The Wife of Bath's Tale*"
Sylvia Tomasch (*Hunter College*)
  "Displacements"

6:00 p.m.—Plenary session: Presidential Address
Presider: Paul Strohm (*St. Anne's College, Oxford*)
Address: Mary Carruthers (*New York University*)
  "Micrological Aggregates: Is the New Chaucer Society Speaking in Tongues?"

Monday, 20 July

9:00 a.m.—Concurrent sessions
Froissart (papers)
Organizer and presider: John M. Fyler (*Tufts University*)
Paule Mertens-Fonck (*University of Liège*)
  "A Continental Chronicler on the Road to Canterbury"
Angela Hurworth (*University of Tours*)
  "The Marguerite Motif in the Poetry of Froissart, and a Reading of the Prologue to *The Legend of Good Women*"
Peter Ainsworth (*University of Liverpool*)
  "Froissart the Historian"

Women's Lyric Voices in Chaucer (papers)
Organizer: New Chaucer Society
Presider: Jane Chance (*Rice University*)
Susanna Greer Fein (*Kent State University*)
  "Chaucer and the English Pastourelle"
Corinne Saunders (*University of Durham*)
  "Women's Laments in Chaucer"
Kara A. Doyle (*Cornell University*)
  "Criseyde's Monologue and Antigone's Song"

Chaucerian Ethics: Connecting the Self and the Good (papers)
Organizer and presider: N. J. Klassen (*Trinity Western University*)
Mark Miller (*University of Chicago*)
  "Naturalism and its Discontents in *The Miller's Tale*"

Alcuin Blamires (*University of Wales–Lampeter*)
  "The Wife of Bath and 'Nigardye': The Ethics of 'Liberality' in Chaucer"
Nicolette Zeeman (*King's College, Cambridge*)
  "Poetic Metamorphosis"

Chaucer's Versecraft (colloquium)
Organizer and presider: Donka Minkova (*University of California, Los Angeles*)
Thomas Cable (*University of Texas–Austin*)
  "The Iambic Tetrameter in Chaucer and in the Seventeenth Century, and Metrical Typology in English"
Martin Duffell (*Queen Mary and Westfield College, London*)
  "Lydgate's Metrics and His Debt to Chaucer"
Christopher McCully (*Manchester University*)
  "Reading Between the Lines: The Qualities of Chaucer's Silence"
Robert Stockwell (*University of California, Los Angeles*)
  "Summation and Evaluation"

Chaucer and Queer Theory (colloquium)
Organizer and presider: Steven Kruger (*City University of New York*)
Glenn Burger (*University of Alberta*)
  "Up Close and Dirty: Chaucer, Flesh, and the Word"
Allen Frantzen (*Loyola University*)
  "The Queer Frontier: *The Man of Law's Tale* and Chaucer's Anglo-Saxonism"
Carroll Hilles (*Union College*)
  "A Material Queer; or, Taillyng the Shipman"
Becky McLaughlin (*State University of New York–Buffalo*)
  "'Deviant' Sexualities on Pilgrimage: The Prioress's Prick, the Pardoner's Perversion, and the Reeve's Revenge"
Ron Scapp (*College of Mount Saint Vincent*)
  "The Queer Thing Is . . . or, The Oddity of Theory"

11:00 a.m.—Concurrent sessions
The Material Body in Chaucer (papers)
Organizer and presider: Jeffrey Cohen (*George Washington University*)
Carol Everest (*King's University College, Edmonton*)
  "Fabliau and Physiology in *The Miller's Tale*"

511

Bruce Holsinger (*University of Colorado–Boulder*)
"The Pauline Body and the Scandal of Apotheosis"
Louise Fradenburg (*University of California–Santa Barbara*)
"Spirit and Bone: Gifted Bodies in *The Canterbury Tales*"

The Griselda Story (papers)

Organizer and presider: Amy Goodwin (*Randolph-Macon College*)
Charlotte Morse (*Virginia Commonwealth University*)
"The Genesis of Kittredge's Marriage Debate"
Wendy Harding (*University of Montpellier*)
"Griselda in Fourteenth-Century France"
Carolyn P. Collette (*Mount Holyoke*)
"Re-presenting Griselda: The Politics of Social Relations and
Social Mobility in *L'Estoire de Griseldis* (1395)"

Authority and Its Discontents (papers)

Organizer: New Chaucer Society
Presider: Tom Burton (*University of Adelaide*)
Daniel Pinti (*New Mexico State University*)
"The *Comedy* of History: Chaucer's Hugelyn and Dante's Trecento
Commentators"
Matthew Giancarlo (*Yale University*)
"Discourse Ethics and Transcendental Counsel in *Troilus and
Criseyde*"
Paul Bernhardt (*University of Exeter*)
"To Play with Mimesis: Considering Chaucer's Ludic Fictions"

The Fabliau in France, Italy, and England (colloquium)

Organizer: Barbara Nolan (*University of Virginia*)
Presider: A. C. Spearing (*University of Virginia*)
Roy J. Pearcy (*University of Oklahoma*)
"Anglo-Norman Fabliaux"
Glending Olson (*Cleveland State University*)
"The *Summoner's Tale* in Its Cultural Context"
Margaret Pappano (*Columbia University*)
"The Priest's Body in Old French Fabliaux"
A. C. Spearing (*University of Virginia*)
"The Matter of Blood in *The Reeve's Tale*"

Tom Hanks, Jr. (*Baylor University*)
"Rough Love in *The Canterbury Tales*"

Neologisms and First-Recorded Usages (colloquium)
Organizer and presider: Christopher Cannon (*St. Edmund Hall, Oxford*)
Juliette Dor (*University of Liège*)
"Policy and Polysemy"
Derek Pearsall (*Harvard University*)
"Chaucer's Experience"
Susan Yager (*Iowa State University*)
"Visual Perception and Chaucer's Terms"
Mary Blockley (*University of Texas–Austin*)
"Rhyme and Collocation"
Nancy Mason Bradbury (*Smith College*)
"'Queynt Termes' in French: Biculturalism in Chaucer's Earlier
Poetry"

6:00 p.m.—Closing plenary session
Who Murdered Chaucer?
Mastermind: Terry Jones (*London*)
Terry Dolan (*University College, Dublin*)
Bob Yeager (*University of North Carolina–Asheville*)
Juliette Dor (*University of Liège*)
Alan J. Fletcher (*University College–Dublin*)

Index